Multilateralism under challenge

This volume is the result of a research project jointly organized by the Social Science Research Council and the United Nations University.

The editors would like to express their gratitude to their colleagues who provided support throughout the course of the project. At the SSRC, Petra Ticha's dedication and hard work were essential to the success of this project. At the UNU, we would like to express our gratitude to Jean-Marc Coicaud and the staff at the Peace and Governance Programme and UNU Press.

The Social Science Research Council is an independent, not-for-profit research organization founded in 1923. Based in New York City, it mobilizes researchers, policymakers, professionals, activists, and other experts from the private and public sectors to develop innovative approaches to issues of critical social importance. The SSRC is committed to the idea that social science can produce necessary knowledge – necessary for citizens to understand their societies and necessary for policymakers to decide on crucial questions. This mandate is carried out through workshops and conferences, research consortia, scholarly exchanges, summer training institutes, fellowships and grants, and publications.

For more information, please visit the SSRC's website: http://www.ssrc.org

Multilateralism under challenge? Power, international order, and structural change

Edited by Edward Newman, Ramesh Thakur and John Tirman

TOKYO • NEW YORK • PARIS

The views expressed in this publication are those of the authors and do not necessarily reflect the views of the United Nations University.

United Nations University Press
United Nations University, 53-70, Jingumae 5-chome,
Shibuya-ku, Tokyo, 150-8925, Japan
Tel: +81-3-3499-2811 Fax: +81-3-3406-7345
E-mail: sales@hq.unu.edu general enquiries: press@hq.unu.edu
http://www.unu.edu

United Nations University Office at the United Nations, New York
2 United Nations Plaza, Room DC2-2062, New York, NY 10017, USA
Tel: +1-212-963-6387 Fax: +1-212-371-9454
E-mail: unuona@ony.unu.edu

United Nations University Press is the publishing division of the United Nations University.

Cover design by Sese-Paul Design

Printed in India

ISBN 92-808-1129-0

Library of Congress Cataloging-in-Publication Data

Multilateralism under challenge? : power, international order and structural change / edited by Edward Newman, Ramesh Thakur, and John Tirman.
p. cm.
Includes bibliographical references and index.
ISBN 9280811290 (pbk. : alk. paper)
1. International cooperation. 2. International relations. 3. Security, International. 4. Environmental policy. I. Newman, Edward, 1970– II. Thakur, Ramesh Chandra, 1948– III. Tirman, John.
JZ1318.M858 2006
327.1′01—dc22 2006018675

Contents

List of figures

Contributors

Amitav Acharya is Professor, Deputy Director and Head of Research at the Institute of Defence and Strategic Studies, Nanyang Technological University, Singapore.

Emanuel Adler is Andrea and Charles Bronfman Professor of Israeli Studies, University of Toronto.

Coral Bell is Visiting Fellow in the Strategic and Defence Studies Centre of the Australian National University.

Trevor Findlay is Director of the Canadian Centre for Treaty Compliance and Associate Professor at the Norman Paterson School of International Affairs (NPSIA).

David P. Forsythe is University Professor and Charles J. Mach Distinguished Professor of Political Science, University of Nebraska-Lincoln.

Richard J. Goldstone is the Muligan Visiting Professor of Law at Fordham University School of Law in New York and formerly Justice of the Constitutional Court of South Africa.

A.J.R. Groom is Professor of International Relations at the University of Kent.

Joyeeta Gupta is Professor on climate change policy and law at the Vrije Universiteit Amsterdam and is professor on policy and law on water resources and the environment at the UNESCO-IHE Institute for Water Education.

Stefano Guzzini is Senior Researcher at the Danish Institute for International Studies, Copenhagen and Professor of Government at Uppsala University, Sweden.

Jorge Heine is the Ambassador of Chile to India and Sri Lanka.

Sirkku K. Hellsten is Counsellor for Governance, Embassy of Finland, Kenya, whilst on leave from the University of Birmingham where she is Reader in Development Ethics. She is also Docent of Social and Moral Philosophy, University of Helsinki.

K.J. Holsti is University Killam Professor Emeritus in the Department of Politics of the University of British Columbia.

Erin P. Kelly is a J.D. candidate at Fordham University School of Law and a scholar in the Joseph R. Crowley International Human Rights Program.

Robert O. Keohane is Professor of International Affairs at the Woodrow Wilson School of Public and International Affairs, Princeton University.

Friedrich Kratochwil is Professor and Chair of International Relations at the European University Institute.

Edward C. Luck is Professor of Practice in International and Public Affairs and Director of the Center on International Organization, School of International and Public Affairs, Columbia University.

Edward Newman is Director of Studies on Conflict and Security in the Peace and Governance Programme of the United Nations University.

Gwyn Prins is an Alliance Research Professor appointed jointly at the London School of Economics and Columbia University, New York.

Beth A. Simmons is a Professor of Government at Harvard University.

Jackie Smith is an Associate Professor of Sociology at the State University of New York at Stony Brook, and a visiting scholar at the McMaster University Institute on Globalization and the Human Condition.

Ramesh Thakur is Senior Vice Rector of the United Nations University and UN Assistant-Secretary-General.

Shashi Tharoor is Under-Secretary-General for Communications and Public Information at the United Nations.

John Tirman is the Executive Director of the Center for International Studies at the Massachusetts Institute of Technology.

Thomas G. Weiss is Presidential Professor of Political Science at the Graduate Center of the City University of New York and Director of the Ralph Bunche Institute for International Studies.

Quansheng Zhao is Professor and Division Director of Comparative and Regional Studies at the School of International Service, and Director of the Center for Asian Studies at American University.

Abbreviations

ABM	Anti-Ballistic Missile [Treaty]
ACDA	Arms Control and Disarmament Agency
AI	Amnesty International
ANZUS	Australia, New Zealand and the United States [Treaty]
ARF	ASEAN Regional Forum
ASEAN	Association of Southeast Asian Nations
AU	African Union
BITs	bilateral investment treaties
BW	biological weapons
BWC	Biological Weapons Convention
CARE	Christian Action for Research and Education
CARICOM	Caribbean Community and Common Market
CBW	chemical or biological weapons
CD/CCD	Conference on Disarmament/Conference of the Committee on Disarmament
CIS	Commonwealth of Independent States
CSCAP	Council for Security Cooperation in the Asia Pacific
CSCE	Conference on Security and Cooperation in Europe
CTBTO	Comprehensive Test Ban Treaty Organization
CTC	Counter-Terrorism Committee
CWC	Chemical Weapons Convention
DPA	(UN) Department of Political Affairs
DSM	Dispute Settlement Mechanism
EAEC	East Asia Economic Caucus
EAPC	Euro-Atlantic Partnership Council
ECHO	Humanitarian Office of the European Community

ECLAC	(UN) Economic Commission for Latin America and the Caribbean
EMP	Euro Mediterranean Partnership
ENDC	Eighteen Nations Disarmament Committee
ENP	European Neighbourhood Policy
EU	European Union
FMCT	Fissile Material Cut-off Treaty
FSNL	Frente Sandinista Nacional de Liberacion
FTAA	Free Trade Area of the Americas
GA	General Assembly
GATT	General Agreement on Tariffs and Trade
GC	Geneva Convention
GC	Global Compact
GSP	Generalized System of Preferences
HEU	highly enriched uranium
HI	Humanitarian Intervention
HIPC	Heavily Indebted Poor Countries Initiative
HRW	Human Rights Watch
HST	Hegemonic Stability Theory
IADC	Inter-American Democratic Charter
IAEA	International Atomic Energy Agency
ICAO	International Civil Aviation Organization
ICC	International Criminal Court
ICI	Istanbul Cooperation Initiative
ICISS	International Commission on Intervention and State Sovereignty
ICRC	International Committee of the Red Cross
ICTR	International Criminal Tribunal for Rwanda
ICTY	International Criminal Tribunal for the former Yugoslavia
IDPs	International Development Programmes
IFIs	international financial institutions
IGOs	intergovernmental organizations
IHL	international humanitarian law
IMF	International Monetary Fund
IOs	International Organizations
IPCC	Intergovernmental Panel on Climate Change
IPRs	intellectual property rights
IR	international relations
MAD	mutual assured destruction
MD	Mediterranean security dialogue
MDGs	Millennium Development Goals
MFNs	most favoured nations
MINUSTAH	Mission des Nations Unies pour la stabilisation en Haïti
MSF	Médicin sans frontières
MTCR	Missile Technology Control Regime
NACC	North Atlantic Cooperation Council
NATO	North Atlantic Treaty Organization
NEPAD	New Partnership for Africa's Development

NGOs	non-governmental organizations
NPT	Non-Proliferation Treaty
NSG	Nuclear Suppliers Group
OAS	Organization of American States
OAS	Organization of African States
OAU	Organization of African Unity
ODA	Oversees Development Assistance
OECD	Organization for Economic Cooperation and Development
OEEC	Organization for European Economic Cooperation
OPCW	Organization for the Prohibition of Chemical Weapons
OSCE	Organization for Security and Cooperation in Europe
PEPFAR	[US] President's Emergency Plan for AIDS Relief
PfP	Partnership for Peace
PRC	People's Republic of China
PSI	Proliferation Security Initiative
R2P	"Responsibility to Protect" ICISS report
SG	Secretary-General
SAPs	structural adjustment policies
SEATO	Southeast Asia Treaty Organization
SIPRI	Stockholm International Peace Research Institute
SORT	Strategic Offensive Reductions Treaty
STDs	sexually transmitted diseases
TPB	(UN) Terrorism Prevention Branch
UDHR	Universal Declaration of Human Rights
UN	United Nations
UNAMIR	United Nations Assistance Mission for Rwanda
UNCIO	United Nations Conference on International Organization
UNDAF	United Nations Development Assistance Framework
UNDC	United Nations Disarmament Commission
UNDDA	United Nations Department of Disarmament Affairs
UNFCCC	United Nations Framework Convention on Climate Change
UNHCR	United Nations High Commissioner for Refugees
UNICEF	United Nations Children's Fund
UNMOVIC	United Nations Monitoring, Verification and Inspection Commission
UNRWA	United Nations Relief and Works Agency
UNSC	United Nations Security Council
UNSCOM	United Nations Special Commission
USAID	US Agency for International Development
WMD	weapons of mass destruction
WTO	World Trade Organization

1

Introduction

Edward Newman, Ramesh Thakur and John Tirman

The values and institutions of multilateralism are not ahistorical phenomena. They are created and maintained in the context of specific demands and challenges, and through specific forms of leadership, norms, and international power configurations. All of these factors evolve and change; there is little reason to believe that multilateral values or institutions could or should remain static in form and nature. The relationship between the distribution of power, the nature of challenges and problems, and the international institutions that emerge to deal with collective challenges is constantly in flux. Like any social construction, multilateralism is destined to evolve as a function of changing environmental dynamics and demands. It is this evolution that we examine in this volume

The challenge to multilateralism

In November 2003 United Nations Secretary-General Kofi Annan observed that "The past year has shaken the foundations of collective security and undermined confidence in the possibility of collective responses to our common problems and challenges. It has also brought to the fore deep divergences of opinion on the range and nature of the challenges we face, and are likely to face in the future."[1] The evidence of problems across a range of international norms and institutions is certainly ample. The United States and its allies undertook a war against Iraq in 2003 without the explicit authority of the UN Security Council, which came on the heels of similarly unauthorized NATO military action in Kosovo in 1999. Some observers have interpreted this, and other developments, as a shift amongst some major powers towards an ad hoc "coalition" model of military action. Some states openly question whether the established rules governing the use of military force (only in self-defence, collective self-defence, or under the authority of Chapter 7 of the UN Charter) remain valid in all circumstances, suggesting that preventive force outside the UN framework may be necessary in response to latent or non-imminent threats. In particular, it is questionable whether existing international organizations have the confidence of major powers for dealing with new security scenarios, such as the threat of weapons of mass destruction in the hands of terrorist groups. And if the major powers are not going to be restrained by existing norms, laws and institutions in their use of force overseas, then the other states in turn will lose confidence in norms, laws and institutions as instruments for protecting their security.

The lack of support extends to other policy areas. The United States, China, Russia and many other countries do not support the International Criminal Court and thus render its jurisdiction very limited. According to a 2004 high-level panel report endorsed by the UN Secretary-General, the main global multilateral regime responsible for promoting and protecting human rights "suffers from a legitimacy deficit that casts doubts on the overall reputation of the United Nations."[2] The Kyoto protocol to regulate climate change is jeopardized by key abstentions. A range of multilateral arms control treaties and conventions are being eroded, including the Anti-Ballistic Missile Treaty and the Non-Proliferation Treaty. Others, such as the International Convention to Ban Anti-Personnel Landmines, are not supported by key states. In their decision-making procedures and their representation, many international organizations do not meet contemporary standards and expectations of legitimacy based upon accountability and democracy. In addition, the future of multilateralism has become embroiled in a transatlantic split and competing visions of world order.

Notably, many of the challenges confronting multilateral institutions have been associated with US military and economic preeminence in a unipolar world, and an attendant pattern of US unilateralism. Are the values and institutions of multilateralism under challenge, or even in crisis?

This volume explores the effectiveness of, and prospects for, contemporary forms of multilateralism in a range of issue areas. There are a number of elements to this. Firstly, the relationship between the distribution of power at the international level – in all its dimensions, hard and soft – and the nature of multilateralism is fundamental. In this respect, several of the volume's contributors question whether institutionalized multilateralism, as currently conceived, can offer a viable basis for international order at the beginning of the twenty-first century in a global power configuration of unipolarity. Multilateral institutions are inherently vulnerable to hegemonic/unilateralist power, demonstrated vividly during the UN Security Council's failure to constrain the US misadventure in Iraq. Many analysts have associated the malaise of multilateralism with American pre-eminence and unilateralism, although this equation is not accepted uncritically in this volume.

Secondly, at the same time, the volume's authors suggest that the difficulties and the legitimacy problems confronting multilateralism do not all stem from the distribution of power in international relations, or from the policies of any particular state or group of states. A number of challenges result from structural and normative changes since multilateral institutions took shape after the Second World War. The challenge to multilateralism is in part the challenge to the state. Security challenges, for example, are no longer mainly those of inter-state war; trade and economic relations are increasingly non-state and present mounting regulatory challenges; civil society and other networks and communities are significant generators and enforcers of global norms, and in many cases are directly challenging and even outperforming multilateral institutions on normative grounds. Moreover, multilateralism is premised upon functioning and autonomous sovereign states, which is in some instances a fiction. Sovereignty as an exclusive norm of domestic jurisdiction is in turn being challenged by universal norms relating to human rights and governance.

Thirdly, in their decision-making procedures and their representation, many international organizations do not meet contemporary standards and expectations of legitimacy based upon accountability and democracy. International organizations emerged from the need to regulate and give predictability to a narrow range of inter-state relations. As a result, international organizations have traditionally been immune from requirements of governance that would generally be applied in the domestic context, such as transparency and public accountability. This is no longer the case, and it presents serious problems of legitimacy.

Other challenges to multilateralism stem from more obvious problems of multilateral performance. There have been a number of security failures in particular: the United Nations was created primarily as a collective security organization, and yet hundreds of conflicts have beset the world since 1945, and even with significant multilateral attention to weapons of mass destruction, the use and proliferation of nuclear, chemical, and biological weapons remain highly threatening. In the perception of important policy makers the prospect of weapons of mass destruction in the hands of terrorist organizations has brought this threat to new heights, which traditional multilateral arrangements have difficulty addressing. Existing multilateral arrangements are unable to guide states to a workable framework of how to deal with egregious and widespread abuses of human rights and civil war. Persistent crises such as HIV/AIDS, failing states, terrorism and environmental degradation, amongst others, pose deep and vexing problems that multilateral mechanisms struggle to address. The state-centric nature of multilateralism and the manner in which states make and implement decisions are arguably inadequate to deal with many of these challenges. Finally, there are policy (and knowledge) failures, such as the World Bank's imposition of structural adjustment policies which have been associated with negative social consequences.

Leading states may be less willing to bear the costs and obligations (and restrictions) of maintaining certain multilateral institutions in the face of declining effectiveness, especially in the area of international security. Smaller states feel alienated by the elitist and power political forms of multilateralism, even though they rely by necessity upon their participation in international organizations. Citizens and non-state actors are frustrated by what they see as a lack of accountability and transparency in multilateralism. As a result, confidence in many of the institutions and values of multilateralism is waning in the early twenty-first century. When the effectiveness of multilateral institutions as well as their constitutive principles fail to meet performance expectations and contemporary norms, legitimacy is, in turn, in doubt. Multilateralism thus appears to be under challenge from two fronts: institutions, forged in the post-1945 environment or during the Cold War, may be exhausted normatively, and their inter-state structure is inadequate for contemporary challenges. This characterizes contemporary multilateralism in a number of issue areas.

Multilateralism: Do the forms and norms remain viable?

This volume begins with the proposition that the post-Second World War systems of multilateralism, in a number of important issue areas, have become out of step with contemporary challenges and demands. It considers which challenges and changes can be absorbed within the existing mechanisms and systems of multilateralism and which cannot. On the basis of this, the volume seeks to highlight what issues might have to be confronted in order to re-envision multilateral arrangements in a number of policy areas.

As a starting point, this volume takes existing definitions and ideas of multilateralism as a form of common action amongst states in international relations. In a fundamental sense, multilateral arrangements are therefore institutions, defined by Keohane as: "persistent sets of rules that constrain activity, shape expectations, and prescribe roles".[3] The principal actors (and unit of analysis) are states. Ruggie provides a more elaborate definition:

multilateralism depicts a generic institutional form in international relations ... [It is] an institutional form that coordinates relations among three or more states on the basis of generalized principles of conduct: that is, principles which specify appropriate conduct for a class of actions, without regard to the particularistic interests of the parties or the strategic exigencies that may exist in any specific occurrence.[4]

He notes two corollaries: the principles of multilateralism "logically entail an indivisibility among the members of a collectivity with respect to the range of behavior in question", and, second, the expectation of "diffuse reciprocity". This applies when "the arrangement is expected to yield a rough equivalence of benefits in the aggregate and over time". As a result, he says, multilateralism is "a highly demanding institutional form".[5]

This demanding institutional form – the state-centric model of multilateralism – can be, and is, contested within this volume, especially with respect to the role of non-state actors such as civil society organizations and multinational corporations, and with respect to the importance of norms and values that constitute international society and community.

The first part of the volume revisits a number of perennial themes which are fundamental to the study of multilateralism: power, legitimacy, order, community, and decision-making processes. These chapters approach these themes in light of recent challenges to various multilateral institutions and norms. The United Nations is the global symbol and embodiment of multilateralism, and all of its promise and limitations. Shashi Tharoor's chapter, "Saving humanity from hell", gives a realistic defence of the organization in the context of the many challenges it faces. Tharoor acknowledges that the Iraq war – without clear Security Council authorization – has led some to evoke a parallel to the League of Nations, but argues that the comparisons are grossly overstated. His main argument is that we live neither in a purely Hobbesian world of anarchy and unconstrained power politics, nor a Kantian world of peace and harmony. But one thing is for sure: the United Nations was not created by naive Kantians; it was established as a progressive response to a Hobbesian world. The United Nations, at its best, is a mirror of the world: it reflects our divisions and disagreements as well as our hopes and convictions. Tharoor observes that the United Nations is both a stage and an actor. It is a stage on which the Member States play their parts, declaiming their differences and their convergences, and it is an actor executing the policies made on that stage. The UN's record of success and failure is better than many national institutions; yet somehow, it is only the United Nations that is apparently expected to succeed all the time.

As Dag Hammarskjöld, the UN's great second Secretary-General, put it, the United Nations was not created to take humanity to heaven, but to save it from hell. During the Cold War, the United Nations played the indispensable role of preventing regional crises and conflicts from igniting a superpower conflagration. Its peacekeeping operations make the difference between life and death for many around the world. And despite the fact that the war against Iraq was pursued without clear UN authorization, the UN was firmly involved in Iraq after the war. Moreover, the innumerable "problems without passports" – problems that cross all frontiers uninvited such as weapons of mass destruction, terrorism, the environment, contagious disease, human rights – make the organization as indispensable as ever.

Emanuel Adler's chapter, "Communitarian multilateralism", problematizes what he describes as "classic forms of universal intergovernmental multilateralism". He suggests that these have been under challenge not only by global hegemonic pressures, but also by underlying structural forces that include the weakening of sovereignty, the growing global role of non-state actors and policy networks, and the transferring of liberal practices and institutions from national to international and transnational spheres. In an attempt to cope with these challenges, multilateralism has been transforming itself and taking new forms.

Adler forwards two propositions: that institutions evolve together with collective epistemic understandings, and that constructivist International Relations theory helps us to understand new, viable forms of multilateralism. On the basis of this, he presents a novel conceptual model, namely, "communitarian multilateralism", which he suggests is thriving. This relies on communitarian practices of collective-identity formation that depend not only on material power, but also on collective epistemic understandings. It involves institutionalized efforts to socially construct multilateral communities of practice amongst like-minded actors which engage in the same practice – for example, security communities. Adler cautions, however, that communitarian multilateralism is unlikely to contribute to global governance because its practices are inherently exclusive.

Robert O. Keohane's chapter, "The contingent legitimacy of multilateralism", questions the presumption which underscores multilateral action –

that agreement by states, according to institutionalized rules, guarantees legitimacy. That presumption, he argues, is a construction of the twentieth century which is becoming increasingly problematic because it is at odds with normative democratic theory. His chapter divides the sources of organizational legitimacy into "output" and "input" legitimacy. Outputs refer to the achievement of the substantive purposes of the organization, such as security or welfare. Inputs refer to the processes by which decisions are reached – whether they have certain attributes regarded as important. Keohane argues that by the standards of both input and output legitimacy, the values and institutions of multilateralism are deficient because they do not reflect democratic values and their performance is questionable. During the twentieth century these deficiencies were not debilitating, since multilateral regimes constituted a supplement to traditional interstate relations, not a substitute for them. However, the reach of international organizations has become so penetrating that this deficiency is now glaring.

From this basis, Keohane contends that an institution has a valid claim to make legitimate policy on a global basis only if it meets three standards: of inclusiveness, decisiveness and epistemic reliability. All valid interests must be represented effectively; the multilateral organization must be able to take effective action, even against the opposition of its strongest member state; and the decision-making process must be sufficiently transparent that it is open to criticism from outsiders as well as insiders. According to these criteria, he claims that the United Nations does not reach satisfactory standards of legitimacy, and that contemporary multilateral institutions such as the UN are contingently legitimate, relative to the currently available alternatives, which are quite unattractive. But their advocates, and their leaders, should begin to reconstruct their legitimacy on a twenty-first century basis – with more emphasis on democratic principles and less on sovereignty.

Coral Bell's chapter, "Power and world order", also rests upon a disharmony at the heart of international relations. She considers how consensus can be built and maintained between the contemporary great powers and revisionist actors which do not see their interests met in the existing world establishment. She asks: What degree of cooperation can be devised to manage the transnational groups or forces which threaten the established order? Can contemporary international institutions be modified to serve those objectives more adequately? The archetypical challenge, Bell suggests, is that of the jihadist networks. What is necessary is a conflict-limiting concert of powers under US leadership, to avoid a complex and dangerous multipolar balance of power that current forms of multilateralism will be incapable of forestalling.

Amitav Acharya's contribution, "Multilateralism, sovereignty and normative change in world politics'', gives great significance to multilateralism in international relations and international order. His chapter examines the role of multilateralism in fostering and managing normative change in world politics, with specific regard to the fundamental norms of state sovereignty. He argues that post-war multilateralism helped to define, extend, embed and legitimize a set of sovereignty norms, including territorial integrity, equality of states and nonintervention. Indeed, the post-war international order would not have been so tightly and universally built upon the norms of sovereignty without multilateralism. Moreover, as the normative order evolves, multilateralism is essential to prevent instability and conflict. Acharya thus argues that multilateralism plays a key role in promoting and facilitating normative change. However, multilateral institutions are under increasing pressure to move beyond some of these very same principles, especially nonintervention, as a part of a transformative process in world politics. Multilateralism is particularly important today because of increased global and regional economic interdependence, the emergence of new transnational challenges, major systemic changes affecting the global distribution of power, domestic change and democratization, and the expansion of global civil society. Acharya concludes that multilateral institutions, whatever their weaknesses, can make fundamental transformations legitimate and peaceful.

Perhaps the most significant factor which conditions the nature and potential of multilateralism in international relations is that of power, in all its forms. Stefano Guzzini's chapter considers the claim, popular after the Cold War, that the decline of multilateralism is a logical outcome of the present distribution of international power, and specifically US power. Guzzini provides a critique of the idea that the distribution of international power (generally now conceived of as unipolar) determines the nature of US foreign policy (unilateralism) and that American unilateralism is inherently antithetical to international multilateralism. Relative superiority in power and hegemony do not necessarily determine policy towards multilateral institutions. Indeed, whilst today many observers suggest that pre-eminent US power is enabling – or perhaps motivating – the country to ignore or undermine institutions, in the past theorists of international relations argued on the contrary that *declining* power resulted in declining support for multilateral institutions and regimes. Guzzini considers the idea that the distribution of power – and ideas of unipolarity – at the turn of the century is somehow unique, and argues that this is analytically problematic. Indeed, we have no objective measure of power. Moreover, the distribution of power resources does not determinate outcomes, and so unprecedented preponderance is not a direct cause of unilateralism. Thus, Guzzini concludes, it is the neoconservative policy of

US unilateralism – bringing with it a certain understanding of power and unipolarity – which explains the policy of the US towards multilateral institutions. It is not a systemic inevitability.

Friedrich Kratochwil, in "The genealogy of multilateralism: reflections on an organizational form and its crisis", considers the definition and scope of multilateralism, and seeks to develop criteria of assessment that might distinguish a "challenge" to multilateralism from a "crisis". The distinction between these two is difficult to establish. Nevertheless, Kratochwil suggests that there is a crisis, and it is not limited to the tendencies of the United States or other powers to fall back on unilateral measures or the challenge posed by "coalitions of the willing" which might circumvent established multilateral arrangements. He argues that the crisis has deeper roots, as the concept of sovereignty has been challenged by non-state actors, such as terrorists, warlords, or even the more constructive elements of "civil society".

In contrast, Edward Newman's chapter, "Multilateral crises in historical perspective", argues that analysts have been too quick to conclude that specific international organizations or multilateralism more generally are in crisis or fundamentally flawed. The current sense of "crisis", at the beginning of the twenty-first century, is shared by analysts of different ideological and theoretical predispositions, and seems to be a "truly" historical turning point. But how do we know? Newman's chapter considers whether such a judgement can be based upon a rigorous methodology, and argues that a more systematic approach to the idea of a "crisis of multilateralism" is necessary in order to put the current challenges facing multilateralism in their proper context. He does this by considering the historical perspective and recalling the sources and manifestations of earlier "crises", and then attempts to construct a framework that may assist in distinguishing a multilateral crisis from "politics as usual".

A second set of chapters explores specific issue areas: weapons of mass destruction, international humanitarianism, human rights, the natural environment, international peace and security, terrorism, civil wars, and the use of force for human protection. These chapters analyse the nature and extent to which the limitations of multilateralism are demonstrated in each issue area. They consider the ways in which these limitations are related to changes in structural factors – such as state sovereignty, the impact and significance of non-state actors, international norms, the distribution of power at the international level, and the nature of security challenges. These chapters also attempt to consider, in each issue area, how the values and institutions of multilateralism might be reformed in order to better meet contemporary realities and needs.

K. J. Holsti surveys a broad range of conflict and security challenges in "Something old, something new: theoretical perspectives on contemporary international peace and security". His analysis combines the "classical" inter-state security problems that emerge from a system of sovereign states in a condition of anarchy, with newer threats emerging from the weakness and breakdown of states and the rise of private armed groups and quasi-religious movements. Holsti argues that the occasional defection of the United States from the majority does not mean that multilateral diplomacy has come to an end. The concern is not so much a United States that acts unilaterally as opposed to multilaterally, but one that takes actions inconsistent with many of the objectives sought by the rest of the international community, one that proclaims rights and actions for itself while denying them to others, one that actually exacerbates the problems it is trying to remedy, and one that manufactures threats.

According to many observers, one of the most critical deficiencies of multilateralism relates to weapons of mass destruction, and the acrimony at the review conference for the Nuclear Non-Proliferation Treaty in 2005 was symptomatic of this. Trevor Findlay's chapter addresses the strains under which multilateral approaches to weapons of mass destruction are currently operating. He argues that the pivotal player in this field is the United States, and the neoconservative agenda has been particularly unilateralist and obstructionist in respect of multilateral activity pertaining to WMD. However, he suggests that it would be wrong to assume that the Bush administration is solely responsible for the malaise that currently faces much multilateral endeavour in the WMD realm, and it is therefore necessary to understand the deeper roots of the problem, both the long-term structural and the short-term circumstantial. In addition to the emergence of a unipolar world and the shock-waves of the September 11th attacks, there is evidence of a general problem in multilateral negotiations on WMD issues that has been building for some years, although compounded by recent events. This is due to both structural flaws and a growing dysfunctionality in the multilateral negotiating machinery. However, Findlay does argue that, despite the deficiencies, there have been successes in multilateral monitoring, verification and implementation bodies.

A further issue which has brought the principles and performance of multilateralism into question in recent years is humanitarian assistance, and this is addressed by David P. Forsythe in his chapter "International humanitarianism in the contemporary world: forms and issues". He approaches this challenge within the conceptual dichotomy of nationalism and cosmopolitanism. Forsythe argues that, within this framework, an emerging trend is to redefine state sovereignty not as an elite privilege and a barrier against foreign scrutiny, but as the responsibility to protect human dignity. His central question is whether humanitarianism in the world today, which is inherently multilateral because of the size of the problems and the vast array of actors involved, can be made effective, particularly with attention to the needs of victims. Focusing on the UN system and Red Cross network, Forsythe concludes that the ICRC represents the international standard for independent, neutral and impartial humanitarianism. UN relief agencies like the UNHCR and UNICEF, as well as the UN Emergency Relief Coordinator, may aspire to those same core values that the ICRC represents, but since they are part of an intergovernmental system they are not able to match the ICRC standards. Ultimately, states control the UNHCR and UNICEF, or any other UN agency. States always have national interests, however subjectively and even erroneously constructed, and they cannot help but project those interests into their foreign policies at the United Nations. Thus, the inherent structure of the international system precludes a truly cosmopolitan approach to humanitarianism, and rigorously impartial and consistent humanitarian relief through the United Nations is rare.

One issue area in which there has been broad criticism of multilateral institutions in recent years is human rights. Richard J. Goldstone and Erin P. Kelly explore the crisis of legitimacy which characterizes human rights multilateralism in "Progress and problems in the multilateral human rights regime". They consider if the human rights regime is fundamentally at odds with the principle of sovereignty and statehood, upon which the multilateral system is built. In so doing, they describe the historical and doctrinal foundations of human rights law, and then consider a series of institutional challenges to the regime. The human rights regime has achieved success in establishing the legal foundation for human rights and creating certain enforcement mechanisms. Nevertheless, they argue that the most threatening challenges to the long-term viability of the human rights regime relate to massive human rights violations committed in failed states and in the context of civil armed conflict.

The record of multilateral institutions in addressing environmental challenges is explored by Joyeeta Gupta. She argues that environmental multilateralism is under challenge in eight ways: the non-participation of hegemons and particularly the United States in key environmental regimes; the nature of public goods and free riding; a lack of good governance at the national level; the weakening role of the state; the rising role of non-state actors; the general capacity problems of developing countries; the rise of hybrid relationships; and the rise of bilateralism.

Gwyn Prins, in his chapter "AIDS, power, culture and multilateralism", similarly argues that multilateral approaches to addressing HIV/AIDS are fundamentally limited. He considers if "new threats", such as HIV/AIDS, by their nature bring into question the viability of multilateralism, and argues that the evidence points in rather unexpected directions. Indeed, he suggests that we are not witnessing traditional state-centric multilateralism being undermined by a unilateralist hegemon; rather we see multilateral opportunities being eroded in spitefulness to the USA by countries which claim to promote multilateralism. Moreover, the USA, via its science and pharmaceutical establishments, its statistical arm (the US Bureau of Census) and its specific funding initiative (the President's Emergency Plan for AIDS Relief), is the prime positive actor. Prins also argues that the pandemic has been allowed to become worse than it might have been by the unwillingness of the state-centric international community to challenge the dangerous exercise of sovereign power – including the self-restraint that "political correctness" imposes on criticism of postcolonial, especially African, rulers and states. Specific obstacles to multilateral progress are, according to Prins, intellectual property rights and market-driven constraints.

Terrorism, too, is an issue area with which existing multilateral institutions have been brought into question. Edward C. Luck's chapter, "The uninvited challenge: Terrorism targets the United Nations", suggests that the UN's response to terrorism has been tentative and even ambivalent, but also in some respects positive. He considers various explanations for this related to geopolitics, US leadership, ambivalence about American power, and constraints imposed by the UN Charter and international law.

To many states, including US allies, the way the Bush administration has framed "the war on terrorism" reflects an over-emphasis on the coercive and military dimensions of what should be a more subtle and multifaceted campaign. At the same time, the US has envisioned only a limited place for the UN in the global struggle against terrorism. In that regard, its view of what the UN can and should contribute is similar to that of other capitals, few of which would want the UN to attempt to play the lead role. Given its chequered history, the UN has come a long way toward embracing the struggle against terrorism. More could be done to integrate and streamline its efforts, but the results would not be measured in great leaps forward. There are real institutional and political limits to what the UN can or should do in this area, regardless of American attitudes and policies. The challenge for the UN is to do the best it can within its circumscribed sphere of action, one that is bound to be more normative than operational.

John Tirman's chapter, "Civil wars, globalization, and the 'Washington Consensus'", adopts a critical approach with reference to the possible links between international organizations and armed conflict. He considers the relationship between civil wars and economic and political globalization, in light of the evidence that many contemporary civil wars are rooted in social and economic factors. He argues that both economic and political globalization are promoted and enabled by multilateral institutions. Therefore, incidences of instability and organized violence linked to social and economic factors in market-based countries raise troubling questions for multilateralism. The rules of international organizations are shaped by powerful states in their own interest, and imposed on weak states that may have different needs and interests, often with negative results for many of these smaller actors. In the push for open markets and bureaucratic accountability, multilateral institutions such the International Monetary Fund and the World Bank have insisted on certain economic and political reforms in developing countries, reforms that may in fact have induced instabilities that are conducive to civil war. If this is borne out, it would be doubly problematic for multilateralism.

The record of multilateralism in giving protection to civilians in extreme danger and preventing or responding to widespread human rights abuse is not impressive. Thomas G. Weiss's chapter, "Using military force for human protection: What next?", considers the potential and constraints of multilateralism concerning humanitarian intervention. His analysis is not at all hopeful: state sovereignty, the pre-eminence of power politics, and the reality of US power all prevent progress on this issue, and multilateral institutions are simply unable to provide human protection in many critical situations. Weiss argues that the "humanitarian intervention fashion" of the 1990s now seems like ancient history, even with the endorsement of the "Responsibility to Protect" in the Secretary-General's 2005 report "In Larger Freedom" and the 2005 United Nations Summit Outcome report.[6] The idea that human beings matter more than sovereignty seemed, albeit briefly, to figure in international relations until the wars on terrorism and Iraq. These current obsessions, both in the United Nations and in the United States, suggest that the political will for humanitarian intervention has evaporated. According to Weiss, the US is the preponderant power, and its inclination to commit significant political and military resources for human protection has faded, while other states complain but do little.

The next two chapters consider how other issues – in particular international social movements and economic justice – raise a significant challenge to the way in which contemporary multilateralism is constituted. Many analysts have observed that multilateral intergovernmental institutions have failed to be accountable and transparent – democratic values that are now integral to good governance in the domestic context – and that this is a part of their weakness. Jackie Smith's chapter, "Social movements and multilateralism", considers this democratic deficit alongside the rise of non-governmental associations. She investigates the rise of a "regressive" and unilateralist model of globalization following the 11 September attacks on the US, and connected to this, the ambivalence of contemporary social movements to multilateral institutions, and anti-democratic responses by governments and UN agencies to these developments. She suggests that efforts to strengthen multilateral institutions are inseparable from attempts to democratize the global system. Social movements were central to the democratization of emerging nation states, and they have played key roles in promoting multilateralism as well.

However, Smith observes that three contemporary trends threaten the mutually supportive relations between social movements and international organizations. First, although global civil society is much stronger than it was in the past, more recent "generations" of activists are less likely to support multilateral institutions. Second, the US-led "war on terror" and unilateralism encourages militant fundamentalism while undermining advocates of more democratic global governance. Third, an anti-democratic backlash, characterized by more militant policing of protests and by restrictions on civil society participation in multilateral institutions, threatens to further polarize both national and international societies. To ensure the survival of both democracy and multilateralism, Smith argues that we must find ways to reverse policies that contribute to the exclusion of less powerful groups from economic and political life.

Sirkku K. Hellsten's chapter deals with "Multilateralism and economic justice". She discusses if and how economic justice can be realized today when a large part of trade and economic relations are handled by private non-state agencies rather than by governments which have traditionally been the formal parties to the multilateral agreements. Secondly, her chapter analyses how civil society organizations and other networks now enforce ethical dimensions of international cooperation by challenging multilateral institutions on normative grounds. Her main argument is that, while the traditional forms of multilateral state collaboration have lost much of their credibility due to the global democratic deficit and due to the weakening of the role of national governments in world politics, multilateralism can still offer a firm basis for international cooperation. However, this requires that the existing multilateral institutions negotiate common values and open a dialogue on both political as well as the social dimensions and goals of globalization and international cooperation in which civil society and developing countries have a chance to get their voice heard and their concerns taken into account. If multilateral cooperation wants to regain its credibility, it has to bring questions of ethics and justice back to the agenda of international negotiations.

In the related area of trade, Beth A. Simmons argues in her chapter that multilateralism has been crucial to an increased international flow of goods and services over the past century. It has also been central to the incorporation of developing countries and non-market "transition" countries into the global trading system, and in managing the changing structural economic balance of power – in particular, the rise of Asia's major economies. In contrast to many of the other contributors to this volume, Simmons demonstrates how multilateralism can work effectively in changing circumstances. In fact, she concludes that the GATT/WTO regime could hardly be more robust, yet flexible, as a mode of rule development. Moreover, the system has also coincided with the most remarkable improvements in human material well-being ever documented.

The "crisis" of multilateralism is seen more clearly at the global level, and not necessarily in the regional context, where cooperation in many areas is deepening and thriving. To explore these different experiences, chapters on Europe, Latin America and East Asia consider regional perspectives and processes: whether and how they differ from global norms and institutions. These three contributions ask, for example, if it is possible to think of regions as a counter-weight to global hegemonic forces.

Europe is important in all of these respects, and A.J.R. Groom explores this in his chapter on "Multilateralism as a way of life in Europe". He claims that, despite the constitutional crisis and the budget problems in the first half of 2005, the idea of "multilateralism under challenge" is rather alien to Europe. Multilateralism is seen as a way of life because it is the means by which Europeans have tried, with a considerable degree of success, to reconcile togetherness and diversity. Moreover, Groom argues that multilateralism is so much a part of the way of thinking that there is no strong conception of a unipolar international system. In addition, the notion of multilateralism as being state-centric does not fit with the experience of many Europeans. This is because Europe is now encompassed by systems of multilateral and multilevel governance in which the role of civil society is an integral part. Groom demonstrates this with reference to four processes: the EU is building towards the joint management of pooled sovereignty; it is building down towards the regions which are displaying a greater degree of autonomy and innovation; it is strongly involved in civil society by building transnational ties, such as in higher education; and finally it is building beyond, not only at the governmental level but also at the level of civil society. Whilst the EU has its internal difficulties and there are tensions between the European project and the US vision of global order, this should not detract from the inherently multilateral nature of European politics.

Jorge Heine, is his chapter "Between a rock and a hard place: Latin America and multilateralism after 9/11", similarly demonstrates how multilateralism is fundamentally important in that region of the world. As mostly small or middle-sized powers in a region traditionally at the margins of the main conflicts in world politics, Latin America has historically placed a premium on a regulated international order, one that will protect the interests of smaller nations, rather than leaving them at the mercy of great powers. The region is the source of innovation in international law, and has shown commitment to the lawful resolution of disputes. Partly as a result of that, Latin America is the region with the lowest number of interstate conflicts and the lowest defence expenditures. Countries in the region have drawn strength from numbers and from their participation in international organizations. Yet the close relationship of many Latin American countries with – and dependence upon – the US has put regional multilateral instincts under some strain in recent years.

Quansheng Zhao's contribution, "From economic to security multilateralism: Great powers and international order in the Asia Pacific", focuses on a region which is characterized by having relatively little institutionalized multilateralism. Nevertheless, Zhao suggests that there is a general trend from bilateral to multilateral cooperation. This development first took place in the economic sphere, and only recently has begun to move toward the security dimension. Zhao's central argument is that, with the shift of power distribution and the new dynamics in the region, increasing attention has been paid to institutional change and multilateral frameworks as a new means for international order. Whilst there are major obstacles to overcome, economic integration may further reduce mistrust in the region and lay a solid foundation for security cooperation.

Overall, the contributors consider the fundamental issues which must be raised in order to understand how multilateralism can better respond to contemporary needs. Is the multilateral "moment", as expressed in the period after the Second World War and affirmed occasionally since, essentially over, or changed in some fundamental way? An overarching conclusion that is supported by most of these chapters is that the fundamental *principle* of multilateralism, with all its limitations, is not in crisis. Indeed, this principle is validated and vindicated by the demands of the contemporary world. However, the values and institutions of multilateralism *as currently constituted* are arguably under serious challenge. The challenge concerns both "input" and "output" legitimacy: how decisions are made and how interests are represented in multilateral organizations, and how well multilateral organizations perform according to their specific missions. The challenge to multilateralism, as nearly all contributors note, is rooted in the challenge to the state and state sovereignty in a world that frequently transcends (or ignores) borders in practice and in principle.

Notes

1. United Nations Press Release, "Secretary-General names high-level panel to study global security and reform of the international system", New York, UN Office of Public Affairs, 4 November 2003.

2. "A more secure world: our shared responsibility", Report of the Secretary-General's High-level Panel on Threats, Challenges and Change, Report of the Secretary-General to the General Assembly, A/59/565, 2 December 2004, p. 14.
3. Robert O. Keohane (1994) "International institutions: two approaches", in Friedrich Kratochwil and Edward D. Mansfield, *International Organization: A Reader*, New York: Harper Collins, pp. 48–49.
4. John Gerard Ruggie (1993) "Multilateralism: The anatomy of an institution", in John Gerard Ruggie (ed.) *Multilateralism Matters: The Theory and Praxis of an Institutional Form*, New York: Columbia University Press, p. 11.
5. John Gerard Ruggie (1993) "Multilateralism: The anatomy of an institution", in John Gerard Ruggie (ed.) *Multilateralism Matters*, pp. 10–12.
6. United Nations Secretary-General (2005) *In Larger Freedom: Towards Development, Security and Human Rights for All*, New York, 21 March 2005; 2005 World Summit Outcome (Draft resolution referred to the High-level Plenary Meeting of the General Assembly by the General Assembly at its fifty-ninth session), 20 September 2005.

Part I

Themes

2

Saving humanity from hell

Shashi Tharoor

In March 2003, as the debates were raging in the Security Council over Iraq, a BBC interviewer rather glibly asked me, "So how does the UN feel about being seen as the 'I' word? Irrelevant?" He was about to go on when I interrupted him: "As far as we are concerned", I retorted, "the 'I' word is 'indispensable'."

It was not just a debating point. Those of us who toil every day at the Headquarters of the United Nations – and even more our colleagues on the front lines in the field – have become a little exasperated at seeing our institutional obituaries in the press. The contretemps over Iraq has led some to evoke a parallel to the League of Nations, a body created with great hopes at the end of the First World War, which was reduced to debating the standardization of European railway gauges the day the Germans marched into Poland. Such comparisons are, to say the least, grossly overstated. As Mark Twain put it when he saw his own obituary in the newspaper, reports of the UN's demise are exaggerated.

And yet we live with a paradox. A Pew Poll taken in 20 countries in mid-2003 showed that the UN had suffered a great deal of collateral damage over Iraq. The UN's credibility was down in the US because it did not support the US Administration on the war, and in 19 other countries because it did not prevent the war. The equivalent polls the following year showed the UN's standing at its lowest ever. Kofi Annan spoke, in 2004, of the world being at a "fork in the road".

In 2005, the UN turned 60. In the UN system, 60 is the age at which we contemplate retirement. Is the UN ready to be pensioned off? On the contrary, we are seizing this occasion to contemplate renewal, not retirement.

Indeed, the 2005 UN agenda was dominated by discussion of wide-ranging proposals for renewal, some suggested by the Secretary-General's High-Level Panel on Threats, Challenges and Change,[1] and others by the Secretary-General himself in his report *In Larger Freedom.*[2] These proposals aimed to update the international architecture built up since 1945, to equip the international system to face the challenges of the twenty-first century. They formed the basis for discussions among Member States at the World Summit of September 2005. And while Member States are yet to agree on several important issues, real progress was made at the Summit – and change is on the way. The UN's 60th Anniversary year was a crucial one in determining which route the world will take. And following the Summit, we are all navigating from the same map.

On the principle that the best crystal ball is a rear-view mirror, it is important to recall that the United Nations was founded during a period when the world had known almost nothing but war and strife, bookended by two savage World Wars that began within 25 years of each other. Horror succeeded horror, until, in 1945, the world was brought face to face with the terrible tragedies wrought by war, fascism, genocide and nuclear bombing. The second half of the twentieth century, though far from perfect, was a spectacular improvement on the first half, for one simple reason: because, in and after 1945, a group of far-sighted leaders drew up rules to govern international behaviour, founding institutions in which different nations could cooperate, under universally applicable rules, for the common good.

The keystone of the arch, so to speak – charged with helping keep the peace between all nations and bringing them all together in the quest for freedom and prosperity – was the United Nations itself. The UN was seen by visionaries like former US President Franklin Delano Roosevelt as the only possible alternative to the disastrous experiences of the first half of the century. As he stated in his historic speech to the two US Houses of Congress after the Yalta Conference, the UN would be the alternative to the arms races, military alliances, balance-of-power politics and all the arrangements that had led to war so often in the past.

Roosevelt's successor, President Harry Truman, put it clearly: "You have created a great instrument for peace and security and human progress in the world", he declared to the assembled signatories of the United Nations Charter in San Francisco on 26 June 1945. "If we fail to use it, we shall betray all those who have died in order that we might meet here in freedom and safety to create it. If we seek to use it selfishly – for the advantage of any one nation or any small group of nations – we shall be equally guilty of that betrayal."[3]

That was then, of course, and this – 59 years later – is now. How many of today's critics of the United Nations would recognize the voice of an American president in Truman's speech that historic day? "We all have to recognize," he declared, "no matter how great our strength, that we must deny ourselves the license to do always as we please. No one nation ... can or should expect any special privilege which harms any other nation ... Unless we are all willing to pay that price, no organization for world peace can accomplish its purpose. And what a reasonable price that is!"[4] Of course, such ideals were expressed by hard-headed realists, including the US president who would, six weeks later, drop an atom bomb on a Japanese city. But the ideals of the UN's founding fathers had been shaped in the crucible of a tormented half-century. As realists, they had seen both the horrors and the limitations of military power: the rules underpinning the UN were the only realistic alternative.

I suspect that there are many in Washington today who would not agree that this is indeed a reasonable price for the world's only superpower to pay in the interests of something as amorphous as "world peace", especially in an era of terrorism. It is in the United States, above all, that the organization has suffered most. Perhaps part of the problem lies in the fundamental American critique of the place of the United Nations in today's world. The notion has gained ground of late, particularly in the wake of Robert Kagan's *Of Paradise and Power*, that the elemental issue in world affairs today is the incompatibility of the American and "European" diagnoses of our contemporary geopolitical condition.

In this view, the US sees a Hobbesian world, rife with menace and disorder, that requires the imposition of order and stability by a Leviathan, while Europe (and much of the rest of the world) imagines a Kantian world of peace and rationality which can be managed by reasonable-minded leaders coming to sensible arrangements through institutions like the United Nations. Since the latter view is a fantasy, such analysts suggest, the institutions underpinning it are equally impractical and ineffectual. In the real world, a Hobbesian Leviathan could not possibly function if it were to be tied down by a system of rules designed to serve smaller states: it would be a Gulliver restrained by, in Charles Krauthammer's words, the "myriad strings" of the Lilliputians "that diminish his overweening power".[5] Hence the answer lies in disregarding the United Nations and, as Michael J. Glennon has argued in *Foreign Affairs*, restoring might to its rightful place in world affairs.[6]

There are many flaws in this argument, but the key one lies in its central premise. For the United Nations was not created by starry-eyed

Kantians; it was established as a response to a Hobbesian world. The UN Charter was the work of the victorious Allies of the Second World War converting their wartime alliance into a peacetime organization.

They saw the Hobbesian world of the preceding three decades, which had inflicted upon humanity two savage world wars, several brutal civil wars, the atrocities perpetrated by totalitarianism and the horrors of the Holocaust and Hiroshima, and vowed "never again". But the Leviathan imagined by the visionary statesmen of that era (notably FDR himself) was not a single power; it was a system of laws that would ensure that the world of the second half of the twentieth century would be a better place than the one that had barely survived the first half.

So great was the perceived American stake in such a system that the US became its principal financial contributor, paying as much as 50 per cent of the United Nations' regular budget in the first years of the organization (a figure astonishing to recall at a time when so much American diplomatic energy was recently invested in reducing its current share from 25 per cent to 22 per cent). Gulliver was to lead the Lilliputians, not feel tied down by them; they provided him with a springboard, not a rack.

So what has gone wrong? It might be useful to confront the misgivings of the sceptics on their own terms. Some portray a UN that passed resolutions but could not agree to implement them, and ask if the Iraq war didn't prove that the US and the UK could not do without the United Nations altogether. Not so: despite the infructuous debates of 2003, the US is firmly back at the UN on Iraq. It came to the Security Council immediately after the war was over, to seek the international community's blessing for the occupation. In May 2003, the Security Council unanimously adopted resolution 1483 (a number redolent of the year of the Battle of Bosworth Field, in which Henry Tudor found the crown of England lying in a ditch) which called on the Secretary-General to establish a Special Representative to assist the people of Iraq – to act independently but also in "coordination" with the CPA. In August 2003, it passed resolution 1500, giving the United Nations significant tasks in post-war reconstruction.

The very submission of these resolutions by the US to the Security Council was an acknowledgement by Washington that there is, in Secretary-General Kofi Annan's words, no substitute for the unique legitimacy provided by the United Nations. Without Resolution 1483, the US-led coalition could not have sold a single drop of Iraqi oil. There would have been nothing to prevent, say, a Russian company from filing suit at the International Court of Arbitration in Paris, saying they had a prior contract on that oil with the legal Government of Iraq, that of Saddam Hussein. It was the Security Council resolution that allowed the new authorities in Iraq to conduct normal commerce. And the acceptance of the two resolutions by other Council Members – even those who led the opposition to the US intervention – demonstrated their understanding of the importance of collective action. The tragedy of 19 August 2003, when we lost 22 of our most valued colleagues in a suicide bombing of the United Nations building in Baghdad, set back our ability to fulfil the tasks given to us. But the UN was back in Iraq in 2004, despite continuing fears about the deteriorating security environment, which have constrained the size and the scope of the UN mission.

Indeed, the key message of President Bush's appearance before the UN General Assembly in September 2002 should not be forgotten. In calling on the Security Council to take action against Iraq, he framed the problem not as one of unilateral US wishes but as an issue of the implementation of United Nations Security Council resolutions. The UN and the earlier decisions of its Security Council remained at the heart of the US case against Iraq.

The second flaw in the argument – that the UN is doomed to failure – is that the League of Nations analogy simply does not apply. By the late 1930s, two of the three most powerful countries in the world at the time – the United States and Germany (the third being Great Britain) – did not belong to the League, which therefore had no influence on their actions. The League died because it had become truly irrelevant to the global geopolitics of the era.

By contrast, every country on earth belongs to the UN, including the world's only superpower, the United States. Every newly-independent state seeks entry almost as its first order of governmental business; its seat at the UN is the most fundamental confirmation of its membership in the comity of nations. The United Nations is now seen as so essential to the future of the world that Switzerland, long a holdout because of its fierce neutrality, decided by referendum in 2002 to end its isolation and join. No club that attracts every eligible member can easily be described as irrelevant.

Third, the authorization (or not) of war in Iraq is not the only gauge of the United Nations' relevance. Just five years ago, the NATO alliance bombed Yugoslavia over its government's conduct in Kosovo, without the approval of, or even reference to, the Security Council. My interviewer's "I" word was heard widely in those days – Kosovo, it was said, had demonstrated the UN's irrelevance.

But the issue of Kosovo returned to the Security Council when arrangements had to be found to administer the territory after the war. Only the Security Council could confer international legitimacy on these arrangements and encourage all nations to extend support and resources to the enterprise. And only one body could be entrusted with the responsibility to run the civilian administration of Kosovo: the United Nations. Whatever the tasks the UN ultimately takes on in a post-war Iraq, it is important to remember that this would not be the first time the United Nations was written off during a war, only to be found essential to the ensuing peace.

The UN offers a legitimacy that no ad hoc coalition can muster for itself. It has been suggested that "coalitions of the willing" can provide the answer, and that there is no need for the formal structures of the United Nations – that Americans might do with "multilateralism à la carte" rather than "multilateralism *à la Charte*". But ad hoc coalitions do require structures: they often need the carapace of an enabling United Nations resolution. Washington's efforts to broaden the support base for its forces in Iraq to include potential troop contributors like India and Pakistan have run up against the preference of those countries to deploy under a UN umbrella and under UN command. International institutions provide potential coalition partners the framework within which they can feel empowered on (at least notionally) equal terms. The difference between a UN operation in which everyone wears blue helmets and a "coalition of the willing" led by one big power is that between a police squad and a posse. Posses can be effective, but police squads have uniforms, salaries and the authority of the law behind them, not just that of the sheriff. The governments which declined a US request to participate militarily in Iraq because they needed the protective shield of a UN mandate underscored this message. Many other countries, in Europe as well as Asia, require UN resolutions before they commit troops abroad.

In any case, Washington has discovered in Iraq that the US is better able to win wars alone than to construct peace: military strength has its limitations in the area of nation-building (as Talleyrand said, the one thing you cannot do with a bayonet is to sit on it). It was not surprising, therefore, that the US-led coalition turned to the UN at various crucial points in Iraq. The first was in January 2004, when a transition of sovereignty was being planned, and a series of missions led by Lakhdar Brahimi – who was able to speak with sections of the Iraqi political class that would not deal with the Coalition – midwived the birth of the new Iraqi transitional government which assumed sovereign responsibility in Baghdad in June. In July, a small team of UN experts worked to create the conditions for a successful outcome to the rescheduled national conference. Another served in Baghdad throughout 2004, helping the authorities draft and pass an electoral law and set up an independent electoral commission to oversee the nationwide elections planned in January 2005.

But whatever happens in Iraq, let us also not forget that the relevance of the United Nations does not stand or fall on its conduct on one issue alone. Even while they were disagreeing on Iraq, the Members of the Security Council were agreeing, at the very same time, on a host of other vital issues, from Congo to Côte d'Ivoire, from Cyprus to Afghanistan. Let us not distort the record by seeing the UN's work on international peace and security only through the prism of one issue, Iraq.

And no, it is not perfect. It has acted unwisely at times, and failed to act at others: one need only think of the "safe areas" in Bosnia and the genocide in Rwanda for instances of each. It has sometimes been too divided to succeed, as was the case with Iraq. And all too often, UN member states have passed resolutions they themselves had no intention of implementing.

But the United Nations, at its best and at its worst, is a mirror of the world: it reflects our divisions and disagreements as well as our hopes and convictions. It is folly to discredit an entire institution for the disagreements of its members; one would not scrap the US Senate (or even the House of Lords) because one bill failed to pass.

It is often forgotten that the United Nations is both a stage and an actor. It is a stage on which the Member States play their parts, declaiming their differences and their convergences, and it is an actor (particularly in the form of the Secretary-General, his staff, agencies, and operations) executing the policies made on that stage. The general public usually fails to see this distinction; to most people "the UN" is a shapeless aggregation, in which the sins of omission or commission of individual governments on the "stage" are routinely blamed on the Organization (and so discredit the "actor"). When government officials blame the United Nations for failing to prevent genocide in Rwanda, overlooking the Member States' own role in ensuring that the Security Council took no action on that issue, the point could not be clearer. Of course, one of the more unpleasant, if convenient, uses to which the United Nations has regularly been put has been to serve as a pliant scapegoat for the failures of its member states. Kofi Annan has often joked that the acronym by which he is known inside the Organization – "SG" – in fact stands for "Scape Goat".

The balance of power in this stage–actor equation rests clearly with the sovereign Member States, not with the Secretary-General. As Brian Urquhart memorably put it:

> For all his prestige, the Secretary-General has little or no power, and while he may be able to influence events, he can seldom if ever control them. It is with and through sovereign governments, which are not always responsive to the hopes and ideals which he represents, that he must deal ... The Secretary-

General is an embodiment of the hopes of mankind for international peace and justice, but when peace and justice are traduced he can seldom, if he wishes to preserve his usefulness, point the finger of judgment.[7]

The latter point underscores the limitations of the Secretary-General's authority: he knows he can accomplish little without the support of the very Member States whose inaction on one issue or another he might otherwise want to denounce. A Secretary-General cannot afford the luxury of allowing his frustration on any one issue to affect his ability to elicit cooperation from governments on a range of other issues. Kofi Annan made the point to this author when he cited the old Ghanaian proverb: "never hit a man on the head when you have your fingers between his teeth".

In some ways, however, the independence of the Secretary-General may have been easier to assert in an era of superpower contention, which provided a nimble diplomat with room for manoeuvre between the two irreconcilables, than in an era of a single dominant member of the Security Council, dubbed by some the "Permanent One". Dag Hammarskjöld, during his second term as Secretary-General, articulated for the first time the notion of an international conscience, finding in the United Nations "an opinion independent of partisan interests and dominated by the objectives [of] the Charter" which he was best placed to express and execute.[8] He did a great deal with what he called "imaginative and constructive constitutional innovations" to pursue this vision, capturing the imagination of the world with his actions over Suez, Lebanon and Laos, but also antagonizing the major powers, notably on the Congo civil war. His more cautious successors during the Cold War – U Thant, Perez de Cuellar and even Waldheim – demonstrated that a Secretary-General could fashion a useful if limited space for himself, given the failure of the political organs to function as envisaged in the Charter; but he could do so only provided he was careful enough not to antagonize either the United States or the Soviet Union (the mistake made, after all, by Trygve Lie and Hammarskjöld himself, who towards the end of his life also got on the wrong side of the French).

The curious compulsions of a single-superpower world place the Secretary-General today in a different sort of difficulty, that of successfully managing a relationship that is vital to the very survival of the Organization without seeming to mortgage his own integrity and independence to the dominant power. The insistent and public demands of the United States (or at least of some of its leaders) that the United Nations prove its utility to the Administration in Washington – demands that simply could not have been made in the same terms at the height of the Cold War – obliged Annan to maintain a paradoxical balancing act: to demonstrate his attentiveness to the priorities and preferences of the United States while at the same time seeking to convince the rest of the world's peoples that he spoke for them all. That he has, to a very great extent, pulled off this feat is a tribute to his personal qualities, as recognized in the decision of the Nobel Committee to award the 2000 Peace Prize jointly to him and the Organization. But it remains a huge challenge to be embraced by the sole superpower without being taken hostage by it, and Annan has had to plead with American audiences to understand that the Secretary-General can only be effective across the world if he "does not appear to serve the narrow interests of any one state or group of states."[9]

It is interesting to note that Hammarskjold saw the UN as serving principally the interests of its smaller Member States, and indeed predicted that that would be its future,[10] while Boutros-Ghali and Annan have found themselves heading a United Nations whose utility to its most powerful member has loomed far larger as a consideration. The Secretary-General must be conscious of the opinions of the smaller members as expressed in the General Assembly, but it is the opinions of the Permanent Five to which he must be attentive – not least in his own public pronouncements.

That said, the Member States and the Secretariat together make up the Organization, and it is their collective performance that vindicates (or discredits) the cause of multilateralism in world affairs. The UN's record of success and failure is better than many national institutions; yet somehow, it is only the United Nations that is apparently expected to succeed all the time. Sometimes it only muddles through. As Dag Hammarskjöld, the UN's great second Secretary-General, put it, the United Nations was not created to take humanity to heaven, but to save it from hell.[11] And that it has, innumerable times. During the Cold War, the United Nations played the indispensable role of preventing regional crises and conflicts from igniting a superpower conflagration. Its peacekeeping operations make the difference between life and death for millions around the world.

And yet the UN is not simply a security organization; it is not a sort of NATO for the world. When the present crisis has passed, the world will still be facing (to use Secretary-General Kofi Annan's phrase) innumerable "problems without passports" – problems that cross all frontiers uninvited. These are problems of the proliferation of weapons of mass destruction and of terrorism, certainly, but also those of the degradation of our common environment, of contagious disease and chronic starvation, of human rights and human wrongs, of mass illiteracy and massive displacement. Robert Kagan's famous, if fatuous, proposition that Americans are from Mars and Europeans are from Venus has gained wide currency these days in the US. If that is so, where are Africans from? Pluto?

The tragic confluence of AIDS, famine and drought in parts of Africa threatens more human lives than the crisis in Iraq ever did.

These are problems that no one country, however powerful, can solve on its own, and which are yet the shared responsibility of humankind. They cry out for solutions that, like the problems themselves, cross frontiers. The United Nations exists to find these solutions through the common endeavour of all states. It is the one indispensable global organization in our globalizing world.

Today, whether you are a resident of London or Lagos or Lima, it is simply not realistic to think only in terms of your own country. Global forces press in from every conceivable direction. People, goods and ideas cross borders and cover vast distances with ever greater frequency, speed and ease. We are increasingly connected through travel, trade, the Internet; what we watch, what we eat and even the games we play. What happens in South America or Southern Africa – from democratic advances to deforestation to the fight against AIDS – can affect your lives wherever you live, even in South London. And your choices there – what you buy, how you vote – can resound far away. Recent history has shown us all that the safety of people everywhere depends not only on local police forces, but also on guarding against the global spread of pollution, disease, illegal drugs and weapons of mass destruction. As someone once said about water pollution, we all live downstream.

The argument is sometimes made, especially in the United States, that the UN suffers from a legitimacy deficit because of the presence in its ranks of a number of non-democracies, and that coalitions of democracies would enjoy greater legitimacy than the Security Council itself. Apart from the fact that many of the most divisive arguments within the UN, notably over Iraq, have taken place amongst the democracies rather than between them and non-democracies, this argument misses the crucial contribution that the UN's universality makes to its legitimacy. The leading role given to the United Nations during the Asian tsunami of 2005 demonstrated yet again that the UN enjoys the support of the world's governments precisely because it does not belong to any single one of them. Whenever donors jostle for attention or national interests threaten to take centre stage, the UN is preferred because it embodies the collective interest. Many organizations must bring their expertise to bear on disasters like the Asian tsunami; only the UN is unchallenged as the coordinating authority. It is a truism that no government likes to give in, or play second fiddle, to another state. But all can serve under a common flag that represents everyone. The same American expert, adviser or aid worker is easier for a sensitive government to admit when he or she arrives as a UN official. That is the essence of what we call the "legitimacy issue". Because of its universality, the UN enjoys a standing in the eyes of the world that gives its collective actions and decisions a legitimacy that no individual government enjoys beyond its own borders. This is no mere theoretical proposition. Hard-headed realists acknowledge that international legitimacy has practical advantages. Why else did the US, flush with its victory in Iraq, return immediately to the Security Council in May 2003 to seek the approbation contained in Resolution 1483?

To deal with the reality of our interdependence, the world needs laws and norms that countries negotiate together, and agree to uphold as the "rules of the road". The "problems without passports" are those that no one country, however powerful, can solve on its own. Finding solutions to these problems requires a forum where sovereign states can come together to share burdens, address common problems and seize common opportunities. That forum is the United Nations.

Some people in the United States and elsewhere ask why the world's sole superpower needs an organization like the UN. The answer is simple: global challenges demand global solutions. One convincing example: immediately after the tragic horror of the 11 September 2001 terrorist attacks on the US the UN Security Council passed two vital resolutions which provided the international framework for the global battle against terrorism. Resolution 1373 required nations to interdict arms flows and financial transfers to suspected terrorist groups, report on the movements of terrorists, and update national legislation. Without the legal authority that comes from a UN Security Council resolution under Chapter VII of the Charter – which is binding on all Member States – the US would have been hard pressed to obtain such cooperation "retail" from 191 individual states.

The fact is that the United Nations helps establish the norms that all of us would like to see the world live by. People and nations around the globe retain the hope of strengthening the foundations of stability, and uniting around common values. The United Nations, for all its imperfections, real and perceived, has built up unique experience. It has brought humanitarian relief to millions in need, and helped people to rebuild their countries from the ruins of armed conflict. It has challenged poverty, fought apartheid, protected the rights of children, promoted decolonization and democracy and placed environmental and gender issues on the top of the world's agenda. In the name of our common humanity, we need to build on that experience. This is why I am proud to use the other "I" word – and to affirm the UN's indispensability, as the only effective instrument the world has available to confront the challenges that will remain when Iraq has passed from the headlines. And I am not alone in that assessment.

In September, some 170 heads of state and government gathered at the

UN to make decisions about proposals for change. Secretary-General Kofi Annan, whose ideas inspired the event, said in his address to the assembled dignitaries in the General Assembly Hall after the Summit, "we did not achieve everything",[12] and there are certainly several serious lacunae in the outcome document.

But for the first time ever we have a clear and unqualified condemnation – by all governments – of terrorism "in all its forms and manifestations, committed by whomever, wherever and for whatever purposes". We have a blueprint for stronger and more efficient international mechanisms to support and protect human rights; acceptance by every country of a collective international responsibility to protect populations from genocide, war crimes, ethnic cleansing and crimes against humanity; a plan for a peacebuilding commission to prevent countries emerging from conflict sliding back into war; and a renewed commitment to assistance for development and trade liberalization. The proof of the pudding, of course, is in the eating, but we now have a recipe that should work.

Dag Hammarskjöld once described the United Nations as an adventure, a new "Santa Maria", to use the name of Christopher Columbus's ship, battling its way through storms and uncharted waters to a new world. But, as he explained, on the shore there were always people who blamed the storm on the ship, rather than on the weather. Five decades later, the metaphor sadly still holds true. The UN continues to sail in uncharted waters, but it is blamed for the squalls that assail it. Yet, if we continue to be guided by the compass of our determination to live in a world governed by common rules and shared values, and to steer together in the multilateral institutions that the enlightened leaders of the last century have bequeathed to us, then indeed we can explore the hopes of the UN's founding fathers, and fulfil the continuing adventure of making this century better than the last.

Notes

1. See *A More Secure World: Our Shared Responsibility*, Report of the Secretary-General's High-level Panel on Threats, Challenges and Change, United Nations, 2004.
2. See Kofi Annan (2005) *In Larger Freedom: Towards Development, Security and Human Rights for All*, United Nations report.
3. The full text of the speech is reproduced in Stephen Schlesinger (2003) *Act of Creation*, Westview Press, Appendix I.
4. Ibid.
5. Charles Krauthammer (2002) "The unipolar moment revisited", *National Interest* 70 (Winter 2002/03): 5–17.
6. See Michael J. Glennon (2003) "Why the Security Council Failed", *Foreign Affairs*, May/June 2003.

7. Brian Urquhart (1971) *Hammarskjöld*, New York: Norton, p. 50.
8. As quoted in Brian Urquhart (1981) "International peace and security: thoughts on the twentieth anniversary of Dag Hammarskjöld's death", *Foreign Affairs*, Fall 1981: 3.
9. Speech to Council on Foreign Relations, 7 January 1999; see www.un.org.
10. Urquhart in *Foreign Affairs*, op. cit.
11. The quote has sometimes been erroneously attributed to Churchill, and also (more accurately) to Henry Cabot Lodge, who expressed the same idea in 1954. It was Hammarskjöld, however, who popularized the thought.
12. For the full text of Secretary-General's remarks, see UN Press Release SG/SM/10104 of 17 September 2005.

3

Communitarian multilateralism

Emanuel Adler

Classic forms of universal intergovernmental multilateralism, such as the United Nations (UN), have been under challenge at least since the end of the Cold War. Whilst global hegemonic pressures account in part for this challenge, it is also (and mainly) a challenge from underlying structural forces, including the weakening of sovereignty, the increasing global role of non-state actors and policy networks,[1] and the transfer of liberal practices and institutions from national to international and transnational spheres, most strikingly in Europe.[2] In an attempt to cope with these challenges, multilateralism has been transforming itself and taking new forms. Unlike "old" multilateral forms, the "new multilateralism"[3] seeks to coordinate state actions; but it also amounts to a primitive yet increasingly elaborate hybrid system of international and transnational global governance[4] that addresses national and transnational societal needs to solve problems – such as cleaning up landmines around the globe[5] – that states have been unable or unwilling to deal with. The new multilateralism may be less amenable to state control and hegemonic power influence. As in the International Criminal Court (ICC), it may be more legally binding than its older interstate counterpart. As in multilateral trade negotiations, the new multilateralism raises concerns of legitimacy, focused on accountability, responsibility, and transparency.[6]

Despite the ideological bias of George W. Bush and the American neoconservative movement against classic and primarily new forms of multilateralism[7] – a bias that grew stronger after 9/11 and the United States' hegemonic-driven response to it – new multilateral practices and institutional forms continue to grow; but so has resistance to them. Because of multilateralism's adaptive capacity, hegemonic powers may now have a better understanding of the limits of their material power and of the opportunities for harnessing regional democratization practices to promote their hegemony. At the same time, as attested by the Bush administration's appointment of John Bolton in 2005 – a strong opponent of the UN – as the US ambassador to the organization, and by the rather disappointing results of the UN's 2005 World Summit, recent drives to reform the UN system are not guaranteed success.

Thus the evolution of multilateralism has been and probably will continue to be contingent, if not non-deterministic and chaotic. Not only has multilateral institutionalization been historically inefficient, it also has exhibited complexity; although new forms of multilateralism have adapted in an attempt to survive, they nevertheless are challenging multilateralism's inclusiveness and sources of legitimacy.[8]

Moreover, national and transnational processes of identity change, often materialized as novel practices, may produce either institutional resistance or innovation, and these "throw off course the presumed linearity of history."[9] Hence it would be presumptuous to pretend to study the evolution of multilateralism in a short article and predict its future direction. Instead, building on two assumptions – that institutions evolve together with collective epistemic understandings and that constructivist IR theory[10] can make new forms of multilateralism visible – this chapter will identify and describe a novel and adaptive institutional form I call "communitarian multilateralism". Although incompatible in part with classical and "new" multilateral institutions, communitarian institutional forms may nevertheless help to provide a bridge between regionalism and multilateralism and establish multilateral relations on firmer ground.

Communitarian multilateralism, which transcends liberal transaction-based relations and relies instead on communitarian practices of collective-identity formation that depend, not only on material power, but also on collective epistemic understandings, is thriving. Not only does it merit our attention, it also illustrates the opportunities and challenges facing multilateralism.

By "communitarian multilateralism", I mean primarily institutionalized efforts to socially construct *multilateral communities*, either as a corollary of the expansion of *communities of practice*[11] – like-minded groups of individuals who engage in the same practice – and/or as inclusive forms of security, which *security communities*, such as the European Union (EU), use in their attempt to stabilize their environments. *Security partnerships*, like the "partnership for peace" of the North Atlantic Treaty Organization (NATO), and *constructed social spaces or "regions"*, like a "Greater Middle East", the "Mediterranean region", the "European Neighbourhood" space, and the area marked by the Association of South East Asian Nations (ASEAN), are communitarian practices par excellence.

The first section of the chapter proceeds from John Ruggie's seminal contribution to our understanding of multilateralism to describe the epistemic challenges posed to old and new multilateralism. The second section briefly explains why a constructivist approach may help make communitarian multilateralism noticeable, although other theoretical perspectives have failed. The third section defines communitarian multilateralism in more detail. The next section applies it to NATO and the EU, with special reference to security partnerships and new social spaces or regions currently under "construction". The fifth section discusses communitarian multilateralism in a normative context, and the conclusion asks where exclusive forms of multilateralism, such as communitarian multilateralism, may be headed.

The epistemic challenges to multilateralism

The main sources of multilateralism's current "malaise" are epistemic. They derive, however, from neither a lack of transparency and expert information[12] nor from the latter's excesses,[13] but from the intersubjective background knowledge that constitutes multilateralism as such. In the early 1990s, when John Ruggie defined multilateralism as a "generic institutional form", he was expressing an epistemic (and early constructivist) understanding of institutional reality, which he had first introduced to the discipline in 1975.[14] To recapitulate, Ruggie argued in 1993 that multilateralism is

> an institutional form that coordinates relations among three or more states on the basis of generalized principles of conduct: that is, principles which specify appropriate conduct for a class of actions, without regard to the particularistic interests of the parties or the strategic exigencies that may exist in any specific occurrence.[15]

By this Ruggie meant that multilateralism can exist, and is what it is, because of states' intersubjective normative and cause–effect knowledge of what are "appropriate generalized principles of conduct."[16] Because the latter are rooted in collective epistemes, which, borrowing from Michel Foucault, Ruggie defined as collectively "dominant way[s] of looking at social reality, a set of shared symbols and references, mutual expectations and a mutual predictability of intention,"[17] multilateralism "logically entail[s] an indivisibility among the members of a collectivity with respect to the range of behaviour in question".[18] It also involves the expectation of what Robert Keohane called "diffuse reciprocity", an "arrangement [which] is expected by its members to yield a rough equivalence of benefits in the aggregate and over time".[19]

In Ruggie's view, moreover, epistemic factors enter international organization with the realization that collective (and thus political) problems exist, through the effects of interdependence, the need for appropriate responses to collective problems (such as international regimes), and the conceptualization of legitimate authority.[20] This epistemic approach to institutional reality means, of course, that generalized principles of conduct do not stand apart from actors' strategic interests but enter into the social construction of these interests.

Building on Ruggie's epistemic foundations of the multilateral approach he helped conceptualize, let us consider contemporary epistemic sources of multilateralism's "malaise". These derive from the non-linear and chaotic nature of the evolution of multilateral institutional forms and from gaps in practitioners' and academic observers' understanding of historical change, power and its limitations, and the role of practice and moral purpose in international organization.

(1) One of the most significant epistemic (and social-epistemological) challenges that confronts multilateralism is the need to overcome practical and social-science knowledge of institutional change as the result of efficient history, weighty objective forces, and rational templates.[21] This type of understanding is bound to lead practitioners and academics doubly astray, by producing over-optimistic expectations which can come crashing down under the weight of practice, and by generating a paralysing inaction and loss of institutional potential for adaptation. A crash of expectations, paralysis of will, and the collective feelings these arouse endanger multilateralism, because they tend to obscure its positive outcomes and may provide the opponents of multilateralism with an opportunity to find fault with it. Avoiding this epistemic challenge requires us to realize that change "may weave among paths rather than speeding down regulated highways",[22] and thus a healthy sense of "epistemic humility".

In addition, thinking about change in linear ways may prevent us from recognizing that multilateralism may actually be strengthened by new emerging collective identities – for example, regional or global non-sovereignty-constituted networks and communities – that, from a narrow interstate perspective, seem to threaten multilateralism. Multilateralism may adapt and be transformed because of the ways in which new identities become embedded in practices, which, in turn, trigger the creation of new social purposes and new rounds of adaptation. What starts instrumentally and in local environments may later evolve into new multilateral practices,[23] such as NATO's security partnership practices, which became the wellspring of new interests and the reason why NATO capabilities are now used collectively and multilaterally. Actors may not realize it, but they may be creating new multilateral orders via their day-to-day practice.[24]

Thus the "poverty of imagination" about multilateralism consists in resisting new forms of multilateralism for short-term reasons, without leaving an opening for the possibilities of inventiveness, learning and persuasiveness that can create new collective goods and solve currently unmanageable national and international problems.[25] Communitarian multilateral practices, for example, are beginning to organize regional orders around socially constructed regional identities, which possess an innovative capacity to broaden institutional choices and solve regional and even global problems. NATO's cooperative-security partnership and region-making practices again come to mind.

(2) Collective understandings marked by notions of sovereign exclusion, military definitions of national security, and a deep suspicion of the ability of international organizations (IOs) to deal with the most pressing security and economic challenges are making a comeback (if they ever lost ground), especially in the United States. The American people's collective identity of exceptionalism, its narrative of possessing *the* ideal political regime, together with their country's material power and territorial insularity, elicit a resistance to institutional innovations that threaten US sovereignty, such as the transfer of identification from national to transnational communities. There are both material and epistemic limits, however, to US resistance to these innovations. It is incumbent on academia to understand whether and how non-sovereignty innovations can reach a tipping point in the US.

(3) The growing disjunction between existing multilateral organizations and the collective knowledge and identities they are based on, on the one hand, and practices and related identities that rely on communities and networks of the like-minded for ordering global relations, on the other hand, poses another major epistemic challenge. This is particularly true because transnational communities and networks are increasingly becoming the locus of international learning and agenda-setting and the source of political actions. As Anne-Marie Slaughter recently stated, "[g]lobal governance is not a matter of regulating states the way states regulate their citizens, but rather of addressing the issues and resolving the problems that result from citizens going global – from crime to commerce to civic engagement."[26] Dealing with this epistemic challenge requires turning functional relations and practices into political ones and endowing functional relationships, not only with democratic values and practices,

but also with fairness. In other words, one of the crucial epistemic problems of multilateralism is how to turn "global governance" into "good global governance" and functional practices into "best practices".[27]

(4) Another important epistemic challenge to multilateralism rests on a widespread misunderstanding of power. Academics and practitioners alike believe that material power gives strong states the ability to create, control, and abolish international and transnational institutions.[28] But power enters international organization not only in the form of material resources, but also as dominant cause–effect and normative understandings and discourses that help construct practices and transform social structures.[29] A misreading of power by political actors may have deleterious consequences for multilateral relations and global governance. When materially powerful or hegemonic states, for example, act without the backing of legitimate authority and of consensual cause–effect and normative knowledge, they risk achieving opposite results because of the resistance they generate. Materially weaker states, on the other hand, can sometimes exert immense power if and when, with the backing of transnational networks, they create epistemic and normative revolutions that legitimate new "practised identities" to the point that practices later come to be taken for granted. In such cases, even hegemonic powers are likely to discover that hegemony "may in fact prescribe moral responsibilities with a constitutive self-enforcing quality".[30]

(5) Multilateralism is threatened by a lack of what Jennifer Mitzen[31] called "ontological security" – the need for a secure identity, order and continuity. Current ontological insecurity arises from the perceived threat to the identities of states and to the basic definition of roles and rules in the present international system. This threat is fuelled by a sense that the current order is breaking down and the future is quite uncertain. This challenge to multilateralism goes deep down to the foundation of our epistemic order. But because "different temporal orders coexist, each with its own propensities to engage with others and to respond to change",[32] solutions may be found to this epistemic challenge when the balance of resistance to and innovation in multilateralism is resolved in favour of the latter, at which time new multilateral practices, rules, and institutions become legitimized.

Constructivism can help

A constructivist approach may help us think through the epistemic problems afflicting multilateralism and identify new multilateral institutional forms. First, constructivism is foremost a *communitarian approach*. As such, it is well suited to explore communitarian multilateralism. Until a few years ago, a communitarian IR approach existed mainly in the normative IR theoretical debate between cosmopolitans, most of whom hold a liberal theory of justice and employ a rationalist or individualist methodology,[33] and communitarians, who take communities as the key to understanding moral action.[34] Ever since constructivism penetrated IR theory, however, the communitarian approach has become a leading contender in analytic IR theory. Because constructivism highlights the dynamic role played by the social construction of knowledge in the construction of social reality,[35] the new turn to communitarian IR has meant not only that political communities and their potential transformation are studied in more appropriate and global perspectives, it has also highlighted the "community-shared background understandings, skills, and practical predispositions without which it would be impossible to interpret action, assign meaning, legitimate practices, empower agents, and constitute a differentiated highly structured social reality".[36] In other words, turning to a communitarian approach in IR attempts to make knowledge, along with the communities within which it develops and evolves and from which it diffuses, one of the leading ontological factors in the study of IR. From a communitarian IR perspective, knowledge means not only the information that people carry in their heads, but also, and primarily, the intersubjective background or context of expectations, dispositions and language that give meaning to material reality and help explain the constitutive and causal mechanisms that participate in the construction of social reality.

Second, via constructivism, *power* enters IR theory not only as material and institutional resources, but also as the ability of collective understandings and linguistic practices to construct social reality, as epistemic authority, and as the remote control exerted by institutions through their determination of the explicit and tacit rules of the game.[37] A more complex and sociologically richer (but also more discriminating) understanding of power can help us understand not only who determines whether, and what, institutions get the action, but also why certain ideas become multilateral institutions and others do not.

Third, constructivism construes *change* not only as historical sequences of events, the replacement of one material structure by another or a transformation of beliefs in people's minds, but primarily as the evolution of the "order of things"[38] or as "cognitive evolution".[39] The latter refers to a collective learning process that consists in the expansion, in time and space, of the background knowledge that constitutes practices and thus in the expansion of communities of practice. Hence cognitive evolution can make room for normative change. Adler and Bernstein,[40] for example, show that combined changes in knowledge, values and material power can lead to better practices and a fairer global governance system. Consequently, studying change entails rooting analytical IR theory in political theory as well as providing normative IR theory with ontological and epistemological tools for arguing why normative futures are not only desirable, but also achievable.

Finally, constructivism sensitizes us to the *construction of new social and geographical spaces* by means of security partnerships. In recent years, a grasp of this mechanism has given birth to a communitarian practice of region-building, including the European Union's attempts to stabilize its "near abroad" with a "neighbourhood" policy and the heroic but probably futile American attempts to construct the "Greater Middle East" as a democratic region.

Communitarian multilateralism

Classic notions of multilateralism assert that states may choose to *coordinate* their behaviour by multilateral institutions when, regardless of short-term instrumental considerations, "generalized principles of appropriate conduct" help fixed preferences converge (neo-liberalism) or help *constitute* states' cooperative *reasons* or *preferences* ("modernist" constructivism). In either case, normative knowledge enters states' calculations of preferences and policy coordination with other states. States, however, may change their preferences and behaviours without having to change their identities and discursive practices first. Politics enters this institutional form in states' efforts to persuade other states of the need to attain collective purposes and to influence institutional dynamics in their favour.

Communitarian multilateralism is both "deeper" or socially "thicker" and more "minimalist" than classic (and "new") forms of multilateralism. It is deeper because cooperation results from a change of and coordination between identities and practices, rather than behaviours, and because collective identities and shared practices help constitute the "common good" of communities of shared identities and practice. The common good can be measured, for example, in terms of stability and peace, economic welfare and good (community) governance. Communitarian multilateralism is also deeper than classic multilateralism, because the construction of multilateral institutionalized reality results not only from collectively shared norms, but also from shared practices. This means that, for example, if practice has evolved to empower non-sovereignty–based actors, such as social movements and NGOs, to play a role in global or regional agenda development, or standard setting, non-state actors then become an intrinsic part of multilateral institutional forms.

Communitarian multilateralism is more minimalist than its classic counterpart, however. First, it exists primarily as intersubjective knowledge and discursive practices and tends to be based on informal organizational structures. Communitarian multilateral institutions may therefore be harder to identify and to describe empirically than classic forms. Second, communitarian multilateralism is more minimalist because, due to its reliance on collective identity and shared practice, it is unlikely at this stage to become universal and inclusive. Politics enters communitarian multilateralism as attempts by state and non-state actors to control collective purpose and identity and to expand the community of those who, in their own view, practise reasonable, normatively appropriate, and internationally stabilizing practices. Politics, in other words, enters communitarian multilateralism's concerted attempts to enlarge communities of identity and practice and thus to change others in one's own image.

Hence we may formally define communitarian multilateralism as the social construction and institutionalization, by means of dialogical and community-building practices, of multilateral communities, which, based on collective knowledge (such as identities, norms, and cause–effect relationships), evolve from informal and formal communities of the like-minded.

The concept of communitarian multilateralism owes much to the concept of "security communities", which, drawing on Karl Deutsch's seminal contribution, Michael Barnett and I interpreted from a constructivist perspective.[41] But it also owes something to the concept of "community of practice", which I recently used to conceptualize institutionalization processes.[42] Security communities, in their pluralistic and more analytically useful form, are "transnational regions composed of sovereign states whose people maintain dependable expectations of peaceful change". Loosely coupled pluralistic security communities maintain the minimum properties of the foregoing definition. Tightly coupled security communities, on the other hand, possess a political regime that is something of a post-sovereign system, comprising common supranational, transnational, and national institutions, and some form of collective security system.[43]

Security communities are a mechanism of international security that is different and in some ways antithetical to the balance-of-power mechanism. Whereas achieving security by means of the balance of power warrants the use of deterrence and pre-emptive force, a security-community mechanism, relying on shared norms and identities, enables states to become secure in relation to one another. It therefore relies on a different and more benign set of practices, such as dialogue and persuasion. Moreover, security communities suggest not merely groups of states that have abandoned war as a means of social intercourse, but also the evolution of a community that practises peace: a security community of practice.

A *community of practice* "consists of people who are informally as well as contextually bound by a shared interest in learning and applying a common practice."[44] More specifically, it is a configuration of a *domain of knowledge* that constitutes like-mindedness, a *community of people* that "creates the social fabric of learning", and a *shared practice* that embodies "the knowledge the community develops, shares, and maintains."[45] The knowledge domain endows practitioners with a sense of *joint enterprise*, which is being constantly renegotiated by its members. People function as a community through relationships of *mutual engagement* that bind "members together into a social entity." Shared practices, in turn, are sustained by a *repertoire of communal resources*, such as routines, sensibilities, and discourse.[46]

Communities of practice can be grasped only analytically, as social spaces that are organized around practices. Still, communities of practice are territorially based;[47] like states, they hold epistemic authority over the physical spaces they happen to influence. For example, global environmentalists help the social construction of national and transnational territory as environmental safe havens, while those involved in global trade play a role in socially constructing territory as tax havens. Communities of practice differ from the often-used concept of network,[48] mainly because they involve not only the transmission of information among individuals, groups, and organizations (which is what networks are about), but also processes of social communication through which practitioners bargain about and set meanings, develop their own distinctive identity, and learn practices. Because the boundaries of a community of practice are determined by people's knowledge and identity, and by the discourse associated with a specific practice – unlike transnational, government, and policy networks, communities of practice are not necessarily "congruent with the reified structures of institutional affiliations, divisions and boundaries."[49]

So if we think about our world as made up of communities of practice we will see, for example, transnational communities of diplomats sharing a diplomatic culture, common values and interests that are intrinsic to their practice. We will also see merchants from different countries, even rival countries, who participate in common trade practices and share an interest, knowledge, discourse, and identity in learning and applying these practices. Like international financial traders,[50] they may never get to know each other, but their intersubjective knowledge and discourse distinguish them from the rest of the world.

Because communities of practice are marked by a domain of knowledge about self and other, a community of people, shared peaceful practices, and a sense of joint enterprise, all of them sustained by a repertoire of ideational and material communal resources, security communities, are communities of practice. Security communities of practice expand their membership by means that generate the "we" feeling – socialization and persuasion – but especially by means of regional partnerships and region-building.

Partnerships are meant to persuade partners that learning the practices of the members of a community will make them part of that community,[51] sharing a common identity with its members, so that they can enjoy the security, economic and cultural benefits offered by the community. Although analytically distinct from security communities, transnational security partnerships are among the most interesting communitarian multilateral developments of recent years. Although regional security partnerships are in themselves unable to attain "dependable expectations of peaceful change", they may nevertheless be able, thanks to an agreement by states to cooperate through multilateral mechanisms, to reduce violence and enhance stability and peace.

A primary objective of partnerships is region-building, where regions are understood not only geographically, but also (and chiefly) cognitively, and regional borders are determined to a great extent by identity. As such, socially constructed regions are not passive objects, but "active subjects capable of articulating the transnational interests of the emerging region."[52] According to Wendy Larner and William Walters, regions are liberal governance mechanisms that work "at a distance ... by implicating their [regional] members in projects (perhaps "missions") of reform, rationalization, and national improvement", and by constructing "states and their publics as choice makers".[53] Power is also evident in the magnetic attraction that "core" states exert on other members of a community and in the pull that a community exerts on its neighbours.

The communitarian multilateralism of NATO and the EU

Communitarian multilateralism and its related practice of cooperative security, with its recognition of the indivisibility, comprehensiveness and inclusiveness of security, as well as its emphasis on dialogue and confidence-building, was born from the Helsinki Process, from the associated Conference on Security and Co-operation in Europe (CSCE),[54] and from CSCE regimes like Confidence-Building Measures (1986) and charters like the Paris Charter for a New Europe (1990).[55] Communitarian multilateralism, together with the practices of cooperative security, diffused across the different European institutions and increasingly became part of their own activities. The EU, for example, has developed a variety of initiatives, including the Euro Mediterranean Partnership (EMP) and the European Neighbourhood Policy (ENP), which, as we will see below, rely on CSCE practices, especially partnerships and region-building.

The North Atlantic Treaty Organization

Although NATO became the institutional representation of the Euro-Atlantic pluralistic security community shortly after its founding in 1949, during the Cold War its primary purpose remained collective defence. The post-Cold War political environment, however, allowed NATO to assume new communitarian multilateral missions and tasks, which were compatible with its members' security community identification and congruent with NATO's post-Cold War goal of eastward expansion.

At NATO's 1991 Summit meeting in Rome, which aimed at socializing former members of the Warsaw Pact so they could join NATO and persuading Russia that NATO was pursuing a community-oriented rather than power-politics–oriented approach, the organization established the North Atlantic Cooperation Council (NACC), a consultative cooperative forum on political and security issues. Comprising the foreign ministers and representatives of the NATO countries (16 at the time), Central and Eastern European states, and all the Soviet successor states, including the Baltic republics (a total of 38 countries), the NACC was NATO's attempt to take over the community-building initiative from the OSCE while adopting OSCE-like cooperative-security practices.[56]

In 1994, NACC was beefed up by the addition of the Partnership for Peace (PfP). By establishing a dialogue between NATO and 30 partner countries (ten of which have since joined NATO), the PfP increased the participants' ability to act in concert. The PfP includes a vast programme of practical activities, such as training and common planning, that (a) facilitate transparency in national defence planning, (b) ensure democratic control of defence forces, (c) maintain the capability and readiness to contribute to peacekeeping operations under UN auspices, and (d) develop cooperative military relations with NATO and forces that are better able to operate with it.[57]

A Mediterranean security dialogue (MD) was created, also in 1994. Three years later, the NACC was replaced by the more ambitious Euro-Atlantic Partnership Council (EAPC), a consultative body of 46 members and partners that increases the role the latter play in joint decision-making and planning and makes the PfP more active. Later, special consultative councils were created with Russia and Ukraine. Taken together, these practices and institutions represent NATO's partial adoption of cooperative security practices – the idea that security threats are best handled through cooperative confidence-building, dialogue and quality-of-life measures, notably the inclusion of neighbouring states in a community of values, as partners or even members. They also reflect the partial mutation of NATO from a traditional institutionalized multilateral alliance to a communitarian multilateral institution.[58]

At the 1999 Washington summit, NATO admitted three new members (the Czech Republic, Hungary, and Poland) and launched a Membership Action Plan to help partners become full members. It also adopted a new Strategic Concept that granted formal approval to NATO's transformation. NATO still performs traditional defence tasks, but it now also classifies target states, their military and their civil societies as "partners" and then "teaches" them how to become good members of NATO.

The identity crisis experienced by NATO since 11 September has not impeded its continued adoption of communitarian multilateral practices, but has actually encouraged it. Recently, for example, NATO turned its focus to the Middle East and began using partnership-building measures there. The Istanbul summit of June 2004 was especially important for NATO partnerships with the Mediterranean and the so-called "Greater Middle East". The Istanbul Cooperation Initiative (ICI) was extended to interested countries of the broader Middle East region, especially the members of the Gulf Co-operation Council. At Istanbul, NATO also decided to upgrade the MD to a genuine partnership; this is to be accomplished through "greater emphasis on practical cooperation" on the model of PfP tools.[59] While NATO's minimal role in Afghanistan and Iraq has received most of the press, it is NATO's security partnerships and communities of military practice that may ultimately have an impact on the "Greater Middle East". In recent months, for instance, there has been a sustained dialogue between Israel and NATO, aimed at embedding Israel in the Euro-Atlantic community.

The European Union

The EU, a tightly coupled pluralistic security community, has recently been working to transform its "near abroad" by using communitarian multilateral practices, backed by "normative power" – the ability "to shape conceptions of 'normal'"[60] or to induce the adoption of desired political and economic policies by attracting states to become members or partners of a political community that can be joined only if they adopt a set of norms, practices and institutions.[61]

As the EU's main Middle East policy instrument and preferred tool for engaging Muslim states in constructive dialogue, the EMP, or Barcelona Process, tries to deal with some of the root causes of the EU's insecurity – immigration from the South, the growth of militant Islamic fundamentalism, and international terrorism – by socially constructing a

Mediterranean-partnership identity. Launched in 1995, the EMP is a broad multilateral cooperative framework for the political, economic, and cultural relations of 26 European, Middle Eastern, and North African countries and the Palestinian Authority, aimed at achieving stability and security in the Mediterranean.[62] It builds on the CSCE understanding that stability and security depend on cooperative "partnership" with non-liberal states, and on the EU's expectations that the southward diffusion of its norms can help stabilize the socially constructed region. To achieve this, the EMP envisioned a loose process of pluralistic integration, structured, like the Helsinki Process, into three "baskets", based on economic cooperation (a free-trade zone by 2010), partnership-building security measures, and a thick web of regional civil-society networks to promote a common culture. Similar processes of region-building have taken place in Asia, mainly through ASEAN, the Asean Regional Forum, and the Asia-Pacific Economic Cooperation.[63]

In retrospect, the EMP failed to fulfil its most ambitious expectations, in part because of the collapse of the Oslo peace process, the Algerian civil war, and, later, 9/11 and its international consequences. A Mediterranean collective identity did not develop, stability in the Mediterranean was not achieved, and the Middle East continues to be a source of insecurity for the EU security community. But the architects of the EMP did not imagine that the development of "partnership-building measures" and region-making techniques would help institutionalize communitarian multilateralism in Europe and in its "near abroad". EU's newest institutional development, the ENP of 2003, and, the next year, the US-inspired "Partnership for Progress and a Common Future with the Region of the Broader Middle East and North Africa", both follow the communitarian multilateral model of the EMP (and, by extension, of the Helsinki Process). As Di Palma wrote, "even when actors are ready to learn and not just adapt and survive, even when intentionality drives them, the contours of their imagined institutional change cannot prefigure, save happenstance, a distant outcome that possible has never before been practised."[64] Thus, while the institutional solutions the EMP suggested did not bear fruit directly, they nevertheless contributed to the institutionalization of communitarian multilateralism in Europe and its "near abroad".

In the rest of this section, I will briefly describe the ENP and the "Partnership for Progress". The ENP is an EU policy initiative "to create a ring of countries, sharing the EU's fundamental values and objectives, drawn into an increasingly close relationship, going beyond cooperation to involve a significant measure of economic and political integration".[65] "The task", adds the recent European Security Strategy,[66] "is to promote a ring of *well-governed* countries to the East of the European Union and on the borders of the Mediterranean with whom we can enjoy close and cooperative relations" (emphasis added). Thus the ENP reflects the communitarian multilateral perspective that "the best protection for ... security is a world of well-governed democratic states".[67]

The ENP, which applies to Russia, Ukraine, Belarus, and Moldova and all EMP countries that are not members of the EU, except for Turkey (which is pursuing EU membership), is an institutionalized means of promoting pluralistic integration without creating expectations of future EU membership. In this it differs from the EU's practice of stabilization and peacemaking via enlargement. Although the ENP will "encourage the participants to reap the full benefits of the Euro-Mediterranean Partnership",[68] it departs from the EMP by setting multilateral relations with neighbouring states on individual tracks, so that each neighbour can develop its relations with the EU at its own pace, according to its own potential and priorities. Priorities are then incorporated in Action Plans – drafts already exist with Israel, Jordan, Morocco, Moldova, the Palestinian Authority, Tunisia and Ukraine – that cover a variety of areas for action, such as: political dialogue and reform; trade and measures preparing partners for gradually obtaining a stake in the EU's internal market; justice and home affairs. The envisioned collaborative relations between the EU and its neighbours build on a mutual commitment to common values, such as the rule of law, good governance, respect for human rights, and the principles of market economy and sustainable development.[69]

EMP and ENP partner states are thus being invited to join a region of peace and stability that does not yet exist. Partners receive the material pay-offs from their affiliation with "regions" and "neighbourhoods", such as access to markets and financial and technological aid. They also have access to human and symbolic capital and to the institutional "software" that is conducive to modernization. The EU side of the bargain consists of inducing partners to accept liberal democracy, the rule of law, human rights, and peaceful change, with the expectation that these normative changes will lead to peace and stability.[70] There is, however, nothing naive and idealistic in the steps and practices the EU uses to build partnerships and neighbourhoods. Rather, these steps and practices help translate normative power into real material influence and, sometimes, political control as well.

Until several years ago, the US maintained a healthy distance from communitarian multilateral practices. Having recently set itself the goal of transforming the Middle East from scratch, however, not only has the US used pre-emptive and coercive military measures – with dubious results – it has also begun adopting communitarian multilateral means that follow the Helsinki Process and the EU models. In parallel to the war in Iraq, the US proposed a partnership with Middle Eastern countries aimed at promoting democracy. It later proposed a free-trade agreement between the US and Middle Eastern countries. In June 2004, with Group of Eight (G-8) support, it launched the "Partnership for Progress". Consisting mainly of a "Forum for the Future" and a "Plan of Support for Reform", this partnership aims to employ money and technical knowledge to modify deep-seated Middle Eastern identities. This latest US-led partnership also shows the opportunities and challenges of communitarian multilateralism. If handled properly, in a way that turns partnership into a meaningful and reciprocal dialogue, communitarian multilateral practices may help mitigate the tensions that fuel conflict and violence. The "Greater Middle East" policy project, on the other hand, shows that communitarian multilateralism can have deleterious consequences if it used as a hegemony-preserving tool.[71]

Normative implications of communitarian multilateralism

This short section asks whether communitarian multilateralism can be both productive and fair, so that *good* international and transnational governance can be achieved. This means finding ways to institutionalize and develop forms of governance for community-based practices and institutions and filling them with normative content: democratic principles of accountability, transparency and responsibility. For space reasons, I will concentrate on one critical issue: joint ownership and the sources of the construction of collective identity. The 2004 EU Commission's ENP strategic document maintains that:

> Joint ownership of the process, based on the awareness of shared values and common interests, is essential. The EU does not seek to impose priorities or conditions on its partners.... There can be no question of asking partners to accept a pre-determined set of priorities. These will be defined by common consent.[72]

Without the "joint ownership" principle – which comes from the economic development field and is now applied by the EMP and the ENP to political and security issues[73] – the communitarian multilateral policies of NATO and the EU might strike partners, especially in the Middle East, as being neocolonialist schemes, raising tough questions about their legitimacy. Many of the organizations' communitarian multilateral practices, in fact, do involve one-way socialization and "teaching" rather than two-way dialogue and persuasion. For example, one of the problems with constructing a democratic "Greater Middle East" is that those on the receiving end believe the practice to be yet another American "hegemonic machination". The EMP and the ENP, in turn, may be caught between the language of postcolonialism and the behaviour of neocolonialism.[74]

The important normative question regarding communitarian multilateral good governance, then, is who should socialize whom, on the basis of which norms, and whose identity should be "diffused" to whom? On the one hand, an attempt to impose liberal identities on states and nations that have suffered from European colonialism in the past and believe that communitarian multilateralism may be the most recent form of hegemonic domination will probably backfire. It is also immoral. On the other hand, one wonders about the reluctance of Muslim countries to adopt the values of democracy and human rights on the grounds that these are Western, and therefore "bad", ideas after they adopted without much resistance other European constitutive ideas, such as the nation-state and the sovereignty principle, modern science and economics, and, recently, global communication technologies and networks.

The crux of the matter, thus, is the adoption of liberal democratic and human-rights values by partners, not by imposition, or even as a quid pro quo for material inducements, but as a result of a legitimate process, wherein both sides of the normative divide arrive at the norms and collectives identities that should constitute their mutual communitarian relations on the basis of an open process of dialogue in "public spheres".[75] NATO's PfP and other partnerships, and the EU's EMP and ENP, need to evolve in such direction.

On a more philosophical level, not only can communitarian multilateralism be based on a compromise between liberal and communitarian philosophies, it must be so based in order to be progressive. On the one hand, it must be liberal – not only in the sense of supporting liberal values, such as democracy and human rights, but also of aiming ultimately in the direction of a cosmopolitan community. On the other hand, it must be communitarian in the deep ontological and epistemic sense that the sources of change and learning lie in communities constituted by intersubjective knowledge. What I have in mind, then, is a blend of the liberal argument – which emphasizes the individual, the micro foundations of change, methodological individualism, and a cosmopolitan society as a normative goal – with the normative and analytic communitarian argument – which locates social change in communities, emphasizes the macro foundations of change, and holds that moral life is possible only within communities. Here it is interesting to note the paradox that some varieties of communitarian multilateralism, especially the EU strands, are liberally oriented and embedded in liberal communities of practice, while classic liberal conceptions of state-oriented multilateral institutions, such as the WTO and democracy-promoting partnership activities led by the United States, are based on philosophical notions of narrow (national) communitarian justice.

There is no question that communitarian multilateralism must be reformed if it is to be made normatively progressive, but some of its varieties are on the right track, at least conceptually. I have in mind, for example, the "best practices" concept of the World Bank and the institutionalization of "cooperative security" and "human security" practices in Europe, Asia and Latin America via multilateral communities.

Conclusion

My concluding remarks refer mainly to the question of whether communitarian multilateralism can contribute to global governance and thus be inclusive. Although global communitarian multilateral practices may not be inconceivable, levels of global solidarity and "we-feeling" are currently so low that, almost by definition, communitarian multilateral practices are exclusive. Moreover, at the present time, communitarian multilateral practices take place in parallel to established inclusive institutions, such as the UN; not only may they not make a positive contribution to these institutions, they may actually weaken them. For example, the Bush administration, which is bent on unilateralism, or at least on "selective multilateralism", has adopted communitarian multilateral measures to help bring democracy and economic stability to the Middle East by side-tracking the UN to a great extent.

Communitarian multilateralism not only can, but also must, aim at inclusiveness. Even if a global partnership and global region of stability and peace – a global security community of sorts – is decades, if not centuries, away, global institutions, such as the UN, may and must adopt communitarian multilateralism to jump-start open social communication processes that can lay the epistemic foundations for future development of global identities. This also applies to most classic multilateral organizations other than the UN and the World Bank, such as the World Trade Organization (WTO), which are exclusive in practice and depend for membership on the acceptance of some basic principles of conduct. In addition, not only is the development of shared practices by means of communitarian multilateralism realistic, it may also fit with the politically instrumental and normative purposes behind reform of the UN and other global institutions. Finally, to reiterate what was said in the first section, history is inefficient. A change toward good global governance will depend less on a master plan or some objective forces than on a conjunction of institutional forms and forces, which, due to contingency, non-linearity and lack of practice, we still cannot totally comprehend, let alone predict. I hope this chapter has helped persuade that the evolution of multilateralism toward communitarian forms addresses multilateralism's "epistemic deficit" and, as such, may, although not necessarily must, help produce the desired "tipping point" towards good global governance.

Acknowledgement

The author would like to thank Itty Abraham and Edward Newman for very useful comments on an earlier draft of this chapter.

Notes

1. Keohane, this volume; Anne-Marie Slaughter (2004) *A New World Order*, Princeton, NJ: Princeton University Press.
2. Groom, this volume.
3. Michael Schechter (ed.) (1998) *Future Multilateralism*, Basingstoke, England: Macmillan/UNU Press; Acharya, this volume.
4. Slaughter, *A New World Order*; Thomas Risse (2004) "Transnational governance and legitimacy", presented at ECPR Standing Group on International Relations Conference, The Hague, September 9–12.
5. For the treaty to ban landmines, see Richard Price (1998) "Reversing the gun sights: transnational civil society targets land mines", *International Organization* 52(3): 613–644.
6. Emanuel Adler and Steven Bernstein (2004) "Knowledge in power: the epistemic construction of global governance", in Michael Barnett and Raymond Duvall (eds.) *Power in Global Governance*, Cambridge: Cambridge University Press; Keohane, this volume.
7. G. John Ikenberry (2003) "Is American multilateralism in decline?", *Perspectives on Politics* 1(3): 533–550.
8. Keohane, this volume.
9. Giuseppe Di Palma (2004) "What inefficient history and malleable practices say about nation-states and supranational democracy when territoriality is no longer exclusive?", in Christopher K. Ansell and Giuseppe Di Palma (eds.) *Restructuring Territoriality: Europe and the Unites States Compared*, Cambridge: Cambridge University Press, p. 260.
10. Alexander Wendt (1999) *Social Theory of International Relations*, Cambridge: Cambridge University Press.
11. Emanuel Adler (2005) *Communitarian International Relations: The Epistemic Foundations of International Relations*, London: Routledge; Etienne Wenger (1998) *Communities of Practice: Learning, Meaning, and Identity*, Cambridge: Cambridge University Press.
12. Keohane, this volume.
13. Kratochwil, this volume.
14. John G. Ruggie (1975) "International responses to technology: concepts and trends", *International Organization* 29(3): 557–583.
15. John G. Ruggie (1993) "Multilateralism: the anatomy of an institution", in John G. Ruggie (ed.) *Multilateralism Matters: The Theory and Praxis of an Institutional Form*, New York: Columbia University Press, p. 11.

16. Ruggie, "International responses", p. 558. See also Kratochwil, this volume.
17. Ruggie, "International responses", pp. 569–570.
18. Ruggie, "Multilateralism", p. 11.
19. Ibid.; Robert O. Keohane (1986) "Reciprocity in international relations", *International Organization* 40(1): 1–27.
20. Ruggie, "International responses".
21. Di Palma, "Inefficient history", p. 247.
22. Ibid., p. 249
23. James G. March and Johan P. Olsen (1998) "The institutional dynamics of international political orders", *International Organization* 52(4): 966–967.
24. Ernst B. Haas (2000) *Nationalism, Liberalism, and Progress*, Vol. 2, Ithaca, NY: Cornell University Press, p. 454.
25. Di Palma, "Inefficient history", p. 248.
26. Slaughter, *A New World Order*, p. 16.
27. Adler and Bernstein, "Knowledge in power".
28. John J. Mearsheimer (2001) *The Tragedy of Great Power Politics*, New York: W.W. Norton.
29. Adler and Bernstein (2004) "Knowledge in power"; Michael Barnett and Raymond Duvall, "Power and global governance", in Barnett and Duvall, *Power in Global Governance*.
30. Di Palma, "Inefficient history", pp. 253–260, 263.
31. Jennifer Mitzen (2003) "Ontological security in world politics: state identity and the security dilemma", draft, Minnesota International Relations Colloquium, available at http://www.polisci.umn.edu/information/mirc/index.php?folder=oldsched/Fall2003Papers/PastPapersfromFall2003.
32. Di Palma, "Inefficient history", p. 249.
33. Charles R. Beitz (1999) *Political Theory and International Relations*, Princeton, NJ: Princeton University Press.
34. Michael Walzer (1983) *Spheres of Justice*, Oxford: Basil Blackwell.
35. Stefano Guzzini (2000) "A reconstruction of constructivism in international relations", *European Journal of International Relations* 6(2): 147–182.
36. Richard K. Ashley (1987) "The geopolitics of geopolitical space: toward a critical theory of international politics", *Alternatives* 12: 403.
37. Adler and Bernstein, "Knowledge in power"; Barnett and Duvall, "Power and Global Governance"; Stefano Guzzini (1993) "Structural power: the limits of neorealist power analysis", *International Organization* 47(3): 443–478.
38. Michel Foucault (1970) *The Order of Things: An Archaeology of Human Sciences*, New York: Pantheon.
39. Emanuel Adler (1991) "Cognitive evolution: a dynamic approach for the study of international relations and their progress", in Emanuel Adler and Beverly Crawford (eds.) *Progress in Postwar International Relations*, New York: Columbia University Press, pp. 43–88.
40. Adler and Bernstein, "Knowledge in power".
41. Karl Deutsch (1957) *Political Community and the North Atlantic Area*, Princeton, NJ: Princeton University Press; Emanuel Adler and Michael Barnett (eds.) (1998) *Security Communities*, Cambridge: Cambridge University Press.
42. Adler, *Communitarian International Relations*.
43. Adler and Barnett, *Security Communities*.
44. William M. Snyder (1997) "Communities of practice: combining organizational learning and strategy insights to create a bridge to the 21st century", available at www.co-i-l.com/

coil/knowledge-garden/cop/cols.shtml; accessed 5 May 1999; Wenger, *Communities of Practice*.
45. Etienne Wenger, Richard McDermott and William M. Snyder (2002) *A Guide to Making Knowledge: Cultivating Communities of Practice*, Boston, Mass.: Harvard Business School Press.
46. Wenger, *Communities of Practice*.
47. Saskia Sassen (2000) "New frontiers facing urban sociology at the millennium", *British Journal of Sociology* 51(1): 143–160.
48. Manuel Castells (1996) *The Rise of the Network Society*, Oxford: Blackwell.
49. Wenger, *Communities of Practice*.
50. Karin Knorr Cetina and Urs Bruegger (2002) "Global microstructures: the virtual societies of financial markets", *American Journal of Sociology* 107(4): 905–950.
51. Fulvio Attinà (2001) "The European Security Partnership, NATO and the European Union", *The European Union Review* 6(2): 135–151; Emanuel Adler and Beverly Crawford (2006) "Normative power: the European practice of region building and the case of the Euro–Mediterranean partnership", in Emanuel Adler, Beverly Crawford, Federica Bicchi and Raffaella Del Sarto (eds.) *The Convergence of Civilizations: Constructing a Mediterranean Region*, Toronto: University of Toronto Press.
52. Björn Hettne and Frederik Söderbaum (2000) "Theorizing the rise of regionness", New Political Economy 5(3): 461.
53. Wendy Larner and William Walters (2002) "The political rationality of 'new regionalism': toward a genealogy of the region", *Theory and Society* 31: 415, 418.
54. John Maresca (1985) *To Helsinki: The Conference on Security and Co-operation in Europe, 1973–1975*, Durham, NC: Duke University Press.
55. Janie Leatherman (2003) *From Cold War to Democratic Peace: Third Parties, Peaceful Change, and the OSCE*, Syracuse, NY: Syracuse University Press.
56. NATO, "Declaration on Peace and Co-operation Issued by the Heads of State and Government Participating in the Meeting of the North Atlantic Council (Including Decisions Leading to the Creation of the North Atlantic Co-operation Council (NACC))", Rome, 8 November 1991.
57. NATO, Partnership for Peace: Framework Document Issued by the Heads of State and Government Participation in the Meeting of the North Atlantic Council, Brussels, 10 January 1994.
58. Steve Weber (1993) "Shaping the postwar balance of power: multilateralism in NATO", in Ruggie, *Multilateralism Matters*, pp. 233–292.
59. NATO, A More Ambitious and Expanded Framework for the Mediterranean Dialogue, Policy document, 9 July 2004, par. 8.
60. Ian Manners (2002) "Normative Power Europe: a contradiction in terms?" *Journal of Common Market Studies* 40(2): 240.
61. Adler and Crawford, "Normative Power".
62. Adler et al., *The Convergence of Civilizations*.
63. Amitav Acharya (2001) *Constructing a Security Community in Southeast Asia: ASEAN and the Problem of Regional Order*, London: Routledge.
64. Di Palma, "Inefficient history", pp. 250–251.
65. EU, Commission of European Communities, "European Neighbourhood Policy Strategy Paper", Brussels, 12 May 2004, p. 5.
66. Council of European Union, "A Secure Europe in a Better World: European Security Strategy", Brussels, 12 December 2003, p. 8.
67. Ibid., p. 10.
68. EU Commission, ENP Strategy Paper, p. 4.
69. Ibid., p. 3.

70. Adler and Crawford, "Normative power".
71. Ibid.
72. EU Commission, ENP Strategy Paper, p. 8.
73. Roberto Aliboni (2004) "Promoting democracy in the EMP: Which political strategy?" *EuroMeSCo Reports*, Working Group I, November, p. 9.
74. Adler and Crawford, "Normative Power".
75. Jürgen Habermas (1984) *The Theory of Communicative Action*, Vol. I, trans. Thomas MacCarthy, Boston, Mass.: Beacon Press.

4

The contingent legitimacy of multilateralism

Robert O. Keohane

Multilateralism can be defined in two different ways. The definition that is more consistent with ordinary usage conceives of multilateralism as institutionalized collective action by an inclusively determined set of independent states. Truly multilateral organizations are open to all states meeting specified criteria. The rules of multilateral organizations are publicly known and persist over a substantial period of time. This definition, defining multilateralism in strictly institutional rather than normative terms, makes it possible meaningfully to ask causal questions about whether multilateral institutions promote norms such as those of diffuse reciprocity. Such a definition also facilitates inquiry into whether strictly institutional forms are normatively legitimate. Since the question of the legitimacy of contemporary multilateral institutions is the central issue addressed by this chapter, I use this definition of multilateralism.

Another definition, due principally to John Ruggie, limits multilateralism to action among three or more states "on the basis of generalized principles of conduct", such as diffuse reciprocity.[1] Ruggie's definition is most valuable for studying possible transformations in world politics. Most multilateralism has been accompanied by discrimination among states, according to power, status, wealth or other characteristics. Whenever multilateralism as defined by Ruggie is found, by contrast, we are in the presence of behaviour – action according to "generalized principles of conduct" – that was almost unknown before the middle of the twentieth century. As Fritz Kratochwil's chapter for this volume suggests, forms of multilateralism in the most general sense were facilitated by the institution of sovereignty and through the Concert of Europe. But these forms of multilateralism discriminate among states, notably between Great Powers and others.

Multilateral institutions by no means supersede states as the most important actors in world politics. On the contrary, they are created by states, and states dominate their decision-making. It is now well-established that institutions such as the World Trade Organization (WTO) and the United Nations perform valuable functions for states. They reduce the costs of making and enforcing agreements, they help to provide information about other states' policies, and they increase the costs of reneging on commitments, thereby increasing the credibility of promises.[2]

Were states the ultimate actors in world politics, this story might be sufficient: organizations that are useful for states would persist. But the contemporary world is one of socially mobilized populations – whether political systems are democratic or not. For state policies to be solidly established and effective, they need to generate at least passive support from the people whom they affect. State policies need, that is, to be publicly *legitimate* to mass audiences.

Broadly speaking, we can think of legitimacy as a normative or as a sociological concept. Normatively, an institution is legitimate when its practices meet a set of standards that have been stated and defended. For instance, on the theory of judicial review in American constitutional law, it is legitimate for the Supreme Court to rule actions of the Executive, or of Congress, unconstitutional. On a strictly majoritarian democratic theory, or a plebiscitary theory, such edicts by the Court would not be legitimate.

In the sociological sense, legitimacy is a matter of fact. An institution is legitimate when it is accepted as appropriate, and worthy of being obeyed, by relevant audiences. When the relevant audiences believe in a particular normative theory, normative legitimacy tends to coincide with sociological legitimacy. For instance, since there is almost universal acceptance in the United States of the legitimacy of judicial review by the Supreme Court, such review is both normatively legitimate (on the basis of a theory of constitutional government) and sociologically legitimate. Often, however, legitimacy is contested, either because people hold different normative theories of it or because they evaluate the facts differently.

Inis L. Claude argued almost 40 years ago that the United Nations provides "collective legitimation" for state policies.[3] Such legitimation is most evident with respect to coercive acts by states, involving the use of military force. Except in situations of self-defence, the UN Charter declares unilateral military actions by states to be illegitimate. Only the UN can provide a globally-based endorsement for action – which Secretary General Kofi Annan refers to as the "unique legitimacy" of the United Nations. In this view, actions such as armed intervention against a state, which would otherwise be subject to condemnation, become legitimate when authorized by members of an organization of states, such as the UN Security Council or the WTO. The presumption is that if there is sufficient consensus by states, acting collectively according to established supermajority rules, legitimacy follows.

In this chapter I will question this presumption. I view it as a social construction of the twentieth century, which is becoming increasingly problematic. The view that agreement by states, according to institutionalized rules, guarantees legitimacy relies on a deeply statist normative theory. Such an argument has always been at odds with normative democratic theory. The general acceptance of statist views until the last quarter of the twentieth century, however, implied the general acceptance of a statist theory of legitimacy. But as democracy has become more widely accepted as the best form of government domestically, its international analogues have also made inroads. Demands for multilateral organizations to become more accountable to "civil society" rather than simply to states have proliferated. Insofar as these views become widespread, the sociological legitimacy of statism will decline and multilateral organizations will need to find new bases for their claims of legitimacy in the twenty-first century.

The twentieth-century theory of multilateral legitimacy

The sources of organizational legitimacy are conventionally divided into "output" and "input" legitimacy.[4] Outputs refer to the achievement of the substantive purposes of the organization, such as security and welfare. Inputs refer to the processes by which decisions are reached – whether they have certain attributes regarded as important by the audience. In the contemporary world, it is typically crucial for the legitimacy of state policy that it be made and implemented by nationals of one's state, not by foreigners. In thoroughly democratic societies, publics demand that governments act according to democratic principles, and courts have the authority to constrain the actions of executives, even on issues of national security.

Claims about the "unique legitimacy of the United Nations" or of multilateralism rely to some extent on output legitimacy. They begin with the premise that under conditions of interdependence coordinated policies are essential to avoid dysfunctional uncertainty and conflict, with negative results for all participants. These arguments also draw on a recognition that since the world is politically decentralized and heterogeneous, no single state or bloc can effectively dictate policies. Hence, it is argued that in general, policies that are developed through multilateral institutions have better prospects of general acceptance and widespread compliance than efforts to make policy unilaterally by a small number of states.

Yet advocates of multilateralism have difficulty claiming that the United Nations or other multilateral organizations are more efficient than states. Indeed, there is a long line of reports on the United Nations, and other literature, describing the bureaucratic weaknesses of the UN. The dependence of the organization on states for financial and other means of support means that the UN needs to negotiate with states for resources when crises arise, ensuring that it will respond slowly and often partially to rapidly changing events. Governments sometimes interfere in UN administrative processes for their own purposes, or introduce their own corrupt practices into it, as illustrated by the Iraqi oil-for-food programme of the 1990s. When peacekeeping operations have required decisive action based on complex logistics, the United Nations has had to rely on states or coalitions of states – NATO in Bosnia, Australia in East Timor, the United States around the world.

Indeed, one of the most striking features of effective multilateralism in the twentieth century is that it has often been precipitated by *unilateral* actions by powerful states. For example, the Bretton Woods monetary system was anchored by a unilateral commitment by the United States until 1971 to exchange dollars for gold at $35 per ounce. The Organization for European Economic Cooperation (OEEC) and its successor, the Organization for Economic Cooperation and Development (OECD) grew out of an American initiative, the Marshall Plan. Effective UN operations in Bosnia and Kosovo depended on military actions by the United States (in 1995 in Bosnia) or by NATO (in 1999 in Kosovo), which were only authorized after the fact by the UN. Finally, the creation of the World Trade Organization in 1995 was made possible by the desire on the part of other countries to limit American trade unilateralism.

Since multilateral institutions are not notably efficient organizations, if they are to be effective their processes of decision-making must be legitimate. That is, for multilateral institutions, output legitimacy depends on input legitimacy. To generate compliance, the political processes that generate resolutions by an organization such as the United Nations must be more acceptable, on issues that affect people in a wide variety of countries, than national political processes combined with coalitional diplomacy. On what basis could such a conclusion be reached?

The fundamental argument for the input legitimacy of multilateral organizations is that of diversity of representation and inclusiveness. The scope of interests involved in decision-making is much broader than for any state, voluntary coalition of states or regional organization. If all voices are heard, more objections will be expressed, deliberation may be enhanced and decisions more widely accepted. As a result, according to this argument, policy outcomes are likely to be superior to those resulting from the truncated discourse within countries or coalitions of states with similar interests and outlooks.

This ideal vision, however, is tarnished by a contradiction between the nominal state-egalitarianism of multilateral organizations and the realities of power politics. In most forums of the United Nations (the Security Council is a notable exception), each state, regardless of its size or power, has an equal vote. Weak states collectively can outvote the strong. But inequalities of power intrude on the expression of preferences by states. Even if weak states have the nominal ability to thwart the will of the strong in international organizations, they may be unable to analyse complex issues or make their voices heard. They may also be unwilling to defy their powerful neighbours, creditors and trade partners. As a result, the apparent diversity of interests in a global organization can be only nominal.

Defenders of multilateral institutions have to recognize this intrusion of power politics as an imperfection, and a potential threat to the legitimacy of their decisions. But this is hardly a new problem. The creators and defenders of these organizations in the twentieth century were not unaware of power politics. On the contrary, they conceived of these organizations as ways to *reduce* the impact of unequal military and economic resources on policy. Public debate and voting – "open covenants openly arrived at" in Woodrow Wilson's phrase – were designed to enhance the impact of principled argument and to increase the reputational costs to governments of cravenly bowing to pressure from the rich and powerful. Hence even if the apparent diversity and egalitarianism of multilateral organizations were tarnished by power politics, they remained greater than that of a world characterized by unilateral state action.

The structure of the UN Security Council makes this defence of multilateralism more problematic. First, its permanent membership does not reflect any principled set of criteria for representation, but rather the power politics of 1945, as negotiated at San Francisco. The five permanent members are not differentiated from other states by any consistent set of contemporary criteria, only by historical circumstance. Britain and France are of only middling size. China is clearly undemocratic and Russia does not meet substantive standards of democracy. Among non-members, India is the world's largest democracy, with a population more than eight times as large as those of Britain and France combined; Japan, with double the population of either Britain or France, has the world's second largest national economy.

Second, giving five arbitrarily selected states absolute vetoes over action cannot be justified on the basis of principles of either democracy or elementary fairness and reciprocity. The result of the veto, combined with the diverse political systems and interests of the permanent members, has often been deadlock. Inaction – with respect to military interventions by superpowers during the Cold War, ethnic cleansing in the Balkans during the 1990s and genocide in Africa in the 1990s in Rwanda and in 2004 in Sudan – has been more typical than precipitous collective action. Neither of the proposals for Security Council reform by the Secretary-General's High-Level Panel, in December 2004, would have alleviated the problem of deadlock, since both proposals retained the veto for the five permanent members while adding other members without the veto.[5]

It is true that the veto does help to protect the United Nations against destruction by angered great powers; and, in any case, it cannot be altered without creating a new organization from scratch, which would surely be an impossible task. Yet critics may well ask: if the United Nations is ineffective against elementary abuses of human rights, how valuable is the Organization? It is fair to point out that the existence of the United Nations somewhat ameliorates what otherwise would be a world of great power dominance unconstrained by UN-related rules. But it is also fair to point out the huge gap between the ideals nominally pursued by the United Nations, on the one hand, and the structures and activities of the Organization, on the other.

By democratic standards, or even on principles of elementary fairness and proportionality, the twentieth-century model of multilateralism is highly deficient. But during the twentieth century these deficiencies were not debilitating, since multilateral regimes constituted a supplement to traditional interstate relations, not a substitute for them. The effects of the actions of multilateral organizations were limited, by and large, to the relations between states. They did not penetrate deeply into domestic political systems. Sovereignty remained a core principle of the United Nations Charter, as inscribed in Article 2 (7). Deadlock on security issues meant that states would often rely on alliances and on ad hoc coalitions, as the United States and Soviet Union did throughout the Cold War. Multilateralism in security was an "add-on". In those relatively rare circumstances where there was sufficient agreement for the Security Council to authorize strong actions, it provided a way to confer legitimacy on a single set of policies. When the Security Council could not act, nothing was lost: political manoeuvres were pursued largely outside of the UN, with the UN simply a forum for the rhetorical echoes of these struggles. Twentieth-century multilateralism was only acceptable – hence legitimate – because it was designed as a limited system.

On trade issues, GATT likewise provided a way to specify, and legitimize, policies to be pursued by all members. When agreement could not be reached, the default option was always national regulation. Until the Uruguay Round and the creation of the WTO in 1994, GATT rules by and large did not intrude within the political economy of states. They pertained to external barriers to trade, not to national regulation. Furthermore, it was not essential to economic development that one accept the rules. Mexico, for instance, was not a member of GATT until 1986.

This twentieth-century model is one of limited cooperation – mutual adjustment of policy – rather than of governance. No one pretended that multilateralism constituted a new mode of governance – its scope was too partial and fragmentary for this. It was recognized as imperfect, but nevertheless as an improvement over the "anarchy" of independent state action. If it failed, the basic state-centric structure of world politics remained, as a fallback position.

The legitimacy demands on such a system of limited cooperation were quite modest. States could refuse to join the GATT yet participate fairly actively in world trade. During the Cold War states that were not diplomatically isolated could usually be assured that one Permanent Member or another would block effective Security Council action against them. Multilateral institutions were useful to states at the margin, without being threatening. There was no need to rethink issues of legitimacy, only to ask whether a given set of multilateral actions would be improvements over strategic interaction uncoordinated by institutions. If the answer was in the affirmative, states would support multilateralism; if it was negative, they could probably block it or otherwise opt out.

Threats to legitimacy: the democratic contradiction

Both on security and on trade issues, this situation changed quite fundamentally in the 1990s. On security issues, the end of the Cold War meant that the Security Council could suddenly act on a wide variety of issues, much less constrained by the veto. Almost as many peacekeeping operations were inaugurated during less than three years between 1991 and 1993 (15) than in the entire previous forty-six years of the United Nations (17). Ninety-three per cent of all Security Council resolutions adopted between 1946 and 2002 under Chapter VII, authorizing Security Council mandatory directives to states, were adopted after the end of the Cold War.[6] For the first time, democratization became part of the UN's operating creed. Standards of protection for human rights were raised, and the United Nations began authorizing humanitarian interventions, in countries where governments had abused their own populations. The system centred on the Security Council was transformed from one designed to help resolve certain conflicts between states, when interests overlapped sufficiently, to a system also intended to prevent extensive abuses of state power – at least where the states abusing power were weak – over their own populations.

No longer was the United Nations viewed simply as an incremental tool for improvement of security at the margin, but as responsible for protecting human rights even when states failed or refused to do so. Increasingly, it was held responsible for inaction as well as action – as in Rwanda. By contrast, during the Cold War, inaction had been the norm and sometimes issues were kept away from the Security Council to avoid futile and bitter argument that everyone knew would not lead to effective action. An indicator of the growing role of the Security Council in continuous governance is that inaction became as culpable as action.

These fundamental changes in the international organization of security politics (which were accompanied by parallel changes in trade politics that I do not have space to discuss) signalled the beginning of the replacement of patchwork cooperation with incipient governance systems. The architecture of multilateralism was becoming both more comprehensive and more intrusive. There were no longer any guarantees that the UN would be prevented from intervening in the internal affairs of weak countries whose governments were seen as guilty of human rights abuses. Although powerful states could still expect to block actions that they strongly opposed, weaker states had no such assurance.

The evolution of cooperative regimes into incipient governance systems quite naturally called into question the legitimacy of the organizations at the centre of these systems. Governance implies the possibility of coercion, which requires justification. Furthermore, rather than being supplementary to domestic governance, true international governance would to some extent replace it, both with respect to treatment of minorities and regulation of trade. On what basis could such international governance be legitimate?

In a democratic era, the obvious answer would be: "on the basis of democratic procedures". But there is no prospect of democracy on a global basis. Even if all other conditions were favourable, organizing a democracy of over six billion people would be extremely difficult. And other conditions are not favourable. National states are still the basic units of political organization in the world, to which the loyalties of most people flow. The diversity of values as well as interests in the world is immense. Relatively few countries have a long history of democratic practices, entailing the active involvement in politics of even a substantial minority of their citizens. There is no global public: that is, no representative, globally distributed set of people who identify with the world as a whole, as a political unit, and communicate freely with each other on the basis of common institutions and practices.

The debates about "globalization and democratic governance" reflect a disconnect between the normative basis for legitimacy, in the contemporary world, and the realities of multilateralism. The advocates of multilateralism emphasize what I have referred to as output legitimacy: in a globalized world, failure to coordinate policies can often lead to uncertainty and conflict, with negative results for all participants. But with respect to input legitimacy, the critics, from both Left and Right, occupy the high ground of democracy. As we have noted, multilateral organizations are not organized democratically – with equal votes for each individual – but on a statist basis. If democratic practices alone could provide legitimacy for institutions that exercise coercion, multilateral organizations would not be legitimate tools of governance.

From this perspective, the conclusion might seem to follow that the scope or level of international governance should be restricted. From the perspective of the American Right, the danger is that social democratic and quasi-pacifist European beliefs and practices will come to be viewed as mandated, by customary international law or by the actions of multilateral organizations. The movements to ban the death penalty or to prevent unilateral military action are examples of the danger perceived from this angle. From the perspective of the Left, the danger is that powerful corporations will control the policies of powerful states, which will then impose them on weak states – as the WTO is thought to have done. To governing elites outside the United States, the danger is that American dominance, combined with the decline of sovereignty norms, will expose them to unconstrained uses of American power with a patina of multilateral legitimacy – in effect, incorporating them within an informal American empire. To all three sets of critics, part of the answer is to reinvigorate and re-emphasize national sovereignty.

Faced with criticism from all sides, the defenders of multilateral organizations are thrown back on anachronistic twentieth-century conceptions to defend their input legitimacy. In this twentieth-century conception, societies, whether democratically governed or not, determine their own preferences through their own political institutions. Their governments then express these preferences in international forums. If the preferences of various governments coincide sufficiently, consensus follows. Legitimacy results from the inclusiveness of the multilateral institutions and the consequent diversity of their memberships. Actions taken in accord with decisions in multilateral organizations are legitimate because of the characteristics of the multilateral organizations themselves.

Yet this argument is undermined by the spread of democracy, since the conventional theory of sovereignty assumes that states, no matter how constituted internally, are entitled to represent and express the preferences of their people. Ironically, the "progressive" supporters of multilateralism rest their claim for the legitimacy of decisions made by multilateral institutions on a doctrine of sovereignty that has profoundly anti-democratic origins.

There is an interesting parallel between what we observe in the twenty-first century and the events of the seventeenth century. In both periods abstract morality was at odds with the fragmentation of power and values in world politics. Then the morality at issue was theological: ideologues sought to spread their brand of Christianity across Europe, generating warfare. Now the morality is more secular: democracy is to be instituted worldwide. The decline in religious fervour in the seventeenth century made it possible to organize the world on the basis of sovereignty and non-intervention. The revival and global extension of ideologies of democratic governance are making it harder to organize the world on the basis of sovereignty. This raises difficulties for organizations such as the United Nations and the WTO, founded on principles not of democracy but of sovereign equality.

The key point is that the normative basis for contemporary multilateralism rests on a fundamental contradiction. Intervention in the domestic affairs of states, undermining sovereignty, is justified on the basis of democratic principles, including the defence of human rights. But the organization of multilateralism itself is profoundly undemocratic.

Reconstructing the case for normative legitimacy

How, then, is a basis for the legitimacy of multilateral governance to be reconstructed? Democracy is infeasible at the global level, but democratic principles undercut the old justification of international legal sovereignty.

The remainder of this chapter will focus on this question. In doing so, I will assume the validity of a cosmopolitan approach to ethics, in which individuals have rights to be treated fairly, without respect to their country of origin or other irrelevant ascriptive characteristics. Second, I will assume both the normative validity of democratic theory for groups of people who identify themselves as a people and have the capacity to communicate with one another in a public space. Third, I will take as given the output legitimacy justification for multilateral institutions. In a world of high interdependence (economic and security), international cooperation is essential to avoid disastrous conflict, and systematic international cooperation is greatly facilitated by multilateral institutions with established rules and practices.

Taken together, these assumptions frame the dilemma on which I wish to focus. It is in principle desirable to achieve three objectives: 1) to ensure that the human rights of individuals are respected regardless of their residency or citizenship; 2) to maximize the extent to which democratic processes determine decisions; and 3) to manage international and transnational cooperation in ways that promote security and welfare. This trilogy of objectives can be summarized as human rights, democracy and cooperation.

The problem is that these objectives are extremely difficult to achieve together. One could imagine rigorous rules, enforced by a world government, that protected human rights; but such a system would, in the present state of the world, be undemocratic and would surely generate intense and violent conflict over the rules. One could also imagine achieving the democracy objective by breaking the world up into thousands of democratic mini-states; but in that case there would surely be very large, morally unjustifiable inequalities as well as unregulated international conflict. Finally, emphasis could be placed on efforts by multilateral institutions to promote security and welfare through cooperation. Yet these efforts will necessarily be biased toward the rich and powerful, and are unlikely to achieve the goals either of global human rights or democracy.

Discussing this set of dilemmas should at least put the problem of legitimacy for multilateral organizations in perspective. The question is not whether one could design a perfect system of multilateralism that would actually work. In the current state of the world, this is impossible. The relevant question is whether, *in light of feasible alternatives*, existing or attainable forms of multilateralism are legitimate *relative to these alternatives*.

As noted above, if multilateralism is to be considered more legitimate than uncoordinated and unilateral state action, it will have to be superior on grounds of input legitimacy – the acceptability of the processes by which institutions make decisions. Since I am assuming the widespread acceptance of cosmopolitan ethical theory, I will confine my investigation to applying it to the actual situation of multilateralism. Elsewhere I have considered the WTO, but due to space limitations I limit myself here to an analysis of the United Nations.[7] Can the decision-making processes of the UN be considered *comparatively legitimate*, in the light of actual conditions in world politics and democratic theory? What changes could increase their legitimacy?

Criteria for comparative legitimacy

One possible line of argument would rely on compromise as a positive value. In this view, the most important danger is that powerful states will behave in arbitrary or despotic ways. Even if deadlock ensues from multilateralism, it is better than precipitous action. When all interests are taken into account, and agreement by a supermajority or by consensus is necessary, the dangers of the multilateral organization acting in harmful ways are reduced. Hence multilateralism per se – institutionalized decision-making by an inclusive organization of states from around the world – confers legitimacy because it ensures that actions will be generally acceptable.

This line of argument has two fatal problems. First, it is too conservative: it assumes that the status quo is sufficiently acceptable that deadlock will not generate disaster. In a world of weapons of mass destruction, actively sought by governments and potential terrorist groups, this assumption is not realistic. It is based not on the world as we know it, but on a more benign, imaginary world. Compromise for its own sake is not a positive good – especially when the compromise is with forces of evil. Sometimes resolute action is necessary.

The second problem with the compromise–restraint argument is related. When powerful states believe that they face fundamental threats to their security or welfare, they will respond unilaterally, if unable to do so through multilateral institutions. Even if they were abstractly to accept the input legitimacy argument for the superiority of compromise, it would be trumped by output illegitimacy: the ineffectiveness of multilateralism in responding to threats to vital interests. The more important the issue, the less satisfactory will be compromise per se as a source of legitimacy.

A more plausible line of argument takes the diversity of interests represented in multilateral organizations as a necessary but not sufficient condition for legitimacy. Organizations, from hegemonic states to "coalitions of the willing" or alliances, that exclude large numbers of people from representation, cannot be legitimate on a global basis. No claim that a given state or organization has superior morality or superior knowledge (for instance, because of its political history or religious faith) can provide a valid basis for people who do not share such beliefs to accept their authority.

But diversity is not a sufficient basis for legitimacy. Compromise with evil is not superior to resolute action against it. Serious problems of collective action that are ignored, do not simply go away harmlessly. Hence the legitimacy of a set of multilateral institutions requires that the institutions respond forthrightly and decisively to present and potential threats to security and welfare. No matter how diverse it was, a multilateral institution that ignored genocide or an epidemic such as AIDs would not be normatively legitimate. And a multilateral institution that *blocked* action on such issues would be positively injurious, hence illegitimate. So the second condition for the legitimacy of a multilateral organization is the capacity to act decisively in response to threats of severe global harm, and the existence of a back-up procedure to ensure that if it cannot act decisively, it does not prevent others from doing so.

A legitimate organization not only needs to be able to act; it must act in ways that are consistent with the best available knowledge of factual realities and causal relationships, as well as with ethical imperatives. At any rate, legitimate institutions should be at least as capable of acting intelligently as the alternatives. What this means is that in addition to being inclusive, multilateral institutions must meet an *epistemic* standard.[8] An institution is *epistemically legitimate* insofar as it has the capacity to generate and properly use new information that can generate new policy responses, reduce bias in standards and implementation, and reduce the risk of opportunistic interventions. According to this view, it is important that institutions promote discussions in which all valid interests are represented, and it is equally important that there be provisions for critical re-evaluation, promoted by diversity. But the process must be knowledge-based and have the capacity for improvement over time. There is little moral justification for simply compromising between positions that are well-founded empirically and morally and those that are not.

I contend that an institution has a valid claim to make legitimate policy on a global basis only if it meets all three standards: of *inclusiveness*, *decisiveness*, and *epistemic reliability*. It may also have to meet other standards, but it would require more space than I have here to elaborate them.

With respect to *inclusiveness*, all valid interests – interests that are based on the welfare of a substantial number of people as they perceive them, rather than on hatred or an urge for dominance – must be represented effectively. These interests must be ascertained by a process that shows respect to individuals, preferably by enabling them, through fair and reasonably frequently elections, to select their representatives. And the political entities included in the global institution must be represented by agents with the capacity to represent them.

Decisiveness ideally means that the multilateral organization could take effective action, even against the opposition of its strongest member state. That is, there would be no veto, either in the organization or, effectively, by one state or a small coalition withholding material support from the organization as it pursued a policy that had been agreed on by a large majority. Conversely, this criterion would also require that there be incentives within the organization to encourage states that would otherwise be passive to support vigorous action. The natural condition of multilateral organizations, without leadership, is entropy.

The obvious problem is that in the contemporary world, multilateral institutions lack the capacity either to override the wishes of the most powerful state in the system, the United States, or to overcome the collective action problems that lead other states to hide from danger, or fail to make contributions to a joint cause. The implication of these facts is that the legitimacy of any global multilateral organization will be tarnished by its weakness. On a strict standard of absolute legitimacy, multilateral organizations will fail. They can only be defended on the basis of *comparative legitimacy*: the normative superiority of partial reliance on them for authorization of action, over other feasible processes.

The third criterion of legitimacy is *epistemic reliability*. Epistemic reliability implies that the decision-making process must be sufficiently transparent that it is open to criticism from outsiders as well as insiders. In particular, there must be provisions for accountability and for revising the rules and practices in light of experience. Accountability implies clear standards for behaviour by agents in authority, the widespread availability of information, to publics, about these agents' performance, and the availability of sanctions when the performance does not meet the standards.[9] Revisability requires that the rules do not unduly favour the status quo: when opinion shifts, there must be an open pathway (not necessarily immediately or by a bare majority) for institutional change.

These provisions for revision should be open-ended. It is impossible now to build multilateral institutions on the basis of democratic principles, but it would be wrong to close off the possibility of a democratic governance system eventually developing, on a global level. Now there are national publics – groups of people who identify with one another and live within common boundaries. They are the relevant collective entities that can be said to have preferences. Aggregation of individual preferences takes place within countries, facilitated by the common means of communication and discourse developed within each of them. At the global level there are only small, fragmented publics of elites with common interests in particular issues such as human rights or the environment. But increases in transnational ties among peoples may some day invalidate the assumption that preferences can only be aggregated on a national basis. A legitimate system for global governance would have an open pathway for the progressive involvement of these fragmented publics – now to be found principally in NGOs and networks of activists – in decision-making.

Implications for the United Nations

How well does the United Nations meet the criteria of inclusiveness, decisiveness and epistemic reliability? And what changes would need to be made to improve its legitimacy?

The UN is an inclusive organization, open to virtually any state. No state has ever been expelled from the United Nations, despite the fact that many states have engaged in behaviour threatening to peace, the preservation of which is the essential purpose of the organization. The importance of the UN and of the security issues that it deals with ensure that on critical issues, states belonging to it will be represented by their most effective advocates. With respect to inclusiveness, the most glaring deficiency of the UN relates not to states but to individuals and minorities. Many of the countries in the United Nations are either undemocratic or only partially democratic. We should not expect that the policies they enunciate will be in the interests of their publics, rather than simply of an unaccountable elite. The UN is therefore too inclusive of states, and not inclusive enough of the views of individuals and potential groups within authoritarian states.

If the UN has a mixed record with respect to inclusiveness, it does poorly on decisiveness. The veto makes it impossible for the UN to authorize military action against the wishes of any of the five Permanent Members, creating the problem of deadlock that was discussed above. Members of the UN, and its agencies, often have strong incentives to avoid or downplay emerging threats. The Report of the High-Level Panel upholds the conventional view that the Security Council, acting with the veto, must approve any military action except under conditions of actual or imminent attack. It therefore does not address the issue of decisiveness.[10]

The third major condition for the UN's input legitimacy is epistemic: its ability to use information, to make decisions on the basis of knowledge, and to revise its practices in light of experience. With respect to these epistemic criteria, its performance is somewhat mixed. Three attributes of the United Nations fall on the positive side of the ledger. The first one is familiar: inclusiveness. The fact that many points of view are represented guards against parochialism and self-deception. The refusal of the UN to endorse the US plan to attack Iraq in 2003 reflects this strength: the Security Council would never have accepted the naive and, for the US, self-serving view that Iraqis would welcome American conquerors as liberators. The second positive factor for the UN is that the rules of the Organization give space for independent statements of views by representatives of states. Protests and demands for policy change by states can be expressed, although non-state voices are not so readily heard. Third, the Office of the Secretary-General provides a potential for epistemic reliability, although the Oil-for-Food scandal has thrown considerable doubt on the Secretariat's ability to fulfil this potential. Since the office of Secretary-General has very little power except the power of persuasion, he is more dependent, for effectiveness, on a good epistemic reputation than are leaders of powerful states.

On the negative side of the epistemic ledger, state policies at the UN are driven by interests. Strategic bargaining, incentives not to reveal preferences or information, and even deception outweigh any objective searches for knowledge. Technical expertise plays a subordinate role to political calculation. Second, some of the supermajoritarian features of the UN make it hard to revise policies. In particular, the Security Council veto ensures that it will be very difficult to reverse decisions, once they have been made. Sanctions against Iraq, for instance, continued for years in the 1990s despite lack of majority support for them in the Security Council. Once in place, they could not be removed even after new information was received about the suffering of Iraqi civilians, due to the threat of American and British vetoes. Third, like any bureaucracy the UN Secretariat can be self-serving and even potentially corrupt, as the Oil-for-Food scandal demonstrates.

Improving the accountability of the United Nations Security Council

The UN's potential for epistemic legitimacy is undermined by the absence, in the Security Council, of a system of accountability to evaluate actions taken under its auspices, to impose sanctions on violators, and to revise procedures in light of experience. To enhance the chances for multilateralism on security issues, the United Nations should be reformed to create such an accountability system.[11]

Currently, the UN Security Council is in the position, when it authorizes military action, analogous to that of someone writing a blank check. Not only does the Security Council not direct the use of the military forces whose use it authorizes, it has difficulty holding the great powers that use them accountable for their actions. There are no systematic procedures for monitoring military activities authorized by the United Nations. There are no systematic procedures for the Security Council to interrogate leaders of the states employing force, or for modifying authorizations in light of such questioning. And the Security Council has no ability to punish powerful member states – which themselves have veto powers – for exceeding the limits of UN authorization.

As a result, it is very difficult to agree on UN authorization for the use of force even when a strong case for action can be made. There are dangers of deception: the potential interveners know more about the situation than governments whose states are represented in the Security Council. Even if the representatives of the potential interveners are believed, there may be reasonable doubts whether the policies they announce will be implemented. Will the interveners respect just war principles to minimize the damage that war would bring to civilians? In occupying the country, will they pursue purposes agreed to by the United Nations, or rather pursue their own interests?

One way to solve this problem of credibility would be for the leader of a coalition, such as the United States, to enter into an explicit agreement with the Security Council before military action occurred. Under such an agreement, the coalition leader would specify the threats to world order that it was acting to combat – such as, in the Iraqi case, the production and storage of weapons of mass destruction. It would specify the political objectives – disarmament or regime change? – of its projected military campaign. It would then agree with the Security Council on benchmarks that it – as the occupying power immediately after the war – would have to meet. These could include:

- Immediate post-war access to the whole country for UN inspectors;
- Acceptance of responsibility, including monetary damages, for actions that violated the laws of war or the principles of just war theory;
- Acceptance of United Nations authority, after a very short time, over the economic resources of the conquered country;
- Acceptance of a rapid transition to a United Nations administration, with civil authority over the country, leading rapidly to a transition to rule by citizens of the country involved;
- Guarantees of support for these regimes for as long as necessary by military forces from the occupying powers.

These measures seem to be costly for the coalition leader. Why should the United States, for instance, accept these constraints if it is to bear the principal costs of military action? The answer is that only by accepting constraints, *ex ante*, could the coalition leader make its own promises credible. Credible promises, in turn, are essential to induce other members of the Security Council to grant authorization to the coalition leader to use force on behalf of world society, thus providing the legitimation that it may sorely need.

For the UN to be fully legitimate as a provider of security, it will have to be able to act decisively, generating output legitimacy, and to operate in a transparent way that holds powerful agents accountable, generating input legitimacy. Although the Security Council may now be more legitimate than the alternatives, it falls far short of what could reasonably be demanded on both the input and the output sides. The "unique legitimacy of the United Nations" could be enhanced by a reform of its accountability system.

One potentially feasible supplement to the United Nations would be a league of democracies. Professor Allen Buchanan and I have elsewhere discussed the attractiveness of instituting a league of democratic states as supplementary to the UN Security Council. Such a league of democracies would not replace the Security Council, to which potential intervenors would have to appeal first for authorization. But if Security Council action were blocked only by a veto or vetoes, those calling for intervention could seek authorization from a supermajority (perhaps 2/3) of democratic states. Such authorization would be in some ways more legitimate than Security Council authorization, because more reflective of democratic opinion; and the presence of this option could provide an incentive for states to refrain from abusing their veto privilege in the Security Council. No Charter amendment would be required.[12]

A net judgement on legitimacy rests on a comparison with feasible alternatives. Reliance on individual great powers is inferior on the grounds both of inclusiveness and epistemic reliability. A closed process such as was evident within the United States – and even within the Central Intelligence Agency – before the war against Iraq, creates a situation in which "groupthink" can thrive. Absent the diversity of views that inclusiveness generates, critical questions can be discouraged and flaws in the analysis overlooked.

For the time being, UN-based multilateralism on security affairs through the United Nations, whatever its flaws, retains a potential for input legitimacy that is superior to the currently available alternative of unilateralism and coalition-building. But it should not be beyond our capability to design superior multilateral institutions to protect the security of the world's people.

Conclusions

Twentieth-century multilateralism provided for institutionalized collective action, where consensus existed, to deal with issues such as interstate military conflict and trade discrimination. The legitimacy demands on this form of multilateralism were modest. If the supermajority or consensus requirements of a multilateral organization were met, it meant that multilateralism was acceptable to states – the units that counted. If these requirements were not met, the situation reverted to the default option of unilateralism or coalition-building among states with similar interests. Multilateralism was a tool of policy for states, useful at least at the margin.

Twenty-first-century multilateralism, however, involves much more intrusive intervention in what have traditionally been considered the domestic affairs of states – notably including both how minorities are treated by governments and the regulation of the economy. For standards of human rights or economic liberalism to be upheld, multilateral action is often advocated to substitute for ineffective or injurious domestic policy, rather than merely to complement domestic measures. Furthermore, preventing weapons of mass destruction falling into the hands of state or non-state actors willing to use them against civilian populations, and not in self defence, may well require pro-active policies, involving potential violations of sovereignty. Both types of situation involve coercion imposed by powerful states, legitimated (it could be claimed) by the resolutions of multilateral organizations.

When rules made non-democratically in multilateral organizations are promulgated as substitutes for rules made democratically by states, questions of legitimacy insistently arise. Leaders of multilateral organizations typically claim that the scope, diversity, and inclusiveness of their organizations' membership provide legitimacy for their actions, as compared to those of states or less inclusive coalitions of states. But in a democratic era, inclusiveness alone is not a sufficient basis for legitimacy. In democratic theory, individuals, not states, are the subjects of political and moral concern. Inclusiveness of states is not an unalloyed virtue if it means that non-democracies can express preferences that are not desired by, or in the interests of, most people residing within their territories.

Ironically, defences of the legitimacy of contemporary multilateral organizations often seem to rely on the political theory of sovereignty, whose origins lie in monarchy not democracy. As sovereignty is increasingly called into question, relying on it for the legitimacy of multilateralism entails a fundamental contradiction.

A defence of the legitimacy of multilateralism begins with an acknowledgement that existing multilateral institutions are seriously deficient. The criteria for the input legitimacy of multilateral institutions include inclusiveness, decisiveness, and epistemic reliability. The United Nations earns mixed marks on the basis of these standards. Its output legitimacy is threatened at the same time by its frequent ineffectiveness. The September 2005 World Summit outcome reflects no progress toward greater input legitimacy and only modest progress – notably, in the acceptance of the Responsibility to Protect – in output legitimacy.

In the contemporary world, global democracy is infeasible. But the world is infused with democratic norms, and to bolster its legitimacy, multilateralism needs to be more consistent with those norms. Multilateralists need to recognize how certain aspects of democracy, such as transparency, accountability, and provisions to limit the role of direct coercion, could be incorporated into multilateral institutions, making them more robust against charges of illegitimacy. The UN Security Council needs an explicit system of institutionalized accountability for the use of force.

However, perfection – or even a close approximation thereto – is elusive in world politics. The issue is not whether multilateral institutions meet ideal standards – they do not – but whether they are superior to the alternative of unregulated state competition. For the moment, the legitimacy of multilateral institutions is protected less by their own merits than by the lack of attractive alternatives. In the absence of an effective coalition of democracies, the alternative to the UN Security Council is unilateralism and "coalitions of the willing", which epitomize the absence of effective institutional constraints on the exercise of power.

I conclude that contemporary multilateral institutions such as the United Nations are *contingently legitimate*, relative to the currently available alternatives, which are quite unattractive. But their advocates, and their leaders, should begin to reconstruct their legitimacy on a twenty-first-century basis – with more emphasis on democratic principles and less on sovereignty. Otherwise, multilateral institutions will be in danger of losing legitimacy to a revival of democratic nationalism, or to new forms of transnational organization that are designed to bypass sovereignty, and that will be in many ways problematic for those of us who believe in the accountability of power-wielders to ordinary people.

Notes

1. John Gerard Ruggie (1993) "Multilateralism: the anatomy of an institutional form", in Ruggie, *Multilateralism Matters: the Theory and Praxis of an Institutional Form*, New York, NY: Columbia University Press, p. 11.
2. Robert O. Keohane (1984) *After Hegemony: Cooperation and Discord in the World Political Economy*, Princeton, NJ: Princeton University Press (20th anniversary edition, 2005).
3. Inis L. Claude (1962) *Power and International Relations*, New York: Random House; see also, Inis L. Claude (1966) "Collective legitimation as a political function of the United Nations", *International Organization* 20(3): 367–379.
4. Fritz Scharpf (1999) *Governing in Europe: Effective and Democratic?*, Oxford: Oxford University Press.
5. *A More Secure World: Our Shared Responsibility*, Report of the High-Level Panel on Threats, Challenges, and Change, United Nations General Assembly A/59/565, 29 November 2004.
6. David M. Malone (ed.) (2004) *The UN Security Council: from the Cold War to the 21st Century*, Boulder, CO: Lynne Reinner, p. 6. See especially Peter Wallensteen and Patrik Johansson (2004) "Security Council decisions in perspective", in Malone, pp. 17–33.
7. For a discussion of the WTO and problems of accountability, see Robert O. Keohane and Joseph S. Nye, Jr. (2003) "Redefining accountability for global governance", in Miles Kahler and David Lake (eds.) *Governance in a Global Economy: Political Authority in Transition*, Princeton: Princeton University Press, pp. 387–411.

8. Allen Buchanan (2004) "Political liberalism and social epistemology", *Philosophy and Public Affairs* 32(2): 95–130.
9. Ruth Grant and Robert O. Keohane (2005) "Accountability and abuses of power in world politics", *American Political Science Review* 99(1): 1–15.
10. *More Secure World*, cited (Note 4) pp. 50–51.
11. See Allen Buchanan and Robert O. Keohane (2004) "The preventive use of force: a cosmopolitan institutional proposal", *Ethics and International Affairs* 18(2): 1–22.
12. See Buchanan and Keohane, "The preventive use of force" (Note 9) for details.

5

Power and world order

Coral Bell

Beneath the most familiar map of the world, which is a map of the society of states, there lies another, less familiar, less mapped cosmopolitan world: that of "non–state actors". Almost impossible to map because it changes so quickly, and the entities which make it up are so variable: everything from the Red Cross to the jihadists. In the last few decades, its membership has been increasing fast, as has its ability to make an impact on the society of states. On 11 September 2001, a hidden hand reached up from that world to inflict savage trauma on the most powerful sovereign state in history.

That was a transformatory moment in the long search for order in a system of independent powers. What it signified was that the traditional sources of disorder – the ambitions and rivalries of sovereign states – were no longer the immediate problem. As late as the end of the twentieth century, it had been assumed that an international order could be based on just creating and maintaining a reasonably cooperative relationship among sovereign states, an effective rule of law, or at least some degree of consensus on norms and conventions between the governments which make the decisions for those states. In these early decades of the twenty-first century, the objective must be larger: to build a world order which will not only operate between existing sovereignties but also survive, contain and (when justified) even accommodate the pressures and tensions which arise from transnational forces. Forces which in many cases are generated by those who feel themselves disadvantaged by the existing order, excluded from its benefits, alienated by its norms – and determined to change it.

The world in which this effort must be undertaken is one in which power has recently been concentrated, to a degree unparalleled since Roman times, in a single sovereignty, and a single political elite, the decision-makers and policy-makers in Washington. That circumstance makes the United States the target not only of the resentment of many governments, but of active hatred among those who see it as the primary manipulator and beneficiary of the system which disadvantages them. And neither the massive high-tech military power in which the United States is unrivalled, nor the economic clout which it enjoys in abundance, are altogether effective against the global network of jihadist cells from which come the chief threats against the world order over which the United States presides.

So the problem resolves itself into four separate but related questions. How is consensus to be built and maintained between the contemporary sovereignties of the society of states, including especially those who do not feel they have much to be thankful for in the existing world establishment? What degree of cooperation can be devised to manage the transnational groups or forces which threaten that established order? What internal or external constraints could, over the next few decades, be effective against the paramount power of a unipolar world? Can contemporary international institutions be modified to serve those objectives more adequately?

A consensus of sovereignties: the jihadists as catalyst

The most important and only constructive side-effect of the challenge which the jihadists present to the existing society of states is that it has concentrated the attention of its national decision-makers on the survival of their own modes of governance, democratic or not. That is, the jihadists have operated as a powerful catalyst in diplomatic alignments, changing them without themselves being changed. Nothing is more conducive to consensus than a common enemy, and the jihadists are clearly that, especially for the most vulnerable of their targets, the governments of Muslim societies. Indeed the jihadists themselves, on the evidence of computer discs captured in Afghanistan, questioned whether their most useful strategy was to concentrate on "near" targets (vulnerable Muslim societies) or "far" targets like the United States, where the "payoff" in terms of publicity, funds and recruits is much greater. As former British Prime Minister Margaret Thatcher once said, terrorists live on the oxygen of publicity, and currently they are exploiting it more ferociously than ever before. And they are helped (more than any earlier groups) by the explosion in the means of communication, especially the Internet.

The common consciousness among the society of states of unexpected danger from outside their own ranks has, for the time being at least promoted consciousness of the necessity of multilateralism and diminished the importance of what before 11 September 2001 appeared real and substantial conflicts of national interests. The most obvious and important of these are in the diplomatic and strategic relations between the United States and China. For the Pacific and Asia, the Washington–Beijing relationship became suddenly more benign than it had appeared since the détente of 1971–72.

During the first eight months of the Bush administration, that had appeared the least probable of developments. Indeed, for much of that time, the United States and China had seemed uncomfortably close to a collision course. A potential *casus belli* had been quite visible: the future status of Taiwan. Ever since the Kissinger-constructed détente of 1971–72, amicable relations had been maintained only by a careful, conscious, diplomatic ambiguity on that point. Soon after Bush assumed office, however, that ambiguity had begun to fray, sometimes appearing almost beyond repair. Taiwan's nationalist leader, Chen Shui-bian, seemed to be indicating that he believed that the time was propitious for seeking *de jure* (as against *de facto*) independence. Washington seemed to be going along with that ambition, providing Taiwan lavishly with advanced weapon systems. Bush himself declared that the United States would do everything necessary to help Taiwan defend itself. A US spy-plane was obliged to land on the Chinese island of Hainan in April 2003, and its crew were held captive by the Chinese military for some days. A little more imprudent crisis-management at that moment might have precipitated serious hostilities.

Both sides retreated from the brink in time, but China nevertheless continued to be defined in the Pentagon's terms as the most likely eventual "peer-competitor" of the United States, the only obvious replacement of the Soviet Union as prospective "national adversary number one". Strategic logic appeared almost to impose that view. Northeast Asia had been an area of spectacular economic growth for some decades, and China had become its "front runner" after the slowing of Japan in the 1990s. With almost unlimited low-cost labour, vast territory, substantial resources, an infrastructure approaching First World standards in some respects, and growing technological sophistication, China appeared only at the beginning of its rise to economic, diplomatic, and in time military power. No one could doubt that it had the potential to become a more formidable rival than Japan had ever been in East Asia and the Western Pacific. Indeed, to many people it appeared the natural claimant in geographical terms to be the hegemonial power of the region, since the United States is an ocean away, and (unlike China) might depart in time.

After 11 September 2001, however, the strategic priorities of the United States were revolutionized for the foreseeable future. The Pentagon's attention had to be directed towards a newly defined arc of crisis, the world of the jihadists, from North Africa round to the southern Philippines, via Afghanistan. Moreover homeland security became a more urgent and more expensive matter than it had been even during the Cold War. Though Soviet missiles might have reached the US heartland, the Soviet government could be (and was) deterred by superior US strike-power, and other factors, none of which applied to the jihadists. So the new threat generated a new and controversial strategy: pre-emption in place of (or in addition to) containment.

Chinese decision-makers may reasonably be assumed to have been relieved by the shift in the Pentagon's preoccupations away from their own region. Ability to sell into the US market is a vital economic asset to China in the drive to modernize its economy, and could have been prejudiced by continued high tension. The well-informed strategists of the PLA were unlikely to have been under any illusion that their forces were as yet in an advantageous position vis-à-vis even Taiwan, much less the Seventh Fleet. Moreover, China had its own reasons to worry about the rise of Islamic fundamentalism in Central Asia, and its implications for Xinjiang. That perhaps is why it accepted with what otherwise would have seemed astonishing equanimity a sharp deterioration of its own strategic position vis-à-vis the United States. Washington almost immediately replaced Beijing as Pakistan's most important ally. US forces moved not only into Afghanistan but in to Kazakhstan, Uzbekistan and Tajikistan, almost encircling China's inner-Asian borders. Washington also worked harder on its relations with India (which still has an irredentist quarrel with China, from the 1962 war) and hastily concluded a strategic deal with Pakistan.

The primary compensation for China, to set against the deterioration of its overall strategic position, has been a redefinition of Washington's stance vis-à-vis Taiwan. In December 2003, while the Chinese Prime Minister, Wen Jiabao, was visiting the White House, Bush said, in a blunt rebuke to Taipei, that "the comments and actions of the Taiwanese President, Chen Shui-bian, indicate that he may be willing to make decisions unilaterally that change the status quo. We oppose that." Given Taiwan's strategic dependence on Washington's protection, it appeared unlikely that any near-term decision-maker in Taipei would push his luck in near-future manoeuvres towards independence, even if endorsed by elections. Long-term, that position may change, but given the present rate of economic integration between Taiwan and the mainland, it seems quite possible that reintegration on more or less China's terms might occur before the end of Washington's concentration on the war with the jihadists.

For the entire Asia-Pacific area, the stability of the United States–China relationship is a vital concern. So even the prospect of postponement of one potential conflict is welcome, though others are emerging.

Since 11 September 2001, the United States has another strong reason for giving higher priority to a good relationship with China: the need to curb the nuclear ambitions of North Korea. Only China has the means to exert really persuasive pressure in that country, since it provides its main lifeline in food and fuel. Though there have been some doubts in expert quarters of the reality of North Korea's development of nuclear weapons, it appears at least probable that it is further along that road than the other main target of the US counter-proliferation policy, Iran.

Counter-proliferation is moreover one aspect of United States policy that most governments can regard with at least surreptitious approval. No acknowledged member of the nuclear club (the United States, Russia, China, Britain, France, India, Pakistan and Israel) wants to see new members of that exclusive grouping, and practically all the other members of the society of states have abandoned ambitions in that regard. Even Iran maintains that its nuclear facilities are aimed only at power-generation, though many find that implausible. Persuading North Korea to give up on nuclear weapons would be an important symbolic milestone. Even ideologically, one can see less reason than in the past for tension between the United States and China. Though officially China is still a communist country, and is certainly ruled by a Politburo, and still very intolerant of those like the Falun Gong who dissent from the official norms, Deng Xiao-ping's maxim "to get rich is glorious" is now much more dominant in national life than "Leninism-Stalinism-Mao Tse-tung Thought", and it is a maxim any US capitalist could endorse. Chinese nationalism seems these days the intellectual and emotional driving force of the political elite. That might obviously provide reasons to challenge Western interests and Western power in the region, but it is not precisely a banner that attracts revolutionary movements elsewhere, as Maoism used to do, for instance, in Nepal and Latin America.

For Washington's relations with Moscow as well, the abandonment of any kind of alternative world vision based on Marxist analysis eased the way to governmental consensus about international order, and the most immediate threat to it. So, like China, in the aftermath of 11 September 2001, Russia showed little or no resistance to the sudden assertion of US strategic interest in the ex-Soviet states of Central Asia. American and other Western interest in the oil resources of the area now rival those of China and Russia. But both Chinese and Russian tolerance of that situation appeared to be fraying by late 2005.[1]

The United States and China, or the United States and Russia, were not the only potential or actual "adversary pairs" who suddenly discovered the advantages of détente in the face of a new threat. India and Pakistan, which for more than fifty years had lived in a state of endemic tension, rising at times to full-scale war, have been on rather more hopeful terms since the threat posed by the jihadists became clearer to them both. For each it is an internal as well as an international issue. India has one of the largest Muslim populations in the world, after Indonesia, and must also be concerned with those of Pakistan and Bangladesh. South and Southeast Asia's Muslims, in total, vastly outnumber those of the rest of the world, so their orientations, for or against the jihadists, are likely to be of vital importance in the outcome of the jihadists' war. The government of President Musharraf in Pakistan found a useful ally in Washington, and the United States a strategically vital one in Pakistan, for as long as the Afghanistan campaign persists, but the orientation of many Pakistanis is profoundly anti-American, and the President is a much-threatened man.

Unfortunately the original post-11 September 2001 diplomatic consensus was disrupted after only a year. By September 2002, as the US Secretary of State was developing his case at the United Nations on Iraq's alleged weapons of mass destruction, most governments and their peoples had become deeply critical of the unfolding strategy of the United States, especially the clear intent by then to effect "regime change" in Iraq. Few other decision-makers were prepared to see that as a sensible approach to dealing with the problem of the jihadists. So the Anglo-American resolution of March 2003, seeking United Nations legitimation for the invasion of Iraq, had to be withdrawn, not merely because it was certain to be vetoed by France, but because it was quite likely to fail to obtain a simple majority of the Security Council, several of whose members would earlier have been regarded as client states of the United States. Nevertheless, the basic point that most of the traditional rivalries which have threatened world order in the past have been "put on the back-burner", as governments contemplate the new challenge, remains true. The arguments between governments have been about strategies and definitions, not objectives.

Defining the challenge to world order

Since 11 September 2001, official Washington has used the phrase "war on terrorism" to describe the policies it has pursued, and is pursuing, in reaction to that intensely traumatic event. But that phrase, however convenient for politicians, does not really convey much about the nature of the threat to world order. "The jihadists' war" is more precise.[2] Terrorism is both their strategy and their tactic, but it is not exclusive to them. It has been used over many years by a great many political movements. Almost all those past and present groups have however been seeking change only in local political or territorial arrangements, or governmental reform of some sort. The jihadists are different. Their objective is global, not local; nothing short of the transformation of power relationships in world politics, and thus overturning the existing world order.

That is to say, the challenge is not merely to the United States, but to the society of states: the contemporary world establishment and its governments as a group, including even a fundamentalist Islamic state such as Saudi Arabia. The choice of the United States and, in particular, the World Trade Center and the Pentagon, as targets was nevertheless significant. They were the prime symbols of the economic and military ascendancy of the United States as the paramount power of a unipolar world. In other words, the most obvious icons of the late twentieth-century world order, which the jihadists believe they have a duty to overturn.

President Bush, at the beginning of his 2004 campaign for re-election, absent-mindedly deviated into realism and candour when he said to an interviewer that the "war on terrorism" could not be won. Obviously, acts of terrorism are always going to be possible to those who know enough chemistry to put together a home-made bomb (like Timothy McVeigh, or the "Unabomber") or even to those who can acquire a rifle (like the Washington snipers). Though Bush hastily retracted his words, they remained true. Terrorism cannot be defeated because it will always be an option to those who believe that their grievances against a government are important enough to resort to violence. But the jihadists as an organized coherent force can be defeated, though it will be difficult. Defining the conflict as "the jihadists' war" has thus the advantage of making the target specific, and of restricting it to its real dimensions. The adversary is not Islamism, or Islamic fundamentalism. Those terms denote only religious or political orientations. The jihadists are those who see themselves as "on active service" in an asymmetric war against the current global order.

A parallel from the past

Several factors clearly distinguish the jihadists' war from the last protracted conflict faced by the West, the Cold War, 1946–89. The importance and reality of the differences between the two conflicts should not, however, be allowed to obscure the points of resemblance. Both are hegemonial wars: wars about the order of power in the world. Both are also wars of doctrine, wars about the norms on which societies should be ordered. In both, the whole world is the battle space, but some areas are more vital and vulnerable than others – in the Cold War, Central Europe and Northeast Asia; in the current conflict, probably Pakistan, Saudi Arabia and the North Caucasus. The jihadists believe they will prevail because Allah is on their side. The revolutionaries of 1917 and their successors, up to Khrushchev's time, believed that they would prevail because history was on their side.

Even the developmental sequence of the two conflicts has been so far quite similar. In both, there have been two actual military campaigns: Korea and Vietnam in the Cold War, Afghanistan and Iraq in the conflict with the jihadists. In both struggles, the earlier of those campaigns was a "necessary war", forced on the West by surprise attacks – in June 1950 for Korea and, on 11 September 2001, by a far more unforeseen adversary. But the other two campaigns, Vietnam and Iraq, were unnecessary wars, "wars of choice". No area vital to the West was under attack. The strategic importance of Vietnam was grossly exaggerated in the late 1950s and early 1960s in Washington, just as the strategic "necessity" of getting rid of Saddam's illusory weapons of mass destruction was in 2002–2003. In both campaigns, the "domino concept" made its misleading appearance, alleged to be the other side's strategy for Southeast Asia in the Vietnam case, and actually the strategic rationale of the neoconservatives in the Iraq case. (Iraq was seen by Washington "insiders" as "the first domino", whose toppling by military action would have a "knock on effect" throughout the entire Arab world.) The Cold War lasted 43 years as far as conscious Western containment was concerned, but the underlying conflict had begun in 1917, so 72 years in all. Similarly, a conscious Western strategy to meet the jihadists' war was not really formulated until after 11 September 2001, but the adversaries' campaign had been under way at least since 1982, according to Osama bin Laden's account in his video just before the US election. We will be lucky if the contemporary overall conflict is any shorter than the Cold War.

Those reflections on some parallels between the Cold War and the current conflict are not intended in any way to diminish the importance of the most vital difference between them. The Cold War was a conflict between sovereign states, drawn up in two heavily armed alliances. The jihadists' war is a conflict between the society of states as a whole and a worldwide loosely connected network of terrorist cells, using effectively and very ruthlessly the tactics of asymmetric war.

The choice of strategies

Nevertheless, the similarities listed appear to suggest that the strategy which saw the West through to victory in the Cold War might have some usefulness in this new conflict. That has not been Washington's official view. The National Security Strategy of 2002 proclaimed that containment must be replaced by pre-emption, because, as the National Security Adviser famously said, if the United States waited for the "smoking gun", it might prove to be a "mushroom cloud". That evocation of the nuclear image as a weapon that might be available to the jihadists was no doubt politically shrewd in reconciling the US public to the notion that war on Iraq without a *casus belli* was legitimate in the interests of US security. But it is difficult to see that anything at all was "pre-empted" by the invasion of Iraq. It could more accurately be described as a preventive war, since in intent and effect it was really "a shot across the bows" for the Arab world as a whole, a warning of what might happen to any of them if they provoked enough rage in Washington.

In that, it has been relatively successful. Libya has been the "poster boy" for change. Syria made an exit from Lebanon, but remained in 2005 under heavy diplomatic pressure. Egypt and even Saudi Arabia have made gestures towards democracy. The objective of effecting a democratic revolution in the Arab world is one difficult to quarrel with openly, even for a practising autocrat. But US strategy is questionable. Can democracy really be exported on Abrams tanks? The analogy of change in Germany and Japan in the aftermath of defeat in the Second World War is quite misleading. By 1945, both Germany and Japan were in states of total exhaustion and incapable of further resistance, which is far from the case with the Arab world, or even Iraq, as has been well demonstrated. Despite the absence of jungles, the parallel with Vietnam is much closer, with urban guerrilla warfare the primary tactic of the local nationalist insurgents, as well as the jihadists, and the great-power backing given by the Soviet Union and China replaced by the militants in the worldwide Islamic community.

A rational and defensible foreign policy requires the prudent choice of lesser evils. Though Saddam's continuance in power would no doubt have been a source of many evils, his removal by outside military force created greater ones, at least in the short term, and possibly in the very long term. Estimates of the Iraqi dead range from 20,000 to 100,000. Add more than 2,000 Americans and other "outsiders" dead, many more wounded or disabled, massive destruction in Iraq, damage to US diplomatic standing all over the world, a heavy financial burden on the US taxpayer, a great deal of blind hatred for the United States and the West in general in the Islamic world. Above all, for the long term, an increased chance of the jihadists' war possibly turning into the worst possible outcome, a war of civilizations.

So, on any reasonable cost-benefit analysis, the one clear benefit of the war so far, Saddam's removal, was dearly bought, especially if it turns him in time to a martyr for Arab nationalism. The necessity for a less expensive strategy became apparent by 2004, even to some of those who espoused the theory of Iraq as the first domino. There was an echo, by 2005, of Dulles' time as Secretary of State in the early 1950s. He had come to office denouncing the allegedly "ineffective" and "cowardly" policy of containment, and proposing an instant recipe for success: the "roll-back" of Soviet power in Eastern Europe by promoting democratic revolutions there. That strategy did not outlast the first feeble attempt, in East Germany in 1953. So there was then a quiet return to containment which finally delivered success, as its original theorist had predicted back in 1946.[3] Admittedly it took a long time, but 40 years on there did occur the "erosion" and "mellowing" of Soviet power originally claimed as the eventual outcome of "a long-term, patient but firm and vigilant containment".

The concept as originally formulated should not be equated with its later military expression in the deployment of troops in central Korea and Western Germany. Any such geographical conception is obviously irrelevant on the context of an adversary whose cells are worldwide, including in some of the cities of the West. But the power to do damage can be contained, limited and eventually eroded in a variety of ways.

Before the decision to invade Iraq, that did seem to be happening on various fronts. The prospect of further proliferation of nuclear "know-how", and maybe fissile material, was inhibited by pressure on Pakistan (the chief actual source) and by close cooperation with Russia in the safeguarding of Soviet-era nuclear "assets". The flow of funds to the jihadists was diminished by blocking their sources, chiefly in Saudi Arabia, and improved checks on money-laundering. The Saudis, after the realization of their own vulnerability, found the resolve to put some restraints on the sermons in radical mosques, and the curricula in radical schools. Other Muslim countries may in time be able to follow that lead. The counter-proliferation campaign appears to be having some effect on its two main targets, North Korea and Iran, mostly through multilateral diplomacy, in the Six-Power Talks for North Korea, and the IAEA for Iran. The failed or failing states deemed by richer neighbours likely to be unable to prevent jihadist cells from establishing training-bases on their territories suddenly found themselves being offered substantial help to establish more effective police and armed forces. Intelligence agencies worldwide, whose past traditions had been of fierce rivalry even with domestic competitors for "turf" (as, for instance, between the FBI and the CIA) suddenly found themselves under orders to cooperate not only with them, but foreign rivals. Many intelligence agencies suddenly were more lavishly funded, new sorts of linguists were hastily trained, and global cooperation became the "in-thing" and seemed to be producing results. Above all, the jihadists by 2004 had lost the enormous strategic advantages of being underrated, and largely lost the advantage of surprise, save on the tactical level of choice of target and timing.

One of the least-noticed aspects of the Western victory in the Cold War has a paradoxical but cheering implication for the current conflict. Military success (or rather the lack of it) in that earlier protracted conflict had little visible influence on its outcome. Both Korea and Vietnam ended very disappointingly for the West. Korea was at best a stalemate: the lines of confrontation remained much what they had been; the northern tyrant was not removed, but like any monarch passed his power to his son. After more than 50 years there is still not even a treaty, and the threat to the South, and now even to the world in general, is rather greater than it was in 1950. Certainly that is the case if the North Korean regime has really managed in the meantime to produce nuclear weapons, as well as missiles than can deliver them. Vietnam in 1975 looked even worse: an unmitigated and undisguisable disaster, the enemy taking over the contested territory. But the West's relations with Hanoi are now much better than those with Pyongyang.

Even the balance of forces, in terms of the actual military status of the two sides in 1989, did not really indicate the eventual outcome. As the Wall came down and the Soviet Union began to vanish into history, Soviet soldiers still stood from the centre of Germany to the far reaches of Afghanistan. More than enough of its nuclear missiles were deployed on near-invulnerable platforms. Its armouries were crammed with tanks and artillery. So what was eroding was not actual military capacity or strategic assets, but the will of the Soviet political elite to use them. That reflection is relevant to the possible eventual fading of the conflict with the jihadists.

Nothing fails like failure. What happened in Moscow was a sort of generation-by-generation change in the norms and assumptions of the political elite. Khrushchev was probably the last "true believer". He once affably assured Eisenhower that their grandchildren would play together as Communists, come the bright new dawn. His first three successors, Brezhnev, Andropov and Chernenko, seem to represent a declining curve of optimism on that point. How else could Gorbachev have come to power? The thirty years between the advent of Khrushchev in the mid-1950s, and that of Gorbachev in the mid-1980s, might be seen as the necessary time-lapse for the slow process of erosion of the Stalinist norms (such as they were) and their replacement by others.

To sum up a hypothesis that requires much more historical background than can be provided in this chapter, containment, détente, engagement and normative shift did their slow-motion work. And the Soviet Union relinquished its original aspirations to overturn the earlier order of power in the society of states.[4] The jihadists now hold that aspiration as fiercely as the revolutionaries of 1917 once did. But, though the Cold War lasted 43 years, its intensity diminished after its most dangerous point, the Cuba Missile crisis of 1962. Despite a final upsurge of tension in 1983, it ended just six years later, in 1989. Some downturn towards diminished hostilities may be likely, though for different reasons, in the jihadists' war.

The diplomacy of the Gorbachev–Reagan period, 1985–88, was important in the final winding-down of the Cold War without a shot being fired. If there is to be any equivalent of the Gorbachev role in the jihadists' war, it would probably have to be by a group of very senior Sunni and Shia clerics. The radical young clerics of the current period, like al-Sadr, as is clear from his 2005 policies in Iraq, are quite conscious that the Shia have a lot to gain from a genuine transition to electoral politics there, since they are a 60 per cent majority. But the Sunni, who have lost a lot with the fall of the old regime, must also be reconciled. The current global conflict is in essence a struggle for the soul of Islam between the "zealots" and the "modernizers". The United States and the West in general, are seen as the "Great Satan" because Satan is seen as the "great tempter", luring the young away from traditional Islamic norms. In the sixteenth and seventeenth centuries, Christendom went through a somewhat similar struggle, international and domestic wars arising in part from doctrinal differences. It came out of that disastrous period in 1648, with the Peace of Westphalia – and in time also with the Enlightenment, and the norm that religion should not dictate domestic political structure, still less international politics. There are plenty of Islamic intellectuals and clerics who could in time mediate that thought to their fellow Muslims. But the West cannot impose the evolution by tanks and bombers.

Power, order and unipolarity

The point was made earlier that one of the fringe effects of the jihadists' war was to induce solidarity among the governments who represent the society of states. Every existing government, as of 2005, had reason to feel that its citizenry, or its interests, were in some way damaged by the jihadists' campaign. The governments of Muslim societies, above all others, have reason to fear that even their very survival may be at stake. None of them wants to see itself replaced by a Taliban-style regime. In countries like Saudi Arabia and Pakistan, where a substantial sector of the population (judging by the street protests and slogans) share the norms, assumptions and aspirations of the jihadists, their jeopardy is a strategic danger also for the West. But many of the supporters or even the members of those governments may in their hearts agree with the jihadists, at least to the extent of seeing the existing international order as an order of entrenched injustice, created by the West, and likely to be perpetuated unless something is done to pull it down.

In effect, therefore, the restoration of a viable world order may depend on the reform of the international order. As a global task, that is somewhat less formidable than the task of defeating the jihadists, because it involves essentially only the decision-makers of those political elites who are in office or prospect of office, among the major powers. Defeating the jihadists, unfortunately, involves changing the world-view of many Muslims: the young men who may decide to go "on active service" as jihadists, and the elderly clerics and teachers who form the opinions of those possible recruits. Even if only one tenth of one per cent of the billion-plus Muslim citizens of the world decide for jihad, that would produce more than a million potential "foot-soldiers". The crucial group however are the mostly middle-class intellectuals, many of them educated in the West, who lead the foot-soldiers, plan their operations and raise their funds. So it is primarily that group that must be influenced.

At its advent, the chief virtue of the unipolar world seemed to be that logically it made war much less likely between sovereign states. Hegemonic wars (like the First and Second World Wars, and the Cold War), were deemed impossible while it lasted. That was just a matter of definition, since a unipolar world was defined as one in which the paramount power faced no direct military challenge from any "peer-competitor" in the traditional form of another sovereign state, or alliance of states. Hardly anyone, even in the intelligence services, contemplated the then improbable scenario of the challenge coming from a "non-state actor", a worldwide web of jihadists' cells. But in terms of traditional international relations theory, those cells now constitute the "revisionist power," challenging the world "establishment". That does raise a few historical echoes, mainly of the challenge to legitimacy in the mid-nineteenth century, or the anarchist movement towards its end, or the far-left terrorists of the 1960s and 1970s. But none of them was anything like so formidable as the present global network of cells, and unfortunately, zealotry in the name of a religious doctrine may prove far more durable than that based on economic or political assumptions.

As far as the durability of the unipolar world is concerned, the erosion of America's economic power has been the usual argument for predicting its end. On that basis, the end is by no means near. Even though the United States spent more on military goods and services than the next twenty major powers combined, that absorbed only 4 or 5 per cent of its GNP. At the height of the Cold War, for comparison, it was spending more than 14 per cent of a much smaller GNP. However America's vast military capacity is still geared to fight a conventional or nuclear war against a sovereign state, or an alliance of states. Against a non-state actor, in an asymmetric war, it has not been doing as well as the strategists responsible for the doctrines on which the Iraq invasion was launched had originally hoped. But the strategic advantages of the United States' geographic position, with wide oceans to east and west, and militarily non-competitive neighbours to north and south, though slightly eroded by technology, remained far greater than Rome enjoyed in its time. The jihadists have obviously the capacity to inflict grief and loss on the American people, and considerable economic damage, but there is no conceivable way they could achieve an actual direct military victory.

The crucial damage to US power since the decision to invade Iraq is elsewhere: to its capacity to induce bandwagoning. Both its formal alliance structure and its diplomatic reputation have taken a considerable battering. But Iraq has not been the sole reason for the rise of anti-Americanism as a sort of political ideology over more of the world than has ever been affected by Islam, and even among the citizenry of its two closest allies, Britain and Australia. The mere fact of unipolarity invites resentment of the paramount power. Every other society has to reflect wryly from time to time that all sovereignties may be theoretical equals, but for the time being one is a great deal more equal than all the others. In the old days of the multipolar balance, resentments at national inequalities could at least be divided among several great powers. Now it is all directed towards Washington, seen as the self-selected manager of the world, and as managing it very badly. In the case of Iraq, inventing a crisis (those non-existent WMDs) as a rationale for regime change, which in reality was sought on the basis of an imprudent, over-ambitious determination to convert the Arab world to instant democracy.

Balance or concert?

Despite the much-resented unilateralism of the period since about 2003, there is one fully-unilateral decision by Washington that could transform the diplomatic disfavour in which it found itself in the Bush second term. The next administration could decide to administer the unipolar world as if it were a concert of powers.

That old European concept has never recovered in the United States from the rather unfair "bad press" it got in Woodrow Wilson's time, during and after the First World War. But with the advantage of retrospect, it is now clear that it did better in restraining and limiting wars between the great powers for the whole hundred years 1815–1914 than the system which succeeded it, and which Wilson himself sponsored.[5] No hegemonial wars occurred in the Concert period, whereas in the 75 years which followed, 1914–1989, there were three hegemonial wars (the First and Second World Wars, and the Cold War, which was the form of the Third World War). Now the world has a fourth, the jihadists' war, which also is a struggle about the order of power in the world.

The most reasonable charge against the old European Concert is that it allowed the major powers of the time – Britain, France, Russia, the Kaiser's Germany, Spain, Portugal, the Netherlands, Belgium – to annex large swathes of Africa, Asia, and the Islamic countries to their respective empires. But any new concert of powers must of course be global, and indeed its major function would be to allow the emerging great powers of Asia, Africa, Latin America and the Islamic world to move more easily to their rightful places in the diplomatic sun, "centre stage" in the world order.

That process could, and theoretically should, take place through the formal institutions of the society of states, like the Security Council. India and Japan, for instance, have long been irritated by their failure to be offered permanent places on that body, and Brazil has lately joined them. The difficulty is that formal structures like the United Nations almost inevitably enshrine long established legal privileges, like the veto, reflecting the order of power at the time they were established. So the Security Council in 2005 still reflected the power balance of 1945. Some of the nations thus originally privileged were never likely to be ready to share that status with a larger group, as the hopeful reform proposal of 2005 had suggested.

Informal structures, like the old Concert, or the current G7, are much more able to expand their membership when it is economically or diplomatically useful to do so. The G7, for instance, becomes the G8, with the addition of Russia. In 2004 it included China, an overdue gesture considering the economic importance of that country. It could readily become the G12 anytime the current members decide to issue the invitations. And it does not have to confine its agenda to economic matters. When presidents and prime ministers get together informally, they can and should discuss whatever is important to the world.

Some Americans have hoped to prolong unipolarity for the indefinite future, or at least the end of the century, but not even the most Machiavellian operator in the Pentagon is likely to be able to bring that off. The issue will be settled far outside the corridors of power in Washington by the ineluctable forces of demographic and economic change. China is already putting on economic power and diplomatic influence with notable speed, and building military capacity. India is beginning to catch up. Indonesia, Pakistan, and Bangladesh, along with India, represent the majority of the world's Muslims, and their future orientation will be crucial for order in the world. Japan may at last be coming out of its long stagnation, and with the rise of China will be obliged to re-think its options. Latin America is beginning to produce candidates for great power status, like Brazil and Mexico. Despite its long string of disasters, Africa also is producing future contenders, in powers like Nigeria and South Africa.

So what used (rather condescendingly) to be called the Third World is catching up, economically and technologically, with the advanced world. Demographically it is far outdoing it. World population is expected to stabilize by mid-century at about 9 billion, and fertility rates to converge, a bit later, at about replacement level (2.1). But in the interim, about 85 per cent of the world's peoples will be non-Westerners. Though America's own population is not expected to decline (indeed to grow to about 400 million) those of its European allies and Japan will age and diminish. So Washington by mid-century will have to share the governance of the world with sovereignties from cultures vastly different from its own. The next two or three decades, while the society of states remains at least militarily unipolar though diplomatically and economically it will be reverting to multipolarity, could thus be regarded as opportunity for a "learning curve", or a useful sort of "practice session": administering the world as if it were a concert of powers, before the changing distribution of power makes it mandatory.

That old diplomatic technique, in the nineteenth century, had as one of its prime objectives, to preserve "the repose of Europe". For the future, that would of course be amended to promoting the repose (peace and security) of the whole world. A potential multipolar world of perhaps twelve great powers (the United States, Europe, China, India, Russia, Indonesia, Pakistan, Brazil, Mexico, Nigeria, maybe Egypt and South Africa, if population, regional influence and economic growth-rates are any guide) could arrange itself as either a balance of power, as in the eighteenth century, or a concert of powers as in the nineteenth century. It may instantly be objected that the United Nations is a better and more recent model. Agreed, and I would expect it to remain the formal and legal structure, with a sort of "updating" in only one vital eventual membership, that of the Security Council. Its importance as a symbol of sovereignty for those nations which cannot hope for great power status will remain crucial. But it would be difficult to deny that the whole 60 years of the United Nations' existence have been dominated by either the bipolar balance of the Cold War, or the current paramountcy of the United States.

Despite the formal legal authority of the Security Council, decisions for peace or war are in reality still made by governments, on the basis of their assumptions about their national interests. The institutions in which they come closest to collective decisions about such vital matters are security communities. The NATO decision, just after 11 September 2001, to invoke its principle that "an attack on one is an attack on all" (even if not fully exemplified in the actual military commitments to Afghanistan of all its members) was at least an approximation to collective security: a "league against the unknown enemy", as it used to be called. No enemy could have been more unknown and unexpected than the Taliban.

For a variety of historical reasons, no anti-hegemonial alliance was ever constructed against the United States in its long rise to paramountcy, 1898–1992. But the prospective new distribution of power will make one far more likely, and would enable a very much larger and more potent alliance to be created than ever in the past. During the worst moments of the Iraq crisis, in 2003, one could see its potential shape hovering in the diplomatic air. Only Tony Blair, of the major decision-makers of the society of states, seemed fully on the side of Washington, and still a true believer in the trans-Atlantic bond. So one of the most significant side-effects of the Iraq crisis was to make more visible the potential tug-of war over the future of Europe: partner or competitor to the United States? As two eminent US political scientists have written "the preservation of an Atlantic zone of stable peace – the establishment of which is perhaps the greatest achievement of the twentieth century – is in question, with balance-of-power dynamics returning to relations between the United States and Europe".[6] The strategic necessities which produced the alliance in 1949 have been gone since 1989. Europe now faces no security challenge other than the jihadists, and a lot of Europeans believe (mistakenly) that severing the trans-Atlantic bond would exempt them from its dangers. The young assume (again perhaps mistakenly) that Stalin and Hitler are less relevant to their future than Charlemagne. President Chirac never bothers to disguise his nostalgia for the multipolar world.

But events do not have to move in that Gaullist direction, nor should they. It would produce a multipolar balance of at least eight nuclear powers (the United States, China, Russia, India, Pakistan, France, Britain and Israel) and probably more. A large potential for catastrophe would reside in that. The decisions taken in Washington in the next few years are what will determine whether the society of states moves towards a complex and dangerous multipolar balance of power, or a more stable and conflict-limiting concert of powers.

Nothing could have appeared more improbable at the outset of the second Bush term than the idea of a global concert. Yet, at the beginning of the second Reagan term, nothing was less expected than that the Cold War was moving towards its end, "not with a bang but a whimper". And at the beginning of the second Nixon term, everything in the two years that followed would have appeared just political-science fantasy. So the possibility of radical surprise should never be discounted. As the second Bush administration began moving into history in 2006, that principle seemed a useful one.

Notes

1. By late 2005, the Shanghai Cooperation Group, which appears to express the common interest of Russia and China in limiting US influence in Central Asia (and was joined for that meeting by India, Pakistan and Iran), was enquiring tartly when the United States proposed to wind up its bases there, and Uzbekistan had given Washington six months' notice to quit.
2. The word "jihadist" has several meanings in Islamic thought. It can mean just the moral struggle of the individual to live by the tenets of the Prophet. But the meaning for those who would at the moment be defined as jihadists is (in the words of the cleric who inspired the first attempt (1993) to blow up the Twin Towers is "do jihad with the sword, with the cannon, with the grenades, with the missiles ... to break and destroy the enemies of Allah ... their high buildings ... and the buildings in which they gather their leaders". Quoted in "America and the New Terrorism", *Survival* 42(1) Spring 2000.
3. George F. Kennan, writing while he was Counsellor at the US Embassy in Moscow in 1946, in a cable replying to an inquiry by the then Defense Secretary, asking what Stalin was up to. The cable was published under the title "The Sources of Soviet Conduct" by "Mr X" in the July 1947 issue of *Foreign Affairs*, and had an enormous intellectual influence on policy makers, even more in Europe than in the United States. For an account of this period in Washington, see Walter Isaacson and Evan Thomas (1986) *The Wise Men*, New York: Simon and Shuster.
4. The collapse of the Soviet Union was not adequately foreseen by Sovietologists, and still needs many more studies. Some authorities theorize that it was due to over-confidence on Gorbachev's part. He believed that the system could survive the impact of *glasnost* and *perestroika*, but events proved him wrong.
5. For an American "take" on the nineteenth-century concert, by an analyst very familiar with the problems of US foreign policy, see Henry Kissinger (1994) *Diplomacy*, New York: Simon and Shuster), and also his earlier work, *A World Restored*, New York: Grosset and Dunlop (Universal Library edition).
6. See "Liberal realism: the foundations of a democratic foreign policy" by G. John Ikenberry and Charles A. Kupchan (2004) in *The National Interest* 77, Fall.

6

Multilateralism, sovereignty and normative change in world politics

Amitav Acharya

This chapter examines the role of multilateralism in fostering and managing normative change in world politics, with specific regard to the fundamental norms of state sovereignty.[1] Post-war multilateralism helped to define, extend, embed and legitimize a set of sovereignty norms, including territorial integrity, equality of states and nonintervention. Today, multilateral institutions are under increasing pressure to move beyond some of these very same principles, especially nonintervention, as part of a transformative process in world politics. Without multilateralism, it is highly doubtful that the post-war international order would have been so tightly and universally built upon the norms of sovereignty. And without multilateralism, argues this chapter, transition from this normative order now would be difficult and chaotic, as may be already happening as a result of the Bush administration's challenge to the current multilateral system.

I begin by briefly outlining the idea of norms and normative change. Then, I offer an overview of the role of multilateralism, both at the global and regional levels, in promoting the norms of sovereignty in the post-war period. Next, I outline the pressures for normative change being faced by multilateral institutions in recent years. Finally, the chapter analyses how multilateralism is promoting normative change, with particular reference to the norm of nonintervention.

What is normative change in world politics?

Realists dismiss international institutions and regard them to be marginal to the game of power politics.[2] Liberal institutionalists mainly stress the functional role of institutions in lowering transaction costs, providing information, enhancing transparency, and monitoring and preventing cheating.[3] Constructivists argue that institutions can have a deeper impact; they do not simply regulate state behaviour, but also help develop collective identities that can ameliorate the security dilemma.[4]

While acknowledging the importance of the functional role of institutions, it can be argued that the main contribution of multilateral institutions to world order has been in the normative domain.[5] In this role, institutions act as agents of norm construction and normative change with a view to regulate and transform state behaviour. The normative role of institutions may include giving global legitimacy to local norms as well as local legitimacy to global norms. Post-war multilateral institutions universalized European legal ideas and practices about sovereignty, which were until then associated only with the "civilized" European nations and deemed inapplicable to the colonies. But even after the European state-system came to recognize the political independence and cultural dignity of non-European societies, European norms of regional interaction, developed by institutions such as the European Union (EU) or the Conference for Security and Cooperation in Europe (CSCE), continued to set a model for other regions trying to cope with the problems of sovereignty in their respective neighbourhoods. At the same time, norms developed at the global level diffused through to the growing number of new states. In this process, multilateral institutions, thanks largely to the role of these new actors, redefined existing norms or created new norms to expand the meaning of sovereignty. More recently, multilateral institutions face the challenge of modifying or displacing older norms which have become delegitimized or dysfunctional in an increasingly complex and globalized world. In the past, international relations scholars were interested in the role of multilateralism in "embedding" norms into post-war economic and security structures (such as Ruggie's notion of "embedded liberalism").[6] But multilateralism now needs to be looked at as an agent of norm displacement and transformation, involving some of the very same principles it once helped to institutionalize. Together, these normative functions of multilateral institutions have been critical to the maintenance and peaceful transformation of international order.

The post-war international order is founded on the bedrock of sovereignty. Sovereignty, according to a widely used definition offered by Hinsley, is "the idea that there is a final and absolute political authority in the political community ... and no final and absolute authority exists elsewhere."[7] The concept of sovereignty cannot be understood without reference to its core norms; as Jackson argues, sovereignty is "essentially a legal order defined by rules".[8] Among the fundamental of constitutive norms of sovereignty, three have been especially important: territorial integrity, the sovereign equality of states, and nonintervention.[9]

Before we turn to an empirical examination of post-war multilateralism in promoting these norms, let me clarify what I mean by multilateralism, norms and normative change. The minimalist definition of multilateralism refers to interaction among three or more states. Ruggie extends this definition to the qualitative domain: "At its core, multilateralism refers to coordinating relations among three or more states in accordance with certain principles".[10] Ruggie's definition acknowledges the normative elements of multilateralism, which is important to this chapter, but does not explore how the norms of multilateralism acquire specificity and meaning through socialization. My central argument here is that while multilateralism or multilateral institutions may well be founded on certain general principles, these norms may not be initially specified or contextualized. Hence, multilateral institutions provide the social setting within which such norms are interpreted and extended. The norms of multilateralism themselves vary, and undergo adaptation and transformation in different historical and regional contexts, something Ruggie's general definition of multilateralism does not demonstrate. Chayes and Chayes offer a generic definition of norms "to include a broad class of generalized prescriptive statements – principles, standards, rules, and so on – both procedural and substantive. The term includes statements that are reduced to writing or some other authoritative formulation as well as informal, tacit, or background norms."[11] This definition allows us to include both legal and institutionalized rules, or norms which have been incorporated into formal organizations, as well as informal and social norms which lack similar institutional support but may be important nonetheless. This is especially important in considering the development of normative orders in the Third World, especially Asia, Africa and the Middle East, where the level of institutionalization and legalization in formal regional organizations remains weak. Second, procedural norms are as important as substantive ones, reflecting underlying political bargains which themselves are shaped by the fundamental beliefs of the actors. Third, this definition does not claim that norms are necessarily "moral". This point needs careful attention. To view norms in moral terms is a well-known tendency of constructivist norm scholars,[12] who generally ignore bad norms, or the bad effects, unintended or not, of norms which have been once regarded as fundamentally good. But not all norms are intrinsically good or moral; in fact a good case can be made that the norms of sovereignty such as nonintervention or self-determination (or for that matter sovereign equality) have always been morally ambiguous. The extent to which they may be judged moral or immoral is a matter of perception, period and place. Nonintervention is a "good" and necessary norm because it offers weak states protection against the capricious intervention by the big powers. But it is a "bad" norm in so far as it fails to protect people from the human rights abuses by their own governments. Similarly, the moral content and functional efficacy norms do not remain fixed or constant, but change over time and in response to new developments. What might have seemed good and necessary in a given historical period may seem bad and dysfunctional at a later period. Turning to nonintervention again, while liberal Third World leaders such as the Indian Prime Minister Nehru (no one's idea of a tinpot dictator) saw nonintervention as a moral and legal protection of the weak in a world of the strong, the growing incidence of Third World human rights abuses and the emergence of a global civil society campaigning for human rights have led to this norm increasingly being seen in a negative light.

Moreover, norms which may seem bad globally may enjoy considerable legitimacy locally. Norms which may be discredited in one part of the world may retain a robust appeal in another. Such variations are hardly unusual. Indeed, as I shall show shortly, the diffusion of the norms of sovereignty in the developing world after World War II was not marked by a single or uniform pattern, and it did allow substantial diversity between the regional orders of Western Europe, Latin America, Asia and Africa. While path dependency is itself an important indicator that norms matter, this applies equally to good and bad norms. When we say "norms matter", we should not simply be looking for evidence of good norms producing behaviour that could not be attributed to power politics or instrumental rationality, and reproducing themselves in state or collective action through a reasonable period of time, but also of bad norms sticking around and shaping outcomes that materialist and rationalist perspectives would find difficult to explain.

Drawing upon my recent work on norm diffusion, I argue that empirical research on norms should account for the contested understandings, spatial variations and the changing moral content and functional efficacy of norms.[13] Moreover, normative change is not always, or mainly, produced and directed by global moral entrepreneurs peddling universal ideas, while local actors remain passive recipients. The latter can be, and are in most cases, active borrowers and constructors. They help to construct new norms of sovereignty to displace old and discredited ones or reconstruct global norms with a mix of existing ideas and practices. In a contest between new global norms and pre-existing local norms, localization rather than displacement, is more likely to occur. To say that is not to argue that local agents and localization are regressive; but only to say that normative change is not often the dramatic, revolutionary transformation.[14] Constructivist norm theorists have spent so much time studying the latter (the collapse of the Soviet Union, the end of Apartheid, the global ban on land mines, the protection of whales, amongst others). But normative change can be, and mostly is, an "everyday form": an incremental, evolutionary dynamic which proceeds through local reconstructions of outside norms in accordance with some pre-existing beliefs and practices, through which actors seek a new legitimacy without losing their fundamental sense of individual or group identity.

Multilateralism and the making of the post-war sovereignty regime

As Ruggie reminds us, "the earliest multilateral arrangements instituted in the modern era were designed to cope with the international consequences of the novel principle of state sovereignty".[15] Post-war multilateralism was instrumental in facilitating the global diffusion of what were essentially European norms of sovereignty. It did so through the adoption of these norms in the constitutional documents of multilateral organizations. For example, the UN Charter universalized the norms of equality of states, territorial integrity and nonintervention. Regional organizations such as the OAS, Arab League, and later the OAU (now the African Union) and ASEAN, also made their contribution by recognizing and institutionalizing these norms. An important point here is not to overstate the norm-promoting role of the UN at the expense of regional organizations. The United Nations Conference on International Organization (UNCIO) which drafted the UN charter is 1945 out of the Dumbarton Oaks proposals, was attended by 50 countries, compared to 21 independent founding states for the OAS (established in 1948), 7 independent states for the Arab League (established in 1945), and 32 independent states for the OAU (established in 1963). Moreover, 29 states attended the Asia-Africa Conference in Bandung, where the nonintervention norm was forcefully articulated by Indian Prime Minister Nehru. And many of the non-European countries at the UNCIO were not fully sovereign yet; the Indian delegation was chosen by the British and 'played a subordinate role" to the British delegation to the UNCIO.[16] Hence the role of regional institutions in creating a conducive political climate for the diffusion of state sovereignty norms should not be overlooked.

Furthermore, the norm-setting role of universal and regional institutions could not have been taken for granted, because international law at that time did not require the adoption of any specific set of rules as a precondition for the founding of international organizations.[17] But multilateral institutions not only just adopted these norms,[18] in some cases, they also clarified their meaning, adapted them to the new circumstances, and extended their scope. The best example of this at the UNCIO was the doctrine of "sovereign equality" of states, which combines the concept of state sovereignty and the principle of equality of states. The idea of the equality of states had evolved as a natural law principle espoused by Grotius and most notably Wolff, but was challenged by the emergence of positive law, which recognized the inequality of states, most starkly due to the impact of the European Concert of Powers. The Concert acknowledged the special responsibility and status of European great powers in managing international order. In view of this alternative way of how to organize international relations, the principle of equality of states could not have been assumed as the basis of the new international order which emerged from the ashes of World War II. At the UNCIO, however, the doctrine of equality of states was transmuted into the doctrine of sovereign equality of states, with the UN charter under Article 1 recognizing the "respect for the principle of equal rights" and Article 2 affirming that the organization "is based on the principle of the sovereign equality of all its Members". An important act of clarification at the UNCIO was to define "sovereign equality" in terms of the following elements: (1) that states are juridically equal; (2) that each state enjoys the rights inherent in full sovereignty; (3) that the personality of the state is respected, as well as its territorial integrity and political independence; (4) that the state should, under international order, comply faithfully with its international duties and obligations.[19]

These principles were important for two reasons: they ensured that sovereignty was "an equal attribute of all the members of the United Nations with no distinction being drawn between the Great Powers and other members of the United Nations".[20] Second, and no less important, they provided the recognition that membership in international organizations such as the UN, and the acceptance of certain obligations which follow from such membership, does not violate sovereignty. "Rather it is by an exercise of this sovereignty that such obligations are assumed".[21] This would be used for the participation of states in international organizations of all kinds, even in the case of such a supranational entity as the EU, in whose case, as Jackson points out, drawing upon Keohane's "bargaining away" of sovereignty thesis, membership is nothing but an exercise in voluntary loss of sovereignty.[22]

The doctrine of sovereign equality of states of course did not mean the political equality of states. This inequality was striking with respect to the UN Charter's adoption of great power permanent membership in the Security Council and the right of veto, indicators of the "inequality of nations with respect to power and political influence".[23] But the UN Charter at the end was essentially a compromise between those who sought the principle of absolute equality of states (this would have been unrealistic) and those who could settle only for the juridical equality of states (which would have been too modest and less empowering to the weaker nations).[24] Moreover, the doctrine of sovereignty equality did lead to the UN charter into accepting the unanimity principle "in the law and practice of multilateral treaties".[25] This would have an enduring influence on decision-making in multilateral institutions at global and regional levels, where unanimity and consensus are seen as key protectors of the traditional norms of state sovereignty.

The UN also institutionalized the territorial integrity norm by disallowing the use of force to alter state boundaries. In addition, it extended the norm. The 1960 UN Declaration on Granting Independence to Colonial Countries and Peoples, as well as the 1970 Declaration of Principles of International Law Concerning Friendly Relations and Cooperation Among States, stipulated that the principle of self-determination applied to existing colonies, and not ethnic groups, and that the national territories were to be protected.[26]

The UNCIO strengthened the norm of nonintervention by giving an expansive meaning to the scope of domestic jurisdiction. It is important to bear in mind that nonintervention was not a "Westphalian" norm in the sense that it was enshrined in the Treaty of Westphalia in 1648. Rather, it emerged much later from the writings of European legal scholars. But many of these very scholars made important exceptions, both geopolitical and humanitarian, to the nonintervention principle. The most notable writer on nonintervention during this period, Vattel, justified intervention to preserve the balance of power. As Vincent writes, Vattel conceived of Europe "as a political system whose members were independent, but were bound together by a common interest in" the maintenance of the balance of power. Hence "[n]ations were always justified in not allowing a powerful sovereign to increase his power by force of arms, and if the formidable prince betrayed his plans by preparations then other nations had the right to check him."[27] Pre-war inter-American multilateralism contributed much in making the nonintervention norm unexceptional. In 1933, it finally succeeded in getting the US to accept the principle and thereby dampen, or even "multilateralize" the Monroe Doctrine. But it was the UN which made the doctrine a universal principle, allowing no intervention even by the UN collectivity in matters of domestic jurisdiction. Although recent arguments in support of nonintervention have claimed exceptions to this original formulation by citing the obligations imposed by the Universal Declaration on Human Rights, the founding documents of the UN made it clear that all matters of domestic jurisdiction would lie outside of the UN's functions with the notable exception of its enforcement role. In fact, originally part of Chapter VIII, the nonintervention norm was moved (at the suggestion of the five sponsoring countries) to Chapter II and thus made "a governing principle for the whole Organization and its members".[28] This was intended to ensure that the broader scope of the organization's functions in economic, social and cultural areas would not be too intrusive for the member states. But the doctrine was further limited, thanks largely to an Australian-sponsored amendment to the UN charter, with respect to the determination of and action against threats to peace and acts of aggression.[29] Here, the authority of the organization was further restricted by specifically excluding binding decisions by the Security Council with respect to settlement of disputes that fell essentially within the domestic jurisdiction of states. This has proven to be one of the most contested aspects of the normative role of the UN, which would shape future debates about humanitarian intervention.

Finally, it was at the UN that self-determination was given worldwide legitimacy. Until 1958, customary international law "conferred no right upon dependent peoples or entities to statehood". The self-determination norm had gathered powerful support at Asian and Afro-Asian conferences, including the Bandung Conference of 1955 of Asian and African nations, which declared that "colonialism in all its manifestations is an evil which should speedily be brought to an end". This determination was to be "reiterated by these countries time and again at every opportune moment".[30] Among these subsequent statements was the UN General Assembly's Resolution on Self-Determination of 1958 and its Declaration of 1960 on Granting of Independence to Colonial Countries and Peoples. Moreover, UN declarations and resolutions in 1970 and 1975 defined the right of self-determination in some detail. The Third World coalition at the UN also played a part in broadening and the further extension of sovereignty to new areas, including development, such as natural resources or even information flows.[31] It sought to develop such auxiliary and subsidiary norms of sovereignty as a code of conduct for multinationals, the right to development, and above all self-determination for states rather than peoples.

At the regional level, the Latin American states played an important role in extending European norms of sovereignty. As noted, they were key proponents of nonintervention and the legal equality of states. Originally a response to their fear of a Spanish reconquest and European meddling, their attention in promoting these norms shifted to the US as it added a Roosevelt Corollary to the Monroe Doctrine. They succeeded in trading their support for a collective defence framework under US leadership for Washington's acceptance of the nonintervention principle. In this process, Latin America developed an extensive legal framework for peaceful settlement of disputes, arbitration which helped to embed the norms of equality and nonintervention in the inter-American context, both bilaterally and through regional institutions such as the Pan-American Union and the OAS.[32]

In contrast to Latin legalism, Asian countries through a series of interactions stretching from the Asian Relations Conference of 1947 to the Bandung Asia-Africa Conference in 1955 advanced the principle of nonintervention politically, especially in the emerging context of a bipolar international system. These interactions, while failing to create a formal regional organization, laid the foundations for the Non-Aligned Movement. Through these interactions, Asia also developed a norm against collective defence, which served to limit superpower intervention in Asia and (through the Non-Aligned Movement) the Third World. These early post-war interactions also shaped the design and purpose of future regional associations in Asia, especially the Association of Southeast Asian Nations, which to date remains a bastion of state sovereignty and which has formed the basis of newer regional organizations including the ASEAN Regional Forum, a grouping that brings together all the major powers of the contemporary international system. Asian regional organizations also gave expression to the process norms of sovereignty; the nonintervention principle was the basis of Asia's somewhat distinctive multilateralism based on organizational minimalism, preference for consensus over majority voting, and avoidance of legalistic approaches in favour of informal and process-based socialization.[33]

Africa may be given special credit for the strengthening the norm of territorial integrity. It is here that the traditional norm of territorial integrity of states became infused with the new idea of the non-violability of postcolonial frontiers. Although this latter principle had developed in Latin America since the 1820s, and was implied in the UN Charter more generally, it was in Africa that this norm had its most direct and crucial impact, given Africa's especially acute problem with artificial postcolonial state boundaries. The first regular OAU summit in 1964 declared postcolonial boundaries as a "tangible reality"[34] and approved a resolution calling on its members "to respect the borders existing on the achievement of national independence".[35] Under this formula, the OAU also disallowed self-determination by Africa's traditional minorities. The inviolability of postcolonial boundaries norm was to become the OAU's most significant contribution to regional order. The Conference on Security and Cooperation in Europe (CSCE), despite its greater concern with human rights and national self-determination, would also adopt the same norm in its Helsinki Final Act (a case of Europe learning from the Third

World!). The Act stated that existing borders could only be changed "in accordance with international law, by peaceful means and by agreement." And both the EU and NATO have accepted new members only on the condition that they had reached border agreements with their neighbours, while the Commonwealth of Independent States (CIS) has accepted territorial integrity as a core principle.[36]

Three points may be highlighted in considering the role of multilateral institutions as promoters of international norms in the early post-war period. First, the main normative focus of multilateral institutions in the early post-war period was to promote and institutionalize the legal norms of sovereignty, rather than to advance humanitarian norms or principled ideas (despite the adoption of the Universal Declaration on Human Rights by the UN). By giving the norms of sovereignty a prominent place in their constitutional documents and subjecting most of their social, political and economic functions to these foundational principles, multilateral institutions helped to lay the foundations of a firmly sovereignty-bound global political-legal order. While revolutionary at its time of origin (the transformative element came from the circumstances and challenges of having a create a new international order after catastrophic European wars and to manage the absorption of a large number of formerly subjugated peoples into the states-system), it also became the basis of a persisting and self-preserving global status quo.

Second, contrary to a popular perception, regional organizations and interactions were not mere followers to the UN in norm-setting. The evolution of the global sovereignty regime has involved both the universalization of regionally-developed principles as much as the localization of globally-negotiated norms. Third, and in a related way, the diffusion of European ideas in the international system has not simply been a matter of Third World states accepting them passively or on an "as is" basis. While Europe contributed a set of foundational legal ideas about sovereignty, the full-scale development of these ideas came about after decolonization, when the Third World countries sought to adapt and employ these norms in the conduct of their international relations. The newly independent countries were keen to assume the identity of "sovereign" states. But they also needed to translate and operationalize ideas about self-determination, equality and nonintervention into specific principles of conduct in international affairs. In that process, they would contest the "true" meaning of equality and nonintervention, and the sort of relationships with other nations would uphold or undermine these. This role of Third World as agents of norm-setting should not be ignored in the literature on international relations, as it explains both the resistance of Third World countries to some of the fundamental currents of normative change in the world politics today. It also explains important variations in the creation of regional orders reflecting local patterns of diffusion sovereignty norms. This explains the contrast between Latin America's legalism versus Asia's "soft institutionalism" and Africa's distinctive emphasis on the non-violability of postcolonial frontiers. Compare also Asia's rejection of collective defence with Latin America and Arab League's acceptance of it. Last, but not the least, as Western Europe turned solidarist in the 1950s, blaming war on sovereignty and challenging nonintervention in domestic jurisdiction, Asia, and later, African states played an instrumental role in preserving state sovereignty. Hence, there is a need to rethink the conception of the global sovereignty regime as a linear or a uniform extension of the Westphalian model.

Why and how does multilateralism promotes normative change?

Why are multilateral organizations promoting normative change now? Let me highlight five drivers of this changing role, although the list is not exhaustive. The first has to do with changing functional imperatives owing to, first and foremost, increased global and regional economic interdependence. The EU offers the most striking example of how functional cooperation leading to incremental institutional adjustments produce a redefinition and dilution of the traditional norms of sovereignty. At the global level, interdependence has created demand for more complex and authoritative institutions, such as the WTO's dispute arbitration and settlement mechanisms. In other regions of the world, economic interdependence and integration have similarly led to the creation of institutional mechanisms that would have been inconceivable in the early postcolonial period. Examples include the free trade areas in Mercousur and ASEAN, and the peer-review mechanisms adopted by the New Partnership for Africa's Development (NEPAD).

Second, the emergence of new transnational challenges (challenges that may originate from within the physical boundaries of states but with international consequences) have also led multilateral institutions to depart from a strict adherence to sovereignty norms. Responding to international financial crises, such as the Asian contagion of 1997, and more recently to Al-Qaeda terrorism, has required more intrusive multilateral monitoring and management. Thus ASEAN now has a macro-economic surveillance process and East Asia has begun to develop regional monetary cooperation, which had been avoided in the past manly due to sovereignty concerns. The UN has adopted new measures to curb terrorist financing, and Security Council's Counter-Terrorism Committee requires states to report on the dangers of terrorist activity, which, though not binding, does leave the door open to mandatory consultations and assistance for states who seem to lack the will or capacity to control terrorist activity within their borders.

Third, major systemic changes affecting the global distribution of power have opened up new roles for multilateral institutions and prompted them to adjust their normative predilections. In Europe, the CSCE/OSCE begun playing a more intrusive role in regional military and political affairs as the Cold War came to an end. Indeed, the CSCE contributed to the lessening of Cold War tensions by developing a set of very intrusive military confidence-building measures and by linking regional security cooperation with the domestic practices of states, including their human rights record. While these mechanisms were developed during the heydays of the Cold War, they became further institutionalized as the CSCE became a more formal organization at the end of the Cold War. Its confidence-building agenda inspired similar attempts in other parts of the world, including within the ASEAN Regional Forum, although not to the same degree of intrusiveness. The post-Cold War NATO, needing a new rationale for its continued existence, adapted to the OSCE's humanitarian missions, and became an instrument of sorts of humanitarian intervention. The United Nations, no longer constrained by the Cold War Security Council deadlock, and facing the need to rebuild states following the resolution of Cold War regional conflicts, could undertake elaborate state-building projects such as in Cambodia in the early 1990s. The OAU, facing ever greater marginalization due to post-Cold War superpower disinterest, had to develop local capacities and roles in internal conflicts which have torn central, west and now east Africa apart since the end of the Cold War period. ASEAN relaxed its norm of excluding great powers from regional affairs by creating the ARF (ASEAN Regional Forum), thereby subjecting itself more directly to pressures from the Western nations on issues such as human rights and democracy.

A fourth factor affecting the normative basis of multilateral institutions is domestic change. The growing trend towards democratization around the world, including east and central Europe and in many parts of the developing world, though neither complete nor irreversible, has created a more conducive international climate for both the UN and regional organizations to develop new roles in domestic governance. The global financial institutions such as the World Bank have expanded their role in developing democratic institutions without being subjected to the traditional barrage of criticism from Third World countries about interference in their domestic affairs. A striking regional example of multilateral institutions promoting democratic governance is the aforementioned Inter-American Democratic Charter (IADC) of the OAS, which carries injunctions not just against coups, but also against "backsliding" by existing democratic regimes. Democratizing states have shown themselves to be more amenable to relaxing the rules of sovereignty; in Southeast Asia, this was indicated in 1998 by an initiative by Thailand, backed by the Philippines (both having gone through democratic transitions) for a "flexible engagement" process that would give regional partners a say over the domestic political and economic policies and practices of fellow ASEAN members. More recently, newly democratic Indonesia has championed the promotion of democracy as a regional norm.

Fifth, the expansion of the global civil society has brought about increased prospects for normative change in multilateral institutions. As Margaret Keck and Kathryn Sikkink's detailed study points out, civil society movements are among the leading norm entrepreneurs of the contemporary era, and their role has redefined the concept of multilateralism.[37] Multilateralism is no longer regarded, as it was at the onset of the post-war period, as a formal inter-governmental organizational framework with founding constitutional documents, legally specified decision-making procedures, and a large permanent bureaucracy. These do remain important of course, but such traditional multilateralism is being challenged by other types of actor-coalitions. Three types of actors are central to the emergence of this "new multilateralism". The first may be termed "counter-hegemonic coalitions" (to borrow Robert Cox's phrase[38]), or social movements whose main target is neo-liberal globalization and its principal national and inter-governmental agents. A second type of actors are "cosmopolitan moral movements" or groups that coalesce around some universal "principled" ideas, or ideas with a high moral and humanitarian content, such as human rights, prohibition on land mines, child soldiers and small arms. A third type of civil society grouping is knowledge-based "epistemic communities" (a formulation we owe to Peter Haas and Emanuel Adler[39]) or "Second Track" processes which bring together both political-bureaucratic policy actors and issue specialists to explore and advance ideas about change in specific issue areas. The Council for Security Cooperation in the Asia Pacific (CSCAP) would constitute a good example of this type of actor

These civil society groups vary in terms of their respect for the norms of state sovereignty. Some may see the role of anti-hegemonic coalitions as ironic when they protest against global financial institutions which themselves have been accused of promoting the erosion of state sovereignty (by encouraging globalization). In general, however, these groups have essentially been challenging existing state sovereignty norms, albeit within a fundamentally different political framework than inter-governmental institutions like the International Monetary Fund (IMF). Cosmopolitan moral movements and knowledge-based epistemic communities lack the visceral anti-governmentalism of the anti-hegemonic coalitions, and are willing, wherever possible, to work with like-minded governments in mobilizing resources and support that would translate their ideas into policy. Many multilateral institutions have started to accept, even encourage, the participation of such groups in a bid to shore up their legitimacy and satisfy the domestic constituencies of their members. (This is true not just of the EU, but also of Mercosur.) But whatever their disagreements about state sovereignty norms, all three types of civil society groups have pushed into the agenda of inter-governmental multilateral institutions a whole host of new issues which had previously been ignored by them, including social, environmental and human security issues. These, in turn, have led these institutions to develop new and expansive roles in the domestic and international affairs of their members. They have also led to a substantial redefinition of the security role of multilateral institutions to include human security, a shift that challenges the traditionally close association of multilateral institutions with state or national security.

A key aspect of the new multilateralism that is relevant here relates to leadership. Multilateralism today is characterized by new types of leadership, going well beyond the "structural leadership" of global hegemons or traditional great powers. It is commonplace to acknowledge the central role of the United States in the creation of post-war multilateral order. To quote Ruggie, "the pronounced shift toward multilateralism in economic and security affairs" in the post-war era was due to "the fact of an *American* hegemony ... not merely American *hegemon*" (emphasis in original).[40] But some of the most creative contributions of multilateralism today – such as the report of the International Commission on Intervention and State Sovereignty – are not American-led (nor is it produced by a formal governmental organization). Even in Latin America, the emergence of such transformative instruments of regional order as the Inter-American Democratic Charter was led by smaller nations, Peru in particular.[41] The US retains the ability to wreck multilateral initiatives it does not like (although by no means all of them, as evident in the case of the ban on land mines and the creation of the International Criminal Court). To a large extent, the US role in multilateralism today may be defined in such negative terms – a far cry from the positive association between hegemony and the promotion of multilateralism in traditional hegemonic stability theory, or the more recent perspective of John Ikenberry which suggests the willingness of hegemonic powers to seek legitimacy through strategic restraint created within a multilateral setting.[42] But the US indifference and opposition to multilateralism has combined with, and might have opened greater space for, the "entrepreneurial" and "intellectual" leadership (to borrow Oran Young's classification)[43] of middle powers such as Canada and Norway, or coalitions of "weak powers" such as ASEAN, to promote important avenues of change in world politics today.

Disembedding nonintervention

The transition of multilateralism to a post-Westphalian normative orientation remains far from complete. To begin with, principles such as sovereign equality of states, and especially nonintervention, continue to hold a powerful sway over developing countries.[44] From the perspective of major Third World nations such as India, Nigeria, Egypt and Brazil, the idea of the sovereign equality of states remains unfulfilled as long as the present system of permanent membership in the UN Security Council holds. Hence, a major normative concern of these states is to plug such loopholes in the post-war global sovereignty regime, rather than to subvert it.

More important, the normative contestation between nonintervention and humanitarian intervention continues, with no immediate victory in sight for the latter. Nonintervention today is the most contested norm of sovereignty. The territorial integrity norm faces no powerful challenge nowadays, having survived post-Cold War challenges in Eastern Europe and Kosovo. And despite the ongoing demands for Security Council reform, states will pragmatically accept inequality in their foreign relations as long as unanimity/consensus remains the principal decision-making rule in most other multilateral institutions, and the nonintervention norm constrains Western intervention in their domestic affairs.

To a much greater extent than the territorial integrity and sovereign equality norms, nonintervention is more directly implicated in some of the most horrendous tragedies of the post-Cold War period. It is also the most difficult norm to change, because in most cases it concerns regime survival. Hence, it is not surprising that the idea of humanitarian intervention – how to define, conduct and regulate it – is today a far more controversial topic than the issue of Security Council reform or changes to decision-making rules, such as shifting from unanimity to majority voting which impinges on the sovereign equality norm.[45]

In this context, the contribution of the International Commission on Intervention and State Sovereignty must be noted.[46] The report, "Responsibility to Protect" (R2P) goes some way towards developing an international consensus on the principles and modalities of humanitarian intervention.[47] It aims to make humanitarian intervention not only more legitimate, but also more efficient, by establishing clear rules, procedures and mechanisms for such intervention. Instead of arguing against the salience of state sovereignty as the basic organizing principle of international relations, the report, the product of a global epistemic community drawn from all continents and cultures, finds the presumed tension between state sovereignty and humanitarian intervention to have been an exaggerated contest. Sovereignty "does still matter", but sovereignty is not to be taken as a right, but as a responsibility, with the understanding that the most basic responsibility "for the protection of its people lies with the state itself".[48] When states are grievously incapable of living up to that responsibility, or are willingly causing severe harm to their own people, the responsibility to protect shifts to the international community. Hence the most significant contribution of the report is its redefinition of humanitarian intervention as a responsibility (first, of the state concerned, and failing that, of the international community), and not a right (of outsiders, however may they represent the international community at large).

No other policy document has gone further in specifying the criteria for humanitarian intervention. The Report sets down six conditions: right authority, just cause, right intention, last resort, proportional means and reasonable prospects. To satisfy the concerns of developing countries that humanitarian intervention may be used indiscriminately and capriciously by the strong against the weak, the report regards humanitarian intervention as "an exceptional and extraordinary" measure to be undertaken only in response to large scale loss of life and ethnic cleansing. Going by this criteria, democratic breakdowns, or conflicts that do not produce "serious and irreparable harm" to human beings, the traditional principle of nonintervention still holds.

The R2P faced obstacles in becoming the standard bearer of a new norm of humanitarian intervention that would significantly reduce the salience of nonintervention. Developing countries remain wary of its recommendations, while on the other extreme, some advocates of humanitarian intervention argue unhappily that it keeps the threshold of intervention too high to cover situations like Burma.[49] The report was sidelined by the 11 September attacks on the US and the consequent preoccupation of the international community over the US-led global war on terror, which severely damaged multilateralism. The war on terror reinstated strategic intervention ahead of the humanitarian variety, notwithstanding the US belatedly and self-serving justification offered by the Bush administration that its invasion of Iraq was a humanitarian action (as it became clearer that evidence could not be found to support the war's original rationale, the Iraqi possession of weapons of mass destruction). More important, American decision-making leading to the attack on Iraq violated almost every criteria of humanitarian intervention laid down by the R2P (which mirror the traditional principles of the "just war" doctrine), including: "right authority", "just cause", "right intention", "last resort", "proportional means" and "reasonable prospects". The report has retained value, however, as a point of reference, if not guidance, by governments and NGOs alike when discussing humanitarian intervention. But the report received a new boost in the 2004 Report of the Secretary-General's High-Level Panel on Threats, Challenges and Change". The panellists "endorse[d] the merging norm that there is a collective international responsibility to protect, exercisable by the Security Council authorizing military intervention as a last resort, in the event of genocide and other large-scale killing, ethnic cleansing or serious violations of international humanitarian law which sovereign Governments have proved powerless or unwilling to prevent". The criteria specified by the report to justify humanitarian intervention correspond closely to the criteria found in the R2P report.[50] This norm of humanitarian intervention was one of the few major substantive items from the High Level Panel Report (and the subsequent report by Secretary-General Kofi Anan, "In Larger Freedom") to survive the 2005 UN Summit in September 2005.[51]

Given the early post-war regional variations in the construction of sovereignty, normative change at the global level remains contingent upon transitions at the local and regional level. In this context, important challenges to the nonintervention norm are emerging at the regional level. The case of the IADC has already been noted. The African Union began its life in May 2001 by assuming the authority (under Article 4) "to intervene in a Member State pursuant to a decision of the Assembly in respect of grave circumstances, namely: war crimes, genocide and crimes against humanity".[52] Although there would be an amendment to this provision that would shift the ground of intervention from humanitarian justifications "to the rationale of preserving order", it is nonetheless a major breakthrough for a continent which has been a strong proponent of "negative sovereignty".[53] And, as noted, the NEPAD initiative, strongly backed by South Africa, seeks to move beyond strict sovereignty concerns by adopting a "peer review mechanism" covering areas of peace and stability, democracy and political governance, and economic and corporate governance.[54] Asia continues to lag behind other regions of the world in departing from nonintervention. But here, too, a regional financial surveillance mechanism in the making and an Indonesian proposal for an ASEAN Security Community calls for democracy as a regional norm and the non-recognition of any unconstitutional custer of governments.

How will the different regions fare in leaving the strict or absolute conception of nonintervention behind and developing new multilateral mechanisms to cope with problems of stability and development? Normative change depends on a set of conditions: chief among them is "local initiative" or the availability of local/insider proponents (and not just global or outside norm entrepreneurs), the present legitimacy of the pre-existing normative order, the existence of a prior receptive norm onto which the new norms can be "grafted", and the prospect that norm diffusion would lead to the legitimation and universalization of local identities.[55] Moreover, normative change is seldom a total displacement of the prior normative order, because local beliefs and practices do matter in shaping socialization processes around a new norm. In the case of the IADC, the insider leadership of Peru complimented the prior democratization of the continent creating a receptive environment for the development of the IADC. Even then, concessions had to be made to the proponents of state sovereignty such as Venezuela, and a high degree of state-centrism characterizes the charter, whose preventive measures such as collective vigilance and crisis missions could be undertaken "by invitation only" or through prior consent. In Africa, NEPAD is seen less as a "local" initiative despite its championing by South Africa, than the new AU, because of strong feelings in the region, especially among civil society groups, that the real norm entrepreneurs of NEPAD are the global financial institutions pushing for the neoliberal norms of the "Washington Consensus". And the prior norms of African development, including "self-reliance" retain legitimacy. Hence, the prospects for NEPAD succeeding are bleaker than those of the IADC. The AU's acceptance of humanitarian intervention is genuine, but not total, there remain an important local constituency for the nonintervention principle who continue to associate humanitarian intervention with a form of neocolonialism. And the organization is constrained by a lack of capacity, which the international community urgently needs to address. And Asia lacks many of the conditions for normative change in so far as nonintervention is concerned. Insider advocacy of the idea of humanitarian intervention is limited (only Thailand under the government of the Democrat Party was an open advocate or a modified version of this norm and then its Foreign Minister Surin Pitsuwan was seen as an "agent" of the West). Whether Indonesia fares better with its ideas about regional norm of democratic polities remains to be seen. China remains a particularly powerful critic of humanitarian intervention. India shows highly qualified support for it.[56] The democratization process in Asia is not widespread or robust enough (especially with China, Vietnam, Burma and North Korea remaining firmly authoritarian) to create a conducive climate for the diffusion of the humanitarian intervention norm through regional institutions. And sections of the ASEAN elite happen to believe that instead of legitimizing its identity and reputation as a regional actor, departing from the nonintervention norm will be ruinous for the organization.[57]

Conclusion

Without multilateralism, the norms of sovereignty would not have become so prominent a feature of the post-war international order. The developing countries, after securing independence from colonial powers, would have found it difficult to adopt and extend the norms of sovereignty and defend them against challenges such as superpower encroachment. Without the bargaining and socializing environment offered by multilateral institutions, the developed countries would not have found it possible to secure the consent of the developing countries that would allow them to enjoy substantive and procedural exceptions to the principle of sovereign equality of states, which in their view was necessary for the sake of more efficient approaches to international peace and security.

Today, state sovereignty, especially its nonintervention norm, is facing challenges from a variety of sources, at intra-state, regional and global levels and in different issue areas.[58] Without multilateralism and multilateral institutions, the international community will find it difficult to manage normative change without substantial chaos. It is possible to argue that normative change could occur, and probably occur more dramatically and quickly, without multilateralism. Perhaps such change could be imposed by powerful states, or brought about by an American empire of the type that some neoconservative intellectuals in the US advocate. But as the case of the Iraq war shows, such attempts, even with a humanitarian justification, could have profoundly destabilizing consequences, not only in terms of realizing the purpose of the intervention, but also in ensuring cooperation and understanding in the international community as a whole. Multilateralism and multilateral institutions may not be the quickest, most efficient or decisive producers of normative change, but they make fundamental transformations legitimate and peaceful.

Notes

1. I would like to thank the Weatherhead Center for International Affairs at Harvard University for providing affiliation to complete this paper, Robert O. Keohane for comments on the draft, and Morten Hansen for research assistance. The focus of this paper is on multilateral organizations, although I consider the role of social movements and other elements of "new multilateralism". I consider regional organizations such as the Organization of American States (OAS), African Union (AU) and Association of Southeast Asian Nations (ASEAN) to be multilateral, despite their limited geographic scope. The scope of this paper is limited to considerations of state sovereignty, rather than popular sovereignty.
2. John Mearsheimer (1994) "The false promise of international institutions", *International Security* 19(3) (Winter 1994/95): 5–49.

3. Robert Keohane and Lisa Martin (1995) "The promise of institutionalist theory", *International Security* 20(1) (Summer): 39–51.
4. Martha Finnemore (1993) "International organizations as teachers of norms", *International Organization* 47 (Autumn): 565–597.
5. Andrew Hurrell (2003) "Norms and ethics in international relations", in Walter Carlsnaes, Thomas Risse and Beth A Simmons (eds) *Handbook of International Relations*, London: Sage; Friedrich Kratochwil (1993) "Norms versus numbers: multilateralism and the rationalist and reflexivist approaches to institutions", in John Gerard Ruggie (ed.) *Multilateralism Matters: The Theory and Praxis of an Institutional Form*, New York: Columbia University Press, pp. 443–474.
6. John Gerard Ruggie (1982) "International regimes, transactions and change: embedded liberalism in the postwar economic order", *International Organization* 36 (Spring).
7. F.H. Hinsley (1966) *Sovereignty*, New York: Oxford University Press, p. 26.
8. Robert H. Jackson (1996) *Quasi-States: Sovereignty, International Relations and the Third World*, Cambridge: Cambridge University Press, p. 34. Jackson views sovereignty as a "normative premise of world politics", or "the basic norm, *grundnorm*, upon which a society of states ultimately rests". Robert Jackson (1999) "Introduction: sovereignty at the millennium", in Jackson (ed.) *Sovereignty at the Millennium*, Oxford: Blackwell, pp. 8, 10.
9. Joseph Camilleri and Jim Falk speak of three fundamental principles as the "accepted norms of international conduct": "a sovereign state could not, without its consent, allow other political entities "to make or apply their own rules on its territory"; a sovereign state had the obligation "not to intervene in the internal affairs of other states or compromise their territorial integrity"; and "states enjoyed by virtue of their sovereignty equal rights and duties regardless of differences in their demographic, economic or strategic circumstances". Joe Camilleri and Jim Falk (1992) *The End of Sovereignty?*, London: Edward Elgar, p. 29. The wording of the first two of the principles is taken from K.J. Holsti (1967) *International Politics; A Framework for Analysis*, Englewood Cliffs: Prentice Hall, p. 84. For Brierly, the core norms of sovereignty are derived from the "rights of states" which include "self-preservation, independence, equality, respect and intercourse", J.L. Brierly (1963) *The Law of Nations*, 6th edition, Oxford: Oxford University Press, p. 49. Jackson identifies the constitutive rules of sovereignty to include: "legal equality of states, mutual recognition, jurisdiction, nonintervention, making and honouring of treaties, diplomacy conducted in accordance with accepted practices, and in the broadest sense a framework of international law including the law of war which attempts to confine even violent conflicts between states within a rule-bounded playing field that protects noncombatants and other spectators". He distinguishes between such constitutive rules and the "instrumental rules" of sovereignty, including foreign policy, and "precepts, maxims, stratagems, and tactics which are derived from experience and contribute to winning play", Jackson (1966) *Quasi-States*, pp. 34–35.
10. John Gerard Ruggie (1993) "Multilateralism: the anatomy of an institution", in Ruggie (ed.) *Multilateralism Matters: The Theory and Praxis of an Institutional Form*, New York: Columbia University Press, p. 8.
11. Abram Chayes and Antonia Handler Chayes (1995) *The New Sovereignty: Compliance with International Regulatory Agreements*, Cambridge, MA: Harvard University Press, p. 113.
12. As Martha Finnemore and Kathryn Sikkink write: "contemporary empirical research on norms is aimed ... at showing how the 'ought' becomes the 'is'. Empirical research documents again and again how people's ideas about what is good and what 'should be' in the world becomes translated into political reality". While they also recognize that "principled commitments and notions of what 'should be' have fuelled xenophobic

nationalism, fascism, and ethnic cleansing", there has been very little research conducted on such effects of norms by constructivist norm scholars, who for the most part remain concerned with such moral transformations as end of apartheid, abolition of slavery, foot-binding and female circumcision, protection of whales, ban on land mines and regulation of small arms, and above all promotion of human rights. Martha Finnemore and Kathryn Sikkink (1998) "International norm dynamics and political change", *International Organization* 52(4) (Autumn): 916.

13. Amitav Acharya (2004) "How ideas spread: whose norms matter? Norm localization and institutional change in Asian regionalism", *International Organization* 58(2) (Spring).
14. Unless "revolution" implies long-term historical change, as in Daniel Philpott (2001) *Revolutions in Sovereignty: How Ideas Shaped Modern International Relations*, Princeton: Princeton University Press.
15. Ruggie (1993) "Multilateralism: The Anatomy of an Institution", p. 15.
16. V.S. Mani (2004) "An Indian perspective on the evolution of international law", *Asian Yearbook of International Law, 2000*, vol. 9, Netherlands: Brill, p. 66.
17. "Legally there is no obstacle to create different international organizations upon any conditions which the member States agree upon", Bengt Broms (1959) *The Doctrine of Legal Equality of States As Applied in International Organizations*, PhD dissertation, University of Helsinki, p. 336.
18. The focus of this chapter is not substantive norms, such as nonintervention or sovereign equality of states rather than procedural norms such as consensus or majority voting. But the two are closely linked. As will be noted, in Asia, the nonintervention principles formed the basis for a number of procedural norms such as avoidance of legalistic dispute settlement procedures, and organizational minimalism.
19. United Nations Information Organizations (1945) *Documents of the United Nations Conference on International Organization, San Francisco 1945*, vol. VI, New York: United Nations Information Organizations, pp. 332, 717–718. Hereafter referred to as *UNCIO Documents*.
20. Broms (1959) *The Doctrine of Legal Equality of States*, p. 165.
21. Leland M. Goodrich and Edvard Hambro (1949) *Charter of the United Nations: Commentary and Documents*, Boston: World Peace Foundation, p. 99.
22. Jackson (1966) *Sovereignty at the Millennium*, p. 31.
23. Goodrich and Hambro (1949) *Charter of the United Nations*, p. 100.
24. Ibid.: 164–165.
25. J.G. Starke (1994) *Starke's International Law*, 11th Edition, I.A. Shearer (ed), London: Butterworths, p. 100.
26. Mark W. Zacher (2001) "The territorial integrity norm: international boundaries and the use of force", *International Organization* 55(2) (Spring): 221.
27. John Vincent (1974) *Nonintervention and International Order*, Princeton, NJ: Princeton University Press, p. 290.
28. *UNCIO Documents* (1945) Vol. VI, p. 507; Goodrich and Hambro (1949) *Charter of the United Nations*, p. 111.
29. *UNCIO Documents* (1945) Vol. VI, pp. 334, 435–440.
30. R.P. Anand (1987) "Attitude of the Asian-African states towards certain problems of international law", in Frederick E. Snyder and Surakiart Sathirathai (eds) *Third World Attitudes Toward International Law*, Boston: Martinus Nijhoff Publishers, pp. 12–13.
31. Hedley Bull and Adam Watson (eds) (1984) *The Expansion of International Society*, Oxford: Clarendon Press, p. 2.
32. Ann Van Wynen Thomas and A.J. Thomas, Jr (1956) *Nonintervention: The Law and Its Import in the Americas*, Dallas: Southern Methodist University Press.

33. On the Asian origins of these norms, see Amitav Acharya (1997) "Ideas, identity, and institution-building: from the 'ASEAN Way' to the 'Asia Pacific Way'", *Pacific Review* 10(2): 319–346; Amitav Acharya (2002) "Regional institutions and Asian security order: norms, power, and prospects for peaceful change", in Muthaah Alagappa (ed.) *Asian Security Order: Instrumental and Normative Features*, Stanford: Stanford University Press, pp. 210–240.
34. Robert H. Jackson (1990) *Quasi-States: Sovereignty, International Relations and the Third World*, Cambridge: Cambridge University Press, p. 153.
35. Zacher (2001) "The territorial integrity norm", pp. 221–222, 229–231.
36. Ibid.: 222.
37. Margaret E. Keck and Kathryn Sikkink (1998) *Activists Beyond Borders: Advocacy Networks in International Politics*, Ithaca: Cornell University Press; Sanjeev Khagram, Kathryn Sikkink and James V. Riker (2002) *Restructuring World Politics: Transnational Social Movements, Networks, and Norms*, Minneapolis: University of Minnesota Press; Thomas Risse, Stephen C. Ropp, and Kathryn Sikkink (eds) (1999) *The Power of Human Rights: International Norms and Domestic Change*, Cambridge: Cambridge University Press; Jackie Smith, Charles Chatfield and Ron Pagnucco (1997) *Transnational Social Movements and Global Politics: Solidarity Beyond the State*, Syracuse University Press.
38. Robert W. Cox (1996) "Multilateralism and world order", in Robert W. Cox with Timothy J. Sinclair, *Approaches to World Order*, Cambridge: Cambridge University Press.
39. Peter M. Haas (1992) "Introduction: epistemic communities and international policy coordination", *International Organization* 46(1): 1–37; Emanuel Adler (1992) "The emergence of cooperation: national epistemic communities and the international evolution of the idea of nuclear arms control", *International Organization* 46: 101–145.
40. Ruggie (1993) "Multilateralism: the anatomy of an institution", p. 31.
41. Andrew F. Cooper (2002) "Negotiating the inter-American democratic charter: a case of 'new' multilateralism?", paper submitted to the Conference on Inter-American Democratic Charter: Challenges and Opportunities, Vancouver, Canada, 12–13 November 2002.
42. On hegemonic stability theory and the ability of multilateral institutions to endure after hegemony, see Robert O. Keohane (1984) *After Hegemony: Cooperation and Discord in the World Political Economy*, Princeton: Princeton University Press. On the institution-binding perspective, see John Ikenberry (2001) *After Victory: Institutions, Strategic Restraint, and the Rebuilding of Order After Major War*, Princeton: Princeton University Press.
43. Oran R. Young (1991) "Political leadership and regime formation: on the development of institutions in international society", *International Organization* 45(3) (Summer).
44. On the historical reasons behind Third World's attachment to sovereignty, see Mohammed Ayoob (1995) *The Third World Security Predicament: State Making, Regional Order and the International System*, Boulder, CO: Lynne Rienner.
45. The European Union is making significant moves towards majority voting. Changes to decision-making procedures adopted by the Constitutional Treaty adopted by the European Council in Brussels in June 2004 ensures that more decisions are reached through majority decision-making, rather than unanimity. Instead of the majority of Member States representing 60 per cent of the population, a qualified majority will require the support of *55 per cent of the Member States representing 65 per cent of the population*. This is accompanied by two further elements. First, in order to avoid the situation where, in an extreme case, only three (large) Member States would be able to block a Council decision due to an increase in the population threshold, a blocking minority needs to comprise at least four Member States. Moreover, a number of Council mem-

bers representing at least three-quarters of a blocking minority, whether at the level of Member States or the level of population, can demand that a vote is postponed and that discussions continue for a reasonable time in order to reach a broader basis of consensus within the Council. The procedures of consensus and veto mechanisms, however, will continue to apply to the politically sensitive issues of foreign policy, security and defence. http://europa.eu.int/constitution/download/oth250604_2_en.pdf; http://europa.eu.int/constitution/download/oth180604_3_en.pdf

46. The Responsibility to Protect: Report of the International Commission on Intervention and State Sovereignty (Ottawa: International Development Research Centre, December 2001). Hereafter cited as the Report or The Responsibility to Protect.
47. The discussion of R2P draws heavily from my article: Acharya (2002) "Redefining the dilemmas of humanitarian intervention", *Australian Journal of International Affairs* 56(3) (November): 373–382.
48. The Responsibility to Protect, p. 7.
49. Ramesh Thakur (2004) "Developing countries and the intervention–sovereignty debate", in Richard M. Price and Mark W. Zacher (eds) *The United Nations and Global Security*, New York: Palgrave Macmillan, pp. 193–208; Ramesh Thakur (2004) "Iraq and the responsibility to protect", *Behind the Headlines* 62:1 (October), Toronto: Canadian Institute of International Affairs.
50. *A More Secure World: Our Shared Responsibility*, Report of the Secretary-General's High-Level Panel on Threats, Challenges and Change, New York: United Nations, 2004, pp. 66, 106. See also the subsequent Report by Secretary-General Kofi Anan: *In Larger Freedom*. http://www.un.org/largerfreedom/.
51. The Resolution of the Summit stated that the world leaders "are prepared to take collective action, in a timely and decisive manner, through the Security Council, in accordance with the Charter, including Chapter VII, on a case-by-case basis and in cooperation with relevant regional organizations as appropriate, should peaceful means be inadequate and national authorities are manifestly failing to protect their populations from genocide, war crimes, ethnic cleansing and crimes against humanity. Resolution adopted by the General Assembly, 24 October 2005 60/1. 2005 World Summit Outcome; http://daccessdds.un.org/doc/UNDOC/GEN/N05/487/60/PDF/N0548760.pdf?OpenElement (accessed 16 December 2005).
52. Quoted in Corrinne A.A. Packer and Donald Rukare (2002) "The African Union and its Constitutive Act", *American Journal Of International Law* 96(2) (April): 372.
53. Evarist Baimu and Kathryn Sturman (2003) "Amendment to the African Union s right to intervene", *African Security Review* 12(2): 38. The Constitutive Act of the African Union adopted 9 July 2002 under Article 13 authorizes the Executive Council to take decisions in areas including "humanitarian action and disaster response and relief". It establishes a Peace and Security Council of the African Union whose objectives shall be to "promote and encourage democratic practices, good governance and the rule of law, protect human rights and fundamental freedoms, respect for the sanctity of human life and international humanitarian law, as part of efforts for preventing conflicts". The Council (under articles covering actions, mandate and powers) would "support and facilitate humanitarian action in situations of armed conflicts or major natural disasters". The Council also provides for an "African Standby Force ... to undertake humanitarian activities and ... facilitate the activities of the humanitarian agencies in the mission areas" (http://www.africa-union.org).
54. International Peace Academy (2002) "NEPAD: African initiative, new partnership?", *IPA Workshop Report*, New York: IPA; Dani W. Nabudere (2002) "NEPAD: historical background and its prospects", paper prepared for presentation at the African Forum for Envisioning Africa, 26–29 April 2002, Nairobi, Kenya; Adebayo Adedeji (2002)

"From the Lagos Plan of Action to the New Partnership for African Development and from the Final Act of Lagos to the Constitutive Act: whither Africa?", keynote address prepared for the African Forum for Envisioning Africa, Nairobi, Kenya, 26–29 April 2002.

55. These conditions are taken from and elaborated in Acharya (2004) "How ideas spread".
56. For review of the Asian attitudes towards humanitarian intervention, see Koji Watanabe (ed.) (2000) *Humanitarian Intervention: The Evolving Asian Debate*, Tokyo: Japan Centre for International Exchange. The chapters on China, India and ASEAN are written by Jia Qingguo, Jasjit Singh and Simon Tay and Rizal Sukma respectively. From this study, it would appear that China remains most opposed to humanitarian intervention, followed by India and ASEAN, while Korea and Japan are most positive about the concept.
57. For further discussion, see Acharya (2004) "How ideas spread".
58. K.J. Holsti (2004) *Taming the Sovereigns: Institutional Change in International Politics*, New York: Cambridge University Press.

7

From (alleged) unipolarity to the decline of multilateralism? A power-theoretical critique

Stefano Guzzini

This chapter[1] deals with the claim that the decline of the institution of multilateralism[2] is but a logical outcome of the present distribution of international power.[3] This claim is inspired by power materialist approaches which assume both a significant impact of international structural change on state behaviour, and that institutions are ultimately just a reflection of the distribution of state power.[4] In case of a large power preponderance, the leading state can be logically expected to pursue a policy of primacy which maximizes its foreign policy autonomy.[5] It will guard itself from international institutions that acquire an autonomous dynamic antithetical to its power position. In such a circumstance, it would unilaterally bypass or retreat from them in order to reassert its primacy.[6] Since multilateralism is an institution based on *generalized* principles and diffuse reciprocity – hence diluting exceptionalist prerogatives simply based on power – it almost by definition clashes with a strategy of primacy. For, although (defensive) realists can envisage the increased use of multilateralism in order to reassure other states,[7] the institution of multilateralism requires the leading power to curtail its autonomy and capabilities. It will have to forego part of its power, if not its preponderance, in the name of its own security and world order.[8] This being unlikely, or so the argument goes for power-oriented realists, common principles will yield to power when primacy faces multilateralism.

In this chapter, I will analyse what amounts to a double causal claim, namely that the distribution of international power (unipolarity) determines the nature of US foreign policy (primacy-plus-unilateralism) and that such policy is antithetical to international multilateralism. My analysis will not question the existence of a unilateralist turn in US foreign policy (accelerating recently, but dating back earlier) which challenges several areas of the existing multilateral order.[9] But on the basis of recent conceptual analyses of power, I argue that the general thesis of a causal relationship between unipolarity and a decline of multilateralism does not hold. Such systemic explanations misconceive the role power can play in social science explanations. I will make this point in three steps.

First, I illustrate the indeterminacy of systemic power analysis for assessing the general causal claim by comparing the present debate with the hegemonic decline debate of the 1980s. This comparison shows that systemic power analyses have explained the same outcome by opposite power dynamics, once a decline and once a rise in US power. It also shows that US unilateralism is not necessarily antithetical to all components of multilateralism. Hence, the causal chain does not work in its two main links.

Second, I show that this contradiction is not fortuitous but intrinsic to the properties of the concept of power in International Relations. For the very assessment of this unipolarity is contingent on a series of often implicit definitional moves which have been discarded in political theory. They end up privileging a view of power as a property concept and not a dispositional and relational concept, and as being unidimensional (mainly military or material) and not multidimensional. Once these assumptions are questioned, two implications follow: it undermines the possibility of an overall concept of power necessary for polarity analysis, as well as the overall assessment of US power which turns out to be much more ambivalent. Linking this finding up with the first section, I conclude that, since power is not measurable, claims to a specific unipolarity cannot be independently checked to save the causal links of a systemic power analysis going from unipolarity to the decline of multilateralism.

In a third step, I will use a constructivist twist to the conceptual analysis of power in order to assess whether a particular conception of power, if shared, has an actual effect on world order. Precisely because the distribution of power resources does not determinate outcomes, but are often understood to do so, the capacity to shape the definitions of power is not mere semantics, but has political effect. This move reverses the relationship between the two central concepts. Rather than seeing unprecedented preponderance as the cause of unilateralism, it shows how a successful (neoconservative) policy of US unilateralism could foster a certain understanding of power which, if it becomes shared by the international society, will have real power effects akin to the alleged effects of unipolarity.

The indeterminacy of polarity explanations: unipolarity, unilateralism and the logic of Hegemonic Stability Theory in reverse

The implicit hypothesis of most observers is that the present preponderance of the US in world affairs explains its increased use of unilateral and bilateral policies. Such a hypothesis trades on a theoretical assumption that power differentials significantly shape the definition of state interests and behaviour, whether directly and somewhat naturally or via the decision making elite's perception of them.[10] This theoretical assumption is flawed, and systemic power approaches with it, as a comparison with Hegemonic Stability Theory (HST) shows.

The causal link between the distribution of power and the nature of the international system (or its regimes) is purely systemic. Its basic causal relationship is not new. It has been played out in the 1980s during the debates about the alleged US decline. But then, its logic ran in reverse. Whereas today it is allegedly obvious that unilateralism is the result of unipolarity, during the heyday of HST, US decline was held responsible for the decline of multilateralism. I will use this curious reversal to illustrate the indeterminacy, if not arbitrariness, of general systemic power arguments in International Relations.

HST had its heyday after the US had started to dismantle the system of Bretton Woods, a system it had significantly helped to inaugurate and manage. The theory drew on a historical analogy with the inter-war period. The inter-war breakdown of the international liberal order was interpreted as the direct result of missing leadership.[11] Then, the UK, seen as the declining hegemon, was no longer able, whereas the US was perhaps able, but not yet willing to support the international liberal order. When the Nixon administration unilaterally declared the fixed Gold–Dollar link suspended, commentators saw the US repeat the British experience.

HST is an extension of a classical realist thesis, that high power differentials are conducive to stability. In the words of Kenneth Waltz, "Extreme equality is associated with extreme instability".[12] It derives its specificity by linking this idea to a rationalist theory of public goods.[13] Such public goods can be understood in the classic realist way as the provision of international order,[14] as an international economic order for mercantilists,[15] or as international régimes for neo-institutionalists.[16] Multilateral institutions are usually connected to the last two. And indeed, that hegemons have been at the origins of multilateral institutions is at the core of standard approaches to multilateralism.[17]

Flowing from its collective good formulation, HST makes three central propositions.[18] First, the emergence of a hegemon is necessary for the provision of an international public good (hegemony thesis). Second, the necessary existence of free riders (and thus the unequal distribution of costs for the provision) and/or a loss of legitimacy will undermine the relative power position of the hegemon (Entropy thesis).[19] Third, a declining hegemonic power presages a declining provision of the international public good (Decline thesis).[20]

Showing with some detail the causal propositions of HST illustrates an obvious puzzle for the causal link between the present unipolarity and the alleged decline of multilateralism in both its causal links. For the US of the immediate post-1945 period had a similar unipolar/hegemonic position and yet did nor pursue a policy which was antithetical to multilateralism.

The logically most satisfying solution to the puzzle would consist in devising a hypothesis in which the optimal provision of an international public good would be connected to a certain equilibrium of power, not more and not less. In one case, the weakened hegemon would be no longer able to go multilateral; in another the emboldened hegemon would, by objective forces propelled, be no longer willing. However, this solution trades on the existence of a general measure of power, which, as the next section shows, is missing.

A special "unipolarity"? The pitfalls of power as aggregate resource analysis

It is a curious feature that the ubiquity of power analysis in IR has largely remained unshaken by the multiple warnings that the concept of power cannot shoulder the explanatory weight assigned to it. This section shows that the "unipolarity breeds the decline of multilateralism" thesis systematically misconceives of the dispositional, relational and multidimensional character of power in the understanding of social interactions and their outcomes. Through the detour of conceptual power analysis, it questions the very possibility of a general polarity analysis and hence of the starting point of the causal link under scrutiny: unipolarity. For this reason, I argue that assigning to the present unipolarity a special quality is eventually arbitrary.

Power: dispositional, relational and multidimensional

The very idea of unipolarity assumes an overall concept of power in which different resources can be consistently aggregated. It moreover assumes that resources as such are sufficient to predict or understand outcomes (such as unilateralism). The critique of such assumptions is legend and I will only briefly rehearse it here.[21]

The difficult relationship between power understood as resources and power as control over outcomes has been an evergreen in IR power debates.[22] On the one hand, power analysis is most interested in the control of outcomes, not resources as such. Yet, defining power in terms of control over outcomes produces an obvious risk of circularity.[23] Hence, mainstream power analysis goes back to resources and basically stipulates its link to control over outcomes in probabilistic terms. The underlying idea of causality with regard to the outcome is kept.

This is either at odds with the dispositional character of power, or needs to be very heavily qualified for the relational character of power. Peter Morriss has shown that in its most general understanding, power is neither a thing (or property, or resource), nor an event (which shows itself only if realized in an outcome), but an ability: a capacity to effect a certain action.[24] Dispositions translate into effects only under specific conditions. In a social context, such a disposition is understood in a relational way. In its Weberian understanding, power refers to the capacity to get others to do something they would not have otherwise done. For understanding the latter, one needs to know the preferences and value systems of the actors at hand.[25] To use an extreme example: killing a person who wants to commit suicide at all costs is usually not understood as an instance of power. Power does not reside in a resource but stems from the particular relation in which abilities are actualized. Hence, in order to find out whether a certain action (*not* just the possession of the resource) indeed realizes an instance of (social) power, the distribution of resources says quite little independently of the specific conditions which apply to the social relations at hand. Power is situation-specific.

Moreover, power is a multidimensional phenomenon. This is linked to the fact that power in political relations cannot be thought in an analogy to money in economic exchange, both in practice and theory. Whereas different preferences and different markets can be gauged through the fungibility of money, which allows also the observer to reduce this multiplicity on a single aggregate scale, no such scale exists for power in real world politics.[26] While (in monetarized economies), money is the real world measure of wealth, there is no equivalent currency to measure power. This is not merely a theoretical problem that would be resolvable with some conceptual work;[27] it derives from the different status in practice. As a result, there is no overarching issue structure, as suggested by polarity analysis. And abilities in one area might not affect from one issue area to another (or the effect cannot be controlled for). The multidimensional character of power goes hand in hand with an issue-specific vision of world politics. It also means that attempts to construct a more general theory of linkage are doomed from the start: such a theory of linkage would assume that we had indeed a measure which would allow us to move from one issue area to another, a measure whose very absence is however the reason why we have different issue areas to start with.

There have been different reactions towards these findings. Although realists are usually committed to neglect or downplay these difficulties,[28] some have contributed to the debate by rethinking the role of power even if it cannot be measured,[29] by accepting that issue-specificity applies to world politics,[30] or arguing that the problem of fungibility is not as big as assumed,[31] yet without really answering Aron's and Baldwin's critiques.[32]

Unipolarity, influence and legitimacy

These characteristics of power have significant implications for the "unipolarity breeds the decline of multilateralism" thesis by questioning the taken-for-granted assessment of unipolarity. On the one hand, it qualifies (and simultaneously widens) the assessment of significant resources. Here, US preponderance appears less clear cut. More importantly, it moves from resources to the analysis of actual influence and then to authority showing that legitimacy is not just a function of resources, even soft ones.

Wohlforth's reference study does acknowledge the difficulty of having a single issue area, and hence bases the assessment on the "decisive preponderance in *all* the underlying components of power: economic, military, technological and geopolitical".[33] Yet, there are several difficulties with this assessment.

First, as in this case, unipolarity analysis tends to concentrate on mere material resources (see below for "soft power") for assessing power. This misses two qualifications. First, the nature of international society affects the respective value of abilities, their resources and the relevant issue areas.[34] This is an old idea, running from Wolfers through Keohane/Nye and the English School to constructivism-inspired approaches.[35] It simply means that, in a context of international relations which can no longer be satisfactorily described as Hobbesian in most parts, but has aspects both of a society of states and a transnational world of societies,[36] power is to be thought of in quite different ways at the same time. It is not obvious that US (or any other) military resources are usable against friends in the same way as against enemies. The important implication is that they then no longer qualify as unconditional sources of "power" in those relations *in the first place*.

A second qualification derives from the reductionist understanding of influence through resources alone, where the distribution of resources is a shorthand for international order or governance. Such an approach assumes that by aggregating instances of influence in particular social interactions, one can get a comprehensive picture of authority relations in the international system.[37] Going this road, however, conflates the aggregation of instances of influence with authority. Authority is linked to legitimate rule which can obviously not be reduced to material matter alone. Indeed, in one school of thought, power is the opposite to violence:[38] the most powerful police is the one which does not need to shoot. In such an Arendtian understanding, it is connected to the capacity to create things in common.[39]

Taking these two arguments together, one can conclude that the link from resource to control over outcomes is only applicable to a situation-specific analysis, and that the link from mere material resources, via influence to general authority is even weaker.

As a result, a more comprehensive understanding of power is needed. This applies both to the bases of power (abilities) and to the more social understanding of power applicable to present international affairs. Stressing the multidimensional character of power, Nye rejects the label of unipolarity for the present world.[40] Sticking to his power approach derived from Weberian sociology,[41] Michael Mann includes economic power in which the US does not have clear lead,[42] as well as political and ideological power on which he finds the present US fundamentally wanting.[43] Focusing directly on the concept of power, Christian Reus-Smit argues that to understand power correctly today, it needs to be conceived as relational not possessive, primarily ideational not material, intersubjective and social, not subjective and non-social.[44] And again, he finds the US wanting in most. In both cases, only the superiority of its military seems to be unquestioned.

Joseph Nye's concept of "soft power" seems to belong to the same category insofar as it does not understand power simply in terms of resources but as actual influence, and includes non-material sources. And yet Nye's use is more ambivalent and at times differs in an important way.

Nye's concept of soft power is akin to attraction and consensus, and used for pointing to the legitimacy component of power. Just as Susan Strange's reconceptualization of power as "structural power", which included a knowledge structure comprising technology and culture,[45] Nye formulated "soft power" as a reaction against the US decline debate of the 1980s.[46] But even in his most recent statement of it, there is a tendency to analyse soft power in terms of objective resources ("objective measure of potential soft power"[47]), based on the relative number of US movies, patents, high-level universities, and so forth. Now, stressing the difference between resources and influence, he does note that some (popular) cultural items, even if diffused, do not imply a political stance in favour of the US. Also, he gives three different sources of soft power in culture, national values and foreign policy. But, or so the argument can be read, since the US has strong resources in culture, and is allegedly leading the West in terms of values, better public diplomacy becomes the only crucial variable for actual US attractiveness – and anti-Americanism the default residual variable, should it fail. The real value of the other resources is more or less taken for granted. That means that the focus of the power analysis does not really engage with the social and intersubjective component of legitimacy, but slides into a classical *conversion failures* study so much criticized earlier by Baldwin in the wake of the Vietnam war. When allegedly overriding power seemed not to translate into influence, that was not because the US lacked sufficient power, but because of conversion failures (lacking political will, that liberal press back-stabbing, etc.). Hence, we have again the curious finding that the same outcome can be explained by opposite causes (power or powerlessness). The problem here is not just indeterminacy. It is what Baldwin called the "paradox of unrealized power" which makes power analysis unfalsifiable and arbitrary. The value of resources is ultimately objectified and all misfits in terms of influence are explained away via incompetent agency: power resources never fail, only politicians do.

Soft power can be read to apply this logic to the issue of legitimacy: soft power resources never fail, only public diplomacy does. It then falls short of taking the social and intersubjective component of legitimacy into account, as Reus-Smit rightly notes.[48] Reminding the US administration that a clever lion knows when to be fox could miss the point. If one takes power seriously, then one would have to look at the problem not just in terms of the packaging (public diplomacy),[49] but more fundamentally of the content, i.e. the legitimacy of the US specific American vision and project of the international order (not to be confounded with the wider Western, let alone the liberal or the democratic, project).

From the missing measure of power to power perception?

In view of the difficult measurement of power, some power analysis has moved from the actual distribution of aggregate power resources to their perception. Applied to our argument here, the causal link would then start from a perceived unipolarity to the decline of multilateralism. Moreover, such an explanation could perhaps answer the contradiction with which this chapter started: the perceived unipolarity in post-1945 is of a different kind to the one today. Although William Wohlforth developed this argument for another context, it could be reapplied for the present one. When discussing US primacy, Wohlforth does see similarities in the preponderance of Britain between 1860–70, post-1945 US and post-1989 US. Yet, according to him, what sets the present situation apart is the perception of power.[50] Whereas the rational expectation in the past was that the respective leadership position would be passing, now it is not. From this, one could derive the argument that the present situation has no historical comparison.

Unfortunately such an attempt seems to beg the question. If the material component of power has no causal force alone – if it does not "impress" itself unambiguously – then the significant part of the causal explanation moves towards perceptions. But why does the expectation of a leadership in decline ask for multilateralism in 1945, but for unilateral retrenchment in the 1970s and 1980s? In other words, a recourse to perceptions opens up an explanatory regress and risks being adjusted ad hoc to save a realist type of power analysis.

What all this shows is that the general argument, although presented in a forward causal link from unipolarity, is in fact running backwards. Changes in US foreign policy outlook and international multilateralism are read back into an assumed and ultimately unquestioned power link, which is then adjusted to serve the explanatory needs of the day.[51] The classical risk of circular power statements resurfaces.

Unilateralism as a strategy to redefine power

The fact that there is no measure of power has posed perhaps more problems to the (realist) observer than to the (realist) diplomat. Whereas the former still look out for a measure that would help to fix systemic analysis,[52] the latter meet those observers who do not deduce power in any objective way, but understand it from the way practitioners understand it. Since we miss a measure of power, practitioners have to rely on secondary indicators and read power from events. Yet events do not determine a certain vision of power, as the above mentioned indeterminacy and hence circularity of such argument shows. Still, since power as a measurable fact is still crucial in the language and bargaining of international politics, measures of power are agreed to and constructed a social fact: diplomats try and need to agree first on what counts before they can start counting.[53]

This moves the analysis of power away from the illusion of an objective measure to the political battle about defining the criteria of power, which, in turn, has political effects. Concepts of power are not merely external tools to understand international politics, but intervene into it. This moves the analysis unto constructivist ground since it is interested how knowledge reflexively interacts with the social world.[54]

Based on such an analysis, I discuss a possible reversal in the relationship between unipolarity and unilateralism: whereas the earlier sections have shown that unipolarity does not cause the decline of US multilateralism, nor international multilateralism (although US power in certain issue areas can be used to such effect, if US administrations chose to do so), this section argues that US unilateralism can become a strategy to attain the diplomatic (social) equivalent of the alleged effect of unipolarity.

Performative and reflexive aspects of the concept of power

Some concepts, such as power, play a special role in our political discourse. They interact with the world they are supposed simply to describe. This means that besides understanding what they mean, their analysis has to assess what they *do*.[55] Two issues stand out for our present discussion. Power is firstly connected in our political discourse to the assignment of responsibility. "For to acknowledge power over others is to implicate oneself in responsibility for certain events and to put oneself in a position where *justification* for the limits placed on others is expected".[56] Moreover, there exists a reflexive "looping effect"[57] of power definitions with the shared understandings and hence working of power in international affairs.

This link to responsibility makes out of power a concept which is closely connected to the definition of political agency, or politics *tout court*. The traditional definition of power as getting someone else to do something he or she would not have otherwise done implies an idea of counterfactuals. The act of attributing power redefines the borders of what can be done. In the usual way we conceive of the term, this links power inextricably to "politics" in the sense of the "art of the possible/feasible". Lukes[58] rightly noticed that Bacharach's and Baratz's conceptualization of power[59] sought to redefine what counts as a political issue. To be "political" means to be potentially changeable; that is, not something natural, objectively given, but something which has the potential to be influenced by political action. In a similar vein, Daniel Frei argues that the concept of power is fundamentally identical to the concept of the "political"; i.e. to include something as a factor of power in one's calculus, means to "politicize" it.[60] In other words, attributing power to an issue imports it into the public realm where action (or non-action) is required to justify itself. In return, "depoliticization" happens when by common acceptance no power was involved. In such instances, political action is exempted from further justification and scrutiny.

Such a performative analysis of concepts is not new in IR, in particular with regard to the concept of security. Barry Buzan and Ole Wæver have proposed a framework of security analysis around the concept of "securitization". According to them, security is to be understood through the effects of it being voiced. It is part of a discourse (for example, "vital national interests") which, when successfully mobilized, enables issues to be given a priority for which the use of extraordinary means is justified. In its logical conclusion, "securitization" ultimately tends to move decisions out of "politics" altogether.[61]

US power and special responsibility: justifying exemptionalism

Connolly's original analysis relates to situations where power holders see none of their power involved. No power means no responsibility, thus discharging actors from justifying their actions. Critiques of their actions almost inevitably end up in challenging the understanding of power: there is supposedly no power only because the narrow definition of power precludes seeing it. Hence, a change in the definition of power, if shared, will affect political discourse and action. A classical example of this usage in IR can be found in Susan Strange's concept of structural power which she developed in the mid-1980s against the backdrop of alleged US hegemonic decline. She showed how "non-decisions", as well as unintended consequences of actions are part of any power analysis.[62] Indeed, making the US aware of such non-intentional effects is consequential: the next time, such effects need to be included into one's justification of action.

But the present debate turns this relationship between power and responsibility onto its head: the power holder no longer downplays its power for keeping aloof of criticism, it heavily insists in its power-thus-responsibility so as to justify a worldwide interventionism. If it were true that the US enjoys a very large power and superiority, then it is only natural that it assumes a large responsibility for international affairs. Insisting on the special power of the US triggers and justifies a disposition for action. Here, the insistence on the special nature of unipolarity gives the responsibility–power link a special twist, not dissimilar to the classical realist view that international politics cannot be apprehended with the same norms as domestic politics.[63]

There are two steps in this argument which can combine responsibility with a justification always already given. A first and direct one is the traditional defence of interventionism. With such preponderance of power, there is no safe way to retreat to one's own shores. A second step is more tenuous, but actually derives from Hegemonic Stability Theory: US unipolarity introduces a hierarchical element into world order. US primacy means that it has different functions and duties (responsibilities) than other states. From there, the final step to a right or even duty to unilateralism is not far. Its role as world policemen is no longer a choice, but actually a requirement of the system.[64] Being compelled to play the world leader means, in turn, that the rules which apply to all the others cannot always apply to the US. The US becomes an actor of a different sort: its special duties exempt it from the general norms. This is the basis of its tendency to exemptionalism, something which is difficult to accommodate within a multilateral framework.[65]

The political implications are clear. The more observers stress the unprecedented power of the US, the more they mobilize the political discourse of agency and responsibility tying it to the US and the US alone, and the more they can exempt US action from criticism, since it responds to the "objective" (power) circumstances of our time.[66] This does not necessarily mean that unilateralism is to follow; but it makes that argument much easier to swallow. Inversely, the more observers see this "special responsibility" or exceptionalism as part of the problem, not of the solution to US security concerns (and international order at large), the more they might be inclined to double-check the alleged unipolarity.[67]

The power of unilateralism

Through the link of power to politics in our tradition of political discourse, definitions of power have a reflexive relationship with the world they are said simply to describe. The definition of power, if shared, has power effects in itself. As discussed above, it defines the realm of political justification and legitimacy. But it also provides practitioners with a socially constructed shorthand for their ranking and hence their leverage in any bargaining. The struggle for the right definition of power is not academic; by its potential effects, it is inherently political. Reaching and keeping definitional power over "power" is more widely consequential. For "the theory of knowledge is a dimension of political theory because the specifically symbolic power to impose the principles of the construction of reality ... is a major dimension of political power".[68]

This leads to the last step in the analysis of the relationship between unipolarity and unilateralism, one in which the poles are reversed. Rather than seeing in the "logic" of unipolarity the cause for unilateralist US action (and the decline of multilateralism), US unilateralism, justified through non-relational and one-sidedly material definitions of power, can be part of a self-fulfilling prophecy leading to the alleged "logic" of unipolarity.

As the discussion of the first two sections tried to show, there is no logic of unipolarity, no inherent necessity in moving from the argument of unprecedented preponderance to the outspoken unilateralism in US foreign policy. Indeed, exactly because the US enjoys such preponderance, it could afford to be much more self-restrained.[69] Yet, if power is defined in mainly military terms, not only the US acquires a very special place, but it also means that the very functioning of the international system is understood as one which is "ultimately" one of military security.

In such a remilitarized environment, questions of legitimacy are redefined. For the sake of this argument, we can follow Fritz Scharpf's understanding that legitimacy derives usually from both responsiveness (input) and efficiency (output). In an international order defined fundamentally by military competition, with no international society worth its name, legitimacy is provided, or so it seems, mainly from the output side. On Mars, force is the only source of a necessarily shallow legitimacy. The contract is purely Hobbesian: authority through security. Joseph Nye is aware and wary of this kind of argument, since it allows (the illusion of) an ex post legitimization of an otherwise illegitimate unilateralism.[70]

The crux of this somewhat paternalist legitimation through some future order is that it can push the verification of the claim indefinitely. Having an interpretation of power that raised the US to the pinnacle as the only country able to do anything, even should it fail, it did the right thing responding to its special duty. There is no way to disconfirm this logic. If order has not yet been found, given the unprecedented (read: military) power position of the US, the only way forward is to do more of the same and let the US try to fix it again, being the only authority there is. The logic is a kind of Microsoft theory of security: the problem is not that there is too much Windows, the problem is that there is still not enough.

At some point in time, repeated US unilateralism would have contributed to reduce the international society to military order, and security to military strategy, and so eventually produce the very vision of unipolarity from which all is supposed to derive. The chain of the self-fulfilling prophecy is this: (1) a presumed but wrong causal link between power (unipolarity) and behaviour (primacy-plus-unilateralism) based on a wrong reduction of power to resources and moreover to material ones, allows (2) a justification for a special responsibility which exempts the sole superpower from the usual rules, hence (3) a remilitarized unilateralism which requires a retreat from the multilateral demilitarizing regime network and (4) by these very actions, increasingly enforces a definition of power in purely military terms, which (5) becomes the accepted and intersubjectively shared meaning and understanding of power in international society, that (6) finally *leads to* a world of Mars in which legitimacy is reduced to efficient coercion. This chain is the effect of a neoconservative understanding of the world which actively changes the world, not just responds to it. And the socially constructed character of the concept of power is crucial in every link of this chain.

Most of the critics of unipolarity mentioned so far are concerned and aware of this reflexivity, that is the very significant real world effect an erroneous definition of power ultimately can have. As Buzan puts it, "The salient point is ... which interpretation of unipolarity gets accepted within the US – and indeed the other great powers – as the prevailing social fact. It is the accepted social fact that shapes securitization."[71] And continuous securitization ("hypersecuritization", as Buzan calls it) would indeed change the nature of international society.[72]

It is hard not to be reminded of the by now (in)famous quote made by a senior adviser to President George W. Bush, reported by Ron Suskind. The adviser insisted that people like Suskind were part of the "reality-based community" which thinks about solutions in terms of the existing reality. "That is not the way the world works any more ... We're an empire now, and when we act, we create our own reality".[73] That sentence acquires an even more fundamental significance when put into the context of a reflexive analysis of power.

As mentioned by Buzan, such self-fulfilling effects are of course contingent on the acceptance of certain understandings. Power discourse in its link to responsibility is open to both its classical use as a critique of power holders, as to its new twist where it exempts the especially powerful from norms applicable to others.

Conclusion

This chapter has applied the recent conceptual analysis of power to the thesis that unipolarity predisposes for a US foreign policy of primacy and unilateralism and hence for a decline of multilateralism as an institution. It found this thesis wanting in both links. More specifically, it made three claims.

First, as a discussion of Hegemonic Stability Theory showed, the decline of multilateralism can as well be connected to an alleged decline in hegemony as to its opposite. This illustrated that there is no determinate link between the distribution of power, the foreign policy of the leading power and its effect.

Second, I argued that this indeterminacy of systemic power analysis is not fortuitous, but results from the very characteristics of the concept of power. Usually the analysis assumes a concept of power which is based on resources not relations, and on the one dimension of the military (including material factors supportive of it, such as economy and technology) not on its multidimensionality. Yet, once these conceptually untenable assumptions are loosened, power analysis becomes relation and situation dependent. This widens the assessment of significant resources which make appear US preponderance less clear cut, indeed any analysis in terms of a general unipolarity difficult to defend.

Third, precisely because we have no objective measure of power, it is crucial to analyse the relationship between knowledge about power and politics itself. Like the national interest, balance of power arguments are part of the common language of the international society.[74] It is important not just because theories are built upon it, but because practitioners understand and base actions on it. This shifts the analysis of polarity arguments further, from what they could mean and explain to what their use, if shared, *does* not just to the common understanding, but also to politics and the social fact of power itself. In this context, this chapter shows the special role power has in our political discourse by linking it to the definition of the political realm, to responsibility and hence the need to public justification. Here, the stress on unipolarity, far from requiring the US to justify its deeds as it had in the past, has been twisted to condone, if not require a US policy of primacy that undermines multilateralism. Moreover, the use of one-dimensional power concepts to support a claim to a special unipolarity mobilizes a discourse which remilitarizes the understanding of international politics. Repeated unilateralism which is informed by this militarized understanding, has the potential to affect the shared understandings of power which actually decide what power means and does. This might indeed end up creating the social fact of "unipolarity" which appears objective and no longer questionable to international actors.

Notes

1. A very rudimentary version of this paper was presented at the volume workshop in Washington. An earlier draft of this version was presented during a guest lecture at the Institut d'Études Politiques de Bordeaux and a research seminar at the Danish Institute for International Studies. For comments and suggestions there and in correspondence, I am indebted to Jens Bartelson, Dario Battistella, Barry Buzan, Aida Hozic, Peter Viggo Jacobsen, Elizabeth Kier, Richard Ned Lebow, Jonathan Mercer, Kuniyuki Nishimura, Gorm Rye Olsen, John Gerard Ruggie, Beth Simmons, Jason Weidner, and the editors of this volume. All the usual disclaimers apply.
2. In the following, multilateralism is understood as a primary or fundamental institution of international society, as distinguished both from secondary institutions like organizations and regimes, as well as from simple acts of multi*national* coordination. See Barry Buzan (2004) *From International to World Society: English School Theory and the Social Structure of Globalization*, Cambridge: Cambridge University Press and Christian Reus-Smit (1997) "The constitutional structure of international society and the nature of

fundamental institutions", *International Organization* 51(4): 555–589. Such an understanding is compatible with Ruggie's more qualitative definition of multilateralism, as an institution which coordinates relations among states on the basis of generalized principles of conduct. See John Gerard Ruggie (1992) "Multilateralism: the anatomy of an institution", *International Organization* 46(3): 561–598.

3. See Charles Krauthammer (1991) "The unipolar moment", *Foreign Affairs* 70(1): 23–33.
4. For one classical statement, see Stephen Krasner (1982) "Structural causes and regime consequences: regimes as intervening variables", *International Organization* 36(2): 185–205.
5. Samuel P. Huntington (1993) "Why international primacy matters", *International Security* 17(4): 68–83 (70).
6. For this argument, see Stephen Krasner (1982) "Regimes and the limits of realism: regimes as autonomous variables", *International Organization* 36(2): 497–510 and his (1985) *Structural Conflict: The Third World against Global Liberalism*, Berkeley: University of California Press, written in the context of the Reagan administration's withdrawal from UNESCO.
7. Michael Mastanduno (1997) "Preserving the unipolar moment: realist theories and US grand strategy after the Cold War", *International Security* 21(4): 49–88 (61).
8. Stanley Hoffmann (1978) *Primacy or World Order: American Foreign Policy since the Cold War*, New York: McGraw Hill; Robert Jervis (1993) "International primacy: is the game worth the candle?", *International Security* 17(4): 52–67 (66).
9. For the unilateralist turn, see for example the essays collected in David M. Malone and Yuen Foong Khong (eds) (2003) *Unilateralism and US Foreign Policy: International Perspectives*, London, Boulder: Lynne Rienner.
10. In other words, the present chapter does not follow Kenneth Waltz in his claim that structural realist approaches can function and yet be indeterminate for state behaviour, a claim hardly shared by any realist and often not followed by himself. For realist rejoinders to Waltz, see for example Mastanduno (1997) "Preserving the unipolar moment", pp. 52–53; Colin Elman (1996) "Horses for courses: why not neo-realist theories of foreign policy?" *Security Studies* 6(1): 7–53.
11. For this analogy, see in particular Robert Gilpin (1971) "The politics of transnational international relations", in Robert O. Keohane and Joseph S. Nye, Jr. (eds) *Transnational Relations and World Politics*, Cambridge, Mass, London: Harvard University Press, pp. 48–69; Robert Gilpin (1981) *War and Change in World Politics*, New York: Cambridge University Press; and Charles P. Kindleberger (1987 [1973]) *The World in Depression, 1929–1939*, Berkeley: University of California Press.
12. Kenneth N. Waltz (1969 [1967]) "International structure, national force and the balance of world power", in James A. Rosenau (ed.) *International Politics and Foreign Policy: A Reader in Research and Theory*, New York: Free Press, pp. 304–314 (312).
13. Duncan Snidal (1985) "The limits of Hegemonic Stability Theory", *International Organization* 39(4): 579–614 (581).
14. Robert Gilpin (1981) *War and Change in World Politics*, New York: Cambridge University Press; and Michael Webb and Stephen D. Krasner (1989) "Hegemonic Stability Theory: an empirical assessment", *Review of International Studies* 15(2): 56–76.
15. Charles P. Kindleberger (1986) "International public goods without international government", *American Economic Review* 76(1): 1–12; and Robert Gilpin with the assistance of Jean Gilpin (1987) *The Political Economy of International Relations*, Princeton: Princeton University Press.
16. Robert O. Keohane (1984) *After Hegemony: Cooperation and Discord in the World Political Economy*, Princeton: Princeton University Press.

17. John Gerard Ruggie (1992) "Multilateralism".
18. For a more thorough presentation from which this is taken, see Stefano Guzzini (1998) *Realism in International Relations and International Political Economy: the continuing story of a death foretold*, London, New York: Routledge, chapter 10.
19. For an explicit use of "entropy", see Charles P. Kindleberger (1976) "Systems of international economic organization", in David P. Calleo (ed.) *Money and the Coming World Order*, New York: New York University Press for the Lehrmann Institute, pp. 15–39 (18, 24).
20. Robert Keohane does not belong to those who subscribe to this aspect of HST, arguing that multilateral regimes, once created, can be perfectly sustained without a hegemon.
21. For more extensive treatment in IR, see in particular David A. Baldwin (1989) *Paradoxes of Power*, Oxford: Blackwell, and (2002) "Power and International Relations", in Walter Carlsnaes, Thomas Risse and Beth A. Simmons (eds) *Handbook of International Relations*, London: Sage, pp. 177–191; as well as Stefano Guzzini (1993) "Structural power: the limits of neorealist power analysis", *International Organization* 47(3): 443–478, and (2000) "The use and misuse of power analysis in international theory", in Ronen Palan (ed.) *Global Political Economy: Contemporary Theories*, London, New York: Routledge, pp. 53–66.
22. An early and still valid statement can be found in Robert O. Keohane and Joseph S. Nye, Jr. (1977) *Power and Interdependence: World Politics in Transition*, Boston: Little Brown, and its revised editions.
23. Realists are perfectly aware of this. See most recently John J. Mearsheimer (2001) *The Tragedy of Great Power Politics*, New York: W.W. Norton.
24. Peter Morriss (2002 [1987]) *Power: A Philosophical Analysis*, 2nd edn, Manchester: Manchester University Press, p. 19.
25. As well known, Steven Lukes would also include a third dimension of power in which this very value system is affected so that no visible conflict arises. See now the revised edition: Steven Lukes (2004) *Power: A Radical View*, 2nd edn, London: Palgrave.
26. The central place of the missing money-power analogy for the use of an economic approach to political science/IR has been discussed in Raymond Aron (1962) *Paix et guerre entre les nations*, 8th edn, Paris: Calmann-Lévy, chapter 3.
27. As attempted by Kenneth N. Waltz (1990) "Realist thought and neorealist theory", *Journal of International Affairs* 44(1): 21–38.
28. See Kenneth N. Waltz (1986) "A response to my critics" in Robert O. Keohane (ed.) *Neorealism and its Critics*, New York: Columbia University Press, pp. 322–345.
29. See in particular the thoughts by William C. Wohlforth (1993) *The Elusive Balance: Power and Perceptions During the Cold War*, Ithaca, NY: Cornell University Press, and (2003) "Measuring power – and the power of theories", in John A. Vasquez and Colin Elman (eds) *Realism and the Balance of Power: A New Debate*, Upper Saddle River, NJ: Prentice Hall, pp. 250–265.
30. Barry Buzan, Charles Jones and Richard Little (1993) *The Logic of Anarchy: Neorealism to Structural Realism*, New York: Columbia University Press.
31. Robert J. Art (1996) "American foreign policy and the fungibility of force", *Security Studies* 5(4): 7–42. See also the ensuing debate: David A. Baldwin (1999) "Force, fungibility, and influence", ibid. 8: 173–183 and Robert J. Art (1999) "Force and fungibility reconsidered", ibid.: 183–189.
32. Stefano Guzzini (2004) "The enduring dilemmas of realism in International Relations", *European Journal of International Relations* 10(4): 533–568.
33. William C. Wohlforth (1999) "The stability of a unipolar world", *International Security* 24(1): 5–41 (7) (original emphasis).
34. This is the way Barry Buzan modifies classical unipolarity analysis in Barry Buzan

(2004) *The United States and Great Powers: World Politics in the Twenty-First Century*, Cambridge: Polity Press.

35. See Arnold Wolfers (1962) *Discord and Collaboration: Essays on International Politics*, Baltimore, London: Johns Hopkins University Press; Robert O. Keohane and Joseph S. Nye, Jr. (1997) *Power and Interdependence*; Barry Buzan (2004) *From International to World Society*; and Alexander Wendt (1999) *Social Theory of International Politics*, Cambridge: Cambridge University Press.
36. Ernst-Otto Czempiel (2002) *Weltpolitik im Umbruch. Die Pax Americana, der Terrorismus und die Zukunft der internationalen Beziehungen*, München: Beck Verlag.
37. De facto, this applies Robert Dahl's strategy for assessing "Who governs?" to the international level. See Robert A. Dahl (1961) *Who Governs? Democracy and Power in an American City*, New Haven: Yale University Press.
38. Hannah Arendt (1969) *On Violence*, New York: Harcourt, Brace & World.
39. Hannah Arendt (1986 [1970]) "Communicative power", in Steven Lukes (ed.) *Power*, New York: New York University Press, pp. 59–74.
40. Joseph S. Nye, Jr. (2004) *Soft Power: The Means to Success in World Politics*, New York: Public Affairs, p. 4.
41. Michael Mann (1986) *The Sources of Social Power, Vol. I: A history of power from the beginning to A. D. 1760*, Cambridge: Cambridge University Press.
42. The assessment of the economic sector is widely debated. For some, the US economic and technological lead is obvious from (recent) growth rates, the health of high technology sectors, and so forth. Those scholars, like Mann, who argue that there exist roughly three poles, tend to focus on other items. First, they stress that in the economic sector, EU member states can no longer be counted individually: to the outside, there is one market of a comparable size to the US; in trade terms, and also to a lesser extent with regard to monetary policies, there is one single representation and one central bank. And then one can add that Japan leads in patents, Germany has just overtaken the US as the world leading manufactory exporter (despite the very high euro), and so on. Since there is no common measure of economic power, one cannot really adjudicate between these positions.
43. Michael Mann (2003) *Incoherent Empire*, London, New York: Verso.
44. Christian Reus-Smit (2004) *American Power and World Order*, Cambridge: Polity Press, chapter 2.
45. Susan Strange (1988) *States and Markets: An Introduction to International Political Economy*, New York: Basil Blackwell.
46. Joseph S. Nye, Jr. (1990) "Soft Power", *Foreign Policy* 8: 153–171, and (1990) *Bound to Lead: The Changing Nature of American Power*, New York: Basic Books.
47. Nye (1990) *Soft Power*, p. 34.
48. Christian Reus-Smit (2004) *American Power*, pp. 64–65.
49. David M. Edelstein and Ronald R. Krebs (2005) "Washington's troubling obsession with public diplomacy", *Survival* 47(1): 89–104.
50. William C. Wohlforth (1999) "The Stability ...", pp. 18–22. Wohlforth also argues that the comprehensive power resources of the US are superior. That argument hinges however on an assumption that power is measurable, on which he himself is critical. Moreover, he uses a definition of power which is only material, and allows the know-how of private firms to be simply capitalized for states. Although this is justified so as to make historical comparisons with earlier periods more coherent, the very understanding of how power is historically contingent, a point Wohlforth does not deal with.
51. For earlier statements of this line, see Susan Strange (1987) "The persistent myth of lost hegemony", *International Organization* 41(4): 551–574.

52. See the ongoing quest from Daniel Frei (1969) "Vom Mass der Macht", *Schweizer Monatshefte* 49(7): 642–654, to John J. Mearsheimer (2001) *The Tragedy of Great Power Politics*, New York: W.W. Norton.
53. Stefano Guzzini (1998) *Realism*, p. 231.
54. For the most recent definitional statement on constructivism, see Emanuel Adler, "Constructivism and International Relations", in Walter Carlsnaes, Thomas Risse and Beth A. Simmons (eds) (2002) *Handbook of International Relations*, London: Sage, pp. 95–118. Constructivists have also a wider understanding of power in international affairs, which goes beyond the Weberian one, but given the focus of the present chapter, this is not further elaborated. See Stefano Guzzini (1993) "Structural power", and now Michael Barnett and Raymond Duvall (2005) "Power in international politics", *International Organization* 59(1): 39–75.
55. For the following and for a more detailed account of this turn in conceptual analysis as applied to power, see Stefano Guzzini (2005) "The concept of power: a constructivist analysis", *Millennium: Journal of International Studies* 33(3): 495–521.
56. Ian Hacking (1999) *The social construction of what?*, Cambridge, Mass.: Harvard University Press.
57. William E. Connolly (1974) *The Terms of Political Discourse*, 2nd ed., Oxford: Martin Robertson, p. 97 (original emphasis).
58. Steven Lukes (1986 [1970]) *Power*.
59. Peter Bacharach and Morton S. Baratz (1970) *Power and Poverty: Theory and Practice*, New York: Oxford University Press.
60. Daniel Frei (1969) "Vom Mass der Macht", p. 647.
61. Ole Wæver, "Securitization and desecuritization", in Ronnie Lipschutz (ed.) (1995) *On Security*, New York: Columbia University Press, pp. 46–86, and Barry Buzan, Ole Wæver and Jaap de Wilde (1998) *Security: A New Framework for Analysis*, Boulder: Lynne Rienner. See also Jef Huysmans (1998) "Security! What do you mean? From concept to thick signifier", *European Journal of International Relations* 4(2): 226–255.
62. On the effect of "non-decisions", see Susan Strange (1986) *Casino Capitalism*, London: Basil Blackwell; on the need to integrate ideas from dependency scholars into a concept of "structural power", see Susan Strange (1984) "What about International Relations?", in Susan Strange (ed.) *Paths to International Political Economy*, London: George Allen & Unwin, pp. 183–198 (191). For the full statement, see Susan Strange (1988) *States and Markets*, chapter 2.
63. For a classical (and moderate) defence of this position, see George F. Kennan (1985–86) "Morality and Foreign Policy", *Foreign Affairs* 64(2): 205–218.
64. For example Robert Kagan (1998) "The benevolent empire", *Foreign Policy* 111 (Summer): 24–35.
65. For a more general argument about US exemptionalism, see John Gerard Ruggie (2005) "American exceptionalism, exemptionalism and global governance", in Michael Ignatieff (ed.) *American Exceptionalism and Human Rights*, Princeton: Princeton University Press, forthcoming.
66. For example, Charles Krauthammer (2002) "The unipolar moment revisited", *The National Interest* Winter 2002–03: 5–17.
67. For example, Charles A. Kupchan (2002) *The End of the American Era: U.S. Foreign Policy and the Geopolitics of the Twenty-First Century*, New York: Alfred A. Knopf.
68. Pierre Bourdieu (1977) *Outline of a Theory of Practice*, transl. Richard Nice, Cambridge: Cambridge University Press, p. 165.
69. Stephen M. Walt (2002) "Keeping the world 'off balance': self-restraint and U.S. foreign

policy", in G. John Ikenberry (ed.) *America Unrivaled: the Future of the Balance of Power*, Ithaca: Cornell University Press, pp. 121–154.

70. Joseph S. Nye, Jr. (1990) *Soft Power*, p. 63.
71. Barry Buzan (2004) *The United States and Great Powers: World Politics in the Twenty-First Century*, Cambridge: Polity Press, p. 171.
72. For a more detailed argument on these lines, see also Stefano Guzzini (2002) "Foreign policy without diplomacy: the Bush administration at a crossroads", *International Relations* 16(2): 291–297.
73. Ron Suskind (2004) "Without a Doubt", *The New York Times Magazine*, 17 October 2004.
74. For this analysis of the national interest, see Jutta Weldes (1999) *Constructing National Interests: The United States and the Cuban Missile Crisis*, Minneapolis: University of Minnesota Press.

8

The genealogy of multilateralism: Reflections on an organizational form and its crisis

Friedrich Kratochwil

Introduction

The task assigned for this chapter is to "provide the genealogy and the values and institutions of multilateralism". Despite its seemingly straightforward charge, there are some difficult methodological decisions that have to be faced. Thus, one could be tempted, according to the canons of "science", to start with a nominal definition, provide the appropriate operationalization of the terms and then cast around for phenomena that have fitted historically this definition.[1] However, definitions that begin with a notion that intrinsic to the phenomenon of multilateralism is the number of actors, might be too restrictive. They would, for example, rule out nearly a priori bilateral arrangements that become by extension multilateral. The best example here is the non-discriminatory trading order that developed in the nineteenth century through the extension of the most favoured nation clause included in bilateral trade agreements.[2]

While such a definition might err on the side of under-inclusion, the opposite error could also occur, that is, erring on the side of over-inclusion. This would be the case when, for example, a declaration by several states at the end of a conference to extend the reach of their internal revenue code, or to recognize a new state would be counted as an instantiation of the concept. Hence nominal definitions relying on stipulations or on descriptive reference are problematic because they mistake the term for a concept. We may have effective multilateral regimes, even if they are not called that way. Here Ruggie's critique of Keohane's conceptualization has clarified matters.[3] He correctly pointed out that the important defining dimension of multilateralism is the reciprocal relationship among the actors (on the basis of commonly accepted norms and diffuse rather than specific reciprocity),[4] not the number of parties involved. What kind of (normative) expectations form among the interacting parties and how they treat deviant behaviour are decisive.

These criteria of assessment help us also to distinguish a challenge to multilateralism from a "crisis", a theme that pervades all papers in this volume. Since multilateralism is an institutional form constituted by rules, any rule violation challenges the order serving as a background for our understanding of what is going on. To that extent "crises" occur when the violation is serious, and the actor violating the norm either denies its applicability, or claims an exemption on idiosyncratic rather than justifiable grounds. Particularly under conditions of high threat and pressing time constraints actors are likely to fall back on unilateral action, as they fear otherwise their existence or standing is at stake. This does not mean that the crises need to persist. Bandwaggoning powers might strengthen the argumentative position of the norm violator, or other powers might accommodate. Thus the crisis might subside and become a challenge. Conversely, a simple challenge might escalate into a full fledged crisis, or – especially with hindsight – challenges might be interpreted as indicators of a long-term transformative change. Since we are here dealing with appraisals and not simple descriptions, the differences of characterization and even their change over time (for example through a "revisionist" historiography) are not that surprising.

Furthermore, by emphasizing that we deal here with an organizational form shaping practice we also become aware that the meaning of the concept derives largely from the way it is linked to other concepts and institutions. The meaning of 'multilateralism' consists not so much in referring to objects existing in the outer world, as in its ability of linking to other practices that let us "go on".[5] Conceptual clarification proceeds thereby not via a description in accordance with the classical taxonomic criteria, or via an operationalization and a subsequent measurement of the "variable". It is rather carried out by tracing and critically examining the extensions and analogies of this concept to a variety of practices throughout history.[6] The meaning of the concept lies thereby in its *use* in accordance to certain criteria, rather than in its capacity to mirror a pre-existing and social reality, thought to be independent of the concepts that constitute the social world.

An analogy with "property" is helpful since it brings out the differences between an understanding of "meaning" emphasizing "reference" and one that foregrounds "use". While the concept of property might at first simply refer to a thing, such as a car or a house, a closer investigation shows that it is not the thing, but the social relations, the "dos and don'ts" that constitute "property".[7] They enable us to act in certain ways and have our expectations protected. Thus entirely intangible elements, such as the goodwill of company, or a patent, can be "owned" and no list abstracted from the various things that count as property is likely to be successful in showing what "property" is. As Wittgenstein reminds us, the meaning of a word is not in the reference to "things" but in its use.[8]

In short, we have to understand how, for example, "property" functions – what its "grammar" informing our practices is, rather than pursue the ideal of an accurate description. Furthermore, since practices are never mere reproductions of some blueprint (iterations of identical instances) but are used by the actors in order to be able *to go on*, applying the rules to often dramatically changing circumstances and contexts is part of their realization. Therefore, any understanding of the concept will have to come to terms with its *historical* dimension. Thus, while in the above example multilateralism as an organizational form might provide a useful heuristics for twentieth-century politics, it should come as no great surprise that "multilateral" politics of former eras exhibited rather different features. While at present much of multilateral actions occur within the framework of international organizations, no such fora existed in the post-Westphalian order.

One way of tapping into these changes is to visit the sites in which claims for a multilateralism are made. In this context it becomes clear that arguments of "having to be taken into account", of "wanting to be recognized" as a coequal partner, are claims for a multilateral ordering. They oppose imperial designs, on the one hand, and unmediated idiosyncratic assertions of self-importance, on the other. To that extent "multilateralism" in its earliest manifestations was part of the "politics of recognition" that characterized the "sovereignty" game subsequent to the Westphalian settlement. While earlier accounts of that period have stressed the radical break with the personalist politics of medieval times and its universalist aspirations,[9] the more recent research shows the continuity of a status society that retained much of its force until well into the second half of the eighteenth century. Nevertheless, the evolving notion of the state as an abstract domain of rule, a rationalist and secular conception of politics, clearly differentiates this form of politics from medieval rule.

Another "site" for claims of multilateral order was opened by the "Concert" system in the aftermath of the French Revolution and the Bonapartist challenge. While notions of a "role" emerged, unilateral action was by no means unknown, and much of the "interest" discourse continued. But with it there was a recognition of the need to have one's policies accepted by others.[10] Here again, the Vienna settlement represents the half-way point rather than the crucial new beginning in which "contract" rather than status became an important ordering device. Finally, I shall look at the two episodes in the move to institutions at Versailles and at the founding of the UN and its network of multilateral institutions. Here functional logic and expertise rather than consent (as in contract), or recognition (as in status) served as a powerful legitimizing formula that authorized the often rather harsh and "unilateral" moves contained in the "conditionality" programmes of multilateral institutions.

With these initial explorations concerning the multi-faceted nature of "multilateralism" in place, the chapter then examines the present "crisis" of multilateralism. As this analysis suggests, the "crisis" is indeed rather deep as present day conflicts comprise issues of "recognition", when non-authorized groups (terrorists) make claims,[11] when hegemonic projects such as "democracy" and "human rights" are contested, and confidence in the expertise of multilateral institutions – when one thinks of the Asian financial crisis – are in serious doubt.

Of course, taking the long view one could also argue that multilateralism is not in crisis. Rather, the present challenges will lead to the evolution of this institutional form, as Adler suggests in this volume. The mechanism for this evolutionary development is the adaptation to changing needs: first recognition, then consensus and now mediation between expertise and consensus, on the one hand, as well as some form of accommodation to non-state actors (see Jackie Smith's contribution), on the other. Similarly one could argue that environmental and health crises challenge (see Prins's article below) so frontally our way of life that only multilateral responses will do and that the unilateral visceral responses are just temporary outliers of a trend that clearly goes in the other direction. This hope is also expressed in Thomas Weiss's chapter vis à vis the US policy stance. Normative progress on human rights, and at least a general awareness of global problems, could buttress such claims. But even here the more optimistic assessments of, for example, Goldstone/Kelly and Heine are balanced by the caution in Forsythe's account (the dilemma of neutrality as a fundamental principle of humanitarian action in humanitarian disasters) and John Tirman's worries that the policies of multilateral institutions as conflict generators, or Hellsten's milder assessment of their ineffectiveness unless remedied by the inclusion of a global ethics. But even beyond this appraisal there remain difficult problems of designing appropriate multilateral responses as the chapters of Gupta and Tharoor show.

While I have certainly no ready-made answers to either the challenges to multilateralism, or the problem of their different assessments, I hope in this chapter at least to provide a useful diagnostic for some of the identified ills. In order to make good on these claims, my argument will take the following steps. In the next section I want to visit these three different sites of multilateral claims, in order to provide a brief analysis of contemporary problems in the third section.

Status and recognition: sovereignty as a multilateral order

It might seem odd to consider sovereignty as part of multilateralism's grammar. The international relations scholar who attempts this is subject to criticism by both realists and liberals. Liberals will charge him or her that multilateralism is precisely the "cure for the dilemmas created by anarchy", and that equating both misses the target by a mile. For liberals it is the realization of joint gains and the redefinition of one's interests in the light of a longer-term perspective that is the decisive reason for a multilateral order. Realists, on the other hand, will argue that the "logic" of anarchy explains why multilateral institutions hold only false promises[12] and that therefore a rational policy would not bother with maintaining such an order had it not by accident been created. But strangely enough, even realists count alliances and the "balance of power" among the important and effective instruments of statecraft, even though in a Hobbesian world no contracts can be binding and, therefore, no rational actor should place his trust in such loose and easily subverted mechanisms.

Thus, although there is a certain surface plausibility to the realist observations, it derives largely from some problematic beliefs about the role of interests in social action and about the varied significance of norms for social order and cohesion. Given that a false dichotomy between a "society" and "anarchy" is set up – and "social anarchies" such as, for example, competitive markets are not seen as social institutions embedded in shared understandings – the constitutive role of norms even for "competitive" games is obfuscated. Therefore the "social" character of such games – that is, a shared understanding of what the game is about, what it means to "win", or even to be an actor – remains obscure. Here the notion of a *constitution* going beyond the familiar patterns of hierarchically ordered and centrally organized institutions is helpful. As Christian Reus-Smit suggested:

> Constitutional structures are coherent ensembles of inter-subjective beliefs, principles and norms that perform two functions in ordering international societies: they define what constitutes a legitimate actor, entitled to all the rights and privileges of statehood; and they define the parameters of rightful action.[13]

Furthermore, by assuming a priori that "interests" are given and that the problem of cooperation consists in identifying joint gains, one misses the forest before the trees. Anything from the altruism of Mother Theresa to the murderous tendencies of assassins is now lumped together without considering whether or nor certain "framing" conditions might or might not make certain "interests" illegitimate and thus affect the status of the actor. This is precisely the Humean argument, that carefully distinguishes between individual preferences and "interests" – in other words, matters that are "between us" and are recognized as such.[14]

What is even more problematic is that "interests" are to work according to the model of efficient causality. This leaves out not only explanations in which formal causes are advanced as reasons for actions, it also assumes that whether something is or is not the case can be decided by the bivalence principle of logic (*tertium non datur*). However, such an assumption is already highly problematic in the natural sciences, as the physicist and philosopher of science John Zinman has pointed out. Even for scientists the alternatives are usually not simply an either/or, but in many, if not most cases, the results belong to the class of "un-decidable", that is, exactly a third category that is ruled out by the very principle.[15] In the social world that does not deal with "natural kinds" such notions prove to be even less helpful since contestation is part and parcel of that world.[16] Nowhere does this become clearer than in the case of "sovereignty". As Wouter Werner and Jaap de Wilde have so nicely shown, the concept does not function as a label for "matters of fact", but represents an ascription of status that is agreed upon and attributed to an actor, which, in turn, entitles him to certain privileges, rights and duties.

> The essence of Westphalian sovereignty is its negotiated nature. This discursive characteristic sets it apart from a more imperial image of sovereignty in which locally accumulated power expands and fades away in concentric circles ... The endurance of Westphalian sovereignty rests in the resilience of the discourse it gave birth to the idea of sovereignty would be completely unnecessary if states were indeed isolated and autarkic.... The essence of the Westphalian system therefore, is not the creation of billiard ball states; rather it is the creation of a structure of de facto interdependent states that accept some basic principles in dealing with each other.[17]

Several important consequences flow from this perspective of sovereignty as status, that is, as an ascription by others. One, although certain resources are necessary to gain recognition and be admitted to the "club", the process is not one in which the capacity to use force effectively translates directly into sovereign status. Much of it will depend on the discursive and symbolic interactions that a "pretender" engages in, that determine acceptance or falling by the wayside. Formerly noble birth was *the* decisive criterion for becoming a member of the club and even Machiavelli's *homines novi*, such as the Medicis and the Sforzas – and still Napoleon at that late age – had quickly to adjust their lowly status. Today power-holders might control certain areas or groups, but as warlords, "Quisling regimes", terrorists, pirates or insurgents they might fail to attain the same privileges and rights accruing to legitimate actors, even if the latter are, for example, only governments in exile and control very little. Having once gained sovereign status makes it unlikely that it can be easily lost even if effective control – for example, the power to exclude or control one's territory or society – is gravely impaired, as in cases of civil unrest, internal war, or military occupation. Here the discussion of "failed states", as well as the reluctance to accept the legitimacy of changes imposed by force, can serve as illustrative examples.

Two, precisely because "sovereignty" is to a large extent an ascription made by others who recognize a member, the analogy to a simple possession needs modification. Thus, giving up certain rights, such as entering into a treaty or accepting the neutralization of one's country, is not diminishing sovereignty, although certain options (to select alliances) are thereby foreclosed. Was Belgium after its creation in 1830 not "really" sovereign? This seems about as sensible as to argue that nobody really "possesses" a piece of property because he has to allow the municipality to run a water pipe under his garden lawn. Or, just to take a contemporary example, is Norway more sovereign than Sweden because it declined to become member of the EU? Although we commonly speak of the "transfer" or "pooling" of sovereignty when we discuss the EU,[18] the descriptivist account attempting to determine sovereignty according to measurable amounts of powers is highly misleading. It treats social reality as independently existing from, rather than as being constituted *by* our concepts. The upshot of this argument is simply that these difficulties are those of our representational understanding of language, rather than of our political practice. Irrespective of whether the EU is becoming a sovereign state, or whether it is simply an association of states, the simple fact is that no sovereignty is being claimed by Brussels while the process of community decision making goes on as "multi-level governance", "comitology", or whatever. In the same vein, the member states do not simply whither away, or consider themselves "failed" states, now that other power centres have developed.

Three, although sovereignty was clearly a new social order, its anti-hegemonic and anti-imperial dimensions are clearly discernible. It is here that the link to "multilateralism" becomes visible. Precisely because one of the constitutive effects of sovereignty is the separation of the "external" relationships from those on the "inside", no policies could be pursued in the name of a religious orthodoxy, a common good, or even on behalf of the *res publica Christiana*, except by consent of the sovereign(s). This had, at first blush, some rather strange consequences. While the individual sovereign could rule by the grace of God – and indeed this formula continued to legitimize traditional rulers well into the nineteenth century – no such pretensions were acceptable in the international realm.[19] Furthermore, while the distinctness of this order was clearly perceived in that outsiders, such as the High Porte were not accepted into the club despite the fact that some sovereigns had to, or chose to interact with them. On the other hand, the sociality of the system was of a rather "unsocial" kind: it entailed recognition and some deference to rights and law, but its actual set up was concerned more with *disabling* rather than enabling common actions. This led to a minimalist notion of social solidarity and it is therefore not surprising that those provisions of the Westphalian settlement that envisaged a type of collective security arrangement remained a dead letter. Instead, "buck passing" and "hiding", exemplified by the growth of neutrality, together with making largely bilateral alliances, became the predominant practice for providing the collective good of security.

The idea of a "republic", of checks and balances, of preventing by structural means the emergence of a superior power, was part of the ensuing political game,[20] as was the attempt to aggrandize one's possession through marriages and dynastic politics. This of course led to the tensions between the well-known maxims of the balance of power and the *amour propre* of individual actors seeking aggrandizement via dynastic politics. Indeed the largest wars were fought when these two principles clashed and when system-wide coalitions formed, as in the case of the War of the Spanish Succession. Similarly, when the missionary fervour of the French Revolution endangered the very existence of the European state system based on dynastic legitimacy, a multilateral coalition opposing Napoleon and his imperial aspirations became necessary. As Fénelon had already pointed out:

> Each nation is obliged to prevent the excessive aggrandizement of each neighbor, for its own security. To prevent the neighbor from becoming too powerful is not to do wrong: it is to protect oneself from slavery and to protect one's neighbor from it.... because the aggrandizement of one nation beyond a certain limit changes the general system of all the nations which have relations with it.[21]

The upshot of this brief historical examination is that although the establishment of sovereignty establishes a rudimentary multilateral order through the politics of recognition, it is only with the more institutionalized forms, such as with the notion of a great power and its "role" that multilateralism attains its distinctiveness. Crucial for these developments was a notion of the "*raison du système*" (rather than solely a *raison d'Etat*) and its manifestation in a grand "coalition" preventing a system transforming hegemony or imperial order.

Contract and consent: the Concert of Great Powers, their interests and role

The distinction between an alliance and a grand "coalition", introduced by the historian of the European balance of power, Ed Gulick, is important. While of course the two great coalitions in the War of the Spanish Succession and against Napoleon were also alliances, they differed in that there was a wide-spread perception among the actors that here "constitutional" issues of the international system were at stake. That even under such circumstances forming such a coalition remained an arduous task will only come as a surprise to those who inhabit the ethereal world of international relations theory – and here, in particular, the imaginary regions of realism. In addition, to the *raison d'Etat*, which slowly displaced the dynastic politics, we also see the emergence of some notion of a *raison du système* which counteracted the common incentives for bandwagoning or "buck passing".

It was recognized that the "repose" of Europe, as expressed in the Preamble to the Treaty of Utrecht (1713), was not the result of a "natural" balance of power, which emerges whenever a multiplicity of actors interact (as Waltz wants us to believe),[22] but that the balance of power had to be institutionalized. This required, on the one hand, some important changes in the actors' "maxims" that included some counter-intuitive moves. Thus the traditional wisdom of "the enemy of my enemy is my friend" does not necessarily apply in balance of power regime if it is to serve as an ordering device, as recognized in the "constitutional" moments of Utrecht and Rastatt. On the other hand, the states increasingly realized that the international system required constant management and attention instead of only the general meetings of peace conferences, a realization that that strengthened cooperation. As Jervis notes, there was an unusually high and self-conscious level of cooperation among the powers immediately after 1815.[23] This was partly the result of the experience of the long and costly war, and this experience in itself impacts on the assessment of whether the multilateral collaborative enterprise can be continued. But it was also the result of the realization that the defeated state, which had to be reintegrated into the system, required continued watchfulness.

Here a second element enters the picture that changes the concept of "multilateralism" from a minimalist to a more institutionalized form: the notion of a "great power". Thus while multilateralism still retains in a way its counter-hegemonic dimension, it is now a multilateralism of a somewhat restricted scope. It is the Great Powers, which, as the managers, of the system have to act in "concert", while the others are mostly bystanders and followers. Such a conception not only solves some of the collective action problems inherent in the strict notion of sovereign equality, it also entails the acceptance of some form of "social differentiation" within the international system. The Great Powers manage and the minor powers focus from now on more on the "codification and development" of international law and institutions for dispute settlement. By the end of the century they result in the "Hague" system and in the (unfortunately) failed attempts of putting disarmament on the international agenda. Nevertheless, even lesser powers often had to play special roles, considered important for the maintenance of the system, as the neutralization of Switzerland and Belgium showed. The purpose of this regime was to prevent a potential French expansion in either the Italian direction via the strategic Alpine passes, or towards the Channel. Thus the role of these countries was to contain conflicts of interests between Austria and France, and between Britain and France. In a similar vein, the role of Sweden and Denmark was to control the Baltic in order to prevent the old Northern questions from flaring up again.

This new form of multilateralism meant that all those with not only the wherewithal but also system-wide interests "belonged" to the Great Powers. This did not prevent unilateral measures, but at least entailed some subsequent vetting of policies within the club for legitimization purposes. It also entailed some mutual recognition of "special" interests in certain regions and set clear limits to the claims connected with them. As the historian Paul Schroeder has shown, the role of, for example, Austria – in order to focus other than on the well-known example of Britain as a "balancer" – was vital for the European state system. Austria was supposed not only to check Russia and France by being present in Italia and the Balkans, but also to provide a counterweight to Prussia and – because of its multi-national composition, it was to mediate the rising tensions between the Germanic and Slavic nations.

> Only Austria could conceivably manage this process within and without its own borders in the interest of international stability; and only if Austria continued to exist could a struggle between the Teuton and Slav for the mastery of Europe be avoided. These special, indispensable functions were imposed by the nineteenth-century international system upon Austria-Hungary, like it or not; and when it proved unable to carry them out and other states proved indifferent to the problem, the stage was set for the destruction of Europe.[24]

However, the demise of the Concert system, and of its distinct multilateral cooperation, can be observed long before the fateful events of Sarajevo led indeed to its destruction. For a while the European peace was secured by a return to bilateral alliances, masterfully employed by Bismarck and by his wise limitation of German colonial aspirations. At the height of his power, Bismarck could host the Berlin Congress in which the German Reich played not only the role of a "satisfied" power but created peace among the others by dividing the spoils of Africa. However, given the growing antagonism between Germany and France, the fear of encirclement was all too real. It resulted in alliance "handicaps" and in a rather ruthless bilateral style of politics.

Instead of the old notion of a role and the need for collective legitimization that limited the pursuit of self-interest, Bismarck decisively broke with a multilateral approach to foreign policy. In 1876 the Eastern Question occupied the European powers and Gortschakoff had argued that the Great Powers had a European responsibility. Bismarck, however, noted on the margin of the dispatch: "Anyone who speaks of Europe is mistaken", adding one line below: "Who is Europe?" In a memorandum Bismarck rather harshly rejects a Concert-style solution by calling Europe an "insupportable fiction" which Germany "resolutely opposes". He is only ready to discuss "Russian interest" ... but not at all the rest of Europe" which to engage he considers an act of "charlatanism".[25] This is not yet the voice of unadulterated self-interest, or the social Darwinist rhetoric legitimizing claims by the right to "survival", that we encounter before the First World War. But it is already a decisive step from defining interest within some multilateral conventions of shared meanings that limit and mediate claims to one in which others interest are at best taken into account on an ad hoc basis.

Functional logic and international organizations: the move to institutions

There is a near universal agreement that the two World Wars and their aftermath significantly changed the international system and its practices. In a way, the period of the two wars with the intermittent "Twenty Years Crisis" – to utilize Carr's characterization[26] – can be read as one instance of a system transformation, and of the defeat of a continental hegemony that would have had rather traditional imperial trappings. Instead, a collective security system was to displace the alliance structure of the pre-First World War era. Moreover, it became increasingly clear that a fundamental change of the scope and domain of institutional norms and of the assembly of practices of international politics was under way. Finally, the legitimizing principle for the international order was also altered.

In terms of the *scope*, we can observe the shift from a Eurocentric world order to one in which the "flanking" states – that is, the US and the Soviet Union were to become the focal points (as already foreseen by de Tocqueville). Within a generation and a half the system truly became a world system with the last vestiges of "non-sovereign" arrangements, such as "suzerainty", having lost their "constitutional" standing. This meant by no means eradicating the gap in power and resources that characterized the former "unequal" treatment of the colonial world or other "dependencies". As a matter of fact, despite the victory of sovereignty as an organizing principle, the emerging "multilateralism" was not a return to a "politics of recognition". It was rather a multilateralism of the "Great Powers" in which the different status of states was finally codified in the right to a veto for the permanent members of the UN Security Council.

Nevertheless, the functional rather than formerly regional definition of their role made spheres of influence, suzerain arrangements, protectorates and the like constitutionally impossible. At first blush the change from territorially defined roles to functional ones seems minor, since it did of course not alter the "interests" of some former colonial powers who were able to preserve thereby their special rank. But, this modification had subsequently dramatic and probably unforeseen consequences. The Great Powers were not entitled to keep their territorial possessions as their *chasse gardée*, as the old Churchillian idea of the British Empire and FDR's notion of the four policemen still suggested. Thereby this change facilitated the emancipation of the colonial world in the 1960s and the emergence of an isle of dense "multilateral" institutions in the North Atlantic area. It not only counteracted isolationist tendencies in the US but encouraged the "binding of the Gulliver" through a "regional" arrangement in Latin America. The different implications become obvious if we look closer at the different nature of the two strategies of engaging the preponderant power. Bilateralism tends to reinforce the differentials of power. A multilateral organizational solution, on the other hand, creates a new "strength in numbers" and commits the *hegemon* prima facie (if not necessarily in actual practice) to exercise much of its power through multilateral channels. Whatever the success or failure of this arrangement might be, historically it has proven to be more resilient than the purely bilateral institutionalization of the Eastern bloc.

In terms of *domain*, the contrast to earlier epochs could not be greater, particularly when we consider the post-Second World War constitutional moment. Although international public unions had grown tremendously already since the second half of the nineteenth century, it is the "externalization" of the regulatory state that is most noticeable in the Bretton Woods arrangements. Here both the internal experiences of the US, adjusting to the devastations of the crash of 1929 and the general interwar experience with the failure of traditional national means to manage "the economy", provided the necessary orientation and the blueprints for the subsequent multilateral organizations.[27] Indeed, the gravest shortcomings of the Versailles settlement were not those identified by the realists – legalism and the utopian belief in the harmony of interests – but the insufficient attention paid to the management of the international economy.

There is no need to rehearse here the arguments for the emergence of the historic compromise that was later dubbed "embedded liberalism".[28] Aside from free trade and convertible currencies, the acceptance of full employment policies as state goals demystified the "power" that had been hidden by making the economy a "private" realm largely exempted from social control. Under the prevailing regime of the Gold Standard the market camouflaged the asymmetry of adjustment costs imposed on different groups and classes. Through the growth of "socialism" this naturalization of the market was no longer accepted. The pursuit of full employment policies without international harmonization measures led, however to the famous beggar-thy-neighbour policies that prolonged the world economic crisis. Furthermore, the use of foreign trade by Nazi Germany to cement strategic dependencies on the basis of non-convertible currencies and barter exchanges, provided another striking lesson for the inadequacies of the classical conceptual apparatus. Finally, as the later discussion concerning the Morgenthau plan for Germany showed, the old logic in which security required that a former enemy be kept weak and economically strapped, in order to prevent any revisionist designs, ran squarely up against the logic of economic recovery. Already the experiences of the interwar period had shown, that only a Germany able to earn money in an expanding international economy could also be expected to pay for the reparations upon which the economic health of the other economies and the entire European economic zone depended.

In short, only during the post-Second World War planning phase did US policy makers hit upon the solution of two dilemmas that had to be solved simultaneously: a liberal trading order that was compatible with a welfare state, and a solution for the contradictory requirements for procuring security and prosperity. A new form of "multilateralism" provided the solution for both dilemmas. It rested on a new mix between the consensus of the politics of recognition and some form of authoritative intervention, which was however not backed by a special "role" but by a (presumably) neutral form of *expertise*. Thus, supervisory institutions like the IMF and the GATT were charged with supplying and maintaining nondiscriminatory liberal regimes and providing processes of conflict resolution in case of national deviations. Instead of bilateral measures, which were based on the manipulation of dependencies, now convertible currencies and the principle of non-discrimination enabled the (re-)integration of all participants in free-trading system. In addition, economies flowing from the complementary endowments in resources were also utilized through the encouragement of the integration and supervision (rather than unilateral control) of entire sectors of the economy (vide the European Coal and Steel Community).

While, of course, the idea of a "neutral" technocratic solution had been inherited from the functionalist ideology and the experience of the international public unions, the experiences with the regulatory state during the New Deal made it clear that administrative measures were hardly ever neutral. Furthermore, it highlighted that policy goals often have conflicting implications for which no technical solution exists but for which a policy choice has to be made. That such choices would be generally accepted, but would also not be against the interest of the leading powers, was in a way the result of fortuitous circumstances and organizational design. As to the former: the convergence on Keynesianism as the ruling economic orthodoxy by the end of the war was crucial. To the extent that no other "expertise" advocating a different set of policy options seemed available, the 'expertise' seemed in fact uncontroversial and neutral. On the design side, these "functional" organizations were not subject to direct political control on the basis of sovereign equality in order to avoid extensive policy discussion about goals, and so forth. Power was effectively disguised through some form of a "property" regime. The votes were weighted according to the subscriptions, giving the US (and other like-minded countries) effective veto power. The more overt form of exercising power according to the sovereign equality principle was called "politicization", which had, of course, to be opposed because it contradicted vested interests and, at the same time, allegedly violated "sound" economic policy based on expertise.

Finally, in order to soften the impact of a supervisory regime that could through conditionality "discipline" a country, a special arrangement was established to legitimize this interference. The idea was that member states had not only to declare their agreement in principle but that the specific conditionality programme had to be "arrived at" through a mutual understanding, that is, through an instrument of "soft law".[29] To that extent the Hobbesian implications of expertise could be avoided in that consent had been entirely replaced by having once and for all authorized some institution of "administering" all pertinent affairs in a certain domain. While, for Hobbes, expertise was not (yet) part of the original contract establishing the sovereign, the legitimacy of the acts of an established authority to rule according to some specialized knowledge is a major element in the development of bureaucratic rule, as Weber has pointed out. With it goes the tendency of attempting to dissolve politics into "rational" administration according to rules and neutral, "objective" expert judgement.

We can see now that two different conceptions of legitimacy have in the meantime become part of multilateralism. On the one hand, there is the old trait of sovereignty requiring recognition and consent. On the other hand, there is "depoliticized" expertise claiming validity in the name of expert/scientific knowledge. The uneasy mediation occurs in a "gentlemen's agreement" in which the political leader is convinced of the "need" to take measures that impose costs on his society and that might undermine his rule. The expert, on the other hand, needs the validation of the political leader who defers to the bitter "medicine" in an "unofficial" act of acceptance. Since both need each other – even if for different reasons – neither can later admit failure when the "medicine" has not worked. The expert accepts "slippage", as it is so euphemistically called in IMF documents, while the political leader submits to "rescheduling" and further measures of "supervision". Particularly in the context of the fiscal and financial, we can observe this type of " ritual dance", which Thomas Callaghy has analysed in the African context.[30] Only during the periodic "crises", as exemplified by the "Asian" crisis, these processes cannot be managed within the game of normal politics or economics. Then the crisis of confidence and of expertise usually work hand in hand and lead to the panicky behaviour that reverberates throughout the international system.[31]

The crisis of multilateralism

With these considerations in mind we are now in a better position to analyse the problem of the contemporary challenges to multilateralism which might have become a crisis. One thing seems clear that this crisis is not limited to the tendencies of the US[32] or other powers[33] to fall back on unilateral measures, or of weakening the existing multilateral structures by coalitions of the willing. As problematic as such actions are, focusing only on the most visible manifestations would provide an incomplete picture. As the above analysis suggests, the crisis has deeper roots, as the project of "sovereignty" and its politics of recognition has been challenged by non-state actors, be they terrorists, warlords, or the more constructive elements of "civil society".[34] They differ, of course, significantly in their political project. A human rights regime is often advocated by the latter and opposed to the predatory politics familiar from "failed states" or to the attempts to establish the reign of true believers through the rejection of "civilized" politics. Nevertheless, precisely because the respective projects sit uneasily with sovereignty and the politics of recognition, the multilateralist agenda based on notions of local autonomy and mutual recognition is under pressure. Both challenges deserve a brief discussion.

While terrorists and warlords most obviously subvert the constitutive rules of the game in regard to the actor status, their political projects also make it virtually impossible to define "roles" and thus mediate conflicting interest. Given the unprecedented threats and the visceral reactions they engender, the likelihood that those who "can" will do whatever they consider necessary is rather plain, even if the economy of force is hard to realize under such diffuse circumstances. Most threatening is obviously that the entire political project upon which the Western political order was built is called into question. The Western project was based on deterrence and the notion of a calculable risk, which presupposed a form of "civil" politics in which excessive goals were ruled out. War or intervention for some orthodoxy were excluded, as were acts of indiscriminate force, senseless cruelty, or measures against "civilians" even if the actual practice often differed.

Nothing could be further from this project than the goals inspiring the recent terrorist violence. It is not states but believers who have to be organized; it is not an order that safeguards rights and informs justice, compatible with a variety of substantive notions of the "good life, but rather a fundamentalist and radical notion of the good is being pursued. The guiding notion is not to ensure a "civilized" life, but glory, and therefore absolute submission is demanded from believers irrespective of the costs to life and limb.[35] Against such a background the foundationalist attempts of much of our Western contemporary political theory seem downright quaint. Having forgotten the heavy conditioning that is part of our project of becoming an "individual", our only worry consists in demonstrating that the rules and practices we utilize "stand to reason" – in other words, would be chosen by all if they were in their right mind.[36] The last flickers of the Enlightenment combine here with a political programme in which production and consumption are the lodestars and in which "efficiency" and expert knowledge are replacing politics. Here, the discourse of "global governance" is indicative of the changes in meaning and of the contradictions of "multilateralism" that we have investigated in the previous sections.

This leads us to the second source of the crisis of multilateralism. It is the problematic notion that politics can be replaced by administration as political choices can be reduced to expertise. Instead of the unilateralist "Wilsonianism in boots" that characterizes present US policy, we should not lose sight of the fact that "multilateral" institutions do much of the intervening and the shaping of states and societies, even if this power is disguised by terms such as conditionality, surveillance and benchmarking. Via the programme of global governance, state institutions – particularly those of rogue or failed states – should not only be reformed, the concomitant interventions are designed to reach deep into the respective societies. The exercise of nearly "capillary control", based on data streams, transparency requirements and surveillance mechanisms, is to ensure that those states and societies are supposed to become more effectively guided in their advance towards "democracy".

At the same time, many of the political levers for change and accountability are disappearing by becoming "private" rights, or they are subsumed and transformed by the "trade regime" and its dispute settlement procedures. Rather than emphasizing the status of an actor or the distributional consequences of an issue, as traditional "politics" does, the emphasis on governance foregrounds practical necessities, best practices and technical competence possessed by an international elite. Since the standing international professionals involved in policy making depends upon their expertise, their validating audience is first and foremost their "profession". To that extent, representative institutions that act in the national context as legitimizers of policy decisions can, in the international context, be nothing but eviscerated institutions. The alibi function of "consultations" with self-appointed elements of "civil society" as practised by some international organizations are, therefore, hardly serious sources of legitimization. The notion of some observers, that they have become "functional equivalents" of the national democratic institutions of former times seems, to me, wishful thinking.[37]

The result is that much of multilateral policy making takes place in a political vacuum and often leads to a disturbing discontinuity between the international and local practices. Even in cases where there is substantive agreement on the need to "do something", as in the case of genocide, and even in a field in which expertise is widely accepted as in "law", the "lessons" learned – for example, in Rwanda – suggest that the preferred policies for international fora, for individual criminal prosecution, and for adversarial proceedings, "may prove inconsistent with and even undermine, international lawyers' goals to preserve collective memory, vindicate and respond to the needs of the victims, affirm the national and international rule of law and promote national reconciliation".[38] In short, as David Kennedy points out, international policy professionals – and here the members of "third sector organizations", such as international advocacy networks, should be also included[39] – err when,

> after inventing international governmental organs as formal and functional imitations of national parliaments, executives, judiciaries, they then make policy in

them as if their Potemkin government would operate like the domestic institutions on which they were modelled. As a consequence they overestimate their own effectiveness. They treat the adoption of a norm as the implementation of a policy, mistake the judgements of the World Court for the decision of a judiciary embedded in a dense and functioning legal culture, mistake treatises and the resolutions of international organizations for statutes, anticipating their implementation, and so forth. They underestimate the diversity of political, legal and social contexts within which their policy initiatives will need to be realized. The policy solutions proposed by international policy makers often have a "one size fits all" quality, which imagines that what works in one place will work in another. The idea here is not only that they fail to respect local cultures, but that they, paradoxically, underestimate the specificity of the culture of international governance itself.[40]

If such mistakes are to be avoided it is necessary to include "local knowledge" more than has been the practice. Contrary to the belief that what works in one place has to work everywhere, we know that this idea represents a fast way to nowhere if we are result-oriented and are not mistaking blueprints for reality. This means not only attention to the special circumstances and traditions of particular societies, it also means the inclusion of those factors, such as shared notions of justice and of the appropriateness of a way of life, that are often short-changed by the exclusive focus on the allegedly universally valid variables that inform the scientific and technical approaches to social problems. True, scientific knowledge is a great legitimizer, but again we must realize that, for practical problems, science hardly ever has ready-made solutions. Not only do scientists often disagree, but even if there is consensus among them the practical dilemmas are not solved. The trade-off between inflation and unemployment might be plottable on a curve; the question at which point we should settle and which strategies and sequences we should chose, however, is certainly not. This also suggests that "voice", as opposed to technocratic decision-making, has to be strengthened if multilateralism is to remain a viable form of organizing politics.

To that extent, it will have to go beyond the ideas of the "new multilateralism", that is, the project of the UNU that sought to engage civil society in both programme-design and in the execution of policies by multilateral agencies.[41] But it also has to go beyond engaging networks and movements in a dialogue or some form of consultation, as in the case of the World Bank, the WTO and the IMF (minimal as it is).[42] Besides, having NGOs increasingly involved in programme execution has its own problem and can lead to perverse effects that are often forgotten.[43] Not only do the present practices of "contracting out" often create severe multiple principal-agent problems between NGOs, donors, and international organizations, leaving the delivery of public goods increasingly to "civil society" and international professionals undermines the chances that political institutions of "voice" and "loyalty" (as well as accountability) are strengthened. Only in this way can societies retain their autonomy in deciding their fate instead of having a Hobson's choice of either submitting to expertise and being administered, or "opting out" (exiting), which obviously is not a real option in international politics.

Notes

1. For a incisive discussion of the shortcomings of such an approach advocated in many "primers" for political science students, see Giovanni Sartori (1970) "Concept mis–formation in comparative politics", *American Political Science Review* 64(4): 1033–1053.
2. See the discussion by Arthur Stein (1984) "The hegemon's dilemma: Great Britain, the United States, and the international Economic Order", *International Organization* (38) (Spring): 355–86.
3. John Ruggie (1992) "Multilateralism: the anatomy of an institution", *International Organization* (46) (Summer): 561–98, as reprinted in John Ruggie (1998) *Constructing the World Polity*, London: Routledge, chap. 4, particularly p. 105f.
4. The difference consists of the fact that specific reciprocity refers to a quid pro quo exchange (with no expectation of further obligations) while diffuse reciprocity refers to situations in which the inequality of the present exchange gives rise to the normative expectation that this inequality will be remedied some time in the future.
5. Richard Rorty speaks in this context of the need to consider "vocabularies" rather than single concepts and to evaluate "re–descriptions" or new vocabularies not in terms of their descriptive accuracy but pragmatic usefulness. See Richard Rorty (1989) "The contingency of language", in Richard Rorty, *Contingency, Irony and Solidarity*, Cambridge UK: Cambridge University Press, chap. 1, particularly p. 12f.
6. For an interesting discussion that these criticisms of traditional logic and taxonomies are indeed justified by the cognitive apparatus that functions differently than is assumed by traditional epistemology, see George Lakoff (1987) *Women, Fire and Dangerous Things: What Categories Reveal about the Mind* (Chicago: University of Chicago Press). For an extensive discussion of the "cognitive revolution" and the implications for social science, see James Davis (2005), *Terms of Inquiry*, Baltimore: Johns Hopkins University Press.
7. Thus even "in rem" rights "work" not through the reference of an owner to a thing but by protecting his entitlements and enjoining others from infringing upon his or her exercise of the respective rights. See C.B. McPherson (ed.) (1992) *Property: Mainstream and Critical Positions*, Toronto: University of Toronto Press; Lawrence C. Becker (1977) *Property Rights*, London: Routledge, Kegan Paul.
8. See Ludwig Wittgenstein (1961) *Philosophical Investigations*, transl. by G.E.M. Anscombe, Oxford: Blackwell, para. 208. For a still more fundamental discussion on the nature of "language games", see Hanna Fenichel Pitkin (1972) *Wittgenstein and Justice*, Berkley: University of California Press, chap. 2.
9. For the discussion on IR, an article by the international lawyer Leo Gross seems to have been seminal for the propagation of the "sharp break" argument. See Leo Gross (1948) "The peace of Westphalia 1648–1948", *American Journal of International Law* 42(1): 20–41. For a critique of the Westphalian myth based on a careful evaluation of the historical sources of the Westphalian settlement and the subsequent practices in the Holy

Roman Empire, see Andreas Ossiander (2001) "The Westphalian myth", *International Organization* 55 (Spring): 251–288.

10. For a further discussion, see my essay (1982) "On the notion of 'interest' in international relations", *International Organization* 36 (Winter): 1–31.
11. See my discussion in (2003) "Moles, martyrs and sleepers: the end of the Hobbesian project?", *Ethnologia Europaea* 33(2): 57–68.
12. See John Mearsheimer (1995) "The false promise of international institutions", *International Security* 19(5): 5–49.
13. Christian Reus-Smith (1997) "The constitutional structure of international society and the nature of fundamental institutions", *International Organization* 51 (Fall): 555–589, quote at p. 566.
14. See the illuminating discussion by Joan Fereira (1994) "Hume and imagination: sympathy and the other", *International Philosophical Quarterly* 34: 39–54.
15. John Zinman (1978) *Reliable Knowledge: An Exploration of the Grounds of Belief in Science*, Cambridge: Cambridge University Press.
16. For a fundamental discussion of the importance of "essentially contested concepts" for our political discourse, see William Connolly (1983) *The Terms of Political Discourse*, 2nd edn, Princeton: Princeton University Press.
17. Wouter Werner and Jaap de Wilde (2001) "The endurance of sovereignty", *European Journal of International Relations* 7 (September): 283–314, quote at p. 288.
18. For a more extensive discussion of the European experience, see John Groom's contribution to this volume.
19. It is interesting that such claims were made only against "outside", i.e. non-Christian, powers, such as when the Czar claimed a special privilege to protect the orthodox Christians in the Ottoman Empire of the French posed as the protectors of the Lebanese Christians.
20. For an interesting discussion of "republicanism" and its arrangement of "negarchy", see Dan Deudney (1995) "The Philadelphia System", *International Organization* 49 (Spring): 191–228.
21. Fenelon, François de Salignac de la Mothe, *Examen de conscience sur les devoirs de la royaute*, as quoted in Edward Vose Gulick (1955) *Europe's Classical Balance of Power*, New York: Norton, p. 50.
22. Kenneth Waltz (1979) *Theory of International Politics*, Reading, Mass.: Addison Wesley, particularly chap. 6.
23. Robert Jervis (1985) "From balance to concert: a study of international security cooperation", *World Politics* 38 (October): 58–79, quote at p. 59.
24. Paul Schroeder (1991) "The neo-realist theory of international politics: a historians view", occasional paper of the Program of Arms Control and Disarmament, Urbana: University of Illinois, April 1991, p. 7.
25. As quoted in R.B. Mowat (1930) *The Concert of Europe*, London: Macmillan, p. 44f.
26. Edward Hallett Carr (1964) *The Twenty Years Crisis, 1919–1939*, New York: Harper.
27. For a good discussion of the New Deal as an institutional blueprint for post-war reconstruction, see Ann Marie Burley (1993) "Regulating the world: multilateralism, international law and the projection of the new deal regulatory state" in John Ruggie (ed.) *Multilateralism Matters*, New York: Columbia University Press, chap. 4.
28. See John G. Ruggie (1982) "International regimes, transactions, and change: embedded liberalism and the post–war economic order", *International Organization* 36 (Spring): 195–231.
29. See, for example, the controversy about the role of "soft law" in international monetary affairs between Joseph Gold and Prosper Weil: Joseph Gold (1983) "Strengthening the soft international law of exchange arrangements", *American Journal of International*

Law 77 (July): 443–489; Prosper Weil (1983) "Towards relative normativity in international law?", *American Journal of International Law* 77 (July): 413–442.

30. See Thomas Callaghy (1984) "The ritual dance of the debt game", *Africa Report* 29(5) (September/October): 22–26.
31. For some important criticism of the IMF programmes that worsened rather than alleviated the crisis, see the criticism by Peter Krugman (1999) *The Return of Depression Economics*, New York: Norton; Joseph Stiglitz (2002) *Globalization and its Discontent*, New York: Norton; Martin Feldstein (1998) "Refocusing the IMF", *Foreign Affairs* 77: 20–32.
32. For a good critique of US unilateral initiatives, see David Malone and Yuen Foong Khong (eds.) (2003) *Unilateralism and US Foreign Policy*, Boulder, CO: Lynne Rienner.
33. Thus, despite France's protests in the Security Council before the second Gulf War, it also had acted without authorization in Africa when its "interests" seemed at stake.
34. For a conceptual clarification of this slippery term, see Simone Chambers and Will Kymlicka (eds.) (2002) *Alternative Conceptions of Civil Society*, Princeton: Princeton University Press; For an optimistic reading, see Mary Kaldor (2003) *Global Civil Society: An Answer to War*, Cambridge UK: Polity Press.
35. For a further development of these thoughts, see my (2003) "Moles, martyrs and sleepers: the end of the Hobbesian project?", *Ethnologia Europaea* 33(2): 57–68.
36. See, for example, John Rawls's original attempt to specify the conditions for such a choice in his (1971) *A Theory of Justice*, Cambridge Mass.: Harvard University Press.
37. James Rosenau (1998) "Governance and democracy in a globalizing world", in Daniele Archibugi, David Held and Martin Kohler (eds.), *Re–imagining Political Community*, Cambridge UK: Polity Press, quote at p. 41.
38. Jose E. Alvarez (1999) "Crimes of states/crimes of hate: lessons from Rwanda" *Yale Journal of International Law* 24: 365–483: p. 369.
39. See Margaret Keck and Kathryn Sikkink (1998) *Activists Beyond Borders: Advocacy Networks in International Politics*, Ithaca: Cornell University Press; Sanjeev Khagram, James Riker and Kathryn Sikkink (eds.) (2002) *Restructuring World Politics*, Minneapolis: University of Minnesota Press.
40. David Kennedy (2001) "The politics of the invisible college: international governance and the politics of expertise", *European Human Rights Law Review* 5: 463–598: 432.
41. See, for example, Michael Schechter (ed.) (1998) *Future Multilateralism*, Basingstoke UK: Macmillan/UN University Press.
42. For a good discussion and evaluation of the actual impact of social movements on these three international organizations, see Robert O. Brien, Anne Marie Goetz, Jan Aart Scholte and Marc Williams (eds.) (2000) *Contesting Global Governance*, Cambridge: Cambridge University Press.
43. See, for example, the critical assessment of NFGO involvement based on an evaluation of several projects by Alexander Cooley and James Ron (2002) "The NGO scramble", *International Security* 27 (Summer): 5–39.

9

Multilateral crises in historical perspective

Edward Newman

In November 2003 United Nations Secretary-General Kofi Annan observed that "The past year has shaken the foundations of collective security and undermined confidence in the possibility of collective responses to our common problems and challenges. It has also brought to the fore deep divergences of opinion on the range and nature of the challenges we face, and are likely to face in the future." Many scholars and policy analysts shared his view, for good reason. The United Nations and other formal multilateral organizations have been under severe strain in a range of issue areas. The most visible sign of multilateral malaise was the war against Iraq in 2003, conducted without the clear authority of the UN Security Council. Whilst many bemoaned what they claimed was a war pursued outside the framework of the UN, others decried the apparent inability of the UN to address the threat of Iraq and its violation of Security Council resolutions. As the chapters in this volume amply demonstrate, the values and institutions of multilateralism more broadly have been challenged in terms of their role in governing the use of force in international politics, protecting human rights, protecting the natural environment, preventing and responding to health epidemics, promoting international justice, and regulating weapons of mass destruction, amongst other things. Whilst some analysts might argue that multilateral institutions are being sabotaged by the forces of power politics, others have concluded that organizations such as the United Nations have moved towards "self-marginalization" as a result of their idealism and ineffectiveness.[1]

In 1982 UN Secretary-General Pérez de Cuéllar similarly wrote of a "crisis in the multilateral approach".[2] His predecessor observed that the forces of change a decade earlier "were destroying the credit of the United Nations and might ultimately even tear it apart".[3] Observers have been quick to conclude that specific international organizations or the values and institutions of multilateralism more generally are in crisis or fundamentally flawed. The current sense of "crisis", at the beginning of the twenty-first century, is shared by analysts of different ideological and theoretical predispositions, and seems to be a "truly" historical turning point. But how do we know? What does a "crisis" mean in terms of a specific international organization or multilateralism in general? How are scholars of international relations to objectively judge if an international institution – or multilateralism more broadly – is in "crisis"? Can such a judgement be based upon a systematic methodology, rather than mere intuition? Does a historical comparison with earlier periods when international organizations appeared to face fundamental challenges help us to develop such a methodology? What variables would we measure in order to consider if the values and institutions of multilateralism are in crisis?

A more systematic approach to the idea of a "crisis of multilateralism" is necessary in order to put the current challenges facing multilateralism in their proper context. This chapter seeks to put the idea of a crisis in multilateralism – especially the UN, as a key multilateral organization – into some historical perspective by recalling the sources and manifestations of earlier "crises". It then attempts to construct a framework that may assist in making judgements on the subject, and finally briefly considers if the current so-called crisis is in reality any more fundamental than in previous experiences.

What is crisis?

What do scholars and policy analysts mean when they talk about multilateralism in crisis? Do they mean specific institutions and organizations, or the whole concept of multilateralism? If we are dealing with specific organizations, is the crisis in every area of the organization's activities, or just particular functions? It may seem unnecessary to consider what a "crisis" is in relation to an international organization or institution, and many analysts and politicians seem to take the "crisis" as a given. Indeed, many observers appear to be satisfied that they know an international organization in crisis when they see one. However, it is reasonable to suggest that judgements about the utility and difficulties of multilateralism are in part an extension of the observers' ideological or theoretical preconceptions of the nature of international relations and the role of international organizations within this. It is thus important to interrogate the concept of crisis to bring some precision to the debate, and as an essential starting point to constructing any sort of objective judgment on the subject. Without such as analysis, the distinction between a crisis of multilateralism and "politics as usual" is not clear.

In this chapter, crisis refers firstly to specific formal multilateral arrangements, rather than the whole concept of multilateralism. In turn, if a significant number of key multilateral institutions are in crisis and a common cause or manifestation appears to run through these crises, then it may be meaningful to think in terms of a broader crisis of multilateralism. A multilateral institution may be objectively judged to be in crisis if it is ineffective and/or obsolete in its current form and with respect to current performance, and is consequently losing diplomatic support and funding; if there is the expectation that the institution is permanently flawed in its existing formulation and requires fundamental revision in its normative and operating principles in order to gain or regain effectiveness; or if a completely new and alternative arrangement is required to achieve the necessary policy objectives. We can borrow from regime theory for a useful observation on the distinction between a crisis and the evolution of an institution: "Changes in rules and decision-making procedures are changes within regimes, provided that principles and norms are unaltered ... Changes in principles and norms are changes of the regime itself."[4]

The incentives that states perceive in creating and supporting multilateral institutions and regimes – which can be both informal arrangements or formal organizations – have been thoroughly explored in the literature of international relations. As a corollary, these incentives provide a starting point as to why multilateral institutions may encounter difficulties. Much of the international organizations' scholarship – which addresses various formulations of multilateralism, regime theory and institutions – approaches the subject of multilateralism within an anarchical model of international politics. Anarchical, but of course "not lacking in rules and norms".[5] Within the broad scholarship of international relations, the institutionalist (or (neo-)liberal institutionalist) approaches have invested the greatest effort in describing and explaining the potential and limitations of multilateralism. A major part of this scholarship has sought to consider how international rules are constituted, how regimes emerge and evolve, and how changes in the international environment are reflected and absorbed by international regimes and institutions. The institutionalist approach clearly believes that multilateralism is fundamentally important to international politics. Multilateralism brings stability, reciprocity, regularity. It is necessary because all states face mutual vulnerabilities, all share interdependence, and all need to benefit from public goods. Even the most powerful states cannot achieve security, environmental safety and economic prosperity in isolation or unilaterally, and so the international system rests upon a network of regimes, treaties and international organizations. Regimes can be defined as "sets of implicit or explicit principles, norms, rules and decision-making procedures around which actors' expectations converge in a given area of international relations".[6] An institution can be thought of as "persistent sets of rules that constrain activity, shape expectations, and prescribe roles".[7] Multilateralism is generally seen as "an institutional form that coordinates relations among three or more states on the basis of generalized principles of conduct ... which specify appropriate conduct for a class of actions".[8] Clearly, these well-established and widely accepted definitions of regimes, institutions and multilateralism are not confined to formal international organizations, and the concept of multilateralism should not be confused with or confined to formal international organizations. This distinction is fundamentally important in order to differentiate a discussion of a crisis in multilateralism as a general principle from a discussion about a crisis in a specific formal international organization. As Ruggie has observed, our conclusions regarding the "success" or effectiveness of multilateralism will not necessarily be the same as our conclusions regarding formal multilateral organizations.[9]

Multilateral institutions involve, in theory, indivisibility among the members in a specific issue area in terms of payoffs and behaviour; and they rely on the expectation of what Keohane calls "diffuse reciprocity", whereby members can expect to receive roughly equivalent benefits over time, if not necessarily on every decision.[10] Keohane also demonstrated that multilateral institutions perform important roles for states by reducing the costs of making, monitoring and enforcing rules (transaction costs), providing information, and facilitating the making of credible commitments.[11]

While the logic of multilateralism is clear, this logic is still problematized by an inherent paradox in international politics. All countries depend upon multilateralism and the maintenance of regularity, reciprocity and public goods in the international system. But the international system is nevertheless basically anarchical in a formal sense. States vary in power, political outlook and interests. They are formally sovereign, and generally driven by self-interests which are frequently in conflict. Leaders and hegemons – invariably the chief sponsors of international regimes – decline or increase in relative power and perceive negative changes in cost-benefit equations. Thus, international organizations are basically a reflection of the dynamics and processes of international power. This does not mean that formal or informal multilateral institutions are not effective or important, or that they cease to be effective in changing circumstances. It does, however, suggest that they are conditioned by the exigencies of changing international power configurations, and by conflicts which exist within the broader international system. Multilateral arrangements are inherently under strain. Institutionalist scholars, therefore, have sought to demonstrate that – in addition to the primary incentives for forming multilateral institutions – multilateral forms endure for a number of reasons, even when the environment which led to the emergence of the institution has changed. These include sunk costs, continued functional utility and institutional inertia.[12] Ruggie adds that the durability of multilateral arrangements is also a function of domestic environments within which constituencies of support develop.[13] What we are asking in this chapter is: despite the durability of multilateral institutions and their continued functional utility in changing circumstances, when do formal multilateral organizations reach a crisis in which their constitutive norms and operating procedures are tested beyond a tolerable threshold?

Multilateral crises in historical perspective

Since the project of universal organizations began after the First World War, international organizations have faced significant challenges to their integrity and effectiveness. In this section we will recall a number of these historical phases.

The League of Nations is best known for its failures that would surely constitute a series of "crises" by any standard. Japanese aggression in China, Italian aggression in North Africa, German aggression in Europe, and finally the Second World War occurred in violation of the League Covenant. A number of organizational weaknesses hampered the organization, but its true crisis must be seen as an extension of the turmoil of inter-war international relations. This saw a struggle between status quo powers – such as France and Britain – and dissatisfied revisionist powers which sought to challenge the norms and rules of the international system, such as Italy, Japan, Germany and the Soviet Union. Within this, the League was a part of the "illusion of peace"[14] which masked over a deep conflict.

Britain, France and, to a lesser extent, the United States sought to operate an unrealistic hegemony/concert and keep Germany, Italy, Japan and the Soviet Union under some sort of control, and the League became embroiled in this game. This international order proved to be unviable. Firstly, the system did not weaken Germany sufficiently enough to dissuade its ambitions because the Versailles treaty which ended the First World War was not fully enforced. Britain and the US wanted to bring Germany back into mainstream international politics as long as it did not represent a threat, even though France was deeply worried. For instance, the reparations payments owed by Germany were softened by the Dawes Plan and the London Conference of 1924. Britain accepted the idea that the economic health of Europe depended upon the integration of Germany. When the Western countries did begin to become worried about Germany's rearmament and recovery, because they had fed the illusion of peace to their publics, it was difficult for them to take serious defensive measures. At the same time, the Western countries had signed a treaty that created enormous grievances in Germany. So, according to many, the worst thing possible happened: the Versailles Treaty injured Germany, but allowed her to become strong again and challenge her perceived injustices. The post-war system similarly failed to accommodate or sufficiently contain the aspirations of Japan and the Soviet Union and also – although less significantly – Italy.

The League depended upon the majority of states – and certainly the most powerful ones – supporting a system of collective security with a common outlook on the rules governing international order. However, after the First World War powerful states shared no such outlook, and some rejected the "rules" and sought to change the system by force. Other states did not wish – or were not able – to support the system of collective security enshrined in the League Covenant. Therefore the League was secondary in importance to, and at odds with, the underlying power political dynamics, the underlying instability, and the deterioration in relations which marked the period.[15] It was a textbook example that an international normative system does not, and cannot, bring stability if it does not reflect – or is out of step with – the underlying power political order.

In the 1970s the United Nations suffered from a malaise which many observers believed was a growing crisis for the organization. A number of historical processes were transforming the organization into something quite different from that which was created in 1945 and something increasingly at odds with key actors in international politics. The influx of new UN members as former colonial territories became independent alienated the organization from its principal sponsors as the organization became embroiled in North–South tensions and revisionist "Third World" campaigns. Thus, what has been called the "minilateralist"[16] or the "club model"[17] of international organizations – whereby an exclusive collective of powerful states created post-war multilateral arrangements in their own image and with their own world-view and interests in mind – was coming under strain and increasingly challenged. The new "Third World" majority – to use the terminology of the time – found a voice in the UN organs and agencies that allowed, through their numerical superiority, expressions of solidarity and bloc voting. This "radically altered the entire character of the United Nations".[18] The new majority demanded economic redistribution and egalitarian systemic changes exemplified by the formation of the UN Conference on Trade and Development and the proposed New International Economic Order. These initiatives, and the militant spirit in which they were proposed, were the antithesis of the prevalent free-market thinking of the West. The "common front" rhetoric of the Non-Aligned Movement – inspired by leaders such as Tito, Nehru, Sukarno and Nasser – reached a crescendo in the General Assembly sessions of 1973 and 1974. The Secretary-General recalled how this reflected upon the UN:

> [t]he new arrivals were overwhelmingly non-white, non-western, underdeveloped and unschooled in the practice of national and international governance. They brought to the UN corridors a burning sense of injustice done them under their former colonial masters, a chip-on-the-shoulder insistence that the west, therefore, owed them the wherewithal needed for economic growth, and a more or less conscious rejection of the tenets of western liberal democracy.[19]

In November 1975, the General Assembly passed a resolution that equated Zionism with racism, and the floodgates of Western condemnation opened. The visit of PLO chairman Yasser Arafat to the UN, complete with (empty) gun holster, and the uproarious welcome he received, further contributed to the alienation of status quo powers from the organization.

The combative US position was epitomized by UN Representative Daniel Patrick Moynihan, who denounced the organization as a "dangerous place" – a vehicle for undemocratic forces and communists to mount diplomatic attacks against the West and set an anti-US tone in international politics.[20] US Representative John Scali was similarly "sceptical, disdainful, and combative" towards the UN.[21] Israeli UN Ambassador Yehuda Blum, in outlining the decline of the Organization's credibility, reflected upon "an unholy alliance of dictatorships and totalitarian regimes".[22] Unsurprisingly, surveys of the American public and of Western governments reflected considerable disenchantment towards the UN in general.[23]

Disillusionment with multilateral organizations on the part of much of the West, and in particular the US under Nixon, meant that the UN was often peripheral to the foreign policy of major powers. The Vietnam war, the maintenance and balances of superpower détente, arms control, the Middle East peace process, and many crises of decolonization, are examples of critical issues pursued or left outside the UN. Although financial and diplomatic sanctions against the UN were more of a weapon later under President Reagan, in October 1970 Congress reduced the US contribution to the ILO by 50 per cent; in 1974, the US contribution to UNESCO was suspended, and the US withdrew from the ILO between 1977 and 1980.[24] The relative decline of US hegemony had, according to many analysts, underpinned this growing antipathy of the US towards multilateralism. The collapse of fixed exchange rates and the soaring oil price increases of 1973 exacerbated the atmosphere of discord and US antipathy.

Observers noted that "at the White House, where Nixon and Kissinger were the architects of American foreign policy, there was little regard for the United Nations".[25] A study by Seymour Maxwell Finger goes into detail on the "Nixon–Kissinger mind set", an approach which was sceptical of international organizations, defensive, and consistent with Kissinger's "negative, almost disdainful attitude toward the UN".[26] Nixon saw no significant part for the UN in the grand design of history. Kissinger was more concerned with great power manoeuvring and power balances. Whilst Nixon's memoirs hardly mention the UN, Kissinger's clearly suggest that the UN was an instrument at his disposal for the pursuance of his own agenda.[27] The Soviet Union was in a similar position to the US. It was basically comfortable with the tacit norms and rules of the game reflected in superpower détente – until the late 1970s – through which it could consolidate its position on the world stage in a structure of bipolar stability. Subsequently, in common with the Nixon–Kissinger attitude, the Soviet Union sought to maintain the mechanisms of this system outside the organs of the UN and the complications which they entailed. However, the Soviet Union was equally happy to incite the challenge to the norms of the international system posed by the militant developing world members of the UN, thus further undermining the effectiveness of the organization.

A further period of crisis for the UN occurred in the 1980s. This was a reflection of political changes connected with an upsurge of Cold War hostility combined with the continuing "Third World" discontent and militancy. Major actors – and most importantly the US – circumvented the UN at critical stages, and proxy Cold War confrontations were impervious to constructive intervention by the organization. In this sense, the 1980s witnessed the culmination of trends that were in evidence in the previous decade but exacerbated in the 1980s by the breakdown of détente and the "nefarious influence" of the Cold War.[28] A number of states reverted to unilateralism, the Security Council was unable to address a number of threats to international peace and security, and a number of key UN members withdrew or de facto abstained from certain programmes and agencies. The absence of new peace-keeping operations between 1978 and 1988, and the precarious financial state of the organization, were indicators of this organizational blight.

In the words of Taylor and Groom, the organization "was on the sidelines and penniless.... The United Nations framework itself had become dilapidated and in gross need of reform. In short, a great experiment was in danger of failure".[29] Anthony Parsons experienced that environment as the British Representative to the UN, observing that by the mid-1980s "the UN was in deep trouble, perhaps at the lowest ebb in its history ... The UN had reached the bottom after a long fall from the pinnacle of exaggerated expectations which had characterised its creation".[30] In the Western imagination, international organizations seemed "out of control".[31]

The United Nations of the early 1980s reflected the continuation of the struggle between revisionist and status quo forces. Developing countries continued to exploit their numerical advantage to exert leverage upon the agenda of UN organs, but without the optimism of the 1970s. Marc Williams suggested that amongst these countries a "shared powerlessness in the face of adverse economic conditions provided the basis for cooperation ... [and] the absence of effective structures through which the developing countries could attempt to redress their grievances".[32] However, by the early 1980s "the North–South dialogue ha[d] been shelved as a result of the debt crisis, increased economic differentiation in the Third World, the negative response of the leading industrialised countries to the Third World demands and the primacy accorded to market solutions".[33] Nevertheless, it was a triumph of collective action that the developing countries managed to influence the final form of the Law of the Sea Convention to the extent that they did, in an attempt to "dismantle the superpowers' monopoly over the sea".[34] The clauses relating to the establishment of an International Seabed Authority in the Law of the Sea Convention clearly reflected an ethos of public ownership of natural resources. Krasner suggested that "[d]eveloping countries have rejected liberal regimes" in a book which is instructively entitled *Structural Conflict: The Third World Against Global Liberalism.*[35] This was perhaps a last vestige of the declining "dependency theory" or structuralist challenge to the systemic status quo. With the grand revisionist schemes of the 1960s and 1970s – such as the New International Economic Order – largely without hope, the "renaissance" of the Third World shifted in the 1980s towards rhetoric and posturing. The cohesion of the "new majority" was waning.

There was still an institutionalized hostility towards South Africa and Israel in the General Assembly, which clearly undermined the role of the Secretary-General in his efforts towards the settlement of conflict in which these two countries were a party. The drifting developing world was exploited by the Arab contingent in this respect, ensuring a constantly anti-Israel tone. The Soviet Union – although since the intervention into Afghanistan somewhat estranged from the majority – was happy to either acquiesce in or encourage this. The politicization of the specialized agencies and the creation of apparently politically orientated and sometimes extravagant programmes were manifestations of the excesses which Ambassador Scali had earlier described as the "tyranny of the majority".[36]

Aside from the developing world, there was also a deterioration in East–West relations as the years of détente gave way to renewed confrontation. This was a result of a number of factors: Soviet adventurism in Africa, Afghanistan and Central America; the Sandinista victory in Nicaragua; the Vietnamese invasion of Cambodia; the Soviet deployment of SS-20 intermediate-range missiles towards the end of the 1970s; and martial law in Poland. On the other side, the ascendancy of the New Right in the US and Britain, the establishment of diplomatic relations between the US and China, the deployment of Cruise missiles and the development of SDI anti-ballistic missile technology, and the imposition of sanctions upon the Soviet Union by the US in December 1981 – all contributed to the "second Cold War". The comfortable bipolar stability of détente was swept away by a resurgence of ideological fervour in the West and by the mismanagement and excesses of the Soviet Union. The United Nations had little impact in terms of alleviating the fallout from this process; indeed, it may have served to exacerbate it. The Security Council failed to fulfil its Charter responsibilities until the late 1980s and a climate of ill-will pervaded the whole organization.

As the primary diplomatic, economic and military sponsor of the United Nations, it is necessary to pay particular attention to the US attitudes and practice towards the organization during the 1980s, something Perez de Cueller described as "very disturbing".[37] During the 1970s the Nixon–Kissinger–Ford attitude had been largely one of sceptical and often scornful circumnavigation of the UN in the sphere of high politics. The organization had little substantive role to play in their agenda, apart from serving as an instrument to aid the balance between East and West, such as in the settlement of the Yom Kippur war, and in the provision of certain functional services. However, the agenda of the New Right in the 1980s, epitomized by President Reagan and US Representative at the UN Jeane Kirkpatrick, was much more combative and largely viewed détente as a mistake which had resulted in Soviet gains. The Kirkpatrick team made quite clear the Reagan administration's intolerance to the Soviet and developing world "antics" at the UN. In fact, "in Reagan's Washington there seemed to be an open season on a variety of multilateral or international arrangements which were the fruit of years of painstaking work and negotiation."[38] Outside the UN the administration was shedding the Vietnam syndrome: it would meet Soviet adventurism head-on and in proxy conflicts, outside the UN framework. According to Franck, in "the space of 40 years, the United States had gone from believing that the United Nations should and could do anything, to believing that it should and could do nothing".[39] From a systemic perspective, the Reagan approach reflected declining "northern commitment to universal multifunctional organisations".[40] Haas applied the concept of regime decay and the declining hegemony thesis to explain the waning capability of the organization in conflict management.[41] From the 1970s, US indignation grew as the UN reflected the apparent decline of American dominance and of Western cultural universalism, yet the US was still shouldering the heaviest financial burden for the organization.

As a result of the hostile majority "[t]he reality of U.S. impotence at the United Nations is stunning", according to Kirkpatrick.[42] Therefore, "[m]y mandate was to go forth and represent the policies of the Reagan administration and certainly those involve a restoration of American influence and an end of the period of American retreat and apology".[43] The Kirkpatrick team at the UN felt that the organization – and especially the General Assembly and the specialized agencies – were "irretrievably politicized",[44] wasteful, bureaucratic, and actually made conflict worse. The latter argument suggested that conflicts were exacerbated by the UN because the number of parties to a conflict became extended as countries felt obliged to take sides, even if they had no direct interest. It was in accordance with this that the frustrations of the US resulted in a resurgence of unilateralism. The policies towards Angola, Israel, Namibia, Nicaragua, El Salvador, the Law of the Sea Convention, the specialized agencies, and the "liberation" of Grenada, are a few examples.[45] In addition, the US began to monitor the behaviour of countries in the organization and to hold them accountable. Deputy Permanent Representative Kenneth Adelman reminded members that when "the United States is being attacked, we respond quite vigorously in various forms".[46] This was somewhat different from the marginalization of the UN by Nixon and Kissinger; whilst the New Right circumvented the organization in the 1980s when necessary, it also confronted it.

In addition to holding individual states accountable for their "antisocial" behaviour, the US – and to a lesser extent the United Kingdom – imposed a number of economic sanctions and withdrew or restricted their diplomatic support of agencies which manifested the worst excesses. The US withdrew from the ILO between 1977 and 1980 and from UNESCO in 1985, and refused to sign the 1982 Law of the Sea Convention. The 1985 Kassebaum Amendment involved a significant reduction of the US share of assessed contributions. The 1985 Sundquist Amendment threatened to withhold some of the US contribution to Secretariat salaries. If Israel was expelled, suspended, denied its rights or credentials, the US would suspend its own participation and reduce its contribution. Finally, the US withheld certain funds from specific UN activities which were disapproved of, such as support for the PLO, SWAPO, and the preparatory commission for the implementation of the Law of the Sea Commission.[47]

It was not just the economic sanctions which defined the adversarial environment. The resurgence of Cold War polarization contributed to the prolongation of regional conflicts in Afghanistan, between Iran and Iraq, in Africa, and in Central America. The US and Soviet Union obstructed efforts by the Security Council and the Secretary-General to address such issues until the latter half of the 1980s, and there was a general reversion to unilateralism and bilateralism. It is interesting to also recall the public manifestations of this. New York Mayor Koch suggested that he might alter the "Swords into Plowshares" inscription outside the UN to "hypocrisy, immorality and cowardice".[48] Similarly, Charles Lichenstein – Deputy US Representative to the United Nations under Kirkpatrick – famously told UN members who felt that the US was failing in its obligations to the organization to leave and take the UN with them: "we will put no impediment in your way and we will be at dockside bidding you a fond farewell as you set off into the sunset".[49] Shortly thereafter, Reagan suggested that Lichenstein probably spoke for most Americans.[50]

In his first annual report on the work of the UN in 1982, the Secretary-General expressed his frustration towards the failure of the Security Council to operate effectively and a climate which was "perilously near to a new international anarchy". He continued,

> I believe that we are at present embarked on an exceedingly dangerous course, one symptom of which is the crisis in the multilateral approach in international affairs and the concomitant erosion of the authority and status of world and regional inter-governmental institutions ... Such a trend must be reversed before once again we bring upon ourselves a global catastrophe and find ourselves without institutions effective enough to prevent it.[51]

After a year in office, he complained that the UN was "kept on the sidelines" and that his greatest achievement to date was to put his signature to the first Annual Report.[52]

With the end of the Cold War the United Nations again faced fundamental challenges. Initially, with the end of the Cold War, there was a climate of optimism and expectation at the UN and real reason to believe that a historical juncture had occurred in the evolution of the organization. The credibility of UN diplomacy was reborn in the late 1980s as the superpowers used the organization to facilitate the settlement of conflicts in which they had directly or indirectly been involved.[53] The reversal of Iraqi aggression against Kuwait, although dominated by the US and to a lesser extent Britain, also bolstered the UN because the operation, at least nominally, represented collective security under the UN Charter. The Security Council Permanent members continued their cohesion into the 1990s, with the "almost sacred principle" of not using the veto.[54] Boutros-Ghali wrote of "the start of a new phase in the history of the Organisation", and a "new chapter in history".[55]

This was short-lived. As a result of misguided experimentation, financial problems, over-reach and crisis in certain peace operations, the fortunes of the UN began to turn in 1993. Earlier pledges of support by many members were forgotten as the cost – in political, material, and even human terms – of the new agenda was realized. A plethora of Security Council resolutions and field operations ran into serious problems. The foundering and costly experiments in the former Yugoslavia and Somalia caused a crisis of credibility and finance in the UN and a decline of confidence and commitment on the part of many states. The realization dawned that early optimism had been premature and "the extent to which the UN relies on political will and not pious rhetoric for the performance of tasks was under-estimated".[56] Ideas of nation-building were abandoned and an environment of cautious realism and multilateral fatigue subsequently pervaded the organization. From October 1993 the US Congress began to cut back its support to the UN following the Somalia disaster. A wave of political attacks was directed against the organization, and when the Republicans retook Congress, they immediately embarked upon further moves to restrict the organization. The fate of Rwanda in 1994 was the worst manifestation of this malaise, and surely stands out as a singular crisis for the UN in the 1990s.

A mixture of unilateralism, and to a smaller degree neo-isolationism, came into play in the US. Republican Bob Dole, although a believer in US leadership and not an isolationist, promised that "when we recapture the White House, no American boys are going to be serving under the command of Field-Marshal Boutros Boutros-Ghali".[57] The Republican majority in Congress backed their words with various financial sanctions – such as the unilateral capping of its contribution to the peace-keeping budget to 25 per cent – and by the beginning of 1996 the Secretary-General announced that the organization was on "the edge of insolvency".[58] In January 1996 the Under-Secretary-General for Administration and Management, Joseph Connor, reported to the High-Level Open-Ended Working Group on the Financial Situation of the United Nations that the organization was owed $3.3 billion; $1.6 billion for the regular budget, $1.7 billion for the peace-keeping budget, and a further $4.9 million for the international tribunals.[59] In response Boutros-Ghali proposed modest levies on certain international transactions – a kind of international tax – to help address the financial crisis so that the UN could operate on a "secure and steady independent financial foundation".[60] All the political parties in the US condemned the idea; Presidential candidate Bob Dole introduced the "Prohibition of United Nations Taxation Act".[61]

Not so long after President George Bush had proclaimed the New World Order and commitment to the UN "mission",[62] many politicians in the US and the West had become acutely wary of collective internationalism as the "slippery slope".[63] The manner in which many US politicians blamed the UN for the US casualties in Somalia in October 1993 (in the context of "irresponsible internationalism", in the words of Dole)[64] was typical of this attitude. The Heritage Foundation called for "no more Somalias" and Kissinger warned of a "recipe for chaos" in US involvement in hazardous situations on the basis of vague ideas of humanitarianism and collective internationalism.[65] The Clinton administration basically also reflected the trend, despite its more friendly tone. The starkest example of this was Presidential Policy Directive 25 of 1994, which imposed severe constraints on the use of US soldiers in UN operations.[66]

Crises in historical perspective

How do we compare these moments of "crisis" in the 1930s, 1970s, 1980s and 1990s and now at the beginning of the twenty-first century? The first point to note is that, when considering "crises" in historical perspective, we see that crises are in fact common – indeed natural – to multilateralism and certainly the United Nations. Crises generally result from environmental variables and particularly environmental changes which bring the values and operating procedures of multilateral institutions into tension with the members of the organization or the nature of their tasks. The environmental factors include changes in the nature and balance of power, the nature of security and of threats to international security; changes in terms of the types of actors which have an impact upon international politics; the ideological outlook of major states; the international norms which regulate the behaviour of actors in the international arena; and the evolving nature of the state and state security. James Caporaso observes that multilateralism is highly demanding: "It requires its participants to renounce temporary advantages and the temptation to define their interests narrowly in terms of national interests, and it also requires them to forgo ad hoc coalitions and to avoid policies based on situational exigencies and momentary constellations of interests."[67] The changing environmental variables can and often do present an insurmountable challenge to this equation.

A number of factors appear to be common to the sense of crisis in different historical contexts. Thus, how would we judge if a particular multilateral institution – in terms of its constitutive principles and performance – is in crisis? The following conclusions suggest themselves:

- The constitutive principles upon which the organization/regime/norm are founded and operate are consistently challenged by the activities and declarations of leading members of the multilateral arrangement. Thus, key members – and/or a numerically significant proportion of members – pursue relevant policy objectives at odds with, and/or outside the framework of, the organization.
- There is epistemic consensus that the values and institutions of a particular form of multilateralism are no longer effective or legitimate, and that the multilateral body consistently fails to achieve the principal objectives for which it was created.
- There is an epistemic consensus that the ineffectiveness and illegitimacy of a particular multilateral form are permanent as long as the constitutive principles of the organization remain the same.
- Multilateral institutions are challenged by significant alternative arrangements which perform the same task, to which member states transfer their diplomat attention and material resources.

Why might a multilateral institution be in "crisis"? The brief survey presented above suggests a number of interconnected and overlapping possibilities:

- The mission of a multilateral institution is simply no longer necessary or viable. An example of this could be the UN Trusteeship Council after all former colonial territories became independent.
- Decision-making processes are, or become, out of step with the balance of power in international politics. This can involve a leading member state declining in relative power and being less willing to accept an increasingly unattractive costs-benefit equation and "free riders". The opposite tendency can involve a shift towards unipolarity in economic and/or military power, whereby a single state is perceived to be preeminent and free from the constraints of multilateralism when such constraints are deemed unacceptable.
- The balance of power *within* an international organization changes as a result of changing members. The best example here comes from the 1970s and the United Nations.
- The attitude of powerful states turns against a multilateral organization for ideological reasons – through a change of government, for instance – and withholds diplomatic and material support. There were signs of this in the US administration under President Ronald Reagan and then under President George W. Bush.
- The constitutive principles upon which the organization or regime was founded and operates are challenged by changing norms or the break-

down of norms. For example, the growing prominence of terrorist organizations and the perceived threat of weapons of mass destruction in the hands of terrorists or "rogue states" have arguably challenged the UN Charter norms regulating the use of military force in international politics (that is, only in self-defence or within the collective security framework of the UN).

- Multilateralism fails to adapt to changing circumstances and challenges; the constitutive principles and policies of the organization are no longer appropriate to deal with the challenges with which the organization is faced. For example, the state-centric and national-interest orientation of many international organizations has been questioned with regard to dealing with transnational challenges such as contagious diseases.

On the basis of this, can we conclude that the challenges that the UN faces at the turn of the century are exceptional and unique? It may seem so today, but according to this framework the crises that the UN faced in the past were also fundamental in scale and nature. But whilst all of these periods reflected symptoms of crisis, none of these crises met the test what would suggest that multilateralism in general could be considered permanently flawed.

A principal difference in the early twenty-first century is that the challenge to multilateralism is found, amongst others sources, in changes in the state and from non-state challenges, more than in the past. It is therefore something of a post-Westphalian challenge. A further difference is that our expectations are today higher. Issues just as critical as the 2003 war against Iraq occurred in the 1970s and 1980s. The Vietnam war, the wars between Israel and its neighbours, the Iran–Iraq war, and too many others – all proceeded with little or no UN involvement. The difference may be that in the post-Cold War world we have higher expectations – we expect the key issues of international relations to be dealt with through the UN, and if they are not, we see a crisis. The fact that states are engaged in a serious reform agenda at the UN demonstrates its continued utility and shows a process of evolution rather than crisis. A greater crisis would be if states disengaged and worked outside the UN in the first instance, as they have far more in the past.

Notes

1. Michael J. Glennon (2005) "Idealism at the UN", *Policy Review* 129 (February/March): 15.
2. J. Pérez de Cuéllar, "Report of the Secretary-General on the Work of the Organization", September 1982.

3. Kurt Waldheim (1980) *In the Eye of the Storm*, London: Weidenfield and Nicolson, p. 121.
4. Stephen D. Krasner (1982) "Structural causes and regime consequences: regimes as intervening variables", *International Organization* 36.
5. Edward D. Mansfield, "The organization of international relations", in Friedrich Kratochwil and Edward D. Mansfield (1994) *International Organization: A Reader*, New York: Harper Collins, p. 3.
6. Stephen D. Krasner (1982) "Structural causes and regime consequences", p. 1.
7. Robert O. Keohane, "International institutions: two approaches", in Friedrich Kratochwil and Edward D. Mansfield, *International Organization: A Reader*, pp. 48–49.
8. John Gerard Ruggie (1993) "Multilateralism: the anatomy of an institution", in John Gerard Ruggie (ed.) *Multilateralism Matters. The Theory and Praxis of an Institutional Form*, New York: Columbia University Press, p. 11.
9. John Gerard Ruggie (1993) "Multilateralism: the anatomy of an institution", p. 26.
10. Robert O. Keohane (1985) "Reciprocity in international relations", *International Organization* 40 (Winter).
11. Robert O. Keohane (2002) "Introduction", in Robert O. Keohane, *Power and Governance in a Partially Globalized World*, London: Routledge.
12. Stephen Krasner (ed.) (1983) *International Regimes*, Ithaca, NY: Cornell University Press.
13. John Gerard Ruggie (1993) "Multilateralism: the anatomy of an institution", p. 33.
14. S. Marks (1976) *The Illusion of Peace. International Relations in Europe 1918–1933*, London: Macmillan Press.
15. E.H. Carr (2001) *The Twenty Years Crisis: An Introduction to the Study of International Relations*, 2nd edn, New York: Palgrave.
16. Miles Kahler (1993) "Multilateralism with small and large numbers", in John Gerard Ruggie (ed.) *Multilateralism Matters. The Theory and Praxis of an Institutional Form*, New York: Columbia University Press.
17. Robert O. Keohane and Jopseh S. Nye, Jr. (2002) "The club model of multilateral cooperation and problems of democratic legitimacy", in Robert O. Keohane, *Power and Governance in a Partially Globalized World*, London: Routledge.
18. K. Waldheim (1980) *In the Eye of the Storm*, London: Weidenfield and Nicolson, p. 111.
19. K. Waldheim (1984) "The United Nations: the tarnished image", *Foreign Affair* 1 (Fall): 96.
20. Daniel Patrick Moynihan (1978) *A Dangerous Place*, Boston: Little.
21. S.M. Finger (1988) *American Ambassadors at the UN: people, politics and bureaucracy in making foreign policy*, New York and London: Holmes and Meier, pp. 218, 227.
22. *New York Times*, 13 September 1979, p. 27.
23. For example, a Gallup survey found that 45 per cent of leading figures in 70 non-Communist states said that their attitude towards the UN had become less favourable than before, *New York Times*, 19 September 1973, p. 2; the *New York Times* reported a negative survey result found by *Foreign Policy*, 4 September 1976, p. 6.
24. See Y. Beigbeder (1988) *Threats to the International Civil Service*, London: Pinter Publishers.
25. S.M. Finger and A.A. Saltzman (1990) *Bending with the Winds. Kurt Waldheim and the United Nations*, New York: Praeger Publishers, p. 33.
26. S.M. Finger (1988) *American Ambassadors at the UN: People, Politics and Bureaucracy in Making Foreign Policy*, New York and London, Holmes and Meier, p. 218.
27. Henry Kissinger (1982) *Years of Upheaval*, London: Weidenfeld and Nicolson and Michael Joseph, pp. 471–474 and pp. 480, 486, 502.

28. J. Pérez de Cuéllar (1995) "Reflecting on the past and contemplating the future", *Global Governance* 1(2): 153.
29. P. Taylor and A.J.R. Groom (1992) *The United Nations and the Gulf War, 1990–91: Back to the Future?*, London: Royal Institute of International Affairs Discussion Paper 38, p. 2.
30. A. Parsons (1993) "The UN and the national interest of states", in A. Roberts and B. Kingsbury (eds) *United Nations, Divided World*, p. 111.
31. Robert O. Keohane and Jospeh S. Nye, Jr. (1985) "Two cheers for multilateralism", *Foreign Policy* 60 (Fall): 148.
32. M. Williams (1991) *Third World Cooperation. The Group of 77 in UNCTAD*, London: Pinter Publishers, p. 164.
33. Ibid., p. 2.
34. L. Yali (1985) "The United Nations and the Third World", *Beijing Review* 28(42) (October): 18.
35. S.D. Krasner (1985) *Structural Conflict. The Third World Against Global Liberalism*, California, University of California Press, p. 65.
36. *New York Times*, 7 December 1974, p. 1.
37. J. Pérez de Cuéllar (1995) "Reflecting on the past and contemplating the future", p. 155.
38. B. Urquhart, *A Life in Peace and War*, New York, Harper and Row, 1987, p. 326.
39. T.M. Franck (1989) "Soviet initiatives: US Responses – new opportunities for reviving the United Nations system", *American Journal of International Law* 83(3) (July): 532–533.
40. S.D. Krasner (1985) *Structural Conflict*, p. 300.
41. E.B. Haas (1983) "Regime decay: conflict management and international organizations, 1945–1981", *International Organization* 37(2) (Spring).
42. J.J. Kirkpatrick in L.M. Fasulo (1984) *Representing America: Experiences of US Diplomats at the UN*, New York: Praeger, p. 284.
43. J.J. Kirkpatrick in L.M. Fasulo (1984) *Representing America*, p. 284. See also R.W. Gregg (1993) *About Face? The United States and the United Nations*, London: Lynne Rienner, pp. 19–20.
44. W.C. Sherman (1984) "Deputy Representative to the Security Council 1981–1983", in L.M. Fasulo (1984), p. 299.
45. J. Kirkpatrick (1984) "The superpowers; is there a moral difference?", *The World Today* (May): 185.
46. K.L. Adelman in L.M. Fasulo (1984) *Representing America*, p. 291.
47. See Y. Beigbeder (1988) *Threats to the International Civil Service*, London: Pinter Publishers, pp. 56–57.
48. *New York Times*, 10 February 1982, p. 1.
49. L.M. Fasulo (1984) *Representing America*, p. 281.
50. *New York Times*, 22 September 1983, p. 1.
51. J. Pérez de Cuéllar (1982) "Report of the Secretary-General on the Work of the Organization", September.
52. *New York Times*, 1 January 1983, p. 1.
53. G.R. Berridge (1991) *Return to the UN: UN diplomacy in Regional Conflicts*, London: Macmillan.
54. J.O. Jonah (1993) "Differing state perspectives on the United Nations in the post-cold war world", *ACUNS Reports and Papers*, no. 4, p. 14.
55. B. Boutros-Ghali (1992) *An Agenda for Peace. Preventive Diplomacy, Peacemaking and Peace-keeping*, Report of the Secretary-General, New York, United Nations, paragraph 6.

56. M.R. Berdal (1994) "Fateful encounter: the United States and UN peacekeeping", *Survival* 36(1) (Spring): 30–31.
57. *Guardian*, 20 February 1995, p. 9.
58. *Washington Post*, 7 February 1996, p. 16.
59. United Nations News Summary, London, NS/1/96, 7 February 1996. By the end of 1995 only 94 countries had paid their regular budget payments in full and 22 had made no payment at all. For the first time in its history the UN had been unable to repay revenue borrowed from the peacekeeping budget.
60. The Secretary-General's Cyril Foster Lecture, Oxford University, 15 January 1996, Federal News Service transcript.
61. Congressional Press Releases, 22 January 1996.
62. Security Council Summit, p. 33.
63. J.R. Gerlach (1993) "A UN Army for the New World Order?", *Orbis. A Journal of World Affairs* 37(2) (Spring). Also, J.G. Ruggie (1992) "No, the world doesn't need a United Nations army", *International Herald Tribune*, 26 September; J. Kirkpatrick (1995) "Refusing to subordinate U.S. policy to United Nations isn't isolationism", *Sacramento Bee*, 12 January.
64. *Boston Globe*, 3 April, 1995, p. 1.
65. T.P. Sheehy (1993) "No more Somalias: reconsidering Clinton's doctrine of military humanitarianism", *Heritage Foundation Reports*, backgrounder no. 968, 20 December; H. Kissinger (1993) "Recipe for chaos", *Washington Post*, 8 September, p. 19.
66. Unofficial US document made available at the United Nations, May 1994.
67. James A. Caporaso (1993) "International Relations Theory and multilateralism: the search for foundations", in John Gerard Ruggie (ed.) *Multilateralism Matters*, p. 56.

Part II

Issues and challenges

10

Something old, something new: Theoretical perspectives on contemporary international peace and security

K. J. Holsti

This chapter explores some generic and structural features of the contemporary international system and links them to the kinds of problems that are most likely to pose a high probability of serious harm, through armed force and other means of violence, to states and societies around the world.[1] I use this characterization of security to distinguish it from the much broader nomenclature of "human security" that has become fashionable, though contested.

The range of possible threats in highly vulnerable modern societies is so great, though of highly variable probability, that to cover all of them adequately would require numerous volumes. Threats might include cyber wars, poisoning urban water supplies, release of poison gases or biological agents, computer viruses, random shooting of civilians, and assassinations, to mention just a few. Everything is possible, but analyses of seemingly random acts or events are less significant than challenges that occur with regularity, that are the manifestations of deep structural social, economic and political problems in broad areas of the world, and that result in widespread loss of life and injury, inflicted by state and non-state actors for political purposes.

The overall argument is that the agenda of international peace and security combines the perennial problems that emerge from a system of sovereign states in a condition of anarchy with newer threats emerging from the weakness and breakdown of states and the rise of private armed groups and millenarian quasi-religious movements. The new security agenda in the early twenty-first century is an addition to, not a replacement of, the old security agenda.

Classical security *problèmatiques*: interstate wars and armed aggression

The systematic study of security and war – aside from some classic non-Western exemplars such as those of Sun Tzu – arose originally in the context of the Peloponnesian Wars (Thucydides). They flourished as a genre in the European states system beginning in the seventeenth century. The related problems of war and security were major concerns of political philosophers such as Hobbes and Rousseau, and international lawyers such as Grotius, Pufendorff, and Vattel. These and other writers trolled through the wreckage of major wars of the era, noting how the emerging states system was also a war system. Formal anarchy, which replaced the more hierarchical medieval order, liberated the states from superior command, but in so doing created two related problems: (1) perpetual fear of attack from neighbours (war and aggression), and (2) the re-establishment of hegemony and empire. If we extrapolate from Hobbes's concept of the state of nature, war would be ubiquitous. On the other hand, in his famous analogy to weather, he claimed that the *state of war* did not refer to constant armed struggle, but as rain in the British winter; it is a *disposition* to fight. War erupts from time to time as states go about their business seeking security, prestige, glory, and other values and interests.

Anarchy is the permissive condition that gives rise to the occasional use of force between states and to the potential for hegemony. But we cannot predict from it – as in the ecological fallacy – when, where, or who will use armed force or which state will seek supremacy over others. We only know that historically war is a relatively rare event if we consider how many states are potential aggressors and victims. Yet it is an event of such momentous consequences that since at least the Napoleonic era, statesmen, publicists and scholars have sought to control its use. For what purpose?

The diplomats who gathered in San Francisco in April 1945, like their forebears at Utrecht, Vienna and Paris, fashioned an eminently Westphalian document. The main purpose of the United Nations is to establish and maintain international peace and security. That was defined – as a response to the serial aggressions of the 1930s and early 1940s – as *protecting the independence and territorial integrity of each member state.*

Many analysts have noted the declining incidence of classical interstate wars since 1945. John Mueller has argued that *major* wars between the great powers are becoming obsolete.[2] However, when we combine interstate wars, characterized by organized campaigns of armed forces against each other, with unilateral armed interventions aimed at overthrowing or supporting established political authority structures or personnel in another state, the raw figures suggest an increase and not a decline or obsolescence in the incidence of these types of armed force. In the period 1496 to 1945, a war or armed intervention started on average once every three years. Since 1945 that figure has increased to a new war or armed intervention every 1.5 years, that is, approximately a doubling of the raw incidence of war.[3] It is thus premature to conclude that the old Westphalian security *problèmatique* has been solved or has become obsolete. Nevertheless, we must acknowledge that from the point of view of probabilities, most states are under less threat of foreign invasion than at any previous time, for the raw figures must be adjusted for the much higher number of states in the system today compared to the eighteenth or nineteenth centuries. In fact, the probability that an average state would become involved in a war or armed intervention in any year has decreased from one chance in seven for the period 1495 to 1918 to one chance in 100 since 1990.[4]

What about aggression, an outright attack on another state that cannot be justified by the usual canons of international law (reprisals, protecting nationals, and the like), and that is usually staged through a phoney incident designed to make the aggressor appear like the aggrieved party (examples would include the famous Ems telegram, the Mainila incident preceding the Russo-Finnish war of 1939, the Gulf of Tonkin incident, or the "weapons of mass destruction" threat concocted by the Bush administration prior to its attack on Iraq in 2003)? If we discount the serial aggressions of Napoleon in the early nineteenth century and those of the dictators in the 1930s, there have been remarkably few outright attacks. Most wars and armed interventions, in fact, were the outcome of long and sometimes protracted crises that escalated to violence (World War I is the paradigmatic example). After Napoleon, there were only two aggressions in the remainder of the nineteenth century (Prussia against France in 1870 and the United States against Spain in 1898). We then come to the period of the 1930s when Japan, Germany, Italy and the Soviet Union went on an orgy of military conquests not seen in the previous three centuries (excluding colonial conquests in the 1880s and 1890s). Regrettably, the situation since 1945 more closely resembles the 1930s than the nineteenth century. I count at least nine major aggressions (not including armed interventions) since 1945, or one every 7.5 years.[5] Those who see a long-run secular decline in the incidence of violence between states overlook such figures, and those who proclaim a "new security era" featuring novel types of threats replacing older ones are looking at only one-half of the picture. While many people in some areas of the world, including Europe, North America, South America, and possibly Southeast Asia, may no longer live in fear of foreign invasion and conquest, for the rest of the world the classical Westphalian *problèmatique* of war remains on the agenda.

Classical security *problèmatiques*: the problem of hegemony

The second classical problem arising from anarchy, after state insecurity and possible war, is the re-establishment of hegemony. We call the states system "Westphalian" because the two peace treaties signed in 1648 in that German duchy symbolically, if not actually, destroyed the intellectual and religious grounds of the two power centres that exercised (often competing) forms of hegemony over the rising European dynastic states. The purpose of the succeeding great wars against Louis XIV and Napoleon were all designed to prevent the re-establishment of "universal monarchy" as hegemony was then called.

Hitler and Stalin were the last historical figures who dreamt of destroying the Westphalian system and replacing it with another, based on totally different principles (in Hitler's case, a racial hierarchy; in Stalin's example, a world of united working-class parties beholden to the secular papacy in Moscow). We have not had universal dreamers since Hitler's suicide in 1945 and Stalin's death in 1952.[6] The world has been better off because of that fact.

But we do have the structural fact of the "unipolar" moment. The United States has both the military and economic capacity to become an overbearing hegemon, if not the core of a new global empire. Despite American assertions that, like all other great powers before it, its intentions are benign and necessary for world peace, the United States can and may become a major security threat to the rest of the world. When military capacities outpace decision-makers' intelligence and judgement, dangers to the states system may result. Reading the literature and pronouncements of the contemporary American "neoconservatives," one cannot fail to be impressed by the number of influential people who have already adopted the imperial mind-set of military omnipotence and celebrate its derivative, the opportunity to act alone without regard to the norms or rules of the international community. During the Cold War, Sir Herbert Butterfield warned against the consequences of this dangerous tendency. Paraphrasing Butterfield, Paul Sharp writes:

> The powerful, and especially those whose power rests on populist claims, are tempted not only to assert, but to believe, that their view of the world is everybody's view of the world or ought to be. A great power that succumbs to this temptation ... becomes a system of organized hypocrisy corrupted by its self-righteousness and pride. It is dangerous, not because its sense of right is subor-

dinated to its interests, but because its sense of right fuels its exercise of power, putting others, itself and, in the nuclear age, the whole world at risk.[7]

In what ways could the United States become a major threat to international peace and security? If we define those terms in the sense of the United Nations Charter, then the probabilities are remote. To date, the United States has never announced a programme of conquest or territorial expansion. The formal sovereignty and territorial integrity of members of the United Nations are not in jeopardy from the United States. The potential for posing threats are more diffuse and of a different order. There are at least five problems with current American policies, all of which could lead to serious threats and possibly to the re-establishment of acute security dilemmas that could eventuate in armed intervention, aggression and war. They are: (1) the promotion of proliferation of weapons of mass destruction, and particularly nuclear weapons; (2) contemporary "defence" strategies that are likely to eventuate in security dilemmas and military responses from other states; (3) the potential "hair trigger" use of force in the form of pre-emption or preventive war; (4) major misperceptions and construction of faulty security threats; and (5) extreme meliorism.

The United States and the promotion of proliferation

The United States government ranks proliferation of weapons of mass destruction as the major threat to its security. NSPD-17, publicly released 31 January 2003, states that "Weapons of mass destruction ... in the possession of hostile states and terrorists represents one of the greatest security challenges facing the United States." The report further asserts that "[w]e will not permit the world's most dangerous regimes and terrorists to threaten us with the world's most destructive weapons."[8] The major security threat to the United States is not a hostile foreign state, as the Soviet Union was throughout the Cold War, but a generic problem of weapons proliferation. The main thrust of American foreign policy, then, is to prevent or even reverse proliferation. The United States, the document continues, "must ensure compliance with relevant international agreements, including the Nuclear Non-proliferation Treaty (NPT), the Chemical Weapons Convention, and the Biological Weapons Convention" (p. 2). Now consider what the United States had done to ensure compliance with these international agreements, all designed to control the proliferation of weapons of mass destruction.

It has branded certain states members of an "axis of evil" or "outposts of tyranny" with the implied threat to attack them. In a memorandum to the American President, his former National Security Adviser asserted "pre-emptive attack against terrorists or tyrants who control rogue states is a legitimate form of self-defense."[9] This posture is almost a guarantee that targeted states would seek to obtain or continue to develop weapons of mass destruction as a deterrent against potential American attack. That these states should fear attack is underlined by the American invasion of Iraq. What would be truly surprising is if the targeted states *failed* to seek a nuclear deterrent, provided they already had some necessary infrastructure and access to fuels.

The United States has failed to ratify the Comprehensive Test Ban Treaty, one of the key pillars of non-proliferation. Why? Because it deems it necessary to undertake future tests in developing new kinds of nuclear weapons. The foundational compromise of the NPT – non-nuclear states would forego the nuclear option in exchange for the great powers' nuclear disarmament – has been ignored by those great powers, led by the United States. For the Americans to argue that they fully support the NPT and expect compliance by all other states, when they violate its fundamental premise, places the NPT under increased stress. The development of new nuclear weapons by the United States is itself a form of proliferation, though one that seems to have been lost on American officials.

The United States, despite its rhetorical commitment to international agreements has walked out of the protocols of the Biological Weapons Convention, has exempted itself from key monitoring elements of the Chemical Weapons Convention, and has unilaterally abrogated the Anti-Ballistic Missile (ABM) treaty.

One can hardly expect to promote non-proliferation by refusing to ratify key international agreements such as the Comprehensive Test Ban Treaty (CTBT) and by building up one's own stockpiles while denying others similar opportunities. In brief, some contemporary American policies are not only failing to prevent proliferation, but are promoting it.

Revitalizing the security dilemma: American strategic doctrines and deployments as threats to international peace and security

As Rousseau famously insisted, steps taken by states to protect themselves are perceived by their neighbours as potential threats to their own security. This is the heart of the security dilemma. Throughout history, policy makers have inferred threats from the build-up of capabilities of others. The United States has launched several programmes that enhance the probabilities of creating security dilemmas between it and states such as China and Russia. For example, the United States Air Force has developed a formal plan to fight a war in space, listing targets that range from weather and communications satellites to spacecraft-launch facilities of other countries. The recently released report, called Counterspace Operations, calls for space-based radio-frequency weapons, interceptors, and airships outfitted with lasers and anti-satellite missiles. In brief, the United States is about to place weapons into space, with a capacity to destroy not just other countries' communications systems, but also a wide array of defensive capabilities. This will be a clear violation of the 1967 Outer Space Treaty. The likely consequence of this plan is some form of arms racing in space. The American initiative, of course deemed only a "defensive" measure against others' potential attacks (a "space Pearl Harbor", as Donald Rumsfeld termed it), provides the ingredients for a classical security dilemma. The American predominance in space in combination with an (dubious) operable missile defence system will make the world safe for an American first strike, negating the deterrent effect of Chinese or Russian retaliatory forces. It is unlikely that such American military domination will go without some form of response by those most threatened by it; then the vicious circle of arms build-up will begin.

The doctrine of extreme preventive attack

As a strategy for coping with the problem of terror, American pre-emptive and capabilities-based strike doctrines go far beyond classical concepts of pre-emption or preventive war. Those insist at least on some evidence of malevolent intent. Under the Rice formula, the United States could attack any state or group of individuals within a state that was just *suspected* of *seeking* to obtain weapons of mass destruction. Does this not seem like an extreme position? Of course, but the United States attacked Iraq in 2003 in similar circumstances. The precedent has now been set. The principal decision-makers in Washington publicly proclaimed that Saddam Hussein possessed weapons of mass destruction, but they must have been aware of the mounting evidence, some within the government itself, that Saddam had essentially "come clean" in 1991 and had not renewed efforts to amass such weapons.

In announcing the attack on Iraq in March 2003, President Bush invoked the eighteenth-century notion of the sovereign right to use military force. The president himself has acknowledged that the Iraq war was one of "choice" rather than necessity. He could not have invoked the "inherent right" of self-defence clause in Article 51 because there was no evidence that Iraq posed a threat to the United States. It had neither the capabilities nor intentions. Thus, the attack was not even a case of preventive or pre-emptive war. It was, rather, a case of aggression. Combined with the formal doctrine asserting the "right" to engage in preventive war in the absence of either known capabilities or intentions, the

United States has unilaterally abrogated the constraints on the use of force that were carefully crafted in the League of Nations Covenant and the Charter of the United Nations, not to mention other multilateral instruments such as the 1990 Pact of Paris, the 1933 Montevideo Convention, and the Charter of the OAS. The proliferation of states asserting similar "rights" now continues apace, as Russia, Israel (much earlier), and Australia have recently followed suit. If the momentum for attenuating the India–Pakistan conflict loses force, then we can expect these two countries to follow the American lead in insisting on a right of preemptive or preventive attack. Here is, then, another contradiction. The United States, which has self-proclaimed itself as a leader in bringing peace to the world, is undermining another of the foundations of that peace, the emerging norm that *all* use of force is illegitimate unless authorized through the processes of international or regional organizations, or under Article 51, the necessity of establishing a reasonably imminent peril. Certainly the enunciation of a "hair trigger" pre-emptive doctrine is more likely to cause mimicry by anyone confronting a potential threat than it is to deter terrorist groups or "rogue" states.

Intellectual flaws, misperceptions, and the construction of threats: the American case

The potential for harm arises also from intellectual limitations, flawed thinking and serious problems of misperception. Should we not be concerned when, for example, the President's National Security Adviser publicly asserts that the threat posed by Saddam Hussein to world peace was as serious as that posed by Adolph Hitler? Or that the occupation of Iraq would present no greater problems than the post-World War II occupations of Germany and Japan? Is there no recognition in official Washington that the rage and charges of hypocrisy that emanate from the Arab countries are actually the *consequences* of American choices and actions, rather than some primordial prejudice about or envy of the United States? Is there much hope for ameliorating serious international problems when American policy makers, in the aftermath of 9/11, claimed that nothing the United States had ever done in the Middle East could help explain the rise of Muslim extremism? One final anecdote summarizes the intellectual sources of hubris. A top adviser in the administration told a critical reporter that "guys like [you] are in what we call the reality-based community", which he defined as people who "believe that solutions emerge from ... judicious study of discernible reality. That's not the way the world works anymore. We're an empire now, and when we act we create our own reality."[10]

Equally disturbing are the mood and knowledge levels of the American public and media. The build-up to the attack on Iraq demonstrated three critical facts: (1) the level of knowledge of Middle East affairs in general and of Iraq specifically is extremely low; (2) the media, for the most part, play a mobilizing and cheerleading role for the use of military force, and (3) the public has a high degree of tolerance for mendacity. Together, these three conditions have helped create an environment in which any American government could use military force without fear of electoral punishment. We need not go into the documentation of each fact; the evidence strongly supports at least two of them. Any population, 70 per cent of whom do not know the difference between Saddam Hussein and Osama bin Laden, cannot be trusted to make critical judgements about a country's foreign policy. Media that mobilize dozens of "experts" advocating war, while systematically ignoring those who have serious questions about it, is not performing its public duty. None of the principals planning the war ever had to face a press conference where critical questions were raised. Only on the claim of mendacity is there room for debate, but there is no lack of evidence. Vice-President Cheney insisted in August 2002 that Saddam Hussein would have nuclear weapons within a matter of months. Paul Wolfowitz in January 2003 insisted that Saddam Hussein was known to have and be hiding vast quantities of mass destruction weapons. Condoleeza Rice, in the same month, wrote in the *New York Times*, in an op-ed entitled "Why We Know Saddam is Lying", that there was no doubt whatsoever but that Saddam was sitting on a massive pile of WMDs. This was despite the fact that to that date the weapons inspectors had come up with nothing more frightening than a balsa wood drone that *could* carry biological weapons and a few missiles whose range was about 10 kilometres greater than allowed under the 1991 armistice agreement ending the 1991 Gulf War. By February 2003, the IAEA proclaimed that Saddam had neither a nuclear weapons capability nor a programme to develop one. Yet, the American people overwhelmingly believed the government line that Saddam Hussein constituted a grave threat to American security and that therefore the invasion of Iraq was a justified act of self-defence. I believe that eventually the evidence will show that numerous people in the Bush administration, and probably most of the principals, knew prior to March 2003 that Saddam Hussein had no weapons of mass destruction. The plan to attack Iraq was a product of the 1990s, among a few notables known as the "neoconservatives" whose ambition was forcefully to "democratize" Iraq as a means of bringing stability to the Middle East, greater security for Israel, and guaranteed access to oil and military bases, both assets that were increasingly under doubt in a volatile Saudi Arabia.

The contemporary mood of the American people has been profoundly shaken by the events of 9/11. It is a mood of intense fear sustained by both government rhetoric and media attention. In this environment, it is easy to construct threats, even when more distant observers would fail to notice them.

The history of imaginary threat construction goes back to colonial times when the settlers in the colonies branded indigenous populations a "threat" because of their crude life style and occasional licentious behaviour. When settlers moved into the traditional lands of the natives, not unexpectedly they were not always welcome. The actions the Indians took to protect access to their lands were frequently gruesome by any standards, but they were essentially defensive. The settlers, however, saw these as a "threat" that then justified massacres, ethnic cleansing and the formal acquisition of territory.[11] The same dynamics occurred in 1898 when the government, supported by the "yellow press", asserted that Spain constituted a security threat to the United States and thus had to be removed from Cuba and the Philippines. In the 1980s, when the Cold War was winding down, numerous analysts and novelists began to portray Japan as a threat to American economic – and, ultimately, military – predominance in the world. The Japanese economic "miracle", had it continued into the 1990s, might well have led to a serious revision of American thinking about threats to security. After 1991, when the world indeed did seem to have no serious security concerns, the senior Bush administration began casting around for new enemies to protect against. The first candidates were the drug lords of Colombia, Peru and Bolivia. New strategies for fighting the "war on drugs" were developed, and even an aircraft carrier was sent off the coast of Colombia to patrol leaky drug waterways. The Clinton administration failed to come up with a new threatening foe, and as a result, defence spending declined significantly. The junior Bush administration began an earnest overhaul of military priorities and spending in 2001 and began to recast China as America's new threat and adversary. The anti-missile defence programme, ostensibly a shield against a rogue state such as North Korea, is really aimed at China. However, the attack of 11 September 2001 changed the artwork of threat construction. Al-Qaeda provided enough evidence of a *real* threat, one that was more actual than just the potential offered by China.

Americans, as Robert Kagan avers, see themselves as living in a Hobbesian world.[12] It is a world of never-ending potential and actual threats. Americans – though I would not argue uniquely so – seem uncomfortable without someone to fear, or someone who has to be bested in ideological, economic and military dimensions. The problem Kagan fails to acknowledge is that it is often American *actions* (not *reactions*) that create a Hobbesian world. As we have seen, contemporary American "defence" policies are likely to become self-fulfilling prophecies. Enemies will emerge simply because they want to protect themselves from American sanctions, attacks and intervention. And in doing this, they will constitute a "threat" to the United States. This characteristic sets a permissive environment where American governments can justify the use of force so long as the threat is painted to be serious enough. A combination of "hair trigger" preventive military doctrines, military deployments with first-strike implications, and a fearful population are the ingredients for future "wars of choice" that are threats to international peace and security.

Extreme meliorism

The United States is another in a list of regimes that have taken upon themselves the universal task of "liberating" the world's oppressed. The armies of the French Revolutionary regime, after 1791, fought deep into the heart of Europe to "liberate" the peoples there from the yoke of monarchical despotism. Napoleon, in his early years of military leadership, fought under a similar banner. European and American imperial programmes in the late nineteenth century were undertaken primarily for strategic and prestige reasons, but they were sold to gullible publics under the rubric of "lifting" and "liberating" the uncivilized world of savages, pagans and barbarians. Lenin's vision of the world he wanted to create also involved the liberation of the proletariat from the exploitation they suffered under capitalism and imperialism. In his rhetoric – and following the neofundamentalism of his entourage – George W. Bush has embraced the same historical role for the United States. It is to serve as the vehicle for God's plan of the ultimate gift of freedom for all. Bush buttresses this historical task with more practical considerations. He has adopted the democratic peace theory, asserting that the best long-term solution to the problem of terrorism is to bring democracy to the world. A world of democracies will be a world at peace. This is not mere campaign rhetoric. It is the universalization of Paul Wolfowitz's more modest scheme for bringing peace to the Middle East via the forceful removal of Saddam Hussein.

These extreme meliorist solutions to the problem of war and terrorism fail to acknowledge the unanticipated consequences of using force to "make the world safe for democracy," and thereby universal peace. The French onslaughts on despotism in Europe brought forth Napoleon's empire and the succeeding world war. Lenin's dreams (though he pursued them mostly through revolution and subversion rather than classical aggression) led neither to peace nor to democracy. Wilson's "war to make the world safe for democracy" resulted in *diktat* of Versailles, the serial aggressions of the 1930s, and World War II, the most destructive war in history. The track record of universal "liberation" is not impressive if both peace and democracy are the desired outcomes. Moreover, there is a fundamental contradiction between military-meliorist schemes and the Westphalian principles underlying the Charter of the United Nations. Those principles embrace political pluralism and tolerance (though not an unlimited tolerance). The non-interference rule is there to protect against those who believe that they know the best political arrangements for *all* societies, and who are willing to use military force to effect those arrangements. Sovereignty and "liberation" cannot coexist. The present administration in Washington has chosen the latter value and, for its troubles, it can expect the real or hypothetical targets of "liberation" to take the necessary means – including weapons of mass destruction – to deter the United States. The "liberation" of Iraq has cost over 100,000 lives as of the time of writing, and thousands more victims are to be expected before anything resembling a stable political order can emerge in that country. Of course "liberation" has to be tempered by prudence. Judging from recent announcements in Washington, neither Iran nor North Korea is under serious consideration for armed "liberation", primarily because the costs would be too great. Indeed, there is mounting evidence that the liberation theology is more an expression of ultimate aspiration than a commitment to repeat the Iraq adventure in any "outposts of tyranny". If the Bush administration were seriously committed to "liberation", then it should be preparing operations against Cuba, Uzbekistan and Saudi Arabia, as well as against rogue regimes. This is unlikely to happen.

Future problems of the hegemon

The greatest structural problem facing the world in the coming decades arises from the dramatic economic and somewhat more muted military growth of China. The American-based literature on China spans a wide range of future possibilities. Some characterize China as increasingly embedded in the institutions and norms of the international system and, aside from the problem of Taiwan, unlikely to provide a serious challenge to United States' supremacy. At the other extreme, there is the argument that China, like all great powers before it, will seek unification through armed force, establish hegemony over Southeast Asia and Korea, challenge Japan, ultimately seek to exclude American influence from Asia, and establish a military capacity with worldwide reach. If we borrow Robert Gilpin's analytical model for great power behaviour, then we can expect either of two outcomes: a China that accepts a position of inferiority to the United States, or an armed conflict between the status quo power and the challenger – meaning a world war.[13] This is not the place to evaluate the various arguments about China's future policies, but it may be germane to refer back to the historical propensity of the United States to construct an enemy, even if it is benign, and to launch a dynamic security dilemma. The possibility of creating self-fulfilling prophecies cannot be underestimated.

The privatization of armed power: a new medievalism?

International peace and security as defined in both the United Nations Charter and in the vast literature on security studies no longer adequately covers the full panoply of acute security problems in the contemporary international system. One set of statistics supports the point. According to the 2002 UN *Human Development Report* (p. 11), in the 1990s, 220,000 people died as a result of classical interstate wars and armed interventions. In the same period about 3.5 million people perished from armed conflicts fought mostly *within* states.[14] The analytical categories of old-fashioned realism continue to have some theoretical utility, but they refer only to a limited segment of the security pie. We increasingly live in a world where its main features include political decentralization, the fracturing of states and the rapid proliferation of armed non-state actors.

Hedley Bull coined the phrase "new medievalism".[15] He referred to a future scenario in which states collapse or weaken to be replaced by a decentralized world in which public authority gives way to multiple loyalties configured around private power centres of criminal networks, non-governmental organizations, and a plethora of quasi public associations built around ethnic groups, cities, churches, and the like. Of all the possible scenarios Bull concocted the "new medievalism" seemed the least likely.

However, in some areas of the world we have witnessed the increasing disjunction between statehood (public authority) and the growth of private power centres, many of them armed. Amnesty International lists 176 armed groups operating in 64 countries. The Federation of American Scientists lists more than 380.[16] An estimated global total of insurgents and other non-state combatants, as well as armed militias, lists 183,000 as active, 150,000 as semi-active, and 234,000 combatants serving in militias.[17] We do not have reliable data on the growth rate of these armed power nodules, but we do have evidence about the steady increase in global trafficking in light weapons. This would be one indicator of the expansion of armed private power centres.[18] Thanks to giant leftovers from the Cold War, the sale of such weapons by states to other states and sometimes to groups within those states, purchases on the open market, and extensive networks of "grey" and "black" arms traffickers, all of these conduits service a multitude of private groups, encompassing secessionist movements, warlords, millenarian movements, militias, terrorist groups, private armies, and private security firms. An estimated $6 to $8 billion worth of weapons provided to the Afghan *mujahedeen* by the United States and China to fight the Soviet Union in the 1980s has flowed into Pakistan and surrounding territories since the Soviet withdrawal in 1988.[19] After the American-led attack on Iraq in 2003, approximately seven million weapons suddenly "leaked" to the population, forming the basis for the armed insurgency against the coalition and its "collaborators" among Iraqi officials and conscripts of the police and new army.[20] Experts who study light arms trafficking conclude that, while such arms do not cause the numerous armed conflicts littering the contemporary world landscape, their huge numbers and easy availability help cause local arms races and dramatically increase the probability of open warfare.

We often underestimate the significance of armed private power as a structural characteristic of the contemporary international system. The phenomenon is thriving and probably escalating primarily in weak, post-colonial states, many of which are or have been wracked by never-ending wars. But it appears elsewhere as well. During the wars in former-Yugoslavia, as many as 80 private militias, only under weak influence of state authorities, roamed the battlefields and villages, cleansing ethnic communities, pillaging, running drugs and arms, raping, and organizing slave labour.[21] In many places, such as the Congo, Angola, Liberia, Sierra Leone, and elsewhere, such groups have plundered national resources, thus turning Clausewitz inside out: war has become a means of conducting business by clandestine means.[22]

Students of armed force agree that since 1945 there has been a dramatic escalation of civil wars of various kinds (secession, taking control of state power, wars to exterminate rivals such as ethnic groups, plunder, ideological foes, and the like).[23] We must not forget that the vast majority of people killed through collective armed violence since 1945 have been the victims of their own governments – a monumental reversal of Hobbes's *Leviathan*, which had the main purpose of maintaining peace within a society.[24] In some contemporary states, the government not only fails to provide security for the state's inhabitants but also has become their main tormentor. In some cases these predatory states have become the instigators of mass killing precisely because they confronted pockets of private armed power that denied them the monopoly over the legitimate use of force that they sought in mimicking European states. Thanks to the growing prevalence of means of acquiring weapons – the drug trade, illegal exploitation and sale of resources, white slavery, gun running, extortion, and other criminal activities – these private groups have the wherewithal to challenge state authorities in a manner that their sixteenth-century European forebears (dukes, cities, pirates) could only dream about.

However, the "new medievalism" is not an accurate moniker for characterizing the contemporary situation regarding international peace and security. The increasing privatization of armed power in the world today is an unprecedented phenomenon. In the medieval era, the highly decentralized authority structure was based upon a well-developed legal system sanctified by time, law and religion. Armed cities, duchies, and church territories had *rights*. The authority structures of the era were part of an *order* that was legitimized by law and often by the church. There were clear distinctions between the legitimate and illegitimate use of force in such a system.

None of the features of the medieval order is to be found in many areas of the contemporary world. In both, to be sure, power was and is decentralized, but there is a vast difference between power and authority. The European medieval system was also a system of authority (legitimate rule over a public domain). In contemporary Congo, Sudan, Tajikistan, Sri Lanka and Myanmar, to take a few examples, power is decentralized but in many areas it is exercised through force and "facts on the ground," not through legitimate authority. Criminality, coercion and corruption sustain many private power centres (one thinks of UNITA, RUK and RENMANO). And unlike the medieval order, the authorities of many contemporary weak or collapsed states cannot do much about this.

Sources of the problem

The literature on these new kinds of warfare practised by armed non-state actors has expanded rapidly during the past decade, so we need not review it here. However, there is considerable disagreement about their sources. Some emphasize greed, criminality, and the attraction of trying to obtain control over resources such as timber, diamonds, minerals and oil.[25] Others emphasize income inequality and poverty.[26] My analysis of the problem focuses on the legacies of colonialism, the inability of many postcolonial states to make a successful transition from what were essentially precolonial political formations and structures to those of a modern state, and the lack of political legitimacy between populations and governments and among distinct population groups themselves.[27] In many, rulers maintain their positions through corruption and discrimination against minorities and outsiders. Some of the features that these polities have in common are multi-ethnic societies, weak state and government legitimacy, the deliberate exclusion of some portions of the population from access to political office and other types of rewards, and tensions between population groups. Each war, of course, has its unique sources and characteristics. But despite these differences, the similarities in the character of fighting and the sources of the problem are clearly akin. There is a general weak state syndrome that encompasses economic, political, weak legitimacy and resource dimensions that combine to create a high probability of armed violence in some areas of the world.

Whatever the case for gaining a better understanding of the sources of the "wars of national debilitation",[28] it is easy to predict that they are going to be with us for a long time. Sierra Leone, Mozambique, Angola and Liberia may be in post-war phases, with something akin to a restored peace, but new problems in the Congo, Sudan, and now Nigeria have appeared since those earlier limited successes. The problems in the north of Uganda, featuring the depredations of the Lord's Resistance Army, are almost incomprehensible to most analysts, but they continue without respite. The Ivory Coast, once an exemplar of successful transition from colonialism, has at best an unstable cease-fire. Insurgents rule parts of Nepal, Tajikistan, Sri Lanka and Mauritania, and Muslim elements in the south of Thailand are once again active militarily. Afghanistan, Kashmir, Myanmar and Assam remain seemingly intractable problems. The list goes on.

But do these problems constitute threats to international peace and security? The 2004 High-level Panel's report to the Secretary-General, "A More Secure World: Our Shared Responsibility", insists that they do.[29] However, in the past, the states with the greatest capacity to intervene in peacekeeping and other conflict-resolving activities have been highly selective in choosing how and where to become involved. For forty years, they have mostly ignored the problems in Myanmar. They did nothing in Rwanda in 1994, which at least brought some expressions of shame and regret from President Clinton and Kofi Annan, but not from others who were complicit. The current involvement in the Congo is probably insufficient to contain the mess there. The United States may be willing to put diplomatic pressure, and possibly even sanctions, on the government of Sudan over the asserted genocide in Darfur, but China and Russia will have none of it.

But it is doubtful that the great powers, the United Nations, or regional organizations can regularly turn their backs on all of these and similar conflicts of the future. Why not? Because in a world of burgeoning transnational relationships, conflicts in one domain may have dangerous consequences elsewhere. The international drug trade, illicit trade in arms, AIDS and illegal immigration are both the sources and legacies of these "wars". All have direct impacts on countries around the world. Many of these issues have not been "securitized" in some countries, but that does not mean that they fail to have deleterious consequences near and afar. And despite realists' claims that human sympathies play no role in defining interests or influencing policy choices, the compulsions to "do something" in cases of egregious violations of the laws of war and human rights cannot be overlooked. Typical conflicts in weak or collapsed states may not pose immediate threats outside their perimeters, but a direct military threat to the homeland is not a necessary condition for intervening in one form or another. The United States would not have intervened in Somalia or Yugoslavia if the only condition triggering this type of response was a direct threat to American interests at home or abroad. Finally, the locales of these wars may become the safe havens for illicit drug cartels and for transnational terrorist groups whose interests *are* to attack various homelands. It is not by coincidence that the staging and training areas of Al-Qaeda were the Sudan and Afghanistan, both fractured states in which violence had debilitated the structures of government authority. Governments are only slowly beginning to realize that weak and collapsing states, all suffering from vast legitimacy deficits and poor governmental capacities, may become the main headquarters for non-state armed groups and terrorists dedicated to causes that constitute threats to international peace and security.[30]

Terrorism

Terror has become a fixation, perhaps an obsession, in academic and policy-making circles in the United States, Russia, and a few other countries. George W. Bush has constantly reiterated that his "war on terror" is a global campaign designed to "root out" the evil-doers who are assaulting "civilization itself". The events of 9/11 have traumatized an entire country; its government has not spared efforts to use the campaign against terror as the defining issue of the administration. Terror is *the* issue of international peace and security, in this view. In his forceful way of portraying the complex world in terms of simple good/bad dichotomies, Bush has laid down the gauntlet: those who do not join the campaign against terror and its hosts are enemies of the United States. International peace and security, in this view, is no longer defined in terms of the United Nations Charter, but according to the priorities set by one government after enduring a traumatizing attack on its homeland.

The loss of thousands of innocent lives, whether in the United States, Israel, Palestine, Iraq, or elsewhere, is not a trivial matter.[31] One cannot fail to act to prevent such acts, as almost all governments have done since that fateful September day in 2001. However, is there a reasonable relationship between risks and costs? The September attacks on the United

States killed almost 3,000 Americans and hundreds of non-Americans. The response has been a homeland security programme that, to date, has cost almost one hundred billion dollars, an attack on Iraq that has cost more than two hundred billion dollars (and rising), a Patriot Act that challenges some fundamental freedoms of the American constitution and Bill of Rights, the systematic use of torture, *contra* the Geneva Conventions, the alienation of American allies, the lowest standing of the United States in world opinion *ever*, and the probable swelling of recruits to various terrorist causes. In contrast, the American response to the 30,000 fatalities caused annually by handguns has been to allow a law banning the public sale of military assault weapons to lapse! Such disconnects confirm the utility of the Copenhagen School's concept of "securitization".[32] Security is what people make of it. Apparently in the United States, a security threat exists only if it comes from outside American borders. For domestic political reasons, no one in the United States defines 30,000 people killed annually by their fellow citizens as a security problem. By the same token, it should not be surprising that many people in the world, particularly in countries that have not experienced a terrorist problem, do not share the American view that terrorism is the ultimate threat to international peace and security.

The literature on terrorism is vast and growing. Definitions abound and categories proliferate. To declare a "war" on something as nebulous and undifferentiated as "terror" will inevitably lead to operational problems and charges of hypocrisy (e.g. declare political opponents "terrorists" while ignoring state-based terror) and double standards. While it may not add much precision, at least we must distinguish terrorist tactics (e.g. the deliberate targeting of innocent civilians) used by political groups such as liberation movements, secessionist movements, and resisters to foreign occupation, from the same tactics used by millenarian and apocalyptic groups whose purposes are as vague as "a new coming", "the elimination of evil from the world", or "jihad". Terrorist tactics have been used in asymmetrical warfare since ancient times. In the modern era, there have been left-wing terrorists, right-wing terrorists, ethnonationalist/separatist terrorists, and "sacred" terrorists.[33] American armed forces, militias, posses, and other quasi-military formations used terror in the extermination and ethnic cleansing of native Indians. The Stern Group and Irgun used terror against the British and selected Arabs in their campaign to conquer Palestine. In Cyprus, Kenya, Vietnam, Malaya, Burma, and countless other colonial territories, terror was an integral part of violent independence campaigns. It continues today in Chechnya, Kashmir, and elsewhere. But when Americans and others use the term "war on terror", what they really have in mind is the need to respond primarily to one network – Al-Qaeda – and to its acolytes and mimics around the world.

Since the attacks of 11 September 2001, there have been many calls to approach the problem of terror through better understanding of its sources, aims, values and appeal. Despite the obvious need for systematic study of such an important phenomenon, at this stage no consensus is even beginning to appear. The main type of terrorism that is truly a disrupter of "international peace and security" is that placed in a millenarian-political category, those individuals and their networks that see themselves engaged in a Manichean struggle of good against evil, who are convinced that they are working according to God's plan, who believe that, therefore, they cannot be constrained by secular laws and values, and whose ultimate purpose is to achieve a vague image of a perfect world built upon the ruins of the evil crusader, modernist culture.[34]

The main candidates for the aetiology of contemporary religious-based terrorism include:

1. Poverty. It is now largely disproved. For example, most of the 9/11 attackers came from middle-class origins and were highly educated. Studies show no correlation between the two phenomena.[35] We must recall, also, that the amount of poverty in the world three decades ago was greater than today, but in that period religiously based terrorism was a rarity.
2. Fear, including the threats to patriarchy, family structure, and the virtue of women arising from the invasion of Western and largely American popular culture into the Muslim world. That popular culture has largely erased the line between pornography and entertainment, promotes violence and homosexuality, impugns female modesty, and denigrates the family in favour of promiscuity. In brief, Western modernity represents an all-encompassing threat to Muslim culture, sensibilities, values and religion.
3. Religiosity, that is, living a life consistent with one's interpretation of religious values and commands. That form of religiosity is not open to interpretation or debate, but is truly revealed as the only *truth*.
4. Culture. Some have suggested that certain characteristics of Muslim culture make it resistant to change. It lacks a tradition of self-criticism. Members of this culture tend to blame their own failures on outside, malevolent forces.[36]
5. Globalization. Economic forces, particularly the free market, contractualist economic order symbolized by the United States threatens the clientelist, traditional forms of economic exchange in many developing countries. According to Mousseau, "To win the war against terrorism, the United States and other market democracies must remove the

underlying cause of terror: the deeply embedded anti-market rage brought on by the forces of globalization."[37]

This is not the appropriate venue to evaluate these competing, but sometimes complementary, explanations of the religious-terrorist phenomenon. Most have their persuasive points if not systematic confirming evidence. However, a *political* explanation is conspicuously missing from this roster. Yet, what is clear from the evidence gleamed about the 9/11 attackers, and from anyone who bothers to consult the media, governments, and innumerable political groups in the Middle East, is the antipathy toward the United States for its policies in the region. From their perspective, the United States has been a consistent supporter of Israeli expansionism into lands populated for centuries by the Palestinians. While proclaiming almost on a daily basis American support for a "just and lasting peace", the United States has failed to censure those Israeli policies that make such an outcome impossible. From this perspective, a form of perpetual hypocrisy characterizes American policy.[38] To take one example. In 2002/2003 President Bush reiterated almost daily the international sins of Saddam Hussein: he attacked his neighbours; he possessed (not "he *may*" possess) weapons of mass destruction; and he defied United Nations resolutions. The problem here is that if these charges are correct, they would apply equally to Israel and to the United States itself. It is not difficult to imagine that when in the Spring of 2004 President Bush and Prime Minister Blair announced their support of Prime Minister Sharon's plan unilaterally to annex some of the occupied territories in the West Bank to save important but illegal Jewish settlements there, dozens, perhaps hundreds, of Muslims joined the terrorist cause. Analyses of the sources of terrorism that focus on psychology, culture, and economics, but fail to include political/diplomatic variables, are of limited explanatory value. One cannot overlook motivation that arises out of strong perceptions of injustice, hypocrisy and double standards. While a more even-handed policy on the Palestine issue would not solve the problem of terrorism, it is certainly a necessary component.

This raises the question whether terrorism, like wars within weak or collapsing states and problems arising from American hegemony, can be characterized as a structural feature of the contemporary and future international system. The High-Level Panel's 2004 report to the Secretary-General of the United Nations lists terrorism as the fifth of six main security problems confronting a reformed UN. We can be fairly certain that wars between and within states, infections, poverty, environmental degradation, proliferation of weapons of mass destruction, and transnational organized crime will constitute threats to many societies in the coming decades. Can we say the same about "jihadist" terrorism? No one can offer a certain answer. However, if we count the number of victims of "jihadist" terrorism as a metric of threat, and compare it to the victims of domestic wars, human rights abuses, and genocide or "politicides",[39] then clearly terrorism of this particular type is not a major threat, comparatively speaking. Since 9/11, there have been major assaults in Indonesia, Spain, Saudi Arabia and London. We may not know for a long time how many other attacks were foiled by police and intelligence agencies around the world. However, annual casualties around the world (again, excluding terrorist incidents associated with liberation movements, anti-occupation forces, separatist groups, and the like) since 9/11 is well under 1,000, whereas the victims of domestic wars surpass that number almost daily.[40] "Jihadist" terrorism arose quickly, only in the last decade of the twentieth century. The terrorists of previous decades – the Bader-Meinhoff gang, the Red Brigade, Italian neo-fascist groups, and their mimics – seldom lasted more than ten years. There is at least some possibility that, as increasing numbers of "jihadists" are captured or killed, and as many of their murderous bombing projects are foiled, the problem will abate to the point where it can no longer be considered a significant threat to international peace and security. This is not a prediction, but a possible projection. Although the United Nations has declared terrorism a threat to international peace and security under Chapter VII of the Charter (Security Council Resolution 1371, 2001), within a decade the persistence of civil wars, armed interventions, and a re-established security dilemma involving China and the United States will likely constitute greater threats.

The security agenda and multilateralism

The first institutionalized mechanism for dealing with the consequences of anarchy – war and potential hegemony – was the Concert of Europe. It developed a set of norms about appropriate great power behaviour. In some cases these norms worked as reasonably effective constraints on shaping interests and ambitions. In many others, they were significantly ignored. The essential ideas of the Concert worked their way into the League of Nations Covenant and the United Nations Charter, where primarily responsibility for the maintenance of international peace and security were lodged squarely in the Council and the Security Council, respectively. But throughout the twentieth century, these mechanisms of multilateralism played only a partial role in dealing with the paramount security issues of the day. In the 1930s, there was an institutional vacuum, as neither the League of Nations nor traditional alliances were effective mechanism for dealing with the dictators' threats to international peace and security. During the Cold War, mutual assured destruction (MAD) was the main instrumentality for limiting the ambitions of the great powers and muffling the occasional crises that occurred in their mutual relations. The United Nations played only a peripheral role in the most dangerous crises of the era, whether over Berlin, Cuba, Vietnam, or in Sino-Soviet relations. It is not appropriate, therefore, to contrast the problem of contemporary multilateralism on security issues with some imagined era of greater international cooperation. The multilateralism of the Cold War era, for example, was primarily *within* alliances, not between them. The American attack on Iraq was nothing new: its structural features found precedents in the Soviet invasions of Hungary (1956) and Czechoslovakia (1968), the Israeli–British–French invasion of the Suez Canal in 1956, and numerous armed interventions by the United States in the Caribbean and Central America throughout the twentieth century. But there was a difference because, unlike these previous cases, in 2002–2003 the United States and Great Britain went to the United Nations and resorted to armed force only after failing to obtain a permissive resolution from the Security Council. We must not assume that multilateralism necessarily results in international consensus. Multilateralism is primarily a process and set of procedures, the outcomes of which are always problematic. Sometimes unilateralism can produce better outcomes for the international community than multilateralism, so long as it supports what John Ruggie calls "generalized principles of conduct" (universal norms).[41] What must be judged is less the processes than the outcomes.

Of the issues on the contemporary security agenda, all but the potential threat posed by the United States lend themselves to multilateral forms of management or solution. The problems of weak and failing states resist collective solutions to some extent (primarily because of indifference and the rule of non-intervention), but the sovereignty norm has not precluded collective action under Chapter VII of the Charter. Simply by constructing any situation as a threat to international peace and security, the Security Council can authorize various forms of collective action, as it has done at least 15 times since the first call to arms in the Korean case in 1950. Moreover, the major players at the UN Summit in 2005 gave guarded support to the principle of a collective responsibility to protect and assist victims of systematic government abuse and human rights violations, with armed force if necessary, without the consent of the government in question. The principle of a responsibility to protect constitutes a major new norm in international relations, but actions would remain reactive rather than proactive.

Governments have not collectively developed joint and comprehensive strategies for dealing with the generic problem of state collapse, civil wars, wars of secession, and the like. By comprehensive, I mean collective and shared foreign aid, trade, arms sales, democracy promotion, and other related policies (including quarantines). Governments continue to fashion aid policies unilaterally, and often proceed on a project-by-project basis without any reference to an overall collective strategy for dealing with the worst problems that are potentially threatening to the international community.[42] To address the fundamental problem of the consequences of weak and collapsing states and the multiplication of private, non-state armed power groups and networks, the international community needs to develop effective diagnostic and early warning tools, plans for collective preventative actions, and joint policies.[43] This requirement smacks of meliorism, but it is different from "liberation". The main purpose is to offer assistance in maintaining statehood so that the luxurious growth of private, armed non-state actors will end or even wither. Effective statehood must precede democratization.

In the case of terrorism, the response has been global in scope, if not in depth. Police and intelligence agencies from numerous countries routinely collaborate in identifying, monitoring and apprehending terrorist suspects. Even President Bush, who invoked the metaphor of the "war on terror", admitted in the days following 9/11 that this "war" would combine numerous capabilities, not just armed force. The general public is unaware of the large amount of multilateral collaboration that takes place, primarily because of the need for secrecy. At the public level, the Security Council has defined terrorism as a threat to international peace and security and it approved the American attack on Afghanistan. These actions indicate clearly the collective view of the international community as regards terror as a political tactic. It has been declared illegitimate. Multilateralism in this domain seems to work both as process and as norm-support.

The problem of the United States is more difficult. In the prevailing mood in the United States (which may, of course, change over time), the uncertainties associated with multilateral procedures and international norms may vitiate effective action. The American preventive attack doctrine reflects awareness that threats can be so severe that lengthy debates, investigations and monitoring – the usual procedures employed in dealing with traditional issues of international peace and security – will amplify rather than help confront the threat. Multilateral procedures will either have to address American security concerns or, as the President himself has threatened, become irrelevant. Moreover, one could argue that in forming a "coalition of the willing", the United States is employing multilateral means for engaging in the "war on terror". As noted, it bypassed the United Nations only when that body, in Washington's view, abrogated its responsibility to deal with Saddam Hussein's chronic disregard of Security Council resolutions. The initial coalition was fairly broad, although only a few countries placed troops on the ground. However, the attack was not in support of universal norms, nor was it consistent with the emerging norm of collective force authorization. International multilateral diplomacy has not come to an end because the United States occasionally defects from the majority. The concern is not so much a United States that acts unilaterally as opposed to multilaterally, but one that takes actions inconsistent with many of the objectives sought by the rest of the international community, one that proclaims rights and actions for itself while denying them to others, one that through its actions actually exacerbates the problems it is trying to remedy, and one that manufactures threats that may not exist in reality. These are serious intellectual problems born of deep trauma caused by 9/11, certain contemporary American social conditions, and a long history of creating the very problems that are then signified as "threats". The best one can hope for is that through the slow procedures of ordinary diplomacy, both bilateral and multilateral, America's friends and allies will vigorously seek to change attitudes and perceptions, and point out the vast costs to American prestige, leadership and "soft power" that continued violation of community norms will extract.[44]

Notes

1. My thanks to the editors of the volume and to Michael Byers, Wade Huntley, Brian Job, Paul Marantz, Dick Price, and Katja Coleman for helpful suggestions on an earlier version.
2. *Retreat of Doomsday: The Obsolescence of Major War*, New York: Basic Books, 1989.
3. Data from K.J. Holsti (2004) *Taming the Sovereigns: Institutional Change in International Politics*, Cambridge, Cambridge University Press, p. 310; Meredith Sarkees, Frank Wayman and J. David Singer (2003) "Inter-state, intra-state and extra-state wars: a comprehensive look at their distribution over time", *International Studies Quarterly* 47(1): 49–79; James D. Fearon and David D. Laitin (2003) "Ethnicity, insurgency, and civil war", *American Political Science Review* 97(1): 75–90. A more recent study, using different categories of violence and different cut-off points, supports the general trend of declining interstate wars but also notes a significant decrease in intra-state wars since the early 1990s. See Andrew Mack (ed.) *Human Security Report 2005*, Human Security Centre, Liu Institute of Global Issues, University of British Columbia, Vancouver, Canada.
4. Holsti (2004) *Taming the Sovereigns*, p. 310.
5. A list of major aggressions since the late seventeenth century is in K.J. Holsti (2005) "The use of force in international relations: four revolutions", in Ramesh Thakur (ed.) *The Iraq Crisis and World Order*, Vol. I. *Arms Control, Disarmament, and Nonproliferation Challenges*, Tokyo: United Nations University Press, in press.
6. Some might claim that Osama bin-Laden is such a dreamer, but I know of no visions of a future world that are as concrete as those of Hitler and Stalin. Mere plans to destroy infidels, Jews, and crusaders do not constitute a coherent political programme.
7. Paul Sharp (2004) "Virtue unrestrained: Herbert Butterfield and the problem of American power", *International Studies Perspectives* 5(3): 300–15.

8. NSPD-17 available at www.fas.org/irp/offdocs/nspd-17.html.
9. United States, The National Security Adviser, Memorandum to the President, "Impact of the 2002 National Security Strategy on Reshaping America's Military", 2002, available at http://www.cfr.org/pdf/Military_CPI_addendum.pdf.
10. Reported in Bob Herbert (2004) "For Bush, real life just gets in the way", *International Herald Tribune*, October 23–24, p. 7.
11. Richard Drinnon (1997) *Facing West: The Metaphysics of Indian-Hating and Empire-Building*, Norman, OK: University of Oklahoma Press.
12. *Of Paradise and Power: America and Europe in the New World Order*, New York: Alfred A. Knopf, 2003.
13. See his *War and Change in World Politics*, Cambridge: Cambridge University Press, 1981.
14. United Nations Development Programme (2002) *Human Development Report*, Oxford: Oxford University Press.
15. Hedley Bull (1979) *The Anarchical Society*, New York: Macmillan, ch. 10.
16. See Amnesty International's 2004 Report. The data for the Federation of American Scientists are available in its report "Liberation Movements, Terrorist Organizations, Substance Cartels, and Other Para-state Entities", available at www.fas.org/irp/world/para.
17. Figures are in Graduate Institute of International Studies (2001) *Small Arms Survey 2001: Profiling the Problem*, Oxford: Oxford University Press, p. 79.
18. Figures can be obtained in the annual publication, *Small Arms Survey*.
19. Tara Kartha (1999) "Controlling the black and grey markets in small arms in South Asia", in Jeffrey Boutwell and Michael T. Klare (eds) *Light Weapons and Civil Conflict: Controlling the Tools of Violence*, Lanham, MD: Rowman and Littlefield, p. 49.
20. Graduate Institute of International Studies, Geneva (2004) *Small Arms Survey 2004: Rights and Risk*, Oxford: Oxford University Press.
21. Vesna Bojicic and Mary Kaldor (n.d.) "The political economy of war in Bosnia-Herzegovina", in Mary Kaldor and Bashker Vashee (eds) *Restructuring the Global Military Sector*, Vol. 1: *New Wars*, London and Washington D.C.: Frances Pinter for the United Nations University, p. 159.
22. Peter Andreas (2004) "The clandestine political economy of war and peace in Bosnia", *International Studies Quarterly* 48(1): 30.
23. For statistics, see the references in endnote No. 4.
24. Rudolph Rummel (1994) *Death by Government*, New Brunswick, NJ: Transaction Books.
25. James Fairhead (2000) "The conflict over natural and environmental resources", in E. Wayne Nafziger, Frances Stewart and Raimo Väyrynen (eds) *War, Hunger and Displacement: The Origins of Humanitarian Emergencies*. Oxford: Oxford University Press, pp. 147–78; David Keen, "War, Crime, and Access to Resources", in Nafziger, Stewart and Raimo Väyrynen (eds) (2000), pp. 283–304. For a more balanced view, see Karen Ballentine and Jake Sherman (eds) (2003) *The Political Economy of Armed Conflict: Beyond Greed and Grief*, Boulder CO: Lynn Rienner.
26. E. Wayne Nafziger and Juha Auvinen (2003) *Economic Development, Inequality and War*, New York: Palgrave-Macmillan. The High-Level Panel's report *A More Secure World* also links poverty to security threats.
27. Cf., K.J. Holsti (1996) *The State, War, and the State of War*, Cambridge: Cambridge University Press; K.J. Holsti (2000) "The political sources of humanitarian emergencies", in Nafziger, Stewart, and Väyrynen (eds) *War, Hunger and Displacement*, pp. 239–281.
28. The expression is introduced in Leslie Gelb (1994) "Quelling the teacup wars", *Foreign Affairs* 73: 2–6.
29. Available at www.un.org/secureworld.

30. Cf., Robert H. Dorff (2005) "Failed states after 9/11: What did we know and what have we learned?", *International Studies Perspectives* 6(1): 20–34.
31. Approximately 100,000 Iraqi dead (combining Sadam's armed forces, insurgents and civilians) since March 2003 might not agree with the American president's assertion that the world is much safer since the capture of Saddam Hussein.
32. Cf., Ole Waever (2004) "Aberystwyth, Paris, Copenhagen: new 'schools' in security theory", paper presented at the annual meetings of the International Studies Association, Montreal, March 17–20, p. 9.
33. Audrey Kurth Cronin (2002/2003) "Behind the curve: globalization and international terrorism", *International Security* 27(3): 30–58.
34. Ibid.
35. Cf., Michael Mousseau (2002/2003) "Market civilization and its clash with terror", *International Security* 27(3): 5–6.
36. Ibid., p. 8.
37. Ibid., p. 24.
38. In a tape released 30 October 2004, Osama bin Laden refers to the 1982 Israeli invasion of Lebanon, supported by the United States, as a defining moment in the development of his view of the necessity to punish America for its pro-Israeli policies.
39. Rudolf Rummel introduced the term in his *Death by Government*, 1994.
40. There is a serious debate about trends in terrorist incidents and victims. US State Department figures reveal a decline in "severe" incidents over the past few years. The State Department report is available at www.state.gov/s/ct/rls/pgtrpt/2003/33771.htm. However, other studies dispute the methodology of these studies and insist that both incidents and victims have increased recently. It should be noted that these studies include insurgency terrorist acts in Iraq in the database. If these were eliminated, there would be no significant increase in the trend. For further details see Mack (ed.) *Human Security Report 2005*, pp. 42–46.
41. "Multilateralism: the anatomy of an institution," in John G. Ruggie (ed.) (1993) *Multilateralism Matters*, New York: Columbia University Press, pp. 10–12.
42. Cf., Dorff, "Failed states after 9/11", p. 30.
43. This argument runs parallel to views expressed in the report, *A More Secure World*, especially paragraph 56.
44. There is evidence that in Bush's second term the verbal hubris of unilateralism and exceptionalism has become more muted.

11

Weapons of mass destruction

Trevor Findlay

The abject failure of the seventh review conference for the 1968 Nuclear Non-Proliferation Treaty (NPT) in June 2005 is but the latest evidence of the stresses and strains under which multilateral approaches to so-called weapons of mass destruction (WMD)[1] are currently operating. Further evidence may be found in the continuing deadlock at the Conference on Disarmament (CD) over its agenda, the collapse of negotiations on a biological weapons verification protocol, the non-entry into force of the 1996 Comprehensive Nuclear Test Ban Treaty (CTBT), the lack of progress in commencing negotiations on the long-heralded fissile material cut-off treaty (FMCT) and uncertainty over the future of the UN Monitoring, Verification and Inspection Commission (UNMOVIC). Most recently, the "outcome document" of the UN Summit in September 2005 contained no reference at all to disarmament or non-proliferation, an outcome that UN Secretary-General Kofi Annan described as "a real disgrace".[2]

The pivotal player in all of these dramas is the United States. The Republican administration of George W. Bush has been particularly unilateralist and obstructionist in respect of multilateral activity pertaining to WMD. It has adopted an à la carte approach, grudgingly accepting multilateral activity where it furthers American interests (sometimes only American interests), while rejecting it if in any way it impinges on US options – sometimes even when there might be net benefit to US political, military and strategic interests.

Yet it would be wrong to assume that the Bush administration is solely responsible for the malaise that currently faces much multilateral endeavour in the WMD realm. The US is only able to act the way it does because of the wider international context. This chapter seeks to understand the deeper roots of the problem, both the long-term structural and the short-term circumstantial. In doing so it will take into account the panoply of treaties, institutions and arrangements that constitute the multilateral arms control, disarmament and non-proliferation regimes dealing with WMD – defined here as nuclear, radiological, chemical and biological – and their associated delivery systems and technologies.

The multilateral WMD world

Multilateralism attempts to deal with weapons of mass destruction and associated issues through a variety of treaties, verification and implementation bodies, secretariats and negotiation and discussion forums. The most notable of the WMD treaties are the CTBT, the NPT, the 1993 Chemical Weapons Convention (CWC) and the 1972 Biological Weapons Convention (BWC), along with their verification organizations (where they exist). These comprise the nascent Comprehensive Nuclear Test Ban Treaty Organization (CTBTO), the International Atomic Energy Agency (IAEA) and the Organization for the Prohibition of Chemical Weapons (OPCW). Although threadbare, the extant institutional elements for the BWC, namely, confidence-building measures and the UN Secretary-General's mechanism for investigating alleged use of chemical and biological weapons, also need to be taken into account. In addition to these universal multilateral institutions, there are regional multilateral arrangements, principally nuclear weapon-free zones and their secretariats.[3]

Among the UN bodies mandated to deal with WMD issues, the most notable are the CD, which is supposed to negotiate new multilateral WMD treaties, the First Committee of the UN General Assembly, which annually considers a range of security and disarmament issues and adopts non-binding resolutions, and the UN Disarmament Commission (UNDC), intended to provide an opportunity for deeper deliberation, but not negotiation. In addition, within the UN Secretariat the Department of Disarmament Affairs (UNDDA) promotes disarmament, services meetings and conferences and provides secretariat support to the multilateral treaties that lack their own organization. Finally, there is the Security Council. As well as having the authority to deal with any WMD challenge that it perceives to be a threat to international peace and security, the Council is also charged with handling WMD non-compliance cases that are too difficult for individual treaty regimes to manage themselves.

There are, in addition, quasi-multilateral arrangements that are gaining increasing prominence and attention as part of the global "regimes" that deal with WMD. They are a species of "coalition of the willing" – groups of countries, invariably led by the US, which coordinate their WMD policies. Their aim is to deny potential or actual proliferant countries the benefits of the know-how, materials and technologies needed for WMD and their delivery systems. Such arrangements include the Nuclear Suppliers Group (NSG), the Zangger Committee, the Australia Group, the Missile Technology Control Regime (MTCR), the Proliferation Security Initiative (PSI) and the various cooperative threat reduction programs, including the Group of Eight's Global Partnership Against the Spread of Weapons and Materials of Mass Destruction.[4] Sometimes known as "plurilateral" arrangements, these will be considered here only in juxtaposition to truly multilateral endeavours that are open to universal membership.

Structural change: the rise of the hegemon

One of the most obvious recent changes in the international environment that has affected the way that WMD issues are dealt with multilaterally is the rise of the US as international hegemon – politically, economically and militarily. In the WMD field US military strengthening is readily apparent. One striking measure is that by 2006 American military spending may exceed that of the rest of the world combined.[5] Most of this budget, it is true, will be spent on conventional weapons rather than WMD, including sizeable operational costs for the continuation of the war in Iraq. But the sheer size of the US military budget, and the high technology-based conventional war machine that it provides, has several implications for multilateral WMD endeavours. First, it will stoke the belief of countries like North Korea and Iran that they can resist US hegemony only by acquiring WMD. Against overwhelming US conventional military superiority (notwithstanding its inability to prevail readily in Iraq), WMD will continue to be perceived as the "poor man's equalizer". Second, it will reinforce US perceptions of its exceptionalism. As the world's most powerful state it is able to portray itself as the universal defender and ultimate guarantor of freedom and democracy for a world of lesser states. From Washington's perspective the implication is that disarmament need not apply to the US, but only to others. Finally, in practice, the US military budget is large enough to accommodate measures that will enhance the leading edge that the US has in WMD capabilities – both offensive and defensive – which, in turn, has implications for the negotiation asymmetry that complicates multilateral negotiations on WMD.

US WMD capabilities

In the nuclear arena the US is by any measure the most capable nuclear weapon state on the planet. Despite significant cuts in its nuclear forces since the end of the Cold War, and plans to halve the current stockpile from 10,000 to 5,000 by 2012,[6] the US has, unlike the Russians, retained an assured, credible deterrent based on a triad of missiles, submarines and aircraft. It is able to afford a sophisticated stockpile reliability programme that permits it to retain, and perhaps even improve, its nuclear arsenal without nuclear testing.[7] Despite the promise of the 2002 Nuclear Posture Review that nuclear and conventional strategies would be integrated, this has not yet occurred.[8] At least part of the US strategic nuclear force remains ready to launch on warning (as apparently does part of Russia's). The US is also the only country wealthy enough to be able to afford a national missile defence system (albeit one that is not yet proven and which will devour increasingly large amounts of money). This may give the impression, if not create the reality, of a US first strike capability against at least some other nuclear powers. Additionally, the US is the only nation able to even contemplate military dominance of space, a venture that it is now, apparently, contemplating.[9]

As a party to the CWC and BWC the US no longer has chemical or biological weapons (CBW). Yet it is able to afford a range of early-warning and defensive measures and is increasing the tempo of its research, development and deployment of such measures, especially in the biological weapons area. US biodefence research is being pursued with such vigour that it will, in effect, give the US a worryingly ambiguous biological weapons capability (while there is no suggestion that this option might be exercised it nonetheless complicates verification of compliance with the BWC and may encourage others to sail close to the compliance edge).[10] American public health capacities and medical research infrastructure, although vulnerable in some respects, boost US defensive capacities in the CBW area relative to other countries.

US capabilities in weapons delivery systems, communications, command and control, strategic air and sea-lift and national technical means of intelligence-gathering and verification (notably satellite imagery and electronic eavesdropping) are all force-multipliers in ensuring US WMD hegemony. American technological prowess, human and financial resources, and geographic size and location make it less vulnerable to WMD advances by other states, giving it a relatively comfortable margin of error for the foreseeable future. Despite recurrent scaremongering,[11] the prospect of China challenging the US for WMD hegemony still seems distant.[12]

US WMD capabilities translated into diplomatic leverage

These fundamental facts set the tone and political context for dealings on WMD between the US and the rest of the world. So powerful has the US become that it is able to flaunt the overwhelming weight of international opinion in respect of many WMD issues. It is often a minority of one or, paradoxically, in the poor company of two members of the "axis of evil", Iran and North Korea. The CTBT is just one example. The US has declined to ratify its signature, despite the overwhelming support of the international community for the treaty, and even when its erstwhile nuclear arch-competitor, Russia, has signed and ratified and its second most powerful nuclear competitor, China, has indicated it will do so if the US takes the lead. It also refuses despite the fact that it alone of the current nuclear weapon states could probably design an entirely new, reliable nuclear arsenal without ever conducting another nuclear test explosion.

In actual negotiations across the range of WMD issues American political, diplomatic and technical weight overshadows that of all but a few countries (the major exceptions being the United Kingdom, France and some of the other European Union states, Russia and China). Although on paper US power in the governance structures of all of the WMD multilateral regimes appears relatively weak compared to its actual power (it only has one vote, like all other states), it is often the determining factor in decision-making on critical issues. In reality, though, these organizations are unlikely to flout strongly expressed US preferences. More tellingly than its single vote, US power and influence is expressed through the size and capacities of its large delegations, its technical expertise and its technological contributions (both voluntary and those provided for a fee by US corporations).

US influence is preponderant even at treaty review conferences where, in theory, it is possible for majority votes to be called. In practice such conferences aim for consensus, in recognition of the impossibility of forcing a minority to bend to the will of the majority – especially if the US is the minority. At the 2005 NPT Review Conference all the levers of US power and influence were on display. It sent an insultingly low-level delegation, instructed not to compromise on any US position in order to facilitate consensus, and seemed little interested in rescuing the conference from deadlock. This provided an opening for Iran and Egypt to promote their own extreme positions, thereby cleverly attenuating perceptions of the US being solely responsible for the conference's failure.

The multilateral treaties that have their own verification secretariats are even more vulnerable to US pressure since they are dependent to a considerable extent on US financial contributions (up to one-quarter of their annual budgets, in addition to sizeable voluntary financial and technical contributions). Such financial power is periodically wielded, more often by implication than outright leverage, to achieve US goals. The ugliest recent example was the threat to OPCW finances that the US unsubtly made in order to secure the premature resignation of the organization's Director-General, José Bustani.

In terms of its share of global gross domestic product, the US in fact wields less financial influence on multilateral budgets than it should. That this is not rectified is partly due to institutional inertia, partly due to the reluctance of the US Congress to pay more, and partly due to the recognition by other states that if the US pays more it will have even more sway over their collective organizations.

A treaty like the BWC that has no secretariat is in some ways more vulnerable to hegemonic presumptions as there is no standing body to call non-compliant behaviour to account or to deal multilaterally with US non-compliance allegations against others. The US thus felt able to quietly disregard the requirements of the BWC's confidence-building measures by failing to declare three biodefence programmes that should have been revealed, an omission that would have triggered outrage and alarm had any other state acted in similar fashion. Washington's logic was undoubtedly that other states, not the US, were a threat to the BWC, and that the US needed to protect itself against non-compliant states by developing defensive measures which, while close to the fine line between offensive and defensive BW research, could not possibly, in the US case, be perceived as offensive in intent. This is the type of thinking towards which hegemons naturally incline.

In the Conference on Disarmament, a potentially powerful organ designated by the UN General Assembly as the "single, multilateral disarmament negotiating body", US power is both protected and frustrated by the consensus rule and by the ever-expanding membership. In theory any member, whether Myanmar, Kenya or Morocco, can block the commencement of negotiations on a WMD treaty or the adoption of the final product of negotiations, so can the US. Such blockage does happen, as witnessed by the current deadlock over the CD's agenda, a result of American unwillingness to countenance multilateral negotiations on nuclear disarmament or on preventing an arms race in outer space, China's unwillingness to drop its demand for negotiations on space, and the opposition of India and Pakistan to a fissionable material cut-off treaty. Notably, though, despite the consensus rule, it is only the more significant powers, including the US, that dare block consensus. Again, of all countries, the US is the least likely to have its will flouted by the CD in the way that India's was in the case of the CTBT's adoption in 1996.[13]

In the Security Council, meanwhile, the US is often able to force through resolutions on WMD issues that other members do not relish through the sheer weight of its influence. A recent notable example was resolution 1540 of April 2003, adopted under the enforcement provisions of Chapter 7 of the UN Charter, which obliges states to strengthen their national measures to prevent non-state actors from acquiring WMD. Many UN member states, including such influential developing countries as Pakistan and Brazil, saw this as a US plot to have the Council "legislate" on WMD issues as a way of bypassing troublesome multilateral negotiations that require consensus. Nonetheless it proved difficult for such opposition to prevail. The US is likely to retain such sway in the Council whatever the mix of new members in a reformed Council and whether or not they acquire a veto.

US power in the Security Council on WMD issues is not, of course, unalloyed. The US still needed (and failed to secure) the votes of Angola, Chile and other relatively inconsequential states in the Council in order to achieve a majority vote for a resolution to formally end the work of UN WMD inspectors in Iraq in March 2003 and to authorize an invasion on the basis of Iraq's alleged non-compliance with the Council's WMD disarmament demands.[14]

Bipartisan hegemony

The rise of US power has affected the behaviour and policies of both major US political parties when in government. Hence, although it was the administration of George W. Bush that killed the BW protocol, the Clinton administration had itself had serious reservations about its likely impact on US options in biodefence and on the competitiveness of the US biotechnology industry. Long before John Bolton (currently US ambassador to the UN) took charge as President Bush's Under Secretary of State for Arms Control and International Security, the US had moved to progressively weaken the intrusiveness of the protocol's on-site inspection arrangements.

Hegemonistic attitudes may, naturally, be characteristic not just of an executive branch of government, but also a legislative one. Belief in US exceptionalism increasingly pervades the US Congress, worsened presumably by the dearth of contact that legislators have with foreign governments and international organizations and the resulting absence of countervailing pressure on them to think and act more multilaterally. The problem is compounded when one party controls both the presidency and the Congress. The Clinton administration, despite being well intentioned towards the CTBT, failed to secure Congressional approval for ratification because it lacked the requisite numbers in the Senate. It is also likely that if any administration agreed to a BW protocol it would be defeated in that chamber. Even while agreeing to US ratification of the CWC the Senate imposed exceptionalist conditions that are considered illegal internationally, notably a ban on samples taken by OPCW inspectors from leaving the continental US. The Senate has also cut US funding for the CTBTO's on-site inspection activities, again in violation of US international legal obligations as a CTBT signatory, as a signal of its disdain for the treaty (although notably continuing funding for the International Monitoring System which the US finds useful for its own treaty compliance monitoring).

The Bush administration as unilateralist hegemon

Hegemons do not, of course, always become self-absorbed unilateralists. American domination of world politics at the end of the Second World War produced a frenzy of multilateralism, notably the Marshall Plan, the United Nations and the Bretton Woods institutions, along with a panoply of regional alliances (among them NATO, SEATO and ANZUS).[15] What is notable about the current era is that a period of hegemony has coincided with a particularly unilateralist administration in Washington.

In its arms control and non-proliferation policy, especially, the administration of George W. Bush has been driven by conservative individuals, some of them so-called "neocons", with a strong bias against multilateralism, international law, the United Nations and arms control and disarmament. While it is beyond this chapter's scope to consider the US domestic roots of such views, it is notable that a small number of key individuals have disproportionately affected policy making on these issues. They include Vice-President Dick Cheney, US Secretary of Defence Donald Rumsfeld, Under Secretary of State for Arms Control and International Security John Bolton, National Security Council adviser Richard Perle and Under Secretary for Defense Douglas Feith.

Proving that a single, persuasive individual can disproportionately shape the tenor and content of an entire area of government policy, John Bolton has been particularly significant in crafting US policy towards multilateralism in the WMD field. As the Senate hearings into the nomination of Bolton as US Ambassador to the UN have revealed, he repeatedly stretched intelligence findings on WMD proliferation to make worst-case WMD allegations against several states, including Cuba, Iraq, Syria and North Korea.[16] He also conducted personalized campaigns against two heads of international verification organizations, IAEA Director General Mohamed ElBaradei and Bustani of the OPCW and helped derail the immediate prospects of talks with North Korea by insulting President Kim Jong-Il. And he opposed new multilateral arms control initiatives outright.[17]

Vice-President Cheney and other senior US officials also attempted to belittle UN inspectors in Iraq and, in particular, the chief weapons inspector, Dr Hans Blix. Quite apart from disagreements on substance, such campaigns have further soured relations between the US and the multilateral community that deals with WMD issues.

Within the federal bureaucracy, the loss of the Arms Control and Disarmament Agency (ACDA) and the decimation of staff with long-term experience in and commitment to arms control, disarmament and verification have left the US bureaucracy without a countervailing voice to the unilateralists.[18] This will allegedly be made worse by the imminent amalgamation of the State Department's arms control and nonproliferation bureaus. Such developments have made dialogue on WMD issues between the US and even its closest allies all the more difficult.

There is some evidence that the appointment of Condoleezza Rice as Secretary of State and the departure of Bolton and Feith from Washington's inner circles will attenuate US unilateralism somewhat, at least in presentation if not substance. This has already been noted in the convergence of US and European policy towards Iran's nuclear aspirations and the attenuation of the war of words with North Korea sufficient to permit a resumption of the Six-Party Talks in September 2005. Another possible light on the horizon is the June 2005 bipartisan report co-authored by Newt Gingrich and George Mitchell on *American Interests and UN Reform*, which contains a raft of sensible proposals relating, inter alia, to WMD and multilateralism.[19]

The end of the bloc system

Along with the rise of US predominance, the end of the Cold War has produced the concomitant demise of the Soviet Union and its bloc system and the subsequent weakening of Russian military power and political influence over the former Warsaw Pact states and Soviet republics. This has led to the absence of a competing, adversarial locus of power in multilateral affairs that is particularly notable in the WMD area.

The US is now in such a strong position vis-à-vis a weakened Russia that it is able simply to ignore Russian demands on WMD issues such as its calls for subjecting strategic arms control to greater transparency, verification and irreversibility. Hence, in the negotiations on the 2002 Strategic Offensive Reductions Treaty (SORT), the US was able to obtain everything it wished for. The treaty has no verification provisions, only the most modest of compliance arrangements, little transparency and permits the US to store non-deployed warheads rather than destroying them. Given the state of the Russian nuclear arsenal – its numbers and the readiness of its delivery systems have been in free-fall for many years – there was no incentive for the US to negotiate. Likewise the US was able to withdraw unilaterally from the 1974 Anti-Ballistic Missile Treaty without major repercussions, knowing that Russia was unlikely to be able to afford offensive countermeasures or penalize the US in some other way. It was also able to ignore China and international opinion generally on the issue without repercussions.

As a result of Russian decline the US no longer needs to wean states of the now rudderless non-aligned camp away from a competing superpower by moderating or compromising its own positions on WMD issues, or offering trade-offs in unrelated areas. When negotiating the CWC before the end of the Cold War the US felt it necessary to offer incentives to the developing world to bring them into a treaty of its own design, notably the promise of cooperation in the peaceful uses of chemistry. Just a few years later it was adamantly unwilling to do this in the case of the BWC protocol negotiations, judging that while the CWC had been useful to it, the BWC protocol was not. Washington felt it had nothing to gain from placating the non-aligned camp on this issue.

The US has also been able to effectively sideline opposition from within the Western Group of countries on WMD issues through a policy of divide and rule. This partly takes advantage of the "Old Europe/New Europe" division that became evident in the debate over Iraq. The European Union (EU) is clearly no match for the US on WMD issues. Apart from its own lethargic approach to forging a comprehensive WMD strategy, which was finally agreed in December 2003, the admission of former Eastern bloc countries with conservative, pro-US inclinations, like Poland, the Czech Republic, Slovenia and Hungary, makes it less likely than ever that the EU WMD policy, described as a work-in-progress, will evolve radically away from US preferences.[20] Western disunity on WMD issues has also resulted from conservative governments being in power in key allied nations, such as Australia, Denmark, the Netherlands, Italy, Spain (until the change of government in 2004) and, most importantly, the UK. This has left Western "progressives" in WMD forums, like Austria, Canada, Japan, Germany, Finland, Sweden, Ireland and New Zealand, some of them grouped in the so-called New Agenda Coalition,[21] isolated and ineffectual. The truth is that none of these states cares as passionately about multilateral WMD arms control and disarmament as the US does about retaining all of its latitude and options in the WMD area.

Unable to stomach lengthy negotiations during which its preferred goals are invariably watered down, the US has been increasingly inclined to launch unilateral initiatives which require only tailor-made coalitions of the willing. These can be assembled initially through a series of bilateral contacts in which states are corralled one by one, rather than through a truly multilateral negotiating process, thereby marginalizing opposition that might arise. The prime example is the PSI, which the US was able to launch with a small number of states, despite widespread concerns that it would infringe the Law of the Sea or potentially disrupt legitimate seaborne trade. The US increasingly attempts to portray this as a form of multilateralism equal to, if not superior, to the traditional type.[22] To other observers it is dangerously over-hyped.[23] Still, the US continues to return to traditional treaty approaches when deemed to be to US advantage. In October 2005 the US strongly supported an amendment to the Convention for the Suppression of Unlawful Acts Against the Safety of Maritime Navigation that would ban non-military ships from being used to transport or launch WMD.[24]

The effects of 11 September 2001

The attacks of 11 September 2001 compounded the impact of both US hegemony and the end of the Cold War on multilateralism in the WMD field, providing an opportunity for US power to more openly manifest itself. Not only did the US now have the capacity to take unilateral action in the WMD arena, but it felt compelled as a matter of national survival to do so. It was also able, for the first time, to link dramatically and convincingly WMD to the threat of global terrorism. Even though the "weapons" involved in the attacks on New York and Washington DC were fuel-laden aircraft rather than any form of WMD, the scale of the assault was easily parlayed into alleged evidence of the increasing danger of WMD proliferation generally and the imminent danger of their use against the US mainland by WMD-armed terrorists specifically. The Washington anthrax incidents that followed soon after 11 September facilitated the case. Widespread fears of such attacks on the US "homeland" could be utilized to strengthen the case for strong unilateral action, as opposed to slow, allegedly timorous, multilateral approaches that had supposedly failed.

Hence the US was able to make a plausible case for invading not just Afghanistan, which had no WMD prospects of its own but was a haven for Al-Qaeda to plan and perhaps research, develop and store weapons and weapons components, but also Iraq, which clearly did have WMD potential and a history of past acquisition and use of at least chemical weapons. Not only was Iraq unarguably in violation of repeated UN Security Council resolutions ordering it to divest itself of WMD, but there was arguably a good chance that Iraqi President Saddam Hussein would countenance providing such weaponry to terrorists. The train of logic was, at face value, persuasive and was swept along by understandable outrage over the events of 11 September. The fact that it was not true seemed to be beside the point, even after it had been comprehensively rebutted by legislative enquiries, press leaks and foreign governments, and even after the British and American governments conceded that they had been wrong.[25] Multilateral processes, notably the debate in the UN Security Council and the patient work of UN inspectors in Iraq, were unable to resist a US administration that was intent on achieving regime change in Iraq regardless of the veracity of the WMD threat from that country.[26]

The anthrax incidents in Washington DC and elsewhere soon after the 11 September attacks bolstered the conviction of the US administration that biological weapons were a particularly challenging new threat. The response was not, as it might have been in other times, to seek concerted international action through multilateral treaties like the BWC. In theory the annual BW experts group meetings held in Geneva since the demise of the BWC protocol provided the perfect forum for rallying the international community into taking concrete collective action. Instead, fear of biological weapons was to propel the US towards intensified unilateral measures, such as vastly increasing the level of funding for research into biodefences and seeking increased levels of actual biodefence through such means as detection systems and stockpiling of vaccines. It also sought reinforcement of the Australia Group's export controls on BW dual-use materials and technology. Its role in the experts' group meetings, meanwhile, was to hold the line against anything that smacked of negotiations. This illustrates well the Bush administration's propensity for unilateralism as the preferred approach, followed by coalitions of the willing, with multilateralism a distant third.

Skilful manipulation by the US of the alleged link between WMD and "global terrorism", combined with the awareness of Western states of their own vulnerability to WMD terrorism, have made them reluctant to oppose US policy on such issues in multilateral fora, or even to suggest proposals and initiatives that might be perceived as too "multilateral", such as resuming negotiations on BW verification or sending UNMOVIC back into Iraq. It also made US Western allies, at least outwardly, eager to join US initiatives such as the Cooperative Threat Reduction enterprise and the PSI. Presumably because WMD counter-proliferation was perceived to be so central to current US security concerns, other states were unwilling to "go it alone" in such areas as BW, in contrast to the climate change area where the Kyoto Protocol parties decided they would proceed with their treaty despite the US refusal to participate.

One should not, however, exaggerate the newness of US willingness to turn to coalitions of the willing when multilateralism is seen as unable to rise to the occasion. In 1985 the US, concerned that it could not achieve the tight import–export controls that it desired through a multilateral treaty process, suggested to Australia that it establish a group of like-minded, initially Western states, to coordinate their respective national controls on chemical and biological weapons-related technology and materials exports. Hence the birth of the Australia Group. The MTCR is a similar animal, born of an eagerness by the US to constrain ballistic missile proliferation while remaining free of any multilateral treaty encumbrances that a body such as the CD might attempt to devise. In the case of North Korea, the Clinton administration, rather than referring the issue to the Security Council, turned to a select group of North Asian states to craft the 1994 Framework Agreement in an attempt to disarm Pyongyang of its nuclear weapon capabilities.

US policy after 11 September also had some beneficial effects for multilateral action on WMD, especially in drawing worldwide attention to the potential link between WMD and terrorism, a possibility that had been neglected for too long. Although the subject is prone to scaremongering, sober analysis has long revealed that terrorists may be able to either seize WMD and/or their components or produce their own WMD, given the necessary financial and technical resources.[27] Evidence that Al-Qaeda had not only aspirations to acquire WMD but was making rudimentary, if naive, plans to produce both nuclear and biological weapons[28] has been a beneficial wake-up call to the international community.

One important outcome of this heightened awareness has been the adoption of several resolutions by the Security Council, at US behest, aimed at forcing states to take action to break the potential terrorism/WMD nexus. They include resolution 1373 of 28 September 2001 on counter-terrorism[29] and resolution 1540 of 28 April 2004 on WMD and non-state actors. The first is extraordinary in the degree of institutional support for monitoring compliance that the Council, at US urging, has been willing to provide. The Counter-Terrorism Committee (CTC) has acquired a substantial expert secretariat and actually conducts visits to states to determine the veracity of their reports on their counter-terrorism measures, including action against money-laundering. Thorough and professional monitoring of compliance with mandatory Security Council resolutions is apparently an idea whose time has come. Unfortunately, although there are similar mandatory reporting requirements of states in respect of resolution 1540, the Council has not been so willing to provide the necessary resources to ensure follow-up and intensified monitoring of compliance. Nevertheless the precedent has now been established. And for some observers, even without the necessary institutional support, resolution 1540 represents "perhaps the most far-reaching multilateral policy reorientation against nuclear proliferation" since the NPT.[30]

The events of 11 September also had a positive effect on two of the jewels in the multilateral verification crown in the WMD field – the IAEA and OPCW. Both organizations sensed at an early stage that their previous neglect of, and lack of tools to deal with, the non-state actor threat could challenge their multilateral monopoly of their respective WMD proliferation fields. Commentators prone to exaggerating the non-state actor threat hinted that these large organizations had been, at least partially, marginalized. This added further fuel to the contentious thesis propagated in the US in some quarters that traditional arms control would soon go the way of the dinosaur.[31]

Both the IAEA and the OPCW responded to 11 September by putting greater efforts into assisting states with their national implementation obligations, on the grounds that states are ultimately responsible for the activities of non-state actors present on their territory. Over the years relatively little attention had been paid to this issue, despite the fact that most multilateral disarmament agreements contain binding obligations on states parties to ensure that domestically and in respect of all of their citizens, wherever they might be, they are in full compliance with their treaty obligations. Such obligations include adopting national implementation legislation that provides for a ban on nationals acquiring or being involved in any way in the acquisition of WMD. Such legislation should ideally provide for stiff criminal penalties for transgressions. Import–export controls and national coordinating authorities are also considered necessary for effective national implementation.

In the case of the IAEA new emphasis was also placed on the previously relatively neglected area of nuclear materials security. This included the Agency participating in creative, cooperative efforts with the US and Russia to repatriate fissionable materials from old Soviet reactors to avoid such material being seized by terrorists. In addition the Agency began to determine and promote best practice in nuclear materials security, in the absence of a binding legal obligation on states to enforce agreed security standards. Negotiations to amend the Convention on the Physical Protection of Nuclear Materials to cover shipment of materials within states as well as between them were successfully concluded in July 2005.[32]

Another positive result of the Bush administration's policy since the attacks of 11 September has been the focus on achieving full compliance by all states with multilateral WMD treaties. The US has laudably been willing to hold countries to account for not complying with their treaty commitments, in the process sweeping away some of the previous shameful reluctance to "name names" even when all the world was aware that treaties were being violated. It is to the credit of the US and the United Kingdom that they ultimately sought, after several years' procrastination, to hold Iraq to account in respect of the obligations that the Security Council had legitimately imposed on it. The impatient rush to war in March 2003, before UN inspectors had been given a chance to fulfil their mission, unfortunately ruined this "compliance strategy".

The US also has a mixed record when it comes to subjecting its allies like Pakistan to the same degree of scrutiny that it subjects foes like Syria. To its credit, it supported a full investigation into the lapses of its ally South Korea in complying with the NPT, even if these pale in comparison to the violations by North Korea. The US too played an invaluable role in verifying and assisting in Libya's nuclear disarmament – essential because the IAEA, as a multilateral verification body, cannot be permitted access to sensitive nuclear weapons information. In doing so, the US demonstrated the utility of quiet, patient diplomacy in achieving verified arms control and disarmament, in stark contrast to its Iraq misadventure. But again this positive role was tarnished by its initial attempt to marginalize the involvement of the IAEA, presumably because it suspected that the multilateral body was not up to the job.[33] On the other hand, it is encouraging that the Bush administration, after reassessing its intelligence analysis procedures in the wake of failures in respect of Iraq's non-existent WMD, recanted the accusations it had made against Cuba of having a biological weapons programme in violation of the BWC.[34]

A general malaise in multilateral negotiations on WMD

Quite apart from the emergence of a unipolar world and the shockwaves of 11 September, there is evidence of a general malaise in multilateral negotiations on WMD issues that has been building for some years but which has been compounded by recent events. This is due to both structural flaws and a growing dysfunctionality in the multilateral negotiating machinery.

Negotiation asymmetry

One structural flaw, inevitable and unfixable in the short term, arises from the fact that multilateral negotiations on WMD are directed towards changing the status quo dramatically: they have as their ultimate goal complete and general disarmament. This is uncontroversial in the case of chemical and biological weapons, since there are treaties which seek to ban such weapons outright and which aim to secure universal membership and compliance. No state today feels able to advocate openly the acquisition of chemical or biological weapons and most would dispute their military efficacy. In the nuclear area, however, the situation is completely different. The nuclear disarmament endeavour is driven by the "have-nots", sometimes with rhetorical support from the "haves", but most often against the latter's wishes. There is neither a consensus nor a universal ban.

At the practical level, none of the states which currently possess nuclear weapons evince any intention of giving them up. This creates continuing tension in multilateral disarmament talks and negotiations that is impossible to circumvent. In terms of negotiation theory, it creates stakes that are so fundamentally different that finding common ground is almost impossible.

For all of the non-nuclear weapon states (the exception being those that benefit from the US nuclear "umbrella"), advocating nuclear disarmament is at absolutely no cost to them. They give up nothing and stand only to benefit from a nuclear weapon-free world, not only in terms of enhanced security, but also in terms of increased national power, given that all states in such a world will be reduced to non-nuclear status. This is quite different from other multilateral negotiations. In international trade talks, for example, the developing world can offer to improve investment conditions in return for developed countries lowering agricultural tariffs on their produce.

For those states with nuclear weapons the stakes are far higher than for those without. They are not only being asked to give up significant sources of national pride and prestige, but they also perceive that their security will be at risk if they dare move towards nuclear disarmament. Moreover, the non-nuclear weapon states have nothing to offer them in return. All of them have already committed themselves to non-nuclear status via the NPT and none would ever consider withdrawing from that treaty, due not least to the dyadic and/or regional benefits they derive from it, simply in order to press the nuclear "haves" to disarm.

This difficulty cuts both ways. The US in particular has for many years, under administrations of various ilks, simply pocketed the nonproliferation aspect of the NPT without giving serious indication that it is willing to fulfil its Article VI obligations, except for reducing its nuclear arsenal to levels which make strategic, military and economic sense regardless of the NPT. Making matters worse is the attitude of the Bush administration which pronounces the NPT to be "largely" a nonproliferation agreement and seeks constantly to impose stronger and more intrusive constraints on the non-nuclear weapon states without any quid pro quo on its part.

Hence the US is highly enthusiastic about the universal adoption of the

Additional Protocol to IAEA safeguards agreements in the firm knowledge that its own protocol is a meaningless piece of arms control theatre – imposing more information requirements in respect of a limited "voluntary offer" of safeguarded peaceful nuclear facilities, while leaving its entire nuclear weapons sector untouched. Similarly, the US strongly advocates a cut-off in production of fissionable material for weapons purposes, knowing that it has stockpiled enough plutonium and highly enriched uranium (HEU) to provide for its future needs. IAEA Director-General Mohamed ElBaradei's proposal for a moratorium on construction of new enrichment facilities met with US disdain as it threatened to foreclose a US option, even though that option might not be needed in the short term. The current Bush administration is, however, simply an extreme case of a long-term trend in US policy that sees the nuclear weapons problem as being one of proliferation, not possession.

The low-hanging fruit syndrome

Another structural flaw in multilateral WMD negotiations, especially in the nuclear realm, is the "low-hanging fruit" syndrome. Hard as the CTBT and the CWC were to negotiate and realize (although the CTBT is still not yet in force), they were among the remaining low-hanging fruit on the multilateral disarmament tree. The vast majority of states are now well boxed in: they are banned from acquiring all types of WMD, banned from testing them, subject to increasingly intrusive monitoring and verification and many, in addition, are members of nuclear-free zones which compound the constraints on their nuclear aspirations. This leaves the "hard cases": the eight or nine existing nuclear weapon states,[35] and the shrinking number of aspirants beyond Iran. Indeed, with Libya and Iraq now removed, it is difficult to see where the next ones will emerge unless there is a breakdown of the NPT.[36]

In the chemical weapons area the universal ban and comprehensive verification system mean that future endeavours simply involve tinkering with this system. In the BW area there is a comprehensive ban but no verification system: but that has already proved impossible to negotiate and is likely to remain so for the foreseeable future.

The next obvious multilateral disarmament or arms control steps in the nuclear field are much more daunting than those taken so far. And despite the multilateralist disarmament credo that all treaties should be universal and negotiated equally and non-discriminately, future treaties will have a real affect on fewer and fewer states.[37]

The FMCT, the next obvious multilateral step, would in practice constrain only emerging nuclear weapon states like India, Pakistan and North Korea (as well as Israel). If and when the FMCT is achieved and the Additional Protocol becomes ubiquitous, effectively putting a global cap on the amount of fissionable material available for nuclear weapons, the remaining obvious steps would be coordinated moves towards complete nuclear disarmament. This could, at most, involve only eight states. Unlike previous strategic arms reductions they will have to focus on numbers of nuclear warheads, not just delivery systems. The problem is that once nuclear weapons themselves are the subject of negotiations there is little or no role for multilateral negotiation or for verification institutions that involve the non-nuclear weapon states, due to the danger of proliferation of nuclear weapons know-how. If and when it occurs, the minutiae of a nuclear disarmament convention will thus not be negotiated by the CD, despite the fact that it has had nuclear disarmament on its putative agenda since its establishment, but by the nuclear weapon states themselves.

Institutional decrepitude

The malaise affecting multilateral negotiations in the WMD field is made worse by the decrepit state of a number of the institutions that handle it. The UNDC has long since slipped into senility. The collective product of its annual sessions, which focus on a limited number of topics, is invariably either non-existent or anodyne and platitudinous, representing the lowest common denominator. The First Committee of the General Assembly, despite repeated attempts at reform, still lumbers along with an overcrowded, repetitive agenda. It has produced few initiatives in recent years. The UN Department of Disarmament Affairs, the smallest of the Secretariat's departments, has never been accorded the institutional support or funding that it needs for even its most basic functions of promoting and supporting disarmament negotiations and treaties. It lacks staff and resources, for instance, to properly collate, translate and distribute, much less analyse, the BWC CBM declarations for which it is responsible. UNDDA does run UN regional disarmament centres in Lima, Lomé and Kathmandu, but they are minuscule and sparsely funded. The Department's most notable achievement of recent years has been to assist the Central Asian states to negotiate a nuclear weapon-free zone.

The Conference on Disarmament is becoming an international disgrace to rival the UN Human Rights Commission. Now bloated to an absurd size of 66 members[38] by endless demands for entry from states with little to say about complex disarmament issues and even less to contribute in substantive terms, this body has negotiated nothing since the CTBT in 1996. For the past eight years it has not even been able to agree on an agenda, much less establish any subsidiary bodies to negotiate anything.

Part of the reason for this is the "low-hanging fruit" problem previously noted. It also has to do with the fact that the need for new WMD mechanisms can be satisfied by other means. The BW protocol negotiations, for instance, rightly occurred in an Ad Hoc Group established by the BWC states parties. Meeting in the Palais des Nations in Geneva and supported by the UN Secretariat, it looked to all intents and purposes like a subsidiary body of the CD. Similarly, moves to strengthen nuclear safeguards have rightly taken place at the IAEA. Other initiatives have, however, deliberately skirted the CD and followed the example of the instigators of the 1999 Ottawa Anti-Personnel Landmine Ban Convention in using other venues than the "single multilateral disarmament forum". Hence the Hague Code of Conduct on missiles was negotiated informally by a group of like-minded states, knowing that missiles were never even likely to make it onto the CD agenda.

Yet there are other factors at work in making the CD dysfunctional. One already mentioned is that the old Cold War bloc system, which in the CD reduced the negotiating parties to three groups (Western and others, Eastern European and the Group of 21 neutral and non-aligned, plus China when it ventured a different viewpoint), has been attenuated. The erosion of previous group discipline makes negotiations more anarchic and difficult. The rise of China as a player has had both good and bad consequences. When China first joined the CD it so lacked confidence and experience in multilateral disarmament forums that it said very little and acted mostly in solidarity with the non-aligned group. Now it participates so confidently that it is willing to block consensus on the agenda.

A further factor, though, is the mutual mistrust that seems to have infected multilateral disarmament negotiations. This is in part due to the broken promises that now litter the landscape. In the nuclear area there is the failure of the nuclear weapon states to move more rapidly towards nuclear disarmament – despite this being a quid pro quo for the definite extension of the NPT agreed to in 1995. American disavowal at the 2005 NPT Review Conference of the deal on 13 practical steps that all parties agreed to in 2000 has exacerbated the situation.[39] The current US argument that these deals did not "amend" the treaty and are merely "politically binding" calls into question the basis on which international relations proceeds not just in the disarmament area but across the board. In the case of the CWC, the developing countries remain aggrieved that what appeared to have been a commitment by the Western states to dismantle the Australia Group and its perceived discriminatory export control arrangements remains unfulfilled more than a decade after the CWC was agreed.

Even its fellow nuclear weapon states must feel bitter that, after they had agreed, signed and in some cases ratified the CTBT, the US simply pocketed that fact and refused itself to ratify, while hinting that it may need to resume testing. This also undermines faith in international deal-making and fair play. Another egregious example was the BW protocol negotiations, where Western nations which had negotiated long and hard to help protect US interests were simply double-crossed by unyielding US opposition to proceeding with any type of agreement or alternative negotiation venue or strategy. In the CD this increasing lack of trust manifests itself in the unwillingness of key players to even agree to set up a subsidiary body on a particular issue lest it be perceived as some sort of trick to draw them towards an inevitable treaty.

Compliance lacunae

Compliance mechanisms for multilateral WMD regimes, in contrast to monitoring and verification arrangements, are underdeveloped, untested and subject to doubt and confusion. While a great deal of attention is paid to what compliance information is to be sought and how it is to be collected, collated and analysed, there is often a reluctance to be clear about how a determination of non-compliance is to be made and what subsequent steps are possible if such a finding is made. Even IAEA safeguards have not been free from this: confusion surrounding the possibility of "special inspections" (essentially challenge inspections) has long dogged the NPT.

The most lively current case of alleged non-compliance with a multilateral arms control treaty, the Iran case, has, remarkably, wound its way through the IAEA compliance process as envisaged by the IAEA Statute: following outside leads and its own investigations the IAEA has drawn the attention of its Board of Governors to the possibility that Iran was not complying with its safeguards and NPT obligations. The Board has slowly increased the pressure on Iran to comply, issuing various requests, followed by demands, to the Iranian authorities, to which they have responded only partially satisfactorily. Technical means have been employed effectively by the Agency to strengthen its case, while at the same time keeping an open mind in investigating Iranian counterclaims. A like-minded group of members of the Board, France, Germany and the UK, has attempted to engage Iran constructively, while another, the US, has issued veiled threats. This "good cop, bad cop" routine is one way of seeking to deal with a non-compliance problem. If Iran fails to comply, however, the question of how it can be induced to do so will soon confront the UN Security Council, since the IAEA itself will have exhausted the range of "carrots and sticks" at its disposal. The cases of North Korea and Iraq followed different trajectories when their non-compliance was determined, although this is not necessarily a bad thing as long as it achieves a return to full compliance.

In the case of chemical weapons there have been only a few cases of alleged non-compliance in which investigations took place, but these related to the 1925 Geneva Protocol and they all ended unsatisfactorily. There has been no experience to date of deliberate non-compliance with the CWC, even though many consider a challenge inspection long overdue. Similarly there has been no alleged violation of the CTBT in its current state of non-entry into force. In the BWC case, allegations ended in one unsatisfactory official compliance process and one inconclusive trilateral exercise involving the US, the UK and the Soviet Union, then Russia. Clearly the BWC compliance process will always be at a disadvantage without an accompanying multilateral verification system with impartial monitoring and on-site inspection capabilities.

Across all international treaty regimes there remains much work to be done to clarify how non-compliance cases should be dealt with and to broaden the range of incentives and disincentives that might be employed. A useful concept here is "compliance management", which implies a clear and well considered process for bringing recalcitrant states back into compliance without backing them into a corner or causing them to lose face unnecessarily. Without a more refined approach to compliance management, the multilateral system will be lumbered with recurring improvisation, which as UN peacekeeping has constantly demonstrated, is potentially disastrous.

The multilateral success stories

Set against the deficiencies of the multilateral forums for deliberating and negotiating on WMD issues is the success in recent years of the multilateral monitoring, verification and implementation bodies.[40] The IAEA, the OPCW and nascent CTBTO are all exhibiting great energy and competence in their allotted tasks. Indeed, apart from the BWC case, multilateral verification regimes are currently better governed, organized, funded and supported by the requisite technical and technological means than ever before. It is easy to overlook the enormous advances that have been made since 1972, when the NPT became the first multilateral arms control treaty with a matching verification system.

Multilateral WMD verification today is a substantial international enterprise.[41] Recurrent annual expenditure for the three major organizations currently totals more than $US300 million. More than 3,000 people are employed by these bodies, not counting the hundreds more employed by national implementing authorities and regional organizations. The number of full-time arms control/disarmament inspectors employed by multilateral agencies exceeds 700, while a further 380 are on UNMOVIC's roster (in addition to a notional number on the roster of the UN Secretary-General for CBW use investigations).

For its part the IAEA has responded well in seeking to strengthen nuclear safeguards following the revelation after the first Gulf War in 1999 that Iraq had come close to acquiring nuclear weapons. It has adopted those measures that were within its legal power to implement immediately and has worked assiduously to promote the adoption of the Additional Protocol by all of its member states. While it is no longer able to verify North Korea's compliance with its nuclear safeguards obligations, the Agency was partly responsible for revealing the extent of that country's violation in the first place. The Agency played an exemplary role in Iraq, helping dismantle that country's nuclear weapons infrastructure, to the extent that Iraq was unable to achieve any significant recovery of that programme during the absence of inspectors between 1998 and 2002. After its inspectors were re-admitted to Iraq the Agency was able swiftly to verify the non-existence of a reconstituted Iraqi programme and rebuff various misleading allegations. This included those relating to purported yellowcake imports from Niger and the intended purpose of aluminium tubes supposedly imported for nuclear centrifuges. Again, the Agency was able to play a useful role, in cooperation with the UK and US, in verifying Libya's decision to disarm itself of WMD capabilities, and in pursuing Iran's non-compliance with the NPT.

The IAEA may in fact have been too successful from the point of view of the US. The assertive multilateralism demonstrated by Director General ElBaradei does not sit well with the world's only superpower. Not only did he contradict the findings of US intelligence agencies with regard to Iraq, but he has attempted to scrupulously maintain his objectivity in respect of US non-compliance allegations against Iran. ElBaradei has proposed measures such as a global moratorium on construction of new uranium enrichment and plutonium reprocessing facilities that do not sit well with a US desire to keep its WMD options completely open. This was undoubtedly a factor in the unsuccessful US campaign, led by John Bolton, to unseat him.[42]

Despite the non-entry into force of the CTBT, the CTBTO has made remarkable strides in establishing the treaty's verification system.[43] The nascent verification body is in place, a global monitoring system is largely functional and exceeding its designers' expectations, and states are already receiving data from the system. While some states are expressing misgivings about continuing to fund a system that lacks a binding treaty framework, to date the CTBTO has managed to sustain its progress towards making the system fully operational for the day when the CTBT does enter into force.

After an impressive beginning, the OPCW encountered management and financial difficulties several years ago that threatened its performance. It was also overburdened by an unexpected abundance of declared chemical weapons for verified destruction (a success of sorts) which led it to neglect its other verification tasks.[44] Under new leadership, however, it has improved its performance and is making steady progress in the unprecedented attempt to apply monitoring and verification to an ever changing global chemical industry.

Notable, too, has been the success of two Security Council-mandated multilateral verification bodies, the UN Special Commission (UNSCOM) and UNMOVIC, which cooperated with the IAEA in verifying Iraqi WMD disarmament. Largely unheralded, the UN, in a relatively short period, has as a result of the work of these two bodies, acquired unprecedented, proven expertise and capacity in monitoring and verification. The two organizations proved that a UN body could plan, organize and rapidly deploy a verification operation in the most difficult physical terrain and conditions and in the most taxing political circumstances – that of enforced, contested disarmament. Not only were UN and IAEA inspectors able to conduct thorough, systematic, on-site inspections and other in-country monitoring and verification activities, but they also successfully dismantled or supervised the dismantling of extensive nuclear weapons and ballistic missile programmes, and other elements of WMD programmes in the chemical and biological fields. Both UNSCOM and UNMOVIC, along with the IAEA, also successfully monitored the arms embargo against Iraq and an import–export regime related to dual-use items.

Both organizations were able to use information, including from national technical means and open sources, wisely and to great effect, as well as protecting confidentiality where necessary. While UNSCOM did have difficulties in its relationship with foreign intelligence agencies, UNMOVIC learned the correct lessons and avoided such difficulties. Both UNSCOM and UNMOVIC successfully withstood the political pressures from the inspected state and from other countries, that could have derailed or diverted their work. Both demonstrated that the UN could organize an effective, efficient and suitably independent verification mechanism outside the structure of a specific treaty regime. Hence all is not gloomy on the multilateral WMD front. These new-found multilateral capacities need, however, to be preserved and nurtured for potential future use.

The great lacuna in the multilateral WMD verification area is BW: attempts to provide the BWC with a verification agency have failed utterly. Without strong US support and advocacy there is currently no prospect of this situation changing dramatically despite the earnest discussion among BWC states parties in their current "new process". Only UNMOVIC has anything approaching what would be needed for BW and it remains mandated only to deal with Iraq. The UN Secretary-General's mechanism for investigating alleged use of chemical and biological weapons in violation of the 1925 Geneva Protocol is hyper-virtual, comprising only outdated lists of experts and analytical laboratories. Nonetheless, there are steps which could be usefully taken and which should be able to attract US support. One possibility is to rejuvenate and upgrade the UN Secretary-General's mechanism, especially since it has the endorsement of both the UN General Assembly and the Security Council. It could usefully draw on UNMOVIC's expertise, experienced inspector cadre, accredited laboratories and wealth of lessons learned. Another, more ambitious, proposal is to create a standing UN verification body that would enhance the UN's overall capacity for dealing with WMD issues.[45]

Conclusions

Multilateralism in the WMD field is currently under great stress. One of the principal causes is the emergence of a hegemon, the United States, which is unrivalled in its ability to affect the WMD agenda. Concomitantly there is no alternative source of power with which the US feels the need to compete in the multilateral marketplace of ideas and influence. The effects of this development are compounded by the fact that the US is currently governed by an administration that is in historical terms unusually unilateralist and, to put it mildly, sceptical of multilateralist endeavours, especially in security affairs. This administration has been able to take advantage of the tragic events of 11 September 2001 to pursue its aspirations either unilaterally or in concert only with like-minded states on an ad hoc basis.

But there are additional factors that exacerbate the state of WMD multilateralism, notably the malaise in the multilateral WMD machinery devoted to consideration and negotiation of new agreements. This is caused by negotiation asymmetry, the fact that the next steps in the disarmament agenda are more difficult to achieve, the mistrust that has been allowed to infect the atmosphere and the decrepitude of the institutions themselves.

The bright light on the horizon is the largely creditable performance of the multilateral institutions charged with monitoring, verifying and helping states implement the existing multilateral disarmament agreements.

This has confounded the sceptics and established foundations on which future multilateral endeavours in the WMD area might be built. In the meantime, the multilateral agenda must await the re-emergence of a hegemon that is pro-multilateral rather than unilateralist in its inclinations and an international community that is prepared to set aside parochial national interests in favour of collective endeavour.

Notes

1. The term "weapons of mass destruction" is in many ways unsatisfying in its grouping of weapons that can be fundamentally different in nature, in their intended and unintended effects and in their impact on international relations. The term is, however, so ubiquitous and such a convenient shorthand that is used here with the qualifier "so-called".
2. Jim Wurst, "Nonproliferation, disarmament matters dropped from U.N. Summit document", Global Security Newswire, 16 September 2005, www.nti.org.
3. Similar arrangements do not exist for chemical and biological weapons.
4. Agreed at the Kananaskis summit in Canada in June 2002. The Group of 8 comprises Canada, France, Germany, Italy, Japan, Russia, the UK and the US.
5. According to the Stockholm International Peace Research Institute (SIPRI) US spending makes up 47 per cent of the world total. See SIPRI, "Recent trends in military expenditure", www.sipri.org. Expenditure has continued to increase in 2005, edging it closer to 50 per cent.
6. Wade Boese (2005) "U.S. weighing nuclear stockpile changes", *Arms Control Today*, May, p. 22.
7. Even while keeping its testing option open in case it needs it by refusing to ratify the CTBT.
8. See "U.S. House Committee urges nuclear weapons review", Global Security Newswire, 31 May 2005.
9. See Frances Fitzgerald (2005) "Immaculate destruction", New York Times, 3 June 2005, www.nytimes.com/2005/06/03/opinion; and "U.S. sets missile defense for Europe, space", *Arms Control Today*, May, p. 30.
10. To be fair we still have no comprehensive idea of the former Soviet BW programme and to what extent it has persisted since Russia inherited it.
11. See, for example, Demetri Sevastopulo, "Pentagon report to portray China as emerging rival", *Financial Times*, 25 May 2005, FT.com.
12. See Jeffrey Lewis (2005) "The ambiguous arsenal", *Bulletin of the Atomic Scientists* May/June, pp. 52–59.
13. In that case, when India refused to join the consensus to forward the agreed treaty to the UN General Assembly, Australia simply tabled it there as a proposed Australian draft, whereupon it was adopted by an overwhelming majority vote.
14. For an account of the machinations, see Hans Blix (2004) *Disarming Iraq: The Search for Weapons of Mass Destruction*, London: Bloomsbury, pp. 205–208.
15. The North Atlantic Treaty Organization, South-East Asian Treaty Organization and the Australia, New Zealand, US Treaty.
16. On Cuba, for instance, see Miles A. Pomper (2005) "Bolton hearings highlight internal differences on Cuba's biological weapons, *Arms Control Today*, May, p. 26.
17. Former State Department colleague Avis T. Bohlen notes that "He was absolutely clear that he didn't want any more arms control agreements. He didn't want any negotiating

bodies. He just cut it off. It was one more area where we lost support and respect in the world". Quoted in Scott Shane, "Never shy, Bolton brings a zeal to the table", *New York Times*, 1 May 2005, nytimes.com.

18. Wade Boese (2005) "State Department reorganization approved", *Arms Control Today*, March, pp. 40–41.
19. *American Interests and UN Reform*, Report of the Task Force on the United Nations, US Institute of Peace, Washington DC, June 2005.
20. The presence of two nuclear weapon states, the United Kingdom and France, in the EU already has a dampening effect on at least the nuclear aspects of the policy. See European Strategy against the Proliferation of WMD, adopted 12 December 2003, European Council, Brussels.
21. Members of the New Agenda Coalition are Brazil, Egypt, Ireland, New Zealand, Mexico, South Africa and Sweden.
22. This has been evident in the campaign for Senate approval of the appointment of John Bolton as US ambassador to the UN, during which his negotiation of the PSI is cited, misleadingly, as demonstrating his commitment to multilateralism. See The Honourable John R. Bolton, Nominee for representative of the United States of America to the UN, Statement before the Senate Foreign Relations Committee, Washington DC, 11 April 2005, US State Department website, http://www.state.gove.t/us/rm/44489.htm.
23. Jo Cirincione, non-proliferation director at the Carnegie Endowment for International Peace describes PSI as "a good little program that has been puffed totally out of proportion" (quoted in "Rice hails PSI WMD interdiction efforts", Global Security Newswire, 1 June 2005).
24. Wade Boese (2005) "Treaty amended to outlaw WMD at sea", *Arms Control Today*, December, www.armscontrol.org.
25. See, for example, Comprehensive Report of the Special Adviser to the Director Central Intelligence on Iraq's WMD, Central Intelligence Agency, Washington DC, 30 September 2004 and Addendum, 25 April 2005.
26. See Memorandum of 23 July 2002, recounting UK Prime Minister Tony Blair's meeting on Iraq with senior UK officials on 23 July 2002, in which Blair's adviser Alistair Campbell reported on his recent talks in Washington DC thus: "Military action was now seen as inevitable. Bush wanted to remove Saddam, through military action, justified by the conjunction of terrorism and WMD. But the intelligence and facts were being fixed around the policy. The National Security Council had no patience for the UN route, and no enthusiasm for publishing material on the Iraqi regime's record." (Downing Street Memo, http://www.downingstreetmemo.com/memo.html).
27. For a work that combines both, see Graham Allison (2004) *Nuclear Terrorism: the Ultimate Preventable Catastrophe*, New York: Times Books.
28. See Charles D. Ferguson, William C. Potter, Amy Sands, Leonard S. Spector, and Fred L. Wehling (2004) *The Four Faces of Nuclear Terrorism*, Washington DC: Monterey Institute of International Studies and the Nuclear Threat Initiative.
29. The resolution requires every state to freeze financial assets of terrorists and their supporters, deny travel or safe havens to terrorists, prevent terrorist recruitment and supply, and cooperate with other states in sharing information and prosecuting criminals.
30. See Alistair Millar and Morten Bremer Mærli (2005) "Nuclear non-proliferation and United Nations Security Council Resolution 1540, *Policy Briefs on the Implementation of the Treaty on the Non-Proliferation of Nuclear Weapons*, Norwegian Institute of International Affairs, Oslo, April 2005, p. 35.
31. See, for example Michael A. Levi and Michael E. O'Hanlon (2005) *The Future of Arms Control*, Washington DC: Brookings Institution Press.

32. "States agree on stronger physical protection regime", International Atomic Energy Agency press release 2005/03, 8 July 2005.
33. Jack Boureston and Yana Feldman (2004) "Verifying Libya's nuclear disarmament", in Trevor Findlay (ed.) *Verification Yearbook 2004*, London: Verification Research, Training and Information Centre (VERTIC), pp. 87–105.
34. Adherence to and Compliance with Arms Control, Nonproliferation and Disarmament Agreements and Commitments, US Department of State, Washington DC, August 2005, pp. 19–20.
35. Depending on whether North Korea is included, the others being China, France, India, Israel, Pakistan, Russia, the UK, the US.
36. Egypt, Saudi Arabia and Syria have all been implausibly mentioned. While Japan might react to definite confirmation that North Korea nuclear weapons by acquiring its own this seems unlikely given the US nuclear umbrella and potential adverse Chinese reaction.
37. Even the CTBT, hailed as the holy grail of multilateral disarmament, was bound to actually affect only a handful of states, since the vast majority had already forsworn the right to conduct a nuclear test by joining the NPT. Non-NPT party Israel probably views the CTBT as no great burden as it has been able to do without nuclear testing anyway – hence it has been willing to sign, although not ratify, the treaty.
38. The CD started out as the Eighteen Nations Disarmament Committee (ENDC) in March 1962 and then became the Conference of the Committee on Disarmament (CCD) in 1969, expanding to 30 members. Both of these bodies were jointly chaired by the US and the Soviet Union. In 1983 it became the Committee on Disarmament and had 38 members until June of 1996 when it expanded to a membership of 61 and became the Conference on Disarmament. In 1999, the membership expanded, once again, to 66.
39. See Rebecca Johnson (2005) "Politics and protection: why the 2005 NPT Review Conference failed", *Disarmament Diplomacy* 80 (Autumn).
40. For a full account see "WMD Verification and Compliance: The State of Play", report no. 19, submitted by Foreign Affairs Canada and prepared by VERTIC, Weapons of Mass Destruction Commission, Stockholm, 2004, www.wmdcommission.org.
41. The following details are provided in Trevor Findlay (2004) "Introduction: the state of play of verification", *Verification Yearbook 2004*, London: VERTIC, p. 20.
42. Dafna Linzer, "U.S. drops opposition to IAEA chief", washingtonpost.com, 8 June 2005.
43. Ben Mines, "The Comprehensive Nuclear Test Ban Treaty: virtually verifiable now", VERTIC Brief no. 3, April 2004.
44. See "Getting verification right: proposals for enhancing implementation of the Chemical Weapons Convention", London: Verification Research, Training and Information Centre (VERTIC), 2002.
45. Trevor Findlay (2005) *A Standing United Nations Verification Body: Necessary and Feasible*, Compliance Chronicles, no. 1, Canadian Centre for Treaty Compliance, December, http://www.carleton.ca/npsia/research_centres/cctc.htm.

12

International humanitarianism in the contemporary world: Forms and issues

David P. Forsythe

In the contemporary world we remain caught between nationalism and cosmopolitanism: between the national interest and the human interest, between state security and human security, between the legal principle of state sovereignty and the moral imperative to protect human dignity based on need if not rights.[1] An emerging trend is to redefine state sovereignty not as elite privilege and a barrier against foreign scrutiny, but as the responsibility to protect human dignity.[2] Still, this useful notion does not tell us exactly what to do when the primary responsibility to protect is not properly exercised because the state is either unwilling or unable to do the right thing. There are abusive states and failed states.

States themselves have produced a cosmopolitan and liberal framework by constructing an international law that mandates attention to universal human rights and humanitarian affairs, whether in peace or war.[3] Within this framework there are different types of mandated multilateral management for persons in exceptional dire straits. This multilateral management entails states, intergovernmental organizations, and nongovernmental organizations. But all too often the states that drive the process choose – or feel compelled to choose – a realist policy reflecting state power politics and expedient state advantage. They preach liberalism but often practice realism.[4] They preach cosmopolitan liberalism but often manifest indifference to "others" beyond their own state.

Contemporary international humanitarianism – the transnational concern to help persons in exceptional distress – reflects the pervasive tension between nationalism and cosmopolitanism. And because the tension is unresolved, for humanitarianism and for international relations in general, the nature and forms of humanitarian action have varied by context. The five main components of international humanitarianism today – states, the United Nations system, the NGO community, the Red Cross network, and the media – have combined in different ways at different times in different places. At the very same time that there was an unprecedented outpouring of humanitarian assistance for the victims of the tsunami disaster in Asia in the winter of 2004–2005, there was widespread indifference to a greater disaster in the Democratic Republic of Congo – where perhaps almost four million civilians died over the course of a few years of political conflict. Whether such inconsistencies can be levelled out in a more just and orderly world is a pertinent question.

Because the global humanitarian challenge is so great, and because so many of the actors involved in the humanitarian enterprise are inherently international or transnational, some type of multilateralism is usually a characteristic of the situation.[5] Even in the case where a state takes the lead in action, whether claiming humanitarian or other motivations, usually other components of the normal humanitarian system become involved, leading to some type of multilateral involvement. Typical was the response to the 2004–2005 tsunami disaster: national militaries worked side by side with NGOs and IGOs; some Asian states welcomed involvement by other states and some did not. It may be chaotic multilateralism, but still multilateralism. As usual, questions of effectiveness and participation must be addressed. After all, the primary value is not multilateralism per se, but effective protection of human dignity for persons in exceptional distress, with perhaps participation of stake holders.[6]

A unipolar world, or more precisely a unipolar military situation in the larger game of international relations, creates certain dilemmas but does not fundamentally alter the central and persistent tension between nationalism and cosmopolitanism – the latter entailing universal standards of human rights and humanitarian norms. This is not the place for an extended discussion of humanitarian intervention, since other authors treat the subject of saving foreigners by military force.[7] I do, however, have to note coercive factors in passing. Paradoxically, while particularly Red Cross humanitarianism arose as an effort to limit the human costs of war, contemporary humanitarianism – including now even the Red Cross – recognizes that there is sometimes a role for political action to deal with the root causes of humanitarian crisis, perhaps even entailing the use of force.[8]

This analysis stresses humanitarianism in war and other political conflict, while largely leaving to others the matter of humanitarian response to natural and industrial disasters.[9] I also do not address persons being in persistent, and thus routine, distress because of a failure of development.

As a general historical trend, there is now greater attention to humanitarianism in world affairs. This is certainly true for war and similar political conflict, which is easily seen if we think back to the plight of individuals, whether combatant or civilian, in situations like the Wars of the Austrian Succession or the Crimean Wars toward the middle of the nineteenth century. Compared to that time, all national military establishments in developed states now have sophisticated medical services, supplemented by a vast array of other humanitarian actors whether public or private, national or international. The same is no doubt true for natural and technological disasters, and in that regard we can note the extensive response not only to the tsunami in the Indian Ocean but other contemporary calamities affecting Kobe, Japan (1995 earthquake) and Central America (1998 hurricane Mitch). As noted, however, this general trend of progress is dotted with exceptions.

The central question is whether humanitarianism in the world today, which is inherently multilateral because of the size of the problems and the vast array of actors involved, can be made effective, with appropriate attention to the needs and desires of victims.

We briefly analyse the components of international humanitarianism today in an inductive process, with a focus on the UN system and Red Cross network, then put the pieces of the puzzle into a larger picture at the end.

The United Nations system

Has the United Nations been able to provide a systematic and multilateral response to humanitarian disasters, particularly in conflict situations? Has "the UN" been able to combine "its own" agencies with private groups and governmental units, in the context of media coverage, to at least coordinate meaningful multilateral humanitarianism? An overview published in 2004 provides the distressing answer:

> There exists no system for triggering and delivering international disaster assistance; there is rather a hodgepodge of public and private agencies. And the independent role of the communications media in covering or ignoring a story is often important. Whether ... actors are motivated to act because of a concern for the human rights to food, clothing, shelter, and health care (which has been rare) or because of humanitarian compassion (more prevalent), all of these actors have proceeded with minimal central coordination – and thus with resulting overlap and confusion. Various UN organizations have been protective of their decentralized independence. The private agencies have resisted coming under the full control of public authorities. Various agencies have competed among themselves for

a slice of the action in a given situation and for credit for whatever accomplishments were achieved – said to be important for fund raising. To be sure, emergency assistance has been delivered and lives have been saved in a vast number of situations.[10]

Some history

During the era of the League of Nations, "the Nansen Office" was created to supplement Red Cross and other private, public, and quasi-public efforts in order to deal with refugee relief – especially given the flood of persons on the move in Europe because of communist revolutions in places like Russia and Hungary. But the League never developed a comprehensive system of response to various humanitarian disasters.[11] An international relief union was stillborn.

Surprising as it may now seem, the United Nations system was very slow to manifest any broad responsibility for disaster response. True, the Office of the UN High Commissioner for Refugees (UNHCR) was created in 1950, as was a legal framework for refugees (1951) which was originally designed to deal in fact with a trickle of persons fleeing persecution from European communist countries – these latter proving very adept at least at sealing borders. But the UNHCR was said to be a protection agency, not a relief agency, meaning that it concentrated on diplomatic and legal representations designed to protect the rights of manageable numbers of refugees. Only in the aftermath of the Israeli–Palestinian contest for control of western British Palestine did the UN General Assembly create an early refugee relief agency – UNRWA (United Nations Relief and Works Agency) – whose mandate was limited to one people in one part of the world.

The UN system was not utilized to help manage a systematic and multilateral response to a broad range of humanitarian disasters until about 1970.[12] In the well publicized Nigerian-Biafran conflict (1967–1970), the major relief players trying to get aid to civilians in secessionist Biafra were the International Committee of the Red Cross (ICRC) and its Red Cross partners, and Joint Church Aid, a faith-based private consortium. While other relief actors like the French Red Cross acted independently, no UN organ or agency was a major player in that drama.

After Biafra, and with other changes in international relations, in 1971 the General Assembly created the UN Disaster Relief Office.[13] By 1992 this office morphed into the UN Department of Humanitarian Affairs. In 1998 this Department was changed into the Office of the Coordinator of Humanitarian Affairs (OCHA), headed by an Under Secretary-General who became at the same time the UN Emergency Relief Coordinator. Other administrative arrangements were created in related developments to enhance coordination of a multilateral process involving different actors.

The UNHCR and UNRWA both continued. The former became more and more a relief agency and not just a legal protection agency.[14] This was in no small measure because Western donor states wanted refugees cared for "over there", rather than become asylum-seekers in the Western states themselves. Other parts of the UN system also developed, or were given, mandates to deal with refugees, internally displaced persons, and others in emergency distress: UNICEF, the World Food Program, the UN Development Program and its Resident Representative in particular countries, the World Health Organization, etc.

Significantly, as the Cold War wound down the UN Security Council (UNSC) began to concern itself more often with humanitarian affairs.[15] During the Cold War, the deployment of military force under UNSC aegis had led to traditional (or simple or first-generation) peacekeeping missions entailing primarily observation and reporting, with only light weapons used for self-defence. The point was to show the UN flag and utilize armed diplomacy to help fighting parties reduce or avoid hostile confrontation. Humanitarian matters were excluded. But increasingly the UNSC in the 1990s began to deploy complex (or second-generation) peacekeeping missions which entailed human rights and humanitarian mandates. The point was not just to limit or avoid conflict, but to create a humane and rights protective situation. Further, on occasion the UNSC would assert a right under UN Charter Chapter VII to engage in enforcement action, not just peacekeeping narrowly defined, and sometimes this was related to human rights and humanitarian affairs.

Thus progressively the UNSC became involved in humanitarian matters because they were seen as linked to international peace and security. Either one had to protect rights and humane values in order to get peace and stability, and/or one had to use force to compel a target party to respect rights and humane standards. The previously low politics of humanitarianism became enmeshed in the high politics of peace and security.[16] The process proceeded inconsistently and selectively with many double standards, because at times "The unwillingness by major powers to spend money was matched by an unwillingness to run risks".[17] Still, in general, the notion of international peace and security in the UNSC was more and more informed by humanitarian concern – that is, by the concern for human security in conflict areas.

Unfortunately the UNSC also played fast and loose sometimes with the language of human rights and humanitarian affairs. Clearly in the Balkan wars of 1992–1995, state members of the UNSC, especially the P-5, and most especially the United States, used the discourse of human rights and humanitarianism to avoid a more disagreeable if more decisive response to atrocities. To these states on the UNSC, it was more agreeable to dispatch the UNHCR to care for those persecuted and uprooted than to commit their military forces to stop the root causes of the forced displacement and other abuses. Likewise to them, it was more agreeable in the short term to create a criminal court (the International Criminal Tribunal for the former Yugoslavia (ICTY) in 1993, then the International Criminal Tribunal for Rwanda (ICTR) in 1994) than to risk blood and treasure in a forceful intervention. Only in the wake of media coverage of the massacre at Srebrenica, and other terrible events, did powerful states finally use UN authority to help bring pressure to bear on Serb parties sufficient to end the worst Balkan atrocities by 1995. But even graphic media coverage of genocide in Rwanda failed to mobilize significant intervention there, particularly by Western states (mainly because of US difficulties in Somalia and a domestic backlash against incurring costs to save "others").

In Bosnia we were treated to the unseemly spectacle of the UN High Commissioner for Refugees, Sadako Ogata, suspending UNHCR relief in order to try to force UNSC members to deal responsibly with the situation, only to have the UN Secretary-General, Boutros Boutros Ghali order a resumption of relief – even though he probably lacked the legal authority to do so.[18] Likewise, when Ms Ogata brought to the attention of the UNSC the fact that Hutu militias, particularly in Zaire, had infiltrated – had even taken over – some of the UNHCR refugee camps, state members of the UNSC refused to authorize a deployment of force to deal with the situation.[19] The UNHCR in particular knows what it means to be left in a sensitive and untenable situation by a UNSC that neglects its proper security responsibilities when faced with a humanitarian disaster.

In places like Bosnia and the Great Lakes region of Africa, UNHCR leaders faced hard choices. They knew their role was being manipulated by various states and non-state parties for "political" purposes. They tried to carve out a zone of relatively neutral humanitarian space for the impartial benefit of innocent victims. But, in the final analysis, key states refused to take decisive action to guarantee that neutral space leading to genuine humanitarian action. A few NGOs, or sections of NGOs, withdrew from the field in protest, but that meant that their efforts for victims were terminated. One may not want relief to reach belligerents, but abandoning victims has moral and material repercussions as well.

Regardless of developments within the UN system, driven by state policy, private aid and relief agencies constituted a cumulative force to be reckoned with regarding humanitarian affairs. Some had rather long histories during which they had built up expertise, name recognition and a donor base. To take the tip of the iceberg, the Save the Children network dates from 1919, the International Rescue Committee from 1933, Oxfam from 1942, Christian Action for Research and Education (CARE) from 1945, World Vision from 1950. Others are more recent (e.g. Doctors Without Borders (Médicin sans frontières (MSF)), 1971) but have brought considerable energy and commitment to their work. Annual budgets as of 2002, however small compared to national militaries, were significant relative to UN and Red Cross agencies: CARE-USA $420m; World Vision, $820m; Oxfam, $390m; MSF, $400m.

Then, too, private human rights advocacy groups like Amnesty International (AI) and Human Rights Watch (HRW), among others, while not providing relief on the ground, provided a running commentary on humanitarian crises (which entailed human rights violations) and tried to pressure states and UN bodies into further action. Their locales, contacts and budgets (AI, $32.5m; HRW, $19.5m) also contributed often to media coverage that sometimes helped set the agenda for other actors. They constantly peppered states with reports and requests, urging more protection of human dignity. Other private actors like the International Crisis Group, an advocacy group for conflict monitoring and resolution, pushed in the same direction.

On the one hand, some of these private groups were sometimes coopted into the UN system in a somewhat systematic way. The UNHCR, which increasingly (some would say disproportionately) became a general relief agency at times, relied on these private groups for grass-roots action. In effect the UNHCR tried to coordinate relief in places like the Balkans and the Great Lakes region of Africa, while the private agencies did the work in the field. On the other hand, sometimes various private relief or development groups went their own way, with little regard for any designation about "UN lead agency". In Cambodia (and Thailand) during 1979–1983, Oxfam intentionally undercut some of the principles and policies of UNICEF, the latter coordinating with the ICRC to try to provide coordinated multilateral relief in that devastated area. Oxfam wanted an independent part of the action, even if this impaired what other humanitarians were trying to do.[20] In and around Rwanda in 1994, some NGO relief agencies operated completely independently, causing major headaches for both the United Nations Assistance Mission for Rwanda (UNAMIR) and the UNHCR.[21]

The UN family was highly fragmented in the matter of response to humanitarian disasters. OCHA or the UNHCR certainly had trouble coordinating the private aid agencies that did the grass-roots work in UN-sponsored programmes.

Global governance, multilateralism, effectiveness

It is states that control the UN system. They get the type of United Nations they authorize and pay for. For the most part, state hypocrisy dominates, not only regarding the principle of state sovereignty,[22] but more generally as well. States profess high-sounding values, but they undercut those values daily. We noted at the outset that states preach a cosmopolitan liberalism, but often practice realism or just plain indifference about "others". It is not unusual for states to provide only a fraction of what they pledge in response to various disasters.

Foundational to the evolution of things are two factors: the weakness of a broad transnational morality despite increasing material globalization, and national elite interest in protecting a preferred position.[23] On the former, even after US Secretary of State Colin Powell declared the Darfur region of the Sudan to be the locus of genocide in 2004, reaction both inside and outside the United States was muted. On the second point, a centralized and powerful United Nations would be seen by many national officials as a threat to that preferred position, not as a primary means to deal with the distress of "others". Thus it is not so surprising that multilateral humanitarianism associated with the United Nations remains essentially in the same spasmodic condition it was about a quarter of a century ago.

There has been some substantive progress. As one author noted, "The prominence of the humanitarian impulse altered the ethical, rhetorical, and military landscapes of Security Council decision-making in the 1990s. The nature and scope of enforcement decisions have amounted, on occasion, to a fundamental increase in the relevance of humanitarian values in relationship to narrowly defined vital interests."[24] Yet the process was not consolidated into systematic and sure practice. And issues of coordination and effectiveness remained much discussed but mostly unaltered.[25]

The major donor countries to UN humanitarianism, who also channel much money through private relief agencies, could certainly insist on a more streamlined and effective UN system. But they do not do so. Above all, we are talking about the US Agency for International Development (USAID) and the Humanitarian Office of the European Community (ECHO). In addition to a lack of interest at high levels of governments, a serious argument can be made that a certain amount of choice in relief mechanisms is a good thing.

There is something to be said for going with UNHCR as lead agency in the field for one situation, but UNICEF or even the World Food Programme (WFP) in another. One may be better situated than the other for that lead role, depending upon contacts, history in-country, and so forth. There is an argument to be made for coordination by consensus among leading relief actors.[26] Many times the UNHCR, UNICEF, the WFP, and others, do in fact work out rather clear divisions of labour for relief. And OCHA is there, plus associated standing committees, to facilitate such arrangements. Of course, when a UN lead agency is designated for relief, that agency should be authorized and empowered to manage rigorously the private aid agencies that contract with the UN. And the relief groups that try to act as Lone Rangers need to be marginalized. But if the Lone Ranger NGO strikes a separate deal with the host state, which is "sovereign", then what?

Can UN humanitarian bodies be independent from state strategic calculations? Many UN officials and other observers call for precisely this type of independence from politics – meaning, in reality, from the strategic calculations of governments.[27] But the UN system is an intergovernmental system. OCHA, as part of the UN secretariat, can properly aspire to that independent status. Even the UNHCR can appeal to its authorizing resolutions and associated conventional instruments to seek independent, impartial and neutral programming. But in the last analysis, UNHCR and UNICEF and WFP will not be fully independent. Their mandates and budgets come from governments. If the United States and its western allies want UNHCR or UNICEF to become a large relief agency caring for refugees and International Development Programmes (IDPs) far away from Western borders, they have the power to make that happen.

It is a fact of life that the United States contributes more money for relief, reconstruction and development in Iraq and Afghanistan, compared to funding for the Sudan or the Democratic Republic of the Congo or northern Uganda. In the former, there is a greater security interest, along with commitments of personal and national prestige. With regard to the latter, and most humanitarian disasters occur in the less-developed countries, the UN system may manifest a limited humanitarian impulse, but not a neutral and impartial moral imperative.[28] Powerful states, and above all the quasi-imperial United States, will ensure that this is so. The UN Emergency Relief Coordinator may be principled and dynamic, a spokesman for a liberal cosmopolitanism, but he will remain powerless to change the dominance of nationalistic decision-making in UN bodies. The two fundamental principles continue to clash; they remain unresolved on a systematic basis.

It does not help matters that the Western-based media outlets are also highly nationalistic – more interested in the fate of a few Western soldiers or journalists than in the hugely greater numbers of those in distress in non-Western poor countries. One has only to look at the lack of sustained Western media coverage of the Democratic Republic of the Congo to see that this is so. And when there is Western media attention to the humanitarian disasters of the Global South, it is mostly short lived. Even regarding the 2004–2005 tsunami in Asia, eventually the media moved on to other stories. In commercial journalism one can only tell about a disaster for so long. The follow-on problems of development and re-development do not make good pictures or stories with mass appeal.

States acting unilaterally would do well to avoid the discourse of humanitarianism. Most of the time (but not always), such state foreign policy debases the notion of humanitarianism. One of the more egregious examples was when the Reagan administration referred to its non-lethal, but nevertheless military, aid to the Contras in Central America as "humanitarian". State unilateral reference to humanitarianism is most often a self-serving cover for self-interested concerns. When the US adopted "humanitarian" policies towards the population in Afghanistan circa 2002, such as emergency food relief, its fundamental goal was strategic and self-interested – to separate the Taliban and Al-Qaeda political factions from the rest of the Afghanistan people, and to show to the rest of the world that its fight was with those political factions, not with Islamic peoples per se.

Moreover, a certain state reference to humanitarianism can endanger the real humanitarians. Both Colin Powell and US AID director Andrew Natsios have called for relief NGOs to get on the US team, to fully support US objectives in places like Iraq.[29] This effort is misguided.

It is bad enough that in places like Iraq Red Cross agencies used the Red Cross emblem in efforts for neutral projects, while coalition forces used the same emblem on certain military equipment and facilities while carrying out their invasion and occupation.[30] The hard fact was that in Iraq there was no automatic neutral space for humanitarian work, and it proved extremely difficult, if not impossible, to construct that neutral humanitarian space. There were repeated violent attacks on a variety of "aid workers". When Secretary of State Powell referred to relief NGOs as force multipliers for the occupying coalition, he helped erase their image of neutrality, impartiality and independence.

When the ICRC and the United Nations independently tried to improve the daily lives of Iraqis through improved sanitation and medical care, inter alia, this inadvertently contributed to what the coalition sought to achieve: a satisfied Iraqi population willing to accept a coalition-inspired government friendly to the West. The best that the ICRC could do was to try to locate and dialogue with the anti-coalition forces, to convince them that the organization was not motivated to support the coalition and its interim government. The same dilemma of how to construct neutrality plagued not only the UN in Iraq, but also NGOs like CARE in Iraq and MSF in Afghanistan, whose personnel were also attacked by radical Islamic elements.[31]

It is no easy thing for many NGOs to chart an independent, neutral and impartial course in humanitarian relief, distinct from the strategic calculations of states. Care-USA receives 40–70 per cent of its budget from the US government in any given year. Save the Children-USA may receive about 40 per cent of its budget from the US government in a particular year. The International Rescue Committee may get about 80 per cent of its annual budget from Washington. World Vision, which receives only about 20–35 per cent of its income from the US government in a given year, is part of the American Christian social conservative movement; it started as part of a broad anti-communist concern and worked closely with the US government during the Cold War; it has worked hand in hand with the US government regarding food aid to North Korea. A former vice-president of World Vision was Andrew Natsios, who became the head of the US AID under George W. Bush, and was the head of AID's Office of Foreign Disaster Relief under George H.W. Bush. Such facts raise questions about independent humanitarianism by these and other NGOs.

UN humanitarianism today

Space does not allow a detailed further examination of UN humanitarianism today. It is sufficient to note, however, the continuing unevenness and unpredictability of the process. In the 2004–2005 tsunami disaster, the UN's Jan Egeland, as Emergency Relief Coordinator, played a valuable if controversial role. He was both an effective (if sometimes irritating) stimulus for greater resources, and also a reasonably effective coordinator, trying to minimizing overlap, duplication and inappropriate donations in kind. Given the size of the disaster, some management and coordination problems were inevitable, and did indeed occur. But on the whole, the international response, led by the UN, was good enough to prevent mass starvation and epidemics.

On the other hand, in Kosovo in 1999, the UN and particularly the UNHCR were pushed aside early on by NATO states. The latter regarded the displaced ethnic Albanians as too important to be left to the care of others–since their plight was the publicized *raison d'être* of the forceful intervention by those Western states. It was also the case that early on the UNHCR was thinly staffed, unprepared, slow in response, and basically unimpressive in that particular case.[32] So whereas particularly OCHA got reasonably high marks for effective coordination in the winter of 2004–2005, particularly the UNHCR was marginalized and ineffective early-on in the Kosovo affair.

At the UN World Summit in September 2005, there were official promises to improve OCHA's Central Emergency Revolving Fund. Otherwise, humanitarian relief did not loom large in talk of institutional reform. There was also little attention to humanitarianism in the Secretary-General's preceding report ("In Larger Freedom"), and none in the report of the Secretary-General's High Level Panel on Threats, Challenges and Change. The World Summit did pay some attention to refugees and IDPs.

Red Cross redux

Long before the United Nations even existed, the ICRC, the lead agency in conflicts for the International Red Cross and Red Crescent Movement (hereafter, the Red Cross, or the Red Cross network), was trying to organize a transnational humanitarian Movement. In the ICRC's view, international humanitarianism involves not only providing food, water, clothing, shelter, and health care, but also supervising detention conditions and protecting family cohesion in a variety of ways (tracing of missing persons, reunification of family members, reintegration of former child soldiers into civilian society, providing for orphans because of killed parents). Since about 1970, after the Nigerian–Biafran conflict, the ICRC has been reinventing itself so as to better its performance. Where there are persons in distress because of war and other types of political conflict, the ICRC is always present – often in highly important ways. It stresses its independence from the UN system, in the name of neutrality, while cooperating with it at times according to its own decisions.[33]

Some history

From its beginnings in 1863, the ICRC focused on persons in distress because of war – and later other forms of political conflict. Starting with a focus on wounded combatants in international war, because of the work of its founder Henry Dunant in caring for the wounded after the battle of Solferino in 1859 in northern Italy, the ICRC later took up the plight of individuals in internal conflicts, as within the Ottoman Empire. During World War I it gave great attention to prisoners of war, and immediately after that war it started visiting political prisoners in situations of internal troubles and tensions in places like Hungary and Russia. World War II brought recognition for both civilian relief and prisoner protection, as well as the tracing of missing persons. Basic ICRC functions did not change during the Cold War or the following unipolar period.

The ICRC's original intent, not fully consistent with Dunant's direct action, was to help develop a legal framework for humanitarian action by others. It drafted the 1864 Geneva Convention (GC) for victims of war, under which wounded soldiers were neutralized, along with the medical personnel who cared for them. The wise course of action was to place the primary obligation on public authorities for the care of victims of war. This was the first full treaty in international humanitarian law (IHL), with other core treaties following in 1906, 1929, 1949 and 1977.[34] Particularly in the four interlocking GCs of 1949, the ICRC is recognized and even given certain rights – such as the right of detention visits to combatant and civilian prisoners in international armed conflict. In modern IHL there is a right to humanitarian assistance in war, although it is not clear who exactly is supposed to implement the right, under what conditions.

From its start the ICRC also promoted the development of national relief or aid societies, which over time evolved into today's 182 National Red Cross or Red Crescent Societies.[35] But the Franco-Prussian War of 1870 and then World War I showed the strength of narrow nationalism, the other side of which was the weakness of Red Cross cosmopolitanism as envisaged by Dunant. Various national aid societies were not able to rise above nationalism to practice neutral and impartial humanitarianism. They cared mostly for co-nationals. Over time these official national aid societies increasingly were nationalized and militarized by their chartering governments.[36] So the ICRC, based in neutral Switzerland, became more of an actor in the field and less of a rearguard storage depot and mailbox. The ICRC was well positioned to practice independent, neutral and impartial Red Cross humanitarianism (as long as Swiss national interests did not come into play).

After World War I the large and influential American Red Cross tried to push aside the all-Swiss ICRC by creating a League of Red Cross and Red Crescent Societies. The ICRC was not able to block the creation of the League, now the Federation, as a union of all the National Societies. But the ICRC was able to limit the Federation's mandate to natural (and industrial) disasters and development of the National Societies, thus preserving for itself the realm of Red Cross humanitarianism in conflicts. After much organizational competition and some confusion during 1920–1990, the components of the Red Cross have reaffirmed and codified this basic division of labour.

In the Seville Agreement of 1997, the Movement again stipulated that the ICRC was the network's lead actor in armed conflict for the roles of detention visits, relief, and family reunification efforts. The ICRC also maintained its lead role concerning detainees and their families in situations of internal troubles and tensions. The Federation took on work with refugees and IDPs in countries not characterized by armed conflict, and well as continuing its coordination regarding the international response to natural and industrial/technological disasters. National Societies were to support both the ICRC and Federation internationally, as well as continuing a broad range of domestic social programmes. A National Society might even become the lead agency for the Movement in an international action, but only with the "concurrence" of the two (separate) headquarters in Geneva.

This Seville Agreement has reduced friction between the ICRC and Federation, or more accurately codified an improvement in relations that was already occurring, as well as encouraging a more orderly relationship between the ICRC and its natural "local partners", the National Societies. Officials of the latter are now regularly seconded to the ICRC (and Federation) for short-term contract work.

The significance of Seville is that the Red Cross network is relatively more integrated than in the past, with the ICRC better able to tap into the resources of the stronger National Societies without being undercut by the Federation. A division of labour has been clarified particularly regarding refugees and IDPs, where the ICRC has ceded some ground to the Federation. The ICRC, having too often ignored the National Societies in humanitarian field work between about 1914 and 1990, now is relatively more interested in a better integrated Red Cross network, at least for relief but not for detention visits.[37]

The fact remains, however, that most National Societies are often more aligned with their national governments than with the ICRC. Like the American, British, or French Red Cross Societies, most of these National Societies are more nationalistic than cosmopolitan. They are more patriotic than neutral and impartial. For example, they followed their governments into Northern Iraq in 1991 without much coordination with the ICRC. They may enthusiastically support some ICRC humanitarian operations when their governments do not object or interfere. In the Darfur regions of the Sudan, for example, there is a loose coordination between the ICRC and various Western National Societies that have taken an interest in that conflicted country.

At the International Conferences of the network, which occur in principle every four years, and at which states that are parties to the Geneva Conventions also attend and vote in addition to Red Cross or Red Crescent agencies, there is some renewed discussion of cosmopolitan neutrality for the National Societies as compared to nationalistic deference to their governments. But almost 150 years of fragmented and nationalized history will be difficult for the Red Cross network to completely change, to understate matters.

Mono-nationality, multilateralism, effectiveness

ICRC statutes, reinforced by Movement statutes, establish the ICRC as a private Swiss organization ultimately governed by a Committee of not more than 25 Swiss citizens, which, when meeting in formal session, is called the Assembly. It is the Assembly, not the Red Cross conference or any other body, that is responsible for ICRC governance, or the basic rules and doctrine (strategy) of the house. The ICRC is democratic internally, with votes in its Assembly on general policies. It also bears noting that even democratic processes often manifest undemocratic elements. In the United States one has not only appointed judges but also the Federal Reserve System that is largely shielded from democratic pressures in the interest of effective monetary policy. In the same way it can be said that the ICRC is shielded from outside democratic pressures manifested through the Red Cross network or the United Nations. The self-governing nature of the ICRC has been approved by votes in the Red Cross Conference, with states parties to the GCs participating.

Arguably it is ICRC mono-nationality that is foundational for its independence, neutrality and impartiality. The all-Swiss Committee, linked to permanent Swiss neutrality, in the last analysis does ensure that when belligerents fight, or factions in a civil war, or persons generating internal troubles and tensions, no member from any such group will be on the Committee.[38]

The ICRC now has a headquarters agreement with the Swiss Confederation, as if it were an international organization, making its premises and records off-limits to Bern. The organization has similar agreements with dozens of states where it maintains rather more permanent offices. Since 1992 the ICRC manifests a multinational staff, drawn overwhelmingly from the North Atlantic area. The Global South is hardly represented at all (approximately 5 per cent). In the future, important ICRC officials such as the Director-General, the Director of Operations, and the heads of various delegations and offices may be non-Swiss. On occasions there are joint programmes with the multinational Federation, and, as noted already, personnel from various National Societies are seconded to the ICRC. So the ICRC is now a blend of mono-nationality at the top and a certain type of multinationalism in its professional staff.

The all-Swiss Committee/Assembly has reduced importance today. It meets only five times a year. The daily operations are managed by the Director-General, who has personal responsibility for the Directorate, a five person "cabinet" that coordinates the professional side of the house. However, the ICRC President and the Council of the Assembly, a subgroup of the Assembly, remain both Swiss and influential. In reality, the leadership of the organization is shared by the President and the Director-General, with the Council of the Assembly as a periodically important body. At the time of writing, all of these latter elements are Swiss. (These offices and bodies are also dominated by white males, but that is another question.)

The Swiss connection at the ICRC has indeed led to considerable independence, neutrality and impartiality over time in its humanitarian endeavours, not to mention an impressive record of accomplishment that has led to three or four Nobel peace prizes, depending on view.[39] No organization is perfect, and a reasoned argument can be made that the ICRC was not as independent, neutral, impartial and effective as the organization projects, especially prior to about 1970.[40] The ICRC was carefully supervised by Bern during World War II to ensure that its activities did not unduly antagonize Nazi Germany. This situation constituted the major blight on its record of independence. The organization was not totally neutral during the cold war, tilting towards the United States in the Korean War, and towards France in Southeast Asia during the 1947–1954 period. During the cold war, indeed from 1917, the ICRC leadership, overlapping with the political elite in Bern, was almost as anti-communist as Bern. There were times, especially during its early history, when it was less than impartial in responding to human distress based on need. In World War I it gave more attention to the Western front than other theatres of war. In World War II it gave more attention to Europe than to the Far East.

Still, we should not establish impossible standards of perfection for organizations, which of course are comprised of fallible human beings. Particularly since 1970, after reviewing its defects in the Nigerian–Biafran conflict, the ICRC has paid careful attention to ways of establishing and improving a record of independence, neutrality and impartiality in its humanitarian work. As for independence, it now keeps a greater distance from Bern. Also, the ICRC did not hesitate to oppose the United States, a major donor, over the desirability of an absolute prohibition on the deployment of anti-personnel land mines.[41] As for neutrality, while there are always charges of bias in any emotion-laden conflict, to give but one example, the ICRC has worked on both sides of the Israeli–Palestinian conflict since 1948, and virtually without interruption since 1967. As for impartiality, when much of the Western press wanted to focus on Afghanistan and Iraq after 11 September 2001, the ICRC tried to remind the international community of pressing humanitarian needs elsewhere, as in the Democratic Republic of the Congo.

At the moment, there is no drive under way to change the mono-nationality of the ICRC.[42] This is primarily because of the reduced importance of the Committee/Assembly relative to other parts of the house, and because of the organization's mostly impressive record since about 1970.

Red Cross humanitarianism today

The ICRC is one of the major humanitarian actors in international relations today by any standard. It is one of the big four relief agencies (the others being the UNHCR, UNICEF and the World Food Programme),[43] operating on a par with these major intergovernmental agencies. It achieved this status by 1979–1980 when it teamed with UNICEF (and in some ways was more dynamic than UNICEF) to run a major relief programme in Cambodia (and parts of Thailand). To indicate but one aspect of its relief work, the ICRC recently won an award for its efforts regarding prostheses around the world, as it determinedly used its medical relief to cope with the physical and psychological traumas of landmines, unexploded ordinance, and the other detritus of conflict which continued to maim long after active combat.[44] It is also the premier agency for detention visits around the world regarding international and internal armed conflict, and also situations of internal troubles and tensions. And it still does more than any other agency to restore family ties interrupted by conflict, working often in partnership with various national societies.

Two thumbnail sketches indicate its primary and direct contribution to international humanitarianism in conflicts.[45] In Somalia in the early 1990s, when the complexities and brutalities of that failed state led to a situation of massive malnutrition and starvation, the ICRC was central to breaking the back of that humanitarian disaster by 1994. While most UN agencies and NGOs retired to the sidelines, the ICRC stayed in the country despite the dangers and frustrations. For the first time in its long history it accepted to organize relief under the protection of military forces.[46] Teaming with the Somali Red Crescent, which the ICRC itself rejuvenated and made into an important and reliable partner, it had the best access of any agency to those in dire straits in rural Somalia. It displayed the size, resources, creativity and expertise to save perhaps 1.5 million lives in that era. It was not bureaucratic or stodgy. It required the US military and others to keep weapons out of neutralized planes and premises, then turned around and hired local security forces to protect against theft.[47] To reduce theft of rice, which had become the currency of the nation, it provided cooked food in a network of soup kitchens. For a time, faced with kidnappings for ransom, it moved to Nairobi but ran relief convoys under the protection of local Somali groups identified as reliable partners by the Somali Red Crescent. It took journalists on tours of the country at its own expense, in order to generate public pressure that could ameliorate the situation. In a setting where almost no one with a weapon had ever heard of international humanitarian law, the ICRC out-performed most others, and certainly surpassed the UNHCR, in responding to civilians in extreme distress.

In the US "war against terrorism", the ICRC played its usual role with regard to detention visits. The organization was faced with two contradictory policies established by Washington. First, the ICRC was allowed in principle to conduct detention visits at Guantanamo Bay, in Afghanistan, and in Iraq (but was denied access to certain prisoners held secretly either under US or foreign jurisdictions). Second, the United States instituted a policy of coercive or abusive interrogation of certain prisoners deemed to be of high intelligence value.[48] This latter policy involved the techniques of terrifying with dogs, removal of clothing, sleep deprivation, subjection to loud noises, and other measures designed to break resistance to interrogation. Some measures, such as simulating drowning, clearly amounted to serious violations of human rights and humanitarian law. The other measures were clearly violations of standards against mistreatment. This latter policy led to the widely publicized abuses at the Abu Ghraib prison in Iraq, where abuse and humiliation occurred unrelated to interrogation. There the policy of selective abuse ran out of control because of insufficient training and supervision.

While asking repeatedly for access to those held in secret, the ICRC reported to US authorities discreetly what its delegates witnessed. Particularly at Guantanamo, where relations became strained between ICRC delegates and prison authorities because of ICRC repeated challenges to prevailing practices. Regarding Guantanamo, and consistent with the Organization's doctrine, starting in mid-2003 it went public with its concern about the effect of indefinite detention without charge or trial on the mental health of detainees.[49] Regarding Guantanamo and Afghanistan, President Kellenberger went to Washington and spoke privately with high officials in both mid-2003 and early-2004. The ICRC, at the time of writing, had not gone public with regard to detention in Iraq, partly because the scandal about abuse erupted in 2004 through other sources, and partly because the ICRC believed US authorities had shown sufficient will to institute beneficial changes. The ICRC repeatedly commented in public about its lack of access to secret or ghost detainees.

The ICRC largely left to others the public debate about legal issues, preferring to concentrate on practical improvements "on the ground". President Kellenberger did tenaciously continue a private dialogue with various US officials about the protections afforded by IHL, some of which the ICRC believed applied to various detainees held by the United States. At the time of writing, many of these practical and legal matters remained unresolved, with US courts slowly taking up many issues of prisoner rights in the US "war on terrorism". There remained room for debate about whether the Geneva headquarters had been dynamic enough in making timely representations to senior Bush administration officials about continued mistreatment of prisoners, especially in Guantanamo and Afghanistan, not to mention in the US secret gulag.

Conclusion

The ICRC represents the international standard for independent, neutral, and impartial humanitarianism Whatever its defects of the past, no other actor in the contemporary world is as independent from state strategic calculation, as neutral in power struggles, and as impartial in its interest in protecting human dignity based strictly on need in conflict situations.[50] At times in the past, as in Southeast Asia or East Africa, it has withdrawn from an area or a situation when it decided that the humanitarian good it was doing was not commensurate with the contribution it was inadvertently making to a fighting party's strategic objectives. Such were the hard choices involved in protecting an independent, impartial and neutral role.

As much as the ICRC has increased its human and material resources in the past decades (annual budget at the time of writing of approximately $600 million), it remains too small however to handle the big relief emergencies alone, so there will continue to be a need for UN and NGO roles in that domain. (The UNHCR budget seems to have peaked several years ago at about $1 billion.)

ICRC prison visits remain unaffected as UN measures for prison visits have yet to come into force, while European measures (patterned on the ICRC) are limited to that geographical area. No NGO does systematic prison visits, nor should they.[51]

How the ICRC constructs its budget projections, based on a thorough and bottom-up review of anticipated problems starting with sub-delegation in-put, actually constitutes a reliable early-warning system for humanitarian crises. A few alert diplomats know this.

Of course if one is talking about non-neutral or forceful intervention in response to humanitarian crises, then one has to look elsewhere for the appropriate response. The ICRC may call for such approaches, but its neutrality forbids it from participation.[52] There are no neutral solutions to the root causes of humanitarian disasters.[53]

Regardless of notions like lead agency and public responsibility, the essentially private ICRC remains an important point of comparison for all humanitarian actors. Its claims to independence, impartiality and neutrality remain a yardstick, both for those who make the same claims and for those who would strike a different course. Doctors Without Borders, for example, does not generally claim to be neutral, and, at least in official doctrine, attempts to both "blow the whistle" on violations of human rights and humanitarian law and provide assistance to victims on the ground. But in Rwanda and other places, MSF has had to move toward the ICRC policies of discreet neutrality in order to operate in these violent and complex situations.

UN relief agencies like the UNHCR and UNICEF, as well as the UN Emergency Relief Coordinator, may aspire to those same core values that the ICRC represents, but since they are part of an intergovernmental system they will not be able to match the ICRC record in this regard. Ultimately, states can tell the UNHCR and UNICEF, or any other lead UN agency, what to do. States always have national interests, however subjectively and even erroneously constructed, and they cannot help but project those interests into their foreign policies at the United Nations. Rigorously neutral and impartial humanitarian relief through the United Nations is rare. State foreign policies cannot completely escape the pull of parochial and self-serving domestic elements that question the wisdom of national sacrifice for "others", or advocate advantage for one's own side.

The UN Secretary-General, as well as the UN Emergency Relief Coordinator, and even various UN agency heads, can articulate the cosmopolitan and liberal view of coherent and consistent multilateral humanitarianism. They can personify the international moral imperative to help strangers. But particularly the follow-on policies at the United Nations, because of state values and power, are likely to reflect more of an inconsistent humanitarian impulse than a genuine and thus consistent moral imperative. After all, if states want to advance a genuinely neutral and impartial humanitarian endeavour, they can give more resources to the ICRC, although in that case they will lose control of the operation, given the independence of the ICRC. The ICRC remains private, even if recognized in IHL, and its Assembly does not take instruction from public authorities.

One can dwell on the defects of the one remaining superpower or hyperpower, and the United States was certainly slow to act in the Balkans and never acted constructively at the time of the genocide in Rwanda. The United States also misused the humanitarian argument in its invasion of Iraq.[54] Further, even in the 1999 case of Kosovo, US leadership for action was partially driven by concern for its own reputational costs – its shame at not having acted better in Bosnia earlier.[55] Moreover, the George W. Bush administration was slow and relatively miserly in its response to the 2004–2005 tsunami crisis, until UN officials and others induced changes in Washington.[56] But we should recall that the Dutch were not eager to suffer costs for the defence of Srebrenica, nor the Belgians for staying the course in Rwanda. And when the Japanese did help in Cambodia, or the Australians in East Timor, certain expedient national interests drove those policies as much or more than humanitarianism.[57]

This record but confirms our core point about the continuing weakness of transnational morality. Thick morality reflects nationalism in that the group of genuine and intense and sustained humanitarian concern is the nation, while thin morality continues to characterize reaction to the suffering of "others".

Whether a continuing material globalization will deepen social globalization in the future is an interesting question. Only if more persons identify with foreign suffering, and see that it has relevance to them, morally or expediently, is the situation likely to change. Some social science evidence suggests that when persons view foreign suffering as related to them, either for moral reasons (my own humanity is diminished) or expedient reasons (an abusive or failed state may breed terrorists that may attack me), then one might see the institutionalization of cosmopolitan liberalism through systematic and reliable humanitarianism.[58] This is not going to happen tomorrow.

Still, there has occurred in bits and pieces, and often at great human cost, a stronger and inherently multilateral humanitarian impulse in the world. The process can certainly be depressing. It took the slaughter of World War I to establish firmly the Red Cross network (even if disjointed), not to mention the 1929 Geneva Convention for Prisoners of War. It took the disaster of World War II to produce the 1949 Geneva Conventions. It took ethnic cleansing and genocide in the Balkans and Rwanda to move the international community towards greater attention to criminal justice, in an effort to deter future atrocities. Likewise, it took the Asian tsunami disaster to move the discussion forward about a global disaster alert system.

So there has been a certain, if costly, humanitarian progress. The issue is to tame the process – which is to say to manage it efficiently, and to make it responsive to the needs and sensitivities of those in dire straits in a timely way. The central challenge comes from the continuing strength of narrow nationalism, and the selfish state power on which it is based, and the inherent difficulty of coordinating diverse if often well-intentioned partners.

Notes

1. For a new analysis of this old tension, see Barry Buzan (2004) *From International to World Society? English School Theory and the Social Structure of Globalization*, New

York: Cambridge University Press. For an older example of this same type of analysis, see Robert C. Johansen (1980) *The National Interest and the Human Interest: An Analysis of U.S. Foreign Policy*, Princeton: Princeton University Press.
2. *The Responsibility to Protect*, Report of the International Commission on Intervention and State Sovereignty, Ottawa: International Development Research Centre, 2001.
3. See further, the chapter by Robert Keohane in this volume regarding widespread acceptance of a cosmopolitan liberal ethics.
4. David P. Forsythe (1995) "Human rights and US foreign policy: two levels, two worlds," *Political Studies* XLIII(Special Issue): 111–130. Also in David Beetham (ed.) (1995) *Politics and Human Rights*, Oxford: Blackwells.
5. Here I use multilateralism in a sense broader than Keohane's essay in this volume. His conception of multilateralism centres on states. Mine allows, for example, for a multilateral Red Cross Movement or Red Cross Federation reflecting many actors active in a policy making process, some or all of them not being states. Global humanitarianism today almost always involves actors beyond the state.
6. See further, Keohane in this volume on the importance of three core values: human rights, democratic process and effectiveness.
7. See the chapter by Thomas G. Weiss in this volume.
8. I thank Ramesh Thakur for this insight.
9. For starters, see *World Disasters Report 2003*, Geneva: International Red Cross and Red Crescent Federation, 2004.
10. Thomas G. Weiss, David P. Forsythe and Roger A. Coate (2004) *The United Nations and Changing World Politics*, 4th edn, Boulder: Westview, p. 187.
11. See especially, Claudena Skran (1995) *Refugees in Inter-War Europe*, Oxford: Oxford University Press.
12. In the late 1960s and early 1970s a number of states were concerned not only with growing numbers of refugees and other displaced persons, but with the continuing Israeli control of territories taken in the 1967 war, and with preparations for the 1974 session of a diplomatic conference on IHL, so there was increased attention at that time to many aspects of humanitarianism, not just emergency relief. For example, there was the UN conference in 1968 in Teheran concerning human rights in armed conflict, and reports on that subject by the UN secretariat. These events did not entirely reflect neutral or purely humanitarian concern, for a number of parties were interested in using humanitarian norms as constraints on, and impediments for, adversaries. Thus a number of parties sought to use "humanitarian" rules against, particularly, Israel and South Africa. Some versions of "humanitarianism" were combined with realpolitik.
13. Thomas W. Stephens (1978) *The United Disaster Relief Office: The Politics and Administration of International Relief Assistance*, Washington: University Press of America.

    In 1971 India intervened with force to dismember Pakistan, in the context of much forced displacement on the Indian sub-continent. In general, the UN's involvement was unbelievably complicated and messy during the period 1971–1973. In so far as UN involvement had a focal point, it was the UNHCR. The UN Secretary-General created an office supposedly to coordinate humanitarian matters, whose head was in fact borrowed from the ICRC (Walter Umbricht). These developments on the Indian subcontinent helped propel the UN into humanitarian relief on a more continuing basis.
14. Gil Loescher, among others, argues that the UNHCR gave such priority to relief than its traditional protection work suffered, see Loescher, G. (2002) *The UNHCR in World Politics: A Perilous Path*, Oxford and New York: Oxford University Press.
15. See Thomas G. Weiss (2004) "The humanitarian impulse", in David Malone (ed.) *The U.N. Security Council: From the Cold War to the 21st Century*, Boulder: Lynne Rienner, forthcoming. According to Weiss, during the Cold War the UNSC was mostly "missing

in action" regarding humanitarian affairs. The first mention of humanitarian matters in a SC resolution was in 1968 regarding Israeli occupied territory. The ICRC was not mentioned until 1978.

16. This was broadly characteristic of the situation throughout international relations that Robert Keohane and Joseph P. Nye called complex interdependence.
17. Weiss (2004) "The humanitarian impulse".
18. Even though the High Commissioner for Refugees is nominated by the UN SG, the High Commissioner is selected by the UN GA and does not report to the SG but to the GA. Nevertheless, Ogata, having made her political point to no avail, agreed to a resumption of UNHCR relief.
19. Some relief NGOs, or parts of relief NGOs, withdrew to protest against caring for les génocidaires, even though this withdrawal meant that genuine refugees would suffer the consequences. Most relief NGOs stayed.
20. David P. Forsythe (2005) *The Humanitarians: The International Committee of the Red Cross*, Cambridge: Cambridge University Press; and William Shawcross (1984) *The Quality of Mercy: Cambodia, Holocaust and Modern Conscience*, New York: Simon and Schuster.
21. See, Romeo A. Dallaire (1998) "The end of innocence: Rwanda 1994", in Jonathan Moore, *Hard Choices: Moral Dilemmas in Humanitarian Intervention*, Lanham, MD: Rowman & Littlefield, pp. 71–86.
22. Stephen D. Krasner (1999) *State Sovereignty: Organized Hypocrisy*, Princeton: Princeton University Press.
23. See, Keohane in this volume about how loyalty still flows mostly to the nation state.
24. Weiss (2004) "The humanitarian impulse".
25. It is striking how much the older literature on aspects of humanitarianism resembles the discussions of the contemporary world. See, for example, Lynn H. Stephens and Stephen J. Green (eds) (1979) *Disaster Assistance: Appraisal, Reform, and New Approaches*, New York: New York University Press; and Bruce Nichols and Gil Loescher (eds) (1989) *The Moral Nation: Humanitarianism and U.S. Foreign Policy Today*, South Bend: Notre Dame University Press.
26. See further, Larry Minear (2002) *The Humanitarian Enterprise: Dilemmas and Discoveries*, Bloomfield, CT: Kumarian Press.
27. Jan Egeland (2004) "Humanitarianism under fire," *Christian Science Monitor*, 5 August 2004, available at www.csmonitor.com/2004/0805/p09s01-coop.htm; Gil Loescher (2004) "An Idea Lost in the Rubble", *New York Times*, 20 August 2004, p. A25; Edward Giradet (2004) "A disaster for humanitarian relief", *International Herald Tribune*, 2 August 2004, available at www.iht.com/articles/532107.html.
28. This distinction is developed by Weiss (2004) "Humanitarian impulse".
29. See, John S. Burnett (2004) "In the Line of Fire", *New York Times*, 4 August 2004, available at www.nytimes.com/2004/08/04/opinion/04burnett.html.
30. Likewise in Bosnia, the UNHCR used the UN emblem while presenting itself as a neutral relief agency, at the same as the UNSC and UNPROFOR were acting under the same emblem when sometimes employing coercion.
31. From one point of view, both sides fought a total war disdainful of many conventional humanitarian restraints. Radical Islamic elements attacked civilians. The United States tortured and mistreated prisoners. With regard to the latter, many memos surfacing from the Bush administration featured an effort to make null and void much of the UN Convention against Torture and the 1949 Geneva Conventions and 1977 Protocols.

    We do not in fact know the motivations of those who attacked the UN and ICRC headquarters in Iraq, or killed MSF workers in Afghanistan. Was the violence because the work of these actors inherently fit with US objectives, or was a blind rage at work against all actors seen to be Western? The former reasoning was articulated by certain Taliban elements claiming responsibility for the attack on MSF in Afghanistan.

32. See, for example, A.J.R. Groom and Paul Taylor (2000) "The United Nations system and the Kosovo crisis", in Albrecht Schnabel and Ramesh Thakur (eds) *Kosovo and the Challenge of Humanitarian Intervention*, Tokyo: UNU Press, pp. 291–318. See further, Larry Minear, Ted van Baarda and Marc Sommers (2000) *NATO and Humanitarian Action in the Kosovo Crisis*, Watson Institute for International Studies, Brown University, Occasional Paper #36.
33. This section draws heavily on Forsythe (2005) *The Humanitarians*.
34. There is no agreement on the precise boundaries of IHL. Parts of the Convention on the Rights of the Child pertaining to child soldiers might qualify as part of the international law protecting human dignity in armed conflict. The ICRC considers various legal instruments pertaining to the means and methods of combat, such as the land mines treaty, to be part of IHL.
35. Two emblems emerged for the movement when the Ottoman Empire in the 1870s refused to use the Red Cross emblem for its aid society, but rather chose the Red Crescent emblem, a move supported by Persia and Egypt and a few other Islamic states. Thereafter, to make a long, complicated and still unfinished story short, the movement, and even more so states meeting in a diplomatic conference, saw the problem of a multiplication of emblems. It is states that determine neutral emblems in international law. Theoretically the movement could do as it pleases, but then movement emblems might find no recognition in international law. Moreover, many National Red Cross or Red Crescent Societies are not independent from their governments when voting in Red Cross conferences.
36. The best treatment is by John F. Hutchinson (1996) *Champions of Charity: War and the Rise of the Red Cross*, Boulder: Westview.
37. See Caroline Morehead (1998/1999) *Dunant's Dream: War, Switzerland and The History Of The Red Cross*, New York: Harper Collins. ICRC doctrine on relations with National Societies regarding detention visits is that the relationship depends on the context. The ICRC may bypass, or work with, or partially involve the NS, depending on what will prove effective in protecting the dignity of detainees.
38. For a full discussion of ICRC mono-nationality, see Forsythe (2005) *The Humanitarians*. There one finds an analysis of the effects of the Confederation's joining the United Nations and other factors that might undermine the logic of essential ICRC mono-nationality. In the author's view, certain factors in the contemporary world undermine the argument for an all-Swiss ICRC Assembly. On the other hand, if the current system works well, why try to fix something that is not broken?
39. 1906, to Henry Dunant and Fredric Passy; 1917 to the ICRC; 1945 to the ICRC; 1963 to the ICRC and League, now Federation.
40. See Forsythe (2005) *The Humanitarians*.
41. The ICRC receives about 85 per cent of its approximately $600 million annual budget from state voluntary contributions. The largest donors are the United States, Switzerland, the United Kingdom and the European Union.
42. The last major effort was after World War II.
43. Andrew Natsios (1997) *U.S. Foreign Policy and the Four Horsemen of the Apocalypse: Humanitarian Relief in Complex Emergencies*, Westport, CT: Greenwood.
44. The International Society for Prosthetics and Orthotics awarded the Brian Blatchford Prize to the ICRC in 2004 for outstanding service in developing countries. ICRC news release No. 04/91, 6 August 2004.
45. For detailed treatment, see Forsythe (2005) *The Humanitarians.*
46. At about the same time, in the Balkans, it organized the release and movement of some

detainees under the guns of UNPROFOR, the UN security field operation, because of snipers in that area.

47. Contrary to some speculation, the ICRC contribution to the war economy and prolongation of conflict in Somalia was extremely slight.
48. See Amnesty International, "The United States of America: Human dignity denied – torture and accountability in the 'war on terror'", available at http://web.amnesty.org .library/print/ENGAMR511452004; Seymour Hersh (2004) *Chain of Command: The Road from 9/11 to Abu Ghraib*, New York: Harper Collins; Mark Danner (2004) *Torture and Truth: America, Abu Ghraib, and The War On Terror*, New York: New York Review Books; Karen J. Greenberg and Joshua L. Dratel (eds) (2004) *The Torture Papers: The Road to Abu Ghraib*, Cambridge: Cambridge University Press.
49. ICRC doctrine on discretion/publicity is that the organization will make representations about violations of IHL discreetly to authorities, give those authorities reasonable time to make proper changes, but reserves the right to go public about violations if proper changes are not made, and if such public comment will benefit detainees.
50. David Reiff wrongly presents Doctors Without Borders (MSF) as the primary neutral model in Reiff (2002) *A Bed for the Night: Humanitarianism in Crisis*, New York: Simon and Schuster. Bernard Kouchner, founder of MSF, continues to say that MSF is impartial but not neutral. "The Future of Humanitarianism: Remarks of Bernard Kouchner", Carnegie Council on Ethics and International Affairs, available at www.carnegiecouncil .org.viewMedia.php/prmTemplateID/8/prmID/4425. In Rwanda in 1994, MSF had to be incorporated into the ICRC delegation in order to survive in-country. Progressively MSF, which started out believing it could engage in whistle-blowing while operating medical relief inside countries, has in fact moved toward the ICRC position of cautious neutral humanitarianism – at least in certain situations.
51. In Kennedy (2004) *The Dark Sides of Virtue: reassessing international humanitarianism*, Princeton: Princeton University Press, David Kennedy shows the defects of Lone Ranger and amateurish prison visits by well-meaning do-gooders. HRW asked to do prison visits in Afghanistan after 2001. It was properly ignored by US authorities, at least on this one issue.
52. For an example of precisely such a call, see Jakob Kellenberger, President of the ICRC, "Too little, too late for the victims of Darfur", *International Herald Tribune*, 30 August 2004, www.iht.com/articles/536321.html.
53. See further, David Rieff (2002) "Humanitarianism in crisis", *Foreign Affairs* 81(6) November–December: 111–121. And Michael Barnett (2003) "What Is the future of humanitarianism?", *Global Governance* 9: 401–416.
54. See particularly Kenneth Roth (2004) "Was the Iraq war a humanitarian intervention?", available at www.globalagendamagazine.com/2004/kennethroth.asp.
55. Adam Roberts, "NATO's 'Humanitarian War' Over Kosovo", in Larry Minear, Ted van Baarda and Marc Sommers (2000) *NATO and Humanitarian Action in the Kosovo Crisis*, Occasional Paper #36, Watson Institute, Brown University, pp. 121–151.
56. It is likely that Washington increased its assistance once it realized that it was presented with an opportunity to show Muslim Indonesia and elsewhere that its attacks on Islamic radicals did not preclude positive relations with Islamic communities.
57. Among other concerns, the Japanese wanted to show that they deserved a seat on the UN Security Council, and the Australians wanted stability in East Timor in order to staunch a flow of unwanted asylum seekers.
58. See further, Kristen Renwick Monroe (2004) *The Hand of Compassion: Portraits of Moral Choice during the Holocaust*, Princeton: Princeton University Press; and by the same author, (1998) *The Heart of Altruism: Perceptions of a Common Humanity*, Princeton: Princeton University Press.

13

Progress and problems in the multilateral human rights regime

Richard J. Goldstone and Erin P. Kelly

Introduction

In the twentieth century, international law underwent a breathtaking transformation characterized by a vast expansion in the scope of issues it encompasses as well as the institutional machinery through which it is made and enforced. Increasingly, international law encompasses not only formal relations between states, but their domestic actions, as well as the actions of non-state actors. One of the most extraordinary elements of this transformation is the development of international human rights law. This body of law encompasses the range of rights guaranteed in leading multilateral conventions and customary international law as well as humanitarian law and international criminal law. It is innovative in the extent to which it is concerned with protecting individuals, whether they are threatened by the actions of their own government or non-state actors.

Human rights law also exerts a powerful moral force because it espouses a universal ideal of human security that has increasingly become accepted as the goal of international cooperation. This ideal is expressed in the concept of an international rule of law in which ensuring the enjoyment and protection of human rights is the fundamental obligation of national governments, and their legitimacy is measured by the extent to which they achieve this goal. Human rights law draws its legal force from its universality, which is formalized in the widely accepted legal obligations of international conventions and the recognition that some norms have ripened into customary law.[1] In the 1990s, the international community demonstrated its acceptance of the legal force of human rights norms through its repeated recognition that the UN Security Council was justified to invoke its Chapter VII enforcement powers to protect human rights and prevent ongoing violations.

In the early 1940s, momentum for a new international organization grew and many nations, as well as religious and civil society groups, pushed for an international bill of rights as a central component of what eventually became the United Nations.[2] At the first session of the UN General Assembly, it delegated drafting of an international bill of human rights to the Commission on Human Rights. Two years later, what would become the international human rights regime was launched with the adoption of the inspirational and non-binding Universal Declaration of Human Rights (UDHR). The Declaration urges states and all "organs of society" to work toward ensuring that all people enjoy human rights protections. Consistent with this charge, efforts to realize the goals set forth in the Declaration have not been the exclusive province of states. The UDHR itself was promoted by visionary individuals, such as Eleanor Roosevelt and René Cassin, who pushed governments to see the value in such a declaration.[3] Individuals and organizations have continued to be indispensable advocates of the international rule of law. Nongovernmental organizations (NGOs) such as Amnesty International and Human Rights Watch have done the critical work of documenting violations and galvanizing global public opinion to shame governments that perpetrate gross or systematic violations. They have also lobbied multilateral institutions both within and outside the United Nations to strengthen their commitment to protecting and promoting human rights. At the national level, judges and lawyers have played a crucial role in domesticating international standards. Progress in this regard is illustrated in the extent to which new national constitutions, such as that adopted in South Africa, reflect strong commitments to human rights and international norms. In particular, judges in domestic courts increasingly look to the law of other states in interpreting the scope and meaning of particular rights. The importance of these developments should not be underestimated because domestic implementation of human rights is the ultimate goal of international law and the best assurance that individuals will actually enjoy the rights promised in international conventions.

The current widespread acceptance of human rights is the result of the efforts of many stakeholders, including states, individuals, NGOs and judges. This chapter will focus on institutions that form the international human rights regime. The international human rights regime refers to the legal framework embodied in the UDHR, the Geneva Conventions and several major international treaties and conventions, as well as the institutions, such as the UN bodies and regional courts, that oversee state implementation of and compliance with these treaties. Active multilateral institutions, including UN organs and regional courts of human rights, encourage national exchanges and advocacy. Multilateral bodies and international courts also contribute to the legal authority of international norms cited in domestic courts by clarifying the scope and application of such norms.

Notwithstanding substantial progress in establishing a body of international human rights and humanitarian law in the past 50 years, criticism of the international regime is growing. While some assessments hail international human rights law as one of the greatest successes of the twentieth century, others impugn it as a failure that only masks the international community's refusal to prevent continued widespread violations of human rights. These divergent assessments generally reflect the commentator's primarily normative or rationalist perspective.

Those with a normative outlook tend to measure the success of human rights law by the proliferation of rights instruments and the encouraging, if not adequate, willingness of states to ratify such conventions and comply with their requirements.[4] There is ample evidence that human rights norms have come to the forefront of international concern. A leading example is the evolution of the UN from its primary focus on relations among states to include a central role for human rights and the protection of the individual.[5] The Secretary-General and the High Commissioner of Human Rights have undertaken to coordinate and strengthen human rights protections throughout the work of all UN agencies.[6] At the domestic level, advocates both within government and civil society rely on international human rights law to push for reform. In this context, domestic groups benefit from the legal force of human rights law in its capacity to bolster the moral force of their cause and ability to galvanize domestic and international public opinion. Consequently, lawyers and some scholars recognize human rights law as having a central, though not exclusive, role in advancing state compliance with its stated norms.[7]

In contrast, commentators with a rationalist outlook point to widespread violations of rights and argue that human rights law does not, perhaps cannot, adequately constrain non-compliance. The rationalist view recognizes the role of international law to the extent that it shapes the system of incentives and disincentives that enable states to engage in cooperative relationships but denies that it exerts a normative force able to constrain state behaviour.[8] The efficacy of human rights law, then, must be assessed not by the generality of the professed norms, but by the level of state compliance with its rules. In practical terms, this view results in focusing more on enforcement and the regime's ability to impose costs on non-compliant states and gives less attention to supporting or maintaining the foundation of universality on which it built.

Whichever point of view one adopts, it must be conceded that the current regime has not generally succeeded in preventing serious human rights violations globally and that this failure threatens the legitimacy of the regime. The current human rights regime is suffering from a serious decline in what Robert Keohane defines in his chapter in this volume as output and input legitimacy.[9] The system lacks output legitimacy due to its failure to stem the massive crimes perpetrated in recent times, such as the 1994 genocide in Rwanda and the current crisis in Darfur, and suffers further from the perception of bias in selectively intervening in such crises.[10] Other failures of multilateral organizations to respond to systematic human rights violations, such as occur in Myanmar, North Korea and China, contribute to this perception of failure. In addition, the UN organs charged with monitoring compliance with the major international conventions lack output legitimacy because of their inability to stem the widespread non-compliance with their reporting requirements and their inability to take adequate steps to investigate or remedy violations. The system lacks input legitimacy because the political machinations of several members of the Commission on Human Rights have eroded confidence in the human rights regime and the entire UN.[11]

Adding to these institutional challenges is the potential deterioration of the norms themselves precipitated by the manner in which democratic countries have wavered in their commitments to human rights in their pursuit of the "war on terror". Recent actions of the United States, which has played a leading role in promoting human rights, have dealt a particularly serious blow to the strength of international commitment to human rights. These actions include the US rejection and undermining of the ICC, its curtailment of domestic civil liberties, and tolerance for torture abroad in prosecuting the "war on terror". Because of its unique historical role, the apparent defection of the US from its commitment to a human rights regime has serious implications not only for the vitality of multilateral institutions, but for the viability of the basic norms they uphold. Without strong US commitment to affirming human rights even as it faces the challenges of terrorism, the normative and legal force of human rights law will be eroded. If the US rejects human rights standards, economically and politically weaker states, who are most threatened by the perceived sovereignty costs of participation in the human rights regime, will turn away from human rights and reject their very legitimacy. Repressive regimes will use, and have used, the example of the US war on terror as a justification to further restrict civil and political rights.[12] Finally, international support for humanitarian intervention to stop gross violations will wane if human rights are seen as a political chip easily cast aside in pursuit of national self-interest.

There are clearly significant challenges facing the international human rights regime. This paper addresses each of these challenges and considers its effect. Part I addresses the threshold question of whether the human rights regime is fundamentally at odds with the principle of sovereignty and statehood on which the multilateral system is built. Part II presents key historical and doctrinal foundations of human rights law, and then considers a series of institutional challenges to the regime. These challenges include charges that human rights are a Western cultural tradition which is at odds with the values of other cultures. Part II ends with a discussion of proposals for institutional reform of UN human rights organs. Part III considers the leadership challenge that is perhaps most threatening to the long-term viability of the human rights regime – that is the failures of the US and other democracies in responding to the threat of terrorism and massive human rights violations in the context of military conflict or resulting from failed states.

Part I. Normative challenges: sovereignty

Human rights law faces a significant threshold question in the debate over its efficacy and power as an issue of international concern, which is: are human rights and the international rule of law compatible with the current international system based upon a concept of state sovereignty? Commentators have credited human rights, both approvingly and disapprovingly, as a major contributor to the decline of sovereignty.[13] Rationalist critiques of the human rights regime assert that it is ineffective precisely because it has the power to undermine sovereignty and that therefore states will not participate willingly in a regime that imposes such long-term sovereignty costs. Critiques from a normative perspective tend to welcome the rise of the concepts of individual sovereignty and human security and the constraints they place on the scope of state sovereignty. It is not necessary to take sides in these debates and to answer the question posed because the law of human rights is not incompatible with the multilateral system in its current form. Historically, the principle of sovereignty has included a set of internal constraints on state behaviour based first on natural law and later on the concept of a "common morality". Contemporary human rights, international criminal law and humanitarian law originate in this tradition, which can be traced from the work of early jurists, based in the natural law tradition, through the rise of positivism. The best examples of the persistence of humanitarian concern in the development of international law can be seen in nineteenth-century treaties concerning the conduct of war, which frequently make reference to considerations of humanity reflected in the customary law of war.[14]

The Peace of Westphalia in 1648 ushered in the modern era of territorial sovereignty. This historic agreement effectively restricted the reach of the Holy Roman Empire and elevated a secular notion of statehood based on a system of territorial sovereignty that granted autonomy to the numerous new sovereigns. Though they wielded supreme authority, these new sovereigns were not understood to possess unfettered discretion. For example, jurist Jean Bodin, who coined the term "sovereignty" in the late sixteenth century, described the sovereign as subordinate to fundamental law.[15] Thomas Hobbes challenged this view, asserting the unfettered authority of the sovereign. By contrast, in international relations, Hobbes argued that because of the absence of an ultimate sovereign, states exist in a state of nature. Consequently, Hobbes's legacy for international relations is ambiguous. While his view of domestic sovereignty came to dominate law and philosophy and gave rise to positivism, his view of international relations foreclosed the possibility of positive international law and left open the possibility that states were governed by natural law in their relations with each other.[16] International jurists continued to recognize limitations upon the sovereign and natural law theories continued to dominate. For example, Hugo de Groot, the leading jurist of the seventeenth century, offered a secular theory of international law as a subset of the larger body of natural law that binds all people, including sovereigns. In his view, natural law was the foundation for all law and governance and sovereignty was constrained by its commands.

The just war doctrine is a prominent example of the limitations on sovereignty. According to this doctrine, a sovereign is justified in making war only for a just cause, such as a response to an injury or attack. Today, the doctrine is generally limited to self-defence, but from the sixteenth to the eighteenth centuries serious violations of natural law were considered just cause, even if the harm affected only subjects of another sovereign. International jurists at this time recognized a right to intervene in such cases in order to punish or stop violations of the law of nations.[17] European nations waged numerous wars under claims of a right to intervention.[18] In reaction to perceived abuses of the doctrine, jurists began to denounce the right of intervention and restrict the scope of the doctrine.[19] By the end of the nineteenth century, there was growing consensus that individual states were not entitled to engage in military intervention for humanitarian purposes. Rather, it was required that the intervention was authorized by reference to a general moral or legal principle agreed upon by the society of nations and was commonly undertaken collectively. The just war doctrine persisted in this restricted form and became known as humanitarian intervention, the formulation of which demonstrates that despite the subsequent rise of positivism in international law, the concept of a shared moral responsibility continued to play a significant role in international law.[20]

Contemporary human rights law developed within the positive law tradition and it draws its legal force from the wide accession by states to several major multilateral conventions. Humanitarian law, which identifies the protections that apply to various groups in times of conflict, is embodied in the Geneva Conventions, which has achieved near-universal accession. The advent of the United Nations has provided an infrastructure to support and encourage the development and codification of positive law in the areas of humanitarian law and human rights. In recent years, in response to massive human rights violations such as genocide, war crimes and grave breaches of the Geneva Conventions, UN organs and member states have expressed a vision of sovereignty that seeks to reconcile common morality with the sovereign equality upon which the institution is based. This is a vision of sovereignty that affirms the right of states to be free from interference from other states while simultaneously recognizing that states have obligations to their own people.[21] This development is most apparent in the acceptance of the legitimacy, under certain conditions, of humanitarian intervention.

An example of such acceptance is the response to the NATO intervention in 1999 to stop the ethnic cleansing of the Albanian population of Kosovo, a province of Serbia and Montenegro. The government of Slobodan Milosovic was not prepared to tolerate people who followed the Muslim faith living in their country. The Serb army introduced a policy of ethnic cleansing. The NATO powers felt obliged to protect the Albanians in Kosovo. A threatened veto by the Russian Federation resulted in the NATO powers using military force without the authority of a resolution of the Security Council. It was thus in violation of the United Nations Charter and illegal. The intervention was for one purpose only – a humanitarian effort to save the lives and property of the victims. There was no ulterior motive. The global community generally approved of that intervention. When, after the military campaign was over, Russia proposed a Security Council resolution to condemn the intervention it was overwhelmingly defeated in a vote of 12 to 3.[22] The problem that remained was a gap between international law that made the intervention illegal and the morality of protecting innocent people from war crimes perpetrated by a sovereign government.

Two international commissions have considered this question. In 1999, the Prime Minister of Sweden, Goran Persson, established the first of them, the Independent International Commission on Kosovo.[23] The

Commission concluded the NATO intervention to protect the Muslim community of Kosovo to have been "illegal but legitimate". The Commission set out principles that it suggested should govern the use of military force against a sovereign state to prevent or stop the violation of fundamental human rights. The Secretary-General of the United Nations received the report. The Kosovo Commission was followed in 2000 by a Canadian initiative called the International Commission on Intervention and State Sovereignty. It developed a theme that it called "The Responsibility to Protect" and sought to shift the debate from a focus on the right or duty to intervene to a focus on meeting the needs of those people in need of protection. This included state responsibility to prevent populations from large-scale abuses such as genocide, war crimes, ethnic cleansing and crimes against humanity.[24] It also defined responsibilities with respect to state behaviour in evaluating, planning and carrying out military intervention, and rebuilding the affected state following intervention. That report was also delivered to the Secretary-General.

Those reports laid the intellectual groundwork for the consideration of this issue by the UN High Level Panel on Threats, Challenges and Change.[25] The High Level Panel embraced the idea of a responsibility to protect, affirming the legitimacy of intervention when the citizens of a sovereign state are the victims of serious human rights violations by their own government. It recommended that the Security Council and anyone else involved in deciding whether and how to respond to such crises should be bound by five guidelines or criteria of legitimacy, namely:

1. *Seriousness of the threat* – Is the harm sufficiently serious to justify the use of military force? In the case of internal threats, does it involve genocide and other large-scale killing, ethnic cleansing or serious violations of international humanitarian law, actual or imminently apprehended?
2. *Proper purpose* – Is it clear that the primary purpose of the proposed military action is to stop or avert the threat?
3. *Last resort* – Has every non-military option for meeting the threat been explored, with reasonable grounds for believing that other measures will not succeed?
4. *Proportional means* – Are the scale, duration and intensity of the proposed military action the minimum necessary to meet the threat?
5. *Balance of Consequences* – Is there a reasonable chance of the military action being successful in meeting the threat with the consequences of action not likely to be worse than the consequences of inaction?

The Panel suggested that both the General Assembly and the Security Council should embody these guidelines or criteria in a declaration. The 2005 UN World Summit embraced this part of the Panel's report, affirmed the developing norm of the responsibility to protect and encouraged the General Assembly to continue efforts toward a declaration on this topic. Such affirmation by the assembled heads of government of nearly all the states in the world constituted an important step to narrowing the gap between morality and the law relating to humanitarian intervention. The current state of the debate thus appears to have converged on a consensus regarding the legitimacy of humanitarian intervention. The remaining issues concern the practical and procedural aspects of intervention.

Part II. Multilateralism in the human rights regime: institutional challenges

Development of international human rights and humanitarian law

The roots of positive human rights law can be traced to developments in the law of war from the seventeenth century through to the nineteenth century. Grotius defined the law of war to include prohibitions on taking hostages or enslaving defeated soldiers.[26] The prohibition on slavery was later included in the Peace of Westphalia in apparent conformity with Groatian law.[27] Emerich Vattel reaffirmed the idea that considerations of humanity and moderation were the basis of laws of war that applied to sovereigns and soldiers alike.[28] The nineteenth century ushered in a new era of treaty-making sparked by the rise to prominence of positive law as the foundation for international law. The tremendous growth in international commerce and communications required a heightened level of international cooperation. This led to the innovation of the multilateral treaty, one that is left open for accession after the initial signing. By ratifying such instruments, states accept obligations to all other signatories. The first such treaty was the 1856 Declaration of Paris, a naval treaty that outlawed privateering and clarified certain maritime rules of neutrality. The treaty was first signed by Britain, France and a small number of other states, but was left open for accession by other states.[29]

Technological advances in weaponry also encouraged states to make treaties circumscribing their use in the context of military conflict. The first such treaty was the 1861 St Petersburg Declaration, which outlawed the use of certain exploding bullets and used the multilateral form pioneered in the Paris Declaration. States adopted several other arms control treaties in the next decades, including updated prohibitions on exploding bullets and the arms control provisions of the Hague Conventions of 1899 and 1907.

Increasingly, international action focused on the treatment of combatants and non-combatants in war. Such considerations had long been considered part of natural or customary law, but in the nineteenth century, treaty-based law assumed a favoured position, and a drive to codify humanitarian law began to emerge. Henry Dunant can be credited with a major contribution in this area for his efforts in establishing the International Committee of the Red Cross in 1864. Horrified by the battlefield suffering he witnessed, he assembled representatives of several states and proposed the idea that a private, non-partisan group be established to provide medical care to victims of war. States supported the recommendation and several entered into a multilateral agreement specifying their obligations to allow the new organization, a non-state actor, to function within their territories. This development illustrates recognition by states of the need to yield sovereignty to gain protection for their own nationals who might fall into the hands of an enemy.

The Hague Conventions of 1899 included laws respecting the treatment of belligerents, prisoners of war, and residents of occupied territories. The obligations in the Hague Conventions reflected the emphasis on reciprocity that was a pillar of conventions on the law of war during this period. Consequently, the protections of the Conventions were limited to conflict in which all belligerents were parties. However, in keeping with the "interest of humanity and the ever increasing requirements of civilization" that animated the agreements, the reciprocity clause was replaced with the unilateral and universal obligations of the Geneva Conventions of 1949. Regrettably, it took the horrors of two world wars to move states to accept such universal obligations. The success of the Geneva Conventions of 1949 was built upon the groundwork laid in the steady development of the first modern multilateral agreements in the nineteenth century, which were, importantly, aimed at the protection of all victims in war, including civilians and other non-belligerents.

World War II was a watershed in the development of international humanitarian and human rights law. One of the most significant developments in this regard is the advance of international criminal law and its enforcement mechanisms through the tribunals in Nuremberg and Tokyo. The horror of the Holocaust shocked the conscience of people around the world. The Allied leaders were faced with a dilemma – should the leadership of the Nazi regime be summarily executed, as Churchill preferred, or should they be granted a fair trial, as was the preference of the United States? Fortunately, for the future of international criminal justice, the Allies chose the latter option. They drew up the London Agreement, which laid the foundation for the trials in Nuremberg by the International Military Commission. The basis for the jurisdiction of that tribunal was a pooling of their individual domestic jurisdictions to put the alleged Nazi criminals on trial. There was no resort to any form of universal jurisdiction. The strategy of using a trial to address war crimes accomplished several strategic objectives. These included the promotion of healing among the war-torn countries by providing a public forum for the re-establishment of the rule of law, and avoiding collective guilt and punishment by focusing on the culpability of the Nazi leaders.

The Military Commission's most important contribution to the development of human rights law was its establishment of *crimes against humanity* as a new classification of international crime. These are crimes of such magnitude that they are considered crimes not only against the victims but against the whole of humanity. They are crimes that violate fundamental standards of humanity such that they can never be the legitimate acts of government. They led to the development of *universal jurisdiction* – jurisdiction for crimes so egregious that they are an affront to all humanity. As such they may be prosecuted in any country. Such jurisdiction flows not from the location of the crime or the origin of its perpetrators or victims, but from the nature of the crime committed. The development of universal jurisdiction has historically been motivated by the desire that perpetrators of heinous crimes should not escape punishment, as well as by the practical considerations of the need for international cooperation needed to punish and deter certain crimes. The doctrine of universal jurisdiction was long recognized for the international crime of piracy, considered a heinous crime, as well as one that was not committed in the geographic jurisdiction of any court. In recent decades universal jurisdiction has been applied in an increasing number of multilateral agreements, especially those designed to combat international terrorism.

The Geneva Conventions of 1949 provided the first explicit recognition of universal jurisdiction in an international instrument. They conferred jurisdiction in respect of a new species of war crimes called *grave breaches*. These were defined to include the most egregious of war crimes and their terms enabled acceding states to authorize universal jurisdiction to prosecute any person suspected of committing a grave breach. If the domestic laws of the suspect's nation made prosecution impossible, or if a national authority refused to do so, such a nation accepted the obligation to deliver the suspect to a country that was willing or able to prosecute.

The 1984 Convention Against Torture also included a provision for universal jurisdiction for crimes committed during times of peace. It was this provision that influenced the British House of Lords in 1998 to uphold the legality of the extradition order made against General Pinochet. General Pinochet was indicted in Spain under that country's exercise of universal jurisdiction. It could hardly have been imagined a decade before that a former head of state of a South American country might be arrested in London at the request of a Spanish judge for crimes committed in his home country some twenty years earlier.

The Pinochet affair had important and unanticipated consequences. Indonesia's former head of state, Suharto, was reported to have cancelled medical treatment in a German clinic because he feared arrest under a German warrant for war crimes committed in his country. In 2000, a Senegalese court indicted the exiled former dictator of Chad, Hissene Habre.[30] Mengistu Haile Mariam, the former dictator of Ethiopia, was in South Africa for medical treatment when Human Rights Watch publicized his whereabouts; Mengistu beat a hasty retreat to Zimbabwe where, inappropriately, he had been granted asylum. Such developments demonstrated the final break in the long tradition of impunity for former heads of state in the last decade of the twentieth century. It was not long before a sitting head of state, Slobodan Milosovic, was indicted. These indictments signalled the end of the era of impunity for massive human rights violations, creating a new international legal and political context for the world's worst criminals.

Universal jurisdiction also provided jurisdiction for prosecution in the 1973 convention that declared apartheid to be a crime against humanity.[31] The apartheid convention, which entered into force in 1976, was the first to apply universal jurisdiction in a situation not characterized by open conflict. The Convention recognized that a government's actions against its own people, even outside the context of conflict, could constitute a crime against humanity such that its officials could not hide behind a claim of sovereignty. The convention was an important attempt by developing countries to apply human rights standards to universalize their struggles. However, the Western nations did not ratify the Apartheid Convention and it was rendered practically ineffective. It is unfortunate that the Convention was not taken seriously and no South African officials were ever indicted as such actions may well have ended apartheid a decade or more earlier. The failure of the Western countries to implement the Apartheid Convention indicated to many newly independent countries the hypocrisy of the West's commitment to human rights and was an opportunity missed to promote the rule of law.

National and regional incorporation of human rights norms

Although the multilateral human rights regime gains its legal force through the universality of the norms, the goal of international lawmaking is to obligate states to protect individual rights at the national level. The conventions oblige states to harmonize domestic law and policy with international obligations. States, therefore, retain the discretion to fulfil their obligations in a way that is consistent with their cultural and political traditions.[32] Some states have, however, mounted a challenge to the universality of human rights norms, charging that they are a

Western idea that is out of step with the cultural ideals of other parts of the world. This cultural relativist argument became prominent in the lead up to the 1993 World Conference on Human Rights in Vienna when, at a regional preparatory meeting, China led a group of Asian nations to challenge human rights norms as out of step with "Asian values". Asian values have been characterized as espousing a strong community ethic with an abiding respect for tradition.[33] However, the charge that human rights norms are compatible only with Western traditions finds no support in practice. In the first instance, the UDHR was adopted by the United Nations in 1948 with support from member states in all regions of the world. The current arguments for cultural relativism come only from non-democratic leaders who violate the rights of their own citizens. Leaders of democratic nations have not made such arguments. In addition, the NGOs and activists within Asia continue to use human rights law to bolster their democratic and human rights advocacy such that any blanket characterization of these norms as incompatible with Asian culture and values is incorrect.[34] Domestic activism by human rights defenders has led to the establishment of national human rights commissions in several Asian nations.[35]

Domestic advocacy for democracy and human rights is strengthened by international activism and through multilateral mechanisms. For example, the UN has supported efforts to establish human rights commissions at the national level. In October 1991, it convened a workshop in Paris to explore ways of increasing the effectiveness of human rights institutions. This workshop produced a set of standards for national human rights institutions known as the Paris Principles, which were eventually adopted by the Commission on Human Rights in 1992 and the General Assembly in 1993. The Paris Principles require that national institutions must be independent, have as broad a mandate as possible, be characterized by regular and effective functioning, have a pluralistic and representative composition and adequate funding, and be easily accessible to the public. Several Asian countries have established human rights commissions over the past 20 years, including India, Indonesia, Sri Lanka, the Philippines, Malaysia and Nepal. Bangladesh and Thailand are in the process of establishing them. In Africa, the African Commission on Human and People's Rights, a regional body charged with monitoring and interpreting the African Charter on Human and People's Rights, forged formal ties with a number of national human rights commissions. Using the criteria of the Paris Principles, the Commission has recognized commissions from Algeria, Rwanda, Malawi, Niger, Sierra Leone and Senegal. At a recent session, the Commission criticized the Government of Niger for interfering with the independence of the Niger Commission.

When leaders of non-democratic nations disregard international human rights norms, the norms remain significant to the extent they are adopted by domestic constituencies and help shape reform movement advocacy. South Africa is a prominent example of the value of such international norms in bolstering reform and contributing to the transition to democracy. For decades, Apartheid leaders consistently violated the fundamental human rights of the majority black population. Human rights were spurned and identified with "Communism". Support for human rights often attracted the interest of the security police. South Africa's black leaders, and especially those of the African National Congress, regarded the Universal Declaration of Human Rights as their "bible" and both inside South Africa and internationally, the anti-Apartheid campaign was in essence a human rights movement. When, in 1956, the African National Congress drafted a model charter (the Freedom Charter) for a free and democratic South Africa, it reflected all of the important values enshrined in the Declaration and especially racial and gender equality.

When South Africa began its transition from oppression to democracy, the white minority, almost overnight, became committed supporters of human rights and saw in a generous bill of rights their own protection from majority rule. So, from opposite ends of the political spectrum, all the main negotiating partners agreed on the terms of a bill of rights with only one exception – the death penalty. Its compatibility with the Bill of Rights was left by them for determination by the newly established Constitutional Court. In 1995, its eleven members unanimously declared the death penalty to be unconstitutional.

South Africa's Constitution reflects a deep regard for international law and the domestic laws of foreign democratic nations. The freedoms enshrined in the Bill of Rights may only be limited by a law of general application "to the extent that the limitation is reasonable and justifiable in an open and democratic society based on human dignity, equality and freedom". In the interpretation of the Bill of Rights, all courts and tribunals:

(a) must promote the values that underlie an open and democratic society based on human dignity, equality and freedom;
(b) must consider international law; and
(c) may consider foreign law.

In addition, when interpreting any legislation "every court must prefer any reasonable interpretation of the legislation that is consistent with international law over any alternative interpretation that is inconsistent with international law".

The Constitutional Court of South Africa has taken these constitutional provisions seriously and has held that the reference to "international law" is not limited to laws ratified by parliament but includes the whole body of international law including non-African regional human rights conventions. Comparative constitutional law is a useful tool for all students and practitioners of the law. For a country in transition, and especially if its courts have the power to review legislation, comparative constitutional law can provide an essential reference for creating domestic precedents. The result is that more and more frequently, judges from democratic nations are meeting formally and informally and influencing, directly or indirectly, their own approach to difficult or complex new situations.

The tendency of national courts to look to international standards can be seen in numerous recent decisions from courts around the world. The African Commission on Human and People's Rights has also demonstrated a heightened tendency to survey the jurisprudence of national courts in its own decisions. A 2001 case submitted by an NGO in Sierra Leone protested the denial by a military court of an appeal in a death penalty case. The Commission surveyed the standards applied by military courts in several African nations and held that the Sierra Leonian court's denial of an appeal "was a serious offence as this falls short of the requirement of the respect for fair trial standards expected of such courts".[36] A recent decision by Britain's House of Lords, which struck out the provisions on indefinite detention in that country's anti-terrorism law, cited recent decisions by the United States Supreme Court that addressed issues related to detention of terror suspects.[37] The US Supreme Court has surveyed the practices of other nations in several recent decisions concerning civil rights.[38] These decisions result from the increased interaction of judges and advocates across national lines and are encouraged by many factors, including the efforts of individuals, NGOs, and legal and other civil society organizations acting at the national and international level. The processes by which these standards are incorporated are complex and multifactoral.[39] Multilateral organizations play an important role in this process, both in interpreting the norms and providing a forum for focusing international pressure to observe them.

UN human rights institutions and proposed reforms

Human rights norms have become a central issue of international concern both within and outside the UN, a development that is reflected in the recent report of the UN High Level Panel, which affirmed that protecting human rights is one of the organization's central missions.[40] However, despite this stated emphasis, UN human rights institutions suffer from a crisis of legitimacy that casts doubt on the entire UN system.[41] The treaty-monitoring bodies, which function as expert bodies monitoring state compliance with the treaties that form the legal foundation of the human rights system, are faced with their own operational crises.[42] Serious reform of the UN human rights bodies is needed if they are to enjoy the legitimacy they require to carry out their mandates.

The human rights bodies within the UN have performed a vital task from their inception and have made major contributions to the level of legitimacy that human rights norms currently enjoy. One of their most important contributions has been opening the system to civil society participation. Human rights NGOs have, in turn, promoted the observance of human rights through their domestic and international advocacy. NGOs do important work outside the framework of the UN and the multilateral system provides an important means of directing civil society participation into policy development and action at the international level. The multilateral human rights regime must be strengthened in order to maintain the integrity and vitality of universal human rights standards.

The High Level Panel report recommended reform of the Commission on Human Rights, the oldest and largest UN human rights body. The Commission is a political organ which makes decisions by majority vote and whose members serve in their representative capacity. The Commission currently has 53 members elected on the basis of regional representation. In recent years, state members, some of whom are known to have poor human rights records, have been using their positions on the Commission to shield themselves from criticism and to make politically motivated attacks on other countries. In several cases, state representatives have been unqualified to serve due to their lack of experience in human rights law and policy.

To address some of these glaring threats to the Commission's legitimacy, the High Level Panel has recommended that the Commission be opened to universal membership. However, this recommendation is not likely to achieve the focus on substantive issues that the Panel anticipates. A Commission with universal membership would run the risk of simply replicating the problems of ineffectiveness and lack of focus that the Panel criticized in the General Assembly. Simply expanding the Commission would also fail to address the problem of serious human rights violators as members.

The Commission on Human Rights should be a deliberative body in which members have expertise in international human rights law and policy. State membership should not be automatic. Rather, it should be linked with demonstrated commitment to the multilateral human rights regime. Membership could be predicated on such criteria as ratification of relevant treaties and compliance with reporting requirements. Some human rights groups have recommended additional criteria, such as co-operation with investigations or the absence of condemnations by the Commission.[43] Though membership criteria may be desirable, such criteria and the process for evaluation compliance and eligibility for membership must be carefully considered. The process of removing non-compliant states from the Commission would have its own problems and needs for procedural safeguards. The human rights monitoring regime should also provide incentives for participation and assistance with compliance, particularly for small states that may find it difficult to comply with onerous reporting requirements. Tighter restrictions without other reforms may risk marginalizing the Commission through non-participation, rather than revitalizing it through vigorous application of membership criteria.

The Secretary-General recently offered an alternative to reforming the existing Commission. In a recent report on UN reform, the Secretary-General recommended replacing the Commission on Human Rights with a smaller Human Rights Council.[44] According to his proposal, the Human Rights Council would be a standing body and its members would be elected directly by a two-thirds majority of the General Assembly. The Secretary-General suggested that such a standing body of human rights experts would give to human rights the prominence that was envisioned in the UN Charter. The proposal for a Human Rights Council has been well-received by human rights organizations.[45] World leaders resolved to create a Human Rights Council as part of the 2005 World Summit and requested the General Assembly to establish the mandate and working methods for the Council in its 60th session. This is an encouraging development with the potential to give human rights an organizational mandate aligned with its centrality to the UN mission. In creating the mandate for the Human Rights Council, the General Assembly should retain the most effective parts of the Commission, including its ability to examine human rights situations in specific countries and particular types of violations worldwide. The Council should also support greater coordination of human rights mechanisms with other UN organs, such as the Security Council, the proposed Peacebuilding Council and development programmes.

The treaty bodies, those charged with monitoring compliance with the major human rights conventions, face challenges of a different sort, but of similar gravity with regard to maintaining the integrity of the human rights regime. The UN has been pursuing a strategy of universal ratification of the major human rights conventions and covenants. The priority given to universality is significant in two ways. First, ratification provides the legal force under the dominant theory of international law based on consent. Universal ratification also demonstrates the moral force of the underlying norms in a manner that will promote a culture of compliance whilst legitimizing intervention to enforce the norms in situations of serious violations. While accession to the treaties has seen a significant increase as a result of this strategy, universal accession has infrequently been accomplished. The strategy of universal ratification has been criticized on two grounds. Some have argued that this goal leads the monitoring bodies to lower standards and ignore non-compliance in order to encourage ratification, while others charge that ratification does not change state behaviour and may simply provide cover for states that have no intention of changing their non-compliant behaviour.[46] These analyses lead to prescriptions for a more disciplinary stance for the treaty regime. However, this prescription, in the absence of other reforms, runs the risk of alienating states from accepting legal obligations under the treaty system. Non-participation in the system will lead to the atrophy of the regime and eventually of the human rights norms themselves.

According to a study on reform of the treaty bodies, many states fail to ratify human rights treaties because of inadequate resources to address the requirements of passing domestic legislation and meeting the reporting requirements.[47] Given the concerns of many countries that either do not ratify or do not comply with reporting requirements, reform of the treaty monitoring regime should focus on streamlining reporting requirements and providing the technical assistance necessary to ratify treaties, educate government agencies implicated by treaty obligations, and meet reporting requirements. A more robust reform would also provide technical and advisory assistance to countries that are not complying with particular treaty obligations. Linking the treaty bodies with relevant UN agencies and other institutions could do this. Such reforms would demonstrate the same approach in the human rights regime that has been applied in other areas, in which the regime provides a more direct system of costs and benefits.

It is impossible to discuss these reforms without emphasizing the need for a rationalized system of funding. The Office of the High Commissioner for Human Rights (OHCHR), which is responsible for the operations of the Commission and the treaty bodies, is currently funded from less than a 2 per cent regular budget allocation.[48] In 2003, over two-thirds of OHCHR's operating budget came from voluntary contributions and much of this money is earmarked for particular projects.[49] The reforms described above cannot be successful without an adequate provision for reliable funding for the OHCHR. Such funding will depend upon the leadership of the industrialized countries and the General Assembly in supporting a comprehensive reform of the human rights mechanisms at the UN.

World Leaders addressed these three concerns – regular budget allocation, improved and streamlined reporting requirements and closer coordination between the High Commissioner's Office and all relevant UN bodies – favourably at the 2005 World Summit. The Summit pledged to double the regular budget allocation for the High Commissioner's Office over the next five years, provide streamlined reporting requirements and increase technical assistance, and to better integrate human rights throughout the UN system. These reforms, if carried out, will make significant strides toward improved monitoring and preventing human rights violations.

Measuring human rights

Since the early 1990s, UN agencies, civil society organizations and national governments have all developed instruments that measure various aspects of the overall achievement of human rights. Such instruments can contribute to the protection of human rights by strengthening the legitimacy and effectiveness of UN mechanisms and by promoting a culture of accountability for states and the international community generally. Indeed, such measurement may be a necessary response to demands that international organizations be held accountable for making measurable progress in implementing human rights conventions.[50] The high level of interest in developing effective measurement strategies was reflected in the recent High Level Panel report, which recommended that the High Commission for Human Rights publish an annual report surveying human rights worldwide. This report would form the basis for deliberations by the Commission on Human Rights and as such would be likely to form the basis for remedial actions by the UN organs.

The Panel gave no specific criteria for the contents of the report but suggested that it be drawn from the treaty monitoring bodies, special mechanisms of the Commission and any other sources the High Commission considers appropriate. The range of potential sources is greatly increased by the integration of development and human rights concerns at the UN. The UN Development Programme includes human rights indicators in its annual Human Development Report.[51] The UN Development Assistance Framework (UNDAF) contains human rights indicators in its Common Country Assessment. Other international organizations, such as the World Bank and IMF have also begun to consider such factors such as governance and human rights in their decision-making. The Millennium Development Goals (MDGs) also contain indicators of progress on economic and social rights. In addition, the United States prepares a comprehensive and influential annual survey of human rights.[52] Despite the great progress in developing methods and approaches to measure the status and progress of human rights, many thorny issues of substance and process remain.

We do not propose specific indicators here, but rather recommend a few principles for consideration in developing a comprehensive reporting system. First, it is important to recall the recommendations for improving the reporting process within the treaty bodies and to look for ways to integrate reporting requirements whenever possible. There are heavy reporting obligations associated with the UNDAF and MDG and the integration of human rights and development concerns at the UN should exploit an opportunities for integrating reporting requirements in meaningful ways. Every effort to ease the burdens on developing countries should be taken, including financial and technical assistance. Second, because human rights reporting will optimally help the international community achieve a wide range of goals, measurement should be multidimensional and aim at assessing the current status of particular rights within a particular state, the state's commitment to protecting the right, and its capacity to fulfil its international obligations.[53] Such reporting will assist in holding particular states accountable and help the international community intervene to promote compliance through means such as investigations, technical assistance and even coercive measures. Finally, the reporting process must be transparent and open to substantial participation from civil society. In some cases, only such reporting can provide information necessary to evaluate the effects of state action on the most vulnerable members of a society.

The High Commissioner can play an important role in promoting accountability in protecting human rights through developing accurate and reliable reporting mechanisms. The reporting process should reflect the strong commitment of the international community at every step, from gathering information, to follow-up investigations, to remedial actions.

Part III. Erosion of universal norms: leadership challenges

The criminal trials following World War II marked a new era of international humanitarian law. However, in the decades that followed, Cold War politics prevented the Security Council from taking action even against massive and systemic human rights violations. International covenants such as the Genocide Convention of 1948 and the Geneva Conventions of 1949 were effectively ignored. Following the Cold War, in the 1990s, the Security Council demonstrated a greater willingness to take coercive measures pursuant to its Chapter VII powers in order to maintain international peace and security. In addition, these coercive measures, such as sanctions, criminal prosecution and military intervention, were increasingly justified by reference to violations of human rights.

In order for humanitarian law to be effective, it must be enforced. However, in order for enforcement measures to be considered legitimate, they must be applied in a manner that comports with standards of substantive and procedural justice accepted by the international community. It is necessary for governments to provide the moral and material support and cooperation needed to carry out such measures. There is currently a crisis of legitimacy for coercive enforcement measures that is caused by several factors. First, the perception that military intervention to prevent massive war crime has been biased and based solely on the interests of the Western nations has benefited those who oppose such intervention generally. Secondly, the United States exceptionalism in regard to international law is seriously undermining the normative foundation of universalism upon which human rights and humanitarian law is based. Together, these factors have undermined support for intervention for human protection.

Furthermore, there is considerable concern that the perception of biased and self-serving application of human rights norms will undermine the norms themselves. As described in the first section, multilateral institutions perform a critical function in clarifying and promoting human rights norms and providing a forum for international action. Such institutions have historically benefited from the leadership of democratic states, particularly the United States. If such institutions wither, international NGOs and national movements will find it increasingly difficult to advocate upholding and enforcing human rights norms.

An international criminal court is a necessary part of an effective regime to enforce humanitarian law and address the worst human rights violations. Until 1993, there was wide agreement that such a court could only be established by treaty. It came as a surprise, therefore, when in May 1993, the UN Security Council established the International Criminal Tribunals for the former Yugoslavia. Creating the court was an imaginative and effective way to apply the Council's Chapter VII powers. By the terms of Chapter VII, the tribunals were instituted as a mechanism aimed at restoring international peace and security. In establishing the tribunals, the Security Council made the all-important link between peace and justice. The United States provided essential support in establishing the tribunal and the prosecutor's office.

Less than a year after the establishment of the ICTY, there were warnings of an even more deadly genocide brewing in the Central African state of Rwanda. The Security Council failed to respond to repeated warnings and even failed to respond during the killings carried out pursuant to a planned genocide that resulted in the deaths of nearly one million people. The international community called for intervention, demonstrating strong support for the international obligation to respond to prevent or mitigate genocide. Unfortunately, the Security Council's failure to respond to the genocide was seen as an example of biased commitment to human rights by Western powers. Having been subjected to strong international condemnation for its failure to intervene to prevent or mitigate the genocide, the Security Council quickly agreed to Rwanda's request to establish a criminal tribunal. The ICTR accomplished the world's first conviction for the crime of genocide and was the first tribunal to establish that systematic mass rape could constitute the crime of genocide. The international response to the genocide in Rwanda therefore leaves a mixed legacy. The criminal tribunal has provided an important contribution to the re-establishing of the rule of law in a country devastated by the violence. By establishing the tribunal, the international community demonstrated that massive human rights violations need not go unpunished.

The UN criminal tribunals were successful in important respects. They resulted in a substantial advance in the interpretation and effect of humanitarian law. They also demonstrated that international tribunals could result in fair trials. These and other successes encouraged the United States to press for steps to be taken to establish a permanent international criminal court. In particular the Secretary General of the UN, Kofi Annan, was encouraged by Washington to call the diplomatic conference in Rome in the middle of 1998 to consider a statute for the International Criminal Court. The successes of the ad hoc tribunals also encouraged the establishment of other forms of international justice such as the tribunals for Sierra Leone and East Timor. Those developments had not been anticipated when the ICTY was established in 1993.

The ICTY had another unexpected consequence – the manner in which some Western military commanders have sought to respect humanitarian law. This began with the NATO intervention over Kosovo. Never before had military lawyers advised senior military leaders continuously on the propriety of targets. Never before had the safety of innocent civilians been so carefully considered in the choices of military targets. It is not sufficiently acknowledged that relatively few civilian deaths resulted from 78 days of intensive air bombardment. Where there were civilian deaths and injuries, they were largely the result of error and not by inattention or design.

In the military campaign in Afghanistan, the military coalition led by the United States continued to demonstrate care to protect civilians as persons protected under the Geneva Conventions. The international community largely supported the military campaign in Afghanistan as a legitimate and legal response to an attack on the US by terrorists harboured by the de facto Afghanistan government. The policy of protecting civilian lives as a central concern of the military strategy represents a new and stark change from the past practices, such as the intentional targeting of civilians in both the Korean and Vietnam wars. We would suggest that the change is a direct consequence of the establishment by the Security Council of the International Criminal Tribunal for the former Yugoslavia. As a result of this development, the laws of war had become widely disseminated and political leaders in the democracies were increasingly under pressure to prevent the commission of war crimes.

The 1998 UN diplomatic conference was unexpectedly well attended. Even more surprising was the wide support for the ICC evinced in Rome – 120 nations voted in favour of the treaty while only seven voted the other way. There are currently 100 ratifications of the treaty deposited, and four African countries, and now the Security Council, have referred cases to the Court. It is clear then that international support is strong for multilateral institutions capable of addressing the most heinous crimes. It is a matter of great regret that the US was one of the seven countries to oppose the treaty and that it is now actively attempting to undermine the Court by pressuring countries not to ratify the Rome Treaty or enter into bilateral agreements with countries that have ratified it. These developments are particularly regrettable because the US was the champion of the UN tribunals and was instrumental in encouraging Secretary-General Kofi Annan to call the diplomatic conference in Rome. This unfortunate change appears to have been the result of the fear of the US military that its members would be subject to unjustified or politically motivated indictment for war crimes in the international court. The prospect of the US supporting the ICC in the near future appears to be remote

Given the historic role of the US in promoting the international rule of law, it comes as a further grave disappointment that the US has been guilty of serious human rights violations with regard to the treatment of persons detained in the "war" against terrorism. The muted reaction from the Bush administration to the use of torture and humiliation is not only inconsistent with the values traditionally respected by the US, it has seriously diminished the leadership role of the US in the field of human rights.

The 1990s witnessed the rapid development of multilateral efforts to enforce fundamental norms of humanitarian law. The international community demonstrated widespread support for both humanitarian intervention and the use of international courts to re-establish the rule of law in countries devastated by violence. Humanitarian intervention offers the hope of deterring massive violations of human rights. The ICC and other international and hybrid tribunals offer the hope of punishing perpetrators and restoring a sense of justice in society. Together, these compulsory mechanisms provide hope for deterring future violations. The Western countries have shown the willingness and capability to abide by ever-higher standards of humanitarianism in military campaigns. On the other hand, there are negative recent developments, such as the decision by the United States to withdraw support for and to actively oppose the ICC as well as its efforts to avoid compliance with the Geneva Conventions in its pursuit of the war on terrorism. In order for commitment to human rights and humanitarian law to be maintained, the international community must have the assurance that the law applies to all states. The equal application of the law to all members of a society is a fundamental tenet of the rule of law. The cost of the exceptionalism of the United States may well be the erosion of international commitment to the rule of law, a consequence that is likely to be much more costly than any benefits the United States hopes to gain in consequence of its own non-compliance or non-participation.

Conclusion

All in all, the human rights regime has reached a curious position. On the one hand, the regime has achieved enormous success in establishing the legal foundation for human rights and creating certain enforcement mechanisms. The multilateral conventions have also created the conditions by which civil society, national judiciaries, and others, have adopted international standards domestically. Criminal sanctions have been enforced in several cases, demonstrating the wide acceptance of a set of fundamental norms. On the other hand, the regime faces serious challenges. It suffers from an institutional crisis at the UN stemming from lack of funding and growing political illegitimacy of the Commission. It also faces a broader crisis of legitimacy as the US, long a leading proponent of human rights, seeks to undermine the ICC and seems to subordinate human rights concerns in the war on terror.

Despite these challenges, it is doubtful that multilateralism will be abandoned as a means of achieving human rights. Our world is characterized by the march of economic globalization and the extension of communications and technology to all parts of the earth. In this context, it will be increasingly in the interest of all nations, large and small, to use multilateral institutions to manage global challenges and achieve peace.

Towards this end, stronger enforcement measures including a robust ICC are critical to enhancing the effectiveness of the human rights. It is promising that the Security Council made its first referral to the International Criminal Court by authorizing investigations into the situation in

Darfur. This welcome development is all the more surprising considering the stiff opposition of the US to the ICC. President Bush could have vetoed the referral with little cost domestically. In this situation, the US agreed to the referral largely because the foreign policy costs of opposing allies and appearing to thwart justice for such massive crimes were simply too great. The US took a leading role in focusing international attention on the horrible situation in Darfur and now, with the ICC investigation, the responsibility of seeking justice will be shared.

Most importantly, criminal prosecution of the worst criminals in Darfur will contribute to the possibility of peace and national reconciliation by individualizing guilt. Concerted international action to prosecute war crimes will also send a strong message to other leaders in repressive regimes that the era of impunity has truly come to an end.

Notes

1. The goal of universal ratification was endorsed in the Vienna Declaration and Programme of Action, which 171 States adopted by consensus at the 1993 World Conference on Human Rights in Vienna. Vienna Declaration and Programme of Action, adopted 25 June 1993, UN Doc. A/CONF.157/23 (12 July 1993).
2. At the Inter-American Conference on War and Peace, held in Mexico City in 1945, a group of 21 countries promoted the idea that a bill of rights should be part of the Charter of the United Nations. Johannes Morsink (1999) *The Universal Declaration of Human Rights: Origins, Drafting and Intent*, Philadelphia PA: University of Pennsylvania Press.
3. Eleanor Roosevelt served as the first Chairperson of the Commission on Human Rights. Rene Cassin served as the French representative to the Commission and wrote the first draft of what would become the UDHR. Other leading participants in negotiating the text and securing its adoption included Dr. P.C. Chang (China), Charles Malik (Lebanon), Hernan Santa Cruz (Chile), Omar Loufti (Egypt), Hausa Mehta (India), Carlos P. Romulo (the Philippines), Mr. Bogomolov (Soviet Union) and Mr. Ribuikar (Yugoslavia). For a historical view of the development of the UDHR, See, Asbjorn Eide, et al. (eds) (1992) *The Universal Declaration of Human Rights: A Commentary*, Oslo: Scandinavian University Press; Mary Ann Glendon (2001) *A World Made New*, Mississauga, Ontario: Random House; and Morsink (1999) *The Universal Declaration of Human Rights*.
4. As an independent expert to the Commission on Human Rights on reform of the human rights treaty bodies, Philip Alston has argued that lack of universal treaty ratification is not attributable to rejection of human rights norms, but to inadequate efforts to achieve it. He asserted that the highly successful campaign for ratification of the CRC demonstrated that concerted political will can achieve the goal of universal ratification. The campaign for CRC ratification was characterized by promoting ratification through multilateral institutions, mobilizing domestic constituencies to lobby their own national governments and providing technical assistance from relevant international agencies to interested national governments. Final Report on Enhancing the Long-term Effectiveness of the United Nations Human Rights Treaty System, UN Doc. E/CN.4/1997/74 (27 March 1996). There are currently 151 States Parties to the International Covenant on

Economic, Social and Cultural Rights and 154 to the International Covenant on Civil and Political Rights. Each Covenant has 7 signatories that have not yet ratified it. The Convention on the Rights of the Child, with 192 ratifications, has the highest number of States parties. Only the US and Somalia have not ratified it. The current status of ratification for human rights treaties is published on the web site of the Office of the United Nations High Commissioner for Human Rights, available at http://www.ohchr.org.

5. See, address of Secretary-General Kofi Annan to the General Assembly, 20 September 1999, transcript produced in Press Release, UN Doc. SG/SM/7136 (GA/9596); Kofi Annan (2000) *We the Peoples: The Role of the United Nations in the 21st Century*, Secretary General's report to the General Assembly.
6. The Vienna Declaration and Programme of Action called for all UN specialized agencies and international development and finance agencies to make concerted effort to take human rights concerns into account in planning and assessing their policies. Vienna Declaration (1993), Section II, paragraphs 1–3. Later that year, the General Assembly created the post of High Commissioner of Human Rights, which was charged with, among other things, coordinating human rights activities throughout the UN system. UN GA Resolution, UN Doc. A/RES/48/141 (20 December 1993). The integration of human rights is most explicit in the UN Development Programme, which includes a human rights index in its annual human development report.
7. Louis Henkin espouses the view that international law strongly influences state behaviour. This view is famously summarized in his assertion that "almost all nations observe almost all principles of international law and almost all of their obligations almost all of the time", Louis Henkin (1979) *How Nations Behave*, Council on Foreign Relations, p. 47.
8. See, Robert O. Keohane (2002) "Rational choice theory and international law: insights and limitations", *Journal of Legal Studies* 31: 307–320; Kenneth W. Abbott (1999) "International relations theory, international law, and the regime governing atrocities in internal conflicts", *American Journal of International Law* 93: 361.
9. See, Robert Keohane's chapter in this volume.
10. High Level Panel on Threats, Challenges and Change, *A More Secure World: Our Shared Responsibility*, UN Doc. A/59/565 (2004), paras. 13, 36, 40–43, 87 (hereinafter High Level Panel Report). Regarding bias in enforcement, the report states that "When the institutions of collective security respond in an ineffective and inequitable manner, they reveal a much deeper truth about which threats matter. Our institutions of collective security must not just assert that a threat to one is truly a threat to all, but perform accordingly" (ibid.: para. 43).
11. The High Level Panel Report states that the Commission on Human Rights "suffers from a legitimacy deficit that casts doubts on the overall reputation of the United Nations", High Level Panel Report, p. 78 (Synopsis of Part 4).
12. On 28 September 2001, the Security Council adopted Resolution 1373, a legally binding resolution adopted under the Council's Chapter VII powers, which requires states to take actions to suppress the financing, planning and commission of terrorist acts (UN Doc. S/RES/1373 (2001)). The responses taken by individual states include adopting new legislation to combat terrorism, stepping up repressive policies already in place under existing legislation, or acting within the existing legal framework with relatively little change. Several states, including China, Russia and Uzbekistan recast long-running campaigns against domestic groups in the language of the new war on terrorism. Richard Goldstone, co-author of this chapter, served as Co-Chair of the International Bar Association's Task Force on International Terrorism, which produced a report that documents these national legal responses: *International Terrorism: Legal Challenges and Responses*, A Report by the International Bar Association's Task Force on

International Terrorism, Transnational Publishers, 2003. Human Rights First, a non-governmental organization, has also documented responses to the US example in anti-terrorism law, and argues in a series of reports that the US example is being used by many governments to support draconian laws and repressive actions and to justify curtailment of civil liberties; see, *A Year of Loss: Reexamining Civil Liberties Since September 11*; *Imbalance of Powers: How Changes to U.S. Law and Policy Since 9/11 Erode Human Rights and Civil Liberties*; and *Assessing the New Normal: Liberty and Security for the Post-September 11 United States*, available at http://www.humanrightsfirst.org.

13. Compare, Louis Henkin (1999) "That 'S' word: sovereignty, and globalization, and human rights", *Fordham L. Rev.* 68: 1; and Jack Goldsmith (2000) "Should international human rights law trump US domestic law?", *Chi. J. Int'l. L.* 1: 327 (arguing against incorporation of international human rights law into US domestic law). For a descriptive analysis of contemporary sovereignty, with attention to the role of human rights, see Anne-Marie Slaughter (2004) "Sovereignty and power in a networked world order", *Stan. J. Int'l. L.* 40: 283.
14. The most notable example is the Martens Clause, contained in the preamble of the 1899 Hague Convention II (War on Land) which states in situations not covered by the treaty, "populations and belligerents remain under the protection and empire of the principles of international law, as they result from the usages established between civilized nations, from the laws of humanity, and the requirements of the public conscience". The 1868 Declaration of St Petersburg banned the use of certain exploding bullets because the framers believed that the increased death and suffering caused by such arms was "contrary to the laws of humanity". These signatories understood that the treaty "fixed the technical limits at which the necessities of war ought to yield to the requirements of humanity". These treaties were reproduced in *Laws of War and International Law*, R. van der Wolf and W. van der Wolf (eds), 2002.
15. Bodin's concept of *res publica* conceived of an "absolute" sovereign who was subject to the laws of God, nature and common humanity (Helmut Steingberger (1992) "Sovereignty", in R. Berhardt (ed.) *Encyclopedia of Public International Law*, vol. IV, pp. 500, 505. Writing in the late seventeenth century, Emerich de Vattel applied this concept of sovereignty constrained by natural law to international relations in *Law of Nations*.
16. Jurist Samuel Pufendorf later asserted this view (Wilhelm G. Grewe (2000) *The Epochs of International Law*, Michael Byers (trans.), New York: Walter de Gruyter, pp. 351, 352–355.
17. Terry Nardin (2002) "The moral basis of humanitarian intervention", *Ethics and International Affairs* 16(1) (April): 57, 58.
18. Danish Institute of International Affairs, *Humanitarian Intervention: Legal and Political Aspects* 79 (DUPI 1999); International Commission on Intervention and State Sovereignty, research essays in preparation for *The Responsibility to Protect* 17 (December 2001).
19. For example, Samuel Pufendorf made early objections to the "right of intervention" as it had developed and introduced the requirement that victims of oppression must request intervention. In the nineteenth century, Emerich Vattel denounced the right of intervention because it was misused as a tool to initiate wars of national self-interest, but accepted the exception when an oppressed people request aids. Nardin (2002) "The moral basis of humanitarian intervention", pp. 62–63.
20. Nardin (2002) "The moral basis of humanitarian intervention", p. 64. For a further discussion of humanitarian intervention and its collective character, see also Grewe (2000) *The Epochs of International Law*, pp. 487–496.
21. See, High Level Panel Report (2004) *A More Secure World*, para. 29; International Commission on Intervention and State Sovereignty (December 2001) *The Responsibility*

to Protect, para. 1.35, available at http://www.iciss.ca/pdf/Commission-Report.pdf (arguing that sovereignty implies a "dual responsibility" to respect sovereignty of other states and to "respect the dignity and basic rights all people within the state"); Secretary-General Kofi Annan also expressed this view in his 1999 and 2004 annual addresses to the UN General Assembly.

22. *Security Council Rejects Demand for Cessation of Force Against Federal Republic of Yugoslavia* (press release 26 March 1999), UN Doc. SC/6659.
23. Richard Goldstone served as the Chairperson for this panel of international experts.
24. The ICISS report explained that "the responsibility to protect acknowledges that the primary responsibility in this regard rests with the state concerned, and that it is only if the state is unable or unwilling to fulfil this responsibility, or is itself the perpetrator, that it becomes the responsibility of the international community to act in its place", see *The Responsibility to Protect*, para. 2.29.
25. See, High Level Panel Report (2004) *A More Secure World:*.
26. Grotius conceived of this prohibition in natural law as revealed by reason. He believed that reason would reveal to nations that submitting to law would secure long-term security. This is why Grotius recorded these prohibition as law despite their continued practice, see J. Craig Barker (2000) *International Law and International Relations* Continuum 5 (quoting Grotius from *De Jure Belli ac Pacis* (1625), "[J]ust as the national, who violates the laws of his country in order to obtain an immediate advantage, breaks down that by which the advantages of himself and his posterity are for all future time assured, so the state which transgresses the laws of nature and of nations cuts away also the bulwarks which safeguard its own future peace").
27. *Laws of War and International Law* 14 (R. van der Wolf and W. van der Wolf (eds) 2002); Wilhelm G. Grewe (2000) *The Epochs of International Law*, Michael Byers (trans.), New York: Walter de Gruyter, p. 107.
28. Emerich Vattel, *Law of Nations*, Thomas Pomroy (trans. 1805), Book III, Chapter VIII (Of the Law of Nations in War, and first, of what there is a Right of doing, and what is permitted in a Just War Against the Enemy's Person) and Chapter III (of the Just Causes of War).
29. Van der Wolf (2002) *Laws of War and International Law*, p. 20.
30. Senegal's highest court, *Cour de Cassation* later held that Senegal lacked jurisdiction because Senegal had not passed legislation granting jurisdiction in torture cases as called for in Article 5 of the Convention Against Torture. *Aff. Habré*, Arrêt n° 14 du 20.03.2001, Cour de cassation, available at http://www.icrc.org/ihl-nat.nsf/0/90e26efa1bb31189c1256b21005549b0?OpenDocument.
31. International Convention on the Suppression and Punishment of the Crime of Apartheid, 30 November 1973, 1015 U.N.T.S. 243, 13 I.L.M. 50.
32. The European Court of Human Rights has applied the principle of the *margin of appreciation* to acknowledge a certain level of variation in national implementation of human rights.
33. See, Tatsuo Inoue (2003) "Human rights and Asian values", in Jean-Marc Coicaud, et al. (eds) *The Globalization of Human Rights*, (Tokyo: UNU Press. For a discussion of various relativist perspectives, see Yash Ghai (2000) "Universalism and relativism: human rights as a framework for negotiating interethnic claims", *Cardozo L. Rev.* 21: 1095.
34. See, Yash Gai (1998) "Human rights and Asian values", *Public L. Rev.* 9: 168, cited in Louis Henkin et al. *Human Rights*. See also, Li-ann Thio (1999) "Implementing human rights in ASEAN countries: 'Promises to keep and miles to go before I sleep'", *Yale H. R. and Del. L. J.* 2(1) (chronicling developments in addressing human rights issues at the national and regional level in ASEAN nations).

35. See Abdul Hasnat Monjural Kabir (2001) "Establishing national human rights commissions in South Asia: a critical analysis of the processes and the prospects", *Asia-Pacific Journal on Human Rights and the Law* 2(1): 1–53.
36. African Commission on Human and People's Rights, Resolution on the Right to Fair Trial and Legal Assistance (2001).
37. *A (FC) and Others (FC) v. Secretary of State for the Home Department*, [2004] UKHL 56 (16 December 2004), available at http://www.publications.parliament.uk/pa/ld200405/ldjudgmt/jd041216/a&others.pdf.
38. See, for example, *Lawrence v. Texas*, 539 U.S. 558 (2003) (addressing same-sex sexual activity) and *Atkins v. Virginia*, 536 U.S. 204 (2002) (addressing death penalty for people with developmental disabilities).
39. See, Harold Hongju Koh (1996) "Transnational Legal Process", *Neb. L. Rev.* 75: 181, 183 (describing this complex interaction as transnational legal practice).
40. High Level Panel Report (2004) *A More Secure World*, para. 15.
41. Ibid.: 64 (synopsis of Part IV).
42. For a full discussion of the challenges facing the treaty bodies, see Philip Alson and James Crawford (eds) (2000) *The Future of UN Human Rights Treaty Monitoring*, Cambridge: Cambridge University Press.
43. Human Rights Watch advocates such criteria, see Human Rights Watch Press Release, U.N.: Good Diagnosis, but Poor Prescription (2 December 2004), available at http://hrw.org/english/docs/2004/12/02/switze9760.htm. Amnesty International recommended a set of five criteria for membership, see Amnesty International (2003) *UN Commission on Human Rights: A Time for Deep Reflection*, 13 March 2003, AI Index: IOR 41/004/2003, available at http://web.amnesty.org/library/index/ENGIOR410042003.
44. Report of the Secretary-General, *In Larger Freedom: Towards Development, Security and Human Rights for All*, 21 March 2005, UN Doc. A/59/2005.
45. See, for example, "Joint letter on the U.N. Human Rights Council: Letter from Forty-One Civil Society Leaders to the President of the U.N. General Assembly", 1 November 2005, available at http://hrw.org/english/docs/2005/11/01/global11955.htm
46. See, Anne F. Bayefsky (1994) "Making the human rights treaties work", *Stud. Transnat'l Legal Pol'y* 26: 229; Oona A. Hathaway (2002) "Do human rights treaties make a difference?", *Yale L. J.* 111: 1935.
47. Final report on enhancing the long-term effectiveness of the United Nations Human Rights Treaty System, UN Doc. E/CN.4/1997/74. 27 March 1996, paras. 9–36.
48. High Level Panel Report (2004) *A More Secure World*, para. 290.
49. See, OHCHR Annual Report 2003 (reporting that 33 per cent, US$25.8 million, came from UN regular budget and 67 per cent came from voluntary donations, with 88 per cent of those funds earmarked for particular uses). For a discussion of the effect of this budget mix on OHCHR, see Amnesty International, "United Nations Proposals to Strengthen Human Rights Treaty Bodies" (September 2003), available at http://web.amnesty.org/library/index/engior400182003.
50. For a debate over the efficacy of using data to measure state progress in implementing the rights guaranteed in international covenants, see the response to Oona Hathaway's (2002) article *Do Human Rights Treaties Make a Difference?* (note 46) in Ryan Goodman and Derek Jinks (2002) "Measuring the effects of human rights treaties", *European Journal of International Law* 14: 171. Hathaway answers the response in (2003) "Testing conventional wisdom", *European Journal of International Law* 14: 185.
51. See, UN Development Programme, Human Development Report 2000 (including a section discussing "indicators for human rights accountability").
52. The State Department Human Rights Reports are generally acknowledged to provide comprehensive and reliable information on nearly every country in the world. See, Hu-

man Rights Watch, United States: Critique of State Department's Human Rights Report (4 April 2003) (assessing the 2003 reports as "largely honest and hard-hitting"); Lawyers Committee for Human Rights, *Holding the Line: A Critique of the Department of State's Annual Country Reports on Human Rights Practices*, September 2003 (charging that while the report was reliable overall, reporting on certain allies in the war on terror was biased). It is widely viewed through the State Department's web site. See, Harol Hongju Koh (2002) "A United States Human Rights Policy for the 21st century", *St Louis L. J.* 46: 293 (stating that over 100,000 people downloaded parts of the 1999 report on the first day it was posted online). Unfortunately, the United States leaves itself open to criticism because it does not extend its reporting to its own human rights practices.

53. See, Hans-Otto Sano and Lone Lindholt (2000) *Human Rights Indicators: Country Data and Methodology 2000*, Danish Centre for Human Rights (discussing the importance of indicators of state commitment to human rights as well as outcomes).

14

Environmental multilateralism under challenge?

Joyeeta Gupta

Introduction

Countries have been cooperating for centuries on resource related issues and in the twentieth century they began to cooperate in the area of environmental challenges.[1] It has often been argued that multilateralism is the instrument of choice in the international resource and environmental arena, since multilateralism allows for a political and legal framework for cooperation between countries.[2] Multilateralism is seen in general to work in a number of fields of international cooperation.[3]

The success of multilateral cooperation is demonstrated by the veritable proliferation of multilateral instruments in resource and environmental regimes. There are presently more than 400 bilateral and multilateral instruments negotiated in relation to water,[4] and 900 instruments in the area of environmental issues. The very proliferation shows that multilateral instruments are indeed the tool used by countries to solve potential and existing environmental and resource related problems.

However, in many fields of international relations, existing multilateral institutions are under threat.[5] The elites of some countries are convinced that multilateralism is beset with so many problems over and above the diffuse reciprocity embodied in it, that it is not an effective tool to promote national policy. In the US this particular view is dominant. The difference in view between the US and the European Union (EU) on multilateralism and international law can perhaps be explained by the difference in ideologies and expectations about how international law should develop. In trying to explain these differences, Kagan argues that the EU is inspired by the Kantian ideal of eternal peace and focuses on developing a rule-based world. The development of the supranational European Union framework, the common currency, and the expansion of the EU to include 25 countries shows how the EU countries are slowly moving towards an increasingly structured multilateral order. On the other hand, Kagan argues, the US is inspired by the Hobbesian view in which the world is seen as an anarchic space. As a consequence, the perspectives in the US tend to be far more sceptical about multilateralism,[6] and instead there is a tendency to see the US as being at the hub of international governance with spokes of bilateral cooperation with other countries.[7] At the same time, literature within the EU tends to talk more in terms of multi-level governance and integrating various fields of governance. The G-77 recently announced in its ministerial declaration that it sees a major role in "enhancing economic and social multilateral diplomacy".[8]

Is environmental multilateralism under challenge? In order to answer this question, this chapter takes an inductive approach. It will first suggest that there are eight facts that could be used to show that multilateralism is under challenge in the environmental field. At the same time, it argues that there may be strong reasons to conclude that there is nothing inevitable about these challenges, and many of these challenges may evaporate over time. The chapter then analyses the material in an integrated manner to draw some conclusions.

Environmental multilateralism under challenge

Introduction

As each year sees the birth of a large number of international agreements or follow-up agreements, protocols and/or decisions of the Conference of the Parties, those of us working in environmental governance in Europe are not preoccupied by bald statements about the failure of multilateralism.[9] Instead, we work in our own way to attempt to improve incrementally political, economic and legal design flaws in regimes, while trying to suggest ways and means to enhance international coalition building. We even try to explore opportunities for structural change. Some negotiators argue that they are seeing the birth of a new diplomacy for sustainable development where multilateral discussions and treaties are leading to the development of norms and rules that are often science-driven and are being negotiated within the context of new actors (both non-state and state actors). They argue that from their perspective despite the strongly neo-realistic stance of some countries, especially post-9/11, there is a momentum in the area of international environmental discussions and negotiations that is leading to collective learning.[10] Nevertheless, for the purpose of this book, I re-examined the historical data and literature to see if there is evidence to support the idea that multilateralism is under challenge.

The non-participation of hegemons: US Co. Ltd.

One of the major challenges in many multilateral environmental regimes is the non-participation of the United States in these regimes. The United States did not ratify the 1982 United Nations Convention on the Law of the Sea, the 1987 Basel Convention on the Transboundary Movement of Hazardous Wastes and their Disposal, the 1992 Convention on Biological Diversity or the 1997 Kyoto Protocol to the United Nations Convention on Climate Change, to name a few.[11] This is in line with the facts shown in other chapters about the non-participation of the US in several other multilateral agreements and organizations.

The non-ratification of the US of these conventions can clearly be traced to its commitment to the Hobbesian ideology. However, it is also an indication of the need of the US not to accept what it perceives as unnecessary shackles to its own development prospects and to limit its responsibility and possible liability in a number of issue areas. Thus, the US does not see the necessity of reducing the absolute level of its greenhouse gases because such efforts are expected to be very expensive in relation to the anticipated benefits of climate change policy to the United States.[12] Nor does it see the necessity of being tied down to the conditions expressed in the Convention on Biological Diversity.

The non-participation of the US in these regimes raises three questions. Does this non-participation per se lead to ineffective implementation of the regimes? Does it have a domino effect leading to a crumbling down of the regime? And, finally, is the current non-participation reflective of an irreversible political trend? One can argue first that US non-participation does not always lead to the collapse of a regime. The Law of the Sea, which entered into force in 1994, is being effectively implemented by the parties to the treaty, and the US appears to observe many elements of the regime, even though it did not ratify it.[13] The Basel Convention, too, has entered into force with 149 parties and is being implemented by the participating countries, despite US non-participation. In the climate change regime, the issue is more complicated. The US has very high emissions of greenhouse gases,[14] and its non-participation in the Kyoto regime reduces the impact of the agreement on global concentrations. At the same time, since the climate policy measures to be taken in the other developed countries might lead to a rise in the cost of production, these countries fear that the competitiveness of their industry will be lower vis à vis US industry. This fear might, in fact, reduce the willingness of these countries to actually take measures. That is why most political scientists and game theorists have tended to ague that developed countries are unlikely to allow the Kyoto Protocol to go forward. On the other hand, the Kyoto Protocol has entered into force, and the Protocol has sent a clear message to industry, and industry in the Western world is seeking ways and means to comply with the new rules. Since much of industry is global or multinational in nature, if these industries comply with the new rules in the EU, it becomes a little difficult, if not counter-productive, to maintain two sets of standards in different parts of the industrialized world. Some US industry is reportedly trying to find creative ways of participating in the flexible mechanisms being developed within the regime in order not to lose out on the benefits in the regime. In other words, despite the non-participation of the US state, US industry may feel obliged to change its productive processes.

The domino effect has also not quite played out as one may have expected. The US is the only developed country that is not participating in the Basel Convention regime. The Biodiversity Convention has 188 parties and is a near-universal regime. While in the late 1990s, the EU declared that it would not ratify the Kyoto Protocol until the US and Japan did so, when the US withdrew in 2001, the EU went ahead all the same and ratified, followed rapidly by Japan. Although Russia delayed ratifying and linked the climate change negotiations to other deals in the trade arena, it too has ratified the agreement and the Protocol entered into force on 16 February 2005.[15] The countries that followed the US lead were Australia and Monaco, and so the domino effect turned out to be less real as a threat.

But there are perhaps other incentives that might also push the US to find a way back into the large and influential regimes. The rise of domestic litigation in the US is likely to be a major factor. There are at present several cases in US courts where non-state actors, cities and provinces, as well as individuals, are separately and jointly developing different legal arguments to base their claims against the US EPA and industry in the area of climate change. One such claim is on whether the companies financing and insuring oil fields, pipelines and coal-fired power plants had done so in violation of the impact assessments required by the US Environment Policy Act.[16] Another claim is with respect to the question of whether carbon dioxide should be seen as a pollutant under the Clean Air Act. Other cases base their claims under the Law of Torts.[17] Furthermore, the Inter-American Commission on Human Rights has also received a case against the Bush government where the cause of action is an allegation that the rights of indigenous peoples have been impaired by the (potential) impacts of climate change.[18] Although each of these cases is evolving differently and it is too early to see how these cases will fare in court, there can be no doubt that they will add to the political pressure on the US government to reconsider its position. As Kilaparti Ramakrishna of the Woods Hole Research Center puts it: "The most important impact of this case internationally will be to send another signal to the rest of the world that they do not have to give up on the US as a potential future partner in combating greenhouse gas emissions."[19]

There are a number of public opinion surveys that also indicate a greater support for climate change policy than the administration is apparently aware of.[20] The US is home to a majority of the world's top climate change scientists and their combined knowledge is likely to have some effect on the government. The US has also had its own share of climate- and weather-related disasters. Fifty-three disasters have occurred since 1988 with total costs of about 260 billion dollars.[21] In the summer of 2005, hurricanes Katrina, Rita and Wilma have exposed the Bush administration to the global public as Katrina showed that the poor and vulnerable to climate change are not just located in the developing world, but also within the United States. This, too, is likely to influence public opinion. The combination of domestic political pressures and foreign pressure from the entry into force of the Kyoto Protocol and the global media may indeed push the US to take action.

It is perhaps the combined effect of these elements that has ensured that the US has developed a complicated foreign policy on climate change. The US Department of State has released a fact sheet showing the extent to which the US is engaging in bilateral activity in the area of greenhouse gases. The US will commit some 50 million dollars to a Methane-to-Markets Partnership with Australia, China, Colombia, India, Italy, Japan, Mexico, Ukraine and the UK. This partnership will aim at recovering waste methane (a greenhouse gas) from coal mines and landfills and utilizing these in energy markets. The US has launched an International Partnership for a Hydrogen Economy with 15 countries and the EU to promote research, development and deployment of hydrogen and fuel cell technologies. A Carbon Sequestration Leadership Forum has been launched with 15 other countries and the EU to promote carbon dioxide capture and storage projects. A Generation IV International Forum to promote proliferation-resistant nuclear energy systems has been developed. A Renewable Energy and Efficiency Partnership has been formed with 17 other countries to promote renewables. The US is entering into a number of bilateral and regional agreements on climate change with Australia, Brazil, Canada, China, Belize, Costa Rica, El Salvador, Guatemala, Honduras, Nicaragua, Panama, the EU, India, Italy, Japan,

Mexico, New Zealand, Republic of Korea, the Russian federation and South Africa. The US is promoting a Tropical Forest Conservation Act and has made agreements with Bangladesh, Belize, Colombia, El Salvador, Panama, Peru and the Philippines; and the President has launched an initiative against illegal logging.[22] This indicates that the US does not wish to lose out on all the opportunities that may be inherent within the climate change regime.[23] In July 2005, the US initiated the Asia Pacific Partnership for Clean Development and Climate which includes, *inter alia*, China and India.

The question is: is the US undertaking all these measures to bypass the global multilateral regime and to undermine its effectiveness while still taking the opportunities in the regime not only to reduce greenhouse gases, improve its press relations, and exercise bilateral and regional control over agendas with smaller countries, or is it in fact simply acting in accordance with its commitment to the United Nations Framework Convention on Climate Change? The White House puts it as follows:

> The United States is engaged in extensive international efforts on climate change, both through multilateral and bilateral activities. Multilaterally, the United States is by far the largest funder of activities under the United Nations Framework Convention on Climate Change (UNFCCC) and the Intergovernmental Panel on Climate Change (IPCC). We remain fully engaged in multilateral negotiations under the UNFCCC, and have created or worked to revitalize a range of international climate initiatives within the last two years.[24]

The nature of public goods and free-riding

One may be tempted to argue that while resource regimes are more conducive to cooperation, environmental regimes have an in-built problem. Many of these regimes are about public goods. "Global public goods are public goods with benefits – or costs, in the case of such 'bads' as crime and violence – that extend across countries and regions, across rich and poor population groups, and even across generations".[25] In dealing with such public goods, countries may be tempted to free-ride on the policies of other countries. While there are design mechanisms that may prevent smaller countries from free-riding by excluding them from the benefits of the regime, there may be no design considerations large enough to force an unwilling hegemon into compliance.

Free-riding is also imminently compatible with the current institutional design of international relations, where states are sovereign entities and have to give their consent before they can be bound by any multilateral agreement. From a realist and neo-realist perspective, one could argue that state sovereignty is likely to remain a dominant trend, and hence as long as certain environmental goods have a public nature, the incentive to free-ride will be dominant.

Further, the diffuse nature of reciprocity in multilateralism is particularly obvious in the area of environmental and resource management. An upstream country does not necessarily have much to gain from not causing substantial harm to a country that is much further downstream. In the case of climate change, those who have very high rates of greenhouse gas emissions may not be those who are likely to suffer the most from the impacts.

At the same time, there are some trends that push in the opposite direction. Environmental disasters and their impact on vulnerable communities may not be something that countries can turn their back on. The 2004 tsunami disaster and its coverage in the media shows that. There is also an increasing perception if not evidence that poorer communities can be wiped out by such disasters and that the impacts can be worse than war.[26] Civil society and the fourth power may thus together put pressure on governments to behave more responsibly. Where that fails, the rise in environmental litigation in domestic and foreign courts may increase the pressure, especially in common law systems, to curb the free-rider instinct. The further development of the *erga omnes* principle may counter the political and economic theories that predict free-riding in a Hobbesian world. The literature also shows that new tools are being developed to deal with the problem of public goods. These include appointing national issue ambassadors on key global public goods, designating a national agency to deal with these public goods, linking foreign and domestic politics through matrix management and integrated budgets, establishing councils for implementing multilateral agreements and, among others, creating second-generation global public policy partnerships.[27] Finally, although it is politically challenging to design mechanisms to compel compliance from hegemons, the possibility of using border tax adjustments as a tool to "punish" the US may make the Washington policy makers listen very closely to the multilateral argument.[28]

Lack of good governance at the national level

Multilateralism is often questioned because state parties are not always characterized by good governance and the rule of law. If government authorities are not elected and legitimate, this can often raise questions of their legitimacy, and hence their legitimacy as partners at the international level. This may be because they are seen as quasi-states or as failed states exhibiting some form of neo-patrimonialism (concentration of power and clientelism).

On the other hand, one may argue that there is a slow and steady process of permeation of some basic norms both at the domestic and international levels, and the mere absence of these norms should not deter countries from undertaking multilateral initiatives. The inclusion of quasi- and failed states in the process of multilateral negotiations may serve directly to promote political norms in these countries, but also indirectly through the process of inviting non-state actors to these processes. Kjaer[29] argues that there is literature to show that developing countries can develop where there is coalition building and compromise, a focus on broad-based growth and limits on the power of the vested interests. Leonard argues further that if one compares the US strategy of bringing democracy to countries with the European Union's strategy, then one can see that the strategy of the latter is more successful. "These days in the Balkans, it's the prospect of EU membership that's driving political and social transformation".[30] He argues that this recipe of driving change will prove successful and the twenty-first century will be seen as a new European century. "Not because the EU will run the world, but because the European way of doing things will become the world's".[31]

The weakening role of the state in the developed world

Another argument that is often made to demonstrate the weakness of multilateralism is the diminishing role of the state in the developed world. It is argued that many bureaucracies are being down-sized in the West,[32] and this notion is equally being exported to the developing countries. A down-sized government may have neither the authority to represent the views of society, nor the power to actually implement the promises it makes at the international level. In the environmental field, Hurrell argues that the state cannot provide a political framework for collective management of global issues.[33] The limited practical control of a state over environmental management within its border also erodes the normative legitimacy of the state.[34]

At the same time, it is increasingly clear that in order to manage modern risks, perhaps a stronger state is necessary. This has been realized in the field of terrorism and state defence, where many countries are increasing their human and financial investments to protect themselves from possible terrorist attacks. In the environmental field, it is becoming obvious that a more empowered state is necessary in order to negotiate and implement policies. However, Western governments are reluctant to recognize this. When and if governments realize this, we may see a return to a call for a stronger state to protect its citizens from the problems of the twenty-first century. Oddly enough, however, in the context of developing countries, a popular instrument of many treaties is the notion of institutional capacity building to help states in developing countries deal with these environmental problems. This, however, goes hand in hand with advice to these countries to reduce their bureaucracies. It remains to be seen if the two types of advice are in fact conflicting or whether they can be synergetic. The point, however, is that the evolution of dominant economic theories over the last century shows that the ideology over the need for a strong state seems to fluctuate from decade to decade.[35] In other words, the current commitment to a lean mean state may not be irreversible.

The rising role of non-state actors

Another argument that supports the idea of multilateralism in crisis is the rise of civil society. There is a vast literature on the role of non-state actors and the increasing importance of civil society (in policy making).[36] The rise of such non-state actors and civil society questions the legitimacy and accountability of state authorities to represent national interests in a multilateral setting, and these actors have been actively negotiating in favour of an increased role in global politics and decision-making. Such non-state actors are lobbying their positions with states, while also feeling that states should not be the locus of power.

On the other hand, while non-state actors have been able to move from mere observers of international processes to a much more active collaborative role in international negotiations, these non-state actors and the mechanisms they use are not necessarily more democratic. Such bodies are neither by definition more legitimate nor are they accountable to the general public. As such, one may be justified in arguing that the increased role of the non-state actor in international policy making may lead to a stakeholdercracy with all its inherent limitations.[37] In such a stakeholdercracy, those with larger resources are likely to have a larger impact in the long run. This may in itself call for a return to multilateralism as we now know it.

The general capacity problems of developing countries

There is also evidence that developing countries are unable to actually implement their side of the bargains in many international environmental agreements. This reflects the structural problems of developing countries in terms of low economic growth rates, poverty and debt, low institutional capacity and low access to information and technology.[38] This also reflects the fact that many of the agreements include instruments that have been designed by the developed countries on the basis of the knowledge available in the West that may not always be suitable for developing countries.[39] In order to address these structural problems, many new multilateral agreements have adopted commitments with respect to capacity building, technology transfer and scientific cooperation.[40] However, it is more than likely that with each new agreement, aid fatigue is setting in and the motivation to provide structural support to a group of more than 150 countries is diminishing.

At the same time, some of these countries are developing rapidly and may be the locus of new scientific and technological knowledge.[41] These changes may shape the face of global politics in the years to come. Globalization may also lead to large-scale investment in the developing countries by multinational corporations which may also accelerate growth in these countries. Mobility of humans across the globe as well as outsourcing may also lead to enhanced welfare. The globalization of media and the Internet may also lead to increased solidarity with those that are poor, especially because their vulnerability to environmental shocks is high and their involuntary negative influence on the environment may also be irreversible.

The rise of hybrid relationships

The reduced powers of governments and their reduced willingness in general (which possibly go hand in hand) to negotiate binding multilateral agreements can be traced through a historical overview of treaty negotiations in the area of environmental issues. While, since 1972, there has been an inordinate increase in the use of multilateral treaty negotiations as a tool to address global environmental problems, one may be tempted to argue that 1997 and 1999 were high points in treaty negotiations. For example, however unwilling countries may have been to take on binding quantitative targets, the Kyoto Protocol to the Climate Change Convention not only included binding targets, but also established mechanisms to allow for the participation of non-state actors. While in the last decade there have been several negotiations, by the time of the 2002 World Summit on Sustainable Development, a hybrid form of multilateralism had developed. In this hybrid form, the lack of enthusiasm of some governments served as a reason to push for Type 2 agreements or agreements between social actors on how they will try to achieve sustainable development. (Type I agreements referred to the classic multilateral agreements between states). The initiation of these Type II agreements allowed for the delegation of responsibilities to non-state actors and thus served to empower them.

However, these hybrid systems are not self-enforcing and most often do not include mechanisms to guarantee their implementation. The agreements made thus far do not include the most powerful social actors nor do they deal with the problems of free-riders. While such a process may in theory lead to thousands of initiatives, thus far only 300 initiatives have been registered,[42] and it is not clear what the actual impact of these initiatives will be as it is not clear what the driving force behind these impacts is.[43]

The rise of bilateralism

One may see the crisis of multilateralism reflected in the rise of bilateralism and/or unilaterally steered agreements of like-minded countries. Such bilateralism may aim to circumvent, substitute or act as an impediment to multilateralism.

There are situations where bilateralism was used as a means to ignore the legitimate needs of others leading to the establishment of historical legal rights which may take decades of negotiations to unravel (for example, the agreements on the Nile).[44] There are situations in which bilateral relations are explored as a means to break the multilateral unity being garnered (for example, the attempts of the United States to develop bilateral agreements on climate change and hydrogen to weaken the multilateral climate change negotiations). However, it cannot be ruled out that the US is also using the bilateral framework in order not to be excluded entirely from the implementation process, which may have some lucrative business opportunities for US industry. There are also situations in which countries pursue bilateral agreements to circumvent the possibility of developing countries pooling their resources together to come up with a strong negotiating position. There are a number of bilateral fisheries agreements that have been made by Western countries, and also some Eastern countries, with countries of the South to gain access to fishing rights in the territorial waters and the waters of the Exclusive Economic Zone of these countries. Most of these agreements were made in the 1990s following the coming into force of the Law of the Sea. There is increasing literature on the negative impacts of these agreements on the access to food (fish protein), livelihood of those engaged in the fish-based industry and the ecosystems of the host countries to these agreements.[45]

However, where bilateral approaches are undertaken to circumvent, substitute or impede multilateral efforts at problem-solving, it is more than possible that the negative press and research reports that accompanies these approaches may serve in a globalizing world to embarrass governments. Especially since such agreements are transparent and open to the public, there are sufficient opportunities for civil society to expose any hypocritical efforts. On the other hand, there may be many bilateral efforts undertaken that actually serve to strengthen and support multilateral efforts, or may be justified by the nature of the environmental problem or the principle of subsidiarity. These clearly do not expose the weaknesses of multilateralism.

Revisiting environmental multilateralism

Let us now revisit the arguments made earlier in this chapter. One can submit that despite the tendency towards hybridization, the aberration may not necessarily be a trend. In other words, there is sufficient evidence of growing multilateralism in the area of environmental agreements. The evidence is visible in the number of treaties being negotiated on environmental issues, and the number of global conferences that focus on global issues.

However, the threats to multilateralism in other fields of endeavour have spilt over to the environmental field. This chapter has tried to show that there are eight empirical reasons that may demonstrate that environmental multilateralism is under threat. These include the non-participation of a major hegemon in many recent agreements, the nature of public goods and the potential for free-riding, the general decline in the power and potential of the nation state, the rise of non-state actors and civil society, the lack of good governance at the nation-state level in many developing countries, the poor implementation record of developing countries in environmental issues, the evolution towards hybrid agreements and the rise of bilateralism. These facts could indicate that environmental multilateralism is seriously under challenge.

Ideologically, there are three global discourses that would be happy to accept this conclusion, but for very different reasons. The neo-realist discourse would see this conclusion as inevitable since at the global level we have anarchy, and individual states should make decisions based on a rational assessment of what is good for them. Hence, since multilateralism can be a threat to national interests especially because of their interactional nature[46] and the slippery slope argument,[47] such multilateralism should be shelved. The anti-globalization discourse would also be happy with this conclusion, since they see the state as increasingly unable and unwilling to represent pluralist interests and feel that only inclusion of non-state actors at all levels will serve to redress this problem of decreasing legitimacy of state actors. The global capitalist discourse, too, would support this outcome because it is in their interest to have a lean state, to optimize freedom for industry to operate in the global market and because with the rise of stakeholder dialogues and discourse, industry is likely to have a bigger say simply because the power of the wallet is bigger than the power of the ballot.

On the other hand, I would argue that despite the fact that three different and, to some extent, opposing discourses would see multilateralism as being under challenge in the environmental field, there are sufficient incentives that may ensure that environmental multilateralism is likely to remain a preferred choice.

This is because, first, environmental degradation, accidents and impacts are likely to hit not only the poor and vulnerable, but also affect the business opportunities of the growing community of multinationals in their worldwide operations. Not only can the tourism industry be affected by the melting of glaciers and the rise in storm surges, but the international food and health industry can be affected by the vulnerability of grains to pests and the degradation of biodiversity. Where environmental impacts increase the vulnerability of communities, it may reduce their purchasing power and this affects the markets of global industry. It is in the interests of big industry to have economic prosperity everywhere. It is in their interests to ensure that the environmental options are protected. That industry is also under pressure from civil society to present a green front to society is just an additional incentive.

Second, since most environmental goods and services are public goods, there is an incentive to free-ride. At the same time, this very incentive will need to be countered if environmental goals are to be met. The only way to counter free-riders is to adopt multilateralism with a series of inbuilt incentives to create a level playing field. The epistemic community is now working in this direction and new ideas are being generated.

Third, although civil society and non-state actors have been questioning the legitimacy of government and have till now wanted to have a larger role to play in international policy making, there is increasing literature that questions the accountability and legitimacy of the new forms of governance that are emerging.[48] This literature shows that the very goals that civil society wants to achieve are undermined by the huge number of institutional processes being generated. Ultimately, if civil society and non-state actors want more legitimate and accountable governments they will themselves ask for more durable centralized structures that are more accountable. But they will also ask such structures to focus on dematerialization as a concept, the idea that we are *Globo sapiens*, and to promote transition to a transmodern life that combines intuition, spirituality and rationality.[49]

Fourth, while in many ways industry and business actors may ask for less control from governments and more freedom to operate, industry and business have more to gain from a strong and common multilateral regulatory framework because they do not wish to have different operations in different countries with vastly different rules and conditions. Nor do they wish to work under uncertainty. It is cheaper for them to try to find solutions that lay common ground rules and to operate in circumstances that are clear and predictable over the short- to medium-term and that are not left to the whims and fancies of different institutions and different governments. The rise of market mechanisms itself calls for a stronger multilateral regulatory framework than ever: for example, the rise of stronger trade laws to protect the idea of "free trade", the rise of multilateral agreements on intellectual property laws, the rise of bilateral investment agreements on disputes between states and companies. The World Bank website lists some 1,100 recent bilateral investment treaties,[50] and explains that 155 countries are parties to such agreements. The UNCTAD website lists 1,800 such treaties.[51]

While issues such as security, trade and economics may lead countries to compete with each other, environmental challenges may lead to more cooperation because of the realization that we share one climatic system, one hydrological system, and that if our ecological wealth is squandered we may have less to enjoy in the future. The ecological benefits are so interlocked across countries and continents that this will have a stronger tendency to force cooperation – at least at technical, if not at political, level.

The United Nations itself is pushing for a revival of the role of the UN at the centre of multilateral activity in the area of international security, environment and development. In 2004, the Secretary-General's High-Level Panel on Threats, Challenges and Change reported that making the world more secure would imply coping with the threats of war, violence, human rights abuse, poverty, infectious disease and environmental degradation, weapons, terrorism and transnational organized crime. Development, disease and environmental degradation were seen as major threats to human security.[52] It argued that a "threat to one is a threat to all", calling for shared responsibility and a multilateral response. The recent report of the Secretary-General entitled: In Larger Freedom: Towards development, security and human rights for all, emphasizes at least three environmental challenges – desertification, loss of biodiversity and climate change that call for an inclusive international framework to ensure a concerted globally defined action.[53] At the recent meeting to commemorate 60 years of the UN's existence, countries pledged to support the UN and to taking multilateral action, and also to taking action on climate change within the framework of the UN Convention.[54] However, despite these reports, the recent disagreements at the 60th anniversary that blocked many substantive and procedural reforms reflect the struggle between "international Keynesianism and neoliberalism" and "may be evidence of the growing loss, not betrayal, of the sense of international community on which the U.N. is predicated".[55]

In the global environmental context today, the EU clearly wants a world of multilateral diplomacy – so do developing countries, as expressed by the G-77. The key actor on the global stage that has doubts about multilateralism is the US. However, if the newly emerging economies of China and India were to follow the lead of the US in this area, we may face major challenges to multilateralism in the coming decades. But as Hoffmann puts it: "Washington has yet to understand that nothing is more dangerous for a 'hyperpower' than the temptation of unilateralism".[56] Put differently, Nye argues that the very processes of globalization[57] may in fact dilute the power of the US.[58] The recent entry of the Kyoto Protocol into force was seen by the European Director General for the Environment as a sign that multilateralism has triumphed in environmental issues.[59] It could also be seen as a dilution of power of the US. Perhaps it was this that drove the US to promote a number of bilateral and regional initiatives on climate change. In the environmental field, one is tempted to conclude that multilateralism is here to stay. The process of globalization itself may "drive the values transition needed for a future sustainable society".[60] This does not mean that multilateralism as we know it today will not evolve. It is more than likely that the new multilateralism will take a different form where ministries of foreign affairs are renamed as ministries for foreign affairs and international cooperation,[61] where such multilateralism is embedded within the context of a multi-level governance system, nested sets of institutions and competing networks of governance and regionalization.[62] That, however, may have a strongly instrumental, functional and rational feel to it.[63] It no doubt also probably reflects a little bit of wishful thinking.[64]

Acknowledgements

This chapter has been written in the context of the project – the VIDI project on inter-governmental and private environmental regimes and compatibility with good governance, rule of law and sustainable development, supported by the Netherlands Scientific Organization.

Notes

1. More than 3,200 instruments have been negotiated since the eighth century, Oregon State University (2002) *Atlas of International Freshwater Agreements*, Nairobi: UNEP.
2. Harris argues that: "the multilateral treaty remains the best medium available at the moment for imposing binding rules of precision and details in the new areas into which international law is expanding and for codifying, clarifying and supplementing the customary law already in existence in more familiar settings", Harris, D.J. (1991) *Cases and Materials on International Law*, 4th edn, London: Sweet and Maxwell.

3. Henkin, L. (1979) *How Nations Behave: Law and Foreign Policy*, 2nd edn, New York: Columbia University Press, p. 47; and Arend, A.C. (1996) "Towards an understanding of international legal rules", in Beck, R.J., Arend, A.C. and Vander Lugt, R.D. (eds), *International Rules: Approaches from International Law and International Relations*, Oxford: Oxford University Press, pp. 289–310, at p. 306.
4. Oregon State University (2002: 6) *Atlas of International Freshwater Agreements*.
5. See Chapter 1, this book.
6. Kagan, R. (2004) *Of Paradise and Power: America and Europe in the New World Order*, New York: Vintage Books.
7. Payne, A. (2000) "Globalisation and modes of regionalist governance", in D. Held and A. McGrew A. (eds) *The Global Transformation Reader: An Introduction to the Globalization Debate*, Cambridge: Polity Press, pp. 213–221, at pp. 217–219.
8. Ministerial Declaration on the occasion of the 40th anniversary of the Group of 77, 11–12 June 2004, ⟨http://www.g77.org/40/declaration.htm⟩.
9. The constant flow of articles to the Journal of International Environmental Agreements: Politics, Law and Economics that discuss ways to improve these regimes shows that there is considerable faith in the inevitability of multilateralism in environmental issues.
10. Kjellén, B. (2005) "Diplomacy and governance for sustainability in a partially globalised world," in I. Lowe and J. Paavola (eds) *Environmental Values in a Globalising World: Nature, Justice and Governance*, Oxford: Routledge, pp. 179–196.
11. United Nations Convention on the Law of the Sea, (Montego Bay) 10 December 1982, in force 16 November 1994, 21 I.L.M. (1982) 1261; Convention on the Control of Transboundary Movement of Hazardous Wastes and Their Disposal (Basel) 22 March 1989, in force 24 May 1992; 28 I.L.M. (1989), 657; United Nations Framework Convention on Climate Change, (New York) 9 May 1992, in force 24 March 1994; 31 I.L.M. 1992; Convention on Biological Diversity, (Rio de Janeiro) 5 June 1992, in force 29 December 1993, 31 I.L.M. 1992.
12. See, for example, the Byrd Hagel resolution and Senator Hagel's speech in the Congressional Record: October 3, 1997 (senate) page S10308–S10311; available at ⟨http://www.microtech.com.au/daly/hagel.htm⟩.
13. The Senate Foreign Relations Committee and the US Commission on Ocean Policy reportedly support the US ratification of the Law of the Sea as it protects many US interests with respect to the seas and oceans. See ⟨http://www.unausa.org/newindex.asp?place=http://www.unausa.org/policy/NewsActionAlerts/info/dc032204.asp⟩.
14. For the purpose of the targets in the Kyoto Protocol, the US's emissions amounted to 36.1 per cent of total carbon dioxide emissions of the developed countries in 1990.
15. See, for an analysis of the deal, Kotov, V. (2004) "The EU–Russia ratification deal: the risks and advantages of an informal agreement", *International Review for Environmental Strategies* 5(4): 157–168.
16. There is a case involving cities and NGOs who are suing the US export credit agencies for financing fossil fuel projects under the National Environmental Policy Act.
17. The state of California has launched climate change litigation against private companies, inspired by the decisions from tobacco related litigation. A record of the different litigations and legal initiatives is being maintained by the Climate Justice Programme.
18. The Inuit Circumpolar Conference announced this decision, see Roderick, P. (2004) "Private Climate Change Litigation has got Started with a Vengeance", *Taipei Times*, 23 December 2004; ⟨http://www.taipeitimes.com/news/edit/archives/2004/12/23/2003216383⟩.
19. Interviews with experts in the article entitled "States File Suit Against major US Utilities", The Climate Group, ⟨http://www.theclimategroup.org/index.pjhp?pid=490⟩.

20. Brewer analysed more than 40 public opinion surveys undertaken from 1989 to 2002 and concludes that two-fifths of the US public are seriously concerned about global warming, a majority of the US public wants the government to do more on global warming and to participate in the Kyoto Protocol, and that the Bush administration is not in touch with public opinion on the subject, Brewer, T. (2003) *U.S. Public opinion on Climate Change Issues: Evidence for 1989–2002*, Washington, DC: Georgetown University McDonough School of Business.
21. See US Billion-Dollar Climate and Weather Disasters, NOAA News Online, Story 2380, ⟨http://www.noaanews.noaa.gov/stories2005/s2380.htm⟩.
22. US Climate Change Policy: The Bush Administration's Actions on Global Climate Change, Fact Sheet released by the White House, office of the Press Secretary, Washington DC, 19 November 2004; ⟨http://www.state.gov/g/oes/rls/fs/2004/38641⟩.
23. Sindico, F. and Gupta J. (2004) "Moving the climate change regime further through a hydrogen protocol", *Review of European Community and International Environmental Law* 13(2): 175–186.
24. See fact sheet on US Climate Change Policy, note 22.
25. Kaul, I., Conceição, P., Goulven, K.L. and Mendoza, R.U. (2003) "Why do global public goods matter today?", in I. Kaul, P. Conceição, K.L. Goulven and R.U. Mendoza (eds) *Providing Global Public Goods: Managing Globalisation*, Oxford: Oxford University Press, pp. 2–20, at p. 3.
26. The reporting of the tsunami disaster in the press tended to emphasize this point.
27. Kaul, I., Conceição, P., Goulven, K.L. and Mendoza, R.U. (2003) "How to improve the provision of Global Public Goods?", in I. Kaul, P. Conceição, K.L. Goulven and R.U. Mendoza (eds) *Providing Global Public Goods: Managing Globalisation*, Oxford: Oxford University Press, pp. 21–58, at p. 52.
28. Thomas Brewer made this point at a Conference at the European Parliament on the occasion of the entry into force of the Kyoto Protocol on 16 February 2005. The issue of border tax adjustments has been the subject of many articles, but it appears as if this is now being considered in political circles.
29. Kjaer, A.M. (2004) *Governance*, Cambridge: Polity Press.
30. Leonard, M. (2004) "Why the U.S. needs the E.U.", *Time*, 28 February, p. 31.
31. Ibid.
32. See, for example, Strange, S. (2000) "The declining authority of states", in D. Held and A. McGrew (eds) *The Global Transformation Reader: An Introduction to the Globalization Debate*, Cambridge: Polity Press (see note 7 above), pp. 127–134.
33. Hurrell, A. (1994) "A crisis of ecological viability? Global environmental change and the nation state", *Political Studies* XLII: 146–165.
34. Ibid. Hurrell (1994). In general authors argue that technological and financial integration have reduced the powers of governments to actually control what happens within them.
35. Kuik, O. and Gupta, J. (2002) *Development Dialectics: An Overview of Theoretical Approaches to development and Implications for Climate Change Scenarios*, Amsterdam: Institute for Environmental Studies, Working Document.
36. See, for instance, Mathews, J. (2000) "Power shift", in D. Held. and A. McGrew (eds) *The Global Transformation Reader: An Introduction to the Globalization Debate*, Cambridge: Polity Press, pp. 204–212, at p. 204.
37. Gupta, J. (2003) "The role of non-state actors in international environmental affairs", *Heidelberg Journal of International Law* 63(2): 459–486.
38. Jacobson, H.K. and Weiss, E.B. (1995) "Strengthening compliance with international environmental accords: preliminary observations from a collaborative project", *Global Governance* 1(2): 119–148. At a more general level, Hurrell, A. (1994: 155) "A crisis of

ecological viability? global environmental change and the nation state" (see note 33 above), argues that this has to do with the fragility and corruption of governments, their lack of resources, deep-rooted structural problems and the power of vested interests.

39. Gupta, J. (2004) "Capacity building and sustainability knowledge in the climate regime", proceedings of 2002 Berlin Conference on the Human Dimensions of Global Environmental Change, Berlin, pp. 157–164.
40. See, for example, the treaties on climate change, biological diversity, desertification and depletion of the ozone layer.
41. China and India are seen as possible new areas where science will develop fast.
42. See the UN Department of Economic and Social Affairs website on Partnerships for Sustainable Development, ⟨http://www.un.org/esa/sustdev/partnerships/partnerships.htm⟩.
43. See, for example, the analysis by Tom Bigg (2003) *The World Summit on Sustainable Development: Was It Worthwhile?*, Winnipeg: International Institute for Sustainable Development, ⟨http://www.iied.org/wssd/pubs.html⟩.
44. The Nile treaty of 1929 between Egypt and the British Government gave Egypt the exclusive rights to the waters of the Lake Victoria and the Nile. Although revised in 1959, it included a clause that other countries may not use the waters of the Nile for large-scale projects without consulting Egypt. This has been a source of much dispute on the Nile.
45. See, for an analysis, Gupta, J. (2004) "Global sustainable food governance and hunger: traps and tragedies", *British Food Journal* 5: 406–416.
46. The theory of interactional law-making argues that the negotiating process of international environmental treaties is taking the form of continuous negotiations, even though it may appear that decisions are taken only at discrete moments. This implies that countries have to be continuously aware of the decisions being prepared during the preparatory meetings and that, since these preparatory meetings are mostly undertaken by scientists and policy networks, the decisions move continuously incrementally forward. See, for example, generally Brunée, J. and Toopé, S.J. (2000) "International law and constructivism: elements of an interactional theory of international law", *Col. J. Trans. Law* 39: 19–74.
47. The slippery slope argument refers to the fact that once countries join a framework agreement they become party to an institutional process that relentlessly moves forward and there is no easy way for countries to withdraw from the process.
48. Gupta, J. (2004) "Non-state actors: undermining or increasing the legitimacy and transparency of international environmental law", in I.F. Dekker, and W. Werner (eds) "Governance and international legal theory", *Nova et Vetera Iuris Gentium*, pp. 297–320.
49. Lowe, I. (2005) "Environmental values in the globalizing world: grounds for cautious optimism", in I. Lowe and J. Paavola (eds) *Environmental Values in a Globalising World: Nature, Justice and Governance* (see note 10 above), pp. 236–245, at p. 243 citing Patricia Kelly on *Globo sapiens*, and Marc Luyckx and Harlan Cleveland on trans-modernity.
50. www.worldbank.org/icsid/treaties/intro.htm.
51. The rise in bilateral investment agreements can be explained by the failure of the Multilateral Environmental Agreement. This idea was pushed by the OECD but ultimately did not lead to an agreement because of opposition from civil society. However, since then countries that compete with each other for foreign investment have been negotiating such bilateral agreements with potential investor countries.
52. Report of the Secretary-General's High-Level Panel on Threats, Challenges and Change (2004) *A More Secure World: Our Shared Responsibility*, United Nations.

53. Report of the Secretary-General (2005) *In Larger Freedome: Towards Development, Security and Human Rights for All*, United Nations A/29/2005.
54. Report of the 2005 World Summit, 14–16 September 2005, United Nations A/60/L.1.
55. Thakur, R. (2005) "U.N.'s 'Einstein' moment", *Japan Times*, 3 October 2005.
56. Hoffmann, S. (2000) "Clash of civilizations", in D. Held and A. McGrew (eds) *The Global Transformation Reader: An Introduction to the Globalization Debate* (see note 36 above), pp. 106–111, at p. 111.
57. Globalization has led to the rise of economic and financial integration, multinationals, the world wide web, global media, globalization of criminal behaviour, use of non-conventional warfare (terrorism; guerrilla warfare), and, *inter alia*, the rise of civil society. Junne, G. (2001) "International organisations in a period of globalisation: new (problems of) legitimacy", in J.-M. Coicaud and V. Heiskanen (eds) *The Legitimacy of International Organizations*, Tokyo: United Nations University Press, pp. 189–220.
58. Nye, J.S., Jr. (2000) "Globalisation and American power", in D. Held and A. McGrew (eds) *The Global Transformation Reader: An Introduction to the Globalization Debate* (see note 36 above), pp. 112–115, at p. 112.
59. See the presentation made by Catherine Day, Director General, DG Environment of the European Commission to the European Parliament at the Conference on Leadership on Climate Change in a Changing Political Climate, on the occasion of the entry into force of the Kyoto Protocol, 16 February 2005.
60. Lowe, I. and Paavola, J. (2005) "Environmental values in a globalising world", in I. Lowe and J. Paavola (eds) *Environmental Values in a Globalising World: Nature, Justice and Governance* (see note 10 above), pp. 3–14, at p. 12.
61. Kaul, I., Conceição, P., Goulven, K.L. and Mendoza, R.U. (2003) "How to improve the provision of global public goods?" (see note 27 above), at p. 52.
62. Cf. Rosenau, J.N. (2000) "Governance in a new global order", D. Held and A. McGrew (eds) *The Global Transformation Reader: An Introduction to the Globalization Debate* (see note 36 above), pp. 223–233, at p. 232.
63. Hurrell, A. (1994) "A crisis of ecological viability? Global environmental change and the nation state" (see note 33 above), p. 165, argues that such a thought is shallow but concludes that: "There is no obvious reason for believing that an alternative to the state system would prove a better means of achieving this (already extremely difficult) end".
64. As Lowe argues: "*all* significant social reforms have been seen at the time as utopian"; see Lowe, I. (2005) "Environmental values in the globalizing world: ground for cautious optimism", in I. Lowe and J. Paavola (eds) *Environmental Values in a Globalising World: Nature, Justice and Governance* (see note 10 above), pp. 236–245, at p. 243

15

AIDS, power, culture and multilateralism

Gwyn Prins

This chapter seeks to answer three important questions.[1] Do "new threats", of which the HIV/AIDS pandemic is taken to be one, *by their nature* bring into question the viability of multilateralism? Buried in this question there is an assumption about the nature of "new threats" which should be dug up and identified at the outset. It is that, because such threats are in no way confined to state boundaries, trans-state or non-state solutions are likely to be more effective than state-derived or state-dependent ones? The second and third questions flow from that assumption. If multilateralism is found to be deficient as a way of handling such new threats, is this because the state-centric nature of contemporary multilateralism, containing a presumption of sovereign equality, is vitiated either by that presumption or by return to a uni-polar world in which the imperial hegemon scorns collaboration with smaller powers? The third asks whether the need to combat a "new threat" such as AIDS, catalyses new forms of multilateralism.

The chapter also engages three more far-reaching and underlying questions of this volume. They are, respectively, about process, about motives and about forms of agency. About process – does strong unilateral leadership produce multilateral action in fact? Indeed, is it prerequisite? About motive – whose motives are pure, and in particular, are the motives of American actions malign or benign? About agency – will the strong forms of twenty-first century multilateralism be coterminous with the UN, or found elsewhere?

The answers both to the initial and to the elaborated sets of questions which emerge from the story to be told here are not what casual assumption might lead one to expect. The evidence points in rather unexpected, counter-intuitive directions. The history of the science of the pandemic shows that there has been as much difficulty in transcending loyalties other than to the advancement of understanding as in other, earlier, great scientific challenges. The threat of AIDS is certainly global in its microbiological potentials. Its physical spread has also been considerably assisted by the dense networks of modern transport: a Boeing-boosted threat, which is part of what makes it genuinely new. But the material and psychological responses have mainly been compartmentalized into state-sized – or at most region-sized – units. The principal attempt to create a new form of multilateral agent to address the essential global nature of the threat of pandemic disease – the Global Fund has been in part hijacked for surrogate balance-of-power competition; and the decisive interventions to date have been by the dominant world power. The United States has successfully catalysed much of what multilateral agency there now is. The evidence also shows that the sovereign power of states is pivotally important in the story of the AIDS pandemic to date in negative ways. The pandemic has been allowed to become worse than it might have been by unwillingness of the state-centric international community to challenge mad, bad or dangerous exercise of sovereign power because of the self-restraint that "political correctness" imposes on criticism of postcolonial, especially African, rulers and states, of which maintenance of the fiction of sovereign equality of states is a part.

This fiction has being challenged with increasing vigour since the later 1990s in another sector of global political mobilization through the series of military interventions in exercise of the responsibility to protect human rights which began after the genocidal killings in Rwanda and Srebrenica; but to date, that responsibility has not pursued its own logic to its conclusion in this original field, as Tom Weiss nobly and sadly documents in this volume; still less, more widely. So we find no new form of multilateralism flourishing. Nor do we see traditional state-centric multilateralism being undermined by a unilateralist hegemon; rather we see multilateral opportunities being eroded in spitefulness to the USA by countries which claim, sometimes extravagantly, to promote multilateralism. Conversely, we see the USA, via its science and pharmaceutical establishments, its statistical arm (the US Bureau of Census) and its specific funding initiative (the President's Emergency Plan for AIDS Relief), as the prime positive animator.

This finding, which creates a jarring discomfort of cognitive dissonance for more stringent critics of America in general and the Bush administration in particular, conveys us directly to answers about the deeper questions. The story of humanity's response to AIDS provides a plain example of the power of a strong unilateral lead to engender reciprocal responses which together compose a multilateral regime of action in the end. And the USA is the principal force for good in this regard. Together these answers direct us towards two of the weightiest hypotheses about the future shape of multilateralism to be found in this book. They are Coral Bell's eloquent and prodigious thesis of the return of a Grand Concert, conducted by the USA, as the emerging dominant form of multilateralism in the twenty-first century, and Robert Keohane's more narrowly expressed but harmonious proposal of the League of Democracies. Standing behind these theses one observes the more or less gradual transcendence of the mid-twentieth-century models of formal multilateral organization, of which the United Nations is the most robust.[2] The response to AIDS as described below, is a precursor case substantiating in terms the Coral Bell hypothesis.

The chapter will first explain the specific ways in which AIDS is a new threat for our times. Then it will show how the history of the pure science of the pandemic conforms to past practices and breaks no moulds. The history of attempts to combat the disease through applied science reveals two categories of further obstacles to coordinated multilateral action. The first category is of institutional blockages: over the costs of therapies; over Intellectual Property Rights; over inadequate market-driven priority to providing therapies for poor people. The second category of obstacle has been in the difficulty that Rich World bodies have in conveying messages about changing risky behaviour to people at risk in the Poor World: issues of cultural translation at the least. In fact there are fierce forms of resistance to these well-intentioned Rich World material and admonitory medical interventions. Three are mentioned: a raft of visceral conspiracy theories about the origins of AIDS; a more cynical set of conspiracy theories about the motives of the multilateral AIDS research and relief community; and a toxic mixture of both these to be found on the front line, in South Africa, today. Given these many blockages to traditional multilateral actions, the chapter goes on to argue that, in practice, action is being driven forward by individuals and then, importantly on their initiative, in an attempt at a new form of multilateral agent in the Global Fund. But that, in turn, is currently frustrated by diffusion or lack of will; and it has needed the intervention of the dominant world power of the day to restore momentum. Finally, the chapter raises the question whether any forms of extensive multilateral collaboration beyond the normal exchange of information between scientists will be needed in confronting the next waves of the pandemic, in India and China. So perhaps the unhappy experience so far, principally in confronting the African episode, has only limited future relevance?

AIDS as a new threat

AIDS is a strange and unexpected affliction. It has special characteristics which make it exceptionally difficult to manage through conventional mechanisms of public health control. First, and most fundamentally, AIDS is a classic example of a long-wave event in history. It is unlike previous epidemic diseases which humanity has confronted and of which we have knowledge. The Black Death in Europe (1346–1351) was rather like a bush fire in that it entered communities with startling virulence and killed large numbers of people at a single sweep. Some recent estimates suggest that between one-third and one-half of the population of continental Europe may have died within a span as short as two months. But like a bush fire, the disease does not recur with the same virulence thereafter. A modern example on a much smaller scale is of the Ebola haemorrhagic disease in Central Africa, which contained itself by its speed of action and its deadliness.

In contrast, AIDS is the product of a much older type of virus. The HIV/AIDS virus is a retrovirus – a lentivirus – a form of virus which is probably as old as humanity. The origins of the disease lie in cross-species infection. In this case, HIV most probably entered humanity as a result of people in the Central African rainforest killing and eating apes carrying SIV. Regression analysis of the differentiation of viral types suggests that this transfer to humans may have occurred in the first third of the twentieth century. The virus enters the very DNA of the individual's organism. At present there is no suggestion that we have even a medical model for a cure. But having entered the human subject, and sero-conversion having occurred (usually marked by a bout of fever), the victim appears symptomless for possibly quite long periods of time: symptomless but nonetheless infectious.

The effect of this unusual mode of transmission meant that the disease was able to spread stealthily before HIV was identified by Doctor Montagnier and his team at the Institut Pasteur in Paris in 1983. Long latency means that, as a consequence, a second generation can be infected before the first has died; and in the African episode of the AIDS epidemic we now see that it has achieved a third generation effect. There are grandchildren of the first generation of those infected who are now themselves infected.

Long latency has also been responsible for the distinctly modern way in which the AIDS pandemic presented, geographically. One of the earliest positive identifications of HIV has been made in subsequent assay of preserved body fluids taken from a merchant seaman who died mysteriously in the early 1950s. Transport systems have often shaped epidemics, and people and places involved with them are frequently among early victims: the bubonic plague which was the Black Death came to Europe in ships and spread out from ports. In the case of AIDS, the combination of slow transition from initial infection to final crisis with fast and frequent mass air transport was the key to its special modern novelty. Unusually in epidemiology, thorough contact tracing analysis means that it is now established that the so-called "reference case" which transferred the infection from central Africa to America was almost certainly a homosexual airline steward. He carried the virus into the bathhouse culture of San Francisco homosexuals which provided it with a congenial medium for explosive reproduction. Highly promiscuous multiple high risk (anal) sexual contacts were common: circa 1,000 per person per year in some documented cases.

Long latency, giving long-wave impact in the Poor World and the Boeing boost to global spread, means that the social impact of such a disease is therefore evidently significantly different from the Black Death. It is also different from another modern form of killing, the wholly voluntary anthropogenic plague of selective killing of the brightest and best male specimens, which is the peculiar characteristic of the twentieth century's mass industrial wars. AIDS has one similarity with the battles of Verdun and the Somme. Both are demographically selective. The Great War removed the flower of those generations with long-wave effects such as the drive to create a federal European Union, that have rippled into the contemporary politics of continental Europe. However, it only occurred once. AIDS does it repeatedly, generation by generation, thereby "hollowing out" the demographic profile of afflicted communities. It also kills young women in equal or greater number, given that women are usually socially and always physiologically at greater risk of infection than men. Communities that are thus affected may find it increasingly – indeed, we may suggest, extraordinarily – difficult to manage the impact on their own.

Botswana is one of the leading test cases today. It is a country with a small absolute population and one of the world's highest HIV infection rates. Every other woman tested last year in antenatal clinics was found to be HIV positive (49.7%). It is also a democratic and tolerant society, endowed with great wealth as a result of diamond mining. It therefore has an autonomous access to resources of money and political will that are unusual in sub-Saharan Africa and thus a potential to defend itself. These resources have been further amplified by extensive and early intervention of the outside world (specifically through the agency of the Bill and Melinda Gates Foundation). The AIDS epidemic has now reached a stage where the question arises of what happens when that "hollowing out" of the productive age group has reached the point that the society can no longer sustain social coherence. Botswana has not reached this threshold yet. Neither has Swaziland, the other highly infected small southern African state. Swaziland is involuntarily pioneering this miserable experiment for humanity. In 2005 it has a reported prevalence rate of 55 per cent among young women. This situation has been described by Professor Richard Feachem, Director of the Global Fund to fight AIDS, TB and Malaria, as "viral genocide".[3]

One legacy of the different but severe adversities of the era of apartheid and colonial rule has been the remarkable fortitude of southern African societies and peoples, which may explain how the corrosive effects of AIDS are being resisted up to now. But both Botswana and Swaziland are countries which, on present projections, look likely to cease to exist at some point in the not too distant future, as a direct result of AIDS and regardless of currently known interventions.

This deeply insidious and difficult long-wave effect is, in fact, a characteristic shared with most of the most serious threats to global security. The greatest challenge of long-wave events of this sort is that they are hard to understand in their full potential consequences and even harder to translate into recommendations for specific actions that could be taken by existing agencies of power and political action, whether national or multilateral. The irony is particularly intense because there seems a well-demonstrated rule of thumb that the attention span of power structures is in inverse relationship to the extent to which they are democratic in nature. Mussolini made the trains run on time. So, for structural reasons, AIDS poses a severe ethical as well as practical problem of governance.

But it does not end there. The governance problem is compounded by two other qualities of the matter. The first is that since AIDS acts through the most intimate aspects of people's lives it is not easy to disentangle the two in the public debate. The principal mechanism of transmission in the first (African) wave of the epidemic is through heterosexual sexual intercourse and there are strong social constraints on discussing any part of it for that reason. Death certificates in South Africa are an unreliable source of evidence for the scale of the epidemic if the cause of death is taken as evidence: for doctors, out of consideration to families, frequently mention the immediate cause of death, which is usually an opportunistic infection, rather than the underlying cause of death which was AIDS.

Secondly, as mentioned already, AIDS cannot be cured. There is no "magic bullet" available now or for the foreseeable future, which will cure the disease or even that will vaccinate people to prevent them getting it. As will be described later, certain categories of drugs are available, which do have some mitigating effect: but none of them is a cure or anything close to one; and the drugs are by no means an uncomplicated benefit. In fact, as we shall see, a new class of medical intervention is now, late in the day, beginning to receive substantial attention. But it is not a cure; it is only a way of helping to prevent infection in the first place; and since this mechanism is, like all other means of preventing infection, deeply controversial for one or another community, this does not offer an easy message for any institution, multilateral or otherwise, to carry.

Blocks to multilateralism in the pure science

While the unusual and frightening long-wave nature of the AIDS pandemic makes it a daunting task for public health interventions, one might, nonetheless, expect it to stand more conventionally in a framework for multilateral collaboration when we look at it through the perspective of pure science. Here again, things are not quite as they might appear at first glance.

There is, and has been through most of the twentieth century, a working assumption, both among practising scientists and among lay people, that science stands above and beyond politics. Accordingly, the commitment to knowledge overrides differences of creed or nationality. In this sense, the great set piece tragedy in which these propositions were tested was within the context of the Manhattan Project. Once it had become clear to the participating scientists that their combined enthusiasms to develop the "technologically sweet" (in Robert J. Oppenheimer's celebrated phrase) concept of an atomic weapon could now be translated into reality, a ferocious moral debate broke out among them over the degree to which they should assert authority over the potential uses to which their knowledge might then be put. The case was made in June 1945 by seven of the leading atomic scientists in the Franck memorandum. The case which they launched, most prominently against the scientists' director, Oppenheimer, was that in just the same way that the community of science shared a transcendent responsibility to advance knowledge regardless of its provenance, when that knowledge had the potential to be as deadly as that which had now been created at Los Alamos, they also had a responsibility to speak of its potential use. Oppenheimer, it will be recollected, argued against this. He asserted that the product of their knowledge was owned by the country which had made it possible for them to obtain it and the decision on how that knowledge should be used in practice explicitly did not lie with the scientists. Specifically it did not do so in democracies.

This central drama, at the high water mark of the scientific age, was bracketed before and after by other, different, episodes. The norm during the period of the emergence of modern science until the early twentieth century was more accurately represented by Galileo's appearance before the Inquisition under demand that he renounce his view of the heliocentric universe, since it did not conform with the ruling belief of the Catholic church. At the other end, a strengthening force today, we can see a challenge to the supremacy of scientific knowledge arising from the "creationist" and fundamentalist interpretation of Genesis by strong evangelical sects. So the conventional wisdom about science being above politics, about it being an epitome of multilateral collaboration under the guiding star of Truth, is actually doubly qualified. It is bracketed by periods where other criteria than scientific truth contend with that truth for authority over action; and within that era, even at the high tide of the scientific age, a moral debate about the rights of scientists to control the product of their knowledge was in practice resolved by conscious subordination of a transcendent duty to all mankind to a national interest.

The science of HIV/AIDS presents a startlingly close microcosm of that general history of the tension between scientific and other belief systems and, within science, between a transcendent duty and a national interest. The insidious, intimate and pervasive nature of HIV/AIDS, especially in the African episode, has made it fertile ground for a wild undergrowth of conspiracy theory and alternative explanation to that which science provides: to this I will return below. Here, however, we must recollect that the early history of the science of HIV/AIDS contains an episode as fraught as was the debate within the Manhattan Project over the decision to use the atomic bomb and, in its different way, as decisive in the impact which that debate had upon the way in which scientific knowledge came to be used in interaction with the pandemic.

In 1984, Robert Gallo and others published a paper in the journal *Science* which argued that the retrovirus HIV, which had been identified in patients by Luc Montagnier and his colleagues at the Institut Pasteur the previous year, was indeed the cause of AIDS. A dispute over who actually should be recognized as the principal discoverer – Gallo and his team or Montagnier and his – preoccupied and diverted energy at what we now know to have been a critical early moment in the development of the global pandemic. It was a moment when intervention could have been disproportionately more important and efficient than greater intervention at a much later stage. The dispute over discovery was poisoned by an even more bitter dispute over intellectual property rights. Gallo had discovered a way to grow cultured T lymphocytes *in vitro*. The helper T cells are in the front line of the battle with the virus within the body and this discovery of Gallo's underlay the development of a viable blood test (the ELISA test). As the epidemic burgeoned in numbers and also acquired a degree of political clout through its first wave of discovered victims, the American homosexual community, the intertwined contested issues of primary discoverer of the mechanism and primary discoverer of the test became such that it was only resolved by political intervention at the highest level. President Reagan and the then French Prime Minister, Jacques Chirac, devised a political formula under which Gallo and Montagnier were declared to be "co-discoverers" in an attempt to resolve principally the dispute over patent rights.[4]

Institutional blocks to multilateralism in the applied science

Opportunity/costs and intellectual property rights

After the resolution of that initial and difficult dispute, the pure science of research on HIV/AIDS has much more closely matched the normative expectation of multilateral collaboration on the principle of the sharing of science among scientists. But at the applied end of the science there has been no such harmony. Disharmony and the difficulty of producing agreed multilateral actions has been more the norm than the exception in the fields both of prevention and of mitigation of the symptoms of the disease.

It became rapidly evident that complex cocktails of drugs could be employed to prolong the period of remission between initial infection and the arrival of full-blown AIDS, especially if the administration of the drug regimens could be coupled to regular and careful measurement of the patient's viral loads, so that as soon as one in the triple cocktail began to lose effect, another could be brought in. Furthermore, if the patient could be kept free of stress and provided with a plentiful and healthy diet and much exercise, then, as has been the case for some of the Californian homosexual patients, the period of remission can begin to look almost like the reduction of the disease to a chronic status. However, as this simple description indicates, the drugs are part only of a complete treatment of all aspects of the patient's lifestyle; and the drugs are relatively costly within the advanced Western pharmacopoeia and extremely costly in comparison to the much more parsimonious pharmacopoeia available to doctors in most of the Poor World. Thus the middle decade in the 25 years' history of humanity's encounter with AIDS was caught up in a tremendous legal battle over the terms and means by which AZT and subsequent anti-retroviral therapies could and would be made available to the majority of victims who did not have the – in global ranking – relatively affluent lifestyle and opportunities of Californian homosexuals. And there may be a nasty sting in the tail, described below.

Market-driven constraints

The production and sale of anti-retrovirals was an issue swiftly and angrily infused with the politics of the international market in advanced medical drugs. Under great political and legal duress, it came to be resolved by the later 1990s in terms of two solutions: one, subvention and subsidy for the drugs' originators and patent holders to provide their products cheaply to Poor World markets and, at the same time, as part of that pressure, the opening of a market for generically manufactured anti-retroviral drugs: a process driven principally by Indian entrepreneurs and the Indian medical drugs industry. The sale of Indian generic drugs to South Africa, at prices well below those of the world market, became both an issue in the anguished debate in that country over the correct way to deal with its epidemic, and also a potent signal in the "anti-globalization" dimension of the critique of American power, which was strengthened from the later 1990s and especially from 2000 with the election of President George W. Bush.

Lack of a sufficiently attractively profitable market has obstructed efficient actions against the advance of the AIDS pandemic and the creation within that management of efficient multilateral alliances. It has touched all three of the principal routes to more (or less) efficient prevention of infection. The most medical of those interventions, microbicidal preparations to be used by a woman before unprotected sexual intercourse, has suffered from the same market-mediated constraint which slowed the development and marketing of anti-retrovirals. A conference convened at the Royal Society of Medicine in London in September 2004 that reviewed all bio-medical avenues of research, revealed that microbicides are the most promising of currently available medical interventions in the whole spectrum of the AIDS pandemic. They can kill the virus before it has the chance to enter the person's body. Also aiming to block the virus at entry is development work on gene therapy: genetically-targeted "awakeners" of the body's protective mucosa, which can block off access to the receptors on which the virus wishes to bond. This is work inspired by the discovery that certain prostitutes in Nairobi and Phnom Penh appeared to have a genetic resistance to infection despite heavy exposure.

The global medical drugs market has not given these preparations high priority; and the reflexive instinct of the European Commission blindly to regulate everything that moves as a covert way of extending its powers has recently halted for many months drug trials being conducted by academic institutions.[5] As with the production of cheaper anti-retrovirals, it has taken external "pump-priming" interventions, again initially by concerned NGOs led by the Gates Foundation, to initiate action to accelerate development of these preparations by creating a market which the market unassisted would not do on its own.

Inter-cultural blocks to effective multilateral actions

A second category of dispute, of inter-cultural blocks to effective multilateral actions, has impeded the acceptance of a general prescription for preventative action. This is better known to the general public than the category of institutional blocks and is principally to be seen in the modest success of a 15-years' campaign to encourage the use of barrier contraceptives in populations at risk.

The history of the condom in the front line of defence against the AIDS epidemic is neither fully documented nor fully understood. But aspects of it are known and present a confusing picture. On the one hand, in populations which have no prior religious or other objection to the use of condoms, and which knew and felt themselves to be at extreme risk of infection, condom use was rapidly and successfully increased. The best example here was of American homosexuals of the first generation at risk in the San Francisco bathhouse society. They transformed their behaviour swiftly and extensively. Indeed, the very success of that first generation response became the cause of a problem for the next generation of young homosexuals: for these men saw as evidence that the risk was diminished the relative success of early retroviral treatments in producing the appearance of a reduction of the disease to chronic status; and therefore risky sexual practices (as practised by the index case of the so-called "superstrain" or "superinfected" virus, to be encountered below) began to return. Possibly the best example of the efficient use of condoms to cap an epidemic which had every potential to become disastrous was in Thailand. Here, the use of condoms was recommended by the multilateral AIDS prevention community, accepted and strongly promoted by the government. The use of condoms was both demanded by sex workers and accepted by clients. The profile of the Thai epidemic which did *not* occur thus stands in contrast to the southern African epidemics which did.

Here, the much praised Ugandan programme advocating – in succession – Abstinence; faithfulness within monogamous relationships ("Be faithful"); Condoms – the ABC strategy – has not been replicated in other parts of the region. Indeed, for a variety of cultural reasons, southern African men are strongly resistant to the use of condoms and there seems persuasive evidence to suggest that condom use has simply not increased, and is certainly nowhere near to the scales achieved by the first wave of American homosexuals affected or in Thailand. Yet the message from the multilateral expert community was the same.

What has made the difference in those countries which appear to have managed to reduce the rates of increase in the epidemic is one of the most important and least well-understood research questions in the social (as distinct from medical) study of AIDS. Another conundrum appears when we start to look for answers, one which is the contradictory effect of the Catholic Church. In much of the devoutly Catholic world, the formal position of the Vatican, to oppose the use of condoms, was presented as both socially irresponsible and deeply unhelpful. Yet interestingly, strongly Catholic countries, such as Brazil and others with a presence of formal Catholicism as a result of their histories in francophone Africa, have far better records of social control of the spread of the epidemic than the case in places where those apparent religiously produced constraints on the use of barrier contraceptives are not present. Why? We cannot rightly say.

There is some evidence from Uganda which suggests that the success of the Catholic church in inspiring young Ugandans with the moral and social strength to maintain chastity may have been an important component in that country's encounter with the disease. But whether some other social variable, such as the strong sense of ethic identity felt by Baganda, amplified that or was actually more important, we cannot yet say with any confidence. The necessary fieldwork has not been done. The sources of the social discipline which underlay the behavioural changes that occurred in Thailand is a matter on which I have no detailed information: merely the observation that something in the field of socialized norms, including frank coercion at times, has played an important role. In the case of a country like Cuba, with an overt policy of segregation and containment of HIV-infected people and with a high degree of overt social control, we can see that reason more visibly. Yet, whatever they are, all these forces changing intimate social behaviour are immensely politically sensitive, either to advocate or even to discuss.

Thus, when the administration of George W. Bush advocated the promotion of sexual abstinence as one of its higher priorities, it provoked strongly hostile counter-reactions in many parts of the world. Whether this was to do with the message or the messenger is a moot point, to which I shall return at the end of this chapter.

Grounds of resistance to multilateral Rich World interventions

Attempts to produce a coordinated multilateral regime for the containment and reversal of AIDS are obstructed by the institutional and cultural blocks already mentioned, but also by three more, all of which are built on conspiracy theories. The first is an angry accusation that the rich

North is deliberately denying the poor South access to treatments out of a strategic motivation to let AIDS deepen the immiseration of the poor so that they cannot challenge its suzerainty. The second is a criticism of the manner in which the international community institutionalized its response to the epidemic after 1986 when the WHO founded its Global Programme on AIDS – the precursor of UNAIDS. In particular, a critique of that institutional response was mounted which has resonated in two communities: parts of the global South and among "anti-globalization" critics of American power. This critique is that the international bureaucracy created to combat AIDS has become more concerned with the preservation of its own salaries and privileges than with the task in hand. Unfortunately, this accusation is not wholly groundless; and even more well founded is the observation that the institutional turf wars between UN agencies, notably WHO's resentment of the up-start UNAIDS, has corroded the efficacy of both. Thirdly, and particularly in South Africa which has also been a source of the second critique, the development of effective multilateral (or indeed national) action has been obstructed by a profound and powerfully toxic rhetoric, which combines both of the previous two elements in strongly racist terms.

In the past, there have been scientific doubts expressed and debate to be had about the links from HIV to AIDS; but the advance of knowledge has comprehensively dismissed them. We are now left with conspiracy views that come in various forms.

An extreme version, which appears to be believed by the 1994 Nobel Peace prizewinner from Kenya, Wangari Maathai, is that in some dreadful manner the AIDS virus was a consciously created organism, created by white people and likely to have the welcome effect of killing lots of black people. Variants of that view locate the source of the invented virus in Fort Dettrick, Maryland, the biological weapons laboratories of the American military, or with Dr. Wouter Basson and his team under the previous South African regime, who certainly did attempt to design racially specific infectious agents. A second and less exotic view takes the undoubted fact of the difficulty over pricing and anti-retroviral drugs to imply that this is also conspiratorially motivated: also intended to make the effect of the disease worse in Africa than it need otherwise have been.

The second type of antagonism to Rich World attempts to combat AIDS also implies a conspiracy, but of a quite different sort. Here, the argument tends in a different direction. From the mid-1980s, medical statisticians have been attempting to collect data on the actual nature and possible future course of the AIDS pandemic in different places. This is not easy work to do because in many parts of the most heavily infected areas, the physical capacity to gather accurate statistics has been absent until rather recently. Also, for reasons mentioned at the beginning of this chapter, often the actual presence of the disease will be concealed in formal data such as death certificates under euphemisms and partial truths such as "heart failure" or "sudden death".

The best way to survey an epidemic of this sort is by a national sero survey; but such studies are both logistically difficult to conduct and expensive to do. In fact, Uganda did conduct a national sero survey quite early in the course of the pandemic, although, as a consequence of the war with the Lord's Resistance Army in the North of the country, it was not possible to carry out field research there. Many more national surveys have now been conducted or are in prospect. But in the absence of such comprehensive data, statisticians have been obliged to take representative materials from other sources and attempt to extrapolate from them.

Of these, by far the most important have been the time series made available through blood tests taken from pregnant women presenting at antenatal clinics. Of course, such people are by definition an abnormal cross section of the society. Whereas they are (by definition) women who have had unprotected sex, they are much less likely to represent the full scope of HIV infection, simply because HIV-infected women are less likely to become pregnant and hence to appear in such a clinic. However, from these data over a ten-year period the WHO programme, initially run by the late Jonathan Mann (he and his wife Mary-Lou Clements-Mann were passengers on the Swissair flight which crashed off the coast of Nova Scotia in September 1998), attempts have been made by medical statisticians to represent the general pattern of the epidemic from the fragmentary data available. In the case of the one country which has been heavily infected but which also possesses a competent national statistical service and an actuarial profession, namely South Africa, models have been constructed and have been progressively refined. The result of these attempts to portray the progress of the epidemic have been, broadly speaking, to show estimates during the early stages erring on the side of caution (i.e. high estimates) and, more recently, as the quality and amount of data have improved, to adjust those estimates, sometimes down and sometimes up and in all cases to give indications of ranges of possibility and of certainty. This, in fact, became standard practice in the Fourth UNAIDS report that was published in July 2004 at the Bangkok AIDS conference.[6]

All this looks and, in my opinion actually is, perfectly normal practice in an attempt to investigate a fragile and difficult epidemiological picture. None of the research has been specifically secret and in all cases there has been a normal practice of international peer review. The demographic background, and in many ways the metronome to this work, has been provided by the United States Bureau of Census figures, which are generally accepted as being the state of the art by those in the field. In practice, effective multilateral demographic research work depends as so often upon the lead given by a competent independent actor.

However, as the epidemic undoubtedly worsened in sub-Saharan Africa, and as the actuarial and medical statistical community attempted to refine its picture of the epidemic, a particular group chose to represent their modelling and suggestions in a hostile and sceptical light. Prominent in leading this dissident campaign has been the South African journalist Rian Malan, whose consistent view has been to maintain that apparent contradictions in the data are not a result of the normal practice in a necessarily imprecise field but are indications of deliberate and malicious cover up. What would be the reason for a systematic over-estimating of the level of HIV infection in sub-Saharan Africa, he asks? In order to ensure that the "AIDS industry", as he persists in calling it, will continue to draw its fat tax-free salaries and diplomatic perks both in the field and, more especially, in the flesh pots of Geneva and New York, because an anxious world public will not deny them funds. Their interest, writes Malan quite directly and often, is not in combating the disease, merely in protecting their own position; feathering their own nests.

In fact, it is not difficult to demonstrate the reason why Rian Malan (to take the principal miscreant in this regard) is baffled by the nature of the figures produced by the Actuarial Society of South Africa and others. It is not that there is anything inherently suspicious or surprising about the variability in the statistics. It is simply that he does not understand how statistics are made and why they have the qualities which they do. Yet, as I and two colleagues discovered when we attempted to correct Mr. Malan's misunderstandings in an article in the London *Spectator* recently – placed there deliberately because that journal had originally given Malan international space to make his deeply unhelpful observations – he can neither understand nor accept correction.[7]

His is quite a clever line of attack for it exploits the undoubted fact that the picture presented, particularly presented over the span of a number of years, has not been consistent. In fact, to repeat, it has been modified as data have become available to cause such corrections to be made. Such is the expectation in any unpoliticized field of scientific enquiry. But here the conspiracy view of investigative journalists such as Malan and those who associate with him has had a double effect. For it has also served to cast doubt on the attempts of principal figures in the multilateral AIDS research, prevention and treatment community to express a position in the way that they see it. Thus, against the background of Malan's and the London *Spectator*'s promotion of scepticism about the motives of the multilateral agencies, speeches by Peter Piot, or Steven

Lewis, ring hollow in the minds of many in the international media that have resonated easily with the suggestions of bad faith made by Malan and those like him.

The Malan tendency makes a second type of argument also. This is ingeniously populist because it seems to place the critics on the side of the common man against a vaguely elitist and plainly greedy "AIDS establishment" whose motives have already been excoriated on the first line. As mentioned, there is some fire beneath this smoke. The second argument is that the diversion of scarce money to AIDS actually allows more people to suffer and die. It diverts money and effort from the real cause of African suffering, its poverty perniciously increased by "underdevelopment" – that fashionable *marxisante* 1970s notion of Walter Rodney and André Gunder Frank, before he recanted it.

Certainly, there is a difficult opportunity/cost calculation to be made in the treatment of HIV, for there are other diseases which kill far larger numbers of people and much more quickly. After all, the single largest source of childhood death in sub-Saharan Africa is not AIDS but perinatal diarrhoea. Malaria is a huge killer and tuberculosis is a disease which has, literally, come back from the dead as one of the principal opportunistic infections that carries off people who are suffering from full-blown AIDS. If the mitigation of the effects of AIDS is so expensive and so problematic, goes this argument, then why not spend the money more reliably and more efficiently on much simpler medical interventions, which will uncontroversially save many lives right now: lives which will certainly be lost if these modest interventions with rehydrating salts and other life-savers are not made? Whereas Malan had earlier (and, in our view, disgracefully) explained that among his motives for entering this debate he found that baiting the Treatment Action Campaign and other of the AIDS activists in South Africa was a sort of sport which gave him his kicks, Mr. Malan's adolescent behaviour has had much deeper and more irresponsible consequences than a bit of fun.

It cannot be said whether the injection of this particular strain of scepticism into the international press coverage of AIDS has had the effect of dampening the willingness of contributing governments to commit to the principal funding vehicle, namely the Global Fund for the Prevention of AIDS, TB and Malaria, which opened for business in 2002. Certainly, as will be mentioned again below, the fund's target for increasing pledges and, more to the point, obtaining payment on those pledges, is falling behind what was expected and hoped for. But the other area in which the journalistic scepticism about the statistical representation of the epidemic has been particularly noxious and material in effect is the degree to which it has reinforced the third ground of resistance to multilateral, or indeed any, actions. This block is to be found powerfully and most damagingly in the country which is currently at the forefront of risk in the global pandemic – namely, South Africa.

The epidemic in South Africa is difficult to control because it exists within a toxic mixture of sex, race and power. It was not always so. When the Mandela government came to power after the great transformation of 1994, it was presented with indications of where the AIDS pandemic might take the country at a time when prevalence rates were round about 1 per cent. The decision taken by that first government of democratic South Africa was one that was perfectly moral and entirely comprehensible, although it turned out, in hindsight, to have been tragically wrong. This argument was one of offset choices. On the one hand, the country was faced with the possibility of a major epidemic which had not yet occurred but which, to prevent, would require very substantial expenditure of limited public finance in the short term. Set against that were the demands of immediate expenditures on housing, on sewage and water provision and other politically important social expenditures, with reliable short-term gains for many. The government could not responsibly choose the long term over the short. However, this is not the argument that is now to be found at the highest levels of the South African government where President Thabo Mbeki has been prominent in legitimating a range of reasons for taking no action or minimal action to deal with the AIDS epidemic that is now sweeping over his country.

No one can be exactly sure of President Mbeki's present views, but certainly he has in the past been closely associated with those who argue that HIV does not lead to AIDS, as well as to a range of other views, notably that the illnesses which people call AIDS are produced in patients by the powerful poisons administered in the form of anti-retroviral drugs. He has used his position to give comfort to eccentrics in the scientific community who subscribe to views of this sort and he has taken demonstrable and repeated comfort from the type of scepticism about the statistics which have been peddled by Mr. Malan and other journalists associated with him. But underlying President Mbeki's anger on the subject is what he believes to be an implied accusation of association. On 21 October 2004, he was asked a question in the South African parliament by an opposition MP about government policy on AIDS given the very high incidence of rape which occurs in the country. Rape is an efficient way of spreading the disease. The reply was astonishing.

Mbeki ignored the question and said this: "I for my part will not keep quiet while others whose minds have been corrupted by the disease of racism accuse us, the black people of South Africa, of Africa and the world, as being, by virtue of our Africanness and skin colour, lazy, liars, foul-smelling, diseased, corrupt, violent, amoral, sexually depraved, animalistic, savage and rapist."[8] No one had actually suggested any of these things but the President chose to represent the subject in these terms. What is sadly but undoubtedly the case is that the high prevalence of HIV/AIDS which has occurred in Southern Africa over the last 15 years is importantly a result of the breakdown of the family life of black Southern Africans and most particularly the inability of Southern African women to negotiate or control their sex lives.[9]

One response to the fact that Southern African men will, by and large, refuse to use condoms has been the promotion of microbicidal foams and creams which give women a technical means to protect themselves during intercourse, preferably without the man's knowledge. But another response is that represented by the President's astonishing outburst, which has had the effect of first delaying any large-scale public health measures in the one country in sub-Saharan Africa that would be technically competent to conduct such a campaign efficiently. Then, when reluctantly forced through the courts to agree to actions, to undertake actions which may well be too late and of the wrong kind.

It took the doggedness of the Treatment Action Campaign over the government's refusal to provide the Nivirapine one-shot treatment that can prevent HIV transmission from mother to child at birth (since compromised by poor practice) to bring about a change in the direction of South African government public health policy on HIV. The Nivirapine case went to the constitutional court, where, in a path-breaking judgement, Chief Justice Chaskalson and his colleagues adjudicated between the rights of the mother, the child and the wider community.[10] The court found that the government's refusal to provide this drug at the public expense was perverse and, bending to the will of the court, the government has begun to provide it. Equally, it committed itself to preparation for the "roll out" of a comprehensive anti-retroviral treatment campaign for all HIV positive sufferers to begin during 2005. But a serious and potentially tragic consequence of the delay in the implementation of actions in South Africa – a delay now ten years' long since first warnings were given to the newly-independent government – means that this move is being taken just at the moment when the epidemic is making transition from its primary phase to the so-called "death phase", when very large numbers of people may be expected to die in the next few years.

The moot question is what the balance of cost and benefits of a large-scale ART campaign will be at this point in the history of such an epidemic. On the one hand, it will undoubtedly alleviate the suffering of present infected individuals; but, on the other, as virologists morbidly but accurately observe, the single most likely predictable consequence of the large-scale use of ART at this point will be to accelerate the arrival of a drug-resistant virus. It may also encourage it to mutate. If the HIV/AIDS virus follows the logic of previous infectious diseases, that pathway may be anticipated. Syphilis began as a disease transmitted through skin-to-skin contact. But after the opportunities through close contact in squalid living conditions were diminished, it moved to a more reliable passageway of transmission through the genital tracts. From there, its logical next steps to protect its own reproductive potential was to embed in those parts of the body where it could best protect itself from the effect of drugs which sought it out. These places were the eyes and, most efficient of all, to hide behind the blood/brain barrier in the brain.

Such transformation may be now occurring with the HIV. Initial use of single therapy anti-retroviral drugs in the 1990s contributed directly to the development of acquired resistance in individuals and possibly to the appearance of transmitted resistance, as documented in the February 2005 announcement of the multi-drug resistant, dual-tropic HIV-1 virus in a patient in New York, resistant to three of the four existing categories of anti-retroviral medications and considerably more virulent than wild type virus. (136 per cent replication capacity) It also kills more quickly: in the index case, the period from infection to AIDS was 20 months. The index case acquired infection from multiple high-risk homosexual contacts in a context of recreational drug (metamphetamine) use. The case may therefore be one of dual or superinfection. The authors and the NY Public Health authorities regarded it as having great public health ramifications, as did Dr. Webber reporting the development in South Africa.[11]

The delay in intervention during President Mbeki's stewardship of South Africa so far may well have accelerated the possibility of this further development of this most dreadful of viruses. President Mbeki's unpleasant racial fantasies have been allowed to hold sway for as long as they have and to stand unchallenged because they found an unintended ally in the plague of "political correctness" which settled on the minds of many of the liberal persuasion after the 1970s. "Political correctness" made it difficult for people to name the paralysing combination of a preoccupation with race and bad science for what it was. The same set of constraints silenced the necessary criticism of frequently pathological behaviour which compounded state failure, whether in the Congo or in Zimbabwe. This paralysis affected most particularly the formal multilateral contexts in which interstate and intergovernmental cooperation could occur.

The indispensability of crucial individuals for new forms of multilateral venture

Accordingly – I would suggest consequentially the history of real and effective intervention against the AIDS pandemic shows the prominent role of a small handful of crucial individuals. Pre-eminent among these are Bill and Melinda Gates. Their decision to employ his enormous computer software fortune to public service, and within that vision to devote particular priority to the AIDS issue, stands already in the annals of philanthropy as one of the great histories on a par with the actions of Rockefeller and Carnegie in earlier generations. The Gates Foundation has been indispensable, both in promoting particular lines of action which otherwise might not have come forward as quickly as they did and in catalysing different forms of political action. The former is illustrated by the early and strong commitment to the development of new therapies. Without the stimulus of the Gates Foundation, there is little doubt that research on several fronts – ARTs, microbicides and gene therapy – would not have proceeded as they have done to date. In terms of political action, the decision by the Gates Foundation to focus heavily on Botswana was indispensable to the political and financial mobilization of the resources of that country as it seeks to protect its present and future generation in the very eye of the storm of the epidemic. The depth of the failure of conventional formal multilateralism has thus, ironically, been screened to a degree by the arrival of this reinforcement; and a purpose of this chapter is to alert this point. The example of the Gateses (and indeed others in the philanthropic community who have joined them) was also influential in the manner in which the Global Fund for the Prevention of AIDS, Tuberculosis and Malaria was conceived and deployed.

As another of the small group of key mobilizing individuals, Richard Feachem, Director of the Global Fund, explains it, the fund's philosophy is quite different from that of previous enterprises. They have usually invested in finding answers to problems, and then promoting the adoption of those answers. In contrast, the Global Fund deliberately refuses to be directive in setting priorities for action. On the contrary, it is "radically passive" in its attitude, investing its money and effort in extensive and high-quality peer review of all the proposals brought to it. Proposals for actions once adopted are then funded and will be reliably refunded if they show promise and success. But, equally, if they fail to thrive, then they will be allowed to wither. This, it was felt, would be a more efficient way of ensuring a viable mix between good science and local legitimacy: for underlying the philosophy of the fund is recognition that, as a provider of global public goods for health, for reasons rehearsed earlier in this chapter, any intervention must command the support and the active promotion of the community within which it is intended. Such local legitimacy – "ownership" of the solution – is as prerequisite as a brilliant drug or other technical intervention might be. However, the initial enthusiasm of many governments to pledge money to the fund has not carried forward to further rounds, and some, having made pledges, have found reluctance or difficulty to actually pay up.[12]

A further key individual who galvanized multilateral action was Ambassador Richard Holbrooke. It was Holbrooke who, on a visit to Zambia during his period as US Ambassador to the United Nations, was horrified by the sight of AIDS orphans on the streets of Lusaka and initiated the process which led in 2000 to the passing of Resolution 1308 at the Security Council: the first resolution to recognize AIDS as a threat to international peace and security.

The five years since Resolution 1308 was passed have seen a growing if reluctant recognition that the narrow ground upon which the resolution had suggested there was a link to international peace and security is indeed well-founded. This narrow ground has recently been described in the first comprehensive evidence-based review of the subject of AIDS and security as the "condenser" function of military forces as soldiers, as the governments of many states which have succumbed to military coup d'états and also, more directly in the context of the United Nations, as peacekeeping forces.[13] The condenser can either absorb virus from the surrounding environment or, if at a higher prevalence than the surrounding population, vector it into that population. There is evidence of military forces performing both functions, depending on time and context. Peacekeeping forces can themselves become victims of the virus during operations in infected areas and also, if they themselves are infected, can be vectors for the disease to people who they are supposed to be there to protect. The obvious difficulty for the United Nations has been that, since the discussion of infection in state militaries touches directly their strong sense of national sovereignty, many African countries in particular have been deeply reluctant to see this issue engaged. So, therefore, Holbrooke's initiative has carried the matter into the Security Council, but there is a moot question as to whether it can further progress there.[14]

The centrality of American money and action

In those circumstances, what other sources of initiative could there be to stimulate both action on the epidemic and, at the same time, to galvanize multilateral institutions principally through support for the Global Fund? The answer came in the State of the Union speech in 2003 and the announcement in April of that year of the President's emergency plan for AIDS relief (PEPFAR). To the considerable surprise of a world that was not expecting it, this was a commitment of US$15 billion including $10bn of new money over the period 2001–05 by the George W. Bush administration to a five-year programme for AIDS relief. The programme would be administered directly through the State Department, but with externally recruited leadership. The Senior Administrator, Randall Tobias, was CEO of the Eli Lilley company,[15] and its Executive Director, the Deputy Global AIDS Coordinator, is an energetic apolitical doctor, Jo O'Neill. It acts bilaterally in 80 countries, and focuses specifically on 15 where 50 per cent of HIV cases are to be found. It does not act in China, India or Russia, nor will it do so, despite the impending very large episodes expected there, for reasons congruent with those given in the last section below.[16]

PEPFAR was immediately controversial because the administration announced it with a set of decided preferences for policy interventions led by primary prevention through sexual abstinence. In consequence, the motivation behind the PEPFAR initiative has been much discussed and much criticized. The role of the evangelical Christian community, and in particular of the Samaritan's Purse Foundation, run by Billy Graham Jnr, was important. But it has been the impact of some of the American investment that has been particularly striking. What is not in dispute is that PEPFAR has provided, by a substantial margin, the largest single stimulus to the Global Fund. It made a founding donation of $200m, represents 40 per cent of all pledges to 2008 and 30 per cent of the Fund's cash in hand and, as such, has successfully leveraged promises at least of increased pledge from countries in Europe. There is a statutory limitation that after 2004 US funds may not represent more than a third of the Fund's resources. In May 2005 it remains the case that the USA still provides 32 per cent. At the time of writing, it is hoped to "challenge" other G8 states at the Gleneagles summit to step up to the American example; but the Global Fund continues to be underfunded. To date, in four rounds of funding, the Global Fund has approved $3.4 billion of grants and as of 13 May 2005 has disbursed $1.2 billion. As Bezanson's independent assessment notes, it is rapidly running out of money on present performance, a view broadly confirmed by Bernard Rivers of the authoritative NGO watch-dog AIDSPAN.[17]

Whether President Chirac's enthusiasm to engage in "European Union" matching of United States' funding is prompted by motivations other than a concern for AIDS cannot be known.[18] However, past performance by this long-serving, never particularly popular and, since the May 2005 French rejection of the EU Constitution, functionally politically dead politician, who experienced the thrill of public adulation for his recent anti-Americanism, provides a context for interpretation. Certainly, the impression is that a powerful unilateral step by the world's single most wealthy and powerful country does appear to have had the effect, much predicted by negotiation theorists, of triggering a series of beneficial and possibly competitive counter bids. This pattern is reported in other chapters of this volume, and composes one of the three deeper themes which have surfaced as the authors worked together.

No doubt one day the inside story of why President George W. Bush chose to make this large move in 2003 will be told. Until then, it is merely a matter of speculation from its observed effects, effects which clearly include a degree of cognitive dissonance for those who believe that action on AIDS is a global security priority; that such action should be naturally taken and led through the multilateral institutions, but who now observe that the single most powerful intervention to date has not been multilateral but unilateral and has been taken by a state whose president is presumed to be hostile in an extreme degree to multilateral institutions and arrangements, as a matter of political principle. The evidence might be thought to bring that widespread European presumption into question.

Will multilateralism be important in combating future waves of AIDS?

Looking to the future, we can see from the statistics already that the largest epidemics on the planet will most likely not be those we have already witnessed in Africa. They will be, respectively, in India and China. In each of these two cases, there are different blocks to multilateral action: blocks which come in different ways but from the same source – a sense of national pride and unwillingness to see sovereignty compromised or diluted through external interventions. Mrs Meenakshi Datta Ghosh, who directed the Indian National AIDS Control Council until early 2005, has made this explicitly clear in her impatient irritation with what she believes to be extravagant extrapolations of the likely AIDS impact in India made by bodies such as the Centre for Security in International Affairs in Washington.[19]

The Chinese government, for different but well-known reasons, had until the SARS epidemic resisted all invitations to share data or to permit external scrutiny through field research. Accordingly, the story of the peculiar aetiology of the Chinese epidemic was only sketchily known. It was known to be different from both African and Indian, in that the sexual route of transmission was less important than the transmission through intravenous drug in injection, on the one hand, and the bizarre story of the commercialization of blood supplies to Chinese hospitals that was an aspect of the market liberalization of the economy, which followed the decision to open the capitalist road after the events of Tienanmen Square in 1989. However, the shock of SARS spread further than that epidemic alone. It triggered a general opening of the Chinese Department of Health. In a landmark speech at the Royal Society of Medicine in September 2004, Yiming Shao, of the Chinese Centre for Disease Control and Prevention, made clear that the Chinese government's position was now reversed from that which it had previously held. It welcomed foreign researchers; it welcomed suggestions for remedial action; it sought actively partnerships on best practice from experience in handling the epidemic in other parts of the world.[20]

In the case of both India and China, the risks of state failure and of social implosion which are being run in southern Africa are much less likely because the prevalence rates are so much lower, and likely to remain so. This is a function of the dilution of the HIV positive percentage within total populations of 1.1 and 1.3 billion respectively. The importance of multilateral mechanisms is likely to be much less in any case in either India or China. This is because, as the two rising and potentially dominant Asian powers of the twenty-first century, India and China already possess an adequate indigenous base of advanced research capacity, as well as medical, pharmaceutical and industrial capacity. So, the forms of partnership that will be required and beneficial to deal with this numerically larger portion of the AIDS epidemic are likely to be quite different from those which were desirable, but too often not forthcoming, during the African phase. Of greatest importance may be attempts to harness the indigenous intellectual and technological resources of India and China to an efficient learning of the lessons of what went wrong in the handling of the southern African phase of the epidemic, not forgetting what went right in the successful Brazilian, Cuban and Thai episodes of that same period.

This chapter has suggested that on the evidence to date the likelihood is not great that the demonstrably new threat of the AIDS pandemic will elicit an equal and opposite newness of multilateral response mechanism, but also that the flaws in modern multilateralism are not produced by the nature of the new threat posed by the AIDS pandemic. The power of some Poor World states, assisted unintentionally by the self-inflicted constraints of "politically correct" attitudes in the Rich World, to block the road to relief of the pandemic, has been illustrated. To speak truth to power still looks like the safest strategy. Likewise one of the central propositions of game theory has been seen to be underscored. The ability of strong unilateral leads to trigger reciprocal responses and thereby to establish momentum towards multilateral action seems to be the lesson of the short period since the Global Fund and PEPFAR were created. These coalitions are not based on formal status; they are coalitions of the willing and able: based on evidence of active political will and real committed resources. The deficiency of contemporary multilateralism is not to be attributed to an uncooperative hegemon in this area of study. Rather the reverse. The presumption of sovereign equality is more heavily implicated. In these findings, this chapter provides empirical support for the broader expectation advanced by Bell and Keohane, that whereas some attenuated forms of mid-twentieth-century multilateral structure expressed through the UN may continue, one should expect – and on the case evidence here, should welcome positively – the coalescence of the new Grand Concert that is patently forming before our eyes as the driving force in many of the most intractable but urgent areas of global security.

The UN role in this may still be large if the society of states is prepared to accept the formula for the reconciliation of the divergent concerns of the Rich and the Poor Worlds that has been provided by the High Level Panel which reported to Kofi Annan on 1 December 2004. It is, in my opinion, without question the most intellectually robust and politically important report of its type since 1945: a view echoed in other contributions to this volume.[21] However, I do not expect the UN to emerge from the attempt to enlarge membership of the Security Council in September 2005 undiminished.[22]

What are the lessons of this history for the likely future of the pandemic? India and China are unlikely to require or to welcome assistance framed in the mission or rhetoric of "development aid". They will benefit more from a genuinely free market in advanced pure and applied science. Questions of intellectual property rights are likely to bulk larger than issues of international drug pricing. Interestingly, the attempt by the Blair government, helped by pop stars and cardinals, to push for huge increases in aid for Africa, has aroused educated interest, which is paying attention. As so often in politics, the result may be the reverse of what was intended; for it seems likely to produce the longer-term effect of finally undermining this, the last hurrah of 1960s *marxisante* political analysis, also expressed in the now quickly fading Millennium Development Goals. Inspection shows that a combination of lack of capacity and corruption vitiate the aid-driven solution, and that proper tariff reform and free trade are both more robust and efficient solutions to the problem of poverty. What has worked for China and India can work for Africa too; but dismantling the Common Agricultural Policy of the "EU" and curbing Bush's grotesque US farm tariff protections, not grandstanding hand-outs to diminishingly legitimate postcolonial governmental apparatus, are what is required. This will be more painful for the Rich World and therefore less likely to occur, but nonetheless necessary. My guess on the recent record of facts on the ground is that it will more likely be another push from the global philanthropists that will make the Rich World governments pay attention.

However, before this next phase opens, humanity must be witness to the death phase of the African episode of the AIDS pandemic and the prospect that the medical interventions will be of the wrong sort and at the wrong times, leading to temporary relief for some and the promise of a drug-resistant virus for the many in the near future. Insofar as the willing and able are permitted to override the various conspiracy-based objections to their proffered help, this trajectory can be deflected, but probably not reversed.

The most important contribution from multilateral action to the future phases of humanity's long struggle with AIDS may be to learn as well as we can the reasons for the failures of multilateral actions in its recent past.

Notes

1. I wish to express my thanks to my friends and colleagues in LSEAIDS, Tony Barnett, Colette Clement and John Harriss, and as always to my indispensable assistant Alison Suter, for their astringent and swift criticism of the first draft of this essay. However, I absolve them entirely, severally and singly from responsibility for the arguments advanced here, some of which they agreed with, some of which they did not. But such clarity of form as the essay has, it certainly owes to their help. I also wish to thank colleagues in the authors' discussion at the SSRC in Washington in December 2004, equally exonerated, for many careful and fruitful questions and observations, and the editors for their subsequent observations.
2. The simultaneous draining of power from all three of the mid-twentieth-century enterprises is a notable feature of the contemporary General Crisis. Of the three, NATO has already been functionally dead since the failure by the USA to exploit at once and in Afghanistan the declaration of Article V in response to 9/11. It has been smoothly and successfully superseded in practical military operations by the informal "intelligence special relationship" based upon the anglosphere (Australia/Britain/Canada/New Zealand/USA) with the important shadowy additions of Israel and Japan and some eastern European countries from time to time (see further, G. Prins (2002) "9/11 and the Raiders of the Lost Ark", *Cornell International Law Review* December 2002). Coral Bell correctly notes how 9/11 has galvanized closer working with China. The "European Union" – the most recent name for Monnet and Salter's post-World War I project covertly to create a federal European state, is now clearly entering its last days. It is being destroyed by twin forces. Ironically one is produced by the country in whose principal interest and benefit the whole project was begun: French over-anxiety to compensate for German resumption of active foreign policy in 1991, led to a fierce acceleration (the Euro, the Federal Constitution) both of which are shaking the vehicle to pieces. The Constitution is dead and the Euro will, in my expectation, soon fail. The second force is pervasive corruption within the Commission, whose accounts year by year auditors refuse to sign, and the massive disjuncture between the opinions of the European "Parliament" and the people's views. As a result it has failed to achieve either the democratic legitimacy or cultural relevance for the "European Union" in the eyes of most Europeans, especially younger cohorts, that Pascal Lamy correctly notes is indispensable. The mortal blow was delivered by the people of the Netherlands in their "two-thirds Nee" by two-thirds of the electorate, on 1 June 2005: the arrival of "people power" in western Europe on that day was as dramatic an event as the breaking of the Berlin Wall in November 1989. See further on these points: L. Siedentop (2001) *Democracy in Europe*, Harmondsworth: Penguin; G. Prins, "The end of the European Union", 25 May 2005; "The Euro: the beginning of the end", 6 June 2005, *Open Democracy* www.opendemocracy.co.uk/ democracy-europe_constitution/EUconstitution_2542.jsp;

idem, /content/articles /PDF /2576.pdf; G. Stuart (2003), "The making of Europe's Constitution", *Fabian Society*, December (the definitive account – and denunciation by the MP who was Britain's member of the drafting Praesidium); C. Booker and R. North (2003) *The Great Deception: The Secret History of the European Union*, London: Continuum.

3. Briefing to the private sector, Anglo-American Corporation Offices, London, 8 June 2005.
4. G. Prusiner (2002) "Discovering the causes of AIDS", *Science* 298: 1726.
5. This was because, in its frenzy of trying to regulate everything from the curvature of bananas to this case in point, it was not noticed that by redefining the duties of care of university researchers from civil to criminal codes, the EU would, logically enough, cause insurers of clinical trials to withdraw cover. This they did, bringing field trials to a halt until alternative arrangements could be made. (Information in discussions at the Royal Society of Medicine Conference, "Biomedical prevention of HIV: current status and future directions", 9–10 September 2004).
6. D.A. Stefanski (2004) "Bangkok: The end of broken promises? XV International AIDS Conference 2004", *Sexual Health* 1: 1–6 (CSIRO Australia), September 2004; Peter Doyle (CEO Metropolitan SA) and N. Nicholay (2005) "The battle over HIV and AIDS statistics: Do the models reflect reality?", joint lecture to Pugwash Conferences workshop on Threats Without Enemies: HIV/AIDS and Security", Gordon's Bay, Cape Town, 1 May 2005 (Pugwash Conferences Working Papers Series, forthcoming 2005).
7. R. Malan (2003) "Africa isn't dying of AIDS", *Spectator*, 13/20 December 2003; A. Barnett, G. Prins and A. Whiteside (2004) "AIDS denial costs lives", *Spectator*, 25 September 2004; R. Malan (2004) "Pugwash hogwash", *Spectator*, 2 October 2004; J. Boutwell (2004) "Rian Malan all at sea", *Spectator*, 23 October 2004.
8. In the National Assembly, 21 October 2004, in reply to a question from Ryan Coetzee (DA), cit. A. Quintal (2004) "Break silence on disease of racism – Mbeki". *Cape Times*, 22 October 2004.
9. Sorios Samura (2005) "Living with AIDS", Channel 4, 27 June 2005; "Africa's fatal sexual culture spreads AIDS", *Mail & Guardian*, (Johannesburg) 19 June 2005.
10. *Minister of Health et al.* vs. *Treatment Action Campaign et al.*, South African Constitutional Court, Case CCT 8/02, 5 July 2002.
11. M. Markowitz, H. Mohri, S. Mehandru, et al. (2005) "Infection with multidrug resistant, dual-tropic HIV-1 and rapid progression to AIDS: a case report", *Lancet* 365 (19 March): 1031–38. Correspondence, *Lancet* 365 (4 June 2005): 1923–26. The arrival of such a development was expected: L. Webber (Lancet Laboratories, Pretoria) (2005) "Preventative strategies and vaccine developments", lecture to Pugwash Conferences workshop on Threats without Enemies: HIV/AIDS and security", Gordon's Bay, Cape Town, 30 April 2005; Professor Jonathan Weber (2005) "How is science proposing to prevent HIV transmission – what social scientists need to know", public lecture at LSEAIDS, London School Economics, 16 May 2005, available at: www.lse.ac.uk/collections/LSEAIDS/pdfs/Weber_scienceoftransmission.ppt.
12. The Global Fund to fight AIDS, Tuberculosis and Malaria: "Pledges, 2001/2–2008", 8 November 2004, at www.globalfundatm.org.
13. A.S. Barnett and G. Prins (lead authors) (2005), LSEAIDS report for UNAIDS, *AIDS and Security: Fact, Fiction and Evidence*, (evidence-based report for presentation to the UN Security Council at the 5th anniversary of resolution 1308, 18 July 2005).
14. The fully documented history of how the world got Resolution 1308 is given in G. Prins (2004) "AIDS and global security", *International Affairs* 80(5) October 2004.
15. For those who enjoy adding two and two to make five, there are the makings of a benign

conspiracy theory surrounding some of these key individuals in that there is a common denominator: Melinda Gates is a double graduate of Duke University and was a member of the Duke Board of which Randall Tobias was Chairman. I am indebted for this inside knowledge to another of the authors in this volume, Bob Keohane, until recently a professor at Duke and husband of the former President of Duke University.

16. D. Brown (2004) "AIDS in India, China and Russia nears 'tipping point' UN says", *Washington Post*, 30 November 2004.
17. The Global Fund, Monthly Progress Update, 13 May 2005; K.A. Bezanson (2005). *Replenishing the Global Fund: An Independent Assessment*, February 2005, ISBN 92-9224-021-8, p. 34 (report commissioned for Kofi Annan and Sven Standström, co-chairmen of the replenishment panel); The Global Fund, *Annual Report 2004*, Financial Statements, pp. 63–74.
18. Chirac's peremptory announcement of French public health funding commitment was only accommodated by disruptive reallocation and hence curtailment of other activities within the budgetary cycle (personal information from senior French health officials on the receiving end of the *ukase*).
19. On-the-record meeting, Prins/Datta Ghosh, New Delhi, 25 March 2004. This situation is changing with the new Congress government.
20. Yiming Shao (2004) "HIV/AIDS epidemic and control in China: Current situation and future challenges", lecture given to Royal Society of Medicine conference "Biomedical prevention of HIV: current status and future directions", 9–10 September 2004.
21. The High Level Panel on Threats, Challenges and Change, UN GA A/59/565, 29 November 2004.
22. G. Prins (2005) "Lord Castlereagh's return: the significance of Kofi Annan's High Level Panel on Threats, Challenges and Change", *International Affairs* 81(2): 373–91.

16

The uninvited challenge: Terrorism targets the United Nations

Edward C. Luck

Global terrorism is both a challenge to and a challenge for multilateral institutions. Underlining the former, Secretary-General Kofi Annan has noted that terrorism "is a direct attack on the core values the United Nations stands for: the rule of law; the protection of civilians; mutual respect between people of different faiths and cultures; and peaceful resolution of conflicts".[1] When faced with such a direct assault, manifested most painfully in the bombing of UN headquarters in Baghdad on 19 August 2003, most organizations or communities would be expected to come together in a common front against the perpetrators. Where terrorists hope to divide, they more often unify. At least that has generally been the case for individual states and for bilateral state-to-state cooperation. That is one reason why terrorist successes are usually modest and unsustainable. The story has been rather different for the United Nations and other multilateral mechanisms, however. For the world body, the terrorist challenge to its purposes, principles and patterns of cooperation has been perceived more vaguely and distantly, despite the Secretary-General's decisive words. Some in the UN community, in fact, seem to view counter-terrorism as more of a threat to the UN than terrorism itself. As a result, the UN's response to terrorism has been tentative, halting, even ambivalent.

By looking at historical and institutional developments before and after the events of 11 September 2001, this chapter offers some hypotheses about why this has been so. It favours explanations related to geopolitics, US leadership, and ambivalence about American power over those based on constraints imposed by the UN Charter and international law. Its focus will be on the United Nations, as both the centrepiece and symbol of multilateral cooperation, though references will also be made to the extensive network of international collaborative counter-terrorism activities outside of the world body. The US and the UN, the paper concludes, are the ultimate odd couple. The nature of contemporary global terrorism drives them together, yet their mutual misapprehensions guarantee a most difficult and awkward marriage with equal measures of necessity and inconvenience.

History and context: pre-9/11

The international community may have been shocked by the scale, ambition and sophistication of the terrorist strikes on the United States of 11 September 2001, but collective efforts to grapple with terrorism long preceded those fateful events. In the mid-1930s, the League of Nations drafted a Convention for Prevention and Punishment of Terrorism, along with a Convention for the Creation of an International Criminal Court to try those accused of crimes, such as political assassination, covered by the counter-terrorism convention.[2] Though neither convention ever took effect, delegates in 1937 voiced concerns – about the implications of globalization and mass communications for spreading terrorist dogma and about related problems of counterfeiting and drug trafficking – that still resonate seven decades later.[3]

For the delegates to the UN's founding convention in San Francisco in 1945, however, terrorism was the least of their concerns. With a world war still raging, the second in two generations, their focus was understandably, and rightly, on preventing inter-state conflict. That orientation, however, did not lead them to design, as some have suggested, security mechanisms and principles fit only for dealing with conflict between states. The founders, as pragmatists and realists as well as idealists, were intent, above all, on creating international machinery that would be more effective and flexible than the League had proven to be. While their thoughts may not have been of intra-state conflict and transnational terrorism, the mechanisms they created would not be constitutionally inhibited from dealing with such threats.

The delegates in San Francisco repeatedly emphasized the importance of addressing the economic and social roots of conflict and of upholding human rights. These themes are highlighted in the Preamble, Purposes and Principles, and Chapters IX and X of the Charter. Article 55, for example, speaks of economic and social progress, development and human rights as contributions "to the creation of conditions of stability and well-being which are necessary for peaceful and friendly relations among nations". Though the oft-quoted Article 2 (7) begins by cautioning that "nothing contained in the present Charter shall authorize the United Nations to intervene in matters which are essentially within the domestic jurisdiction of any state", it goes on to stress that "this principle shall not prejudice the application of enforcement measures under Chapter VII". Not only do the Security Council's enforcement powers under Chapter VII extend beyond borders, so do its investigatory powers under Chapter VI, such as in Article 34.

True, the Charter never mentions terrorism, but neither does it refer to peacekeeping, peacebuilding or weapons of mass destruction. Rather than listing the kinds of security issues that the new organization should tackle, the founders wisely gave its principal organs unprecedented powers and the flexibility and authority to respond to emerging threats to international peace and security as they would arise over the years.[4] For instance, under Articles 11 (3) and 99, respectively, the General Assembly and the Secretary-General may bring to the attention of the Security Council any situation or matter that may endanger or threaten international peace and security. The Charter's recurring references to the primacy of preventing armed conflict, moreover, imply a proactive stance that privileges early intervention before intra-state disputes take on an inter-state character. Obviously none of these provisions and principles obligate the Security Council to act against terrorist threats, but neither do they inhibit it from doing so when sufficient political will exists among its members.

Political and strategic factors, much more than constitutional constraints, have shaped how and whether the world body has taken on the challenge of terrorism. The degree of UN involvement has also been determined by the tactics of terrorists themselves, particularly by the extent to which they have defined their field of operations in local or global terms. Since the UN's founding, and arguably beforehand as well, most terrorist incidents have stemmed from separatist, irredentist, or other dissident movements with roots within the societies of individual member states. Though several of the groups that have plagued Western Europe, such as the Red Brigades, the Irish Republican Army (IRA), and the Basque Fatherland and Liberty (ETA), crossed borders for sanctuary, support, and occasional strikes, their targets and purposes have been geographically circumscribed. The same could be said of the Tamil Tigers in Sri Lanka or of the Aum Shinrikyo cult, with its use of sarin nerve gas on the Tokyo subways in 1995. None of these groups or strikes has threatened to bring about war between states. Nor have any of the states victimized by such attacks chosen to bring any of these cases to the attention of the UN Security Council despite their claims to UN-centric foreign policies.

Likewise, India, Russia and the United Kingdom have worked to keep the Council out of Kashmir, Chechnya and Northern Ireland, respectively, despite the terrorist violence associated with those conflicts. As a general rule, most Member State governments have preferred to keep the kinds of sensitive matters linked to terrorist agendas out of global fora – particularly the UN's political bodies – where they fear further politicization of the local issues in dispute. Once the General Assembly or even the Security Council becomes seized of such an issue, the course of deliberations tends to become increasingly difficult to control or even to predict.

As a result, over most of its existence the United Nations has been discouraged by those Member States most affected from dealing with the bulk of the terrorist incidents in the world. (Incidents related to the Middle East, discussed below, have been something of an exception to this rule.) Despite a passing reference to terrorism in a Council resolution condemning the 1948 assassination of Count Folke Bernadotte, the UN mediator in Palestine,[5] neither the Security Council nor the General Assembly addressed terrorism directly during the UN's first quarter century. In 1968 and 1969, Secretary-General U Thant employed his good offices in cases of airline hijackings for the first time.[6] Though the increasing pace and destructiveness of terrorist incidents in the 1970s led to growing UN involvement, the results were ambiguous at best. The Council did manage to pass – without a vote – its first anti-terrorism resolution in September 1970, calling on "states to take all possible legal steps to prevent further hijackings or any other interference with international civil air travel".[7]

The UN's tepid response to the massacre of Israeli athletes at the 1972 Olympics in Munich reflected how deeply divided the Member States were over how to respond to terrorism, particularly when it was related to the situation in the Middle East.[8] In the Security Council, a US draft was not even put to a vote, a much weaker Western European draft was vetoed by China and the Soviet Union, and the US Permanent Representative, George H.W. Bush, vetoed a non-aligned draft that failed to mention either terrorism or the Munich events. This was only the second veto – and the first lonely one – cast by the US in the world body. Secretary-General Kurt Waldheim then urged the General Assembly to take up the matter of terrorism. There, neither US nor Western European drafts were put to a vote and the Algerian alternative that was adopted condemned not terrorism but "the continuation of repressive and terrorist acts by colonial racist and alien regimes in denying peoples their legitimate right to self-determination and independence and other human rights and fundamental freedoms".[9]

For the rest of the 1970s and much of the 1980s, the General Assembly was primarily concerned with such so-called "root causes" of terrorism and the Security Council seemed more worried about the perceived excesses of the counter-terrorism tactics employed by Israel and the United States than about the terrorist strikes that spurred them in the first place.[10] Only as the end of the Cold War approached did the world body begin to grapple with terrorism as a serious threat to international peace and security. In 1989, two unanimous resolutions, 635 and 638, marked a watershed in that regard. The first condemned all acts of terrorism against civil aviation and urged states to assist ICAO (the International Civil Aviation Organization) in its efforts to devise a system for marking sheet or plastic explosives.[11] The second unequivocally condemned all acts of hostage-taking and abduction and urged Member States to become party to the Convention Against the Taking of Hostages and other relevant conventions.[12] Both their unambiguous content and the consensus support they received marked major advances in the willingness of Council members to come to grips with the terrorist threat.

Even during the politically charged Cold War years, the General Assembly and relevant UN agencies made critical contributions to the development of international norms against specific kinds of terrorist acts. Nine of the thirteen global anti-terrorism conventions were adopted prior to 1989. The 1973 Convention on the Prevention and Punishment of Crimes against Internationally Protected Persons, including Diplomatic Agents and the 1979 International Convention against the Taking of Hostages were adopted by the same General Assembly that had seemed much more concerned with root causes than violent acts against civilians.[13] As M.J. Peterson points out, however, those conventions adopted prior to 1985 were less sweeping and generally had "saving clauses" that declared that "the commission of acts in the course of resistance to colonial, racist, or foreign domination ... should not be regarded as a criminal act".[14] The first ten conventions, moreover, failed to use the term "terrorism" in their titles.[15] The three most recent accords, and arguably those most relevant to current circumstances, both included the term and were adopted by the General Assembly without votes: 1) the International Convention for the Suppression of Terrorist Bombings; 2) the International Convention on the Suppression of Financing of Terrorism; and 3) the International Convention for the Suppression of Acts of Nuclear Terrorism.[16]

With the 1990s, the weight of the UN's counter-terrorism efforts shifted from the normative to the operational side, from occasional exhortations to repeated enforcement actions. The demise of the Soviet Union led to new power relationships inside and outside the Security Council, and indirectly to a more global and virulent form of terrorism as well. Three times during the decade, the Security Council imposed sanctions on states accused of aiding or abetting terrorism.[17] These cases included Libya in 1992 for its role in the bombing of Pan Am and UTA flights, Sudan twice in 1996 for refusing to extradite suspects in the attempted assassination of President Hosni Mubarak, and the Taliban regime in Afghanistan and the Al-Qaeda network for the bombing of the US embassies in Kenya and Tanzania.[18] The Security Council, it should be recalled, had not voted for that many sanctions regimes over its first 45 years.

Ironically, the impetus for this new era of Security Council activism in resisting terrorism came from Washington DC rather than from one of the capitals more commonly associated with advocating a larger role for the world body. Three factors would appear to account for this development. One, with the end of the Cold War, the Security Council had become a much more propitious place to pursue American strategic objectives. Russian officials were eager to demonstrate their break from earlier Kremlin support of or tolerance for terrorist tactics by so-called national liberation movements, and Moscow's support for the Council's authorization of the use of force to expel Iraqi forces from Kuwait was seen as a major breakthrough.[19]

Two, as the lone remaining superpower, the US felt greater confidence in its capacity to use the Security Council and other multilateral mechanisms to build supportive coalitions, to gain greater political authority for its actions, and to consolidate and sustain its position of global leadership. As John Ikenberry has contended, such a strategy would replicate Washington's assumptions behind creating the UN in 1945 – at an earlier hegemonic moment.[20] In this sense, the Cold War had postponed the fulfilment of the US vision for the UN of 1945.

Three, by the late 1980s and early 1990s, some of the more ambitious terrorists, with state sponsorship in some cases, began to target more frequently American assets around the world. The United States was becoming less of an observer and more of a victim of terrorism. As more traditional strategic threats began to fade, terrorism moved up the ladder of US security concerns. US officials began to appreciate, as well, that they had a global struggle on their hands.[21] During those years, the US was becoming a more attractive target for global terrorist networks based in the Middle East, both because it represented the global political establishment they sought to upset and because US support for Israel and for conservative Arab regimes frustrated their more immediate objectives. As Coral Bell notes elsewhere in this volume, sympathizers share the jihadists' perspective "at least to the extent of seeing the existing international order as an order of entrenched injustice, created by the West, and likely to be perpetuated unless something is done to pull it down". So, striking at the US and its far-flung assets – including the UN – made sense from both a regional and a global perspective.

History and context: post-9/11

The events of 11 September 2001, therefore, reflected an escalation of these well-established patterns more than they represented a radical departure. The UN's response, likewise, both confirmed the trends established in the previous decade and took them a step or two further down the path to greater involvement and activism. The day after the attacks, the General Assembly and Security Council both condemned them in unanimous resolutions (A/RES/56/1 and 1368, respectively). The Security Council version was particularly far-reaching, as it employed the wording of Article 51 of the Charter on the right of individual and collective self-defence to justify a victim state's right to respond forcefully to such a provocation, which it labelled a threat to international peace and security. While the Council never pronounced itself one way or the other on the subsequent use of force by a US-led coalition against the Taliban regime in Afghanistan, it was generally accepted that resolution 1368 provided a blanket authorization for such a response against those who sheltered Osama bin Laden and his Al-Qaeda operatives.[22]

Just over two weeks after passing 1368 unanimously, the Council, still under a French Presidency, was again unanimous in approving 1373, the most comprehensive and intrusive counter-terrorism resolution to date. Generic in form and scope, 1373 required Member States to "refrain from providing any form of support, active or passive, to entities or persons involved in terrorist acts". They were to freeze the assets of such individuals or groups, prohibit their raising or transferring funds, and bar them sanctuary, safe passage, arms or any other form of material support. Importantly, governments were to share information on suspected terrorist activities, bolster their capacities for counter-terrorism, and report to a new subsidiary body of the Council, the Counter-Terrorism Committee (CTC), on their progress in implementing the resolution's wide-ranging provisions. Introduced by the United States, 1373 readily found broad support among the Council members despite its unprecedented sweep and ambition.

Initially, the CTC achieved some impressive results.[23] All 191 Member States submitted reports to the Committee during the first round, though admittedly some were far more candid and detailed than others. These suggested that a substantial number of Member States were reviewing and/or revising their domestic laws and administrative structures to better implement the requirements of resolution 1373. Soon one of the chief activities of the CTC and its staff was to identify where assistance in capacity building was most needed, whether on the legislative or administrative side, and which government or organization might be best placed to provide it. In addition, the reporting and monitoring process helped to spur a marked acceleration in the number of states signing and/or ratifying the then dozen global counter-terrorism conventions.[24] These interactions have also put the Committee in a good position to encourage a best-practices-based learning process among the Member States. The early signs of success were aided by the consensus-based processes within the CTC, the relative transparency of its procedures, its non-coercive style, and the vigorous leadership of its first chair, Sir Jeremy Greenstock, then Britain's Permanent Representative to the UN.

The CTC, however, has also had its weaknesses. Over time, with recurring reporting–assessment–reporting cycles, grumbling among the Member States about reporting fatigue has begun to grow as the portion of countries responding to each subsequent request has shrunk.[25] The limitations of depending on the written reports of Member States have become more obvious over time, especially since the states of greatest concern have tended to say rather little of fresh substantive value in their declarations. With the host's consent, the CTC has begun to take fact-finding visits to selected Member States to supplement the written submissions and to inform capacity-building efforts. In 2005, visits were undertaken to Albania, Kenya, Morocco and Thailand, with planned visits to Algeria and the Philippines. While most states have been quite responsible in their reporting, some have lacked the bureaucratic capacity to respond regularly and others appear to have the capacity but not the will to do so. Whether to begin a process of naming and shaming such Member States has been debated among the Committee members, but a decision to go that route seems unlikely in view of the group's consensus rule. Given these concerns, subsequent chairs have found it difficult to sustain the CTC's initial momentum. The worry is that, while the CTC may be making headway, it may be proceeding up a cul de sac.

In any case, the CTC was neither the first nor last subsidiary body established by the Security Council to help implement its counter-terrorism policies. As noted above, resolution 1267 of October 1999 imposed a ban on flights and an asset freeze on the Taliban and Al-Qaeda, as well as authorizing the establishment of a subsidiary body of the Council to oversee their implementation.[26] Largely based on information provided by Member States, the 1267 Committee has compiled a Consolidated List of individuals, groups and entities associated with the Taliban and Al-Qaeda and hence subject to the 1267 sanctions.[27] A Monitoring Team was created to assist the implementation of the sanctions regime and to assess the results achieved, including through visits to selected Member States. According to the Committee, more progress has been made on carrying out the assets freeze than on implementing the travel ban or arms embargo.[28] Like the CTC, the 1267 Committee has relied to some extent on written reports from Member States and has begun to identify capacity gaps where international assistance could be helpful.

During 2004, the Council created a third committee and a working group on counter-terrorism, for a grand total of four subsidiary bodies working side by side on particular aspects of the issue. Since all four are committees of the whole, each of the fifteen members of the Council has to assign staff to participate in the four counter-terrorism groups, as well as the Council's twenty other subsidiary bodies. Resolution 1540, adopted unanimously by the Council on 28 April 2004, affirmed that the proliferation of nuclear, chemical or biological weapons, as well as of their means of delivery, constitutes a threat to international peace and security. It called on states to take legislative and administrative steps to ensure that these weapons would not be transferred to non-state actors or terrorists. Once again, the new Committee would call on Member States for reports about what they were doing to implement the provisions of 1540, would identify where technical assistance could be helpful in plugging gaps, would hire experts, and would cooperate with relevant international agencies for the sharing of information and technical expertise.[29] While the US was among the prime advocates of 1540, it initially favoured only a six-month tenure for the committee and then agreed to the two-year term it was eventually granted.

The Russian Federation, spurred in part by the tragic loss of life when a school in Beslan was occupied by terrorists, was the chief sponsor of resolution 1566, adopted unanimously by the Security Council on 8 October 2004. The resolution sought to provide a further working definition of terrorism, to urge closer cooperation among the existing counter-terrorism bodies, as well as by Member States, and to establish a working group to consider (1) ways of enhancing "practical measures" for cracking down on terrorists and (2) the possibility of establishing an international fund to compensate victims of terrorist acts and their families.[30] As a step towards improving coordination, as called for in resolution 1566, the chairs of the three operational counter-terrorism committees (1267, 1373 and 1540) provided joint briefings to the Security Council in April, July and October 2005, and the chair of the 1566 Working Group added further comments.[31] In its search for lessons learned, best practices, and other steps that it might recommend to the Council as a whole, the 1566 Working Group in the first half of 2005 held a session open to non-members of the Council and another one at which this author was invited to provide an independent perspective.[32]

The pace and breadth of Security Council activity on counter-terrorism since the events of 9/11/01 have raised several institutional concerns. One, noted above, is whether these various initiatives have been sufficiently coordinated and form a coherent package. Two, a number of Member States – including Germany, which served as a non-permanent member in 2003–2004 – have complained that the Council in this field, as well as in some others, has been assuming legislative and even judicial roles best left to more representative bodies, such as the General Assembly or ECOSOC.[33] Three, given the Council's lack of Charter-based authority for appropriating expenditures, the funding of these efforts has tended to be voluntary, ad hoc and uncertain, with the Committees gaining a stronger reputation for identifying capacity gaps than for producing funds or technical assistance to fill them. And, four, the staffing of these exercises, like their funding, has been relatively modest, unpredictable, and not well integrated into the regular staffing rules, procedures and patterns of the Organization.

Initially, the CTC was largely staffed by short-term experts on loan from Member States, particularly from the United Kingdom, the first chair of the committee. Seven months after its establishment, its chair, Sir Jeremy Greenstock, complained that, in terms of secretariat support, "the CTC tends to be allocated the resources that are left over when everything else has been covered".[34] The Department of Political Affairs (DPA) was named the UN's focal point for the struggle against terrorism after 9/11/01, but assigned no staff for the task. The UN's grandly misnamed Terrorism Prevention Branch (TPB) in Vienna finally received General Assembly authorization at the end of 2002 for a staff increment to fulfil its new mandate for administrative and legislative capacity-building. The TPB staff was doubled, but this meant only the addition of three professionals and two support staff. The augmented counter-terrorism staff of five professionals and three support personnel compares to the four hundred posts authorized for the Office for Drug Control and Crime Prevention (ODCCP), which provides a home for the tiny TPB.[35] Both report, by the way, not to the DPA "focal point", but to the Office of Legal Affairs.

To begin to address the growing gap between the mandates being adopted at the inter-governmental level and the much slower pace of staff expansion, the second chair of the CTC, Ambassador Inocencio F. Arias of Spain, proposed a revitalization of the committee, revolving around enhanced staff capacity. Specifically, he proposed the creation of a Counter-Terrorism Committee Executive Directorate (CTED), with an Information and Administrative Office (IAO), an Assessment and Technical Assistance Office (ATAO), and an overall staff of some 40 posts to handle the growing demands for technical assistance and capacity-building.[36] Javier Ruperez of Spain was recruited to be CTED's first Executive Director at the level of Assistant-Secretary-General. Though without the powers of a UN czar for counter-terrorism, he can at least claim to be the occupant of the UN's first senior post dedicated to the issue. Whether CTED and the smaller staffs of the 1267 and 1540 Committees will be further integrated remains to be seen, though the report of the 1566 Working Group, expected by the end of 2005, would provide a prime vehicle for addressing problems of coherence and overlap.

At the time of the 9/11/01 attacks, the UN was missing another key part of the puzzle: an articulated doctrine or strategy for dealing with terrorism. There was no white paper on the UN's place in the struggle against terrorism, due both to the divisions within the membership on the subject and to the fact that the UN had not played, and did not anticipate playing, any operational role in this field. Unlike peacekeeping, conflict resolution, disarmament, development, humanitarian affairs or human rights, there was not even a significant academic or think tank literature on how the UN might contribute to the effort to deter and/or defeat terrorism. As a first step, the Secretary-General convened in October 2001 a Policy Working Group on the United Nations and Terrorism to consider policies and strategies for the world body, based on its purposes, principles and areas of comparative advantage.[37] In its report of 6 August 2002, the group proposed a tripartite strategy to "(a) dissuade disaffected groups from embracing terrorism; (b) deny groups or individuals the means to carry out acts of terrorism; (c) sustain broad-based international cooperation in the struggle against terrorism".[38]

Though he readily approved of his Policy Working Group's report, the Secretary-General did not make much use of his bully pulpit for rallying support of a UN-led campaign against terrorism for most of 2002, 2003, or 2004. This disuse contrasted to his vigorous and courageous statements following the events of 9/11/01. Though one can only speculate on his motives, it could well be that the palpable misgivings that he and most of the UN membership and secretariat felt about President Bush's sabre rattling over the course of 2002 about the use of force in Iraq made the Secretary-General reluctant to appear to side with Washington's version of the war on terrorism. Following the initial phase of the war in Iraq, the terrorist bombing of UN headquarters in Baghdad on 19 August 2003 left many secretariat officials wondering more about how to avoid being caught up in the war on terror than about how to win it. Increasing concerns about the violations of human rights and due process that were being justified by some national leaders in the name of fighting terrorism added to the reluctance to be associated with or co-opted by national counter-terrorism campaigns that did not seem to respect or reflect the Organization's basic purposes and principles.[39]

Yet neither the Secretary-General nor the organization he leads could afford either to sit this one out or to let others offer the sole recipe for responding to the terrorist challenge. As noted at the outset, the global breed of terrorism represents both a challenge to and a challenge for multilateral institutions. The Baghdad bombing provided bloody evidence that some terrorists, at least, were not prepared to allow the UN the luxury of observing from the sidelines. Carping about how others conducted a struggle that would have far-reaching implications for the future of multilateral cooperation was not enough. What alternative, it would be asked, could the UN offer? Did it have a better way of getting the job done, one that would promise wider popular support and less compromise of rights and values? In a policy realm as demanding and politically charged as terror, in other words, could multilateralism be operationalized? Is there, in short, a multilateral alternative?

The Secretary-General's High-Level Panel on Threats, Challenges and Change, building on the groundwork laid by the Policy Working Group, in December 2004 called on him to enunciate and promote a comprehensive global strategy that "incorporates but is broader than coercive measures" and that "addresses root causes and strengthens responsible States and the rule of law and fundamental human rights".[40] Four months later, the Secretary-General offered a five-part strategy to the International Summit on Democracy, Terrorism and Security in Madrid. His five pillars included: 1) dissuading disaffected groups from choosing terrorism as a tactic to achieve their goals; 2) denying terrorists the means to carry out their attacks; 3) deterring states from supporting terrorists; 4) developing state capacity to prevent terrorism; and 5) defending human rights in the struggle against terrorism.[41] While some delegations were unhappy with the Secretary-General's endorsement of the High-Level Panel's effort to short-cut the protracted Assembly debate over a definition of terrorism, most found multiple elements of this "5-Ds" strategy to embrace. At the very least, it represented the first reasonably coherent and compelling statement of UN doctrine for the long-term struggle against terrorism. Whether prevailing political and strategic factors will permit its full realization, however, remains to be seen. For the UN, as always, the big question is the unspoken sixth "D" – delivery: will the institution fulfil the promise embodied in the new strategy?[42]

The September 2005 World Summit produced a relatively strong statement against terrorism. In its Outcome Document, the hundreds of heads of state and government declared that:

- Paragraph 81. "We strongly condemn terrorism in all its forms and manifestations, committed by whomever, wherever, and for whatever purposes, as it constitutes one of the most serious threats to international peace and security".

- Paragraph 82. "We welcome the Secretary-General's identification of the elements of a counter-terrorism strategy. These elements should be developed by the General Assembly without delay".
- Paragraph 83. "We stress the need to make every effort to reach an agreement on and conclude a comprehensive convention on international terrorism during the Sixtieth session of the General Assembly" [i.e. by mid-September 2006].[43]

While the political repercussions of continuing problems in the Middle East have so far prevented the completion of either a comprehensive convention or an agreed definition, the Assembly reportedly has agreed on almost all of their elements.

The politics of mutual ambivalence

As the preceding chronology confirms, the pattern of the past two decades has been one of expanding and deepening UN engagement in counter-terrorism. There have been pauses, perhaps a retreat or two, but the overall direction has been unambiguous. Continuing differences over a comprehensive definition have not prevented either the General Assembly from endorsing an ever-expanding set of proscribed actions or the Security Council from adding – through unanimous votes – one layer of counter-terrorism mechanisms after another. These efforts have involved an unprecedented degree of intervention in and monitoring of the legislative processes of the Member States.

Despite the breadth and vigour of these innovations, the United Nations still occupies a modest, some would even say marginal, place in the global campaign against terrorism. It has had to run hard just to retain any role at all in the fast-moving drama of counter-terrorism. There are inherent limits to what the UN can usefully contribute in this sphere. Three broad and largely immutable constraints serve to limit the UN's possibilities: 1) its highly circumscribed and under-resourced functional capacities; 2) the ambivalence of many Member States and secretariat officials toward the US-led war on terrorism; and 3) American doubts about putting too many eggs in the UN basket, especially when matters of urgent national security are at stake. The politics of mutual ambivalence – defined by the latter two factors – serve to discourage thoughts of significantly enhancing the first factor, the world body's functional capacities.

The UN is ill-suited to perform several of the more prominent tasks involved in fighting terrorism. On this, US and UN officials see eye to eye. The Secretary-General's Policy Working Group readily acknowledged that it "does not believe that the United Nations is well placed to play an active operational role in efforts to suppress terrorist groups, to pre-empt specific terrorist strikes, or to develop dedicated intelligence-gathering capacities".[44] As a body of 191 sovereign Member States, some of them with a history of sponsoring terrorism, the UN would neither seek nor be entrusted with sensitive intelligence information.[45] In his Madrid speech, the Secretary-General applauded the Bush administration's Proliferation Security Initiative (PSI), designed to interdict the illicit transfer of materials or components of weapons of mass destruction. Though the PSI aims "to fill a gap in our defences", according to the Secretary-General, the UN is not expected to play any direct role in its implementation. Indeed, it has become core UN doctrine – enunciated by the past two secretaries-general – that the world organization no longer conducts military enforcement operations.[46]

Enforcement, of course, can be undertaken by a range of sanctions short of the use of force. As detailed above, the Security Council invoked economic, financial, travel and/or arms sanctions three times in the 1990s against states and groups that were alleged to have aided and abetted terrorists. At Madrid, the Secretary-General based his third "D", deterrence, solely on such measures, as follows:

> In the past the United Nations has not shrunk from confronting States that harbour and assist terrorists, and the Security Council has repeatedly applied sanctions. Indeed, it is largely thanks to such sanctions that several States which used to sponsor terrorists no longer do so. This firm line must be maintained and strengthened. All States must know that, if they give any kind of support to terrorists, the Council will not hesitate to use coercive measures against them.

Indeed, it does seem that states, even of the so-called rogue variety, are reluctant these days to show any sympathy for global terrorism. The 100 per cent response to the CTC's first round of queries attests to this tendency. Yet the kind of certainty of response by the Council called for by the Secretary-General is far from being attained.[47] The Council, if anything, appears less inclined to consider sanctions this decade than last. Controversies over their effectiveness and humanitarian consequences spawned a concerted effort to develop a new generation of better targeted sanctions.[48] To date, none of the Council's counter-terrorism subsidiary bodies – each apparently preferring the carrot to the stick – have recommended even the naming and shaming of any state. Deterrence may be working, but more likely propelled by the unilateral enforcement steps undertaken by powerful countries than by the UN.

Though few Member States would openly question the importance of stemming terrorism, a number appear to have misgivings about devoting growing portions of the UN's time, attention and resources to the effort.

Their concern is that a hegemonic United States, obsessed with the threat posed by terrorists since the events of 9/11/01, is trying to dominate the Security Council and distort the world body's programmes and priorities to the detriment of the pressing needs of the developing world. According to this perspective, two glaring asymmetries are at work. One asymmetry relates to the distribution of hard-power capabilities between the US and the rest. The second asymmetry concerns the much greater likelihood – real and perceived – that American assets will again be the target of highly sophisticated and destructive terrorist attacks. With such different threat perceptions and capacities to respond among the membership, it would be difficult to find much common ground on the best counter-terrorism strategy for the UN, even if there was a consensus on a comprehensive definition and convention. The qualms expressed about the legislative role played by the Council on these issues stems, in part, from the perception that this has been a US-dominated effort to legislate.

To many states, including US allies, the way the Bush administration has framed "the war on terrorism" – even its employment of that phrase – reflects an over-emphasis on the coercive and military dimensions of what should be a more subtle and multifaceted campaign. According to Rick Coolsaet of Brussels' Royal Institute for International Relations, "within the EU, there is a widely shared belief that the war in Afghanistan was and will remain the only part of the post-9/11 counterterrorism effort where military means played a significant role".[49] In his view, "the international mechanisms of sanctions and suppression have been very effective immediately after 9/11, but are gradually becoming less and less relevant, because – as a result of the decentralisation and atomization of jihadism – they address a set of circumstances which no longer apply".[50]

Along similar lines, Paul R. Pillar, former Deputy Chief of the CIA's Counterterrorist Center, warns that "global cooperation against terrorism is already fragile" and that "foreign cooperation will become more problematic as the issue moves beyond Al-Qaeda".[51] To the extent that the war on terrorism succeeds in breaking up Al-Qaeda's global network, in other words, the pre-9/11 tendency among UN Member States to see terrorism as largely a localized issue unsuitable for Security Council action is likely to re-emerge. This would reinforce the preference of many in the UN community for a focus on root causes.[52] Fuelling that tendency would be the prevalent belief – in the US, as well as in other Member States and the secretariat – that the UN's comparative advantage lies in that direction in any case.

The ambivalence that many others seem to feel towards American power and counter-terrorism strategies is fully reciprocated by Washington's fabled ambivalence toward international law and institutions.[53]

Even a hegemonic power with long-held exceptionalist impulses, like the US, prefers to have the political support of other states and global institutions, especially the Security Council, when confronting significant security threats. As José Alvarez has put it, "even in an increasingly unipolar world, the collective can influence what the hegemon can achieve through the Council and it behoves the hegemon to permit itself to be influenced – if it wants to have a legitimating and effective Council around for a long time to come".[54] The hegemon will consult with others, but will not cede to them ultimate authority over its security choices. Washington's power gives it a wider range of options for dealing with threats than others will have, with multilateral or UN routes seen more as an option than as an obligation.[55] Washington has thus tended to see the UN in instrumental terms.[56] The UN's, and particularly the Security Council's, unprecedented activism in seeking to curb terrorism, both during the 1990s and since 9/11, testifies to the American desire for the world body to play a larger role in this sphere.

At the same time, however, Washington, to date, has envisioned only a limited place for the UN in the global struggle against terrorism. In that regard, its view of what the UN can and should contribute parallels that of other capitals, few of which would want the UN to attempt to play the lead role. The US and its chief partners participate in a wide range of international bodies and arrangements, most with broad but not universal membership, that deal relatively effectively with specific aspects of the challenge. Prominent among these are Interpol for cooperation on policing matters, the Financial Action Task Force (FATF) on terrorist financing, the G-8's Counter-Terrorism Action Group (CTAG) on resources for capacity-building, the various regimes and agencies seeking to stem the proliferation of different types of weapons, and any number of initiatives by regional and sub-regional organizations, as well as the Bretton Woods institutions and more specialized functional agencies. As a result, the UN's own operational efforts, including those of the Security Council, remain understaffed and under-funded, as most of the resources for international cooperation go elsewhere. Certainly the proliferation of international counter-terrorism efforts raises worrisome questions about coordination and coherence. But it also suggests that this issue does not present a simple choice between unilateralism and multilateralism, between going it alone and working with others.

Given its chequered history, the UN has come a long way towards embracing the struggle against terrorism. More could be done to integrate and streamline its efforts, but the results would not be measured in great leaps forward. There are real institutional and political limits to what the UN can or should do in this area, regardless of American attitudes and policies. The challenge for the UN is to do the best it can within its circumscribed sphere of action, one that is bound to be more normative than operational. The challenge to the UN has been pressed and defined by the new breed of global terrorists themselves, for they will not let the world body quit the field of battle over values, principles and purposes. The UN has little choice but to commit to this struggle for the long haul. But do not look to the UN for leadership: Washington is not pushing for it and New York is not volunteering.

Notes

1. Address to Madrid Summit, 10 March 2005, SG/SM/9757.
2. League of Nations, *Convention for the Prevention and Punishment of Terrorism*, L.546(1).M.383(1).1937V, Geneva, 16 November 1937; and, for the draft convention on the ICC, see League of Nations, *Committee for the International Repression of Terrorism*, C222.M.162.1937.V, Geneva, 26 April 1937, Appendix II.
3. League of Nations, *Proceedings of the International Conferences on the Repression of Terrorism*, C.94.M.47.1938V, Geneva, 1–16 November 1937, p. 50; League of Nations, *International Repression of Terrorism, Draft Conventions, Observations by Governments, Series III*, A.24(b).1936V, Geneva, 21 February 1938, p. 2.
4. It is worth recalling, in this context, that the Charter was signed prior to the first use of atomic weapons and came into effect after Hiroshima, Nagasaki, and the end of the war in the Pacific.
5. Resolution 57, 18 September 1948.
6. Sydney D. Bailey (1993) "The UN Security Council and Terrorism", *International Relations* 9(6) (December): 536 and U. Thant (1978) *View from the UN*, Garden City, New York: Doubleday, pp. 302–308 and 317–318.
7. Resolution 286, 9 September 1970.
8. For a fuller discussion of how the politics of the Middle East have shaped the Security Council's response to terrorism, see Edward C. Luck (2004) "Tackling terrorism", in David M. Malone (ed.) *The United Nations Security Council: From the Cold War to the 21st Century*, Boulder, CO: Lynne Rienner Publishers, pp. 88–93 and 97–98.
9. Robert Alden (1972) "Strong Legal Action to Combat Terrorism Is Rebuffed at U.N.", *New York Times*, 12 December 1972.
10. For broader accounts of the roles of the Security Council and General Assembly in addressing terrorism, see Chantal de Jonge Oudraat, "The role of the Security Council" and M.J. Peterson, "Using the General Assembly", in Jane Boulden and Thomas G. Weiss (eds.) (2004) *Terrorism After September 11th*, Bloomington, Indiana: Indiana University Press, pp. 151–172 and 173–197, respectively, and Edward C. Luck (2004) "Another reluctant belligerent: the United Nations and the war on terrorism", in Richard M. Price and Mark W. Zacher, *The United Nations and Global Security*, New York: Palgrave Macmillan, pp. 95–108.
11. Resolution 635, 14 June 1989.
12. Resolution 638, 31 July 1989.
13. Resolution 3166 (XXVIII), 14 December 1973, and resolution 34/146, 17 December 1979, respectively.
14. Peterson, op. cit., p. 184.
15. In contrast, the titles of all seven regional conventions use the word terrorism, and three

of them – by the Organization of American States (OAS), the Council of Europe, and the South Asian Association for Regional Cooperation – were adopted before 1988.

16. Resolution 52/164, 15 December 1997, resolution 54/109, 9 December 1999, and resolution 59/290, 13 April 2005, respectively.
17. David Cortright and George A. Lopez (2000) *The Sanctions Decade: Assessing UN Strategies in the 1990s*, Boulder, CO: Lynne Rienner Publishers, pp. 107–133.
18. Resolution 748 of 31 March 1992; resolutions 1054 of 26 April 1996 and 1070 of 16 August 1996; and resolution 1267 of 15 October 1999; respectively.
19. Resolution 678, 29 November 1990. China abstained, while Cuba and Yemen opposed the resolution.
20. G. John Ikenberry (2001) *After Victory: Institutions, Strategic Restraint, and the Rebuilding of Order After Major Wars*, Princeton, NJ: Princeton University Press, pp. 163–214 and "Getting hegemony right", *National Interest* 64(Spring): 17–24.
21. Secretary of State George P. Shultz spoke about "the war against terrorism" as early as 1984 and Secretary of State Madeleine K. Albright declared in 1998 that terrorists 'have basically declared war on all Americans". See "Shultz Says U.S. Should Use Force Against Terrorism" and "Excerpts from Shultz's Address on International Terrorism" both in *New York Times*, 26 October 1984 and Brian McGrory and Chris Black, "US Hits Suspected Terror Sites", *Boston Globe*, 21 August 1998.
22. The US had not been shy about using force against terrorists or those who sponsored them before, including once in the Reagan administration and twice in the Clinton administration. This was, however, the first time that the US had sought or received the Security Council's authorization. See Edward C. Luck, "The U.S., counterterrorism, and the prospects for a multilateral alternative", in Boulden and Weiss *Terrorism and the UN*, op. cit., pp. 84–86.
23. For a useful summary, see Eric Rosand (2003) "Security Council Resolution 1373, the Counter-Terrorism Committee, and the fight against terrorism", *American Journal of International Law* 97(2) (April): 333–341.
24. For a breakdown of signatories and parties by convention and by country, as of 1 November 2004, see Annex VI and VII of S/2005/83, Second Report of the Analytical Support and Sanctions Monitoring Team appointed pursuant to resolution 1526 (2004) concerning Al-Qaeda and the Taliban and associated individuals and entities.
25. According to the CTC, 191 Member States and 6 others responded to the first round, 164 Member States and 2 others to the second, 124 plus one to the third, and 88 to the fourth. S/2005/266, 22 April 2005, para. 3, Work Programme of the Counter-Terrorism Committee, 1 April–30 June 2005.
26. These measures were later expanded to include an arms embargo, a broader travel ban, and wider financial measures. See resolutions 1333 (2000), 1363 (2001), 1390 (2002), 1452 (2002), 1455 (2003), and 1526 (2004), as well as Eric Rosand (2004) "The Security Council's efforts to monitor the implementation of Al-Qaeda/Taliban sanctions", *American Journal of International Law* 98(4) (October): 745–763.
27. Questions of due process have been raised concerning the consolidated list. For a critique, see the December 2004 report of the Secretary-General's High-level Panel on Threats, Challenges and Change, *A More Secure World: Our Shared Responsibility*, A/59/565, 2 December 2004, p. 50, paras. 152–153.
28. S/2004/1037, 31 December 2004, p. 4.
29. S/2004/958, 8 December 2004, and Briefing by the Chairman of the Security Council Committee established pursuant to resolution 1540 (2004), 25 April 2005, S/PV.5168, pp. 7–8. In part because of differences among its members on how it should go about its work, the 1540 Committee got off to a slow start. While the resolution called for states to present their first reports by 28 October 2004, as of 16 December 2005 the chair

reported that just 124 states and one organization had submitted them, SC/8591, 19 December 2005.

30. The statements of Council members at the time of the adoption of 1566 suggest markedly different perspectives about what was valuable about the resolution. Some stressed the normative side (operational paragraph 3), others the "practical measures" in operational paragraph 9, and others the possible victims fund in operational paragraph 10. S/PV. 5053.
31. S/PV.5168, S/PV.5229, and S/PV.5293.
32. 25 May 2005, talking points for the latter session are available at http://www.sipa.columbia.edu/cio.
33. Eric Rosand cites similar statements from a range of developing countries as well; see "The Security Council as 'Global Legislator': *Ultra Vires* or Ultra Innovative", *Fordham International Law Journal* 28 (May 2005): 542–590.
34. S/PV.4512, 15 April 2002, p. 4.
35. Luck, "Another reluctant belligerent", op. cit., p. 102.
36. S/2004/124, Annex, 19 February 2004.
37. This author served as a member of this group from its inception. To tap the ideas and expertise of independent specialists on terrorism and on the UN, the Policy Working Group asked the Center on International Organization of Columbia University to commission a number of papers and to convene a series of round table discussions at which Member States, secretariat officials, and outside experts could consider the papers' conclusions and recommendations. These can be found at: http://www.sipa.columbia.edu/cio.
38. A/57/273, S/2002/875, Annex, p. 1.
39. See, for example, "Human Rights, the United Nations, and the Struggle Against Terrorism", report of a conference co-sponsored by the International Peace Academy, the United Nations Office of the High Commissioner for Human Rights, and the Center on International Organization of Columbia University, November 7, 2003.
40. High-level Panel Report, op. cit., p. 48, para. 148.
41. SG/SM/9757, 10 March 2005.
42. To provide advice on how to implement the Secretary-General's Madrid Strategy, an inter-agency Counter-Terrorism Implementation Task Force (CTITF) has been created. Also see the report of the Secretary-General on *Uniting Against Terrorism: Recommendations for a Global Counter-Terrorism Strategy*, A/60/825, 27 April 2006.
43. 2005 World Summit Outcome, A/RES/60/1, 15 September 2005, p. 22, paras. 81–83.
44. A/57/273, S/2002/875, Annex, op. cit., p. 4, para. 9.
45. UNSCOM, the UN's first substantial effort to identify, locate, and destroy Iraqi programs to develop and deploy weapons of mass destruction and their delivery systems, was something of an exception. In the end, this mix proved to be a factor in the demise of what had been a largely productive mission. See David Kay (1997) "Information resources for assessing emerging threats to international peace and security", New York: United Nations Association of the USA; Daniel Byman (2000) "A farewell to arms inspections", *Foreign Affairs* 79(1) January/February; and Richard Butler (2000) *The Greatest Threat: Iraq, Weapons of Mass Destruction, and the Crisis of Global Security*, New York: Public Affairs.
46. Secretary-General Kofi Annan, *Renewing the United Nations: A Programme for Reform*, A/51/950, 14 July 1997, p. 36, para. 107, and Secretary-General Boutros Boutros-Ghali, *Supplement to An Agenda for Peace*, A/50/60, 3 January 1995, pp. 18–19, paras. 77–80.
47. One proposal by the High-level Panel that got little traction among the Member States spoke to the question of automaticity, as follows: "If confronted by States that have the capacity to undertake their obligations but repeatedly fail to do so, the Security Council

may need to take additional measures to ensure compliance, and should devise a schedule of predetermined sanctions for State non-compliance." High-level Panel Report, op. cit., pp. 50–51, para. 156.

48. For the debate on arms embargoes and travel sanctions within the "Bonn-Berlin Process", see Michael Brzoska (ed.) (2001) *Smart Sanctions: The Next Steps*, Baden-Baden, Germany: Nomos Verlagsgesellschaft, and for the "Stockholm Process on the Implementation of Targeted Sanctions", see Peter Wallensteen, Carina Staibano, and Mikael Eriksson (eds.) (2003) *Making Targeted Sanctions More Effective: Guidelines for the Implementation of UN Policy Options*, Uppsala, Sweden: Uppsala University.
49. Rik Coolsaet, "Between al-Andalus and a Failing Integration: Europe's Pursuit of a Long-term Counterterrorism Strategy in the Post-Al-Qaeda Era", Egmont Paper 5, Royal Institute for International Relations (IRRI-KIIB), Brussels, May 2005, p. 7.
50. Ibid., p. 6.
51. Paul R. Pillar (2004) "Counterterrorism after Al-Qaeda", *Washington Quarterly* 27(3) (Summer): 106.
52. For evidence of European leanings in this direction, see Coolsaet, op. cit., pp. 6–8.
53. See Edward C. Luck (1999) *Mixed Messages: American Politics and International Organization, 1919–1999*, Washington DC: Brookings Institution Press for the Century Foundation.
54. José E. Alvarez (2003) "Hegemonic international law revisited", *American Journal of International Law*. 97(4) (October): 888.
55. See Edward C. Luck (2003) "American exceptionalism and international organization: lessons from the 1990s", in Rosemary Foot, S. Neil MacFarlane and Michael Mastanduno (eds.) *US Hegemony and International Organization: The United States and Multilateral Institutions*, Oxford: Oxford University Press, p. 27; and (2001) "The United States, international organization, and the quest for legitimacy", in Stewart Patrick and Shepard Forman (eds.) *Multilateralism and US Foreign Policy*, Boulder, CO: Lynne Rienner for the Center on International Cooperation.
56. Rosemary Foot, Neil MacFarlane, and Michael Mastanduno, "Conclusion: instrumental multilateralism in US foreign policy", in Foot, MacFarlane and Mastanduno, *US Hegemony*, ibid., pp. 266–272.

17

Civil wars, globalization and the "Washington Consensus"

John Tirman

Over the last quarter century, two of the more prominent global phenomena have been civil wars and globalization. The incidence of civil wars rose sharply in the 1980s, and while those numbers have receded somewhat, they are now accompanied by another outbreak of organized violence, terrorism. Globalization is not a new phenomenon, of course, but has taken new forms, enabled by the instant transferability of capital, a strong push by the industrialized countries for open markets in the global south, and other compelling forces. The two trends – "new wars" and globalization – would not seem to have much to do with each other. It is sometimes noted that the export of American and European pop culture to traditional societies, particularly Islamic societies, is one of the irritants in the supposed clash of civilizations. The relationship between civil wars and economic and political globalization, however, runs much deeper. And because economic and political globalization are braced and often enabled by multilateral institutions, and relevant policies forged within such institutions, this complex relationship between the urge to nurture open societies and the incidences of instability and organized violence is a troubling one for multilateralism.

In the realm of finance, particularly, the rules of international organizations are shaped by powerful states in their own interest, and imposed on weak states that may have different needs and interests, with deleterious results for many of these smaller actors. In the push for open markets and bureaucratic accountability, multilateral institutions such the International Monetary Fund (IMF) and the World Bank (WB) have insisted on certain economic and political reforms in developing countries, reforms that may in fact have induced instabilities that were conducive to civil war.

Should this conjecture be true, it would be doubly problematic for multilateralism. It first raises the spectre that multilateralism's emphasis on normative values is fraught with contradictions of a very fundamental kind. In John Ruggie's reckoning, "multilateralism is an institutional form that coordinates relations among three or more states on the basis of generalized principles of conduct: that is, principles which specify appropriate conduct for a class of actions, without regard to particularistic interests."[1] But particularistic interests are very much in play with the donors' insistence on marketization, and the inability of those policies to achieve economic growth while also exposing the client countries to heightened risks of civil strife is a serious failing. The UN system is nominally dedicated first and foremost to peace and stability, and it is that bargain – that membership and playing by the rules provide protections – which is being violated. Second, this outcome of poor growth and more violence exposes how satisfying hegemonic power within a multilateral context poses practical as well as normative problems. The Bretton Woods institutions, created mainly by the United States to stabilize the post-war world economy, have done far less well in stabilizing the post-independence developing world. The financial policies not only do not work as advertised, but they rearrange social, economic and political conditions within countries in ways that produce instability.

Arguably, this failure is so grave that armed conflict has been one result. Multilateralism's economic agenda, very much shaped by the hegemonic power of the United States, has muddled multilateralism's security agenda, which involves the United States less directly. Among the questions this raises is how the one influences the other, and how the normative power and legitimacy of the multilateral project is consequently affected. For the actions of international organizations to intervene on behalf of the well-being of people – "the responsibility to protect", in Francis Deng's phrase – with military force, in addition to longer-standing traditions of peace operations, reconstruction and refugee protection, imply a large moral claim. The claim is embedded in the UN Charter and decades of precedent. The desirability of examining this claim and the effectiveness of the actions has for some years been scrutinized and a lively debate is ongoing. But there are many forms of intervention, not just those with blue helmets. Health interventions, ecological protection interventions, and ordinary economic activities like building infrastructure have been on the international agenda for years, too. They also have unintended impacts, and considerable effort has gone into uncovering such consequences and devising corrective measures, as with the environmental impacts of World Bank-funded construction projects. The moral basis of multilateralism is not only that a collective will or permission is being expressed, but that actions of the international community are beneficial in some clearly agreed upon way. The impact of multilateralism's most pervasive projects – those of its financial actors – very directly challenges that claim.

The civil war discourse and multilateral action

The dominant ideas explaining the incidence of civil war over the last fifteen years have gradually shifted from "ancient hatreds" to "rebel greed", reflecting a shift in the venues of the most closely watched conflicts. The wars stirred in the break-up of Yugoslavia were seen as throwbacks to the 1912–13 Balkan Wars and the earlier hostilities along the fault line of the Ottoman Empire. The Rwandan genocide also seemed rooted in long-standing tribal rivalries. Later in the 1990s, a new discourse on civil wars was generated by econometric analyses of World Bank economist Paul Collier and his colleagues, and seemed verified in the carnage of places like Liberia and Angola.[2] In less than a decade, the explanatory juggernaut spanned the deep psychological wounds of millennium-old feuds and grievances to the cool calculations of rebel leaders seeking to maximize personal gains. In these theories, and many others that never gained such a foothold, the role of the international community was frequently viewed as too indecisive in response, or too willing to chase the CNN coverage, or too lethargic in post-conflict peacebuilding. Virtually all studies of the involved multilateral agencies located their responsibilities as preventers or responders to war. Now it is time to consider whether certain habits and policies of major international organizations are contributors to conflict.

Such an assertion stems from three sources. First is the apparent inadequacy of the alternative explanations. The "ancient hatreds" perspective was rooted in weakly derived historical lessons, as with Robert Kaplan's sensationalizing accounts of the Balkans, to provocations like Samuel Huntington's *Clash of Civilizations*, to more measured and modest theories about psychological and cultural frames and narratives that are useful but incomplete. All relied on rather complex causation paths that could be confounded by counter examples – for every case of deadly conflict in places where ethnic or religious groups have long lived in tension, there are cases where they lived quite peaceably. The econometric approach to conflict has yielded many valuable insights, but relies on inadequate data and correlations that are at least empirically questionable if not mere guesswork, and that contradict much field research on rebellion. Missing in these two dominant discourses are large-scale structural influences such as economic and political policies promoted by the international community that are temporally coincident with the high-volume period of civil wars since the 1970s.

The second source for viewing the policies of multilateral institutions as conflict generators comes from a critical discourse on humanitarian intervention. The sheer scale and number of "complex humanitarian emergencies" in the post-Cold War world has taxed the resources and ingenuity of the international community. The responses to famine, massive refugee crises, ecological disasters and war itself bring together a ménage of global actors that cross lines of the state, intergovernmental agencies and non-governmental organizations (including the news media). This phenomenon has begun to yield a number of perceptive accounts, as in the work of Mark Duffield, Alex De Waal, and Fiona Terry (all of whom are in some sense practitioner theorists),[3] among others, which focus attention on the harmful role often played by the responders. Amidst the foibles and miscues, in these analysts' view, are intentional policies of political and economic development shoved onto the rescue and reconstruction activities, with highly problematical effects for development and peace.

That critique of humanitarianism is linked to the third interrogatory source: globalization. While it is fraught with multiple meanings and controversy, globalization is a useful concept in several ways, not least – as used here – to describe worldwide structural forces that are significantly the consequence of intentional policies. Typically, we speak of economic, political and cultural globalization. While cultural forms are strong, and indeed may affect conflict in numerous ways, the more potent expressions of globalization for conflict are economic and political reforms driven by the major powers – the United States being the primary engine – and the multilateral institutions that are often of the same mind, not least because they tend to be dominated by those same countries. The policies at issue are those that have fostered, or insisted upon, "marketization" and "good governance" in the developing world in exchange for loans, trade, aid, and the like. These policies have powerful effects on the conditions that lead to instability and conflict, or, conversely, greater stability, prosperity and peace.

The forces of political and economic globalization should likewise be scrutinized for the impact they have upon stability and peace, aside from their primary economic consequences. Policies such as anti-corruption measures and democratization are laudable in themselves, but their application may not be timely or appropriate. Free markets may be desirable from the standpoint of economic growth, trade vitality and individual choice, but marketization can create other effects that may destabilize certain countries. Yet the "Washington Consensus" on these kinds of measures – which is also a consensus of the policy making actors in the international financial institutions (IFIs) – is such that their impact is rarely gauged for destabilizing tendencies. What are set out as a simple good – democracy or growth – is also the intended outcomes of a broad range of interventions by multilateral institutions (among others), a primary goal of multilateralism generally. By some accounts, the World Bank, the International Monetary Fund, and the World Trade Organization (WTO), which are the multilateral institutions most directly involved in economic policies, not only promote a certain development strategy but use their financial and regulatory power to impose conditions on aid, loans and trade that many countries have little choice but to accept. So, in this regard, multilateralism is a coercive instrument (indeed, a coercive regime) and one in which decision-making is itself non-democratic.

In short, the multilateralism of globalization, so to speak, is every bit as important as the multilateralism of arms control, peacekeeping, human rights, and other more typical activities examined for the effectiveness of collective action. With regard to armed conflict, particularly civil wars, the evidence of impacts is mixed. A number of cases seem to reveal an effect of globalization, such as income inequality, which could be an important contributor to conflict. Another potentially decisive destabilizer is the undermining of the legitimacy of the state. Many analyses dispute broad generalizations, however, and correlations are difficult to make. What is most likely is that different manifestations of globalization combine under certain circumstances to raise the likelihood of conflict in countries that suffer from other vulnerabilities. Understanding the role of multilateral organizations in these deadly combinations is essential to promoting more foresightful policy formation and implementation.

Economics and civil wars

The relationship of international economic policies to the causes of internal conflict is not well understood. Two general schools of thought are prominent. The first stems from the Collier *et al.* analyses that utilize statistics on economic growth, trade, income inequality, etc. as indicators of a country's predisposition to, or relapse into, armed conflict. This set of econometric studies has drawn a tentative conclusion that economic globalization – that is, as measured by trade openness – reduces the probability of civil war, mainly through economic prosperity. A second school, drawing on dependency theory of the 1960s, sees the economic policies associated with globalization as increasing inequality and thereby setting the stage for civil war. This so-called structuralist argument sees a major role played by transnational corporations, whose direct foreign investment, resource extraction and other practices – enabled or facilitated by the new rules of global economics – tend to create greater inequality within those countries. Inequality, in turn, is regarded as an engine of conflict. While the analysis herein accepts the necessity of the structuralist perspective, the devil is no less in the details: not merely *which* structures are at work (IFIs), but precisely how their policies are dynamically conducive to conflict. To some important extent, all civil wars are consequences of challengeable states – the key variable is when and in what way states become vulnerable to weakness.[4]

There is relatively little disagreement that the structural adjustment policies (SAPs) of the 1980s and 1990s promoted principally by the World Bank and others – a momentous and sizeable economic intervention – have in many countries produced greater income inequality as well as lower overall wealth, and even growing inequality worldwide.[5] The question regarding the role of inequality in the onset of armed conflict, however, sharply divides scholars. Here, the Collier contribution, particularly his 2002 article with Anke Hoeffler, is particularly influential: their calculations essentially rule out income inequality as a factor in the onset of civil war. (They also say, however, that inequality can prolong civil wars once started.) Other econometric studies have a more mixed result on this score. But the conclusion from this analytical method largely declaims income inequality as a primary cause of conflict, and, implicitly, that destabilizing inequality could stem from economic globalization.

The econometricians do not have the stage to themselves, however, and a sizeable chorus of scholars asserts inequality as a key variable. Most importantly, the assertion is qualified by reference to other factors: viewing inequality alone is not the proper perspective, but rather seeing it in combination with other factors – identity politics, political disenfranchisement, restraints and opportunities – provides a fuller picture. What seems to be a particularly powerful motive for rebellion is horizontal inequality, the inequality of one group relative to others, rather than the vertical inequality favoured by most economic measurements. The State Failure Task Force, for example, describes a similar phenomenon as "unbalanced development" – high urbanization coupled with low GDP per capita. There are also different possible measurements of economic well-being; the same study found, for example, that countries with high infant mortality rates are likely to suffer from state failure twice as often.[6] And horizontal inequality can indeed be exacerbated by the processes of economic globalization.

Natural resource wealth introduces a potent aspect of economic policy into the conflict equation. The Collier and Hoeffler formulation finds countries with export dependence on natural resources to be much more likely to experience conflicts. The wealth is there for the taking, it seems, and this can stir the revolutionary heart of many a would-be warlord. This assertion has its challengers, but natural resources do open a window to view, however uncertainly, how global economic rules may create instabilities. Multilateral institutions have encouraged open markets, including foreign ownership, of natural resources. Is such ownership a stimulus to conflict? It is not wholly clear. Commercial development of valuable resources like oil or timber can introduce a number of destabilizing elements: new opportunities for official corruption, horizontal inequality, ecological degradation and forced migration, and "sons of the soil" resistance – the last being those groups on the geoperiphery who feel exploited by the centre.[7]

Consider how land reform has altered the social landscape in East Africa. Privatization of land, some done as part of aid or loan conditionality, has in some cases closed off pasture and other traditional uses that support the large populations of pastoralists in the Ilema Triangle, an expanse in Kenya, Uganda, Somalia and Ethiopia. The reduced opportunities for grazing have apparently increased conflicts that have grown quite violent. Privatization alone does not adequately explain these small wars.[8] The introduction of small arms, criminal syndicates and transnational meat markets has intensified the consequences of intentional policies of increased takings for private use (including wildlife parks) and fitful attempts to settle the pastoralists into agricultural livelihoods. The social structure is undermined in the process, further eroding one of the constraints available to resolve conflicts between tribes. Here we see the combination of several intentional policies and several illicit practices that are part and parcel of what we now consider to be globalization.

The example of the pastoralists in East Africa serves to illustrate another caution, however: globalization has many dimensions and effects, and not all of them are wrought by the designs of multilateral institutions. Not only are there many illicit aspects, such as stolen-meat markets, private armies or corruption, but there are large-scale effects that are not only "legal" but necessary in some sense for the global economy as now constituted to operate efficiently – international migration being one good illustration. Migration is a complex phenomenon mainly regarded as a matter of people moving to seek opportunities to work and thrive. Its impact on conflict can be very powerful, as with sudden surges of people, usually as refugees, or when immigrants organize as politically charged diasporas that support organized violence in their countries of origin. While such phenomena qualify as outgrowths of globalization, with unintended policy consequences, they are perhaps second and third order effects that are not central to this case, although migration has a lot to do with globalization, often a lot to do with conflict, and is generally now regulated by multilateral agreements.

Some observers caution against confusing multilateralism and economic globalization, and note the paradox of greater openness in trade and communications occurring at a time when multilateralism seems to be losing its traction.[9] But that again equates openness and globalization in a way that tends to oversimplify the latter, and may be looking at the wrong multilateral agencies. Borders may be open in some new sense, but that does not mean the effects are only about legal trade. Those discussing conflict and globalization often make this same mistake,[10] and it can apply equally to the effects of multilateral decision making of the kind the IFIs are associated with. The relationships, even just the economic ones, are far more complex, and it is that complexity – typically tied up with politics – which must be parsed more thoroughly.

Political globalization and instability

Another set of claims about globalization revolves around changes in political rules fostered by the international community. This runs a broad gamut, from policies promoting or insisting upon anti-corruption measures, smaller state bureaucracies, and expanding democratic practice, to the very structure of international governance and promotion of "global" norms – for example, pooled sovereignty in multilateral organizations. The arguments about potential effects on conflict are quite different in each case.

A set of political reforms often accompanies economic liberalization measures in international lending, "convenants" aimed at reducing the size and scope of the state to disencumber the functioning of markets. These reform measures include significant shrinkage of state institutions, which may involve not only regulatory agencies but security, education and health ministries, for example. The logic is simple and, in economic terms, compelling: such bureaucracies not only may impede the natural functioning of markets with excessive and confusing regulations, but impose formal and informal taxes on the system, all of which increase inefficiency and reduce competitiveness in world markets. Reducing the size of bureaucracies reduces the possibility of cronyism and corruption as well.[11]

At the same time, "good governance" includes democratization, another hedge against cronyism and desirable in and of itself. The global surge toward democratic governance in the 1980s and '90s was braced not only by multilateral institutions but by a growing global civil society interested mainly in the promotion of human rights. As a result, the pressures to democratize have been strong. Definitions of democratic practice suffer from some ambiguity, however, with elections typically held high as the standard.[12] But the demands of the international community for elections and some protections for pluralism and political rights are apparent. Taken together, the political reform agenda – smaller states, more democracy – is now a central tenet of globalization.

The implications for conflict arise in several ways, but pivot on the possibilities for instability. The reduction of bureaucracies can also mean the reduction in resources for education and health, and even security (as in border controls or policing certain areas). Anti-cronyism measures may remove an employment safety valve for social pressures that build with sudden changes in economic conditions, such as commodity price fluctuations or catastrophic losses in exports; privatization or closing of state industries precipitously increase unemployment, too, and in some cases affect particular ethnic groups. And, to top it all off, in this period of uncertain and (for some) sudden impoverishment, governance is made contingent, in a sense, by the introduction – possibly for the first time – of elections. Elections in such situations can be occasions for demagoguery and polarization, and, if things go badly, an excuse for taking up the gun.

Partial democracies are more prone to conflict than full democracies or autocracies, with "partial" usually meaning strong executives and weak legislatures. And while weakness or incompleteness in democratic institutions and practice can arise for many reasons, outside insistence on elections is one prominent source.[13] Countries moving from autocracies to elections often suffer conflict as political leaders implement strategies to maintain power, which can include a wholesale assault on political institutions that provide order. William Reno observes:

> Rulers facing such [democratization] threats systematically undermine the cohesiveness of other collectivities, including state agencies, preemptively disrupting power bases of potential competitors ... This effort also hindered the development of truly autonomous non-state social organizations, as patronage networks and other informal mechanisms of control moved into commercial, religious, generational and other channels that otherwise would be foundations for a societal counterbalance to state power.[14]

Reno has shown how autocratic rulers, under international pressure to reform, undermined state bureaucracies and created new ways to dominate via economic predation, backed by private military force, with catastrophic consequences for peace.

The consequences of "good governance" is perhaps more visible in specific sectors of the state's responsibility, for example, education and health. Among SAPs' notable effects on health, and on the provision of health care, are rising prices for medications, increasing inequality in the distribution of health care facilities, labour migration and forced migration, cutbacks in public health services generally. As one study puts it, "cuts in spending on health and education have left these [developing] countries without an adequate health infrastructure to implement STD [sexually transmitted disease] treatment and HIV prevention programmes. For example, during the period of structural adjustment in the first half of the 1980s, per capita health expenditure fell by 40 per cent in Jamaica and 23 per cent in Ghana."[15] The impact of privatization in particular came to Africa at the same time as the HIV/AIDS pandemic and explains the failure to contain the virus more than any other single factor. The most promising ameliorative medical treatments, moreover, have been restricted by patent laws that continue to be protected by multilateral agreements and the WTO, despite some attempts to renegotiate the terms of such protections.[16] The pandemic now has broad implications for social dissolution and conflict.

The picture of education is similarly troubled. Reductions in education spending, or charging fees for students – both often a consequence of IFI loan conditions – depressed enrolment in primary and secondary schools. A broad reform of the educational policies fostered by the World Bank, driven by macroeconomic policies, altered education policies worldwide and "have not been as effective as postulated, and in some cases have created significant educational distortions in a nation's education sector", according to an empirical study. These results stem from the decision-making culture of the World Bank: "the education sector does not establish operational priorities", says the study, because "the allocation of internal resources and the establishment of operational priorities are solely in the hands of the country economists."[17] The consequences of these policies have a strong link to organized violence. Probably the most important of these links is the "angry young men" thesis of rebellion, in which the availability of a large reserve of unemployed or unemployable young men fuels the labour needs of warlords, revolutionaries and others intent on civil war. Education and per capita income are highly correlated statistically, and there is much field research supporting the idea that a decline in educational opportunities contributes to instability.[18] This has been rather well documented in war zones like West Africa, particularly Sierra Leone. As one account puts it, "When interviewed, young combatants of all factions, almost without exception, represent themselves as victims of educational collapse."[19]

The relationship between education policies, IFIs and conflict is not limited to the warlord venues of Africa, however. It emerges as a likely factor in newer forms of organized political violence. Consider Pakistan, where the large debt repayment burden constrains investments in public education. The alternative – the privatization of education, in effect – are the Koranic schools, which have grown as public sector vigour declined. "The general boom in the Madrassah system indicates a decay in governance that may ultimately affect regional stability", notes a Brookings Institution study. "That is, the religious schools are filling a void in a basic area of social services where government has failed ... In essence, the secular welfare state has been privatized to those with a dangerous agenda of their own."[20] That agenda often includes religiously inspired warfare against the West and India, in Kashmir, Afghanistan, Iraq, Sudan, and elsewhere.

Three other aspects of political globalization deserve mention. First, is the impulse of the international community to promulgate norms fostering human rights, which in its most active form has spurred the imposition of sanctions. In some places, of course, sanctions proved to be powerful instruments of global opprobrium and subsequent political change. But the overall record is mixed.[21] Reno points out how sanctions on the trade in weapons can in fact result in more violence when they deny needed arms to stabilizing groups hoping to restore order.

Second, the involvement of the United Nations and other regional security organizations in failing states and in conflict management can also be viewed as problematic. The looting of aid is now widely believed to be a major failure of the international community's efforts in this regard (although much of it is conveyed bilaterally), and aid can also lead to destabilizing horizontal inequality. The recipes for state building and rescue from humanitarian emergencies include an emphasis on development and stability – that is, marketization packages and political reform that may not be appropriate to a given situation, and in fact may make things worse. Peace processes themselves are fraught with development and aid pledges, technical advisers, new constitutions, and so on. In some cases, the stakes may be raised so high that an incentive for violent behaviour is created to earn a seat at the table.

Political globalization has come to mean, perhaps above all, the set of relationships between states that has evolved in the current period of multilateralism, the shared or pooled sovereignty in which certain functions, responsibilities and capabilities of individual states evolve into those of the collectivity. For the control or prevention of conflict, the concern in this regard is the state's monopolization of security assets and privileges – the monopolization of the means of legitimate violence. To some degree, this monopolization has been eroded by the diffusion of political authority or the displacement of politics beyond the arena of the state. While this is typically expressed with reference to private armies, diasporas, insurgencies, and so on, it can also apply to multilateral institutions. They are, in effect, new arenas of politics about the use of force.[22] And these arenas, when "legitimate", are often multilateral fora, whether the permanent kind, such as the UN Security Council or NATO, or the occasional kind, as with peace conferences. In either case, among others, the beleaguered state may give up some crucial element of its authority, or monopoly, with respect to violence, and embolden those who operate in the shadows of legality.

Legitimacy, sequencing and integrity

The notions laid out above – that multilateral governance in economics and politics can at times unintentionally create conditions conducive to conflict – are largely hypothetical or anecdotal. Evidence is sketchy or partial because the question is not often asked. When it is asked, the variables are narrowly defined and causal relations too simple – for example, the relationship between trade openness and conflict, or the democratic peace thesis. There is nonetheless a significant body of empirical work that does suggest that poorly conceived multilateral policies, often imposed from different directions, can weaken states or create inequalities that are conducive to conflict. These are compounded by a decline in the legitimacy of national political authorities. The entire enterprise of economic and political development becomes a patchwork of imposed conditions, poor implementation or strategies of avoidance, declining vigour of responsible national and local institutions – altogether, a disintegration of the elements needed for prosperity, equity and stability.

The primary argument stems from a widespread acknowledgement regarding the failure of structural adjustment policies of the 1980s and '90s to reduce poverty or stimulate growth that benefited publics broadly. The consequential inequalities – new kinds of economic and social disruptions, not just a decline in incomes – are not likely to be a sufficient condition for organized violence. But such inequality makes societies vulnerable to other triggers. Inequality contributes to a triggering event, potentially, in combination with other phenomena: ethnic fragmentation, "sons of the soil" resistance, or external shocks. And those conditions, in turn, are exacerbated by the inability of states to cope successfully with these stresses. So, as Frances Stewart puts it

> trigger events may include ... changes brought about by the success or failure of the development model resulting in absolute and relative access to employment and incomes ...; adjustment/stabilization policies involving changes in terms of trade ...; external developments [such as] market access, the international terms of trade; debt and interest payments, and capital flows (including aid).[23]

Among the triggers should be added weak or failed democratization efforts. The State Failure Task Force found that the worst kind of regime for conflict onset is a strong partial democracy in which elections may be held but other democratic processes were weak or non-existent. An extensive set of case studies commissioned by the World Bank also found that political instability increases the risk of civil war, and, significantly, that risk escalates with financial turbulence. "The risks associated with political instability", writes the study leader, Nicholas Sambanis, "seem to be magnified with economic transition.... Economic decline weakens political institutions and makes them even less able to respond to crises."[24] The crisis will not always be mass violence. It can be social unrest that is nonetheless indicative of desperate conditions and, if not addressed, an escalation to civil war.

These explorations – looking for triggers in unstable situations – perhaps are too stark as well. The critique of econometric approaches, which has grown alongside the growing prominence of Collier *et al.* leads us back to a need for heuristic analysis that draws on the insights of statistical correlations but situates them in richer, qualitative accounts. After a particularly deft critique of the inequalities-and-conflict literature (mainly on grounds that most econometric methods are fraught with inconsistencies and crudeness), Christopher Cramer notes that "economic inequality *is* hugely important to explaining civil conflict, but only insofar as the economic is considered inseparable from, part of, embedded in the social, political, cultural, and historical. This allows for greater explanatory depth but less claim to predictive power or generalisation across contexts."[25]

Such in-depth, multidisciplinary studies would likely yield considerably greater appreciation for the complex relationships fostered by exogenous influences in developing countries. We do know, on the basis of broad economic data, that inequality increased in the global economy around the same time that structural adjustment and changes in global finance kicked in, and that the incidence of civil wars increased. While eschewing globalization as a sufficient explanation, Susan Woodward maintains that something in the global environment changed:

> (1) the global approach to macroeconomic disequilibria in the foreign sector (balance-of-payments and current account crises) that resulted from the change in official economic ideology, first in the UK, then in the US, and as a result of the latter, in the IFIs; and (2) the American approach to the Cold War and superpower competition. The fact that the changes happened in both the economic and the security fields is crucial because as external shocks to developing countries, they created contradictory pressures on their policy choices that had no happy solution. Moreover, the externally prescribed policy changes required fundamental

and radical changes in the arrangements on which most countries had built domestic stability (within the elite and between state and society) since the late 1940s, early 1950s (or since independence, if it came later). Even if the policies were not adopted as prescribed or correctly implemented, they still generated domestic consequences that dominate the literature on armed conflict and civil war.[26]

What we have, then, is a set of relationships – what I have been calling policies fostering economic and political globalization – whose effects are not well understood individually, but are particularly opaque in combination. How to parse this is a difficult problem of method.[27] But there is at least a strong likelihood of deleterious impacts by multilateral organizations, and it is that probability with which we must contend.

One way to contend with it is to regard how policies emanating from different sectors of the international community affect one another. This simple step would perhaps alone make an enormous difference in how imposed reform affects political and social stability. Joseph Stiglitz makes a parallel point convincingly about *sequencing*, "the failure to be sensitive to the broader social context". Stiglitz means this mainly as economic administration – getting the reforms to work properly, to be capable of implementation. What is striking about his discussion of this problem is that, in his view, it grows out of the IFI's own blindness to how ideological predispositions unfold on the ground. "Many of the sequencing mistakes reflected fundamental misunderstandings of both economic and political processes, misunderstandings that were particularly associated with those who believed in market fundamentalism."[28] Privatization and foreign ownership, shrinking state bureaucracies, closing social institutions, reducing the security of borders – such activities are disruptive and in many cases impoverishing, at least in the short term. When the policies are pushed aggressively by multilateral donors (often in combination with bilateral donors and private banks), without a sensible regard for how they affect each other, the sequencing problem can become acute. Richard Sandbrook puts the same problem another way – "the tensions that emerge between economic adjustment and political democratization" – but it speaks to the same matter of cross purposes.

Three principal contradictions arise: adjustment policies, by adversely affecting the interests of the early urban supporters of the democracy movements, risk alienating vocal constituencies from democratic institutions; the technocratic, top-down style of adjustment programmes blocks the participatory, accountable and open style which should underpin democracy; and a resurgence of clientism under the pressures of democratic competition contradicts adjustment's emphasis on improved governance, in particular the efficient and transparent allocation of public resources.[29]

The results of these policies, so often deleterious, become then a crisis for the state in another way: the erosion of legitimacy. When the most basic functions of the state are not being fulfilled, or are clearly in decline, then the legitimacy of the state and its leaders is in peril. Sandbrook, Dani Rodrick, and others have shown the destabilizing tendencies of the adjustment programmes, and posit the stabilizing capacities of the state as bulwarks against widespread violence – channelling, absorbing, deterring or punishing dissent. With diminished capacity, however, that stabilizing function is contestable, both on the ground and in the perceptions of the public. When "alternatives" – rebel groups, in particular – are poised to challenge that weakened state, often based on the grievances globalization has caused or exacerbated, then a particularly worrisome situation is at hand. Legitimacy is the lifeblood of any regime, and draining it away by outside forces is especially provocative. In the midst of that haemorrhaging, donors also demand elections. The combination is pernicious, or at least disruptive, and sometimes intentionally so.[30] The decline of state legitimacy is widely understood to be a powerful explanatory factor in the onset of civil war.[31]

The multilateral donors and other lenders have largely ignored the tenets of good development practice, a disrespect for the integrity of the development model driven by a faith in marketization and its anti-corruption handmaiden. This faith has not been rewarded by good results, and indeed the "externalities" have been harsh. It is the culture of the IFIs, more than the fact of multilateralism per se, which appears to be the root of the problem, an ideological fervour that is free of empirical validation. But one must also ask if the structure of multilateral institutions can ever escape the interests of the most powerful players, who can change the internal culture and rules to satisfy interests outside the scope of the institutions normative framework. The problem is not merely an instrumentalist manipulation of the IFIs, but neither are these institutions free from the strong socializing and coercive qualities of the most powerful actors.[32]

Multilateralism and civil wars

The challenge to multilateral institutions with respect to these civil wars is not necessary a challenge to free markets, open borders, pooled sovereignty, democratization, or good governance. Each of these tenets of economic and political policy comes with strong arguments for, including ample empirical evidence of, their virtue for prosperity, well-being, freedom, and so on. The point is something else: the ways in which particularly ambitious policies are formulated, including their implementation, have multiplier and interaction effects that matter a great deal. It would be enough to let it go at that, as many commentators do, and urge better coordination of policy implementation.

Something more fundamental is at stake here, however: it has to do with policies and implementation, but more importantly how policies are formed in the multilateral system. The poor performance of SAPs and the now growing controversy about democratization, good governance, the politicization of disaster relief, et cetera, raise the pivotal question of how decisions of this magnitude and reach are being made. The financial institutions, the public ones under multilateral control and the private ones that have grown with the globalization enabled by multilateral action, are at root non-democratic and to some significant degree an instrument of US economic power, or, to be broader, G-7 economic power. Are the ways and means of these multilateral institutions in keeping with the multilateral project that commenced after the Second World War? When viewing in tandem with these economic powerhouses the dynamics of decision-making in the security instruments of multilateralism – the UN Security Council, most prominently, but also institutions like NATO – one sees a democratic deficit, a transparency deficit, and a tenuous normative claim to "doing good". This is a very considerable challenge indeed, and one that requires both a deeper understanding of policy effects while at the same time a serious and sustained scrutiny of the norms and processes of policy formation in multilateralism's universe.

Notes

1. John Gerard Ruggie (1993) "Multilateralism: the anatomy of an institution", in John Gerard Ruggie (ed.) *Multilateralism Matters: The Theory and Praxis of an Institutional Form*, New York: Columbia University Press, p. 11.
2. Paul Collier and Anke Hoeffler (1998) "On the economic causes of civil war", *Oxford Economic Papers* 50; "Greed and grievance in civil war", World Bank, March 2002; and Paul Collier et al. (2004) *Breaking the Conflict Trap: Civil War and Development Policy*, Washington: World Bank. Collier and his cohorts were drawing on an older tradition in economics that included work by Jack Hirshliefer, Herschel Grossman, Tim Tulloch, among others.
3. Mark R. Duffield (2001) *Global Governance and the New Wars: The Merging of Development and Security*, London: Palgrave MacMillan; Alex De Waal (1998) *Famine Crimes: Politics and the Disaster Relief Industry in Africa*, Bloomington: Indiana University Press; Fiona Terry (2002) *Condemned to Repeat? Paradoxes of Humanitarian Action*, Ithaca: Cornell University Press.
4. The dependent variable in this analysis is the precise weakness of regimes that leads to a collapse or significant deterioration of functionality in key sectors (security, policing, health, education, economic growth) that would then lead to armed civil conflict. The difficulty of quantifying this in any meaningful way is apparent and is not attempted here. Independent variables – IFI conditions, world commodity prices, and other condi-

tions conducive to civil war (ethnic strife, nearby wars, etc.) – are also difficult to situate precisely. But the argument here would hold for all civil wars, and need not be differentiated by civil war type – which, while helpfully suggested by some contributors to this volume in our November 2004 conference, does not shed light on the main argument – that is, that weakening states through globalization policies makes those countries particularly vulnerable to civil wars.

5. Joseph Stiglitz is probably the most prominent critic in this respect, and his most important contribution in this respect is Stiglitz, J. (2002) *Globalization and its Discontents*, New York: W.W. Norton. But studies conducted by the World Bank (see especially those by Elbadawi) point to failures in sub-Saharan Africa particularly. One striking statistic: "In the period 1980–91, 40 of 58 (69 per cent) African and Asian countries experienced negative growth. In contrast, only 9 of 53 had experienced negative growth in the period 1960–1980," and cites the "deflationary impact of structural adjustment programs". Jonathan DiJohn (2003) "Mineral Resource Abundance and Violent Political Conflict: a critical assessment of the Rentier State model", Development Studies Institute Crisis State Programme, London School of Economics.
6. Jack A. Goldstone, Gurr, Ted Robert, Harff, Barbara et al. (2000) *State Failure Task Force Report: Phase III Findings*, MacLean VA: Science Applications International Corporation, pp. 23, 14. For a clear argument on horizontal inequality and conflict, see Frances Stewart (2000) "The root causes of humanitarian emergencies", in E.W. Nafziger, F. Stewart and R. Vayrynen (eds.) *War, Hunger, and Displacement: the origins of humanitarian emergencies*, Oxford: Oxford University Press.
7. James Fearon and David Laitin have developed this particularly interesting explanation. See Fearon, J. (2004) "Why do some civil wars last so much longer than others?", *Journal of Peace Research* 41: 3.
8. Maurice Nyamanga Amutabi and K. Inyani Simala (2004) *Globalization, Pastoralism and Violent Resource Conflicts In East Africa*, Washington: Social Science Research Council, December; Fiona Flinton and Imeru Tamrat (2002) "Spilling blood over water: the case of Ethiopia", in J. Lind and K. Sturman (eds.) *Scarcity and Surfeit: The Ecology of Africa's Conflicts*, Pretoria: Institute for Security Studies; Michael Halderman and Jennifer Hadley (2002) *Assessment and Programmatic Recommendations: Addressing Pastoralist Conflict in the Karamoja Cluster of Kenya, Uganda and Sudan*, Washington DC: MSI and USAID.
9. Diana Tussie (1998) "Multilateralism revisited in a globalizing world economy", *Mershon International Studies Review* 42.
10. The leading example of this is Gerard Schneider, Katherine Barbieri and Nils Peter Gleditsch (2003) *Globalization and Armed Conflict*, Lanham, Maryland: Rowman & Litlefield, esp. chapter 13.
11. A good case for the conflict-inducing tendencies of cronyism especially can be found in J.-P. Azam and C. Morrisson (1999) *Conflict and Growth in Africa. Vol. 1: The Sahel*, Paris: OECD.
12. See, for example, Undersecretary of State Paula Dobriansky (2003) "Principles of good governance", *Economic Perspectives* US Department of State, 8 (March).
13. Goldstone, op. cit., pp. 14–16. Monty Marshall and Ted Robert Gurr call these partial democracies "anocracies", and demonstrate how much more prone they are to civil war than either autocracies or full democracies. See Marshall, M. and Gurr, Ted Robert (2003) *Peace and Conflict 2003*, College Park: Center for International Development and Conflict Management, University of Maryland, ch. 4.
14. William Reno (2004) "The empirical challenge to economic analyses of conflict", prepared for the conference "The Economic Analysis of Conflict: Problems and Prospects", Social Science Research Council, Washington DC, 19–20 April, p. 11.

15. Maryam Shahmanesh, Mohsen Shamanesh and Rob Miller (2000) "AIDS and globalization", *Sexually Transmitted Infections* 76. For other effects on health and health systems, see N.B. Mock, S. Duale, L.F. Brown, E. Mathys, H.C. O'Maonaigh, N.K. Abul-Husn and S. Elliott (2004) "Conflict and HIV: A framework for risk assessment to prevent HIV in conflict-affected settings in Africa", *Emerging Themes in Epidemiology* 1 (29 October); Z.A. Bhutta (2001) "Structural adjustments and their impact on health and society: a perspective from Pakistan", *International Journal of Epidemiology* 30; J.S. Benson (2001) "The impact of privatization on access in Tanzania", *Social Science and Medicine* 52; and J. Lethbridge (2004) "Public sector reform and demand for human resources for health", *Human Resources for Health* 2.
16. On the security aspects, see for example the report of the US National Intelligence Council, *The Next Wave of HIV/AIDS: Nigeria, Ethiopia, Russia, India, and China*, September 2002. The issue of intellectual property rights is complex and unresolved, but squarely in the realm of multilateral responsibility. See, for example, Carsten Fink (2003) "Implementing the Doha Mandate on TRIPS and Public Health", Trade Note 5, Washington: World Bank Group. The patent protections and vows to provide drugs to poor countries have been entwined with the negotiations and controversies on other issues, such as agricultural protections. But patent protections are only one piece of the problem for getting cheap drugs to HIV patients. For example, one study at Harvard suggesting that patent rights were not primarily responsible for poor access to life-extending drugs, notes:

    We conclude that a variety of de facto barriers are more responsible for impeding access to antiretroviral treatment, including but not limited to the poverty of African countries, the high cost of antiretroviral treatment, national regulatory requirements for medicines, tariffs and sales taxes, and, above all, a lack of sufficient international financial aid to fund antiretroviral treatment.

    A. Attaran, and L. Gillespie-White (2001) "Do patents for antiretroviral drugs constrain access to AIDS treatment in Africa?", *Journal of the American Medical Association* 286, abstract; and see also the rebuttal, asserting that patents do restrict access, online in "Comment on the Attaran/Gillespie-White and PhRMA surveys of patents on Antiretroviral drugs in Africa", Consumer Project on Technology Essential Action, Oxfam, 16 October 2002, ⟨http://www.cptech.org/ip/health/africa/dopatentsmaterinafrica.html⟩. On the decisive impact of social movements, and domestic production of generic drugs and their positive impacts, see the interview with Paulo Teixeira, director of the Brazilian Ministry of Health's STDs and AIDS programmes, on the "News Hour with Jim Lehrer", 16 July 2003. ⟨http://www.pbs.org/newshour/health/aids/brazil/teixeira.html⟩.
17. S.P. Heyneman (2003) "The history and problems of education policy at the World Bank 1960–2000", *International Journal of Education Development* 23: 315, 319. This is one of the few pieces of research that correlates the IFI culture to actual results, and echoes some of Stiglitz's criticisms. Heneman concludes that the "Bank has been recommending faulty education policies since the beginning of the sector in 1962" (p. 331).
18. On the income–education link, see Indra de Soysa (2000) "The resource curse: are civil wars driven by rapacity or paucity?" in M. Berdal and D. Malone (eds.) *Greed and Grievance: Economic Agendas in Civil Wars*, Boulder: Lynne Rienner, pp. 130–131.
19. Paul Richards (1999) "New political violence in Africa", *GeoJournal* 47. See also Ibrahim Abdullah (1998) "Bush path to destruction: the origin and character of the Revolutionary United Front/Sierra Leone", *Journal of Modern Africa Studies* 36. It must be

noted, however, that enrolments per se should not be taken as a definite indicator of the decline of educational opportunity; enrolments can be artificially inflated but without a corresponding improvement in education, an insight I owe to by MIT colleagues Rachel Glennerster and Esther Duflo.

20. P.W. Singer (2001) "Pakistan's Madrassahs: Ensuring a system of education not Jihad", Brookings Institution Analysis Paper 14 (November). On this there are several other well-researched papers: S.V.R. Nasr (2000) "The rise of Sunni militancy in Pakistan: The changing role of Islamism and the Ulama in society and politics", *Modern Asian Studies* 34; Rukhansa Zia (2003) "Religion and education in Pakistan: An overview", *Prospects* 33 (June); Government of Pakistan Ministry of Education and UNESCO (2003) "Islamabad financing of education in Pakistan: An estimation of required and available resources to achieve EFA goals", *Preparatory Document for the Ministerial Meeting of South Asia EFA Forum, May 21–23*, (May 2003).
21. Two recent entries in the sceptical side of this voluminous literature, are Robert A. Pape (1997) "Why economic sanctions do not work", *International Security* 22(2) (Fall); and Thomas G. Weiss (1999) "Sanctions as a foreign policy tool: weighing humanitarian impulses", *Journal of Peace Research* 36(5).
22. For a powerful articulation of this theory, see Anna Leander (2001) "Globalisation and the eroding state monopoly of legitimate violence", Copenhagen: Copenhagen Peace Research Institute, COPRI Working Papers 24/2001, among others of her papers at COPRI. See also Anna Leander (2005) "The market for force and public security: The destabilizing consequences of private military companies", *Journal of Peace Research* 42(5): 605–622.
23. Stewart, op. cit., p. 17 (in typescript).
24. Nicholas Sambanis (2003) *Using Case Studies to Expand the Theory of Civil War*, CPR Working Paper No. 5, Washington: World Bank, May, p. 31.
25. Christopher Cramer (n/d) "Economic inequalities and civil conflict", CPDR Discussion Paper Center for Development Policy Research, School of Oriental and African Studies, University of London, p. 18. See also his article, (2003) "Does inequality cause conflict?", *Journal of International Development* 15(4).
26. Susan Woodward, "A Memo on the Former Yugoslavia", prepared for the conference, "The Economic Analysis of Conflict: Problems and Prospects", Social Science Research Council, Washington DC, 19–20 April 2004.
27. Case studies that unpacked IFI conditions on countries with certain vulnerable characteristics – histories of violence, wars in neighbouring countries, natural-resource export dependencies, certain kinds of ethnic fragmentation – and traced the impact of those conditions on the state's functionality and legitimacy, would yield the most useful results. Superficially, what we do know of this involvement is suggestive: for example, William Easterly (2002) in *The Elusive Quest for Growth*, Cambridge: MIT Press, notes that 12 of the 15 countries that had earned the most number of loans from the World Bank suffered from civil wars. Examining these cases more closely would likely yield the causation paths more clearly.
28. Stiglitz, p. 73.
29. Richard Sandbrook (1997) "Economic liberalization versus political democratization: a social-democratic resolution?", *Canadian Journal of African Studies* 31(3): 482–516.
30. An official of a development agency involved with democratization efforts once remarked to me that its programmes were meant to challenge authorities and even be destabilizing. Remarkably, however, there is very little assessment of multilateral or bilateral development agencies' programmes to promote democratization. The many tens of millions of dollars spent over decades have never earned a suitable, comprehensive evaluation. See Kenneth Bollen, Pamela Paxton and Rumi Morishima (2003) "Review

of USAID evaluations on democracy and governance", Social Science Research Council, August 2003.

31. P.S. Douma (2003) *The Origins of Contemporary Conflict: A Comparison of Violence in Three World Regions*, The Hague: Institut Clingendael, provides an especially well-grounded explanation of the central importance of legitimacy.
32. Martha Finnemore and Michael N. Barnett (1999) "The politics, power, and pathologies of international organizations", *International Organization*, make the point that IOs develop their own autonomy and power, but they also note the norm diffusion function with, of course, very practical means: "The IMF and World Bank are explicit about their role as transmitters of norms and principles from advanced market economies to less-developed economies" (p. 714). They develop very useful arguments about "pathologies" of IOs that demonstrate how bureaucratic culture can lead to poor decisions, and while this insight is immensely valuable (not least because of their central point that IR theorists ignore this behaviour), bureaucratic norms and behaviour, while formally autonomous, can also be an expression of the interests of powerful states – all the more so in IOs that the powerful states care about.

Using military force for human protection: What next?

Thomas G. Weiss

No idea has moved faster in the international normative arena than the "responsibility to protect" (R2P), the title of the 2001 report from the International Commission on Intervention and State Sovereignty (ICISS).[1] The September 2005 World Summit, for example, provided the latest endorsement.[2] At the same time, the Security Council's painful dithering over Darfur demonstrates the dramatic disconnect between multilateral rhetoric and reality.[3] As Roméo Dallaire, the Canadian general in charge of the feeble UN force in Rwanda when civil war turned to genocide in 1994, lamented, "Having called what is happening in Darfur genocide and having vowed to stop it, it is time for the West to keep its word".[4]

Where are we exactly – at the dawn of a new era, or in the dusk of the bullish days of humanitarian intervention? This chapter's answer is the latter.

R2P: Where do we stand?

The basic idea behind R2P doctrine is that human beings sometimes trump sovereignty as enshrined in Charter Article 2 (7) with its emphasis on non-interference in domestic affairs. As Kofi Annan graphically told a 1998 audience at Ditchley Park, "state frontiers ... should no longer be seen as a watertight protection for war criminals or mass murderers".[5]

Over time, a blurring of domestic and international jurisdictions has taken place, which became more evident with the willingness to override sovereignty by using military force to save threatened populations in the 1990s. The rationale came from Francis Deng's "sovereignty as responsibility" to help internally displaced persons and Annan's "two sovereignties".[6] As a result, the three characteristics of a sovereign state – territory, authority, population – spelled out in the 1934 Montevideo Convention on the Rights and Duties of States have been complemented by another, a modicum of respect for human rights. State sovereignty seems less sacrosanct today than in 1945.

Amidst modest achievements, the World Summit's treatment of R2P suggests that consensus-building can sometimes occur around even the most controversial issues and with opposition from the strangest of bedfellows – in this case, the United States and the Non-Aligned Movement (NAM). The summit's final text reaffirms the primary roles of states in protecting their own citizens and encourages international assistance to weak states to exercise this responsibility. At the same time, it makes clear the need for international intervention when countries fail to shield their citizens from or, more likely, actively sponsor genocide or war crimes.

The NAM will continue to reiterate its rejection of the so-called right of humanitarian intervention and the US its refusal to be committed to military action by others, but the proverbial bottom line is clear: when a state is incapable or unwilling to safeguard its own citizens and peaceful means fail, the resort to military force (preferably with Security Council approval) remains a possibility. In short, there is an unambiguous acceptance by governments of the collective responsibility to protect. Political will remains problematic and the threshold for military intervention high – not merely the existence of substantial human rights abuses but such massive and conscience-shocking events as genocide, war crimes, crimes against humanity and ethnic cleansing. However, that military force for human protection remains a policy option at all represents new middle ground in international relations.

Consensus-building around R2P should be seen in context. Two years earlier, the UN was sidelined in the war against Iraq, and everyone was unhappy – the UN could not impede US hegemony, and the UN could not approve requisite action against Saddam Hussein. Annan asked 16 former senior government officials – the High-Level Panel on Threats, Challenges and Change (HLP) – to describe what ailed the UN and propose a way forward. The blue-ribbon panel's December 2004 report, *A More Secure World*, contains a laundry-list of recommendations – unkindly described as the "101 Dalmatians" for that number of proposals.[7] In March 2005, the HLP's propositions, including its enthusiastic support for R2P and rules for the use of force, were endorsed by Kofi Annan's *In Larger Freedom*.[8]

Once seen as a window of opportunity to revisit the United Nations in light of changes in world politics since 1945, instead summit negotiations exposed the debilitating political and bureaucratic conflicts that regularly paralyse the organization.[9] "A once-in-a-generation opportunity to reform and revive the United Nations has been squandered",[10] said the lead editorial from the *New York Times*. Partisans of R2P were relieved even if the overall results constituted considerably less than Kofi Annan's prior plea that "the UN must undergo the most sweeping overhaul in its 60-year history".[11]

Where does that leave us? Critics and sceptics alike of humanitarian intervention should get serious. Overzealous military action for insufficient humanitarian reasons is not the danger but, rather, standing on the side-lines as we watch Sudan's slow-motion genocide (some 2–300,000 dead black Africans and over 2 million forcibly displaced) and massive suffering in the Democratic Republic of the Congo (an estimated 4 million people, or four Rwandas, have died since 1998 largely from the famine and disease accompanying armed conflict).[12]

The crucial "So what?" question jumps to mind for the ground-breaking work on R2P. What is the value of normative progress? Will support for UN-centred multilateralism wane if the world organization repeatedly fails to act?

David Kennedy worries about the unacknowledged and unanticipated costs of humanitarian action, or "the dark sides of virtue".[13] David Rieff wonders whether the revolution of moral concern "has actually kept a single jackboot out of a single human face".[14] My own sombre lament is collective spinelessness in the face of normative advances – appallingly sparse responsibility to protect those suffering from atrocities that shock the human conscience, as great a threat to international society and global justice as pre-emptive or preventive war.

The humanitarian intervention fashion of the 1990s now seems like ancient history. The notion that human beings matter more than sovereignty radiated, albeit briefly, across the international political horizon until the wars on terrorism and Iraq became UN and US obsessions.[15] The political will for humanitarian intervention has evaporated. The United States is the preponderant power, and its inclination to commit significant political and military resources for human protection has faded while other states complain but do little.

Using R2P as the lens, this chapter addresses two central questions. What is the relevance of contemporary multilateralism to changing perceptions and norms of international security in light of Iraq? What are the implications for international society when power is concentrated in the United States? In short, what kind of world organization is desirable and feasible in the current era, for humanitarian intervention or anything else?[16]

R2P: An introduction

For Adam Roberts, the 1990s were a period during which "humanitarian issues have played a historically unprecedented role in international politics".[17] Secretary-General Annan's own speeches were widely debated because "the age of humanitarian emergencies" had led to "saving strangers".[18] An academic cottage industry grew, and governments sponsored a host of policy and evaluation initiatives.

As suggested by the 2005 World Summit decision, future policy debates and actions will be framed by *The Responsibility to Protect*, which since its publication in December 2001 has been greeted by a host of largely positive reactions, including academic reviews.[19] The former *New York Times* columnist Anthony Lewis described it as "the international state of mind",[20] and even one of its harshest opponents, Mohammed Ayoob, admits its "considerable moral force".[21]

What were the findings? The ICISS identified only two threshold cases, large-scale loss of life and ethnic cleansing, under way or anticipated. Humanitarian intervention should be subject to four precautionary conditions: right intention, last resort, proportional means and reasonable prospects of success. And finally, the Security Council is the preferred decision-maker.

The ICISS pushed the normative envelope in two ways. The first is in the report's opening sentences insisting that sovereignty also encompassed a state's responsibility to protect populations within its borders. Even committed advocates of human rights and robust intervention now see state authority as elementary to enduring peace and reconciliation and recommend fortifying failed, collapsed, or weak states. This realization does not reflect a nostalgia for the national security state of the past, but a realistic appraisal of a new bottom line.

The second ICISS contribution consists of moving away from the rights of outsiders to intervene toward a framing that spotlights those suffering from war and violence. Abandoning the picturesque vocabulary of the French Doctors' Movement[22] shifts the fulcrum away from the rights of interveners towards the rights of affected populations and the responsibilities (if not legal obligations) of outsiders to protect them. The new perspective prioritizes the rights of those suffering from starvation or systematic rape and the duty of states and international institutions to respond.[23] Rather than authorizing states to intervene, R2P specifies that it is shameful to do nothing when conscience-shocking events cry out for action.

Were the commissioners more timid than they could and should have been? They set the bar for humanitarian intervention very high. Although their double-barrelled justification addresses two triggers, the "just cause threshold" is lower than many would have hoped. For instance, it falls short of the 1998 Statute of the International Criminal Court (ICC), whose "crimes against humanity" mention everything from murder and slavery to imprisonment.

There were at least two other obvious candidates for the ICISS's short list of threshold conditions: the overthrow of democratically elected regimes (especially favoured by states and regional institutions in Africa as well as in parts of Latin America) and massive abuses of human rights (favoured by many in the West). Compromise among enthusiastic and sceptical commissioners required a low common denominator, but the insertion of "actual *or* apprehended" after both of its conditions opens the door to earlier rather than tardy action.

Multilateral legitimacy: a balance sheet

The decision by the North Atlantic Treaty Organization (NATO) to use force in Kosovo without a Security Council mandate raised hackles. Notwithstanding legal arguments in a highly political forum,[24] and the opinion of an independent commission of human rights specialists that it was "legitimate" even if "illegal",[25] Kosovo provided additional evidence for many of the council's inconsistency. The world's most powerful states can break the Charter's rules with impunity. That perception has been compounded by Washington's and London's decisions to go to war against Iraq in March 2003 without a Security Council blessing.

It is no secret that many sceptics, especially in the Third World, have always been uneasy with intervention, for humanitarian causes or any other purpose. The reservations were captured by Algerian president Abdelazia Bouteflika's remarks during the UN's 1999 general debate: "We do not deny that the United Nations has the right and the duty to help suffering humanity, but we remain extremely sensitive to any undermining of our sovereignty, not only because sovereignty is our last defence against the rules of an unequal world, but because we are not taking part in the decision-making process of the Security Council".[26]

History counsels caution to anyone even vaguely familiar with so-called humanitarian interventions of the colonial period – or more recently of Washington's on behalf of the contras in Nicaragua or Moscow's on behalf of comrades in Budapest and Prague. Concerns about the degradation of sovereignty often come from those whose borders have been breached by countries that now champion protecting human beings and ignoring borders. At the same time, repressive regimes hiding behind the shield of sovereignty should also be obvious to any student of history.

Hence, an honest debate about motivations and likely costs and benefits is required, not visceral accolades or rejections because of a qualifying adjective. Such a discussion is even more relevant because outside assistance can do more harm than good or can become entangled in a local political economy that favours war.[27] The beginnings of such a debate were started by the ICISS but cut short by 9/11.

US rhetoric about the wars in Afghanistan and Iraq suggests a heightened necessity for clear-headed analysis. There is a danger of contaminating the legitimate idea of humanitarian intervention by association, especially with George W. Bush and Tony Blair's spurious "humanitarian" justifications for invading Iraq. As a result, it is harder today than in 2001 to gainsay those who are reluctant to codify norms about using military force for human protection purposes. Many regard the new doctrine itself as such a threat that it requires renewing the principle of nonintervention rather than any downgrading of sovereign prerogatives.

The *National Security Strategy of the United States of America*,[28] unveiled in September 2002, is bound to influence future discussions about using force. The Bush doctrine "has had the effect of reinforcing fears both of US dominance and of the chaos that could ensue if what is sauce for the US goose were to become sauce for many other would-be interventionist ganders", according to Adam Roberts. "One probable result of the enunciation of interventionist doctrines by the USA will be to make states even more circumspect than before about accepting any doctrine, including on humanitarian intervention or on the responsibility to protect, that could be seen as opening the door to a general pattern of interventionism".[29]

Sceptical or hostile diplomats from developing countries view "human rights hawks" with deep suspicion, seeing humanitarian intervention as a convenient sleight of hand to conceal hidden Western agendas. Their worst fears have hardly been assuaged as mainstream American academics have pointed to the ethical underpinnings of pre-emptive and even preventive war. Lee Feinstein, and Anne-Marie Slaughter, for instance, argue for a new "duty to prevent" while Allan Buchanan and Robert Keohane are calling for the "cosmopolitan" use of preventive military force.[30]

That said, humanitarian intervention is hardly a worry these days because the rescue of humans under duress has been swept away by the concerns about the wars on terrorism and Iraq. For instance, a special section of *The Nation* in July 2003, "Humanitarian Intervention: A Forum", had virtually nothing to do with the announced topic. The preoccupation was the slippery slope facilitating actions by the Bush administration, or in Richard Falk's opening salvo: "After September 11, the American approach to humanitarian intervention morphed into post hoc rationalizations for uses of force otherwise difficult to reconcile with international law".[31] Hostility has resulted from countries that earlier would have supported the concept along with the possibility that "the Iraq war has undermined the standing of the United States and the U.K. as norm carriers ... [and] the process of normative change is likely to be slowed or reversed".[32]

In spite of incantations from the High-level Panel, Kofi Annan and the World Summit, humanitarian intervention is no longer on the side of the angels for fear that the Bush administration could manipulate any imprimatur. The rigorous application of R2P does not lend itself to be a veiled pretext to intervene for pre-emptive or other purposes.[33] However, Washington's loose application of humanitarian rhetoric to Afghanistan and Iraq *ex post facto* suggests why care should be given to parsing the ICISS's criteria, and why it is impossible to dismiss out-of-hand the fiercest claims by some developing countries that R2P conceals an imperial agenda.

Reforming the Security Council: a contemporary pipe dream[34]

For more than a decade, policy makers and academics have debated the possibility of reforming the anachronistic composition of the Security Council. Secretary-General Annan's opening statement to the General Assembly in September 2003 joined this chorus. After charging his HLP to return to the tired theme of Security Council reform, the panel obliged with a series of proposals to increase membership.[35] The ICISS too had judged this topic of "paramount importance" to address its uneven performance, double standards, veto, and unrepresentative character.[36] A larger and reformed council, however, would contribute nothing to enforcing the emerging R2P norm.

Most governments routinely support the call for increasing membership and eliminating the veto. The council does not reflect the actual distribution of power in the early twenty-first century, but reform skirts the main problem – the discrepancy between seats on the Security Council and available firepower. It would be easier to take proposals for reform more seriously if a successful candidacy – either continued or new, with or without a veto – were to entail signing an R2P pledge and the obligation to contribute troops or finance as part of membership qualifications.

The ICISS's obligatory references to the council's reform were part of getting commissioners to agree, but they were largely irrelevant to follow-up.[37] Everyone can agree that if the council's decisions are to have greater political clout, they must have greater legitimacy. How to get there from here has been the irresolvable problem.

From the outset, the clearest candidate for inaction by the 2005 World

Summit was the Security Council. Both the HLP and the Secretary-General made tactical blunders in making changes in the council's numbers and procedures the *sine qua non* for their sales pitches. Of course, the Security Council reflects the world of 1945 and not today's. Every potential solution, however, brings as many problems as it solves.

The debate about the Security Council presents a microcosm of a perpetual problem: the UN is so consumed with getting the process right that it neglects consequences. Allowing the Security Council to expand into a "rump" General Assembly of two dozen or more members would not stimulate activism. The council would be too large to conduct serious negotiations but too small to represent the membership as a whole. None of the possible changes would foster decision-making about the use of force in Darfur or the Congo. They would inhibit it. In addition, a larger Security Council would provide an American administration looking for reasons not to consult other governments with yet another excuse to skip New York.

Significantly, no other previous blue-ribbon international group had ever dressed up an option as a "recommendation", but the HLP produced two "models", each with 24 members but differing as to new permanent seats. If 16 individuals could not formulate a single way forward, how can 191 states and their parliaments? Even the Secretary-General did not take a stand, urging "member States to consider the two options ... or any other viable proposals".[38]

Apparently World War II is not yet over because, spurred by street demonstrations against Japan's campaign for a permanent seat, China dealt a peremptory blow to the notion of expansion. Beijing told the General Assembly in April that it was unwilling to rush a decision. The next day Washington echoed the sentiment with specific references to "artificial deadlines".

Nonetheless, three more options were put on the table in mid-July. Germany and Japan, ever more impatient about their roles as ATM's for the UN budget, joined forces with Brazil and India in the "G-4" – the "Group of 4", or less affectionately the "Gang of 4". They initially appeared willing to push for a showdown in the General Assembly in the hopes of a symbolic but pyrrhic victory of 128 votes – that is, two-thirds of the member states present and voting – on their proposal to add ten new seats (four non-permanent and six permanent, including four for themselves and two for Africa).

Meanwhile, a group of their regional rivals – Argentina, Mexico, Italy, Pakistan and South Korea – which had been caucusing for years as the "Coffee Club", rechristened themselves "Uniting for Consensus". Taking umbrage with the G-4's claim to permanent status, they proposed instead increasing the membership to 25 by adding 10 new two-year non-permanent seats with provisions for re-election, but no new permanent members. Simultaneously, African states proposed 26 council seats with six new permanent seats with veto power (including two for Africa but without specifying among Nigeria, South Africa or Egypt) along with five new non-permanent seats with two earmarked for Africa. And still other options were also being floated.

After postponing a June vote because they had too little support, the G-4 switched gears. They first dropped a demand for a veto, but then sought to woo the 53 members of the African Union, which was still insisting that the veto be given to new permanent members. Late in July the foreign ministers of the G-4 met in New York with 18 counterparts from Africa to reconcile the irreconcilable. Shortly thereafter in Addis Ababa, African states met and nine out of ten rejected the G-4's proposal. At that point, the Secretary-General postponed any vote in order not to sink the coming summit totally.

In the end, the heads of state and government could merely agree to "support early reform of the Security Council" and "continue to adapt its working methods".[39] The cacophony, jealousies and vested interests that have plagued this issue since 1995 remain intact and will for the foreseeable future.

The logic of "if it ain't broke, don't fix it" should find more resonance at the UN, where process almost always trumps substance. The authority of the international political process, however flawed, is at least regulated. For the Security Council, more than other principal organs, practical effectiveness should be more important than representation. Humanitarian intervention would be less likely with a larger council than at present. Inconsistency and double-standards but occasional action would be replaced by the old single-standard – do nothing everywhere.

The long-lasting unipolar "moment"

Continued jostling about Charter reform is a distraction because what Charles Krauthammer first called "the unipolar moment"[40] 15 years ago has lasted considerably longer. If military intervention to protect human beings is desirable, the critical task is to engage the United States in multilateral efforts because, as David Malone quips, "the United States [is] no longer a permanent member *comme les autres*".[41]

Conventional wisdom now holds that terrorism and the attacks of September 2001 altered international relations. The crossroad is not born solely of terrorism; it is multi-sourced and of long gestation. Terrorism, and UN responses to it, accentuate the implications of the post-Cold War trend towards a system based on superpower. The preponderance of the United States – militarily, economically and culturally – is ever more striking. What kind of collective security organization is possible when Washington's gear, according to former European Union commissioner of external relations Chris Patten, is "unilateralist overdrive"?[42]

While the ICISS met with him during a preliminary consultation, they failed to integrate adequately the implications of what French foreign minister Hubert Védrine dubbed the *hyper-puissance*. Bipolarity had given way to what was supposed to be US primacy, but the military prowess in Afghanistan and Iraq makes "primacy" an understatement. Scholars speculate about the nuances of economic and cultural leverage in the international system resulting from US soft power,[43] but the hard currency of international politics undoubtedly remains military might. Before the war on Iraq, the "hyperpower" was already spending more on its military than the next 15–25 countries (depending on who was counting); with additional appropriations for Afghanistan and Iraq, Washington now spends more than the rest of the world's militaries combined.[44]

Security Council efforts to control US actions resemble the Roman Senate's attempts to control the emperor. UN diplomats almost unanimously described the debate surrounding Iraq as "a referendum not on the means of disarming Iraq but on the American use of power".[45] Today, there are two world "organizations", the United Nations (global in membership) and the United States (global in reach). Critics of US hegemony, and several members of the ICISS are among them, argue that enforcement decisions should be based on UN authority instead of US capacity. But the two are inseparable.

As its coercive capacity is always on loan, UN-led or UN-approved operations with substantial military requirements take place only when Washington approves or at least acquiesces. Although small battalions of British and French soldiers had positive demonstration effects in toning up UN operations in Sierra Leone in 2000 and the eastern Congo in 2003, US air-lift capacity and military muscle and technology are required for larger and longer-duration deployments. For enforcement (as opposed to traditional peacekeeping), the value added by other militaries is more political than operational.

The stark reality of US military hegemony in the contemporary international system will put a damper on humanitarian intervention unless Europeans invest more in an independent military capacity; and to date neither populations nor parliaments on the continent have demonstrated any willingness to do so. Andrew Moravcsik argues persuasively for a division of labour between American enforcement and European peacekeeping.[46] But Europe's failure to develop a truly independent capacity – indeed, its military capabilities continue to decline vis-à-vis those of the United States – further constrains bullish notions about humanitarian intervention.

Moreover, downsizing of the armed forces over the last 15 years means an insufficient supply of equipment and manpower to meet the demands for humanitarian intervention. There are bottlenecks in the US logistics chain – especially in airlift capacity – that make a rapid international response improbable to a fast-moving, Rwanda-like genocide.[47] With half of the US army tied down in Iraq and a quarter of its reserves overseas, questions are being raised even about the capacity to respond to a serious national security threat let alone "distractions" like Liberia or Haiti.

Mass starvation, rape, and suffering will reappear in a post-September 11 world, and we will know about them rapidly. It is hard to imagine that there will not be calls to do something to halt or attenuate some conscience-shocking cases of mass suffering. In many situations there is simply no viable alternative to military coercion for human protection purposes.

Lawyers as well as political scientists examine the unparalleled power of the US and employ "hegemony".[48] This word should not necessarily have pejorative connotations because one definition means that the strongest member exerts natural leadership within a confederation. Indeed, many Americans and non-Americans have often rued the lack of US leadership within international institutions.

Washington's multilateral record in the twentieth century conveys "mixed messages", as Edward Luck reminds us. The United States sometimes has been the prime mover for new international institutions and norms, but just as often it has kept a distance.[49] This historical pattern is not about to change. Yet, the first George W. Bush administration's "in-your-face" style was distinct, and his second administration is unlikely to be more inhibited or diplomatic, as evidenced by the August recess appointment of conservative firebrand John Bolton as US ambassador in New York.

What next?

In spite of recent normative advances – indeed, in spite of a century and a half of steady development of international humanitarian law – we are unable to rescue all war victims. With the possible exception of genocide, there is no legal and certainly no political obligation to act, but a moral one. Security Council decisions since 1991 often have reflected the humanitarian "impulse", the laudable desire to help fellow human beings threatened by armed conflict.[50] Multilateralism has played a surprisingly large role, by historical standards, in contemporary decisions about the use of military force for human protection purposes.

Invariably, this urge translates into a limited political momentum and a sliding scale of commitments, reflecting the stark international political reality that we rescue some, but not all war-affected populations. When humanitarian and strategic interests coincide, a window of opportunity opens for coalitions of the willing to act on the humanitarian impulse. The last 15 years provides ample evidence of this impulse but not of an "imperative", the preference of those who are dismayed by the unevenness of Security Council decisions and international efforts to succour war victims. The humanitarian imperative would entail an obligation to treat all victims similarly and react to all crises consistently – in effect, to deny the relevance of politics, which proceeds on a case-by-case basis by evaluating interests and options, weighing costs, and mustering necessary resources. The humanitarian impulse is permissive, the humanitarian imperative would be peremptory.

Interestingly for the larger debate in this volume and unlike other issues under discussion, the state-centric nature of old-fashioned multilateralism is adequate for humanitarian intervention. State decisions are really the only ones that count regarding the use of military force. The 2005 World Summit's endorsement of R2P and the first Security Council use of the term in resolution 1674 provide building blocks.

Concerned diplomats, scholars, and activists should try to understand when Washington's instrumental multilateralism, and especially its humanitarian impulse, might kick in. While the US position towards R2P at the summit was unenthusiastic and even hostile, the roller coaster of past humanitarian interventions suggests that US participation often has been essential and helpful. In this regard, Edward Luck notes, "other states and international secretariats will largely determine whether US policy-makers and legislators find international bodies to be places where America's exceptional potential is welcomed and embraced or is resented and restrained".[51]

The prediction that major powers other than the US would not respond at all with military force to a new humanitarian emergency after 11 September proved somewhat too pessimistic. France's leading a EU force into Ituri in summer 2003 halted an upsurge of ethnic violence and perhaps demonstrated to Washington that the EU could act outside of the continent independently of NATO. This possibility was reinforced by Europe's take-over of the Bosnia operation in December 2004 and its collaboration with the UN force in Haiti.

Is the European glass half full? These efforts provide some hope that a EU security identity could more operationally undergird the responsibility to protect. *A Secure Europe in a Better World*[52] lacks the crispness of its American counterpart. While spending on hardware falls considerably short of targets, nonetheless the number of European troops deployed abroad has doubled over the last decade and approaches the so-called Headline Goals.[53] As two Europeans have noted: "This incremental approach may move some way further yet, but it will come up against budgetary ceilings, against the unwillingness of some governments to invest in the weapon and support systems needed, and against the resistance of uninformed national publics".[54] There is little doubt, however, that US air-lift capacity, military muscle and technology are required for larger and longer-duration deployments. With Washington's focus elsewhere, the danger is not too much but rather too little humanitarian intervention.

The ICISS was originally established because of the Security Council's failure to address dire humanitarian crises in Rwanda and Kosovo. In 1994 intervention was too little and too late to halt or even slow the murder of what may have been as many as 800,000 people in the Great Lakes region of Africa. In 1999 the North Atlantic Treaty Organization finessed the council and waged its first war in Kosovo. But many observers saw the 78-day bombing effort as being too much and too early. In any event, the Security Council's inability to authorize the use of deadly force to protect vulnerable populations linked the two cases.

However, the absence of meaningful military might in Rwanda – like the do-nothing approach in Darfur and the Congo – represents a more serious threat to international order and justice than the council's paralysis in Kosovo. The repeated failure to come to the rescue mocks the value of the so-called emerging R2P norm and ultimately may further erode public support for the United Nations in spite of 60th anniversary celebrations.

Not all claims to justice are equally valid, and NATO's was greater than Serbia's or Russia's. At least in the Balkans a regional organization took a unanimous decision to enable human protection. Justified criticism arose about timidity: Washington's domestic politics meant that military action remained at an altitude of 15,000 feet when ground troops would have prevented the initial mass exodus. Nonetheless, past or potential victims undoubtedly would support NATO's decision. An early survey of victims in war zones reports that fully two-thirds of civilians under siege who were interviewed in twelve war-torn societies by the International Committee of the Red Cross want more intervention, and only 10 per cent want none.[55]

It would be soothing, but premature, to agree with John Ikenberry that "the neo-conservative moment is over".[56] Nonetheless, the morass in Iraq and continued nettlesome relations with allies suggest a possible return to his "strategic bargain". As such, the previous record of the Bush administration may be an aberration. While it succeeded in the re-election of George W. Bush, this major experiment in foreign policy involved Washington's moving against enemies, perceived and real, almost entirely on its own. "This approach looks less attractive in the aftermath of the war in Iraq", writes former NATO ambassador Robert Hunter. "The American people seem reluctant to embrace the diplomatic, financial, and psychological costs of a brusque unilateralism. They do not necessarily agree that the United States should do whatever it wants simply because it can, without embedding its action in a framework of international institutions and law and without sharing the burdens with others".[57]

In the past US policy has systematically tied itself to democratic allies and sought common approaches. It is not unthinkable that we could witness a return to that time-tested approach for humanitarian intervention and other issues. As such, giving up small amounts of procedural and operational flexibility was more than compensated by burden-sharing allies and functioning international institutions and regimes that served US national interests.

In fact, the Bush administration provides an anomalous contrast to the image and actions of the Clinton administration's "assertive multilateralism", two words unlikely to be uttered any time soon by another American politician. On the one hand and in spite of its rhetoric, the Clinton administration's missile strikes against Afghanistan and the Sudan in 1998 were launched without recourse to the United Nations. On the other hand and also in spite of its rhetoric, the Bush administration went immediately to the world organization in the aftermath of 11 September. It also persisted with protracted and difficult negotiations in the Security Council with a unanimous decision in resolution 1411 in November 2002. While it proceeded to war in the following March without the council's imprimatur, it has returned at several junctures to seek help with the internationalization of the much contested occupation that is an increasing political liability.

In many ways, resolution 1546 tied Washington's future in Iraq to the interim and transitional governments, both owing much to UN involvement.[58] Indeed, the world organization once again may be left to pick-up the pieces after having drunk from what Brian Urquhart speculates could be "the mother of all poisoned chalices". The UN has much to lose as it risks playing another traditional role "as scapegoat for disasters created by national policies".[59]

The UN still matters for the US. In spite of its unilateralist rhetoric and image, Washington could be tempted by "tactical multilateralism".[60] Washington's military predominance exists side-by-side with a growing presumption in virtually every other country in favour of more inclusive decision-making in multilateral forums. Although the results may be more conditional and constraining than the US might ideally like, such an outcome is preferable to circumventing the process altogether. International legitimacy counts, even for the remaining superpower. Multilateralism is an essential tactic in carrying out successfully the strategy of projecting and protecting American power.

Indeed, post-war (if that is the term) Iraq has demonstrated that recovery, reconstruction and rebuilding are not US strong suits. Former US Assistant Secretary of State James Dobbins and a Rand Corporation evaluation team have argued that the world organization's performance in post-conflict effectiveness is remarkably good in comparison with Washington's – they attribute success to seven of eight UN operations versus only four out of eight for the US.[61] The UN has accumulated substantial experience over several decades, and this comparative advantage makes plausible the Peacebuilding Commission proposed by the World Summit and then established by a Security Council resolution in December 2005.

With specific reference to humanitarian intervention, there was little difference between responses in January 2003 and those four years earlier when US citizens were asked whether they thought that their country and other Western powers have a moral obligation to use military force in Africa, if necessary, to prevent one group of people from committing genocide against another.[62] US public opinion still accepted the idea of a responsibility to protect after 11 September and the military action in Afghanistan and Iraq; and there is no reason to believe that public support for such operations elsewhere has changed significantly since.

Conclusion

There is a general and growing international consensus that multilateral decisions about using force for human protection are preferable to unilateral ones; but the devil, as always, lies in the details. Reliance upon the Security Council can mean too little too late even in the face of genocide, or the necessity to finesse the Council and not be hostage to lowest common denominators. The long-standing fears about humanitarian intervention being a "Trojan horse" to conceal big power agendas, exacerbated by Washington's and London's pursuit of the Iraq war, are beside the point.

The remedy most often at the top of the agenda, changing the composition and procedures of the Security Council, is not a panacea but a distraction. A Charter amendment is a pipe-dream – politically impossible and irrelevant in light of US power. The solution for proponents of humanitarian intervention is two-fold, increased military expenditures in Europe and coaxing the second Bush administration back to the UN. In the longer run, upgrading African regional capacities could help.

Joseph Nye points to the "paradox of American power"[63] – the inability of the world's strongest state to secure some of its major goals alone. Unless Washington is prepared to bend on occasion, governments are unlikely to sign on when their helping hands are necessary for US priorities. Washington's short list for the UN should include not only post-conflict reconstruction in Afghanistan and Iraq but also fighting terrorism (sharing information and the fight against money laundering), confronting infectious diseases, pursuing environmental sustainability, monitoring human rights, providing humanitarian aid, rescheduling debt and fostering trade.

Indeed, these items figured in President Bush's opening address to the 2005 World Summit in September 2005.[64] And, of course, humanitarian intervention is a quintessentially multilateral task. Nonetheless, more than lip service to the interests of other countries must be paid to secure collaboration on such efforts.

Multilateralism will never be an end in itself for the US, but working through the UN can occasionally help achieve Washington's objectives. UN legitimacy and authority are important enough to attract the most powerful state in the system even when it appears hell-bent on minimizing international legal and political constraints on national security decisions. This reality provides some leverage in Washington, without whose participation humanitarian intervention effectively disappears from the international radar screen.

Notes

1. International Commission on Intervention and State Sovereignty (2001) *The Responsibility to Protect*, Ottawa: International Development Research Centre, hereafter *R2P*; and Thomas G. Weiss and Don Hubert (2001) *The Responsibility to Protect: Research, Bibliography, and Background* (Ottawa: International Development Research Centre. An updated bibliography and both volumes are available at http://web.gc.cuny.edu/RalphBuncheInstitute/ICISS/index.htm (1 February 2005).
2. *2005 World Summit Outcome*, UN document A/60/L.1, 15 September 2005, paras. 138–139.
3. Hugo Slim, "Dithering over Darfur? A preliminary review of the international response", (2004) *International Affairs* 80(5): 811–833. See also Cheryl O. Igiri and Princeton N. Lyman (2004) *Giving Meaning to "Never Again": Seeking an Effective Response to the Crisis in Darfur and Beyond*, New York: Council on Foreign Relations, CFR No. 5.
4. Roméo Dallaire (2004) "Looking at Darfur, Seeing Rwanda", *New York Times*, 4 October 2004. See his (2004) *Shake Hands with the Devil: The Failure of Humanity in Rwanda*, Toronto: Brent Beardsley.
5. Kofi A. Annan (1999) *The Question of Intervention: Statements by the Secretary-General*, New York: UN, p. 7.
6. See, for example, Francis M. Deng (1995) "Frontiers of sovereignty", *Leiden Journal of*

International Law 8(2): 249–286; and Kofi A. Annan (2000) *"We the Peoples": The United Nations in the 21st Century*, New York: UN.

7. UN Report of the High-level Panel on Threats, Challenges and Change, *A More Secure World: Our Shared Responsibility*, New York: UN, 2004.
8. Kofi Annan, *In Larger Freedom: Towards Development, Security and Human Rights for All*, UN document A/59/2005, 21 March 2005.
9. See Thomas G. Weiss and Barbara Crossette (2006) "The United Nations: post-summit outlook", *Great Decisions*, New York: Foreign Policy Association, pp. 9–20.
10. "The Lost U.N. Summit Meeting", *New York Times*, 14 September 2005.
11. Kofi A. Annan (2005) "In larger freedom: decision time at the UN", *Foreign Affairs* 84(3): 66.
12. Data compiled by the International Rescue Committee available at http://www.theirc.org/mortality/.
13. David Kennedy (2004) *The Dark Sides of Virtue: Reassessing International Humanitarianism*, Princeton: Princeton University Press.
14. David Rieff (2002) *A Bed for the Night: Humanitarianism in Crisis*, New York: Simon & Schuster, p. 11.
15. See Jane Boulden and Thomas G. Weiss (eds.) (2004) *Terrorism and the UN: Before and After September 11*, Bloomington: Indiana University Press; and Thomas G. Weiss, Margaret E. Crahan and John Goering (eds.) (2004) *Wars on Terrorism and Iraq: Human Rights, Unilateralism, and U.S. Foreign Policy*, London: Routledge.
16. See Thomas G. Weiss (2004) "The responsibility to protect in a unipolar era", *Security Dialogue* 35(2): 135–153.
17. Adam Roberts (1999) "The role of humanitarian issues in international politics in the 1990s", *International Review of the Red Cross* 81(833): 19.
18. Raimo Väyrynen (1996) *The Age of Humanitarian Emergencies*, Research for Action #25, Helsinki: World Institute for Development Economics Research; and Nicholas J. Wheeler (2000) *Saving Strangers: Humanitarian Intervention in International Society*, Oxford: Oxford University Press.
19. For a review of the reviews, see S. Neil MacFarlane, Carolin Thielking and Thomas G. Weiss (2004) "The responsibility to protect: is anyone interested in humanitarian intervention?", *Third World Quarterly* 25(5): 979–994.
20. Anthony Lewis (2003) "The challenge of global justice now", *Dædalus* 132(1): 8.
21. Mohammed Ayoob (2002) "Humanitarian intervention and international society", *The International Journal of Human Rights* 6(1): 84. For the context that drives Ayoob's scepticism, see Simon Chesterman, Michael Ignatieff and Ramesh Thakur (eds.) (2005) *State Failure and the Crisis of Governance: Making States Work*, Tokyo: UNUP.
22. Mario Bettati and Bernard Kouchner (eds.) (1987) *Le Devoir d'ingérence: peut-on les laisser mourir?*, Paris: Denoël and Mario Bettati (1987) *Le Droit d'ingérence: mutation de l'ordre international*, Paris: Odile Jacob.
23. See Gareth Evans (2004) "When is it right to fight?", *Survival* 46(3): 59–81.
24. Ian Johnstone (2003) "Security Council deliberations: the power of the better argument", *European Journal of International Law* 14(3): 437–480.
25. Independent International Commission on Kosovo (2000) *Kosovo Report: Conflict, Interventional Response, Lessons Learned*, Oxford: Oxford University Press, p. 4.
26. Quoted by Kathleen Newland with Erin Patrick and Monette Zard (2003) *No Refuge: The Challenge of Internal Displacement*, New York and Geneva: United Nations, Office for the Coordination of Humanitarian Assistance, p. 37.
27. See, for example, Mary Anderson (1999) *Do No Harm: How Aid Can Support Peace – Or War*, Boulder: Lynne Reinner; and Mark Duffield (2001) *Global Governance and the New Wars*, London: Zed Books; and Peter J. Hoffman and Thomas G. Weiss (2006)

Sword and Salve: Confronting New Wars and Humanitarian Crises, Lanham, MD: Rowman & Littlefield,

28. *National Security Strategy of the United States of America, September 2002*, available at http://usinfo.state.gov/topical/pol/terror/secstrat/htm, 1 March 2004.
29. Adam Roberts (2004) "The United Nations and humanitarian intervention", in Jennifer Welsh (ed.) *Humanitarian Intervention and International Relations*, Oxford: Oxford University Press, p. 90.
30. Lee Feinstein and Anne-Marie Slaughter (2004) "A duty to prevent", *Foreign Affairs* 83(1): 136–150; and Allan Buchanan and Robert O. Keohane (2004) "The preventive use of force: a cosmopolitan institutional proposal", *Ethics and International Affairs* 18(1): 1–22. See also Tom J. Farer with Daniele Archibugi, Chris Brown, Neta C. Crawford, Thomas G. Weiss and Nicholas J. Wheeler (2005) "Roundtable: humanitarian intervention after 9/11", *International Relations* 19(2): 211–250.
31. Richard Falk in *The Nation*, July 2003, p. 12. He was joined by Mary Kaldor, Carl Tham, Samantha Power, Mahmood Mamdani, David Rieff, Eric Rouleau, Zia Mian, Ronald Steel, Stephen Holmes, Ramesh Thakur and Stephen Zunes. Fernando R. Tesón (2005) makes the implausible case that the war could have been justified as humanitarian intervention in "Ending tyranny in Iraq", *Ethics and International Affairs* 19(2): 1–30.
32. Alex J. Bellamy (2005) "Responsibility to protect or Trojan Horse? The crisis in Darfur and humanitarian intervention after Iraq", *Ethics and International Affairs* 19(2): 32–3.
33. See, for example, Gareth Evans, "Uneasy Bedfellows: 'The Responsibility to Protect' and Feinstein-Slaughter's 'Duty to Prevent'", speech at the American Society of International Law Conference, Washington, DC, 1 April 2004, available at http://www.crisisweb.org/home/index.cfm?id=2560&l=1. See also Ramesh Thakur (2004) "Iraq and the responsibility to protect", *Behind the Headlines* 62(1) (October): 1–16.
34. For an earlier discussion, see Thomas G. Weiss (2003) "The illusion of UN Security Council reform", *Washington Quarterly* 26(4): 147–161. For an extended and updated discussion, see Weiss (2005) *Overcoming the Security Council Reform Impasse: The Plausible Versus the Implausible*, Berlin: Friedrich Ebert Stiftung, Occasional Paper No. 14.
35. *HLP Report*, paragraphs 244–260 concern the Security Council.
36. ICISS, *R2P*, p. 49.
37. Ibid., p. 51.
38. Annan, *In Larger Freedom*, para. 170.
39. *2005 World Summit Outcome*, paras. 153–154.
40. Charles Krauthammer (1990) "The unipolar moment", *Foreign Affairs* 70(1) (1990/1991): 23–33; and "The unipolar moment revisited", *National Interest* 70 (Winter 2002/2003): 5–17.
41. David M. Malone (2004) "Conclusion", in David M. Malone (ed.) *The UN Security Council: From Cold War to the 21st Century*, Boulder: Lynne Rienner, p. 637.
42. Chris Patten (2002) "Jaw-Jaw, Not War-War", *Financial Times*, 15 February 2002.
43. See Joseph E. Nye, Jr. (2002) *The Paradox of American Power: Why the World's Only Superpower Can't Go It Alone*, Oxford and New York: Oxford University Press.
44. Center for Defense Information, "U.S. Military Spending, Fiscal Years 1945–2008", available at www.cdi.org/news/mrp/us-military-spending.pdf.
45. James Traub (2003) "The next resolution", *New York Times Magazine*, 13 April 2003, p. 51.
46. Andrew Moravcsik (2003) "Striking a new transatlantic bargain", *Foreign Affairs* 82(4): 74–89.

47. See Alan J. Kuperman (2001) *The Limits of Humanitarian Intervention: Genocide in Rwanda*, Washington, DC: Brookings.
48. See, for example, Michael Byers and Georg Nolte (eds.) (2003) *United States Hegemony and the Foundations of International Law*, Cambridge: Cambridge University Press; and Rosemary Foot, S. Neil MacFarlane, and Michael Mastanduno (eds.) (2003) *US Hegemony and International Organizations*, Oxford: Oxford University Press.
49. Edward C. Luck (1999) *Mixed Messages: American Politics and International Organization, 1919–1999*, Washington, DC: Brookings.
50. Thomas G. Weiss (2004) "The humanitarian impulse", in Malone (ed.) *The United Nations Security Council after the Cold War*, pp. 37–54.
51. Edward C. Luck (2003) "American exceptionalism and international organization: lessons from the 1990s", in Foot, MacFarlane, and Mastanduno (eds.) *US Hegemony and International Organizations*, p. 48.
52. *A Secure Europe in a Better World*, available at http://ue.eu.int/pressData/en/reports/78367.pdf.
53. These goals set targets for the European Union in terms of military and civilian crisis management.
54. See Bastian Giegrich and William Wallace (2004) "Not such a soft power: the external deployment of European forces", *Survival* 46(2): 163–182, quote at p. 179.
55. Greenberg Research (1999) *The People on War Report*, Geneva: ICRC, p. xvi.
56. G. John Ikenberry (2004) "The end of the neo-conservative moment", *Survival* 46(1): 7–22.
57. Robert E. Hunter (2004) "A forward-looking partnership: NATO and the future of alliances", *Foreign Affairs* 83(5): 15.
58. See Tony Dodge (2004) "A sovereign Iraq?", *Survival* 46(3): 39–58.
59. Brian Urquhart (2004) "The United Nations rediscovered?", *World Policy Journal* XXI(2): 1–2.
60. Jane Boulden and Thomas G. Weiss (2004) "Tactical multilateralism: coaxing America back to the UN", *Survival* 46(3): 103–114. See also Mats Berdal (2003) "The UN Security Council: ineffective but indispensable", *Survival* 45(2): 7–30; Shashi Tharoor (2003) "Why America still needs the United Nations", *Foreign Affairs* 82(5): 67–80; and Madeleine K. Albright (2003) "Think again: United Nations", *Foreign Policy* 138: 16–24.
61. James Dobbins, Seth G. Jones, Keith Crane, et al. (2005) *The UN's Role in Nation-Building: From the Congo to Iraq*, New York: Rand Corporation, p. xxxvii.
62. See http://www.americans-world.org/digest/regional_issues/africa/africa4.cfm.
63. Joseph S. Nye, Jr. (2003) "U.S. Power and strategy after Iraq", *Foreign Affairs* 82(4): 60–73.
64. "Statement of H.E. George W. Bush, President of the United States of America, 2005 World Summit, High Level Plenary Meeting, September 14, 2005", available at: www.whitehouse.gov/news/releases/2005/09/20050914.html.

19

Social movements and multilateralism

Jackie Smith

Multilateralism and democracy

Efforts to strengthen multilateral institutions are inseparable from attempts to democratize the global system. Both democracy and multilateralism rely on the displacement of more coercive forms of power by the rule of law and shared norms. Both democracy and multilateralism assume that the participants in the system are interdependent, and therefore they both require protection for the rights of minority groups. Interdependence means that it is in the interest of the strongest to insure that even the weakest members of society have a reason to participate in and support the existing order. Thus, power must be decentralized, allowing for checks and balances to prevent the abuse of power by any group. By building inclusive structures for cooperation that rest upon widely shared goals and values, effective democracies and multilateral systems help curb action by individuals or states acting against the common interests. Such structures can only emerge from routine consultation and dialogues built upon the norms of tolerance, mutual respect, and a commitment to non-violent forms of conflict resolution. Thus, both multilateralism and democracy require mechanisms that foster open debate and encourage respectful dialogue. Finally, decision-makers in both systems must be accountable to their constituents or to their counterparts in other countries, so decision processes must be open and transparent.

Given these connections between multilateralism and democracy, it is appropriate to consider how social movements – important historical agents of democratization during the evolution of the modern national state[1] – have contributed to both the democratization and strengthening of the global multilateral order. A core argument in this chapter is that any attempt to strengthen existing multilateral institutions must deal first and foremost with the problem of unequal power distributions. Today it is common to hear the idea of "networked governance" discussed in policy circles, but most of this discussion leaves out questions about how power operates in these more informal, and presumably cooperative, governance structures. Proponents of multilateralism must take a more active role to empower actors that have been marginalized by the existing and highly unequal global system. An expansion of cooperative alliances between civil society actors and multilateral institutions can help bring necessary pressure on more powerful actors in the system while reinforcing norms and values of multilateralism and collective security.

This chapter reviews the history of relations between social movements and the United Nations system, exploring the challenges confronting this relationship today.[2] Specifically, the chapter investigates how the rise of a "regressive" and unilateralist model of globalization in the wake of the attacks on the US World Trade Centre, the ambivalence of contemporary social movements to multilateral institutions, and anti-democratic responses by governments and UN agencies to these developments threaten both democracy and multilateralism. I propose a number of possible responses to these challenges that could enhance the future prospects for multilateral governance.

Social movements in a global polity

Historical analyses of multilateral institutions reveal important roles of non-state and social movement actors in advancing institution-building and catalysing social change.[3] Specifically, social movement actors have contributed to multilateralism in three distinct ways: by advocating for multilateral solutions to global problems, by cultivating popular constituencies for multilateralism, and by relating national struggles to international norms and institutions.[4]

First, civil society actors have pressed governments to adopt innovative multilateral arrangements as a means of addressing transnational problems. This is evident from the earliest multilateral initiatives, such as the League of Nations and Geneva Conventions, which grew out of efforts by civil society actors to restrain the destructive tendencies of war-making states. More recently, it is evident in the achievement of the Land Mine Ban, the International Criminal Tribunal on the Former Yugoslavia, and the International Criminal Court. Without civil society pressure, most experts agree that these multilateral initiatives would never have happened.

Second, civil society actors help generate grass-roots constituencies for multilateralism. This was a key motivation behind the UN Charter's provision for formal consultative status for civil society groups.[5] Proponents of multilateral initiatives recognized that civil society pressure can help move states towards common, cooperative international policies. In the eyes of international officials, popular mobilization and support helps insure that multilateral organizations and proposals receive a sustained flow of resources and other support from member governments. Also, by cultivating ties to popular organizations, international institutions can enhance their democratic legitimacy. This can act as a powerful lever against unilateralist activities by recalcitrant governments. For instance, during the UN's early decades, international anti-apartheid activism was an important factor in helping generate broad popular and governmental support for multilateral norms and institutions.[6]

Thirdly, social movements help reinforce multilateralism by mobilizing transnational norms and other resources into national level conflicts. This occurs, for instance, when human rights advocates help bring international scrutiny to treaty violations by their governments or when economic justice advocates evaluate governments' progress in achieving the Multilateral Development Goals. It also is seen when activists protesting their governments' multilateral trade and financial agreements appeal to international labour, human rights, and environmental accords. This was powerfully demonstrated when activists at the 2001 talks in Quebec City on the Free Trade Area of the Americas pinned copies of key articles from the Universal Declaration of Human Rights to the chain-link fences that distanced protesters from the official meeting site. Another important example of how citizens groups have reinforced multilateral norms is by their work to establish and to enhance the effectiveness of truth commissions, such as those in South Africa, El Salvador and the former Yugoslavia.[7]

In short, multilateral institutions have been central to long-term power struggles between national governments and their people. They have helped define boundaries between states and citizens while expanding possibilities for resolving the problems that cross territorial boundaries. They have also served as sites for the creation of transnational identities and solidarities. While realists see states as entering international agreements in order to expand their own control and authority, they do not account for what happens when presumably unitary states enter into long-term social commitments within an inter-state system. Once states become part of complex multilateral arrangements, they are embedded in networks of relations that transform their perceptions of their own interests and identities.[8] These networks of relations, over time, have enormous capacities for transforming state behaviour, and they also create openings for less powerful actors to mobilize symbolic and normative resources against actors that are powerful in traditional economic and military terms.

Contested globalizations

Analysts writing in the *Global Civil Society Yearbook*[9] have identified four main categories of responses to globalization: the "supporters" of globalization are pure "free traders" who favour global integration, especially economic ties, without qualification. Supporters might also be called "market fundamentalists", since they generally prefer policies that prioritize market dynamics over public policy making in decisions about the distribution and allocation of resources. "Regressive globalizers" favour global integration only when it is in their own particular interest (or the interests of their supporters), and they are indifferent to any negative consequences for others. They pursue an exclusionary vision of globalization that seeks to maximize globalization's benefits for some (through, for instance, selective trade protectionism), to the exclusion of the interests or preferences of others. "Reformers" or redistributive globalizers approve of global integration that leads to greater equity and fosters the development of international law. Unlike "supporters", they emphasize political rather than economic dimensions of globalization and seek to subordinate global markets to international politics. In the words of some analysts, they promote *internationalization* as opposed to (market) *globalization.*[10]

Finally, "rejectionists" oppose all forms of globalization as infringements on national or local autonomy. They are seen in both right-wing nationalist and religious struggles, such as those fuelled by groups like Al-Qaeda as well among leftists who reject all global agreements on principle without offering a vision of how to address global crises that demand international cooperation. In the aftermath of the World Trade Centre terrorist attacks, the struggle between supporters and opponents of economic globalization has shifted to one between regressive globalizers and rejectionists.[11] Such a struggle can only generate greater polarization and violence, and both are serious threats to democracy.

This contestation among different visions of global integration both fuels and is fuelled by a growing crisis of legitimacy for contemporary democratic institutions. Modern governments derive their authority not from a divine right of kings, but from the fact that they are elected by and accountable to the people they govern. The legitimacy of governments depends upon the broad perception that leaders are accountable and responsive to their constituents, and that leaders who violate public interests can be ejected from office.

Abundant evidence suggests that many governments around the world are finding their legitimacy in crisis. First, people are refusing to participate in the political system and are questioning the fairness and legitimacy of electoral processes.[12] We see consistent and substantial declines in voter participation across the West as membership in traditional political parties declines.[13] At the other extreme we see militant mobilizations by groups like Al-Qaeda, whose claims that the global system is corrupt and fundamentally incapable of addressing people's needs and interests find a more receptive hearing among those who feel marginalized by the global economy. Such groups reject fundamental democratic premises of non-violent conflict resolution and tolerance of diverse views. And the violence often used by governments against militant (as well as non-violent) opponents is seen to provide further evidence of the illegitimacy of the system. When people are asked to participate in a system that is responsive to their inputs, they feel they have a stake in the survival of the system, and they are more willing to accept democratic norms in exchange for security guarantees. But as economic globalization exacerbates economic inequalities and denies more and more people the right to participate in key political decisions as it also restricts access to basic needs such as water, education and health care, more people will support groups advocating violence as a tool of social change. Both declining participation and rising militancy signal a serious crisis for democracy, and they complicate efforts to strengthen multilateral problem-solving.

The crisis of democratic legitimacy not only affects states, but it also affects international institutions. In his address at the opening of the 2003 United Nations General Assembly, Kofi Annan cited the legitimacy dilemma as he urged governments to make progress in efforts to restructure the UN Security Council. His argument highlighted the vast discrepancy between the impacts of Security Council decisions on member states and the scope of input members have on those decisions. Between 1945 and 2003, the United Nations' membership increased by 140 members, while the Security Council gained just 4 additional members. The structure of the Security Council allows the victors of World War II to effectively control all major decisions about how the world will be governed. Annan warned that the 186 member nations who are excluded from this selective club of the "Permanent 5" will be unlikely to continue supporting the global institution if it does not better reflect their interests.[14] Because the UN depends upon the voluntary cooperation of its members, it cannot survive without a belief that all of its members have a stake in the system. At the same time, the global trade regime remains threatened by a stand-off between governments of the global South, who want a fair system of multilateral trading rules, and the leading rich countries – especially the US and European Union – which are refusing to abandon practices that foster their own economic interests at the expense of "free" trade.

There is also an important "democratic deficit" in global institutions in terms of the limited space they provide for popular participation, transparency and accountability. The United Nations and other multilateral institutions depend upon the mostly false assumption that the representatives designated by governments effectively represent the will of the populations within the country. Even if a government is chosen through legitimate democratic elections, it cannot be said that that government has adequately consulted with its constituents and allowed adequate input and public accountability for foreign policy matters. And although global integration means that the significance of global affairs for citizens' daily lives has grown, foreign policy processes are the least subject to democratic controls of all policy domains.[15] Few citizens know the names of their representatives in global institutions or the international policy positions of their governments. And in February of 2003, an estimated 12 million people demonstrating in over 700 cities in 60 countries around the world were unable to derail US plans to invade Iraq. Without systematic efforts to enhance public dialogue about global policy and to increase government–civil society consultations on foreign policy matters, multilateral institutions will continue to be seen as illegitimate authorities, infringing upon the sovereign rights of national and local democratic governments.

The crisis of legitimacy creates openings or vulnerabilities that encourage the kind of surges in popular mobilization (both non-violent and violent) we have seen in recent years. Groups that have been excluded from decision-making are demanding representation in a system that is defined by a growing "democratic deficit".[16] Many see transnational social movements as helping to define a global polity that is more democratic and inclusive than that preferred by either the economic globalizers or by those who mobilize fundamentalist resistance to it.[17]

Against this backdrop of contested globalizations, we see a rapid expansion of public mobilization around global political issues. The numbers of transnational non-governmental associations has grown dramatically since the 1980s especially, and these organizations have developed more dense and diverse networks of transnational ties. Also more and more national and local groups are focusing their energies on global issues and are cultivating ties to international organizations and to transnational non-governmental organizations.[18] The remainder of this chapter examines contemporary transnational social movement mobilization with the aim of evaluating how social movement actors have responded to the existing global political context and, in turn, how governments have reacted to rising citizen activism. In particular, I ask what tendencies in very recent movement mobilizations suggest opportunities for renewed multilateral initiatives and what developments may prevent a constructive role for newly mobilized global movements in promoting multilateral problem-solving and institution-building.

Social movement – United Nations relationships: three generations

Analyses of the trajectory of citizen mobilization in global political arenas have identified important shifts in the character of relations between civil society groups and global institutions since the founding of the United Nations. They point to three distinct periods, or "generations" of UN-civil society relations.[19] In the early post-war years, and even preceding the formation of the UN, we see comparatively little organizing by groups advocating for social change, and the most prominent activities were seen in the area of women's and peace activism.[20] Hill characterizes this "first generation" of relations between non-governmental organizations and the United Nations system as primarily formal and ceremonial rather than political.[21] The high costs of transnational activism and the difficulties of maintaining cross-national communication inhibited organizing and limited participation to relatively privileged individuals.

As new technologies reduced the costs and expanded opportunities for transnational interchanges, we saw a gradual expansion in the numbers of groups that organized across national lines. But until the late 1980s or early 1990s, comparatively few groups directed much attention to maintaining regular ties to international organizations such as the United Nations. At that time, the end of the Cold War and the rapid sequencing of UN global conferences helped focus attention of civil society organizations on the UN and encouraged new organizing initiatives around international agendas.[22] Social change advocates found important allies in global institutions, and they saw opportunities to mobilize legitimacy and support for their causes within global institutional frameworks. Moreover, they could better coordinate international efforts by focusing on global institutional processes, channelling pressures on individual governments and monitoring governments' implementation of agreements made at international conferences.[23]

The conference processes helped expand transnational organizing around a range of issues, and by providing opportunities for activists to interact with their counterparts from around the world, they contributed to shifting understandings of the global system and the problems it faces, and they led to initiatives to expand popular deliberation on global issues.[24] Bringing together activists from a broad range of countries (the period saw a steady expansion in participation by activists from global south countries in particular), global conferences allowed activists to learn from each other and exposed them to alternative interpretations of global issues and priorities.[25] Accounts from observers, participants, and from a survey of NGOs participating in global conferences, document the importance of global conferences as spaces where activists develop their agendas as well as cultivate transnational strategic frames and the collective identities that underlie them.[26] Moreover, conferences helped cultivate a cadre of activists with sustained experience working in international institutional settings, shaping sophisticated understandings and critiques of the UN and its operations.

The protests in Seattle against the World Trade Organization are just the most dramatic marker for the ending of this earlier period of NGO activism in the UN, whose decline began a few years before. By the later part of the 1990s, growing numbers of activists were becoming disillusioned by the United Nations, as neo-liberal policy makers had successfully marginalized that institution while bringing markets and the global financial institutions to the fore.[27] Many activists felt that the negotiating processes embedded in the UN were too slow and narrowly focused to adequately address the urgent crises on which activists worked.[28] The disproportionate influence of the United States also produces suspicion among activists, who are reluctant to support a stronger UN if that organization continues to be dominated by the US.[29] With the rise of more frequent confrontational protests at the site of international negotiations, there seems to be a shift in the character of transnational organizing.

Third generation activists seem to be devoting less energy and attention to the United Nations.[30] In part, this is related to the absence of large-scale UN conferences and the mobilizations that surrounded them.[31] However, another reason for the shift is the sense that the global financial institutions have in many ways eclipsed the UN and undermined its importance. Many found that the treaties on which they focused their energies during the 1980s and 90s were being trumped by international trade agreements that allow trade law to supersede other international agreements.[32] Many in the activist community had also grown wary of a growing corporate influence in the UN, which began during the mid-1990s, and the International Forum on Globalization articulated this fear most directly when it hosted a meeting to parallel the UN Millennium Forum entitled, "Can the UN be Salvaged?". David Korten, a leading activist and intellectual, expressed his own disappointment at this realization:

Those of us who have been studying these issues have long known of the strong alignment of the World Trade Organization (WTO), the World Bank, and the IMF to the corporate agenda. By contrast the United Nations has seemed a more open, democratic and people friendly institution. What I found so shattering was the strong evidence that the differences I have been attributing to the United Nations are largely cosmetic.[33]

Korten further elaborated the significance of this development in a 1997 memo to Razali Ismail, then the UN General Assembly President:

The credibility of the UN is seriously at stake here. Consider the implications for the UN's public image as people wake up to the reality that the scarce UN development funds intended to benefit the poor of the world are in fact being dispensed as corporate welfare to help finance the global corporate take over of the world economy. *It should not be surprising if this eventually pushes the progressive citizen organizations that have heretofore supported the United Nations into a position of organizing against UN funding, as many of them have organized against World Bank and IMF funding.* (Korten 1997, emphasis mine)[34]

While few progressive groups have actively mobilized against the UN, there has been a noticeable decline in attention to the institution within civil society forums such as the World Social Forum.[35] The fact that Secretary-General Kofi Annan has made a practice of attending the World Economic Forum while failing to attend the World Social Forum certainly hasn't helped this situation. In short, one can say that the failures of multilateralism in recent years, coupled with increased corporate influence in the UN have strengthened the appeal of "rejectionists" in global movements, or at least they have contributed to an ambivalence among activists about whether to sustain efforts to support multilateralism. On the positive side, they might have helped fuel new initiatives to seek alternatives to the contemporary inter-state system as the main source of solutions to the world's numerous crises.

Generations of activists and organizations learned and adopted diverse strategies for promoting change, moving from the early days of lobbying by prominent and respected individuals and organizations to more mass-based politics. The second generation took advantage of gains made by their predecessors to permeate the international conference rooms that states jealously defended. The most recent generation has pounded down the doors to demand a seat at – if not to overturn – the table. As governments have moved away from the UN conference process, and as activists have come to question the effectiveness of these mechanisms,[36] some are now looking outside of formal institutional processes to affect change. Little of the expanding energy of third generation activists seems to be devoted to thinking about how to improve multilateralism.

However, by both demanding and creating opportunities for people to participate in global politics, and by mobilizing a wide range of people into dialogue about the nature and shape of globalization, third generation activism is deepening the foundations for more participatory and accountable forms of global governance. And today's generation of activists – equipped with both dense organizational ties and advanced communications technologies – clearly have capacities for global-level collective action that go well beyond those of their predecessors. A key question, then, is how to encourage activism within this vibrant and deepening "third generation" wave of social movement activism that advocates internationalization or "reformist" and redistributive forms of globalization against the destructive "regressive" and "rejectionist" versions being advocated by actually or potentially powerful forces.

Before attempting to address this question, I first explore how governments have responded to changes in transnational mobilizing, since this response plays an important role in determining how social movements will engage in the process of helping to define and strengthen multilateral governance.

Anti-democratic backlash: government and UN responses to transnational challenges

With the widely acknowledged success of transnational activism at gaining access to international institutions and at cultivating broad alliances for change came new efforts by economic and political authorities to limit their impacts. Tarrow documents increasing violence in the policing of international protest in established Western democracies.[37] Governments – including, importantly, the United States – have sought to curb citizen access to international forums,[38] while corporate actors have mobilized "counter-movements"[39] by creating their own "NGOs" to lobby at international meetings and to otherwise influence government and public perceptions of the conflicts.[40]

At the same time as the world's governments were cooperating to restrict public protest at the meetings of global financial elites, they were also closing doors for groups seeking to lobby at UN meetings – even those groups whose aims mirror those in the UN Charter. For instance, in July 2001 (prior to 11 September and the launch of the US-led "war on terror"), John R. Bolton, US Under Secretary for Arms Control and International Security, addressed the Plenary Session of the UN Conference on the Illicit Trade in Small Arms and Light Weapons for the US saying:

> We do not support the promotion of international advocacy activity by international or non-governmental organizations, particularly when those political or policy views advocated are not consistent with the views of all member states. What individual governments do in this regard is for them to decide, but we do not regard the international governmental support of particular political viewpoints to be consistent with democratic principles. Accordingly, the provisions of the draft Program that contemplate such activity should be modified or eliminated.[41]

The US and other governments are at least partly encouraged to criticize civil society groups' engagement in the UN by right-wing and corporate actors who see their interests being threatened by a more participatory and democratic global order.[42] One increasingly hears critics of civil society seeking to delegitimize it by pointing to its limited representativeness and incomplete accountability.[43] Even those who may be sympathetic with the ideals of democracy and the values of global civil society have adopted fairly uncritically some of this rhetoric. At the same time, these critics ignore the fact that most governments and all corporations are equally if not more guilty of these same limitations. Moreover, while governments and corporations deny or ignore their own unrepresentativeness and lack of transparency, civil society groups have actively reflected upon and sought to remedy these deficiencies.[44] At the same time, while civil society groups don't generally claim to be fully democratic in their internal operations or to "represent" broad groups of people, most demand and support inclusive and democratic relations among groups in civil society. States, on the other hand, derive their very authority from their claims to representativeness, and their continued legitimacy will depend upon the widespread acceptance of this claim. By denying the rights of participation to civil society groups, they can undermine their own democratic claims.

Another way governments have sought to limit civil society access is by attempting to shift major policy decisions outside the UN and into the more exclusive global financial arena.[45] The neo-liberal agenda of the United States always left little room for a strong United Nations. The US worked to reduce UN influence principally under the guise of an effort to increase the UN's efficiency and to reduce costs. But an analysis of the changes that were made at the behest of the United States suggests other motives. For instance, in 1992 the UN Centre on Transnational Corporations, which was set up to help developing countries monitor and negotiate with transnational corporations and to develop a code of corporate conduct, was transformed into a smaller agency that matches corporate interests with countries seeking foreign investment.[46] The post of Director-General for International Economic Cooperation and Development was abolished, and the UN Conference on Trade and Development (UNCTAD) was severely constrained by the (Northern-dominated) decision at UNCTAD VIII (1992) to refuse it jurisdiction over matters being negotiated under the GATT (now the WTO).[47]

Global financial negotiations effectively take place outside the United Nations framework, and no serious efforts were made to reconcile these negotiations with existing international law or practice.[48] Indeed, the major goal of trade negotiations has been to eliminate laws that might restrict the flow of goods and services across borders, and this aim is better served when the number of players active in decision-making is limited. The well-established precedent of involving NGOs (other than business interest groups, who are often represented on government delegations) as observers at international meetings has been ignored or severely restricted in trade and financial forums, especially the IMF.[49] Charnovitz's comprehensive review of NGO relations with intergovernmental organizations reveals a consistent tendency for NGOs to be involved in multilateral relief work and in efforts to promote popular support for international agencies, while they were entirely absent from early multilateral meetings on financial matters.[50] The WTO now allows limited access for NGOs, but a substantial number of those granted formal recognition are business interest organizations, and the accreditation process remains much more restricted than in the UN.[51]

The anti-democratic backlash reflected in increasing government repression of popular protest and in the exclusion of civil society groups from global political arenas as well as in the marginalization of the UN from global economic governance has been reinforced by efforts within the UN itself to enhance its ties to business interests.[52] While the motivations for strengthening ties between the UN and the corporate sector are understandable, greater scrutiny must be devoted to this evolving relationship if we are to prevent it from undermining multilateralism. A key site where UN relations to the private sector are being defined is in the recent Global Compact initiative, launched by the UN Secretary-General in 1999.

The global compact initiative

The "Global Compact" (GC) was designed largely to cultivate "partnerships" between the UN and the private sector, and it responds to the increasingly obvious point that transnational corporations have gained immense powers that rival those of most UN member states. No effort at global governance can be effective if it does not account for the power and influence of TNCs. The GC is, in principle, an effort to cultivate what some analysts are referring to as "networked governance", and it has been cast as a conscious response to the emergence of new confrontational challenges to the global economy.[53] Recognizing the limitations of the UN to actually influence the behaviour of member states or other actors such as transnational corporations, analysts and officials are putting forth notions that governance should involve *cooperative* arrangements among diverse "stakeholders" who play more active roles in shaping and enacting policies. The GC network aims to sensitize corporate leaders to the values and norms of the UN system by encouraging them to sign on to its nine core principles. One of the programme's architects, John Ruggie, calls the system a "learning network approach".[54] Corporate "partners" are asked to submit case studies of how they've attempted to implement GC principles, and "the hope and expectation is that good practices will help to drive out bad ones through the power of dialogue, transparency, advocacy and competition."[55] Because its aim is to promote learning, no attempt is made to insure that corporations comply with even the minimal standards of human rights, environmental, or labour practices as defined by the UN guidelines governing its ties to business interests.[56]

The Global Compact's "learning network" aims to engage participants in information sharing, dialogue, and mutual learning so that parties can appreciate the needs and perspectives of other "stakeholders" while they work to come up with mutually acceptable policy responses. In the view of the GC architects, it constitutes "a mixed institutional order of checks and balances in which markets, community members, states and associations share power".[57] In this system of "checks and balances", civil society groups would be expected to "substitute" for governments to help enforce the "self regulation" by monitoring corporate practices. Corporations are attracted to become "partners" in the GC by the possibility of enhancing their reputations and social legitimacy, and in this regard the GC offers an added bonus of efficiency: It offers "one stop-shopping in the three critical areas of greatest external pressure: human rights, environment and labor standards, thereby reducing their transaction costs".[58]

A key failure in the GC is not its notion of how networks of actors can produce learning and improve corporate practices and governance. Indeed, if it actually did facilitate networks where corporate actors, states, and civil society groups would actually "*share* power", it could be effective. But the crucial flaw in the initiative is its failure to ask how the networks it promotes can achieve a system of "checks and balances" *without confronting fundamental inequities of power*. For instance, the failure of the GC to incorporate any mechanism for monitoring corporate compliance with its principles means that the "learning network's" system of "checks and balances" can never be balanced. As GC proponents rightly point out, "[o]f course, the Global Compact will never be capable of preventing companies from issuing misleading statements". But they nevertheless "encourage the public to consult official Global Compact literature and to perform its own due diligence when possible".[59] In practice, however, the GC itself – relatively powerless in comparison to transnational corporate actors – has been less than diligent in promoting information sharing and dialogue among GC partners, and this has led many of the (already very few) civil society groups that initially supported the effort to question their continued participation.[60] The GC has also failed to advance public capacities for critical reflection on corporate claims or to enhance the capacities of civil society groups to otherwise counterbalance the enormous influence of corporations. In fact, reporting on corporate performance regarding GC principles has become more limited since the launch of the initiative, while information has become less public, and dialogues among GC partners less frequent and substantive.[61] Such criticism is heard increasingly from within the UN itself.[62]

Although civil society groups are asked to help govern this system, they are given no resources or support in doing so. In fact, the GC itself has both actively and passively served to weaken civil society groups by helping to strengthen the hand of corporate actors while – in order to sustain corporations' interests in partnership – actively working to constrain and to delegitimize the many groups that are critical of its corporate "partners".[63] How, for instance, can the public make sense of the discrepancies between claims of NGOs and those of corporate UN "Partners" when the GC refuses to implement procedures for monitoring compliance with GC norms and refuses to evaluate competing claims and evidence? Beyond more passive means of discrediting corporate critics by failing to comment on the validity of their claims or to sanction corporate partners, the GC has engaged in more active attempts to undermine the monitoring capacities of civil society. For instance, Bendell points out that in 2003 the GC and the UN Environment Programme lent their names to a highly critical corporate-funded study of NGO accountability conducted by a British consulting firm.[64] The misleading and patently biased report ignored the wealth of impartial, scholarly analyses being done on this topic within the UN and in civil society itself, and it served to discredit and delegitimize the very civil society actors that are needed to counterbalance the overwhelming influence of corporate actors in the GC.

In their defence of the GC initiative, John Ruggie and Georg Kell have offered dismissive caricatures of the GC's civil society critics as "small, radical, and single-issue" NGOs that are bent on confrontation rather than cooperation.[65] They continue to stress the importance of civil society in the "learning network" even as they ignore questions about why the already tiny number of NGO "partners" in the GC is expressing strong reservations about the GC arrangement.[66] Although civil society participation is necessary for this "learning network" to work, its participation is constrained by an unspoken requirement that it doesn't attempt to disrupt existing power arrangements. In fact, the GC reinforces existing power inequities.[67]

Given the extremes of global inequality, the checked-and-balanced network learning process envisioned by Ruggie and his collaborators is doomed to failure unless it is accompanied by efforts to reorganize power relations within the network. For starters, the idea that businesses should be "partners" with the UN suggests an inappropriate parity of status not only between corporations and the UN but also between corporations and governments. Moreover, why should civil society groups – many of which pursue public interest goals that coincide with the aims of the UN charter – have a far more strict set of criteria for becoming GC "partners" than do corporations, which are explicitly devoted to the pursuit of private profit?[68] When the GC gives them equal status and standing with regard to all other social actors, what incentive do corporate actors have to learn better behaviour?[69]

Aside from this rather glaring flaw, the Global Compact actually *weakens* multilateralism in more subtle ways. First, it undermines existing UN regulations that guide its relationships with external actors, including corporations. It was noted earlier that the idea of helping corporations learn good behaviour has led GC architects to abandon attempts to require that GC partners adhere to some minimal standards of behaviour that conform to principles in the UN Charter. But this very practice violates the UN Secretariat's "Guidelines on Cooperation between the United Nations and the Business Community", which state that "business entities that are complicit in human rights abuses, tolerate forced or compulsory labour or the use of child labour, are involved in the sale or manufacture of anti-personnel mines or their components, or that otherwise do not meet relevant obligations or responsibilities by the United Nations, are not eligible for partnership".[70]

Second, the major attraction of the GC to corporations is its ability to help them promote socially responsible images. This attraction is most relevant to companies with poor business practices, and therefore it also threatens to compromise the UN neutrality norm that "the organisation should not work to benefit the particular interests of any one Nation State, its enterprises or citizens, to the detriment of others".[71] The UN's uncritical engagement with the private sector threatens to come at a cost to both civil society actors and to those private companies that don't need the "reputational benefits" of the GC, namely, those that engage in socially responsible business practices. These voices are further marginalized by the GC. Neutrality is an essential component of the UN's legitimacy in the world community, and practices that contribute to the perception that the organization is partial to particular interests constitute a major threat to multilateralism.[72]

Third, and perhaps most importantly, the GC undermines other efforts within the UN to advance a more rigorous model of global corporate governance either through the proposed "Norms on the responsibilities of transnational corporations and other business enterprises with regard to human rights" or through other existing arrangements such as the International Labour Organization.[73] It does so by drawing attention away from the need for more regulation of corporate activity and by serving as an illustration often-cited by corporate actors that self-regulation works and that mechanisms beyond those seeking voluntary compliance with international norms are unnecessary. In other words, it allows policy makers and corporate actors to maintain the illusion that bad corporate practices are simply the result of a few "bad apples", rather than the inevitable outcomes of an unregulated global capitalist system. Because the GC involves no oversight mechanism, it can provide no credible evidence that voluntary compliance actually works, but it has, nevertheless, slowed down efforts to promote more systemic change. Although GC proponents argue that the initiative is designed to complement and promote stronger regulatory mechanisms, they haven't done much to either support specific initiatives like the draft Norms for business or to encourage their "partners" to accept these.

In sum, the US reaction to the terrorist attacks of 11 September only quickened the pace of what was already a systematic effort to curb citizen involvement in global affairs. For several years prior to 2001, governments used both overt repression against mass protest as well as more subtle strategies to undermine the role of citizens' groups in global policy processes. In fact, counter-terrorism laws were already being used in Washington DC during the World Bank/IMF meeting in the spring of 2000, in Quebec City at the Summit of the Americas in 2001, and in other sites of global economic protests to harass and otherwise obstruct the expression of non-violent public opposition to economic globalization.[74] And more overt forms of repression were accompanied by systematic efforts to both marginalize the UN from global economic governance and to marginalize civil society groups within the UN system. Thus, we should see these more recent repressive actions as part of a long-standing effort to maintain the privileges and power of the existing global political and economic elite (e.g. to defend "regressive" visions of globalization) rather than as a specific response to the threats raised by the 2001 attacks.

However, as my earlier discussion showed, the history of decisions to include civil society groups at international meetings demonstrates the important benefits – if not the necessity – of involving the public in multilateral initiatives. Without transparency and openness to public engagement, multilateral institutions won't have popular support or acceptance, and they will lack the resources and skills to carry out their missions. If the UN and other global institutions roll back earlier provisions for NGO access and participation, they risk undermining the democratic claims of legitimacy upon which most of their member governments depend. They also threaten public support for multilateral institutions and governance at a time when such institutions are urgently needed.

Strategies for enhancing multilateralism

United Nations officials and analysts of global governance increasingly refer to the need for network-oriented approaches to global governance. Such approaches require that the UN cultivate more ties to civil society and private business actors while encouraging greater interaction between national governments and their citizens. Citizens' groups and businesses are being asked to play a more self-conscious role in governance, while the UN is seen as playing more of a facilitating role than an operational one.[75] The limited resources of the UN system and the demands of contemporary governance require decentralized structures involving actors with a wide array of competencies and strengths. In contrast to more formal and hierarchical organizing forms, networks are seen as nimble and responsive to uncertain and rapidly changing circumstances.

However, most discussion of networks as a tool for global governance ignores or downplays questions of how power differentials can be managed within these informal and decentralized settings. A notable exception is the work of Korzeniewicz and Smith, who develop the idea of "polycentric development coalitions" – cooperative relationships between governmental, intergovernmental, and civil society actors with the aim of promoting more democratic, equitable, and sustainable development.[76] Central to the idea of polycentric development coalitions is that both civil society actors and international agencies have common interests in fostering a more democratic (and multilateral) order. Thus, both sets of actors should work to enhance their shared leverage within multi-actor networks that include states that may or may not fully support a democratic/multilateral agenda and corporations that most likely will oppose such an agenda.

Proponents of networked governance call on the UN to take the lead by helping to create spaces that nurture global policy networks of government and international officials, civil society, and private sector actors. *If this form of governance is to work, however, it must actively confront the power inequities that prevent effective action on the underlying causes of conflict.* The history of the modern world system is one of increasing inequality. In fact the inequities between the world's richest and poorest have never decreased.[77] It is painfully clear that most of the world's major conflicts result from the fact that many people have been excluded from full participation in the world's economic and political life. Therefore, any attempts to cultivate networks to improve multilateral governance will fail unless they actively expand inclusion in the system and level the playing field on which *all* network actors operate. This requires a stronger management role for governments and international agencies relative to other network players.

The history of transnational social movements in the evolution of multilateral institutions shows that social movements will be central to the development of effective multilateral governance in the twenty-first century, and the articulation of this policy network model of governance explicitly acknowledges the centrality of civil society to multilateral governance. But the widening inequities of the global system, coupled with the expanded political power of transnational corporations, are serving to heighten polarization and obstruct efforts to envision and cultivate support for new and effective strategies for multilateral governance.

Social movements have always been forces for the democratization of our political institutions, and they have been a force for the democratization of the global polity. However, they face important barriers from governments with unprecedented military and surveillance capacities, a concentrated and commercialized global media, a transnational capitalist class with unprecedented access to wealth and coercive capabilities, and an ideological struggle framed in terms of a "war on terror". This repression only fuels support for those rejecting democratic or multilateral responses to the problems of globalization, and it undermines those activists seeking constructive and inclusive solutions to global problems. Yet the democratic deficit in global institutions, exacerbated by a parallel hollowing-out of traditional state authority, challenges the very foundations of contemporary political institutions. This crisis also creates opportunities for those seeking to promote non violent forms of political change. Below I summarize three core strategies that this analysis suggests might enhance the prospects for the development of more effective and democratic multilateral governance.

First, leaders in movements and international institutions should support the development of global polycentric development coalitions (PDCs). These should be conscious alliances between international agencies and civil society actors committed to core democratic and multilateralist norms, working together to enhance their leverage in networks that engage both states and private financial actors in the tasks of global governance. Activities of these "PDCs" should serve to reduce inequalities between civil society actors, states and the private sector and to promote democratic participation and accountability in governance.

Second, PDCs should focus in the near-term on efforts to democratize formal global institutions. An overwhelming majority of UN member states favours a system that better reflects the interests of all its members. Social movements would also benefit from a UN system that is more representative of all the world's governments. And finally, these reforms would enhance the commitment to the UN System by countries and civil societies that have been largely disenfranchised from global policy making. These changes require focused efforts to bring together supportive governments and international officials and movement actors around a strategy for promoting UN and especially Security Council reforms, including, for instance, those recommended by the recent UN High-Level Panel Report on Threats, Challenges and Change. More concerted effort by UN officials to support and encourage activism aimed at subordinating global financial institutions to more democratic and multilateralist UN processes could help strengthen new alliances and support more self-consciously multilateralist activism. An important benefit of enhancing the representativeness of the UN is that even small reforms might serve to strengthen the position of "reformist" globalizers against regressive and rejectionist globalizers. This could be an important first step in strengthening both democracy and multilateralism worldwide.

A third conclusion is that proponents of multilateralism and democracy must be more proactive in their efforts to empower actors who have been marginalized by existing political and economic structures. They must struggle to reign in the power of corporations in the global polity so that states and civil society actors can exert more control over decisions that affect their economic lives as well as their political choices. Serious efforts are also needed to enhance democratic accountability and participation *within* states. The recent report of the Panel of Eminent Persons on UN–Civil Society Relations has some good recommendations around which policy makers and activists can mobilize, such as the call for a new "Office of Constituency Engagement and Partnerships", with its own Under-Secretary-General, a Civil Society Unit, and an Elected Representatives Liaison Unit. Nothing will come of these suggestions without popular pressure at the national and international levels. Steps to incorporate local and national elected officials into international governance are vital, as are conscious efforts to strengthen the capacities and opportunities for marginalized groups to participate. Once policy leaders and activists mobilize to enfranchise their own parliamentarians into the UN system, they will have helped generate the kinds of local–global links that are essential for more effective multilateral governance.

Finally, a more conscious commitment to the promotion of democracy by PDCs and other actors would strengthen possibilities for multilateralism. For many civil society groups, advocating for more democratic institutions is seen as secondary to their work on particular issues. But more coordinated and self-conscious efforts by social movement groups to promote global democracy would enhance the effectiveness of a wide variety of social change campaigns. Similarly, a more conscious commitment among UN officials to encourage more democratic, transparent, and equitable practices in global institutions would help win allies and reduce tensions within the global justice movement between those promoting the reform of existing institutions and those seeking their abolition. A global pro-democracy movement would involve intensive discussion and consideration of the underlying values and principles of democracy, and it would encourage more internally democratic forms of organizing within civil society. This would contribute to the aim of levelling the playing field in the global polity so that citizens of the poorest countries enjoy similar levels of access and influence in the global polity as those of the richest ones. A level playing field is one that both empowers people while seriously restricting the rights, access, and influence of private capital. No serious steps at reducing global poverty and inequality will be possible without ensuring that citizens' voices – and indeed that states themselves – are not eclipsed by corporate political influence.

In conclusion, social movements are key to the survival and effectiveness of multilateral institutions. Third generation global activism has helped deepen citizens' attention to global problems while cultivating transnational solidarities and commitments to helping address pressing global needs. More concerted efforts to encourage grass-roots involvement in global politics, rather than attempts to repress it, will help bolster the waning legitimacy of multilateral institutions. Multilateralists can help stem the growing polarization between those advocating for reforms of multilateral institutions and those unilateralists and fundamentalists who reject existing structures entirely. But this can only happen if efforts are made to advance proposals that will truly enhance democracy and curb the disproportionate influence of capital in global institutions.

The author is grateful to Charles Chatfield, Judge Richard J. Goldstone, John Markoff, and to the volume editors for their thoughtful comments on earlier drafts of this chapter.

Notes

1. Markoff, John (1996) *Waves of Democracy: Social Movements and Political Change*, Thousand Oaks: Pine Forge Press; Tilly, Charles (1984) "Social movements and national politics", pp. 297–317 in *Statemaking and Social Movements: Essays in History and Theory*, edited by C. Bright and S. Harding. Ann Arbor: University of Michigan Press.
2. Because they are most likely to be implicated in the global changes of interest to this project, I direct my focus here on those groups that are explicitly organized to advocate for social or political change. Moreover, I consider those groups primarily engaged in non-violent and inclusive forms of mobilization rather than social movements mobilizing around more particularistic and exclusionary aims. Thus, I am not speaking about the many elements of civil society such as service-providing NGOs and recreational or interest-based organizations that may maintain some ties to the UN system but that don't seek to alter existing social, economic, or political relations.
3. See, for example, Chatfield, Charles (1997) "Intergovernmental and nongovernmental associations to 1945", in J. Smith, C. Chatfield and R. Pagnucco (eds.) *Transnational Social Movements and World Politics: Solidarity Beyond the State*, Syracuse, NY: Syracuse University Press, pp. 19–41. Finnemore, Martha (1996) *National Interests in International Society*, Ithaca, NY: Cornell University Press; Sidney Tarrow (2005) *The New Transnational Activism*, Cambridge, Cambridge University Press.
4. Smith, Jackie, Ron Pagnucco and Charles Chatfield (1997) "Transnational social movements and global politics: a theoretical framework", in J. Smith, C. Chatfield and R. Pagnucco (eds.) *Transnational Social Movements and Global Politics: Solidarity Beyond the State*, Syracuse NY: Syracuse University Press, pp. 59–80.
5. Kriesberg, Louis (1997) "Social movements and global transformation", in J. Smith, C. Chatfield and R. Pagnucco (eds.) *Transnational Social Movements and World Politics: Solidarity Beyond the State*, Syracuse, NY: Syracuse University Press, pp. 3–18; Robins, Dorothy B. (1971) *Experiment in Democracy: The Story of U.S. Citizen Organization in Forging the Charter of the United Nations*, New York: Parkside Press.
6. Klotz, Audie (1995) *Norms and International Relations: The Struggle Against Apartheid*, Ithaca: Cornell University Press; Newell Stultz (1991) "Evolution of the United Nations anti-apartheid regime", *Human Rights Quarterly* 13(1) (February): 1–23; Seidman, Gay W. (2000) "Adjusting the lens: what do globalizations, transnationalism, and the anti-apartheid movement mean for social movement theory?", in J.A. Guidry, M.D. Kennedy and M.N. Zald (eds.) *Globalizations and Social Movements: Culture, Power, and the Transnational Public Sphere*, Ann Arbor: University of Michigan Press, pp. 339–358.
7. See, for example, Tristan Anne Borer (ed.) (2006) *Telling the Truths: Truth-telling and Peace Building*, Notre Dame IN: University of Notre Dame Press.
8. Boli, John and George Thomas (1997) "World culture in the world polity", *American Sociological Review* 62: 171–190; Boli, John and George M. Thomas (eds.) (1999) *Constructing World Culture: International Nongovernmental Organizations Since 1875*, Stanford: Stanford University Press; Finnemore, Martha (1996) "Sociology's institutionalism", *International Organization* 50: 325–47; Meyer, John W., John Boli, George M.

Thomas and Francisco O. Ramirez (1997) "World society and the nation-state", *American Journal of Sociology* 103: 144–181.

9. See, for example, Kaldor, Mary (2003) "Global civil society in an era of regressive globalisation", in H. Anheier, M. Kaldor and M. Glasius (eds.) *Global Civil Society Yearbook, 2003*, London: Sage, pp. 3–33.
10. This distinction between globalization and internationalization is discussed in greater detail in Daly, Herman (2002) "Globalization versus internationalization, and four economic arguments for why internationalization is a better model for world community", www.bsos.umd.edu/socy/conference/newpapers/daly.rtf (accessed 5 April 2004). Sidney Tarrow offers a similar distinction in (2005) *The New Transnational Activism.*
11. Glasius, Marlies and Mary Kaldor (2002) "The state of global civil society: before and after September 11", in M. Glasius, M. Kaldor and H. Anheier (eds.) *Global Civil Society Yearbook, 2002*, Oxford: Oxford University Press, pp. 3–34; see also, Barber, Benjamin (1995) *Jihad vs. McWorld*, New York: Random House.
12. Norris, Pippa (ed.) (1999) *Critical Citizens: Global Support for Democratic Governance*, New York: Oxford University Press; Pippa Norris (2002) *Democratic Phoenix: Reinventing Political Activism*, New York: Cambridge University Press; Hertz, Noreena (2001) *The Silent Takeover: Global Capitalism and the Death of Democracy*, New York: Free Press.
13. Norris, *Critical Citizens*; Verba, Sidney, Kay Schlozman and Henry Brady (1995) *Voice and Equality: Civic Volunteerism in American Politics*, Cambridge: Harvard University Press. This trend is a long-term one, and even the unusually high rates of voter turnout in the recent (and unusual) US election didn't exceed 60 per cent of eligible voters – keeping it below 1968 levels (Committee for the Study of the American Electorate, 4 November 2004, at: http://www.fairvote.org/reports/CSAE2004electionreport.pdf (accessed 19 January 2005)).
14. Roy, Ranjan (2003) "Annan urges world leaders to push for expanding Security Council to reflect new realities", *Associated Press*, 23 September, Lexis-Nexis.
15. Pagnucco, Ron and Jackie Smith (1993) "The peace movement and the formulation of U.S. foreign policy", *Peace and Change* 18: 157–181; United Nations (2004) "We the peoples: civil society, the United Nations and global governance: report of the Panel of Eminent Persons on United Nations–Civil Society Relations", United Nations Secretary-General, New York.
16. Markoff, John (2004) "Who will construct the global order?", in B. Williamson (ed.) *Transnational Democracy*, London: Ashgate.
17. See Benjamin Barber (1995) *Jihad vs. McWorld*, New York: Random House; Florini, Ann (2003) *The Coming Democracy: New Rules for Running a New World*, Washington: Island Press.
18. Smith, Jackie (2004) "Exploring connections between global integration and political mobilization", in *Journal of World Systems Research* 10(1): 255–285 (http://jwsr.ucr.edu); Smith, Jackie (2005) "Transnational social movement organizations", in G. Davis, D. McAdam, W.R. Scott and M. Zald (eds.) *Social Movements and Organizational Theory*, New York: Cambridge University Press; Anheier, Helmut, Marlies Glasius and Mary Kaldor (eds.) (2001) *Global Civil Society Yearbook*, London: London School of Economics.
19. Bennett, W. Lance (2005) "Social movements beyond borders: understanding two eras of transnational activism", in D. della Porta and S. Tarrow (eds.) *Transnational Protest and Global Activism*, Lanham, MD: Rowman & Littlefield, pp. 203–226.
20. See, for example, Chatfield, "Intergovernmental and nongovernmental organizations to 1945"; "National insecurities"; Rupp, Leila J. (1997) *Worlds of Women: The Making of an International Women's Movement*, Princeton NJ: Princeton University Press; Wittner,

Lawrence (1997) *Resisting the Bomb: A History of the World Nuclear Disarmament Movement, 1954–1970*, vol. 2, Stanford, CA: Stanford University Press; Charnovitz, Steve (1997) "Two centuries of participation: NGOs and international governance", *Michigan Journal of International Law* 18: 183–286.

21. Hill, Tony (2004) "Three generations of UN–civil society relations: a quick sketch", *Civil Society Observer*, http://www.un-ngls.org/Three%20Generations%20of%20UN-Civil%20Society%20Relations-%20A%20Quick%20Sketch.doc (accessed 23 September 2004). Even at this time many groups were working to establish formal access to the institution by civil society groups and to expand the range of issues on which the world body would act, establishing important foundations for later activism in the UN. Significantly, the Cold War made multilateral political spheres less effective and more challenging as a target for activism. See, for example, Kriesberg, Louis (1997) "Social movements and global transformation", in J. Smith, C. Chatfield, and R. Pagnucco (eds.) *Transnational Social Movements and World Politics: Solidarity Beyond the State*, Syracuse, NY: Syracuse University Press, pp. 3–18; Tolley, Howard (1987) *The UN Commission on Human Rights*, Boulder, CO: Westview.
22. The 1972 World Conference on the Human Environment in Stockholm was attended by 134 officially registered non-governmental organizations. In contrast, more than 8,000 groups registered to attend the 1992 UN Conference on Environment and Development in Rio. Anand, Anita (1999) "Global meeting place: United Nations' world conferences and civil society", in J.W. Foster and A. Anand (eds.) *Whose World is it Anyway? Civil Society, the United Nations and the Multilateral Future*, Ottawa: United Nations Association in Canada, pp. 65–108; Willetts, Peter (1996) "From Stockholm to Rio and beyond: the impact of the environmental movement on the United Nations' consultative arrangements for NGOs", *Review of International Studies* 22: 57–80.
23. See, for example, Friedman, Elisabeth Jay, Ann Marie Clark and Kathryn Hochstetler (2005) *The Sovereign Limits of Global Civil Society*, New York: State University of New York Press; Keck, Margaret and Kathryn Sikkink (1998) *Activists Beyond Borders*, Ithaca: Cornell University Press; Smith, *et al.* (1997) *Transnational Social Movements and Global Politics*.
24. See, for example, Falk, Richard and Andrew Strauss (2001) "Toward global parliament", *Foreign Affairs*: 212–220.
25. Krut, Riva (1997) "Globalization and civil society: NGO Influence on international decision making", United Nations Research Institute for Social Development, Geneva; Snyder, Anna (2003) *Setting the Agenda for Global Peace: Conflict and Consensus Building*, Burlington, VT: Ashgate.
26. Benchmark Environmental Consulting (1996) "Democratic Global Civil Governance Report of the 1995 Benchmark Survey of NGOs", Oslo: Royal Ministry of Foreign Affairs; Riles, Annelise (2001) *The Network Inside Out*, Ann Arbor: University of Michigan Press; Foster, John and Anita Anand (eds.) (1999) *Whose World Is It Anyway? Civil Society, the United Nations, and the Multilateral Future*, Ottawa: United Nations Association of Canada.
27. Bello, Walden (1999) *Dark Victory: The United States and Global Poverty*, London: Pluto Press.
28. Krut (1997) "Globalization and civil society".
29. Smith, Jackie (2002) "Bridging global divides? Strategic framing and solidarity in transnational social movement organizations", *International Sociology* 17: 505–528; Bennis, Phyllis (1997) *Calling the Shots: How Washington Dominates Today's UN*, New York: Olive Branch Press.
30. See, for example, Clark, Ann Marie, Elisabeth J. Friedman and Kathryn Hochstetler (1998) "The sovereign limits of global civil society: a comparison of NGO participation

in UN World Conferences on the Environment, Human Rights, and Women", *World Politics* 51: 1–35; Lance Bennett "Social movements beyond borders".
31. Indeed a key recommendation of the recent Report on UN Civil Society Relations is for a return to the use of global conferences.
32. They do so in practice if not in actual law, since the global trade bodies have far stronger enforcement mechanisms than do other international organizations, which are often non-binding agreements or legally binding treaties without resources to monitor or sanction non-compliance. The potential costs of trade sanctions creates a chilling effect, and few countries even attempt to challenge the prioritization of trade over other forms of international law.
33. Korten, David C. (1997) "The United Nations and the corporate agenda", People Centered Development Forum, at http://iisd.ca/pcdf/1997/uncorporate.htm Accessed 16 February 2001.
34. Korten, David C. (1997) "Memo to United Nations General Assembly President, Mr. Razali Ismail", vol. 2004: People Centered Development Forum, at: http://www.pcdf.org/1997/UNfacs.htm (accessed 5 August 2004).
35. Early World Social Forums have seen just a handful of their hundreds of sessions devoted specifically to UN reform or other multilateralist initiatives. And in the recent European Social Forum, just two sessions mentioned the UN in their title, one of which was called "UN = US?" and which dismissed the possibilities for meaningful UN reform. However, the 2005 meeting of the World Social Forum devoted comparatively more attention to this question.
36. A survey of NGOs active at global conferences in the mid-1990s reveals the origins of this disillusionment: "NGOs are more interested in creating direct citizen to citizen links at and around international events than in attempting to alter what apparently is perceived to be the relatively weak or weakening existing intergovernmental machinery" (Benchmark Environmental Consulting, "Democratic Global Civil Governance", 54).
37. Tarrow, Sidney (2005) "The new transnational contention: movements, states, and international institutions".
38. Charnovitz (1997) "Two centuries of participation".
39. Maney, Gregory M. (2001) "Rival transnational networks and indigenous rights: the San Blas Kuna in Panama and the Yanomami in Brazil", *Research in Social Movements, Conflicts and Change* 23: 103–144.
40. Bruno, Kenny and Joshua Karliner (2002) *Earthsummit.biz: The Corporate Takeover of Sustainable Development*, Oakland: Food First Books; see also, Sklair, L. (2001) *The Transnational Capitalist Class*, New York: Blackwell. Of course, this issue raises a number of challenges for multilateral institutions regarding the regulation of civil society participation which I cannot address here, such as what criteria should be used to determine which groups merit recognition in international forums?
41. John R. Bolton, Under Secretary for Arms Control and International Security, Address to the Plenary Session of the UN Conference on the Illicit Trade in Small Arms and Light Weapons for the U.S. at: http://www.state.gov/t/us/rm/2001/index.cfm?docid=403 (accessed 5 August 2004). The groups Bolton challenges include those supporting the UN's role in arms control and disarmament, including the then new Nobel Peace Prize Laureate, the International Campaign to Ban Landmines. It also bears noting that Bolton worked in the Clinton administration, and this policy agenda predated the more blatantly anti-democratic Bush regime.
42. Bob, Clifford (2004) "Contesting transnationalism: anti-NGO mobilization and world politics", presented at the American Political Science Association Annual Meeting, September.

43. For just one of many examples, see Sebastian Mallaby (2004) "NGOs: fighting poverty, hurting the poor", *Foreign Policy* (September/October): 50–58. The political right has also been critical of civil society engagement at the UN partly out of its own ideological resistance to the norms of multilateralism and tolerance. On this point, see Buss, Doris and Didi Herman (2003) *Globalizing Family Values: The Christian Right in International Politics*, Minneapolis: University of Minnesota Press.
44. Wapner, Paul (2002) "Defending accountability in NGOs", *Chicago Journal of International Law* 3: 197–205.
45. Bello (1999) *Dark Victory*.
46. Bennis, *Calling the Shots*; Bruno and Karliner, Earthsummit.biz; Karliner, Joshua (1997) *The Corporate Planet: Ecology and Politics in the Age of Globalization*, San Francisco: Sierra Club.
47. Bello, Walden (2000) "UNCTAD: time to lead, time to challenge the WTO", in K. Danaher and R. Burbach (eds.) *Globalize This! The Battle Against the World Trade Organization and Corporate Rule*, Monroe, Maine: Common Courage Press, pp. 163–174.
48. O'Brien, Robert, Anne Marie Goetz, Jan Aard Scholte and Marc Williams (2000) *Contesting Global Governance: Multilateral Economic Institutions and Global Social Movements*, New York: Cambridge University Press; Skogly, Sigrun (1993) "Structural adjustment and development: Human rights – an agenda for change?", *Human Rights Quarterly* 15: 751.
49. Charnovitz (1997) "Two centuries of participation"; Nelson, Paul (1995) *The World Bank and Nongovernmental Organizations: The Limits of Apolitical Development*, New York: St. Martin's Press.
50. See also Porter, Tony (2005) *Globalization and Finance*, Malden, Mass.: Polity, ch. 9; and Nelson, Paul (1995) *The World Bank and Nongovernmental Organizations*.
51. WTO Guidelines for Arrangements on Relations with NGOs state "it would not be possible for NGOs to be directly involved in the work of the WTO or its meetings, because of the politically sensitive nature of trade negotiations". The value of *informal* dialogue and information exchange with NGOs is recognized, but "primary responsibility for taking into account the different elements of public interest which are brought to bear on trade and policy making [lies at the national level]" (WTO guidelines cited in Krut (1997) "Globalization and civil society", p. 32). Given this supposed interest within the WTO to limit debates about public interest to domestic political arenas, it is ironic that the organization cites the fact that it also helps governments "ward off powerful [domestic] lobbies" and "narrow sectoral interests" as one of its major benefits (http://www.wto.org/wto/10ben/10ben09.htm, retrieved 5/11/00).
52. This move cannot be understood outside the larger context of the neo-liberal expansion of the late 1980s and especially in the post-Cold War era.
53. See Kell, Georg and John Gerard Ruggie (2000) "Reconciling economic imperatives with social priorities: the Global Compact", paper presented at Carnegie Council on Ethics and International Affairs, vol. 2005. New York.
54. Ruggie, John G. (2002) "The theory and practice of learning networks: corporate social responsibility and the Global Compact", *Journal of Corporate Citizenship* 2: 27–36.
55. Ibid., p. 31.
56. Bendell, Jem (2004) "Flags of inconvenience? The Global Compact and the Future of the United Nations", *Research Paper Series International Centre for Corporate Social Responsibility*, No. 22-2004, Nottingham University Business School, Nottingham UK, pp. 11–12.
57. Kell, Georg and David Levin (2002) "The evolution of the Global Compact network: an historic experiment in learning and action", paper presented at Academy of Manage-

ment Annual Conference at: http://157.150.195.47/Pubs/chronicle/2002/issue3/denver.pdf (accessed 16 January 2005).
58. Kell, Georg and John Gerard Ruggie (2000) "Reconciling economic imperatives with social priorities", p. 20.
59. Kell and Levin (2002) "The evolution of the Global Compact network", p. 25.
60. Hobbs, J., I. Khan, M. Posner and K. Roth (2003) "Letter to Louise Fréchette raising concerns on UN Global Compact"; Martens, Jens (2003) "Precarious 'partnerships': six problems of the Global Compact between business and the UN", at: www.globalpolicy.org/reform/business/2004/0623partnerships.htm.
61. Bendell, Jem (2004) "Flags of inconvenience?", p. 9.
62. Bendell reports on criticisms of the GC by officials in the UN Research Institute for Social Development (UNRISD), the GC Advisory Council, and three other UN agencies ("Flags of inconvenience?"). The critiques he raises are also reflected in the recent report of the World Commission on the Social Dimensions of Globalization (2004) *A Fair Globalization: Creating Opportunities for All*, at: http://www.ilo.org/public/english/wcsdg/docs/report.pdf (accessed 20 January 2005). The Commission called for "more proactive measures ... to promote the growth of representative organizations of the poor and other socially disadvantaged groups" (p. 55). It also called for a global system of industrial relations including global works councils, social audits of companies, and mechanisms to monitor and verify the implementation of codes of conduct adopted by multinational companies" (p. 22).
63. This implicit deal is necessary because while civil society groups have few other options but to work with the UN, businesses can and do choose to ignore the multilateral system. The UN therefore works to woo business leaders, but it takes for granted the continued support of civil society.
64. Bendell, Jem (2004) "Flags of inconvenience?", p. 20.
65. Kell, Georg and John Gerard Ruggie (2000) "Reconciling economic imperatives with social priorities", p. 21.
66. See, for example, the "Joint Civil Society Statement on the Global Compact and Corporate Accountability" and response from Georg Kell (2004) at: http://www.globalpolicy.org/reform/business/2004/.
67. Robert O'Brien demonstrates a similar effect of IMF and World Bank policies, which systematically enhance the power of capital while reducing that of labour. O'Brien, Robert (2004) "The International Monetary Fund, the World Bank and labour in developing countries", conference paper, Watson Institute, December 2004.
68. Martens, Jens (2003) "Precarious 'partnerships'".
69. Beausang, Francesca (2003) "Is there a development case for United Nations–business partnerships?", Working Paper No. 03-44, Development Studies Institute, London School of Economic, London (May 2003). Beausang analyses partnership arrangements between private and public sector actors, showing that asymmetries of power make such arrangements problematic for development. She sees a need to enhance the role of international agencies and NGOs relative to corporations in the GC structure and to incorporate disincentives for non-compliance into the GC.
70. Bendell (2004) "Flags of inconvenience?", p. 11; Martens (2003) "Precarious 'partnerships'".
71. Ibid, p. 13. Bendell reports a disturbing case where he recommended in response to a UN staff member's inquiry that the agency seek a partnership with companies engaging in fairly traded bananas. He was told that such companies would not be interested in the "reputational benefits" associated with UN partnerships, and therefore did not constitute attractive (lucrative) partnering options.
72. Martens (2003) "Precarious 'Partnerships'".

73. Ibid. See also the World Commission on the Social Dimensions of Globalization *A Fair Globalization*. The Draft "Norms on the responsibilities of transnational corporations and other business enterprises with regard to human rights" (E/CN.4/Sub 2/2003/12/ Rev.2 26 August 2003) was prepared in the UN Sub-commission on the Promotion and Protection of Human Rights, the broader UN Commission on Human Rights has denied the legal standing of this document since it did not explicitly commission the draft.
74. Virtually all of the arrests of peaceful demonstrators were overturned and police use of force was formally sanctioned in many of the cases. Nevertheless, these legal victories occurred well after the events themselves, insuring that the images of dissenters as criminal will linger in the views of much of the public.
75. See, for example, *A Fair Globalization* and United Nations, "We the peoples: civil society, the United Nations and global governance"; Ruggie, John G. "The theory and practice of learning networks".
76. Korzeniewicz, Roberto Patricio and William C. Smith (2000) "Poverty, inequality, and growth in Latin America: searching for the high road to globalization", *Latin American Research Review* 35: 7–54; Lipschutz, Ronnie and Cathleen Fogel (2006) "'Regulation for the rest of us': global civil society and the privatization of transnational regulation", in T. J. Biersteker, R. B. Hall, and C. N. Murphy (eds.) *Private Authority and Global Governance*.
77. Wallerstein, Immanuel (2005) "After developmentalism, what?", in *Social Forces*.

20

Multilateralism and economic justice

Sirkku K. Hellsten

Introduction

The role of multilateral agreements and organizations in world politics has been changing rapidly in the context of globalization. Besides traditional nation-state cooperation, international activity now takes in various different spheres that can be differentiated by the values and goals they aim for. First, there is multilateral collaboration between states, the main goal of which is, for the most part, the mutual promotion of national interests. Second, there is transnational business led by multinational corporations, which are influencing heavily the rules of global economy and politics. The guiding principles of their actions are self-interest and profit making. Thirdly, there are civil society movements and NGOs, which are gaining influence as critical opposing forces to the market-oriented trends of globalization. Many of them aim to promote global as well as local social justice, including environmental values and various other related forms of the "common good".

This chapter will discuss challenges to multilateralism today in relation to economic justice. Firstly, it will discuss if and how economic justice can be realized when a large part of trade and economic relations are handled by private non-state agencies rather than by governments who have traditionally been the formal parties to the multilateral agreements. Secondly, it will analyse how civil society organizations and other local and global networks now enforce ethical dimensions of international cooperation by challenging multilateral institutions on normative grounds due to the lack of any commonly agreed values and norms in the collaboration between sovereign states. The main hypothesis of the chapter is that while the traditional forms of multilateral state collaboration have lost much of their credibility due to the global democratic deficit and due to the weakening of the role of national governments in world politics, multilateralism can still offer a firm basis for international cooperation. However, this requires that the existing multilateral institutions discuss, evaluate and negotiate common values and open a dialogue on political as well as social dimensions and goals of globalization and international cooperation. Within this dialogue, civil society and developing countries must have a chance to get their voice heard and their concerns taken into account. In summary, if multilateral cooperation wants to gain back its credibility, it has to bring questions of ethics and justice back to agenda of international negotiations. This means that there is an urgent need to question the prevalent, determinist view that sees the globalization of economy as an inevitable global adaptation to neo-liberal market capitalism, that sets aside any other values but economic rationality, and which is thus often offered as an inevitable fact about the nature of "globalization" while simultaneously presented as "the only right choice" for global democracy.

These claims are set within a theoretical framework of social contract and its various interpretations: since the moral foundations of multilateral collaboration and international treaties are usually taken to have their foundations in the "contractarian" approach to justice that focuses on reciprocal benefits between equal and autonomous partners, there is an urgent need to reconsider how the international contracts are made today and how a fair access to the bargaining table can be achieved in the global scale. All in all, I argue that we need to reconsider whether the principles of justice that multilateral cooperation promotes today are still valid. In addition there is a need to look for alternative or complementary views that can balance world power relations in economic and political cooperation.

Values and facts in the context of multilateralism

In the context of globalization – in all its meanings – the concept of multilateralism has gained new meanings and interpretations depending on who is using the concept and for what purpose. The traditional interpretation of multilateralism refers to multiple sovereign states working in concert and negotiating mutually beneficial institutional arrangements and agreements between them. This is a descriptive interpretation of multilateralism as an alternative way of collaboration to bilateralism, that is, two countries working together, and unilateralism, which refers to a single state acting on its own.

However, in today's international politics, particularly when the term multilateralism is used by the United States, it appears to have a normative rather than descriptive sense, referring to the "right kind" of international collaboration that aims towards the liberalization of world markets, and, more widely, to the realization of neo-liberal economic and political ideology in the context of globalization. In its simplest sense, globalization refers to the widening, deepening and speeding up of global interconnectedness. In this chapter I shall focus on economic integration as the main feature of globalization and claim that, while a contested concept, globalization is nowadays often so directly related to neo-liberal economics that it appears to carry intrinsic values related to free market economy particularly in the United States.

As the leader in neo-liberal economic policies, the US tends to set multilateralism not against unilateralism, but instead against regionalism, which it sees as a blockage in the way of "the highest state of multilateral collaboration" – that is, "economic globalism". Multilateral arrangements are needed to support the liberalization of economy in capitalist markets worldwide. Despite political rhetoric, multilateral agreements are there, not to enforce "global democracy" or "global ethics" based on mutual agreement on certain principles of justice that are beneficial to all parties agreeing on these principles, but to enforce the globalization of market economy. The US approach to multilateralism is to unilaterally push for policies that are particularly favourable to its own economic, as well as political, goals. When conflicts occur, the US has effectively rejected arrangements which it sees as non-beneficial to its national and/or corporate interests. This happens despite an international agreement that multilateral treaties and agreements should also benefit the world's poor, protect the environment and in general promote a wider or alternative understanding of the social dimensions of globalization and to protect alternative views to social justice. This view includes seeing justice as equality of opportunity in a Rawlsian sense that allows differences in treatment in order to benefit those least advantaged, instead of the neo-liberal view of justice as mutual self-interest.[1]

Historical overview

The one-sided view of economic justice was not in the original agenda of multilateralism. Traditionally, before the US domination and acceleration of "globalization" as a progressive political and economic phenomena, multilateralism was seen as a sign of increased international democracy with a stabilizing influence in international politics. The first instances of multilateral politics occurred in the nineteenth century after the end of the Napoleonic Wars where the great powers met to redraw the map of Europe at the Congress of Vienna. The Concert of Europe, as it became known, was a group of great and lesser powers that would meet to resolve issues peacefully. While the concert system was utterly destroyed by the First World War, after these conflicts world leaders returned to multilateralism in order to attempt to prevent further conflicts. Along with the political organizations such as the United Nations, the post-war years relied on economic multilateralism in the form of the General Agreement on Tariffs and Trade (GATT), the World Bank and International Monetary Fund (IMF). The agencies played an important role also in maintaining world peace during the Cold War.

Originally the main proponents of multilateralism were the middle powers in world politics, for example, Canada and the Nordic countries. This is due to the fact that larger and more powerful states often act unilaterally (or acknowledge their possibility to do so, when needed by their national interests), and the very small countries, for their part, have much less involvement and little influence in international affairs to start with. The attitudes towards the role of multilateral collaboration in world democracy have gradually changed despite the high profile of modern multilateral systems such as the United Nations and World Trade Organization due to the current unilateral power concentration in the world politics and multilateral agreements. Thus, since the end of the Cold War, after the fall of socialism, and the rise of the United States as the world's dominant power, multilateralism has been on the decline. The objection to multilateralism has been the concentration of power within the US and its tendency to enforce policies that promote its own interests that often coincide with interests of profit-making transnational corporations, as well as, its inclination to reject policies that would actually protect the mutual interests of individual states across the world.

Instead of looking for global consensus and democratic agreement between various autonomously and rationally chosen views on social justice, the US has taken the liberty to act unilaterally in most situations when it pleases its political and economic goals. There are many recent practical examples of this. For instance, under George W. Bush, the US has rejected such multilateral agreements as Kyoto Protocol,[2] the International Criminal Court,[3] and the Ottawa Treaty banning land mines. All these incidents have received a heavy opposition from other sovereign states involved, and particularly from the developing world and the "global civil society movements".

Multilateralism and the lack of global economic justice

We can think of multilateral agreements as social contracts in international context. In order to avoid war against everyone else, in a Hobbesian sense, multilateral treaties legitimize transnational and multinational processes and agencies to impose some limits to the state in order to guarantee mutual benefits and to limit unruly and lawless competition that leads into aggressive international conflicts and wars.

Social contract in a global context could be seen as the moral foundation for multilateral organizations and treaties. The purpose of this contract is to find principles of global justice that all parties can agree on and abide with. When we follow the liberal social contract tradition all parties invited to the negotiating table are equal, autonomous and self-interested decision-makers, who are making laws for themselves. Since all parties are considered both as lawmakers and the subjects of the law, the principles negotiated must be legitimate and bind all. However, in reality this does not seem to be the case. Also, if the contract to be negotiated is to take equality and justice seriously, it would seem that the position of developing and poor countries should be in the centre of the negotiations. Instead, developing countries have historically played only a minor role in the multilateral economic agreements and particularly in the multilateral trading system. Until the Uruguay Round (1986–93) their participation was à la carte, with many not making commitments. The Uruguay Round replaced the old GATT trade contract with a new institution – that is, the World Trade Organization (WTO) 1995. The WTO was given a build-in enforcement system more powerful than of any previous treaty. This system, with closed tribunals of trade bureaucrats who determined if a country's laws exceeded the constraints set by the new rules, included automatic, permanent trade sanctions against any country refusing to comply with WTO demands, The WTO took on the role of implementing globally much the same policy agenda that the World Band and the IMF had already imposed on most of the Third world.

The WTO was created because the US senate had blocked the founding of the alternative International Trade Organization 1948 on the grounds that its broad mandate would compromise US sovereignty. Its goals included full employment, protection of worker rights around the world, and process against what were then referred as "global carters" – small groups of corporations that gained too much power over a sector. WTO, for its part, has had much narrower goal of reducing tariffs in goods and services and setting a handful of board trade principles. World trade grew dramatically after World War II, under guidance of the GATT. While initially limited to this trade expansion mandate, the GATT evolved into institutions that promoted corporate rights over human rights and other social and environmental priorities. Pushed largely by US-based global corporations and their allies in the US government, in 1994/5 GATT was replaced by WTO and given a built-in enforcement system more powerful than that of any previous treaty. This system, with closed tribunals of trade bureaucrats, took over the role of implementing globally much the same policy agenda that the World Bank and IMF had already imposed on most of the Third World. With the Single Undertaking, developing countries became subject to most of the disciplines of the many agreement contained in the WTO. A number of these agreements came to be seen as having little or no benefit to the developing world countries, often the opposite. This is particularly so since the United States, who dominates the multilateral economic agreements, has refused to support any comprehensive proposals that would be mutually binding in truly guaranteeing the developing countries more equal access to world markets.

The critics of the US led "economic globalism" based on neo-liberal policies note that WTO has served primarily US government and corporate interests over the Third World and civil-society interests. The US became the dominant lobbyist for the comprehensive Uruguay Round and the founding of the WTO when it felt that more competitive global conditions had created a situation where its corporate interests now demanded an opposite stance.[4] While WTO in general was set up to regulate trade, prevent trade wars, and protect the interests of poor nations, its actions tell a different story.[5] Despite the fact that November 2001 Doha Development Agenda finally put the development concerns at the core of the WTO deliberations, in general, the attempts of the poor countries to improve the terms of their trade in WTO has been less enthusiastically received by the governments of the industrialized countries.[6]

Due to the Western dominance in the world economic policies multilateral organizations have adopted certain policies that influence those countries that have no decision-making power in designing the policies. This imbalance in power has created a backlash against multilateral economic organizations not only by the developing countries but also by the Western anti-globalization and social justice movements.[7] Anti-globalization movements criticize particularly the official multilateral neo-liberal economic policies. In order to return serious considerations about global justice into the world politics, anti-globalization and social justice movements are searching for practical options to capitalist world economics by suggesting alternative concepts of justice to replace or at least to compliment the dominant neo-liberal approach by calling for fairness and equality in political and economic participation as well as in global and local distribution and redistribution of resources. Their criticism is well grounded as we can conclude from the examples presented above.

If we take a serious look at global economics in relation to "global justice", it is evident that the multilateral trade agreements and economic organizations have not narrowed the gap between the rich and the poor, rather the opposite. While economic inequality and poverty undoubtedly are phenomena that has existed throughout the time in one form or another, it appears that current persistence of world poverty, and particularly the increasing mass poverty in Third World countries, is for the most part a result of neo-liberal economic policies. While we can explain poverty partly through environmental problems, geographical location of countries, the global differences in the levels of economic, scientific and political development and the economic dependency of the poor countries are often results of the unequal global power structures in relation to colonial history, as well as the various policies of globalized economy (such as unfair trade relations, foreign investments profits which are not benefiting poor countries, the crushing burden of the Third World debt).

When it comes to the role of multilateral economic organizations in poverty reduction the World Bank and IMF have played a central role, through development loans. In order to alleviate persistent poverty in the year 2000, the World Bank committed over $6.8 billion in concessionary loans targeted directly at facilitating economic development in the world's poorest countries. The problem is that these loans merely add to the debt due to various earlier bilateral and other multilateral agreements. For many developing countries, the repayment of their debt may involve around 8 per cent or more of the country's GNP each year. This means that poor countries have to devote much of their production to the export market and set their emphasis on "cash" crop production instead of producing crops that are essential in meeting the needs of the country's own population.[8] Concurrently, many multilateral trade agreements have blocked the equal access to the world markets from the developing countries, despite the fact that poverty alleviation, democracy and human rights are at least rhetorically on the global political agenda. Thus, while poverty reduction is mentioned as one of the main goals of current economic policies and multilateral development programmes, in practice there has been no political will to seriously promote more equal power relations in production and trade. Nor has there been international commitment to look for alternative solutions and economic arrangements to solve the problems of the world poor. Instead, privatization and liberalization of trade have been offered as a solution to all social evils, from authoritarianism to corruption, and from poverty to lack of political participation.

Simultaneously, when the development cooperation and aid shifted from bilateral collaboration to multilateral agreements, it started to promote neo-liberal politics with calls for structural changes through privatization and liberalization of markets. In recent decades Oversees Development Assistance (ODA) has radically declined. The original OECD target of 0.7 per cent of GNP is currently achieved by a very few members of the international community. Development cooperation is now focusing on trade, investment and loan arrangements, all of which are part of the globalization of capitalist economy. As a result the already weak states in the poor regions of the world have lost even more control over their national economic policies. While in principle sovereign states, most developing countries are fully dependent on the rules of world economy set by the affluent countries.

The transition from state controlled and more centralized economy to privatized markets is, in fact, currently seen as the precondition of "legitimate neo-liberal democracy". However, the core values of democratic governance and the rational choices of economic efficiency do not always go hand in hand. Instead, the sudden rise of market economy with its capitalist and individualistic values tends to promote the sanctity of private property and the maximization of personal profits. While this may not always be the case, the message is sent that only the fittest will survive. Corruption in poor countries, however, is often further fuelled by the offers made by multilateral corporations when they trying to cut deals with the national governments and local businesses.[9]

All in all, while sustained economic growth has been a constant priority in the development plans of developing countries, poverty reduction driven by policies for pro-poor economic growth have not been the main aim of contemporary multilateral organizations and agreements. Such development programmes as the Heavily Indebted Poor Countries Initiative (HIPC) for debt relief, which promises to cancel debts of those poor countries who commit themselves to reduce poverty locally, promotes further the dominant, one-sided view to economic justice.[10] Despite the concern expressed on world poverty, rich countries have been slow in granting debt relief under the HIPC initiative, and even slower to allow the poor countries as real competitors in the world markets. Simultaneously the investments of the wealthy economies in poor countries tend to maximize the profit made by these countries rather than help the poor countries to profit from these investments locally.[11]

Nation state, civil society and plurilateralism

The US-led tendency to equate multilateral collaboration with the wider processes of "economic globalization" gradually created a determinist view of global economy and international politics. Since "choice" in multilateral agreements has apparently become but an illusion created by those in power, citizens of various nations across the world see that there are no prospects for balanced multilateral collaboration.

In order to get alternative approaches to economic justice to be heard, more powerful anti-globalization and social justice movements are emerging, integrating and networking across borders and regions in order to get alternative views to be heard and taken into account. Civil society participation has gained a central role because people have become more aware that today's multilateral politics tend to render democracy and political participation irrelevant at the national level due to the diminishing role and relevance of the nation state and increasing influence of economic agencies. With globalization more and more things become transnationalized, especially economic activities, and the decisions which affect people's lives and shape public policies are made in distant places of economic power, often anonymously by agents and forces which citizens can hardly understand and much less control.[12]

Expressing the view of anti-globalization and social justice movements, Colin Hines describes globalization as "a process by which governments sign away the rights of their citizens in favour of speculative investors and trans-national corporations".[13] Hines relates economic globalization to erosion of wages, social welfare standards and environment regulations for the sake of international trade. What is interesting in this analysis is the distinction that Hines sets between globalization and internationalism. Internationalism is seen as a form of collaboration that can support social justice by the global flow of technology, ideas and information to rebuild sustainable local communities, while in the globalization process all other goals are overridden by the economic agenda. Internationalism is then related to the free flow of ideas, technologies, information, culture, money and goods with the end goal of respecting and rebuilding local economies worldwide, while globalization merely assimilates all economies to "the end state" of global capitalist markets.

This distinction may be useful if we want to reconsider those values originally related to multilateral cooperation and to evaluate the global legitimacy of the dominant neo-liberal principles of justice. The idea of internationalism would then reflect the ideal role that multilateralism was meant to play in world politics as a promoter for world democracy by providing a forum for a democratic search for principles of justice that are beneficial and acceptable to all parties involved. In the context of globalization, however, these values appear to be replaced by "the one and only right choice" that is to be accepted by all. This concept is based on the classical idea of "might is right". Thus, countries are now rather set against each other, because competition and rivalry is the route to maximizing influence and profits in the global markets.

In other words, multilateral collaboration is not based on any shared moral values but on the self-interest of the parties. With neo-liberal market ideology most of the critical debate on values behind the policies suggested has ceased. While there used to be disputes at least over the influence of different forms liberalism (social liberalism vs. market liberalism) on policy choices, these seem to have disappeared when the neo-liberal view is presented as the "only right choice" left. The impact of globalization, as the main means of spreading neo-liberal politics across the world in world, has then been de-socializing and fragmenting rather than democratic and uniting. Nations are drawn in to the processes of globalization by multilateral agreements, while simultaneously the contents of these agreements have already been decided by the "inevitable" and determinist globalization process itself. The results is then "the one choice politics".[14]

All in all, state sovereignty is not called into question by militaries, armies and missiles, but by elements, which escape national government control – be these economic trends, environmental issues, health concerns – or the combination of them all. Traditional response was to create inter-governmental institutions to manage or mediate specific systems (trade, industrial property, nuclear energy or epidemics) is no longer working convincingly partially due to the global democracy deficit. There has been more and more internal critique towards national governments by civil society. In order to try to take some control back over such processes, civil society movements have been looking for alternative channels of influence. Besides the negative outcomes they have also realized the possibilities that the context of globalization creates.

There is an increasingly complex web of bilateral and multilateral agencies, inter-governmental organizations and international regimes for various areas of international economy regulating different aspect of world commerce and financial markets. While it has become less clear how local voters can actually influence decisions on politics, new forums have been created. The state as a political entity, that ideally materialized popular sovereignty, has now less power, thus civil society has gained stronger global authority. This situation is paradoxical by nature because, on the one hand, the multilateral processes are harnessed to accelerate globalization processes, which, on the other hand, are not seen amenable to any direct democratic control. The civil society, for its part, has taken advantage of the shrinking powers of the states and created global forces of resistance. This has led into a situation in which multilateralism is, if not replaced with, at least extended to plurilateralism.

The concept of plurilateralism refers to structural differentiation. In plurilateralism different levels of the system are separated from each other, and at the same time, various functional structures, for instance, security, economy, political and culture, become more distinct.[15] Different agencies of decision-making function in different forums and spheres of influence. In a plurilateral model various cross-cutting links and actions occur across levels, structure and spheres of social interaction. Each actor has a combination of characteristics and overlapping memberships; therefore, the system is pluralistic in nature and, thus, also promoting plurality of values and concepts of justice. The plurilateral model has to take all kinds of actors – not just states – seriously in global governance. For instance, globalization has broken down the previous clear-cut separation of public and private spheres and new types of public/private combinations have emerged at both the domestic and the international level.[16]

Multilateralism and plurilateralism do not have to exclude each other. Rather multilateralism can be seen as a state-based subcategory of organizational forms and actions within the currently broader plurilateral world. In relation to "global ethics" neither multilateralism nor plurilateralism is per se good or bad. Multilateral agreements and forms of organizations can be used to military interventions, or economic dominance of markets, but they can also secure international treaties to protect environment and to promote peace. Plurilateral structures, for their, part can influence state-based treaties and lobby in causes that might not be otherwise dealt by these treaties due to the conflict between dominant state powers.[17]

When it comes to the changes in power in relation to global governance, the positive "side-effect" of the various processes of globalization is the empowerment of also those who oppose the trends of globalization. The failure of traditional forms of multilateralism in the context of globalization has led to increasing regionalism the purpose of which has been to gain back more control over global economy as well as over national economies. Regional arrangements give a group of nations more bargaining power on the international negotiation table against the US hegemony. However, "regionalization" in its current form appears to be an intermediate state in the process of globalization because it ironically tends to weaken the position of individual states as sovereign political actors. This increases the power of the global civil society and lead into further plurilateralization of world politics. Post-materialist social movements and NGOs might have their agenda set particularly against economic globalization, but indirectly they are the ones who have the most to gain in relation to political and practical importance through the very processes of globalized connections and unification, transfer of ideas and actions, spreading information and knowledge, and accessing wider forums to get their voices heard.

Multilateralism and the possibility of global economic justice

Whether plurilateralism is going to replace multilateralism or whether multilateral arrangements can work hand in hand with plurilateral processes depends on the whether there is a common agreement on the values and goals of these parallel arrangement and whether the states can seriously commit themselves to these values and work for economic alternatives that take into account other concepts of social justice besides the dominant neo-liberal one. The failure of the traditional, state-centred multilateralism may be better understood when set within a theoretical debate on the possibility of a (or the) global concept of justice. This current cosmopolitanism vs. communitarianism debate per se, is reflecting the frustration in attempts to find ethical guidelines for international co-operation within the context of globalization.

The debate on the cosmopolitan concept of citizenship was brought to the academic discussion particularly in the second half of the 1990s. This debate between universal "rationality" and a particular "nationality" could be seen as an extension of the individualist vs. communitarian debate on the foundations of justice particularly within multicultural societies.[18] The current cosmopolitanism versus communitarianism debate focuses on the concept of moral agency and its relation to rights and responsibilities within a global context and among the international agents. The proponents of cosmopolitan views challenge the moral authority of state and see the need to give individuals more central role in global governance, though they are vague how this role can actually be implemented; whether it is by creating new formal international institutions or by civil society movements. The main emphasis of this debate is then on the relationship between individual morality and moral responsibility in relation to the concept of citizenship, and to the role of state in relation to local and global justice. The issues disputed are 1) the role of citizenship in relation to moral agency and national identity; 2) citizens' rights and duties towards their fellow citizens as well as towards distant people(s) and in some cases also towards non-human beings and environment at large); and 3) the possibility for world governance and/or cosmopolitan political institutions to place the existing multilateral, regional and national structures.[19]

The cosmopolitan position is that we have some universal moral guidelines, which give us moral rights as well as moral obligations beyond our nation states, and our close communities. Therefore, we should consider global rather than national citizenship. We also need global arrangements for governance, rather than the self-interested politics of nation states, to bring about these universal rights and obligations equally across the globe. The communitarian view, for its part, is that only nation states can be the only serious and influential global actors and duty bearers. The communitarian view is realistic rather than idealistic in the sense that it recognizes the self-interest of the sovereign states. Their duties are primarily to their own citizens, and only secondarily to their international parties of collaboration. Individual citizens, for their part, can best influence the local as well as global politics and ethics through their states and the locally shared values. Their loyalties should lay with the state, rather than any abstract cosmopolitan institutions or to idealistic common values of a global civil society at large.

If we set multilateral cooperation against this framework it may first appear that the multilateral system must be based on communitarian nationalism while the cosmopolitanism world order could easily be seen as a part of globalization processes. However, due to the complexity of our political reality, multilateralism actually has to be placed somewhere in between these apparently competing theoretical positions. On the one hand, based on the model of contractarian agreement on mutual benefits, multilateral agreements appears to promote certain, universalizable principles and goals by setting up rights, duties and guidelines, that all participating nations are to accept and follow. These rights, duties and guidelines are supposed to be the result of democratic negations between autonomous and equal, but competitive and self-interested, parties. In political practice, however, they rely on the role that existing nations have as political actors. The states do not only agree on these rights and duties, but also enforce them globally on each other and on themselves. With the neo-liberal economic agenda of globalization, these principles and guidelines, however, no longer seem to express the autonomous will or rational self-interest of all the parties of the contracts. The principles are no longer chosen, but rather presented as "universal facts" turned into values to be universally accepted by all. In other words, the guidelines and the principles they are based on are presented as objective goals of the negotiations and their foundation is not in reciprocal negotiations but it is based on the demands of "laws of economics" and the invisible hand of the global markets.

The moral legitimacy of the original contractarian approach to justice as a mutual and beneficial agreement is lost. The idea that certain principles are considered fair if no one can reasonably reject them has been proven not to work in practice. The contemporary multilateralism does not follow the contractarian theory, but takes almost an opposite stand by "rejecting" all those who do not mutually agree with the principles that are already set by those whom they benefit the most. Nations no longer democratically choose values – or maintain the original democratic ideals such as equality, autonomy and tolerance. Instead they enforce neo-liberal values of market freedoms and the libertarian concept of justice based on property rights rather than social responsibility. The value of democracy as mutual participation has turned into the practice of unilateral interests, the values of freedom to deterministic free markets, the value of autonomy to the "only one right choice" politics, and equality to necessity of all to compete on these markets. The irony is, like the French social theorist Michel Foucault has pointed out, that in its ultimate form liberal individualism in the context of market economy leads into an "illusion of freedom" that, in the end, makes everyone choose the same and only option in the name of individual liberty. In the case of economic justice, this means that the neo-liberal view of justice is presented as "the universal concept of justice" that does not allow any compromises or accept that there are serious alternatives to be democratically considered.[20]

When neo-liberal principles are theoretically based on contractarian justification (as the mutually beneficial principles freely chosen by autonomous and rational decision-makers) and enforced by practical international treaties (by sovereign and self-interested states) they become exclusive and extremely undemocratic, leaving no room for genuine negotiations or alternative goals. Instead, they exclude all those not agreeing with them as irrational, dependent and, in general, ignorant of the truth of the universal reason.

This results in negotiations that have no moral legitimacy but are based on mere political and economic interests. In the present situation, multilateral agreements are seen as "a rhetoric of global justice and democracy" rather than "a global practice of justice and democracy". The language of morals is used to justify normative recommendations while the goals are economical and political rather than ethical. This presents a form of "neo-Machiavellism", which, on the one hand, detaches ethics from politics while, simultaneously, using all means possible to protect self-interests of the rulers even if this requires using the language of "ethics" to justify unethical and unjust actions and ends. For example, today international intervention and even war can be justified in the name of higher moral values of "democracy", "freedom" and "human rights". Those members of the international community who see themselves as the representatives of "the free world" and "good against evil", claim moral superiority and/or excellence that grants them the right to take the issues of justice into their own hands and violate any multilateral agreements as they see "morally fit". Interventions to stop "bad governance" or "unjust wars" are easily justified in the name of universal moral norms and principles. As the former US Secretary of State Colin Powell said on the invasion of Iraq, the Bush administration will bring the Iraq case to the United Nations, but that doesn't mean "we lose our option to do what we might think is appropriate to do". If the UN Security Council makes a "right" recommendation, it strengthens the case. If not, the US can always ignore it and enforce its own "moral judgement" and take unilateral action whether one talks about war and conflict or trade agreements and environmental accords. The "global" promotion of democracy with undemocratic means leads to multilateral activities, which have no ethical grounds.[21] The same has been true with the multinational trade negotiations and related climate change negotiations undertaken within the United Nations framework convention on Climate Change (UNFCC). The Convention on Climate Change uses concepts like "equity" and asks that developed country parties should take the lead in combating climate change. The current round of world trade negotiations, for its part, was christened the "Development Agenda" and it created a strong pressure on developing countries to use trade activities in development and poverty reduction, while the affluent countries, with the lead of the US, routinely refuse to change their national policies in a manner that would make these efforts globally credible and realistic. Quite the opposite, they base their requirement on their own interests and economic benefits.[22]

If legitimacy is to be gained and democracy to be recognized, not only in principle but also as a relevant means of international politics, there is a need to focus on the alternative values and evaluation of other concepts of justice. The contractarian method can be used to find truly democratic and mutually beneficial agreements on alternative views, as the history of social contract tradition shows. At different times and in different historical contexts, different principles have been presented as "the right choices of reason". In political practice, this requires that the levels of cooperation with various global and local institutions need to be reconsidered and the value conflicts between the states and the civil society movements need to be opened for discussion. While the cosmopolitan theoretical request for taking our universal rights and global obligation more seriously is important, even more important is to be able to define these obligations and the responsible agents in order to make them concrete. The future of multilateralism depends then on our ability to bring in alternative concepts of justice to be part of the multilateral negotiations. Otherwise the values of the three spheres of globalization mentioned in the beginning – the business, the state and civil society – will never meet and reciprocal international collaboration towards global justice can never be reached. This was already clearly shown in the last WTO's Fifth Ministerial conference in Cancun, Mexico 2003. The direct action in Cancun was part of a large and diverse assault on the WTO's attempt to write a constitution that would supersede national and local legislation, and empower transnational corporations to hold down wages, monopolize markets, wipe out small farmers and overlook the environmental concerns. The WTO failed in this effort largely due to a growing spirit of collaboration between NGOs and Third World governments. This latest battle in the struggle between economic and corporate globalization and social globalization with ethical values established some new political benchmarks and challenges to multilateralism in its traditional state-based form. A much greater willingness of Third World governments to stand up to the Western economic powers and multinational corporations is needed, together with a new level of collaboration between NGOs and developing country governments, and a unity among the cross-roots, or street-level, forces fighting economic globalization and its neo-liberal policies. The deficiencies of multilateral aid and development cooperation programmes are nowadays pointed out by both the Third World governments as well as by international NGOs. The wider participation of non-state agencies was evident also in the Helsinki Process Final Conference in September 2005 that focused on the Social Dimension of Globalization inviting not only government representatives of developed and developing countries but also a large number of international and local NGOs to take actions that lead towards globally more fair economic policies.[23]

Further discussions on global cooperation and renewal of multilateral cooperation took place in the UN Summit in September 2005, which agreed to take action on a range of global challenges, such as achieving Millennium Development Goals, maintaining peace, dealing with health and environmental issues, participating in economic activities. The summit also reconsidered the role of UN in international cooperation in today's world, which is very different from 1945 when the UN was established. In general, the summit's goal was to find a ways to make sovereign states with very different interests and value systems accept more global responsibilities in order to deal with the problems that need global rather than merely local solutions.[24]

Conclusion

If multilateral agreements and organizations are to regain their legitimacy and authority, they need to take the challenges created by global civil society, and by the interests of transnational corporations, more seriously. Multilateral agreements have to make room for civil society organizations in national politics and to give them more direct power in negotiating and realizing international agreements. States, for their part, need to regain more control in dealing with business interests and ensuring corporate social responsibility. They also need to accept the current plurilateral nature of world politics and agree to gain control in economic policies by setting their aim to be "global justice" rather than mere financial profit. This presumes that civil society movements and organizations are given more direct influence in national politics as well as a formal position in transnational politics. It also means that agreements based on values other than economic growth need to be taken seriously.

The challenges to multilateralism are, then, the following: how to integrate national interest groups into multilateral negotiations; how to adapt the traditional multilateral systems to take account of new participants; and how to increase the negotiating influence of developing countries in multilateral negotiations as well as in the growing number of bilateral North–South negotiations.

All in all, in order for multilateralism to have a future and to be a useful force in guiding the world economy towards social justice, there is a need to take account of our global rights and responsibilities seriously and equally. States need to take control over the various trends of globalization by adding a social dimension to economic trends. This entails that regionalism is used for balancing the interests of different regions and bringing in the different concerns on the international negotiating table. Multilateral cooperation could then provide a form of world governance that does not have to rely on a cosmopolitan abstract idea of world government. In order to continue to support the ideal of world citizenship and world democracy, it can harness states to follow up on our global responsibilities in a more balanced and a more clearly organized manner. If we can bring ethical debate on values back on the agenda of international politics – and even better, on actual political practices – multilateral arrangements can play an important role in controlling the negative effects of globalization and also to take into account the social dimensions of globalization.

Notes

1. The main problem in discussing justice in relation to globalization and multilateralism appears to be the classic question of the chicken and the egg: it is not clear whether globalization as a world phenomena has enforced the determinist concept of neo-liberal justice or whether the dominant world politics based on neo-liberalism have pushed globalization towards accepting neo-liberalism as the only doctrine of justice, particularly after the fall of socialism. Either way, the challenge of multilateralism today is to allow alternative views of justice to enter in the formal international collaboration and to be able to find genuine democratic consensus on the principles agreed multilaterally.
2. From 1 to 11 December 1997, more than 160 nations met in Kyoto, Japan to negotiate binding limitations on greenhouse gases for the developed nations, pursuant to the objectives of the Framework Convention on Climate Change of 1992. The outcome of the meeting was the Kyoto Protocol, in which the developed nations agreed to limit their greenhouse gas emissions, relative to the levels emitted in 1990.

3. More problems are in sight with the US plans to override the Geneva Convention in the name of combating terrorism.
4. The threat of the United States in the 1950s to leave GATT if it was not allowed to maintain protective mechanism for various agricultural products led to limited coverage of agriculture in GATT rules, so it was US pressure that brought agriculture fully under the GATT–WTO system in 1995. It was also the US that pushed to bring services under WTO coverage with its assessment that in the new burgeoning area of international services, particularly financial services, its corporation had a lead that needed to be preserved. The US pushed to expand WTO jurisdiction to the Trade-Related Investment Measures (TRIMs) and Trade-Related Intellectual Property Rights (TRIPs). The former sought to eliminate countries' ability to shape foreign investment policies to ensure national benefits. For instance, TRIMs targeted domestic laws regulating international cross-border trade of product components among TNX subsidiaries, which developing countries had passed in order to develop new domestic industries. TRIPS was designed to consolidate the US advantage in the cutting-edge, knowledge-intensive industries. See C. Hines (2000) *Localization: A Global Manifesto*, London: Earthscan Publications; and WIDE (2003) "Feminist challenges in a globalized economy", WIDE Bulletin October 2003, reported by Mandy MacDonald, Belgium.
5. WTO panels have ruled against Canada's cultural protections, which taxed US magazines, and India has been told it must change its national constitution because WTO rules do not allow it to provide its people with inexpensive generic drugs since it is considered unfair to foreign drug companies that profit handsomely from branded products. In the 1999 WTO "banana wars", Europeans were told by the WTO that they could not show import preference to banana farmers' cooperatives located in the Caribbean because it was unfair to two giant US agribusiness corporations, Chiquita and Dole, which grow bananas in Central America and control half the world's banana trade. When Europe refused to end its preference, the WTO sanctioned a retaliatory move by the US to impose 100 per cent on a wide variety of European exports. Thus, in a single case, the WTO struck down a preference for the poor and sanctioned a trade war.
6. Bernard Hoekman (2004) "Developing countries and the WTO Doha Round: market access, rules and differential treatment", *Journal of Economic Integration* 19(2) (June): 205–207.
7. See S. Amin (1997) *Capitalism in the Age of Globalization*, London and New York: Zed Books.; C. Hines (2000) *Localization: A Global Manifesto*, see note 10; International Forum on Globalization, Alternatives to Economic Globalization (2002) 'A better world is possible", a report of the International Forum on Globalization, San Francisco: Berrett-Kehler Publishers; World Commission on the Social Dimension of Globalization (2004) *A Fair Globalization: Creating Opportunities for All*, ILO.
8. This is also one of the main reasons why even in many fertile and well-endowed developing countries with natural resources, people are not benefiting from their domestic production, but live in poverty and suffer hunger and malnutrition.
9. S.K. Hellsten (2003) "'Trust me! My hands are dirty also': Institutionalized corruption and the competing codes of public and private ethics", *Professional Ethics* 11(1): 65–68.
10. J. Remenyi (2004) "Poverty and development: the struggle to empower the poor", in D. Kingsbury, J. Remenyi, J. McKay and Janet Hunt (eds.) *Key Issues in Development*, New York: Palgrave MacMillan, p. 191.
11. One criticism from economists has been that the so-called "Conditionalities", including Structural Adjustment Programmes, on which the financial aid is always bound, retard social stability and hence inhibit the IMF's targets. By discouraging the development of infrastructure and demanding austerity, the IMF Conditionalities restrict the economies

of developing countries to simply providing cheap labour and cheap raw materials to the G-7 nations, which critics claim is a disguised form of colonialism.

12. Ake, C. (1999) "Globalization, multilateralism and the shrinking democratic space" in M. Schechter (ed.) *Future Multilateralism. The Political and Social Framework. Multilateralism and the UN system*, New York: Palgrave MacMillan, pp. 180–181.
13. C. Hines (2000) *Localization: A Global Manifesto*, London: Earthscan Publications.
14. Ake, C. (1999) "Globalization, multilateralism and the shrinking democratic space" in M. Schechter (ed.) *Future Multilateralism* (see note 12); and C. Hines (2000) *Localization: A Global Manifesto* (see note 13).
15. P. Cerny (1993) "Plurilateralism: structural differentiation and functional conflict in the post-cold war world order", *Millennium* 22(1): 27–51; and R. Vayrynen (2002) "Reforming the world order: multi- and plurilateral approaches", in B. Hettne and B. Oden (eds.) *Global Governance in the 21st Century: Alternative Perspectives on World Order*, Expert Group in Development Issues (EGDI), Stockholm: Almkvist & Wiksell, p. 110.
16. The plurilateral model, however, can also be unpredictable because it is not stabilized by any directly hierarchical system, see R. Vayrynen "Reforming the world order: multi- and plurilateral approaches" (note 15).
17. P. Cerny, "Plurilateralism: structural differentiation and functional conflict in the post-cold war world order", pp. 49–50 (see note 15); and R. Vayrynen "Reforming the world order: multi- and plurilateral approaches", pp. 110–111 (see note 15).
18. The individualist–communitarian debate, which started in the mid-1970s after the publication of John Rawls's influential *Theory of Justice* (1971), focused particularly on the relationship between political theory and social practice in relation to individuals' moral agency and cultural identity.
19. D. Archibugi (2003) "Cosmopolitical democracy", in D. Archibugi *Debating Cosmopolitics*, London and New York: Verso, pp. 1–15.
20. Michel Foucault (1994) "The birth of biopolitics", in P. Rabinow (ed.) *Ethics, Subjectivity and Truth*, Vol. 1, New York: New Press, pp. 73–85.
21. This ideology could be found in the pursuit of European colonialism that excluded the colonized from being accepted as equals in the European-dominated and Eurocentric international system, as pointed out by the postcolonial critique. See, for example, Pal Ahluwalia (2001) *Politics and Post-Colonial Theory: African Inflections*, London and New York: Routledge.
22. S. Page, "Developing Countries in International negotiations: How they Influence Trade and Climate Change Negotiations", IDS Bulletin 35(1): 71–75.
23. K. Danaher (2003) "Writing a global constitution: report from Cancun", *Review of African Political Economy (ROAPE)* 98: 649. See, for instance, ActionAid/CAFOD/Oxfam (2005) "Do the deal. The G7 must act now to cancel poor country debts", joint agency paper: http://www.xxfam.org.uk/what_we_do/debt_aid/downloads/g7_deal.pdf (downloaded 27.2.2005), which heavily criticized the debt relief programmes and the inefficiency of the ODA and pointed out up to 40 per cent of all aid is tied to overpriced goods or services from the donor country. For details on the Helsinki Process, see http://www.helsinkiprocess.fi/netcomm/ImgLib/24/89/ENews_3%5B1%5D.05.pdf (downloaded 30.10.2005).
24. For details on 2005 World Summit outcome, see http://www.un.org/summit2005 (downloaded 30.10.2005). Other attempts to recognize global interdependence and to take action can be found, for example, in UN Secretary-General's report "In Larger Freedom" of March 2005, that focuses on the issues of development, security and human rights. See http://www.un.org/largerfreedom/contents.htm (downloaded 30.10.2005); see also the report of the High-Level Panel on Threats, Challenges and Change at http://www.un.org/secureworld/ (downloaded 30.10.2005).

21

From unilateralism to bilateralism: Challenges for the multilateral trade system

Beth A. Simmons

We live in a period of economic globalization. Many think this has something to do with the success of multilateral international institutions developed in the post-war period. In particular, the General Agreement on Tariffs and Trade (GATT) and the World Trade Organization (WTO) are credited with (or blamed for) regularizing a set of broadly agreed rules that have stimulated the growth of world trade. In many ways, these institutions have become increasingly robust: membership has grown, coverage of multilateral rules has extended, and multilateral dispute settlement has become increasingly fair and "legalized".

None of this has occurred without stress. In the 1980s, the primary challenge came from what some termed an "aggressive" form of United States *unilateralism*: the desire to unilaterally force US ideas of liberal trade law on the rest of the world.[1] The challenges today are subtler and are associated with forms of *bilateralism*. Increasingly, global consensus is being undermined by semi-consensual bilateral agreements that in some respects push well beyond multilaterally settled norms. These bilateral agreements pull multilateral norms a strand at a time toward the agenda of the most powerful negotiators, especially the United States and the European Union.

Of course, there is nothing new in the observation that the rules of international trade are written largely by the most powerful. Nor is bilateralism new to international commercial relationships; in fact, it is the dominant form these relationships have historically taken. What is somewhat surprising is how well bilateralism has flourished in multilateralism's shadow. To a marked extent, some of the most important decisions in today's globalized world are taken a country-pair at a time.

The first section of this chapter provides some background to the development of the multilateral trade system. The second section will examine United States unilateralism, and argue that in some very important ways it was used actually to support the multilateral regime. This is not the case, though, with the recent explosion of bilateralism. The third section will show that bilateral (and regional) treaties are on the rise, and that these threaten in some important ways consensual multilateral norms. While multilateralism is still at the core of the international trade system, powerful economic interests have the potential to undermine the norms to which most states have committed themselves.

Trade multilateralism in historical perspective

The development of the multilateral trading system

Multilateralism in international trade is a relatively recent phenomenon. The nineteenth century was marked by unilateral liberalization on the part of the major power, Great Britain,[2] as well as clusters of bilateral trade agreements, centred largely among the major European powers.[3] The United States emerged from its civil war with even higher tariffs than *ante bellum*, and stood aloof from the bilateral agreements negotiated as the century progressed. Tariffs shot up (and sometimes were reduced) unilaterally; the McKinley Tariff Act of 1890 and the Dingley Tariff of 1897 are prime examples.[4] Trade cooperation during this period was ad hoc, fragile and plagued by fears of retaliation.[5] Despite the creation of the League of Nations, nothing fundamental changed during the interwar years. The failure of the World Economic Conference is notorious; monetary issues crowded the agenda and the meeting broke up early over the unilateral devaluation of the dollar.[6] To the extent that trade began slowly to reconstitute during the Great Depression, it was the result of recovery and bilateral rather than multilateral efforts.[7]

The historical preponderance of bilateralism in the trade area is not difficult to understand. Trade itself is typically thought of in dyadic terms, and the liberalization of trade is hardly a public international good in the classic sense. Genuinely broad agreements are difficult to reach. Trade issues are subject to temptations to defect, particularly when domestic producers claim liberalization will injure their interests. For all of these reasons, international trade has historically been governed by bilateral and unilateral agreements and decisions, even when most-favoured-nation (MFN) principles have formally been involved.

The post-World War II period represents the first significant effort backed by most of the world's major powers (minus the Soviet Union, who initially declined to participate) to construct a multilateral trade order. Predictably, arriving at some consensus about what this order should look like raised difficulties. An ambitious International Trade Organization was initially proposed, with a wide range of powers and responsibilities from liberalizing trade in goods to regulating commodity prices, to addressing foreign direct investment. This accord effectively died when the US Senate refused to ratify it; still, the stage was set for a series of substantive trade discussions that would significantly lower tariff barriers over the next few decades. The ITO's initial framework agreement, the General Agreement on Tariffs and Trade (GATT) has since evolved into the most important multilateral trade framework of the twentieth century.

In many respects, the GATT multilateral trading regime has been a tremendous success. The regime was built in 1948 on a few simple principles, whose detailed implementation would be carried out over the next several decades. Its essential features were a commitment to liberalize trade (though not a commitment to *free* trade); non-discrimination among members (with some exceptions for customs unions and free trade areas); reciprocity (the idea that concessions should be mutual); and safeguards (allowing for temporary exemptions from GATT rules in cases of serious GATT-induced market disruptions.[8] The regime's membership[9] and the share of world GDP of its members has grown significantly over time (Figure 21.1). Meanwhile, global trade has grown significantly over time from only a few hundred billion dollars the year the GATT was founded to 8 trillion dollars by 2002.

Substantial trade liberalization has taken place since 1948. In the first decade and a half, state parties concentrated on reducing tariffs on industrial goods. For the Kennedy Round of negotiations (1964–1967), anti-dumping measures were added to the agenda. The Tokyo Round (1973–1979) broached the issue of non-tariff barriers for the first time.[10] By the late 1980s, parties were ready to significantly extend negotiations to new sectors: during the Uruguay Round (1986–1994), agreements were reached on services, intellectual property, textiles and agriculture. In 1994, with a significantly strengthened Dispute Settlement Mechanism (DSM), the GATT was transformed into the World Trade Organization.[11]

Members of the club

The GATT began as a fairly homogenous club of wealthy and fairly democratic countries, but it has had to face some important challenges over

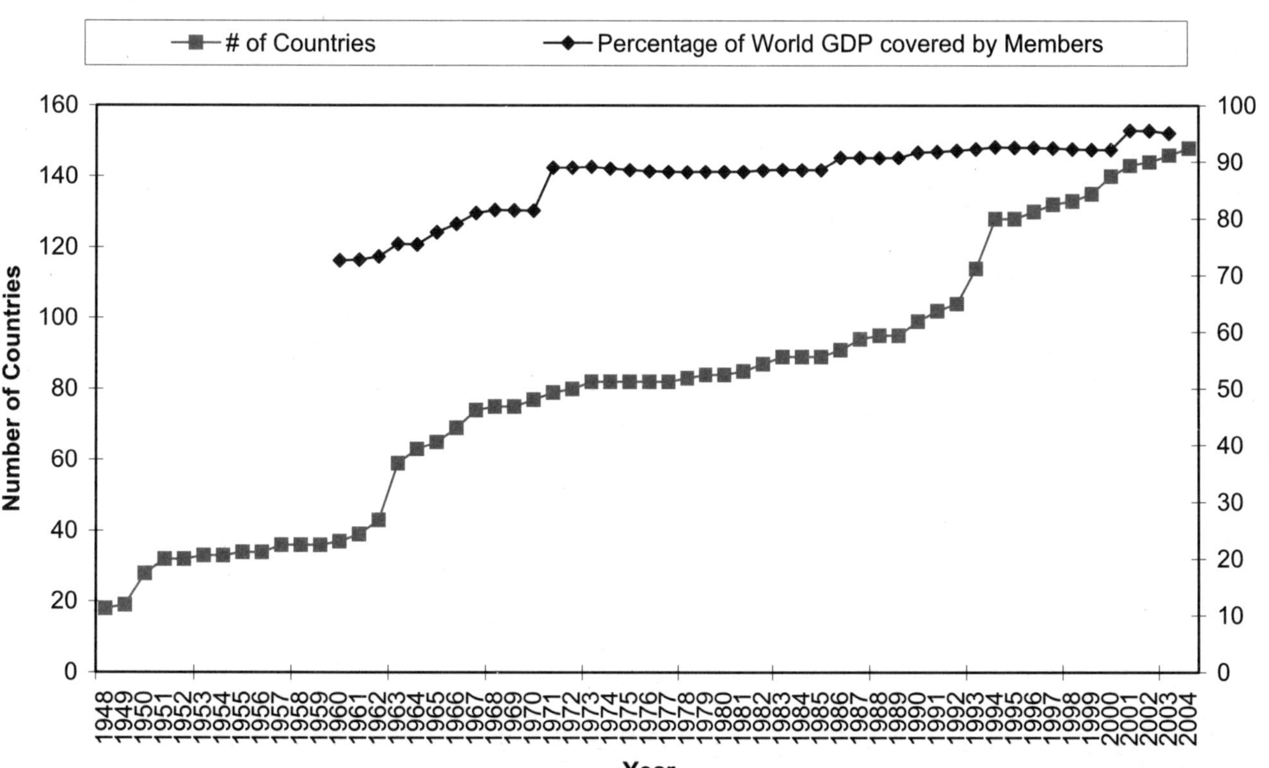

Figure 21.1 GATT/WTO Membership: countries and share of World GDP

the past several decades. A growing membership has required the international trade regime to digest a good deal of diversity. Consider changes in the wealth of the average member over time: Figure 21.2 shows that the per capita GDP of GATT members has, on average, increased ever since the mid-1970s. However, it also shows that the standard deviation of GDP per capita – a measure of the dispersion of wealth among members – is much higher and has increased even faster since the mid-1970s than wealth itself.[12] Wealth among GATT/WTO members is increasing, but is also increasingly *diverging*. GATT/WTO members are also wealthier than the world average, but the gap between members and non-members has closed over time, as more countries are admitted to the club.

The political character of GATT members has changed significantly over time. The original GATT founders were on average much more democratic than the rest of the world (Figure 21.3). In the 1960s and 1970s, new members from Africa and Latin America's turn toward authoritarian rule account for the large dip in the average polity score of GATT members in those years. On the other hand, transitions to democracy in Latin America and Eastern Europe account for the democratic upturn beginning in the mid-1980s. Whereas the GATT members were once much more democratic than the rest of the world, the diffusion of democracy and the growth in GATT/WTO membership has caused global and member averages to converge. Meanwhile, the dispersion of regime types within the multilateral trade system has remained reasonably constant over the years.

Overall, members in the multilateral trading system have become more democratic while diverging in their levels of wealth. This suggests more accountable governments are required to represent polities whose wealth (and possibly interests) have begun to diverge. Taken together, these conditions may help to explain why negotiating rounds have become more ambitious (encompassing a broader range of deals) as well as more drawn out. Negotiating rounds lasted three years in the 1960s, six in the 1970s, and stretched to eight in the 1980s/1990s, reflecting their far greater complexity.

Meanwhile, a structural shift in the relative power and interests of the major economies had taken place: in particular, the economic difficulties of the major Western countries and the rise of the East Asian "Tigers". The signs of relative decline of multilateralism's prime sponsor, the United States, were rife: the end of the Bretton Woods dollar-based monetary system, the energy crisis, and the appearance of a balance of payments deficit in the US accounts reflected and portended basic changes in the structure of global economic relationships. The rise of Asian trade

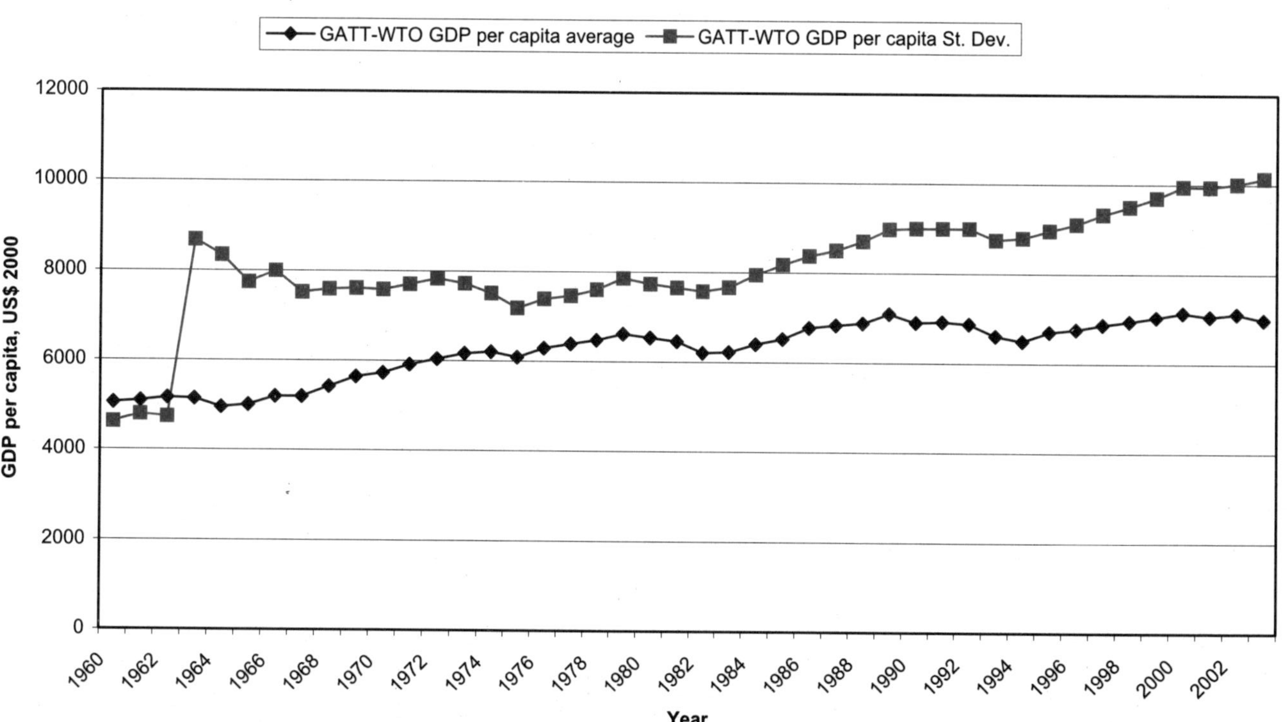

Figure 21.2 Per capita wealth of GATT-WTO members

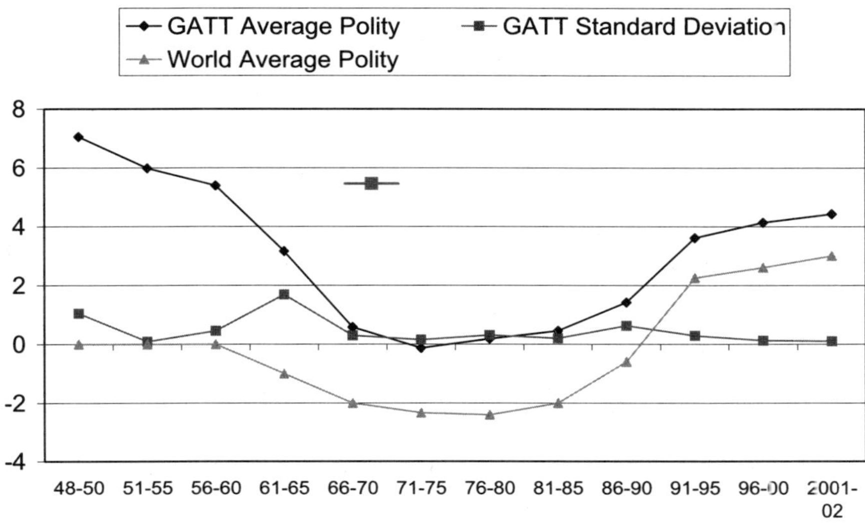

Figure 21.3 Democracy among GATT members

competitors – especially Japan – became the trade issue of the 1980s.[13] Figure 21.4 illustrates the relative magnitude of Asian exports[14] compared to those of the original GATT members. The former comprised only about 10 per cent of the latter in 1960. By the new millennium, the share was well over 50 per cent. In 1960, the United States exported three times as much as the major Asian economies combined. As of 2002, the comparable figure was about two-thirds. These shifting ratios indicate that the multilateral trading system has had to "digest" a good deal of structural change over the past three decades.

Structural change and the risk of unilateralism

By the early 1970s there were widespread concerns in academic and policy circles that the international trading system might not be able to survive the end of US hegemony.[15] These concerns were kindled by a relatively new hawkishness in American trade policy. One of the most important pieces of legislation in this regard was the 1974 Trade Act, whose Section 301 contained a provision that required the US executive *unilaterally* to impose trade restrictions on countries whose trade practices the US found to be "unfair". The United States used this act during

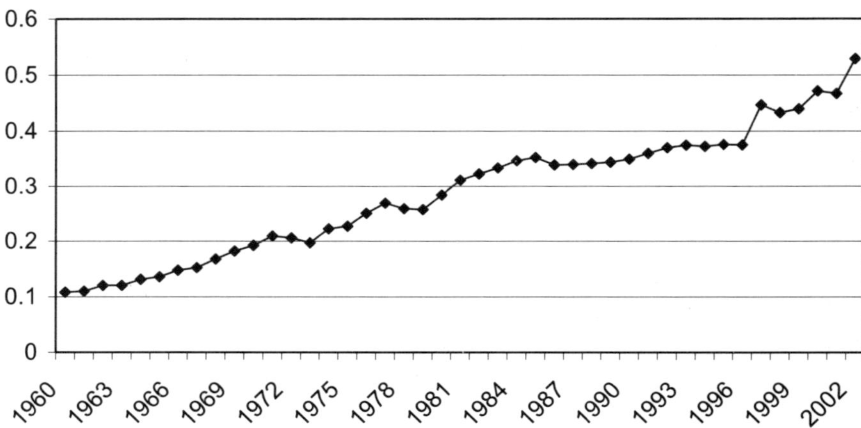

Figure 21.4 Ratio of Asian Tigers' to Original GATT members' exports (*Source*: World Development Indicators)
Note: Asian Tigers: Japan, China, Hong Kong, Malaysia, Korea (data for Singapore and Taiwan are unavailable).

the 1980s and less often in the 1990s to investigate 29 cases of allegedly unfair trade by the European Community (Union). Japan alone attracted 21 Section 301 complaints between 1979 and 1990, while Korea attracted 15 and Taiwan 9. The United States has investigated 3 section cases alleging unfair practices by China, all in the 1990s.

Section 301 represents perhaps the most obvious effort by the United States Congress to hold unilateral policies in reserve in order to secure desired outcomes in international commercial relationships.[16] Some observers have branded the use of this instrument "aggressive unilateralism";[17] others have seen it as a way for the US to encourage the further development of the multilateral system.[18] While the unilateral imposition of sanctions to counter "unfair trade practices" is hardly the only manifestation of unilateralism in trade one might be concerned with, it is the clearest *institutionalization* of self-help by the major trading country in the past few decades.

Contrary predictions notwithstanding, multilateralism has survived the decade of the most intense United States unilateralism. Even as congressmen were bashing Toshiba television sets on the steps of the United States Capitol building, US negotiators were working towards another multilateral round of trade liberalization (the Uruguay Round).[19] The 1980s were the zenith of American trade vigilantism; since the mid-1990s the United States has favoured multilateral trade dispute settlement to unilaterally imposed remedies. We can see this in the relative resort to 301 sanctions compared to dispute initiation through multilateral GATT/WTO channels. Figure 21.5 shows that the ratio of disputes resolved through multilateral mechanisms (the DSM of the GATT or WTO) has drastically risen in comparison to the number of cases handled through 301 sanctioning. (Note that the graph ends in 1999, the last year for which there was any 301 case; with the exception of a "Special 301" sanctioning of Ukraine for "egregious" international property rights violations in 2002 for which the United States imposed $75 million sanctions.)

At first blush, America's unilateral use of Section 301 looks like a desperate move by a declining hegemonic power to preserve its position through unilateral measures. There may be some truth to this charge, but the actual use of 301 is not especially consistent with this interpretation. Consider the hypothesis that 301 cases are a reaction to a growing US trade deficit. While no particular foreign practice is likely to affect the country's balance of trade, the political salience of an allegedly unfair or illegal foreign practice is arguably more likely to receive a sympathetic hearing by US trade authorities when the balance of trade is strongly negative and deteriorating. But the evidence on the use of 301 sanctions relative to use of GATT/WTO dispute settlement tells a different story. The plot of the ratio of multilateral to bilateral disputes bears practically no relationship to the United States balance of trade. The ratio of GATT disputes in which the US was complainant to 301 cases dropped in the late 1980s *despite* the worsening of the deficit. Similarly, the US proved willing to use the DSM in the late 1990s – and forego unilaterally imposed 301 sanctions – despite a worsening deficit. A related hypothesis – that 301 cases reflect concern with a declining share of world exports – also is difficult to sustain. The propensity of the United States to settle disputes in a multilateral framework has *grown in tandem* with the share of US exports in the world total (Figure 21.6).

An alternative interpretation of US 301 patterns would underscore its tactical support of multilateralism. There is some evidence that the United States has favoured unilateral dispute settlement over multilateral approaches during trade negotiation rounds. 301 cases outnumbered GATT dispute resolution during both the Tokyo Round (during which the ratio of multilateral cases to 301 cases was 0.3) and the Uruguay Round (during which the ratio was 0.6). The United States was much more likely to use multilateral dispute settlement when trade talks were *not* in progress: the average ratio of multilateral to unilateral cases was 1.45 when no multilateral rounds were under way. This suggests that the

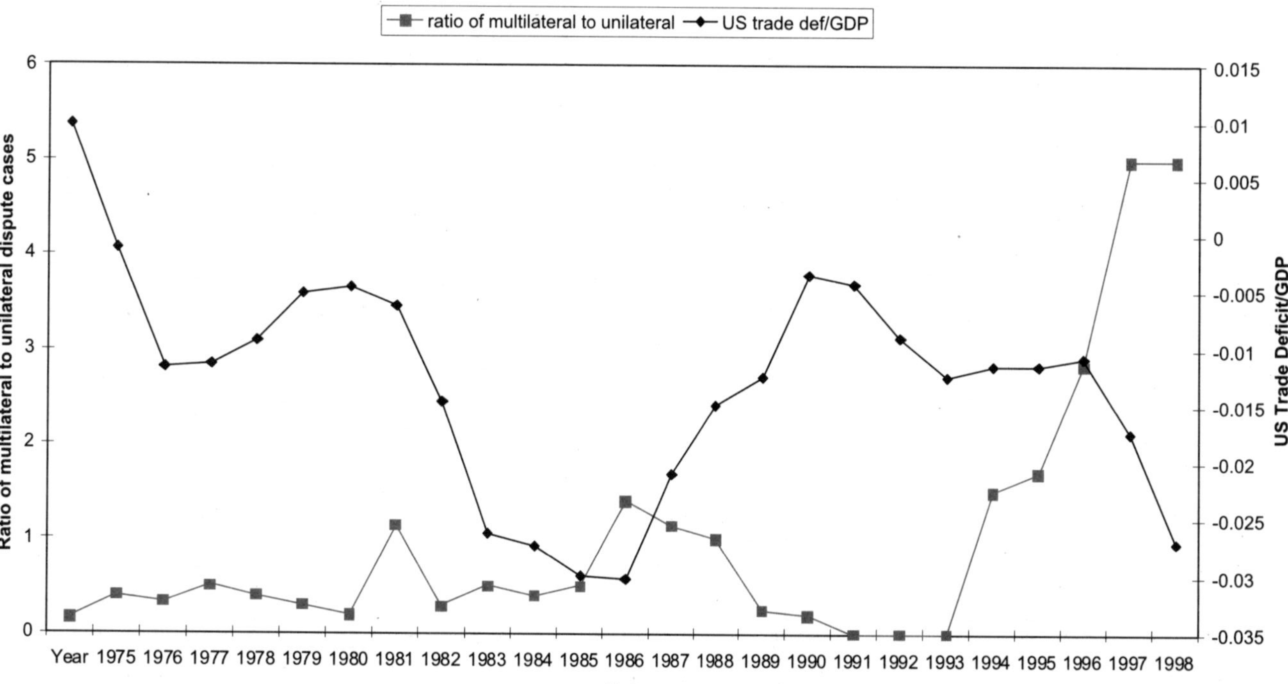

Figure 21.5 Multilateralism and the United States trade deficit
Note: There were no 301 cases from 2000 to 2005. Consequently, the ratio of multilateral to unilateral dispute settlement is undefined.

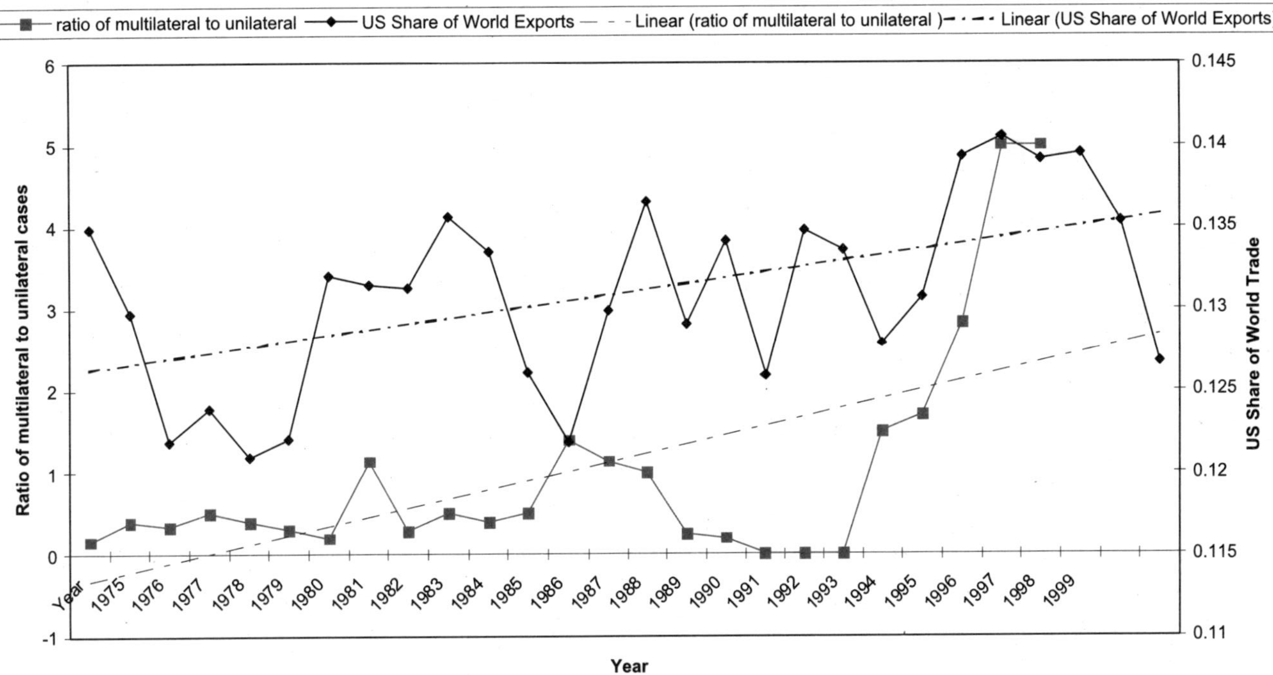

Figure 21.6 US trade share and multilateral dispute settlement

United States may have had a strategy of using unilateral pressures to nudge substantive trade talks in directions favoured by the US.

The United States has drastically curtailed its use of 301 sanctions now that WTO mechanisms are available to assist in settling disputes. For much of the late 1970s and 1980s, the GATT's dispute settlement mechanism was by many accounts in disarray, due largely to a string of "blocked" reports.[20] Dispute settlement rules under the WTO eliminated the possibility of blocking reports, significantly enhancing the right to a multilaterally determined decision. This change seems to have had a significant impact on US dispute settlement patterns. Indeed, the average ratio of multilateral to unilateral 301 cases was 0.46 before 1995 and 3.21 after (excluding the 4 years after 1999 in which there were no 301 cases at all).

On balance, multilateral institutions have endured a tough adjustment period fairly well. The United States has apparently used its power to apply unilateral sanctions in a way consistent with the further development of multilateralism. Section 301 has been used primarily during trade negotiations, not in response to the United States trade deficit or exporting difficulties. Nor is there any evidence that the United States has retreated into unilateral measures with the end of the Cold War. If anything, quite the reverse appears to be true.

With China's accession, all of the major East Asian economies are now formally under the multilateral rules. Ironically, one reason the system may have been able to eventually accommodate this tremendous structural change is it was not forced through strict legal machinery. The United States' tactic of negotiating a series of "voluntary export restraints" and "orderly marking agreements" may have gone against the grain of multilateral values,[21] but may in the end have helped to preserve the system as a whole. Similarly the use of Section 301 may have largely been aimed at encouraging trade partners to further liberalize through multilateral mechanisms.

Bridging the development gap: the bilateral option

Historically, the multilateral trade system was designed to address the trade concerns of the major industrialized economies. Among the original founding members, only two were from Latin America (Brazil and Cuba – the latter later withdrew) only one was from Africa (South Africa), and five were from all of Asia (the former British Empire and the Republic of China (Taiwan)). The early rounds were dominated by the industrial countries' concern to liberalize trade in the manufactured goods they produced. Their dominance has been maintained through the practice of negotiations among major suppliers and major consumers consummating deals that are then passed along via MFN rules to the rest of the GATT members. By "consensus", textiles had been handled outside of the GATT context, in the form of negotiated quotas collectively known as the Multi-Fiber Agreement. The ability to set the negotiating agenda and the process of consensus decision-making has preserved the largest industrial powers' leading role in the multilateral trade regime.[22] As a consequence, developing countries face important challenges in trying to assert their rights in dispute settlement as well.[23] A growing literature is beginning to document the extent to which the gains from GATT/WTO membership has been noticeably asymmetrical in favour of the advanced industrial countries.[24]

This is not to say that the multilateral trade system has utterly ignored developmental issues. The GATT itself contained "special and differential treatment provisions" which allowed for longer time periods for implementing agreements and commitments. The regime respects the developmental needs of the developing members through the Generalized System of Preferences (GSP) meant to encourage favourable access for the products of developing countries to the markets of the developed countries.[25] By at least some accounts, the GSP system has been a relative success for the developing countries participating in it.[26] Still, these agreements are bilateral ad hoc concessions, and can be withdrawn when the country extending preferences so decides.

Several issues dividing developing and developed countries have come to the fore in the 1990s. These have primarily been, on the one hand, liberalization of agriculture and textiles in the industrial countries, and, on the other, investment and intellectual property rights protection in developing areas. The Uruguay Round of negotiations began to address these issues (the Trade-Related Intellectual Property Agreement is an example), but in a largely preliminary way. The Doha Round of negotiations has been difficult to get off the ground precisely because of the remaining bargaining problems associated with reaching agreement on these issues.

Difficulties in the multilateral setting have given rise to a profusion of bilateral economic agreements, largely between developed and developing countries. Bilateral and regional trade agreements, bilateral investment agreements, and bilateral and regional intellectual property rights agreements have all proliferated in the past few years (see Figures 21.7, 21.8 and 21.9).

Bilateral agreements have some real attractions for some countries. From both countries' point of view, negotiating costs are lower, since agreements in the bilateral setting are easier to reach. Bilateral agree-

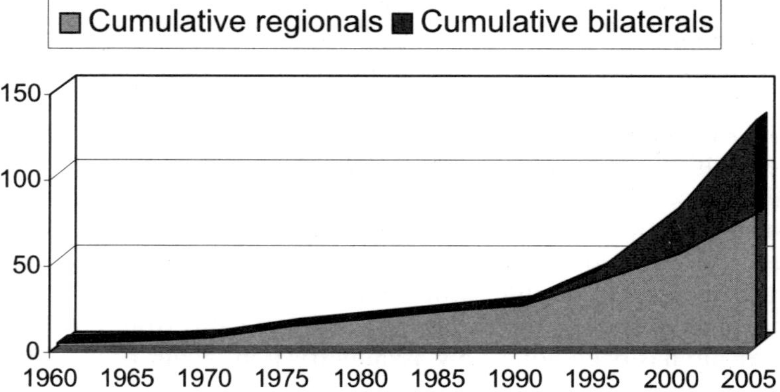

Figure 21.7 Cumulative number of regional and bilateral trade agreements in effect (*Source*: http://www.wto.org/english/tratop_e/region_e/eif_e.xls)
Note: Counts individual accessions to regional organizations as regional agreements.

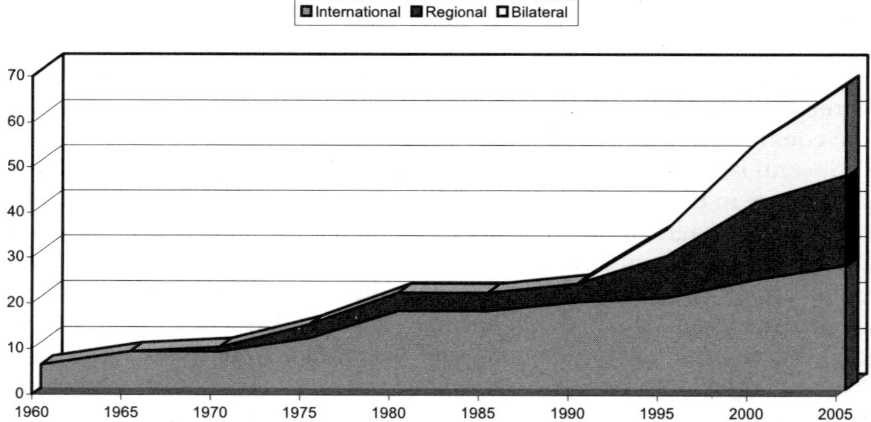

Figure 21.8 Cumulative number of international, regional and bilateral intellectual property agreements (*Source*: http://www.iprsonline.org/legalinstruments/bilateral.htm)

ments can be targeted to the specific issues of primary concern to the two countries. Bilateralism can, however, raise transaction costs, as numerous agreements may take a good deal of time to conclude.

The most important implication of bilateralism is its tendency to attenuate the relative imbalance of negotiating power between larger and

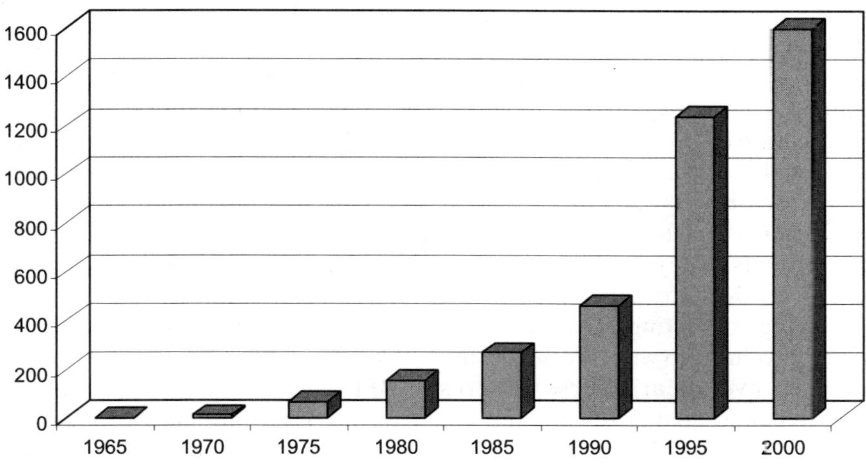

Figure 21.9 Cumulative number of bilateral investment treaties in effect (*Source*: ICSID, UNCTAD; as counted by Elkins, Guzman and Simmons (2005))

smaller economies. Since bilateral agreements are made sequentially, it is more difficult for developing countries to create coalitions with the possibility of balancing the power of the industrialized countries. For this reason, bilateral agreements tend to have the effect of ratcheting up the standards of the global regime in areas favoured by the industrial powers. Competitive dynamics tend to spur the negotiation of bilateral economic agreements, as the swift acceleration over the 1990s in all three figures indicates. Cumulatively, these agreements might support freer trade, but linkage strategies can impose additional costs on the weaker partners in a bilateral negotiation, with important distributive consequences for small countries.[27] Competitive dynamics in a world of exploding bilateral agreements can encourage developing countries to accept conditions that they would not accept were it not for the perceived competition for capital and for market access.

The spread of bilateral investment treaties and bilateral property rights agreements most readily illustrate this point. BITs are agreements establishing the terms and conditions for private investment by nationals and companies of one country in the jurisdiction of another.[28] Virtually all BITs cover four substantive areas: FDI admission, treatment, expropriation and the settlement of disputes.[29] The growing popularity of BITs is puzzling when contrasted with the *collective resistance* developing countries have shown toward pro-investment principles under customary international law and the failure of the international community to make progress on a multilateral investment agreement.[30] On its face, this seems to suggest that BITs do not simply reflect the ready acceptance of dominant international property rights norms. In fact, it is highly likely that the diffusion of BITs – and the liberal property rights regime they embody – are propelled in good part by the competition among potential host countries for credible property rights protections that direct investors require, but have not been able to secure in multilateral forums. Recent research suggests that BITs are likely to be adopted by developing countries when their major trade competitors have negotiated similar arrangements. They are also more likely to be negotiated by developing countries that are dependent on manufacturing capital (for which there are many competing jurisdictions) and less likely to be concluded by primary producers (who are more likely to have a resource advantage to draw in investment). These patterns of BIT adoption suggest a competitive dynamic among developing countries for international manufacturing investments.[31] Arguably, bilateral investment treaties have led to important concessions with respect to the protection of foreign investments without, however, winning developing countries as a whole improved access to the agricultural and textile markets of the rich.

Intellectual property rights have also enjoyed a burst of bilateral legal activity. In contrast to foreign direct investment, however, there is a multilateral regime to protect such rights (the Trade Related Intellectual Property Agreement, or TRIPS). The leaders in the campaign to sign liberal agreements in this area are the United States and the European Union. The United States, for example, has included a higher standard for the protection of intellectual property rights (IPRs) in its preferred version of the Free Trade Area of the Americas, while the Europeans have insisted on enhanced intellectual property rights protection in their negotiations with MERCOSUR. Many bilateral IPR agreements include items that TRIPs does not cover. US agreements with Jordan, Mongolia, Nicaragua, Sri Lanka and Vietnam require patent protection on animals and plants, while the US agreement with South Africa protects "biotechnological inventions" (not mentioned in the TRIPS). Other bilateral agreements accelerate the time tables for TRIPS adoption; still other require the developing country to join multilateral agreements they likely would not have signed in the absence of the bilateral pressure. EU agreements with Morocco, Tunisia and Jordan require these countries to sign the International Convention for the Protection of New Varieties of Plants (1961) as well as the Budapest Treaty on the International Recognition of the Deposit of Microorganisms for the Purposes of Patent Procedure. The upshot of these agreements is the emergence of a "TRIPs-Plus" standard to which most developing countries are reluctant to subscribe. Yet, once a number of countries have signed bilaterals that go beyond the TRIPs, it becomes politically very difficult for developing countries to resist such US and EU proposals in a multilateral forum as Brazil and others did at the WTO Ministerial Conference in 2003.

Conclusion

Multilateralism has been crucial to an enhanced international flow of goods and services over the past century. If the project to develop a broad global trade regime had failed in the middle of the twentieth century, it is difficult to imagine the economic history of the post-World War II period. Multilateral decision-making has been crucial to post-war reconstruction, the incorporation of developing countries, and the integration of non-market "transition" countries into the global trading system. It has also been the central mechanism through which the structural changes associated with the relative rise of Asia's major economies have been accommodated. It is difficult to envision a mode of rule development as robust yet flexible as those reflected in the GATT/WTO regime. Some studies doubt membership in this regime has much improved members' economic circumstances, but the system has coincided with the most remarkable improvements in human material well-being ever documented.[32]

The multilateral trading system has always had a healthy respect for the realities of market power; consensus decision-making initiated by major suppliers and consumers has seen to that. Negotiating outcomes have historically reflected the interests of major economic players, though the broadening of the GATT/WTO membership has placed new issues on the table and allowed for some important bargains across the developmental divide.

The regime has come under particular stress with the rise of Asia and the relatively slow growth of multilateralism's traditional sponsor, the United States. Despite apparent extra-legal "understandings" and unilateral remedies for allegedly unfair practices, multilateralism survived the 1980s. The ideal of a "universal, ruled-based, open, non-discriminatory and equitable"[33] multilateral trading system is largely intact, and yet a parallel world of legal agreements is flourishing at the regional and bilateral level that has the potential to create norms to which many GATT/WTO members would never agree in a multilateral setting. Whether the new bilateralism will be broadly accepted as legitimately norm creating in new areas such as foreign direct investment and intellectual property protection remains to be seen.

Notes

1. Jagdish N. Bhagwati and Hugh T. Patrick (1990) "Aggressive unilateralism: America's 301 trade policy and the world trading system", *Studies in International Trade Policy*, Ann Arbor: University of Michigan Press.
2. Timothy J. McKeown (1983) "Hegemonic stability theory and 19th century tariff levels in Europe", *International Organization* 37(1): 73–91.
3. Robert Pahre (2001) "Most-favored-nation clauses and clustered negotiations", *International Organization* 55(4): 859–890.
4. Andrew G. Brown (2003) "Reluctant partners: a history of multilateral trade cooperation, 1850–2000", *Studies in International Economics*, Ann Arbor: University of Michigan Press.
5. James Foreman-Peck (1995) *A History of the World Economy: International Economic Relations Since 1850*, 2nd edn, New York/London: Harvester Wheatsheaf.
6. Charles Poor Kindleberger (1986) *The World In Depression, 1929–1939*, revised edn, Berkeley: University of California Press.
7. Stephan Haggard (1988) "The institutional foundations of hegemony: explaining the Reciprocal Trade Agreements Act of 1934", *International Organization* 42(1): 91–119.
8. On the GATT provisions generally, see William Adams Brown (1950) *The United States and the Restoration of World Trade: An Analysis and Appraisal of the ITO Charter and the General Agreement on Tariffs and Trade*, Washington DC: Brookings Institution; and John Howard Jackson (1969) *World Trade and the Law of GATT: A Legal Analysis of the General Agreement on Tariffs and Trade*, Indianapolis IN: Bobbs-Merrill.
9. The GATT was succeeded by the World Trade Organization (WTO) in 1995.
10. Alfred E. Eckes (ed.) (2000) *Revisiting U.S. Trade Policy: Decisions in Perspective*, Athens: Ohio University Press.
11. The basic chronology of negotiation rounds can be found at the WTO's website, at: http://www.wto.org/english/thewto_e/whatis_e/tif_e/fact4_e.htm.
12. Note that the large jump in the standard deviation in 1953 is largely explained by the admission of Kuwait, with a yearly GDP per capital in 2000 of US$56,000, to the GATT.
13. Robert S. Walters (1993) *Talking Trade: U.S. Policy in International Perspective, Case Studies in International Affairs*, Boulder CO: Westview Press.
14. Japan, Korea, China (figures available only after 1996), Hong Kong and Malaysia.
15. Robert Gilpin (1975) *U.S. Power and the Multinational Corporation: The Political Economy of Foreign Direct Investment*, The Political Economy of International Relations series, New York: Basic Books; Robert O. Keohane (1984) *After Hegemony: Cooperation and Discord in the World Political Economy*, Princeton NJ: Princeton University Press; Stephen D. Krasner (1983) "Structural causes and regime consequences: regimes as intervening variables", in S.D. Krasner (ed.) *International Regimes*, Ithaca: Cornell University Press.
16. I.M. Destler (1986) *American Trade Politics: System Under Stress*, Washington, DC: Institute for International Economics.
17. Jagdish N. Bhagwati and Hugh T. Patrick (1990) "Aggressive unilateralism", see Note 1.
18. Thomas O. Bayard and Kimberly Ann Elliott (1994) *Reciprocity and Retaliation in US Trade Policy*, Washington, DC: Institute for International Economics; and Robert E. Hudec (1990) "Thinking about the New Section 301: beyond good and evil", in J.N. Bhagwati and H.T. Patrick (eds.) *Aggressive Unilateralism: America's 301 Trade Policy and the World Trading System*, Ann Arbor: University of Michigan Press.
19. For a study that emphasizes the historical commitments of United States executives to favour free trade principles, see Delia B. Conti (1998) *Reconciling Free Trade, Fair*

Trade, and Interdependence: The Rhetoric of Presidential Economic Leadership, Praeger series in Political Communication, Westport, CT: Praeger.

20. Robert E. Hudec (1993) *Enforcing International Trade Law: The Evolution of the Modern GATT Legal System*, Salem NH: Butterworths Legal Publisher.
21. For a sectoral discussion of US trade relations with Europe, which concludes that the "multilateral" system up to the 1980s has never really been multilateral, see Stephen Woolcock, Jeffrey A. Hart and Hans van der Ven (1985) *Interdependence in the Post-multilateral Era: Trends in U.S.–European Trade Relations*, Cambridge, MA: University Press of America.
22. Richard H. Steinberg (2002) "Consensus-based bargaining and outcomes in the GATT/WTO", *International Organization* 56(2): 339–374.
23. Andrew Guzman and Beth A Simmons (2005) "Power plays and capacity constraints: the selection of defendants in WTO disputes", *Journal of Legal Studies* 34(2)
24. Arvind Subramanian and Shang-Jin Wei (2003) *The WTO Promotes Trade, Strongly but Unevenly*, NBER Working Papers, Cambridge MA.
25. For a full chronology of the efforts made under the auspices of the GATT/WTO to improve the trade opportunities for developing countries see http://www.wto.org/english/tratop_e/devel_e/anexi_e.doc.
26. Andrew Rose (2004) "Do we really know that the WTO increases trade?", *American Economic Review* 94(1): 98–114.
27. Giovanni Maggi (1999) "The role of multilateral institutions in international trade cooperation", *American Economic Review* 89(1): 190–214.
28. Automated System for Customs Data (AYSCUDA), http://www.asycuda.org/cuglossa.
29. ICSID Bilateral Investment Treaties, http://www.worldbank.org/icsid/treaties/intro.htm.
30. Andrew Guzman (1998) "Explaining the popularity of bilateral investment treaties: why LDCs sign treaties that hurt them", *Virginia Journal of International Law* 38: 639.
31. Zachary Elkins, Andrew Guzman and Beth Simmons (2006) "Competing for capital: the diffusion of bilateral investment treaties, 1960–2000", *International Organization* (forthcoming).
32. Andrew Rose (2004) "Do we really know that the WTO increases trade?", see note 26.
33. This is the ideal as described by the 2005 World Summit Outcome, 20 September 2005. See http://www.un.org/summit2005/documents.html.

22

Multilateralism as a way of life in Europe

A.J.R. Groom

Introduction

For a European the very title of this volume, "Multilateralism under challenge?", is a shock. Multilateralism is such a way of life that to challenge it is in fact a threat to the very modus vivendi of European politics, both within Europe and in its attitude towards extra European political relationships. Moreover, multilateralism is seen as a way of life rather than as a question of power, international order or structural change because it is the means by which Europeans have tried, with a considerable degree of success, to reconcile togetherness and diversity. There is a process of coming together which is somewhat different from integration because it has the value of rejoicing in and benefiting from diversity. Moreover, multilateralism is so much part of the way of thinking that there is no strong conception of a unipolar international system. There was, to be sure, a unipolar moment, but that has passed and, indeed, even that unipolar moment was severely circumscribed beçause it was never multidimensional. It is true, as the former French Foreign Minister Hubert Vedrine pointed out, that the United States was a hyper-power, nevertheless it was also shackled by countervailing powers in a range of different dimensions, not least in the economic but also in the political, strategic and in the cultural dimensions.

The notion of multilateralism as being state-centric is also not one which fits in with the experience of many Europeans. This is because Europe is now encompassed by a system, or rather systems, of multilateral and multilevel governance in which the role of civil society is an integral part. The EU is an entity which is building simultaneously in four directions: firstly, towards the joint management of pooled sovereignty in the Brussels nexus. Secondly, it is building down towards the regions which are displaying a greater degree of autonomy and innovation. Thirdly, it is strongly involved in civil society by building transnational ties, such as in higher education. Finally, it is building beyond not only at the governmental level but also at the level of civil society through the Mediterranean programmes, amongst others. To be sure, in the European experience multilateralism has its state-centric aspects but that is not the whole story and does not reflect the world as many Europeans experience it. Moreover, this experience goes beyond a dependence upon a rough equivalent of benefits, even over the longer term since higher values, such as the ending of the Franco-German conflict and Europe as a zone of peace, can motivate behaviour that is otherwise difficult to explain in conventional cost/benefit terms. This all serves to provoke the reaction to any challenge to multilateralism with the riposte that it is not what is wrong with multilateralism that should be a prime interest, but what is wrong with those who have difficulties with it, and, in particular, why the United States seems to have such difficulty in conforming to the exigencies of a multilateral world.

Multilateralism has played a key role in the historical processes through which capitalism has spread, particularly as it has reached its apogee with the establishment of a world economy at the end of the twentieth century. Empire, as a vehicle for the spread of capitalism through which multinational corporations and multinational churches worked and in the service of which colonial administrators provided an administrative and military framework, has given way to a nominal independence of former colonial territories and their incorporation, through multilateral frameworks, into a system based on global capitalism which is now being christened, to use an imperial word, as globalization. Moreover, multilateralism has played a key role in handling international crises. For example, the negotiations by Britain, France and Germany with Iran in 2005 over the nuclear question is exemplary of a multilateral approach. Even in the dark days of the Cold War, the London Nuclear Suppliers Club brought together, in a multilateral framework, the antagonists who were at daggers drawn in other dimensions. But they knew that they had to deal with the global problem of proliferation and, despite the antagonisms of the Cold War, they were largely successful in doing so.

In the European experience multilateralism is not about a leadership-power paradox. Such a paradox is certainly not the case domestically within the EU ambit and nor is it the aspiration internationally. Leadership of course there has to be, but leadership is only effective if it is recognized by the constituency which it serves and therefore has a high degree of legitimacy. Multilateralism that is imposed is simply a different technique of imperialism and Europeans know full well, from their own bitter and often shameful experience, that imperialism is costly both for the imperial society and for those who are more the victim than beneficiaries of it in former colonial or hegemonic territories. Indeed, the exercise of illegitimate or non-legitimized power is not efficient in other than the short term because it is simply a down payment and the instalments are never ending as coercion continues to be required to safeguard the advantages seized by force. While, over the subsequent years, a greater degree of legitimacy for the imposed behavioural patters may be conjured up, this often requires the cutting of losses in an effort to gain post-coercive legitimacy. Rather, for Europeans, the question is how can we broach global problems in a multilateral manner.

Global problems are those which necessarily affect everyone and from which there is no escape. The effects of a nuclear war are one such problem and the degradation of the environment and resource depletion is another. The management of the global economy is a further dimension and so is the universal demand for human rights. The list is long and familiar but the underlying approach of Europeans, even if they are not fully cognizant of it, is that "if you don't hang together you will surely hang separately". Europeans have learned this verity the hard way and they hung themselves separately in two devastating civil wars, starting in 1914 and 1939. Thus, it becomes clear that the notion of the common interest is an integral part of national interest. If small actors do not pay their community dues then they will be excluded from the club to their detriment, whilst if major actors do not act in the common interest, then the framework will collapse. While major powers may be able better to defend themselves against global threats on their own than can smaller powers, they do so at greater cost, and the inevitability of the effect of global problems on them will only be postponed rather than pushed aside. In short, multilateralism is a way of hanging together and the alternative, which may be attractive in the short run, only presents us with a bleak future. Western Europeans have seen this at home and learned the lesson. They broach global problems in a like manner.

Definitions and development of the concept

Our thinking on multilateralism owes a lot to John Ruggie who, over a decade ago, first took the lead in attempting to define the term and assessing the importance of the phenomenon both conceptually and also in empirical terms. His definition is as follows:

multilateralism is an institutional form which coordinates relations among three or more states on the basis of "generalized" principles of conduct, that is, principles which specify appropriate conduct for classes of actions, without regard to the particularistic interests of the parties or the strategic exigencies that may exist in any specific occurrence".[1]

A recent European view is to be found in the *Dictionnaire des Relations Internationales* compiled by Marie-Claude Smouts, Dario Battistella and Pascal Vennesson.[2] Their definition suggests that multilateralism is not just a particular form of international activity reflecting the necessity of coming to terms with a world that spills over national boundaries. Rather "le multilatéralisme est censé proposer des principes d'ordre garantissant un minimum de prévisibilité dans les rapports internationaux. L'une de ses fonctions est de construire du sens commun: les réactions face à un événement grave et imprévu ne devraient plus se faire de façon désordonnée selon la façon dont chacun apprécie la situation et les réponses à y apporter mais s'organiser selon des principes acceptés par tous, definis au préalable d'une manière collective." To invoke multilateralism reflects an aspiration to create a value system which condemns unilateralism, conceives bilateral alliances to be dangerous and considers the coordination of national policies as the sole means to create an international order. Smouts and her colleagues also pay tribute to Robert Cox who was one of the leading figures in an UNU project which dealt with multilateralism in the perspective of the 1990s. Cox contends that

The context of multilateralism includes the state system; but the state system is circumscribed and penetrated by other forces. Primary among these is the global economy. Then there are hierarchies, including those arising from social class, gender, ethnicity, religion, and migration. Cutting across these hierarchies are the perspectives of different cultures and civilizations, as well as the constraints imposed by the biosphere. This complex of interacting forces shapes different forms of state and interstate institutions and the problematic of global governance.

Multilateralism, in a long-term perspective, would thus need to encompass all those forces that influence outcomes on global and regional issues. The Westphalian state system puts a theoretical barrier between state-centred multilateralism and the civil society that lies beyond it – a barrier that is breached frequently in practice but still presents a conceptual, and often juridical, obstacle. This realm of civil society consists not only in formally organized groups but is being continually reshaped by political, economic, and ideological pressures that generate new social forces.[3]

This analysis fits quite snugly with the views expressed recently by Franck Petiteville, who like Marie-Claude Smouts, stresses multilateralism from below.[4] Cox and his colleagues also stressed the logic of globalization in terms of its impact upon civilizations. Rather than leading to the expected conclusion of an homogenous global culture based on American roots, Cox pointed out that:

> it is evident that all around the world people are reaffirming old identities against the spectre of homogeneity. Cultural homogeneity through globalization is perceived as the new imperialism. Civilizations endure. One civilization may be overlaid by another dominant civilization for a long time; yet is not extinguished and is ready to be revived when confronted by the right circumstances. Civilizations that have appeared for long to be dormant have now been aroused. This raises new challenges for multilateralism because the official discourse of multilateralism has been a Western, Euro-American, discourse.[5]

Cox further emphasized that the future discourse would have to be one that would recognize the coexistence of civilizations and become pluralist in a multicultural inter-civilizational sense.

All of this implies a rejection of multiple bilateralism or collective bilateralism in which a hegemon acts bilaterally but seeks to cloak it in a multilateral framework, as seems now to be the case with the Bush administration in approaching its European partners. It is also a rejection of a sort of bilateralism where one state negotiates with the collectivity as in the case of Argentina and the IMF. Rather, multilateralism is seen by European states not only as the way in which they manage their own relationships in the framework in and around the EU but also as being a suitable foreign policy framework for states who are of a medium rank. Bertrand Badie in his recent *L'impuissance de la puissance* puts this argument well. "Trop faibles pour triompher sur le mode unilatéral, mais trop solides pour renoncer à tout rôle international et se réfugier dans la passivité du client, les puissances moyennes font des institutions multilatérales le receptacle privilégié de leur demonstration de force internationale." The UN system thus suits them well so that it is the middle Powers which are bringing more power to the UN's elbow. "Mais en fin de compte, les institutions multilatérales deviennent curieusement les instruments d'un nouveau règlement de compte entre une superpuissance qui y perd une part de son ascendant et des puissances moyennes qui y gagnent un rôle nouveau, intermédiaire entre le cavalier seul et le chevalier servant du jeu collectif."[6] Badie points to another change of focus with its emphasis on collective goods. He comments that "ce postulat étant admis, le jeu multilatéral apparaît progressivement comme le plus économique et, en réalité, comme le seul capable d'assurer la gestion des biens".[7]

Contemporary European experience is both multilateral and multilevel. The concentration on the Convention over the last two or three years has perhaps hidden the extent to which practice does not fit easily into conventional moulds. Enrico Gualini helps us to understand how these two factors are creating an innovative process that escapes conventional typologies and categories whether "post-" or "neo-" beyond breaking point. Moreover, these are processes to which there is no known or at least clear final resting point. As Gualini comments:

> Far from constituting a definite "status", however, multi-level governance patterns project their influence on the rules of the game of national politics. Rather than replacing – or "hollowing-out" – nation-states, sub-national empowerment and supra-nationalization are in fact seen as part of a broader dynamic of "power dispersion" in the European Union, in which national states have lost political control to European and sub-national institutions, while retaining significant control over resources and building upon this in introducing measures of institutional restructuring. The constitution of a multi-level governance environment in Europe has been interpreted, in first instance, as a rearticulation of relationships between territorial government levels related to trans-national policy-making rationales. Multi-level governance has been accordingly defined as a system of inter-governmental relationships characterized, on the one hand, by the growing importance of supra-national regulatory patterns and, on the other hand, by the increasing autonomy and capacity of mobilization of sub-national, regional-local arenas in regional programming.[8]

It all seems like a mess, but in fact it works. It is multilateralism within the confines of an entity the form of which is not yet finally delineated and may well never be delineated in a classical sense. It helps to explain why the challenge to multilateralism is such a shock for Europeans since their experience, even if it is not articulated in terms of multilateralism, is in fact that multilateralism works. To be sure, it does not work for everybody all the time nor does it work everywhere. Indeed, there are some fundamental difficulties in that there is a growing challenge to multilateralism from the people, at least in its intra-EU form. This is being crystallized in the referenda on the Constitution since this is really an institutionalization of a process of internal EU multilateralism. International – that is extra-European – multilateralism is not challenged by the people. However, they are not universally ready to follow the elites in the formal institutionalisation of their intra-European mode of living in the form of the Constitution. This domestic multilateralism is not itself under serious challenge, but people do want to have their word to say through referenda and the like. The tension arises from the gap between the daily practice of multilevel and multilateral integration in instrumental activities such as the Euro-zone and single market, which are at a high level, and the failure to develop a commensurate psycho-social community. Such a community exists but not at the same level as instrumental integration, although it is likely to be furthered by significant attempts to build down to regions and across through civil society as in higher education. This tension is exacerbated by a fetish for enlargement to countries which weaken instrumental integration in the economic sphere and do not, as yet, have a deep-rooted democratic culture. Yet such absorption has been successful in the past with countries as diverse as Greece, Spain and Portugal. While there is much to be said against the Constitution in such a context, to argue against the Constitution would, in some cases, such as in Britain, create more difficulties than it would solve. Hitherto the EU has proceeded on the basis of treaties rather than a Constitution – in fact the British mode of constitutional evolution – but it can no longer do so following the Convention. What it can do within the new framework is adopt multilateralism at varying speeds within the EU – a practice which is already much used with the Euro, Schengen and, latterly, defence.[9] Indeed the emergence of an individual European voice in defence and foreign policy, which is increasingly to be heard, although not without discordant overtones, may enhance the degree of psycho-social community as people find that they have a flag to follow which responds to aspirations to play a more independent role in world affairs. What is clear is that no one wants to throw out the multilateral baby with the unilateral bath water. This way of life is confirmed in the rhetoric of leading decision-makers such as Pascal Lamy, Javier Solana and Jacques Chirac.

European views: the "great and the good"

Pascal Lamy, one of the most powerful figures in the Prodi Commission, and as Trade Commissioner a major figure in multilateral negotiations, broached the issue of Europe and the future of economic governance in the *Journal of Common Market Studies* Annual Lecture. His was a powerful plea for multilateralism and a consideration of what Europe has to offer both as a model and as an actor. His priorities are clear: "On substance, we must construct a system that will permit fair and sustainable development at the global level. On process, this system must be built on interconnections between governments, markets and civil society, and count on a central body that can act as its guarantor." To this he added two "organic principles" – transparency and subsidiarity. "Although transparency is a universal value, it has never been more immediate, in all senses of the word, than in the modern information age." Subsidiarity means being "as close to the (wo)man on the street as possible." While admitting that transparency "has been a hard slog", Lamy felt that "few would argue that it has ever been easier for ordinary firms, activists and citizens to know and understand what the EU is doing". Moreover, "European governance is a mixture of local regional, intergovernmental, and supranational practice – even if the debate about subsidiarity has not yet produced agreement on which issues should be addressed at which levels."

Turning to the bases of economic governance, Lamy stressed "underlying values, efficiency and legitimacy. Underlying values are, put simply, the set of values shared by a governed group. But values are, in large measure, responsible for our self-defined 'identity'. It follows that values tend to be vulnerable to attack by the forces of globalization, and worryingly easy to distort into violent forms of exclusion." However it was striking to him how the debate has focused so far almost exclusively on efficiency, to the detriment of legitimacy. "Legitimacy, and the absence – or at least the perceived absence – of legitimacy in different political systems, and different levels of political systems, is a key concept."[10]

Like Cox in an earlier UNU research project, Lamy expressed the idea that NGOs and civil society "can contribute to legitimisation by providing for different channels of activity – including mobilization, advocacy, or indeed simply legal/technical support – and thereby fulfil a demand for new social intermediaries that are not provided elsewhere. We might not always like what they have to say, but they have a legitimising function, and they are pressing for increased legitimacy in the system. They can make a crucial contribution to global governance".[11]

Lamy thinks that Europe has much to offer and he cites the EU dowry to multilateralism due to the fact that

> The EU has long experience, far more than most regional entities, of seeking an appropriate balance between trade liberalization and market integration, on the one hand, and policy integration and solidarity, on the other. The Union's combination of open markets and common rules allows it to go further than any other regional entity towards regulatory co-operation of the kind that is often demanded globally ... The EU, along with other regional entities, has genuine potential to help upgrade multilateralism by functioning as a caucus at the global level that can facilitate decision-making in multilateral institutions.

Ultimately it is trust that is

> the cement that binds an institution into a social contract which, implicitly, constitutes the foundation of the structure. Only through trust that is both shared and built on at each subsequent stage, can progress be made. Yet the important lesson here is that, to build trust, a body is needed that can act as a guarantor of the project and its momentum. Logically, that body should also have the prerogative of generating a consensus proposal that facilitates the emergence of the general interest."[12]

If Europe wishes to preserve its social model of market economy, welfare state and democracy, it must exercise itself at the world level. In facing global challenges,

> Europe is far better placed to act than its individual Member States. Consider its comparative advantage in all of the following areas: safeguarding a democratic society and rule of law at the level of the continent; building a large, competitive market that fosters the emergence of companies that can stand up to global competition: ensuring the capacity and flexibility to resist external shocks and influence economic and political developments in the rest of the world; promoting the security and defence of Europe and sustainable development in developing countries, including those in Europe's own neighbourhood, in the interests of justice and peace.... Europe has to be 'big' to deliver, whether on trade or foreign policy: and yet "small" to embrace subsidiarity fully, and ensure that politics is close, and feels close, to the citizens.[13]

Lamy therefore sees the EU as a part of a multilateral regime for the management of global problems which is a repository of experience in internal matters where the modus operandi is essentially multilateral and based on trust and legitimacy sustained by transparency and subsidiarity. He sees no reason why such an approach cannot form a basis for global governance provided that others will respond in a like manner. For him, and for the EU, multilateralism is not the problem but the solution, and the problem is, by inference, the United States as it wavers away from a multilateralism that had served it so well in the past.

Lamy's experience was in a domain where the EU has an abundance of soft power, whereas Javier Solana's role has been in the area of European security strategy and the imbalance between soft power and so-called hard power in the European context is dramatic. The shock must have been considerable for Solana when he moved from being Secretary General of NATO to being primarily concerned with the EU's foreign and defence policy. But whether the concern has been with the EU as one of the three main global actors in the economic sphere or an embryonic political and security entity, the answer is the same – that is, embracing multilateralism.

Solana's position was set out for and adopted by the Heads of State and Government at the European Council in Brussels on 12 December 2003. For someone who was born in 1938, Solana's first sentence reflects why this writer feels so committed to the European Union.

> Europe has never been so prosperous, so secure nor so free. The violence of the first half of the 20th Century has given way to a period of peace and stability unprecedented in European history. The creation of the European Union has been central to this development. It has transformed the relations between our states,

and the lives of our citizens. European countries are committed to dealing peacefully with disputes and to co-operating through common institutions. Over this period, the progressive spread of the rule of law and democracy has seen authoritarian regimes change into secure, stable and dynamic democracies. Successive enlargements are making a reality of the vision of a united and peaceful continent.[14]

Europe has gone from being the cockpit of global war to being an island of peace, but enjoying a peace that can never be taken for granted and one that is, on a global scale, indivisible. Europe is the anomaly and our task is to contribute to making it the norm for all peoples.

Solana is well aware of this and he states his awareness cogently. The threat is no longer one of invasion but includes proliferation of weapons of mass destruction, terrorist networks, state failure and organized crime. "This implies that we should be ready to act before a crisis occurs. Conflict prevention and threat prevention cannot start too early."[15] Solana, like Lamy, is equally aware of what Europe's answer should be, it is a deep commitment to multilateralism. He set out the European credo that,

In a world of global threats, global markets and global media, our security and prosperity increasingly depend on an effective multilateral system. This development of a stronger international society, well functioning international institutions and a rule-based international order is our objective.

We are committed to upholding and developing International Law. The fundamental framework for international relations is the United Nations Charter. The United Nations Security Council has the primary responsibility for the maintenance of international peace and security. Strengthening the United Nations, equipping it to fulfil its responsibilities and to act effectively, is a European priority.

We want international organisations, regimes and treaties to be effective in confronting threats to international peace and security and must therefore be ready to act when their rules are broken.[16]

The implication is clear. Europe cannot adopt a policy of isolation since peace is indivisible and, in any case, any attempt at isolation, or indeed Fortress Europe, would be tantamount to reversing a trend of engagement on a global basis which goes back in continuous line for at least five hundred years. What therefore is the remedy?

Solana and the Heads of Government point to a basic goal. "The best protection for our security is a world of well-governed democratic states. Spreading good governance, supporting social and political reform, dealing with corruption and abuse of power, establishing the rule of law and protecting human rights are the best means of strengthening the international order." The EU can use its trade and development policies as a powerful tool for promoting reform. Those countries which have placed themselves beyond the pale will be helped to return to the fold either through EU initiatives or through those of individual member states as in the cases of Libya and Iran. But if they persist in their errant ways there is a clear warning – "those who are unwilling to do so should understand that there is a price to be paid, including in their relationship with the European Union."[17] Solana's warning is addressed to conventional rogue states but it could also apply to the United States, although that was clearly not Solana's intention nor that of the Heads of Government, even though some are tempted to move in that direction. However, the consensus remains broad and solid that the way forward will have to be a multilateral way. As Solana put it, "There are few if any problems we can deal with on our own. The threats described above are common threats, shared with all our closest partners. International cooperation is a necessity. We need to pursue our objectives both through multilateral cooperation in international organisations and through partnerships with key actors."[18]

A recent vibrant statement on his commitment to multilateralism by a major European leader was that made by Jacques Chirac in a speech to the International Institute of Strategic Studies in London on 18 November 2004 in the context of his visit to Britain in celebration of 100 years of the *entente cordiale*. Chirac is, of course, an enigmatic figure since there are many who think that he should be in court, if not in jail. There are also many who do not, in general, share his political convictions, but who believe that he spoke for us over the Iraq war and one of our principal problems – the United States. Chirac's analysis is one which will find much favour not only with most European governments, including increasingly those in the so-called "new Europe", but also among the European people whatever their political position with but few exceptions, perhaps on the far right. Chirac rejected organizing the world on the basis of a logic of power because experience suggested that this would produce instability and lead, sooner or later to crisis and confirmation. So he offered an alternative route. "Celui d'un ordre fondé sur le respect de la règle internationale et la responsabilisation des nouveaux pôles du monde, par leur association pleine et entière aux mécanismes de prise de décision. C'est pourquoi nous devons travailler ensemble au renouveau du multilatéralisme. Un multilatéralisme qui doit s'appuyer sur une Organisation des Nations Unies rénovée et renforcée". He advocated an enlarged Security Council together with a new political framework for the economic and social governance of globalization. He commented that "Le dialogue entre les cultures, entre les civilisations, entre les religions est la meilleure réponse aux ennemis de la liberté qui misent sur leur affrontement." This would go hand in hand with support for the process of democratization in a dialogue which would respect diversity. But he warned, "nous devons éviter toute confusion entre démocratisation et occidentalisation. Car si notre mémoire est parfois courte, les peuples jadis soumis à la domination de l'Occident, eux, n'ont pas oublié et sont prompts à voir dans nos actions une résurgence de l'impérialisme et du colonialisme."[19] This was clearly a warning not only for the EU and its member states but also, perhaps, for the United States. While there are many in the United States who share these sentiments, they are not in power. There is therefore a mutual incomprehension between the American administration, on the one hand, and most European governments and peoples, on the other, and it is to that increasingly fraught relationship, which has, as a major bone of contention, attitudes towards multilateralism, that we must now turn.

A dialogue of the increasingly deaf

The American claim to exceptionalism is a cultural norm that goes back to the Puritans. While it may from time to time be hidden under a veneer of multilateralism, at times of tension it rises to the surface and dominates the international scene, or at least the role of the United States on the international stage. Of course, other countries have similar cultural norms, for example, that of neutrality for the Swiss or of liberty, equality and fraternity for France and the inheritors of the French revolution. The United States believes that its exceptionalism should be recognized by others. Indeed it often has been in the past. In the nineteenth century it was recognized by millions of European people for its exceptional degree of political liberty and wide opportunities for economic and social advancement. Again in 1919 thousands of Europeans thronged the streets to welcome President Woodrow Wilson, who was a symbol of the United States's moral authority, economic and political power and, above all, hope for a better world. But after the Second World War there were other visions. Socialism, social democracy and a welfare state rendered the American vision of liberal democracy a free rather than a social market, and individualism based on meritocracy rather than solidarity. These incipient differences were set aside as the Iron Curtain slammed down in Europe and the left was caged up in communist parties which became political pariahs. The moderate left and the centre and right parties on the whole did not challenge American exceptionalism, but tolerated it in multilateral packaging. This acceptance merely confirmed the belief of the United States that not merely was it legitimized but that it did not have to be legitimized, in other words, that it had a right to lead. That leadership was of course accepted by Western Europe both in the political and security fields as well as that of economic ties and a transatlantic, American-led community emerged from 1947 until 1960. Thereafter, in the economic sphere, two other major actors played an increasingly global role and multilateralism was transformed into trilateralism with Japan and the EU joining the United States in the management of the global economy as it expanded to embrace not only the Western world but, by the end of the century, the whole world. In the political and security sphere, the Cold War masked changes although the policy of France towards integration in the NATO military hierarchy was a foretaste of things to come.

Increasingly the European states looked and still look to the United Nations system to fulfil several needs.[20] The first is the conferment, in some raw sense, of legitimacy on norms and behaviour in the international sphere – this ranges from a resolution of the Security Council to the hundreds of standards set by the International Labour Organization. Many of these are merely declaratory, although "merely" is the wrong word, since they set standards to which we all aspire because they reflect a near consensus of values. They provide a target and a goad to attain that target. By accepting them, governments place a rod across their own backs. In this process the United States appears to have a sense of anxiety, or perhaps even a lack of self-confidence. To Europeans, working with others of a like mind is now becoming second nature after half a century's experience, whereas for Americans, despite their manifest power, ability and savoir faire, there is a strange element of inhibition, indeed fear. This sits oddly with the penetration of the United States into all parts of the globe and in all global enterprises. It raises questions about the extent to which Europeans, on the other hand, feel somewhat more comfortable with a multilateral world than an American world, at least in the twenty-first century.

Slowly the question began to arise of whether we really share values, as Europeans, with the United States? The answer in many fundamental ways is "yes", just as we share values with other parts of the world, and perhaps more so, but there is a difference in balance between notions of meritocracy and those of solidarity. A meritocratic society privileges the best and rewards the individual actor with only a minimal concern for solidarity with society as a whole. Margaret Thatcher reflected this point of view when she once exclaimed that "there is no such thing as society". Most meritocrats would not go so far and would admit that there needs to be an element of solidarity with the poorer, weaker and diverse elements of society. Put starkly, unfettered liberalism kills, while an all-pervasive solidarity may suffocate. The US and the EU have different emphases and it shows.

There is therefore a growing value difference between the United States and the EU, although to make the contrast more realistic Canada could perhaps be included in the EU and New Labour with the United States. The difference is crystallized over the essential concern with solidarity which is at the heart of social democracy that dominates European thinking. There is a shared belief across the Atlantic in the fundamental value and rights of the individual. There is equally a firm commitment to the rule of law, although perhaps not always in its practice, and in liberty. The difference lies in the American commitment to an untrammelled meritocracy in the context of a largely unregulated market in many different fields, that is, liberal democracy is seen as the bedrock rather than solidarity. It is of course not a question of one or the other but a matter of degree, but that the degree is now such that it is becoming a matter of differences in kind. Jolyon Howorth points out why this might be so:

> the Europeans have a 50 year apprenticeship in structured multilateralism, and instinctively perceive the international system as a process of genuine institutional bargaining, informed by accepted rules, in which the pooling of sovereignty is recognized as offering more positive rewards than are attainable by its jealous retention or mere assertion. The United States, on the other hand, sees multilateralism as one approach among many, only to be entered into if it clearly yields greater rewards that are attainable by going it alone. Otherwise, unilateralism remains the default position.[21]

The claim for exceptionalism lies uneasily in a multilateral context. To put it bluntly, if you are exceptional it is hard to be multilateral because of your own belief that others are inferior. Edward Luck has commented that "most Americans believe in international organizations, but as a way of propagating American values, not of compromising them in order to get along with the majority".[22] In the end Luck, too, was frustrated that the outside world has not found a way of accommodating American exceptionalism. But the United States had a leading role in drafting the Charter which has, as a central notion, the sovereign equality of members states, albeit with notable exceptions. He does not really broach the issues of why others are unwilling to accept US exceptionalism as a given, but need to be convinced. Americans find it difficult to acknowledge that the United States, as any other leader, must earn the authority of leadership from the constituency which supports that leadership. Without that it may be able to command and coerce, but authority and legitimacy need to be earned. Just as there is no Divine Right of kings, there is no Divine Right of superpowers either.

Europe has evolved in a different direction from that of the United States. For Europeans, everything in life is multilateral since in essence we are social animals and there is no escape from each other. We can, of course, have multilateralized empires, but they are now a thing of the past. We can also have systems of domination, such as that of Napoleon within Europe or the aspirations of a Stalin, a Hitler, a Mussolini or, indeed, of Pax Britannica. Europeans have learned that they cannot impose a system of governance upon themselves unilaterally, they can only evolve one multilaterally. While as some European powers have to learn not to be dominant, others have to learn not to be dominated and to escape from the psychological pit of domination. As a Bulgarian once explained, "After four hundred years of Ottoman domination and fifty years of Stalinist oppression, how do you expect us to do anything?". Generally Europeans are seeking to move, and have largely achieved that movement, from the multilateralism of cooperation within a conflict, that is through the balance of power in Europe, and the multilateralization of adversary relationships, to a multilateralism based on cooperation which reflects a newly perceived shared harmony of values which has given rise to norms and institutions for the furtherance of multilateral ties.

The neo-conservatives in positions of power and influence in the United States have a very different view of the world at least from a European perception. Nicole Gnesotto has set this *Weltanschauung* out cogently, interspersing her analysis with key quotations to illustrate the point:

> the end result is America's claim to complete freedom of action in the name of absolute defence of democracy. As this is a fight for survival, American sovereignty is non-negotiable; as America is a "power for good", it cannot be wrong; because this is an implacable struggle of good against evil, all those who do not support America are considered to be on the side of evil. Hence the various theories on pre-emptive action against an enemy ("We will not hesitate to act alone, if necessary, to exercise our right of self-defence by acting pre-emptively against terrorists"), the warning to partners that "those who are not with us are against us", strategic opportunism regarding alliances ("the mission must determine the coalition, the coalition must not determine the mission"), the defence of national sovereignty ("As we strengthen institutions that allow free nations to cooperate on a multilateral basis, we must take care not to damage the core principle that under-girds the international system – the principle state of sovereignty"), and resort to democratic Messianism a final justification (the concept of "regime change" and the domino theory applied to democracies from Iraq to the Middle East).[23]

This view of the world is profoundly shocking to Europeans, because Europeans have become used to the rule of law based on multilaterally accepted norms. This is not to say that Europeans do not bend and cynically stretch the rule of law, but they try hard not to break it, whereas the United States sees international law as policy rather than as rules to which reference is required. As such the United States is profoundly lawless. In the face of this lawlessness Europeans have been somewhat pusillanimous in the sense that they have not defended the rule of law as a principle – as, for example, when both United States and Australia have violated human rights law. If the rule of law is selective then it is no longer the rule of law. On the other hand, it is strange that the United States should break international law in such a flagrant manner because, after all, international law tends to reflect the values of the dominant powers of the day or of the immediate past and therefore reflects American values. This is all the more so in the case of the United Nations since the United States played a very important part in the drafting of the Charter.

While the European States, and indeed peoples, judging by their reaction to the attack on the Twin Towers in September 2001 accept the right of individual and collective self-defence as set out in Article 51 of the United Nations Charter, they do see this as related to a particular event and not as a permanent general right. In short the war on terror, everywhere, and at any time, outside of any rules, should not be given any countenance and certainly not a permanent exceptional status in the context of international law. It is an old rule of thumb in counter-insurgency struggles that the governing power should not break its own rules. The United States is doing this with flamboyance and insouciance. This causes concern to many countries who wonder when it might be their turn to be the object of the use of overwhelming conventional military power. The United Nations Security Council and the rule of law are their protection against American pre-emptive action, and many in Europe as well are coming to rue the day that they pushed international law aside in the context of Kosovo but, apart from Tony Blair's government, they have not generalized this. Moreover many European powers learned from their struggles as colonial powers that, in the longer term, it profits you little to defend your conception of the rules by breaking them. A willingness of the United States administration to do so has had a catastrophic effect on the esteem with which it is held by the European public. Now only 45 per cent of Europeans look with favour upon a US leadership role, 78 per cent see American unilateralism as a threat, and 71 per cent want to see the EU become a leading world power in some sense to counteract this threat.[24] Perhaps what the average European person thinks is of little importance to the Bush administration. Indeed, it appears to have had little influence upon Tony Blair, although a related decline in trust in him did prejudice his position in the 2005 general election. Otherwise he appears to have got away unscathed by his five wars in six years. This is yet again an example where, in a mature democracy, everyone concedes that the elections are fair but is also driven away from the democratic political system by the refusal of governments to do what the people want them to do. What is more they flaunt it "in your face".

The coming apart?

In the months after the ending of the Second World War in Europe, those parts of Europe which had a choice, and they were mainly Britain, France, the Low Countries, most Scandinavian countries and Switzerland, could exercise that choice with four options. The first was to rest in the slough of despondency caused by the destruction, the atrocities, the moral corruption of being both occupied and occupier and let the outside powers, the United States and the Soviet Union, have their way with Europe. The second option was to look to the Soviet Union which was plainly a system that worked since it was the Soviet armies, or rather the Russian people in the Soviet armies, that took the guts out of the *Wehrmacht*. Moreover, Russians did it largely through their own resources. It was also a system that professed, but did not practise, human rights. Ironically many Western Europeans owe their liberties, in great part, to the Russian people who have not been the beneficiaries of such advantages. The Soviet Union as a model attracted many on the left, but in the centre and on the right it was the American model that was admired. The United States was not only a colossal military power, it was also the largest and most prosperous economy in the world and its people enjoyed the benefits of liberal democracy. There was also another, fourth, model which was that of liberal democracy fortified by a social market and a welfare state, and this was the path that the then free European countries followed. It had much in common with the American model, but was not the same. The two approaches were, however, compatible within a framework of multilateralism. As Paul-Henri Spaak pointed out, the Atlantic community and NATO were the bastard child of Stalin's oppression whereas what is now the European Union was the love child of Western Europe's own making. Allusion has already been made to the historical evolution of multilateralism. The question now cannot be escaped, are we coming apart?

Samuel Huntington may have had his tongue in his cheek when he wrote his piece on the clash of civilizations, perhaps not realizing that it would take off and envelop him in controversial discussions.[25] However if the implication of Huntington, put crudely, was the West against the Rest, then he misses the point. Of course, there are differences and similarities between the West and the Rest but the real dichotomy is between fundamentalists, whether in the West or elsewhere, and cosmopolitans whether in the West or elsewhere. This fundamentalist–cosmopolitan divide is one which underlies many of the current difficulties between the United States and Europe. The fundamentalists seem to have a handle on power in the United States and they can be found in the other major civilizations with theocratic roots – Judaism, the Islamic world and, indeed, the Hindu world even where, as in the United States, there is a formal separation of religious authority and the state. In all of these areas, there is a struggle between those who look for a fundamentalist theocratically oriented-system of governance and those who are essentially cosmopolitan. A prime example of the cosmopolitans is the Western Europeans and multilateralism is the policy face of cosmopolitism. It helps to explain why Europeans have so much difficulty in understanding what is happening in the United States. They are also worried that power disenfranchises thought. Feedback loops are withering on the vine as the fundamentalists chant their mantra. There is little or no communication and just as Europe and the United States are coming apart, so perhaps is the United States over this great divide. Fundamentalists, including those in the United States, look at risks whereas cosmopolitans, especially those in the EU, look at threats. Moreover, the EU generally follows a principle of prudence since it is aware that it lives in a small world. The United States tends towards the principle of the pursuance of goals *à l'outrance*. American policy brooks no rules, whereas Europeans try but do not always succeed to live by the book. If, as has been asserted, power has a tendency to disenfranchise thought, then despite the inefficacy of immediate feedback, the failure of power may enfranchise thought. In the meantime how can the fundamentalists, and particularly elements in the United States administration, be insulated so that no more failed states are created and the policies being followed do not feed the devil they are seeking to exorcize? In short, how can we help to preserve the cosmopolitan process?

As President Chirac observed in an interview on the BBC, "Si vous observez l'évolution du monde, au regard de la sécurité et du terrorisme, vous ne pouvez pas dire de façon crédible que la situation s'est améliorée." He also doubted whether "avec l'Amérique telle qu'elle est, qu'il soit possible à quiconque, même aux Britanniques, d'être un honnête intermédiaire."[26] Nevertheless, like all European leaders, Chirac wishes to compose with the United States and indeed thinks that the British link might be of some benefit to Europe as a whole. But European leaders are not going to compose on a question of principle and their principle is multilateralism not unilateralism or empire. Even Donald Rumsfeld's conception of new Europe has proved to be a passing one as the new members of the EU begin to realize that they do not have to exchange one authoritarian leadership (Russia) for another somewhat less authoritarian leadership (United States) and begin to learn how to play the multilateral game in the European context. The dichotomy between old and new Europe was but a temporary one and, apart from Iraq, even the Blair government appears to be moving towards the old European position on important questions such as defence cooperation and the environment as well as Africa. Perhaps we can use the concepts of old and new in a different manner.

The United States is an old international actor, whereas the EU is a new international actor and is one of several other such actors who are slowly coming on to the international scene. A number of potential major entities have spent the last half century being concerned mainly with their domestic arrangements. This is of course true of the EU with the establishment of a single market, the currency and other things. But it is also true of a number of other states such as China since 1949, India since 1947, Indonesia since 1950, Japan since 1951. All of these have gone through their own process of putting their domestic house in order with varying degrees of success. But they are all equally now concerned with their global political, economic, social and security environments, and this is why the unipolar moment was but a moment rather than a system. We know little about how these new actors will react to the global environment over the next 20 years as they feel their way into new roles. The reaction of the United States to this development will be a crucial one, since it is always difficult for the old to make space for the new and particularly so when the climate is envenomed by fundamentalism. And how will the new react to the old? It is clear that the EU wants to act in a multilateral framework with the other major entities and not least the United States. This is stated time and again. If the United States does not respond what are the options?

We could fall back into the pit of balance of power policies where there is a limited amount of cooperation to manage a basically conflictual world. Another alternative would be to operate a system of multilateralism minus one, although that is hardly efficacious, but it is a possibility if the door is left permanently ajar for the one to join. After all, this was the situation in the League of Nations when the United States adopted a parallel policy to that of the League Powers, at least on some issues. The ideal would be to transfer that form of multilateralism that has proved so beneficial in Europe for Europeans, and more generally was beneficial historically in terms of the transatlantic community, to the new range of world actors, to which one will presumably add Brazil. Fundamentalism is a difficult barrier to overcome in trying to re-establish a genuine multilateralism, one which is not a cloak for empire. Moreover the global street wants its say and has effective ways of making its voice heard. If we are to avoid the consequences of terror, we cannot crush it, but we can alleviate its causes. The fundamentalists revolt is in all its dimensions – political, economic, cultural – and in all parts of the world a condemnation of existing society. We cannot say that we have not been warned. Thus, in our approach to this and to other global problems, we have to learn to hang together or we shall surely hang separately.

Multilateralism is both a state of mind and a process. It has helped in taking Europe from the abyss of the Nazi degradation to a high level of prosperity in a context of the rule of law and the protection and development of human rights based on shared values epitomized by the notions of liberty, equality and fraternity. The European experience suggests that this might be a way towards coming to terms with global problems that necessarily affect us all. But it is not a royal road. The wider Western world has, in the past, embraced such ideas but the United States has always been ambivalent about multilateralism except where it has been a cloak for genteel hegemony. Hence, the current tension in transatlantic relationships and a divergence in some key values. But the difficulties are likely to be greater as the other new entities of the twenty-first century begin to assert themselves on the global stage. The value linkages may be less, but the problems are shared and are inescapable. This gives grounds for hope, but not for complacency. The world can commit suicide. It is most likely to do so if the fundamentalists prevail since multilateralism is anathema to them. They believe themselves to be truly exceptional and seek not even a form of genteel hegemony but the Kingdom of their God even if the Heavens may fall. Europe is, so far, happily free from such phenomena – in part surely because it has embraced multilateralism as a way of life. It has served us well and it may well serve others likewise. It is not perfect but has anyone this side of the fundamentalists got something better?

Notes

1. John Gerard Ruggie (1998) *Constructing the World Polity*, London: Routledge, pp. 109–110.
2. Marie-Claude Smouts (2003) in Dario Battistella and Pascal Vennessen (eds.) *Dictionnaire des Relations Internationales*, Paris: Dalloz, p. 334.
3. Robert W. Cox (1997) "An alternative approach to multilateralism for the twenty-first century", *Global Governance* (January): 107.
4. Frank Petiteville (2004) "L'hégémonie est-elle soluble dans le multilatéralisme? Le cas de l'OMS", *Critique Internationale* 22 (janvier).
5. Cox, op. cit., p. 110.
6. Bertrand Badie (2004) *L'impuissance de la puissance*, Paris: Fayard, pp. 224–225.
7. Ibid., p. 228.

8. Enrico Gualini (2004) "Integration, diversity, plurality: territorial governance and the reconstruction of legitimacy in a European 'postnational' state", *Geopolitics* 9(3) (Autumn): 552–553.
9. See A.J.R. Groom (2005) "Britain and Europe: looking through the defence prism", *Arès* 54(XXI) (January): 2.
10. Pascal Lamy (2004) "Europe and the future of economic governance", *Journal of Common Market Studies* 42(1): 11–12.
11. Ibid., pp. 13–14.
12. Ibid., p. 16.
13. Ibid., pp. 19–20.
14. It has since been widely disseminated in the form of a booklet entitled *A Secure Europe in a Better World*, published in December 2003 by the European Union Institute for Security Studies in Paris, p. 3.
15. Ibid., p. 11.
16. Ibid., p. 14.
17. Ibid., p. 16.
18. Ibid., p. 20.
19. *Le Monde*, 20.XI.04.
20. See A.J.R. Groom (2003) "The United States and the UN", *Journal of International Relations and Development* 6(2) (June).
21. Jolyon Howorth (1998) "Foreign and defence policy cooperation" in John Peterson and Helen Sjursen (eds.) *A Common Foreign Policy for Europe?* London: Routledge.
22. Edward Luck (1999) *Mixed Messages*, Washington: Brookings.
23. Nicole Gnesotto (2003) in Gustav Lindstrom (ed.) *Shift or Rift*, Paris: EU Institute for Security Studies, pp. 26–27.
24. *Transatlantic Trends* (2003) Washington DC: German Marshall Fund of the United States.
25. Samuel Huntingdon (1993) "The clash of civilisations", *Foreign Affairs* 72(3).
26. *Le Monde*, 20.ii.04.

23

Between a rock and a hard place: Latin America and multilateralism after 9/11

Jorge Heine

The so-called crisis of multilateralism has a special resonance in Latin America. As mostly small or middle-sized powers in a region traditionally at the margins of the main conflicts in world politics, Latin America has historically placed a premium on a regulated international order, one that will protect the interests of smaller nations, rather than leaving them at the mercy of the great powers. During part of the nineteenth and the first half of the twentieth century (and to this day) the region was the source of many new concepts and innovations in international law, from the law of asylum to the international law of the sea, and has been strongly committed to the lawful resolution of controversies. Partly as a result of that, Latin America is the region with the lowest number of interstate conflicts. It is also the one with the lowest defence expenditures. Countries in the region have drawn strength from numbers and from their participation in international organizations. Twenty-one Latin American nations were among the founder members of the United Nations. The weakening of the latter would necessarily lead to a further weakening of the former.[1]

Preceded by the pan-American conferences of the nineteenth century, the Organization of American States (OAS), founded in 1948, has been one of the key elements of the region's Inter-American system, and the region's leading multilateral body. Another was the Rio Treaty of 1947, the defence treaty designed to fend off any extra-continental threats (meaning mostly the Soviet Union), supplemented by the Inter-American Defence Board. Today made up of 34 members (including Canada, which joined in 1990), the OAS never really managed to live up to the expectations its creation raised. Headquartered in an ornate white marble building in Washington DC, it was immediately caught up in the perverse dynamics of the Cold War, rendering it largely ineffective to deal with most, if not all international crises in the Western hemisphere, from Guatemala in 1954, Cuba in 1961 (the Bay of Pigs invasion) and 1962 (the Cuban missile crisis), the Dominican Republic in 1965 and Grenada in 1983. The gap between the legal fiction of the "one country, one vote" principle of the OAS charter and the political reality of the "majority of one" exercised by the United States (which also pays for some 60 per cent of the organization's rather modest, if traditionally in arrears, 80 million dollar yearly budget) was simply too big for it to be effective.[2]

Yet, despite these difficulties, some progress was made. In 1979, when President Anastasio ("Tacho") Somoza of Nicaragua faced the final offensive of the Frente Sandinista Nacional de Liberacion (FSNL), the United States mooted the possibility of an Inter-American Peace Force to be deployed in Nicaragua and thus provide a compromise solution between "somocismo" and "sandinismo", an overwhelming majority of Latin American members at the OAS opposed any such initiative, arguing that it was up to the people of each country to sort out their own internal political difficulties and set up their own government. Many observers consider this to have been a true turning point. Another, also in the late seventies, was the strengthening of the Inter-American Human Rights Commission, as well as the setting up of the Inter-American Human Rights Court and the Inter-American Human Rights Institute (both in San Jose, Costa Rica), which were to become instrumental (to this day) in the struggle to defend human rights in the hemisphere, in those days under especially vicious attacks by military regimes.

If the OAS, which in the eighties was also unable to deal with other crises in the region, like those provoked by civil wars in El Salvador and Guatemala and the break down of law and order in Haiti, and had to defer to the United Nations to take care of them, found itself often paralysed by lack of resources or sheer lack of political will (or both), the Rio Treaty has also been seen as a largely obsolete document, designed to fend off a Soviet Union that no longer exists. This was apparent even before the fall of the Wall, as early as in the Falklands/Malvinas War in 1982, when Argentina invoked it, to no avail, against the United Kingdom (a case of an extra-continental power in armed conflict with one of the Western hemisphere, if there has ever been one), as Washington stood steadfastly behind the British.

Not surprisingly, then, the end of the Cold War brought about a veritable flurry of multilateral activity in Latin America, much of it outside the traditional regional institutions, as the new democratic regimes moved to occupy the newly available political space created by the end of bipolarity, one for which the old frameworks seemed quite unsuitable.

From the old to the new Latin American multilateralism

One expression of it has been political cooperation. Triggered by the Central American crisis of the mid-eighties, a group of Latin American countries that did not share Washington's somewhat Manichean view of its origins, formed what was called the Contadora Group (named after an island off the Panama coast where the first meeting of the group took place) in 1986, later joined by a Support Group. This laid the foundations of what came to be known as The Rio Group established in 1989, which ended up bringing together all South American countries plus Mexico, and one rotating representative of the Central American nations and another of CARICOM. With yearly summits, the Rio Group is perhaps the most significant and emblematic product of this "new multilateralism" in the region, and has done much to facilitate dialogue and exchange among governments and leaders. In contrast to the OAS, it does not include the United States, nor does it have a permanent bureaucracy or headquarters. The secretariat rotates, and is run from the Foreign Ministry of whichever country happens to chair it.

It is also another expression of the sort of "summit diplomacy" that took Latin America by storm in the nineties. The Ibero-American Summits, started in 1992 on the Quincentennial of the arrival of Christopher Columbus to the Americas, were another, largely designed to keep the flow of communications between Spain (and Portugal) and her former colonies going, as were the Summits of the Americas.[3] Launched in 1994 in Miami, and held every four years, these bring together all countries of the hemisphere (except Cuba) and have focused mostly (though not exclusively) on promoting free trade and the eventual creation of a Free Trade Area of the Americas (FTAA).[4]

The latter is also a reflection of the new impetus that regional integration underwent in the nineties[5]. Of these mechanisms, MERCOSUR, established by Argentina, Brazil, Paraguay and Uruguay in 1991, is the most significant, but by no means the only one: the Andean Community, the Central American Common Market and the Caribbean Community (CARICOM) should also be added. Based on the principle of "open regionalism" (as opposed to the "closed" variety so popular in the sixties), these schemes looked for new ways in which the Latin American economies could work with each other's strengths, without raising necessarily new barriers to the products and services of extra-regional or subregional economies. Each of these grouping has its own yearly "summit", leading to an often overcrowded calendar of meetings for regional heads of government and foreign ministers, and a certain amount of agenda duplication.

The point is that an extensive multilateral regional network has emerged in Latin America in the post-Cold War era, one that has been nurtured and cultivated by the almost universal establishment of democracy in the region since the early nineties, which has also given a distinct imprint to it, one far removed from the bad old days of "coups and earthquakes". To be sure, in many countries political institutions remain weak; "low intensity democracies" has been one way of referring to them. Yet, multilateralism has also been instrumental for keeping countries on the "straight and narrow": the "democratic clause" in many of these IOs has considerably raised "the cost of coups". The Democratic Charter of the OAS, approved on 11 September 2001 in Lima is perhaps the best known of them, but they also exist in MERCOSUR as well as in the Ibero-American summits.

This increased "multilateral density" in the region should not be surprising. In addition to the end of the Cold War, the twin pressures of globalization and regionalization have put a premium on international collaboration.[6] To face the enormous challenges of a rapidly changing world environment "out there", small and medium-sized countries have joined forces, concluding that there is much to be gained from "bandwagoning".

The United States and Latin America

Yet, having said this, Latin America continues to be highly dependent on the United States, more so, perhaps, than any other region in the world. This is true not only for trade and investment (a country like Mexico sends as much as 90 per cent of its exports to the United States), but also for matters like immigration, something especially valid for the Caribbean Basin nations. To alienate the United States is therefore a high-risk endeavour, and as Washington becomes increasingly leery of multilateralism, there is a problem.

Ironically, in many ways globalization and regionalization, instead of diminishing Latin American dependence on the United States, have actually increased it. The prospect of an FTAA is powerful incentive for countries "to play ball" with the United States rather than to play the "anti-Yankee" card.

Latin America, then, finds itself torn in different directions in these trying times. On the one hand, both its established traditions and the more recent collective state practices that have emerged in these years of increased regional multilateralism push in the direction of standing up for sound international law principles and the defence of proper procedures in international organizations, in the understanding that, ultimately, that is the best hope of the weak in the world of the strong. On the other hand, given the enormous weight of the United States economy and the overwhelming power of the US, there are many incentives not to "rock the boat" and thus simply go along with US policy in multilateral bodies, since doing otherwise might risk market access and other forms of preferential treatment. This, of course, is also related to the basic asymmetry of US–Latin American relations, where the low salience of Latin America in US foreign policy is matched by the high salience the US has for Latin America.

Joseph Tulchin has pointed out that the real challenge to Latin America today is to identify those among the "new threats", beyond the so-called "war on terror", and "hard security" issues more generally (which are far too sensitive to the United States, and where the price for "crossing" Washington would be too high), where there is room for engaging the United States multilaterally.[7] Matters like drug trafficking, international organized crime, international migration flows and international environmental issues would fall into this category. The point is well taken. Yet the very fact that a scholar of his standing makes it, underscores a broader and less differentiated argument that has found increasing favour in the region.

Because one net result of these conflicting pressures has been to make some Latin American countries even more reluctant to take on international responsibilities "out of area" than they were in the past, on the theory that this will only "get you in trouble". Paradoxically, this reluctance by many Latin American nations to engage in broader international issues (Brazil is an exception to this, taking a high-profile role on many global issues, particularly in trade, where it has developed a fruitful working relationship with India and South Africa in the WTO negotiations, and leading post-Cancun G-20+) has not necessarily led to a concomitant strengthening of regional bodies, like the OAS one would expect.

The choices for middle powers

And this speaks directly to the role of middle powers in this new international environment. Between the extremes of the members of the P-5 and some others which have a reasonable claim to join it, on the one hand, and, say, micro-states so small that tourism is the only viable economic activity, or countries so poor, like many in Africa, whose only concern is how to increase the flow of international cooperation, there is a third category, that of middle powers, like many in Latin America (a region that has often been described as the middle class of nations). Whereas the big powers are agenda-setters and the small powers largely agenda-takers, for middle powers (which, of course, are also agenda-takers, but which have a somewhat higher probability of influencing international developments, at least at the margins), the challenge takes a different form.

For such countries, is it at all possible to develop a foreign policy that goes beyond, say, border issues and regional topics? Is it conceivable that some Latin American countries may actually consider making a contribution to the resolution of global issues such as, say, humanitarian intervention (HI), the so-called "war on terror" or world hunger, for that matter?

This dilemma faced by middle powers became especially apparent when Chile joined the Security Council as a non-permanent member in 2003. In half a century, that is, from 1945 to 1995, Chile had been elected to the Security Council only twice – once in 1951 and then again in 1962. It was then elected for the 1996–1997 period, and again for the 2003–2004. This despite the fact that, according to the rotation principle and the existence of 33 Latin American and Caribbean countries that are United Nations members, each country's term in the Security Council should come up only once every sixteen years. Yet, for a variety of reasons, including that one South American country, Uruguay, decided to "skip" its turn (for reasons to be elaborated below), Chile was elected again only six years after the previous term.

There are two ways of looking at this. One, that it is a great opportunity to have "a place at the table of high politics" and thus be able to make a contribution to global governance. Traditionally, a seat at the Security Council has been highly coveted as there are not that many occasions where small and middle powers can regularly sit round a relatively small table with the big powers. Yet, a revisionist view has started to gain ground in Latin America.

According to the latter, by joining the Security Council without the "clout" or the resources to back up such participation, one only exposes oneself to very difficult dilemmas, such as "having to choose between one's principles and one's friends". According to this notion, Latin American middle powers should not get involved at all in the "high politics" issues that come before the Security Council. To do so only risks being caught in the fray of big-power disputes. Given how vulnerable Latin American countries are to US pressures, to join the Council, simply for the sake of what could be described as narcissistic gratification at best, or an ego trip at worst, is to court disaster,[8] Rather, or so the reasoning goes, Latin American nations should concern themselves with "low politics" issues, like international trade, investment and market access, matters that bring tangible benefits to citizens and consumers. If the latter don't care very much about domestic politics, according to this view, they do even less so about international politics, and the less said and done about it, the better. On the face of it, the abrupt changes in US policy towards Latin America after 9/11 would only seem to confirm the need for Latin American nations to tread carefully in the increasingly unpredictable environment of the first decade of the twenty-first century.

Hemispheric politics between expectations and realities

In one of those extraordinary coincidences of history, 11 September 2001 was also the day on which the foreign affairs ministers of the continent gathered in Lima, Peru to ratify the Democratic Charter of the Americas, thus formalizing the commitment to democracy in the hemisphere, in a document that followed up on the OAS Santiago Declaration of 1991. A few weeks later, Latin American nations, invoking the Rio Treaty, gave their full support to the United States in its fight against terrorism. Even countries traditionally cautious about being seen as "automatically aligning themselves with Washington", like Brazil, took the lead in that initiative, joining the "grand coalition" that the United States built to wage war against Al-Qaeda and the Taliban government in Afghanistan.

At that moment, many saw a great "window of opportunity" for Latin America. Even if a slight downturn in the world economy might be expected, in a situation in which the key factor was the devastating action of an Islamic fundamentalist group based in Central Asia, financed from West Asia, trained in Europe and in the United States, and with several "dress rehearsals" in Africa and in the Middle East, Latin America looked like a true "oasis of peace", almost the only region in the world not involved or affected in any way by Al-Qaeda's actions (and, given the absence of any significant Muslim population, with little potential for being so in the future). In a hostile world, the region looked like a bastion of pro-US regimes, ready to take a stand in defence of "the West" in the coming "clash of civilizations".

And beyond the specific 2001 *conjuncture*, the time seemed right for a significant "great leap forward" in the region. For the first time in many decades, 32 of the 33 nation states in the region had established democratic institutions. The various Summits of the Americas mentioned above had proclaimed a commitment to an FTAA by 2005, something personally ratified by President George W. Bush in the third such summit in Quebec in April 2001. Democracy and free trade seemed to enjoy a firm footing in Latin America, thus laying the foundations for what promised to be a decade of progress, peace and prosperity, scarce commodities in a world marked by ethnic cleansing, religious fanaticism and conflicts with centuries-old roots. Presumably, the United States would be the most interested in promoting political and economic stability in the region, as this would allow Washington to take on without major distractions close to home the enormous challenges arising in the Middle East as well as in Central and South Asia.

Yet, in the four years since that tragic Tuesday in September 2001, the situation in the region has been rocked by one crisis after the other, in a far cry from those optimistic predictions.[9] Argentina, a country that in the early twentieth century was among the world's ten richest, defaulted on its foreign debt and went essentially into receivership. Venezuela, applauded for forty years as a symbol of democracy in South America, offered the spectacle of a president forced to leave power on a Friday, only to return the following Monday. And the "Andean Arch of Crisis", far from tapering off, has in many ways deepened. In Colombia, despite the progress and popularity of President Alvaro Uribe and the presence of US troops to fight the insurgents, 80 people a day are the fatal victims of political or criminal violence. In Peru, despite strong economic growth, the popularity of President Alejandro Toledo has occasionally reached single digits. Ecuador and Paraguay continue to be affected by enormous institutional fragility, not surprising in countries where the vast majority of the population, much of it indigenous, has never felt truly part of the political system, which they continue to see as alien and distant from their needs and priorities. This is also very much true of Bolivia, where President Gonzalo Sánchez de Losada was forced to leave office in 2002, not too long after being elected. In fact, the odd situation of civilian elected presidents forced to leave office prematurely, not because of their ouster by military juntas (as in the days of yore), but simply because they are unable to cope, has become a pattern of sorts over the past decade.[10]

And contrary to what one might think, far from actively responding to the difficult challenges faced by Latin American nations in these years, Washington's policies have at times seemed almost expressly designed to make it more difficult for governments in the region to do so.[11]

Latin America and the Iraq issue

And this takes us to the Iraq issue at the United Nations in late 2002 and early 2003, in many ways the trigger for the "whither multilateralism?" debate. Latin America, of course, did not have a common position on it. There was a group of countries that fully supported the United States position. The Central American countries (Honduras, El Salvador. Nicaragua, Costa Rica and Panama), plus the Dominican Republic and Colombia were among these. The exceptions were Guatemala (still traumatized by the 1954 US intervention there to oust President Jacobo Arbenz) and Belize. Costa Rica, despite its long-standing pacifist tradition, had certain doubts, but they were, in due course, resolved once the war started on 20 March 2003.

That the Central American states, historically highly dependent on the United States, would take such positions should be unsurprising. Much the same goes for the Dominican Republic (which in the nineteenth century even applied to become a fully fledged state of the US). Colombia, the only South American country (and the only one of those in the Americas supporting the US war in Iraq that could conceivably be classified as a regional middle-power) faces its own civil war and the government of President Alvaro Uribe has made an effort to strengthen the "Plan Colombia", the US plan according to which Washington has committed US$1.5 billion to fight the guerrillas and the drug lords in that country. Colombia defined the war in Iraq as part and parcel of the "globalization of the war on terror".

On the other hand, Washington's adversaries in the hemisphere, both old and new ones, like Cuba and Venezuela, took very critical positions on the war, rejecting both the military intervention and the application of the "preventive attack" doctrine. During the World Social Forum gathering in Sao Paulo in February 2003, this sentiment became especially manifest.

The vast majority of the countries in the region, however, ended up in a somewhat intermediate position that, without backing US policy, did not reject it frontally either. Among these, the two members of the Security Council, Chile and Mexico, faced the most complex situation, to which we shall return. However that may be, it should be noted that of the 33 countries in Latin America and the Caribbean, only seven fully supported Washington's position on the war in Iraq. This raises an obvious question. Given the enormous support the United States enjoyed after 9/11, how come its calls for broadening the "war on terror" to Iraq found such few takers in Latin America, a region highly dependent on the United States and where almost no Muslims exist, so that sympathy for the cause of Al-Qaeda or Saddam Hussein should be minimal?

One answer has to do with the kinds of policies that Washington has applied in the hemisphere after 9/11, another with the extant commitment to multilateralism and the reluctance to condone the unilateral use of force. It is my argument that even in these times of "multilateralism under challenge", the best course for middle powers is not just to "stick to their guns" and remain wedded to what they always have done – rather than to become "switchers", and "go with the flow", as it were, that is, to behave opportunistically – but in fact to *increase* the issue areas in which they participate in multilateral fora as, in the end, that will raise their leverage and bargaining power. This goes both against the revisionist view emerging in the region that Latin American states should stay away from "high-politics" fora, and more modest proposals like Tulchin's, somewhat along the same lines. To illustrate this, a brief case study of the foreign policy behaviour of one such middle power in this period, Chile, is provided in the next section of this chapter.

Testing the limits of foreign policy principles

On 1 March 2003, a Saturday, Chilean President Ricardo Lagos got a phone call from the White House at his home in Santiago. President George W. Bush was on the line. His question was a simple one. The United States was planning to submit a second resolution on Iraq to the United Nations Security Council to pave the way for the deployment of US forces there under the umbrella of international law. There were four Security Council members publicly committed to vote favourably on that resolution and three more that, in his view, would eventually come around to do the same. This meant only two additional votes were needed to reach the magical number nine with which such a resolution would be approved. Would Chile (and Mexico, another member, with which Chile had been closely coordinating its position at the Council until then) come around as well?[12]

This, of course, was a foreign policy nightmare come true. As if the pressure from a personal phone call of the President of the United States (something always and everywhere rather strong, but especially so in Latin America) was not enough, for Chile the timing could not have been worse. Right then, a Free Trade Agreement (FTA) between Chile and the United States was pending in the White House, waiting for President Bush to send it to Congress for its approval, an FTA Chile had been pursuing for 13 years. Moreover, under the circumstances, Chile's vote could make the difference between approval or rejection of the second Security Council resolution on Iraq.

Rarely are Latin American countries presented with such stark foreign policy choices on matters involving the "high politics" of superpowers. In this case, the dilemma was clear-cut. On the one hand were certain key principles that had traditionally informed and inspired Chilean foreign policy for much of the twentieth century: the peaceful resolution of conflicts and controversies, non-intervention in other countries' affairs and many international law principles that were being sidelined by the new "pre-emptive attack" doctrine recently coined in Washington. Chile's position until then, criticized by some as "sitting on the fence", was that Hans Blix needed more time and that a second resolution on the matter of Weapons of Mass Destruction (WMD) was premature as there was not sufficient evidence of their presence in Iraq. On the other hand, there was a quite concrete and specific economic interest – getting an FTA with the United States, a long-time project, and one especially significant for an economy as heavily dependent on exports as Chile.

In Chile, the public debate leading up to all this had been intense. Particularly in some sectors of the press and especially among those "jack of all trades" that are the economists of today, both from the government and the opposition, strong views were expressed along the lines of, "Who cares about principles, when we are talking about trade, which means growth and development? Why should Chile care about what happens in Iraq? If the United States, which in today's world is the only superpower left, needs our support, why should something as vague and elusive as foreign policy principles interfere with concrete economic interests which would be put at risk? Isn't in this a case of the diplomatic tail wagging the all-important economic dog?"[13]

To make a long story short, President Lagos stood his ground and told President Bush that Chile was not in a position to vote for a second resolution – and, given the close coordination between the two Latin American members of the Security Council at the time, neither was Mexico. In the end, given that the nine votes weren't there, the second resolution was never tabled, and the rest, as they say, is history.[14]

We will return to the effects Chile's stand on this matter had on US–Chile relations, but there is little doubt that however removed Latin America may be from the main West and Central Asian theatres of the so-called "war on terror" unleashed by the United States after 9/11, the effects on the region of the drastically changed international scenario were far from negligible.[15] They have certainly forced Latin American governments to re-evaluate their foreign policy priorities and their approaches to multilateralism. Unfortunately, much of the debate has not been about the specific features any future multilateral order should take – although there have been glimpses of that – but rather about whether Latin American nations should even join the fora where such debates take place.

And this takes us back to our initial story and the reverberations of Chile's stance against the war in Iraq in March 2003. In Santiago, all hell broke loose. Angry editorials denounced that this had been a fatal mistake, one brought about exclusively by misplaced ideological proclivities, at a time when a cold, hard look at Chile's national interest would have dictated otherwise. A statement from United States Trade Representative Robert Zoellick to the effect that the national security interests of the United States could not be divorced from international trade policy only fanned the fire, and a number of analysts predicted that the FTA with the United States would never be sent by the White House to Capitol Hill for approval, and that even if it did so, it would be rejected by a US Congress angry at the veritable "betrayal" by a country that until recently had been a trusted ally and friend, and suddenly had turned its back on Washington. According to this reasoning, this would drive a permanent wedge between Chile and the United States. There have not been many occasions when the United States has actually needed Chile's support on an issue of war and peace, and when it did so, Chile failed to come through, or at least this is the way the argument went.[16]

Yet, incredible as it may sound, once the dust settled, the White House did send the FTA to the Congress, where it was ratified quite quickly. The one thing Chile did not get was a photo op of both presidents in the White House signing the treaty, something that was left to the United States Trade Representative and the Chilean Foreign Minister to do in Miami. In the course of 2004, Presidents Bush and Lagos met on three occasions, including one for lunch in the White House and another for dinner at La Moneda, Chile's presidential palace. According to some observers, Chile is today considered to be "Washington's best friend in South America". What happened?

Actually, the Chilean case is a good illustration of how middle-powers can in fact *increase* their influence in world affairs by participating more actively in a wide range of international fora and issue areas, including so called "hard" security issues – which is the opposite from what the "revisionist" school or, in a less extreme form, scholars like Joseph Tulchin have postulated.

On building "soft power"

The different emphases of the three successive governments in Chile since the return of democracy in 1990, all led by the same centre-left coalition, nicely illustrate this expanding foreign policy "outreach", which has led Chile to play an increasingly relevant role in hemispheric and world affairs, incrementally building up its "soft power" and projecting itself way beyond what could have been normally expected from a small-to-medium-sized country located *finis terrae*.

President Patricio Aylwin's (1990–1994) main foreign policy priority was that of "reconnection" – that is, reconnect Chile once again to the international system, from which it had largely been isolated during the seventeen-year-long military regime of General Pinochet. From 1982 to 1989, not a single head of state actually visited Chile, except for the Pope, whereas 20 did so in 1990 alone.[17] From 1990 to 1994, diplomatic relations were re-established with countries that had broken them, embassies that had been closed were reopened, Chile joined APEC, and took the lead in conceptualizing and proposing the United Nations Social Summit, ultimately held in Copenhagen in 1995.[18]

From 1994 to 2000, on the other hand, during the government of President Eduardo Frei, the main priority became what I have called the "Latin Americanization" of Chile's foreign policy. Chile's leaving the Andean Pact in 1976, as well as the notion of "bye, bye, Latin America" expressed by officials of the military regime, underscored Chile's progressive distancing from the region, based on the notion that Chile did not need regional integration, since it was already integrated into the world economy. This needed redressing, which Chile did by joining MERCOSUR as an associate member in 1996, overcoming a number of border disputes with its neighbours, signing all sorts of FTAs with many countries in the region and actively participating in regional summitry – the Rio Group, the Ibero-American Summit and the Summit of the Americas, the latter actually held in Santiago in April 1998.

The notion that Chile had to formulate its foreign policy *from* Latin America became quite firmly established in those years. Yet, the limits to a foreign policy circumscribed *to* Latin America became obvious when Chile's attempts to become a full member of MERCOSUR failed in 2000, upon which it embarked on FTA negotiations with the United States instead, and later with the European Union and with South Korea, all of which were successfully concluded. Thus, from *reconnection* and *Latin Americanization*, Chile, during the presidency of Ricardo Lagos (2000–2006), moved into its *globalization* phase – one in which an export-led economy realizes its links to the major world markets are a key component of its international relations, and to stabilize them and make them as fluid and predictable as possible a fundamental requirement.

Three foreign policy objectives emerge in these years as paramount:[19]

1. The promotion of an international economic policy that generates a dynamic insertion into the world economy;
2. The strengthening of democratic institutions in Latin America, as well as regional political cooperation and integration;
3. The support of a regulated and stable international system

And it is to this latter point that I now turn to. As opposed to the more pragmatic approach that reduces foreign policy to trade policy, the underlying notion here is that Chile has a certain degree of responsibility for the "maintenance and upkeep" of the existing international order. The latter is based on established conflict resolution mechanisms that seek to maintain international peace and avoid wars and confrontations in which the smaller and weaker powers will generally have the most to lose. According to this reasoning, countries like Chile, which, in the developing world are among the main beneficiaries of a peaceful international order, should be especially keen on keeping it so. That means an active collaboration in the tasks this entails.

This, of course, does not arise in a vacuum, or *ex novo*, but is also the product of a long and established twentieth-century Chilean tradition. In accordance with its own internal political practices and the stability and continuity of its democratic institutions for much (albeit, alas, tragically not all) of this period, Chile has been a strong proponent of international law, international organizations and multilateralism, the peaceful resolution of controversies and respect for international treaties and obligations. Chile is one of the founding members of the United Nations, hosts the headquarters of the United Nations Economic Commission for Latin America and the Caribbean (ECLAC), provided the founding president of the Inter-American Development Bank and has otherwise made a significant contribution to international institutions and the practice of multilateralism.[20]

In the nineties, then, after a tragic 17-year break, Chile took on, once again, its duties of "international citizenship" – in other words, it took part in some peacekeeping operations, but still in a rather modest and timid fashion, that only slowly started to come to terms with the enormous challenges posed by the post-Cold War world and the plethora of internal conflicts it released.[21]

In this decade, however, there have been three instances in which Chile has had to come to terms with what it actually means to have to take on these responsibilities, having to make some very difficult decisions and each of them exemplifies the sort of tough choices middle powers are confronted with in the international scene. The first is the case of Chile's participation in the United Nations Security Council and the choice it had to face on the Iraq issue (2003) a subject already examined, and which requires no further elaboration. The second, one of troop deployment in a peace enforcement operation (2004), and the third, that of the election of a new OAS secretary-general (2005). Although apparently unrelated, they in fact are not as they build on each other, further enlarging Chile's international standing and "soft power", each of them risky and, at the time, controversial decisions that aroused considerable opposition at home and abroad, but that, in the end, paid considerable dividends and left the country in a stronger position than it was before. We will now turn to analysing the second and third of these "critical choices" in Chilean foreign policy.

The Haitian crisis

Almost exactly a year after the heated deliberations on Iraq at the Security Council, a less prominent but by no means insignificant crisis erupted in the Caribbean, in February 2004. President Jean-Bertrand Aristide, who had been in power in that country for on and off 15 years, and who was unable to assert full control over his country or deal with a rebel uprising coming down from Northern Haiti to the capital, Port-au-Prince, ended up leaving in the middle of the night in a plane chartered by the US State Department, seeking asylum in, of all places, the Central African Republic.

Haiti, of course, has been a bit of a Caribbean basket case. For long dominated by one dictator or another, it was for many decades in the hands of the Duvaliers – first François, the father, and then Jean-Claude, "Baby Doc", the son, until the latter was finally ousted in 1986. Aristide, a Catholic priest with great popular appeal, was elected in December 1990 in the first truly democratic elections ever held in that country, and enormous expectations were raised as to what "Titide" (as Aristide is popularly known) would do. The fact that, fifteen years later, the country was in much worse shape than when he took over speaks for itself.

Haiti, the poorest country in the Western hemisphere, with a per capita income of U$300, has caused great frustration to the international community in general and the United Nations in particular. Yet, in March of 2004, the will "to take the bull by the horns" seemed to be there finally, and after Aristide left for Central Africa the United Nations Security Council unanimously passed Resolution 1529 that authorizes the presence of a Provisional Multinational Force for a three-month period, to re-establish peace and security and provide humanitarian assistance.

This time, the US Secretary of State Colin Powell called the Chilean Minister of Foreign Affairs, Soledad Alvear to find out whether Chile was willing to send troops. This was by no means an easy choice. The conditions under which Aristide had left the country were still somewhat doubtful. CARICOM in fact questioned it, and some people argued that a "soft coup" had taken place. Aristide himself intimated that he had been forced to leave the Presidential Palace against his will, although this was disputed by others. Aristide had for long been a darling of the Left, and many organizations, including the Black Caucus in the US Congress came out in his defence.

Moreover, this would have been the first time that Chilean troops had participated in what was to be, *de facto*, a peace-enforcement operation, as opposed to the peacekeeping operations with small contingents – as a rule no more than fifty men – in which it had been engaged until then.[22]

Latin American diplomacy has a strong herd instinct, and no one else, including Brazil (which said it would wait out the first three months "to see what happens"), was willing to send troops to Haiti.

There was also a constitutional obstacle. According to the Chilean Constitution the deployment of troops abroad has to be approved by the Senate.[23] Yet events in Haiti were escalating so quickly that there was no time for the type of reasoned deliberation among senior legislators such a momentous decision seemed to demand. In many ways, then, it would have been easier to pass, or to follow the Brazilian example to "wait and see".

Yet, within 24 hours Chile accepted the invitation to deploy a sizeable military force in Haiti, and within 48 hours some 350 Chilean military men found themselves on their way to Port-au-Prince. They ended up joining the US, French and Canadian contingents for a mopping-up operation that, in the end, went well. After the three-month period was over, the latter forces all left, with only the Chilean forces staying on, this time increased to some 600 men and women from all three services as well as the national police. Argentina, Bolivia, Brazil, Ecuador, Guatemala, Peru and Uruguay have sent troops as well, to what has become the first ever United Nations peacekeeping operation manned by a majority of Latin American forces. A Brazilian general, Augusto Heleno Ribeiro Pereira, is in charge of the UN peacekeeping force, and a former Chilean Foreign Minister, Juan Gabriel Valdés, is the UN Secretary-General's Special Representative in Haiti, the first time a Chilean has taken on such responsibilities.

This is a major nation-building task, which is by no means easy, but Chile has finally started to "walk the talk" of its "international citizenship duties", and, in so doing, it has also exercised a measure of leadership. The presence of Chilean troops in the initial Provisional Multinational Force (otherwise formed exclusively by Northern countries), contributed to the legitimization of that initial operation, and, after their three-month mandate was over, facilitated the incorporation of troops from many other countries in the region into MINUSTAH (Mission des Nations Unies pour la Stabilisation en Haïti), the more permanent forces tasked with keeping peace in the land of Dessalines.

With its quick reaction to the United States' invitation to participate with troops in Haiti, Chile demonstrated not only its military capabilities (it is by no means easy to produce 350 men to be deployed at 48 hours' notice), but also that its stand on the Iraq issue in the Security Council had not been triggered by anything other than specific international law principles and the facts of the matter (the absence of evidence for any WMD in Iraq). It also showed the way for other Latin American countries, especially those in the Southern Cone, which although not directly affected by anything that could happen in Haiti, did see the wisdom of Latin Americans taking care of troubles in their own hemisphere, no matter how far removed from their own borders.

Electing a new OAS secretary-general

As mentioned earlier, one of the weaknesses of multilateralism in the Americas has been the relative ineffectiveness of the leading regional body, the OAS, which, for a variety of reasons, has never really been able to live up to the expectations raised when it was created in 1948. These troubles reached a new low in October of 2004 when its newly elected secretary-general, former Costa Rican President Miguel Angel Rodríguez, had to quit and return home from Washington scarcely three weeks after taking office in order to face corruption charges.

Interestingly, Rodríguez had faced no opponents as he ran for the position of top executive of the organization in the first half of 2004. Former Chilean Foreign Minister (and then Home Affairs Minister) José Miguel Insulza briefly considered doing so, but in the end decided not to, as many countries were already committed to the Costa Rican candidacy (a country that, ten years earlier, had lost another bid to occupy that position, as the United States managed to prevail with the candidacy of former Colombian President César Gaviria).

Yet, Rodríguez had scarcely arrived back in San José (where he was promptly arrested), when the jockeying for the position started. The White House made it known that it favoured former Salvadorean President Francisco Flores, who had backed President George W. Bush on the Iraq issue, and had been very much part of the "coalition of the willing" in the Iraq war. This time around, the Chilean government decided to "throw its hat into the ring" with what it considered to be a very strong candidate, Minister Insulza. And in a somewhat surprising move, Mexico did the same, submitting the name of its foreign minister, Luis Ernesto Derbez.

For Chile, this election was in many ways much more than about the OAS itself. Chile's economic accomplishments, and its international economic policy, one strongly oriented towards Northern markets, had often raised the issue of Chile's true commitment to Latin America,[24] Wasn't Chile really much more interested in Europe and NAFTA, in joining the OECD (the "rich man's club") and in continuing to attract high amount of FDI from the developed world, than in truly engaging with its neighbours? If nothing else, submitting a candidate for secretary-general of the OAS would seem to indicate a true interest in the region, and a willingness to expose oneself to the risks any such venture entailed. It would certainly put paid to the notion that Chile didn't seem to care about the region, busy at it was negotiating all these FTAs with the developed countries.

However that may be, the conventional wisdom on OAS elections is that no secretary-general has ever been elected against the wishes of the United States, which, in theory, should have strengthened the candidacy of Flores. In fact, the latter never really picked up any steam, with his supporters being confined to the half-dozen Central American nations.[25] What was seen as a big asset by the White House (El Salvador's support of the US position on Iraq, and its actual participation in the war there) was in fact a handicap to the region, where the war was and is deeply unpopular.

In a three-way race, many gave Insulza, who had managed to enlist much of South America as well as the CARICOM nations behind his name, the upper hand, if not necessarily to win the majority of 18 votes needed to elect the new secretary-general. In a second round, he would presumably have had the advantage of having won a plurality of the vote and thus a good chance of coming out on top. Yet, 72 hours before the election on 11 April 2005, Flores withdrew from the race, and the United States swung behind Derbez. After five rounds of voting in a row, the Chilean and Mexican candidates could not break a 17–17 tie, and a new date was set for the election, to be held on 2 May.

Most observers considered that Washington made an all-out effort to block the Chilean candidacy, on the basis that it was supported by Venezuela, with whose government the Bush administration has had serious differences. At least two countries which had committed themselves to vote for Chile were thus enticed to switch their votes.

Once again, Chile was faced with a difficult choice. Would it be advisable to insist on a candidacy against the manifest preferences of the United States? Even if the Chilean candidate were to win under such conditions, would he be able to accomplish anything in an organization based in Washington DC, 60 per cent of whose budget is provided by the United States?

In Chile itself, voices objecting to keeping up Minister Insulza's candidacy were raised in various quarters. One argument against it was that, in so doing, Chile risked alienating the countries of North America (in addition to the United States, Canada had also backed the Mexican candidate) with which Chile had "thrown in its lot" long ago (presumably because of the FTAs with these countries). Another was that by being backed by populist governments like those of Argentina and Venezuela, Chile risked being associated with them.

Elsewhere, calls were made for a compromise, one that would entail a new candidate from a third country. Yet despite the frustration of not having been able to win the first time around, Chile decided to insist on Insulza's candidacy, continuing to cultivate its initial, largely South American and Caribbean, coalition, while also reaching out to its opponents, and especially to the United States. It insisted that this was neither a North–South nor a Left–Right issue, but simply one of the best candidate and of willingness to reform the OAS and make it into the sort of IO the Americas needs. President Lagos got on a plane and, in a whirlwind tour of South American cities, visited President Lula in Sao Paulo (where he secured Brazil's message to Paraguay to change its vote), President Chávez in Caracas (in his first visit to Venezuela) and President Uribe in Bogotá (thus signalling his ability to keep the communication channels open with all parties, as Colombia had backed Derbez).

The Panamanian Foreign Minister Samuel Lewis asked for a meeting with President Lagos in Bogota, where further strategizing took place. Needless to say, such high-profile presidential "canvassing" for an election in a multilateral body is quite uncommon in Latin America (and elsewhere), and entails high reputational risks for whoever undertakes it.

In the end, the fact that Chile was hosting the Third Summit of the Community of Democracies held in Santiago on 28–30 April 2005, just two days before the second round of voting on the election of the OAS Secretary General was to take place in Washington DC, was decisive. The presence of many Western hemisphere foreign ministers (including US Secretary of State Condoleezza Rice and Mexican Foreign Minister Derbez) made it possible to reach an agreement designed to avoid another divisive scenario that would split the hemisphere in half.

With crumbling support at home (where many saw him as little more than a "stand-in" for the previous US candidate, former Salvadorean President Flores) Mexican Foreign Minister Derbez was increasingly debilitated. Paraguay announced that it would switch its vote from the Mexican candidate to the Chilean one (thus breaking the tie) and Panama intimated it would do the same if no consensus on Insulza was reached. On 29 April, in Santiago, Colombian Foreign Minister Carolina Barco announced that Derbez had agreed to withdraw his candidacy and that the only remaining candidate was Insulza, who, in Washington DC on 2 May 2005, was promptly elected with 31 votes.[26]

Instead of going for the "low-risk" strategy of withdrawing its candidate and searching for a third alternative, Chile, as in the case of the UN Security Council resolution on Iraq and on the issue of deploying troops in Haiti, pressed on with what it set forth as "the right thing to do", on the strength of what it considered to be not only the best candidate, but also the country's proven record of commitment to multilateralism and its key principles.

By way of conclusion

In hindsight, two-and-a-half years after the invasion of Iraq, and as the WMD have yet to be found, Chile's decision not to back a second resolution on Iraq turns out to have been the right one. The same goes for the decision to deploy troops and play an active role in peace-enforcement operations in Haiti, and having insisted on what seemed to many a losing proposition, that of the candidacy to the OAS secretary-general. But this is not simply a factual issue. Rather, it underscores a broader concern.

For middle powers like Chile, one of their most significant assets is the credibility that comes from its democratic traditions, on the one hand, and, on the other, the principles it has applied more or less consistently in its foreign policy through much of its history. Although Chile has a strong and well-performing economy, at the end of the day its greatest capital in international affairs does not stem from that (which remains rather small at a GDP of US$90 billion) but from its political standing and reputation – what Joseph S. Nye has called "soft power".

To behave opportunistically and according to what is most expedient at any given point in time, as opposed to doing what is considered "the right thing to do" – which basically is what applying a foreign policy according to certain principles is all about – is, of course, the easiest way to squander this capital away and devalue your main asset.

Another issue is how middle powers should relate to the one remaining superpower. There is at least one school of thought which considers that, given the current overwhelming power and predominance of the United States, the best and most advisable option is simply "to go with the flow", and just follow the instructions that come from Washington. Material incentives should provide handsome rewards for those who behave accordingly, and no purpose is served in hanging on to bankrupt ideologies, let alone such outmoded principles as multilateralism, with its whiff of *déja-vu*.

Yet, such a brazen notion implies essentially the abdication of having a foreign policy at all, a sort of self-inflicted *capitis diminutio*, and a self-assumed attempt to minimize Latin America's role in world affairs that would be incomprehensible both for regional public opinion and for the rest of the world.

Moreover, at a time when we are going through tectonic changes in the international system, Latin America would be ill-advised not to participate in the deliberations leading to the reshaping of this new order. Humanitarian intervention (HI), the new requirements of the world's financial architecture and those of an emerging universal justice system are only some of the issues on the table, all of which point in the direction of a much more interventionist world order. Latin American countries, of course, are free not to participate in the deliberations about these issues, but this will only mean that the new order will emerge without the region's input – hardly a desirable outcome.

Chile's foreign policy after 9/11 would seem to confirm the notion that, far from being highly vulnerable countries that are, almost by definition, precluded from engaging in "high politics" issues in universal IOs, Latin American middle powers can have a voice and make a difference in world affairs. The art of foreign policy, ultimately, lies in being able to balance principles and interests. The case of Chile, arguably the country in the region that had the most to lose by opposing US policy on Iraq (given its then pending FTA), indicates that it is possible to do so in today's complex environment. Far from having lost out as a result of its principled stance, it gained much – not only was it not "punished" but it now has an enhanced role in the region.

Crucial to the latter, however, has also been Chile's participation in MINUSTAH, the United Nations peacekeeping operation in Haiti initiated in March 2004. While Chile had been participating in various UN peacekeeping operations since the early nineties, its contribution had been small, even symbolic sometimes. Several Latin American countries, including Argentina, Brazil and Uruguay had done so with much larger contingents, and Chile, while active in organizations like the Human Security Network and the Community of Democracies, was lagging behind in its actual manpower contribution to the duties of international citizenship. At first, Chile's policy had been to take part only in peacekeeping operations and to stay away from peace-enforcement. Yet this was changed in the late nineties, though no actual participation in such operations had taken place. In Haiti, Chile was first willing to be the only Latin American country to send troops (going in with United States, French and Canadian contingents) sending 350 men within 48 hours, and then, three months later, stay on with a force of 600 in an overwhelmingly Latin American-manned operation, which would have been much more difficult to deploy had Chile not been ready to take the initial "plunge" in March 2004.

As this experience would seem to suggest, in this age of "multilateral crisis", it is not withdrawal from IOs and reluctance to take part in their principal bodies that would seem to be the best way forward for Latin American nations, and middle powers more generally. By engaging on their merits the issues of the day, and doing so in a variety of fora, including most prominently the Security Council, but also by being willing and able to participate actively in building up regional bodies like the OAS, they may do better than by simply "staying home" and nurturing an international low profile. Contrary to the revisionist view that has been gaining ground in the region lately, to continue to stand up for the principles that have guided their international behaviour for much of the twentieth century (quite apart from the obvious need to bring them up to date with the requirements of this new era) may be the best way to defend not only those very principles, but also national interests.

Acknowledgements

The author would like to thank the participants of the workshop at which this paper was first presented, especially Edward Newman and Gwyn Prins, as well as Richard Fagen, Emilio Pantojas-García and Ramesh Thakur for their comments on an earlier version. The usual caveats apply.

Notes

1. On multilateralism in Latin America, see Francisco Rojas Aravena (ed.) (2000) *Multilateralismo: Perspectivas latinoamericanas*, Caracas: FLACSO-Chile and Nueva Sociedad.
2. On the OAS, see Luigi Einaudi and Joseph S. Tulchin (eds.) (1991) *The Future of the Organization of American States and Hemispheric Security*, Washington DC: Woodrow Wilson International Center for Scholars. See also Monica Herz (2001) "Managing security in the Western hemisphere", in Michael Pugh and Wahageru Pal Singh Sedu (eds.) *The United Nations and Regional Security: Europe and Beyond*, Boulder, Colorado: Lynne Rienner.
3. On the Ibero-American Summits, see Raúl Sanhueza Carvajal (2003) *Las Cumbres Iberoamericanas: Comunidad de Naciones o Diplomacia Clientelar?*, Santiago: FLACSO-Chile and Editorial Universitarial; and Francisco Rojas Aravena (ed.) (2000) *Las cumbres Iberoamericanas: Una mirada global*, Caracas: FLACSO-Chile and Nueva Sociedad.
4. On the FTAA, see R. Devlin and A. Esteverodal (eds.) (2003) *Bridges for Development*, Washington DC: Inter American Development Bank; and A. Esteverodal, D. Rodrik, A. Taylor and A. Velasco (2004) *Integrating the Americas*, Cambridge, Mass: Harvard University Press.
5. On regional integration trends in the nineties, see Victor Bulmer Thomas (ed.) (2001) *Regional Integration in Latin America and the Caribbean*, Washington DC: Brookings Institution. See also Robert Devlin and Ricardo French-Davis (1999) "Towards an evaluation of regional integration in Latin America in the 1990s", *The World Economy* 22(2): 261–290.
6. See Robert O. Keohane (2002) *Power and Governance in a Partially Globalized World*, New York and London: Routledge.
7. Joseph S. Tulchin (2003) "Estados Unidos-América Latina: Nuevos espacios y temas estratégicos. Posibilidades y obstáculos en una relacion cada vez mas compleja", in Francisco Rojas Aravena (ed.) *La seguridad en América Latina pos 11 de septiembre*, Caracas: Nueva Sociedad, pp. 45–58.
8. See, for example, the editorial "La arriesgada apuesta de Chile de ingresar al Consejo de Seguridad", *La Tercera* (Santiago), 3 March 2003.
9. Christopher Marquis, "US Hasn't Kept Promise on Latin America, Critics Say", *New York Times*, 19 May 2002.

10. See Jorge Heine (2002) "Los avatares de nuestras (incompletas) democracias", *Foro Chile 21* (Santiago) 2(13) (May): 21–24.
11. Jorge Heine (2002) "Que pasó, Tio Sam? Los Estados Unidos y América Latina después del 11 de septiembre", *Estudios Internacionales* (Santiago) 35(138) (July–September).
12. This paragraph and the following one draw on my (2003) "Nuevo imperio, viejo patio trasero? Los Estados Unidos, América Latina y la guerra de Irak", *Estudios Internacionales* 36(142) (July–September): 97–112.
13. This debate, of course, was not confined to Chile. For a Mexican expression in a somewhat crude version of this argument, see the column of Enrique Krauze in the weekly *Proceso* (Mexico City), 23 February 2003. For a more sophisticated version of the economic reasons for supporting the US position on Iraq, see Edgardo Boeninger (2003) "Iraq: una decisión complicada", *La Tercera* (Santiago), 11 March.
14. For a well-documented analysis of the decision-making process in Chile that led to all this, and how it played at the United Nations and elsewhere, see Heraldo Muñoz (2005) *Una guerra solitaria:La historia secreta de EEUU en Irak, la polémica en la ONU y el papel de Chile*, Santiago: Random House–Mondadori. The author is Chile's Permanent Representative to the United Nations.
15. See Claudio Fuentes (ed.) (2004) *Bajo la Mirada del Halcón: Estados Unidos-América Latina post 11/09/01*, Santiago: FLACSO.
16. For a subsequent elaboration of that argument, see Hernán Felipe Errázuriz (2003) "La diplomacia chilena en la segunda guerra de Irak", *Estudios Internacionales* 36(142) (July–September): 113–120.
17. See Jorge Heine (1991) "Timidez o pragmatismo? La política exterior de Chile en 1990–1991", in Jorge Heine (ed.) *Hacia unas relaciones internacionales de mercado: Anuario de políticas exteriores de América Latina 1990–1991*, Caracas: Nueva Sociedad.
18. Carlos Portales and Alberto van Klaveren (1994) "La política exterior chilena en un mundo en cambio", in *Proposiciones* 25 (Santiago) (October).
19. José Miguel Insulza (1998) *Ensayos sobre política exterior de Chile*, Santiago: Editorial Los Andes.
20. For a good discussion of these traditions, see Heraldo Muñoz (1989) *Chile: Política exterior para la demoracia*, Santiago: Pehuén.
21. Paz Milet (2000) "Chile en el escenario multilateral", in Rojas Aravena (ed.) *Multilateralismo*, pp. 193–203.
22. Jorge Heine (2004) "Siete razones para enviar tropas chilenas a Haití", *La Tercera*, 3 March.
23. In the end, despite strong misgivings by a number of senators, including many from the government benches, Senate approval was given *ex post facto*.
24. On Chile's development diplomacy, see Alberto van Klaveren (1998) "Inserción internacional de Chile", in Cristián Toloza and Eugenio Lahera (eds.) *Chile en los noventa*, Santiago: Dolmen, especially pp. 122–127. Difficulties with several neighbouring countries in 2003 made many raise the question whether Chile's global economic success was not being matched by regional political isolation, leading to a lively debate on the matter.
25. Marcela Sánchez (2005) "La importancia de distinguir una izquierda de la otra", *Washington Post*, 21 April.
26. See Joel Brinkley and Larry Rohter (2005) "Chilean, once opposed by US, is elected Head of the OAS", *New York Times*, 3 May. See also Alvaro Vargas Llosa (2005) "Voto de EEUU a favor del ministro surge tras nuevos cálculos estratégicos", *La Tercera* (Santiago), 3 May; and José Rodríguez Elizondo, (2005) "Panzer habemus", *La Tercera*, 3 May.

24

From economic to security multilateralism: Great powers and international order in the Asia Pacific

Quansheng Zhao

Since the end of the Second World War, Europe, East Asia and the Middle East have been the foci of major powers both in terms of conflict and cooperation. With the post-Cold War disintegration of the former Soviet Union, the intensity of focus in Europe has more or less been reduced in terms of international conflict, but East Asia and the Middle East continue to draw world attention as major sources for international conflict and cooperation. There has been noticeable mutual influence between East Asian regionalism and global multilateralism in economic, political and security dimensions.

Mutual influence between global and regional settings

The Korean peninsula provides a prime example of a focus of major powers in East Asia. Historically, it has been known as a shrimp among four whales – China, Japan, Russia and the United States. It was the case a century ago; it is still the case today. Therefore, conflict and cooperation in the region has inevitably had its impact on global governance.

The best way to look at the mutual influence in regional and global settings is to examine policy orientations of the United States – the only superpower in the world – which is believed to exercise under a principle of unilateralism, particularly under the second Bush administration.

In his recent comments on the US's Asia policy under the second Bush administration, former US Ambassador to Japan, Michael Armacost, argued that "continuity rather than change is likely to be the watchword".[1] Keeping this thought in mind, it is essential to understand the main characteristics of Bush's policy during his first term, upon which policy in the second term has been built. In a *Brookings Review* article entitled "America unbound: the Bush revolution in foreign policy", Ivo Daalder and James Lindsay present the three practices of American foreign policy under the guidelines of the Bush revolution: (1) a disdain for multilateral arrangements and institutions, (2) the full consideration of pre-emptive military actions, and (3) the forcing of regime changes in rogue states.[2]

These foreign policy practices are based on two strains of revolutionary thought in foreign policy: first, in order to ensure American security, Washington may have to shed the constraints imposed by friends, allies and international institutions; and, second, the US should utilize fully its strength to change the status quo in the world. These new ideas are labelled as "the new neoconservative framework" in US foreign policy. Under these guidelines, the United States has launched its wars in Afghanistan and Iraq in the post-9/11 period. These two wars are very much along the lines of the above-mentioned three guidelines of US foreign policy in the Bush era.

When one looks at Bush's Asia policies, specifically his policy towards East Asia, one may find that they are quite different from those guiding US actions in other parts of the world. In almost every foreign policy practice in Asia, Washington has been the one to promote a multilateral institutional approach for major events in the region, and specifically the North Korea nuclear crisis. The six-party talks, consisting of China, Japan, Russia, South Korea, North Korea and the United States, were directly constructed and pushed by the US, in close consultation with other players, particularly Beijing. In the presidential debates toward the end of 2004, Bush put forward the view that only a multilateral framework could deal with the North Korea crisis, as if he would not consider unilateral action at all (as the US did in Iraq), and there was little discussion of a pre-emptive attack on Pyongyang. One does not often hear public remarks from Washington for regime change in the Asia Pacific, including North Korea. People may then wonder why there are such distinct differences between US policy towards East Asia and towards Iraq. It is the author's view that in its global strategy, the Bush administration considers Iraq a higher priority than East Asia, which causes and accounts for different perceptions and strategies in Washington in terms of unilateral versus multilateral approaches. Now let us look at general trends in regional development in East Asia.

In my 2001 article, "The shift in power distribution and the change of major power relations", I analysed the trends of international relations in the Asia Pacific in the post-Cold War era.[3] This chapter is, in a way, a follow up to that previous article to depict further regional development in terms of general trends from bilateral to multilateral cooperation. This development first took place in the economic dimension – only recently did the development begin to move towards the security dimension. I should first clearly define that this chapter will only cover the Asia Pacific, in terms of East Asia and Southeast Asia, plus the United States. It will not deal with other parts of Asia, such as the South, West and Central, although these regions are by no means less important. The general argument of this chapter is, with the shift of power distribution and the new dynamics in the region, increasing attention has been paid to institutional change and multilateral frameworks as a new means for international order. Having said this, there are nevertheless major obstacles preventing the region from deeper development in the direction of multilateralism.

In the Cold War era, particularly since the Asian financial crisis of 1997–1998, there have been increasing demands for regional cooperation in East Asia. These demands first began as calls for economic cooperation and gradually expanded to the security dimension. Entering the twenty-first century, the North Korea nuclear crisis and the 11 September terrorist attacks on the United States have brought new incentives for not only medium and small players, but also major powers, to focus on a security framework in the region. A win–win mindset has gradually developed and in some ways replaced the zero-sum game of the Cold-War era. This chapter will not only examine the dynamics of two great powers – China as a rising power, and the United States as the world's only superpower – but also other key powers such as Russia, Japan, the two Koreas and ASEAN.

There were three noticeable and fascinating developments in East Asia from the latter part of 2003 to the end of 2005. The first was the six-party negotiations over the North Korea nuclear crisis, which was hosted in Beijing, beginning in August 2003, and included North and South Korea, China, Japan, Russia and the United States. The second round of the high-profile talks commenced in Beijing on 25 February 2004.[4] This involved much behind the scenes manoeuvring among the main actors, particularly between Pyongyang, Beijing and Washington.

The second event was the ASEAN-plus-three summit in October 2003, which included the ten ASEAN countries together with China, Japan and South Korea. In this meeting, China signed the Treaty of Amity and Cooperation with ASEAN, bringing the prospects for an East Asia community one step closer to actualization.[5] The latter development indicates progress towards regional community building, whereas the former development indicates that a new security framework may be evolving. This chapter will argue that the two processes are closely linked. The community building process in East Asia primarily concentrates on economic integration, whereas a new security framework considers strategic security issues, increasingly moving from bilateral to multilateral security arrangements.

The third development was the East Asia summit to held in December 2005 in Malaysia. In May 2005, East Asian nations met in Kyoto, Japan, and decided upon the participants of this summit: the ten ASEAN countries, three Northeast Asian countries (China, Japan South Korea), India, Australia and New Zealand. This kind of regional summit targets on the establishment of a multilateral framework facilitating an East Asian community. The United States was conspicuously excluded from this summit and Washington expressed its uneasiness with this development. Although Japan proposed an observer status for the US, Washington did not accept this prospect and expressed an ambivalence toward this summit.[6] On the one hand, Washington understood this as the trend of development in the region. One the other hand, it was concerned that this trend might diminish US influence there. In a way, the new summit will force Washington to rethink its unilateral approach in its foreign policy orientation.

Any discussion of a new security framework must first examine characteristics of the old one. In East Asia, the post-war security framework was primarily built upon the Cold War reality. That is, the world was bipolar, divided into the Communist camp (headed by the former Soviet Union) and the West (headed by the United States). It is natural that the prevailing security frameworks were formed also along the lines of these two different camps. And more noticeably, in each camp the security framework was basically bilateral in nature. For example, in the Communist camp, one can point to the China–USSR Friendship Treaty signed in 1950, as well as other arrangements between then socialist states. Along similar lines, US-led security regimes were also bilateral, unlike the European security framework. In Asia, there was no overarching security organization like NATO, but rather a number of US-led bilateral security arrangements, many of which were initiated in the 1950s. These included US security arrangements with such countries as Japan, South Korea, Australia, New Zealand, the Philippines and Thailand.[7] To better understand the newly emerged multilateral potential for security arrangements, we should first look at the evolution of regionalism in East and Southeast Asia.

Regionalism in East and Southeast Asia and post-Cold War reconfiguration

In the Asia–Pacific region, there has been an increasing call for regionalism. As the process of globalization continues, one can see rising regional integration and the formation of regional economic blocks. There are three major economic zones in today's world: Europe, North America and East Asia. The first two regions have rapidly progressed towards regional economic integration, as well as political cooperation and security coordination. The most well-known organizations are the European Union (EU) and the North American Free Trade Agreement (NAFTA). Despite enormous efforts, East Asia is far behind in terms of regional integration.

Although the effort for regional community-building in Southeast Asia began as early as the 1960s, the movement did not gain real momentum until the post-Cold War era. The whole process of integration is an incremental one, which began with the formation of several sub-regional institutions. The most significant development was the Association for Southeast Asian Nations (ASEAN), established in 1967. The current members of ASEAN include all ten members of Southeast Asia: Indonesia, the Philippines, Malaysia, Singapore, Thailand, Brunei, Vietnam, Cambodia, Laos and Burma. The three major countries in Northeast Asia – China, Japan and South Korea – have also increased consultations and coordination in the economic sphere. Furthermore, the Asia–Pacific Economic Cooperation (APEC), established in 1989, has become a regional force and counts such countries outside of Asia as the United States, Mexico, Canada, Russia, Chile, Peru, Papua New Guinea, Australia and New Zealand among its members. The creation of the ASEAN Regional Forum (ARF) and Asian European Summit are also significant developments. Most notable, perhaps, is the effort to integrate Northeast Asia and Southeast Asia, namely through such mechanisms as ASEAN-plus-three (China, Japan, Korea) or ASEAN-plus-one (China).[8] These regional organizations have achieved major progress in bringing the countries together and have produced tangible results, primarily in the economic dimension. However, it is widely believed that the ARF was far from the ideal organization to effectively deal with regional security issues. The passive nature of the organization has produced more talk than action. Therefore, one cannot say that, with these regional organizations, the region has already developed a multilateral framework, particularly in the security dimension.

East Asian international relations and regional community building efforts have been greatly affected by the reconfiguration of power relations in the region since the beginning of the post-Cold War era. It is a common belief that the end of the Cold War in the late 1980s – especially the collapse of the Soviet empire – significantly altered the configuration of major power relations in the Asia–Pacific region. These changes have generated new major-power relations in the region and redefined bilateral relations among China, Japan, Russia and the United States. The rise of the United States to sole superpower status has given Washington a dominant role in all four dimensions of world affairs: political, strategic, economic and technological.

As the United States assumed its role as the sole superpower in the world, China also increased its standing. Since 1978, when it initiated economic reforms and the Open Door economic policy, China has achieved spectacular economic performance, sustaining high growth rates (even with the slowdown from 11–12 per cent to 7–8 per cent since 1998) and escaping the Asian economic crisis of 1997–1998. This expansion has greatly increased China's influence in regional and global affairs.

On the other hand, there has been a noticeable "down turn" in influence with regard to Russia and Japan. With the collapse and dismemberment of the former Soviet Union in the early 1990s, Russia experienced major setbacks in all respects, and it has a long way to go to return to its previous status and influence in the region. The nature of Japan's downturn is quite different, as it is reflected only in economic terms and is a result of consecutive economic recessions rather than a major financial crisis such as befell Korea and Southeast Asia.[9]

Competition and cooperation are the two dominant modes of behaviour among major powers in the economic dimension. An important element that characterizes post-Cold War international relations is the trend towards globalization, or economic interdependence. The shift in distribution of power, and the rise of China in particular, has placed major emphasis upon economic integration – take China, Japan and the United States, for example. In terms of top trading partners, each one of the three countries places the other two high on its list. Trade between and among East and Southeast Asia has also increased dramatically. This development has further advanced the rapid trends toward interdependence in the region, and for the last decade economic integration has developed at an unprecedented pace. This kind of momentum has created a foundation for further development of community-building and a platform for the possible development of a new security regime.

The changing security concerns of the two great powers – China and the US

A major shift of security framework took place in the post-Cold War era, mainly after the collapse of the Soviet empire in 1990. A bipolar world became a unipolar one – that is, the United States was left as the only superpower. Under these new circumstances, each country's security framework had to begin taking the "US factor" into consideration. Another major development is the "rise of China" as discussed previously. In terms of regional and even global security, a key issue confronting all powers in the Asia–Pacific region is how to manage the relationships with, and between, the two ascendant powers – the United States and China. Virtually all regional controversies, such as cross-strait relations between Taiwan and the People's Republic of China (PRC), the resolution of the tensions on the Korean Peninsula, and the evolving nature of the US–Japan security alliance (and the future direction of Japanese foreign policy) are all closely linked to major power relations, particularly the ongoing dynamics of China and the United States. In terms of security perspectives, the old realist school of zero-sum games – namely, "I win, you lose", and vice versa – has remained the dominant paradigm in the region. Thus, given the post-Cold War developments in the Asia–Pacific region, some people suggest that if the influence of the United States and Japan declines, China may enter into the power vacuum.[10]

Thus the strategic concerns of the major powers can easily evolve in diametrically opposed directions, thereby promoting a polarized division of the world into enemies versus allies, as was the case during the Cold War. As Barry Buzan argues, it is also important to look at internal developments within China and the US.[11] During the early stage of the first term of George W. Bush Jnr's administration, American priorities in East Asia shifted to emphasize the US's relationships with its allies in the region, most notably Japan. In fact, Deputy Secretary of State Richard Armitage was one of the first people to argue that the US should pay more attention to the US–Japan alliance.[12]

There were three factors at that time (the late 1980s throughout most of the 1990s) encouraging bilaterally oriented arrangements. First, the two great powers – United States and China – preferred bilateral arrangements at that time. Second, was the historical legacy. Japan, the US's major security partner in Asia, has yet to resolve the problems rooted in the invasion of its Asian neighbours during World War II. The third factor is an ideological consideration: despite the dissolution of the Soviet Empire and the decline of communism, major socialist countries in the region such as China, North Korea and Vietnam still remain. That factor, in many ways, could provide difficulties for other players to move in multilateral directions.

These three factors have all been gradually eroded over the years and are being replaced with other considerations. Facing new developments in the region, China and the United States have begun to change their attitude towards multilateral framework. China, for example, has long stopped viewing ASEAN as a security threat, but rather as a good vehicle to strengthen the security environment on its southern borders.[13] Although the history factor with Japan is still strong, in China and South Korea, in particular, it is no longer a dominating factor in foreign policy considerations. And ideological considerations are also in great decline. Both China and Vietnam enthusiastically embraced a market economy and encouraged private entrepreneurship, thus rendering ideology a lesser factor in terms of multilateral cooperation. The decline of these three factors is conducive to more multilateral arrangements, but that alone will not provide enough impetus for major powers – which may need more incentives for the momentum to develop.

Such incentives include the terrorist attacks of 11 September and the new developments in North Korea's stated nuclear capabilities which came to light in October 2002. In the wake of 11 September a US-led anti-terrorist campaign was launched and Asia became a key point of interest and concern, second only to the Middle East in importance. It became evident to Washington, including the most hawkish thinkers and unilateralist advocates, that a multilateral effort and a broader anti-terrorist coalition was necessary. In this case, not only are traditional allies such as Japan and South Korea essential, but new partners such as China and ASEAN countries are also necessary for the success of this anti-terrorist association.[14] This is a clear signal for the formation of a collective security framework, in place of the traditional approach of bilateralism.

Let us now concentrate on examining the two most significant players in Asia–Pacific security arrangements – China and the United States. China's active attitude towards regional community building began in the wake of the 1997 Asian Economic crisis. During that crisis, China stood out in its role as a reliable partner and leading player in guiding the region out of the economic crisis. One of the strong stances which was helpful for China's Asian neighbours was Beijing's persistent policy to maintain the stability of its currency, the *renminbi*. In other words, China resisted frequent attacks from financial speculators regarding its currency, and withstood enormous pressure to devalue it. China's role in the economic integration process appeared even more active at the turn of the new century, particularly after joining the WTO in 2001, and began to participate in the process of establishing Free Trade Area (FTA) agreements with ASEAN countries.[15] China also showed real interest in developing a similar FTA agreement between itself and the two other East Asian powerhouses, Japan and South Korea. This multilateral approach seemed to work smoothly for China's interests as the country's economy continued to boom.

In the security dimension, however, the picture is much more complicated. Traditionally, China prefers a bilateral approach in its discussions or negotiations on security measures with other countries. This is particularly true with regard to the issue of Taiwan. By insisting that this is an internal affair, China has made it clear that the issue should be dealt with only through a Beijing–Taipei dialogue and has thus prevented it from becoming an international concern. According to Beijing, any multilateral security arrangement in the region should therefore not include the Taiwan issue. This consideration has become a major obstacle for Beijing to move into a more active multilateral security arrangement. But one does see some signs of flexibility for China to make security arrangements along the lines of multilateralism in dealing with issues other than Taiwan.

Since the beginning of the twenty-first century, China has developed a new line of thinking regarding its security framework known as a "new security concept". This notion was elaborated by Chinese Vice Foreign Minister Wang Yi as a "comprehensive, common, and cooperative" security framework.[16] Under this new conception, China emphasizes gentler and friendlier relations with its neighbouring countries, as well as more agreeable policies on multilateral security arrangements in the region.

One obvious example of this shifting approach is the South China Sea islands dispute. There are conflicting territorial claims made on these islands among China and several ASEAN countries, such as Vietnam, the Philippines, Indonesia, Malaysia, and Brunei. Previously China insisted on negotiating over these islands in a bilateral manner and avoided talking with these countries in a collective way. It was relatively easier for China to negotiate with a single, smaller country, rather than with a collective effort that would increase the ASEAN countries' bargaining power. But this attitude has changed over the past few years. China agreed to sign the Code of Behaviour with ASEAN countries regarding the dispute over the islands. Furthermore, China began to advocate a programme of joint development of the disputed area with these countries, some in a bilateral way, some in a multilateral way, when the area had multilateral claims.[17]

Another successful development for China's multilateral security arrangements is the case of the Shanghai Cooperation Organization (established in 2001), which includes China, Russia, Kazakhstan, Kyrgyzstan, Tajikistan and Uzbekistan. A primary function of the Shanghai Cooperation is to fight against terrorism, and there has already been the slow development of joint military exercises among its member countries in recent times. The latest development of the "Shanghai Six" has seen the establishment of its permanent headquarters in Beijing in January 2004.[18] One of the main purposes of this multilateral organization is to target terrorist groups in the Central Asia area. There are also domestic considerations for Beijing, particularly within its own Xinjiang autonomous region where some of the Uyghur minority are actively engaged in a separatist movement.[19] Therefore, placing these domestic issues into the international multilateral coalitions, such as the Shanghai Six and the anti-terrorist coalition with the United States, is in line with Beijing's own security interests, both externally and internally.

Despite this development of a multilateral approach, a number of major security areas still pose difficulties in their inclusion in the multilateral security arrangement. The first is another flash point in Northeast Asia – that is, relations across the Taiwan Straight. Beijing regards Taiwan as a vital national interest and firmly resists the internationalization of the issue. China has so far emphasized a bilateral approach between Beijing and Taipei and would not want the Taiwan issue placed in an international context.

The most complicated region for China still lies in Northeast Asia. Although China has struggled in its bilateral cooperation with Japan and South Korea, including military cooperation, it is still difficult to work out a comprehensive multilateral arrangement with these countries. One reason is found in the US factor. Any multilateral security arrangement must consider the United States since it has long-standing security ties with both Japan and South Korea.

In sum, there has been a noticeable shift in China's attitude toward multilateral security arrangements. While there is still much concern over the issue of Taiwan, Beijing has begun to put a more positive light on multilateral frameworks. China's active role in hosting the six-party talks over the North Korea nuclear crisis and the new flexibility toward ASEAN countries both demonstrate a new approach. At the same time, many of China's basic concerns still remain. The future evolution of Beijing's attitude, therefore, deserves continued careful examination. Now let us look at the other crucial player in the region – the United States.

As the only superpower in the post-Cold War era, the United States has played a vital role in virtually every part of the globe. The Asia–Pacific region is no exception. There have been two parallel strategies under the first George W. Bush administration and this has continued into his second term. One line of thinking, perhaps represented by the US Department of Defense, emphasizes the unipolar nature of the world, with the US having the utmost responsibility for maintaining world order. Unilateralism, according to this school of thought, is most suitable for maintaining US interests and getting things done. The best example is the war in Iraq against the Saddam Hussein regime. In the Asia–Pacific region, advocates of this line of thought emphasize already existing bilateral arrangements, such as the US–Japan Security Treaty and the US–South Korea Security Alliance. Security arrangements with other countries, including China, can only be given lesser importance after these military allies.[20] In other words, because of this kind of mentality, it will be quite problematic for the Pentagon to develop a multilateral security regime that may include China.[21] As a matter of fact, some commentators even advocate for the US to regard China as an enemy.[22]

Another line of thinking, perhaps represented by the mainstream members of the State Department and the National Security Council, is more inclined to rely on multilateralism. It continues to call for active participation in the regional economic integration, such as the role of the United States in APEC activities. This school believes a multilateral arrangement is more suitable for solving security issues such as the North Korea nuclear crisis. In this regard, a more cautious State Department approach has prevailed over the views of hardliners who believe that a pre-emptive strike on North Korean nuclear sites would solve this issue. The US has encountered increasing difficulties in the post-war occupation of Iraq which have highlighted the limits of US forces and the desirability of a multilateral participation in the process of rebuilding Iraq. This fresh experience may, in turn, enhance the influence of multilateralists within the US foreign policy apparatus. This new approach may also increase the necessity for Washington to seek a constructive and consultative partnership with major powers, especially China, in maintaining a peaceful environment in the region.[23] At the same time, however, the US will continue to rely on existing bilateral security arrangements with such allies as Japan and South Korea. The alternating situation between old and new approaches – in other words, between bilateralism and multilateralism – may continue in Washington under the second term of the Bush administration.

One major obstacle for Washington in developing an even closer strategic relationship with Beijing lays in the issue of Taiwan. In 1996, China's missile exercise across the Taiwan Strait, and the subsequent move into the area by two US aircraft carriers, highlighted the potential military confrontation between the two great powers over Taiwan. Beijing has so far made it clear that a war with Taiwan would be adverse to its economic modernization. However Beijing may deem military force an acceptable means of preventing Taiwan from moving towards independence should it be necessary.

There is also a dilemma for Washington. On one hand, the United States has viewed Taiwan as a loyal ally and a newly democratic society, and therefore the continued division of Taiwan and the mainland would be in line with US interests. On the other hand, Washington is clearly aware of the potential military conflict with China, and has so far adopted a balanced yet clear policy towards the Taiwan issue. That is, it does not support Taiwanese independence, but insists on an eventual peaceful resolution fostered by both Taiwan and China. In December 2003, in his meeting with Chinese Premier Wen Jiabao, President Bush made a clear statement of the US position on the Taiwan issue: "We oppose any unilateral decision, by either China or Taiwan, to change the status quo of Taiwan's relationship with the mainland".[24] This referred to Taiwan President Chen Shui-bian's call for an unprecedented referendum – asking voters to demand that China remove its missiles – on the day of next presidential election.[25] President Bush, for the first time, rebuked Chen's referendum action as a move that would change the status quo. At the same time, he warned Beijing that the US will intervene if the mainland attacks Taiwan. More recently, the then Secretary of State, Colin Powell, after meeting with Chinese leaders in Beijing in late October, issued an unambiguous statement in interviews on CNN and Phoenix TV that "the United States does not support independence for Taiwan" and "those who speak out for an independence movement in Taiwan will find no support from the United States". Furthermore, Secretary Powell said that "Taiwan is not independent. It does not enjoy sovereignty as a nation".[26] One can see clearly that China and the United States have overlapping concerns over the issue of Taiwan. Yet, there are also clear differences between the two powers. This mixture of overlapping national interests and differing concerns between the two powers may prevent them from developing a more comprehensive multilateral security regime.[27] But that is not to say that a more flexible multilateral consultation will not be well developed in the security dimension – one in which both Washington and Beijing actively participate.

The case of security dialogue on North Korea can serve as a good example in this regard. The Bush administration has developed a proposal for a multilateral security guarantee in exchange for North Korea's termination of its nuclear weapons programme.[28] The situation in North Korea is apparently different from that in Iraq, although to a certain degree they share a terrorist nature. The Pyongyang regime is perceived differently from the Baghdad regime in terms of its capacity and ability to lead a major war. Moreover, there are major powers who have a stake in the development of the Korean peninsula (a reminder of the Korean War of 1950–1953 and China's involvement at that time), whereas virtually no major powers were supportive of Saddam Hussein. Furthermore, there are no well-developed economic resources in North Korea, compared to the rich oil reserves in Iraq. It is not difficult to imagine that enormous difficulties may result if the US chooses to send its military alone into North Korea. It is virtually assured there this would be another Vietnam War. There is a plan to withdraw about one-third of US troops in South Korea (approximately 12,500) and shift them to Iraq. Although there is still a large US military presence in South Korea, this decision signals the new global reconfiguration of US military strategies.[29] All of this has prompted Washington to actively seek a multilateral framework, particularly one including China, to solve the North Korean crisis.

Other players – Japan, Russia, the two Koreas, ASEAN and Taiwan

In addition to China and the United States, other crucial players – Japan, Russia, the two Koreas, ASEAN, and Taiwan – in the region may have their own perceptions and preferences in a variety of policy areas. This is therefore an appropriate juncture at which to discuss each of their attitudes and policies in this regard.

Japan

Japan, with the second largest economy in the world, has a major stake in both East and Southeast Asia. It has long regarded the countries in this area as its primary trading partners (in addition to the United States). Japan's Overseas Development Assistance (ODA) has long put this region as its top priority, holding steady at 60–70 per cent. Japan has not, however, lived up to the expectation for its leadership role in the community-building process for two reasons. First, the possibility of a resolution of historical issues between Japan and its Asian neighbours, China and Korea, (in particular, full recognition from Tokyo of its wartime behaviour) has been difficult to come by. This unsettled historical legacy has time and time again been triggered by the provocative actions of leading Japanese politicians, such as Japanese Prime Minister Junichiro Koizumi's repeated visits to Yasukuni Shrine to pay tribute to the war dead, including Class-A war criminals. This kind of action not only prevented an official state visit between China and Japan up to the end of 2004, but also created unfriendly, and even hostile, feelings among the countries' younger generations. One illuminating example of such tensions comes in the anger towards Japan displayed by Chinese soccer fans following the Asian Cup final in August 2004.[30] The concerns of Japan's neighbours were further heightened when the Japanese government sent its troops to Iraq under the US-led military coalition.[31] The second reason is the decade long economic recession, beginning in the early 1990s. This prolonged recession has had an adverse impact in terms of damaging both Japan's confidence and its credibility in the region.

On the other hand, Japan has made an effort to participate in the economic integration process. The best example comes from the 1997 financial crisis, during which Japan made a proposal to establish Asian monetary funds. Although the idea did not work at the time, it is still being considered. Japan's recent effort to establish an FTA with several ASEAN countries has demonstrated a real effort from Tokyo to strengthen the trends. With the rise of China, Japan has harboured deep suspicions of China and regarded it as a threat in both economic and security dimensions. For example, with regard to the East Asia FTA arrangement, Japan attempted to establish such an agreement with South Korea first and then with China, but South Korea was only lukewarm to this idea and made the counter suggestion that the beginning stage should also include China.[32] Japan has, however, recently begun to shift from viewing China as an economic threat to an economic opportunity, and has as a result been more willing to cooperate with China.

In the security dimension, Japan has very much relied on bilateral agreements, particularly in the US–Japan security treaty. Discussed earlier were the controversies between Japan and China around the treaty's new guidelines. These kinds of controversial items may become obstacles for further multilateral security arrangements with China, particularly if they include such sensitive topics as the Taiwan issue.

Recently, however, Japan has begun to bring South Korea into this security framework more actively, which can be considered a multilateral approach. The degree of openness to a more equal military security arrangement between Japan and South Korea may be different in Tokyo and Seoul, since the public perception of Japan in South Korea still contains some reservations and scepticism due to historical legacies. Although both Japan and South Korea are military allies of the United States, for a long time South Korea refused to have joint military exercises with the Japanese, only relenting in August of 1999, when Seoul and Tokyo held joint naval exercises for the first time since World War II.[33] In order to avoid any sensitive issues arising from the historical legacy, these joint exercises were featured as search and rescue operations in the ocean areas between the two countries. In the end, the two ROK destroyers made a goodwill call at the Japanese port of Sasebo, the first such visit in Japan–Korean relations.[34] Yet, it is still clear that South Korea is not prepared to allow Japanese military units to enter its land, even under the name of military exercises.[35]

It is nevertheless important to pay attention to Japan–US relations. Indeed, cooperation between the United States and Japan has been so close it is said that if "one party coughs, the other gets sick". An example of this collaboration is that the two countries have shared intelligence through a coded system. Together, the US and Japan will spend millions of dollars to change this communication system due to the Hainan incident of April 2001, in which the Chinese military examined the top-secret equipment of the US EP-3 surveillance plane.[36]

Another illustration of the close ties between the United States and

Japan is related to the controversial visit of Taiwanese President Lee Teng-hui to the United States in 1995 for the stated purpose of attending an alumni reunion at Cornell University. There were similar preparations made for Lee Teng-hui to visit Japan, also under the guise of attending an alumni event at Kyoto University (where he attended as an undergraduate). However, this plan did not get very far since Beijing immediately gave a stern warning against such an action. Even so, Lee Teng-hui was granted a visa in April 2001 to visit Japan for heart treatment in a hospital in Okayama prefecture.[37] This situation indicates close coordination between the US and Japan, as the US also issued a visa to Lee Teng-hui at the same time.

One may notice that in the strategic arena a major problem between Japan and its Asian neighbours, China in particular, is a lack of mutual trust and confidence. In the long run, Tokyo and Beijing have to overcome the obstacles discussed above and develop new mechanisms for a possible multilateral framework in strategic terms. Obstacles also arise from the issue of territorial disputes between Japan and its neighbours, including a territorial dispute over the Diaoyu/Senkaku islands with China, the Northern Islands with Russia, and Takeshima/Tokudo with South Korea. Although these issues are different in nature, they still constitute in varying degrees obstacles, to the development of a multilateral security framework where it relates to territory issues.

One other obstacle for Japan's smooth integration with the East Asian community is the rise of the so-called "new nationalism". Although it is generally believed that the mainstream of Japanese society is moving away from militarism, nevertheless, one may notice the rise of nationalism, particularly in light of the recent, decade-long economic recession. It is not unreasonable to some Japanese politicians, including Prime Minister Junichiro Koizumi, to call for upgrading its military force so that Japan can become an "ordinary country". It is, however, alarming when someone such as Shintaro Ishihara argued that Japan has faced a wolf (i.e. China) at his front door, and a tiger (i.e. the United States) at his back door. The development of this nationalistic sentiment may continue to hurt Japan's ability to assume a leadership role in the community-building process and limit Japan's acceptance into a multilateral security arrangement.[38]

As discussed earlier, the issue of Taiwan has been a consistent problem in China's consideration for a multilateral security framework in the region, and Japan tends to be a "loyal follower" of the United States in this respect, prompting Beijing's concern over the new security guidelines for the US–Japan Security Treaty announced in 1997.[39] Specifically, China's concern is over Part V of the "Guidelines for US–Japan Defense Cooperation" as to whether "surrounding areas" are meant to include

Taiwan itself. Although the document specifically indicates that this term reflects the situation rather than the geography, conflicting statements have been made by a variety of Japanese government officials, such as the announcement made by then Chief Cabinet Secretary Kajiyama Seiroku in August 1997 that the guidelines were indeed considered to include Taiwan.[40] In February 2005, a "two plus two" meeting took place in Washington, which included Secretary of State Condoleezza Rice and Secretary of Defense Donald Rumsfeld from the US, and Foreign Minister Nobutaka Machimura and Defence Agency Director Yoshinori Ono from Japan. The meeting issued a statement on 19 February indicating that the countries had produced a "revised US–Japanese strategic understanding", which for the first time included security in the area around Taiwan as a "common strategic objective".[41] As a number of scholars also argue, this presumption may still shift; for example, if Sino–US relations spiral downwards to a level of hostility, as occurred at the time of the EP-3 incident, then Taiwan's strategic position may move up in the US's global calculation.[42] In fact, it is reported that an informal anti-Chinese alliance has been formed between the United States, Japan and Taiwanas a result of the Chinese submarine intrusion into Japanese waters in late 2004.[43] This apparent coordination of policy understandably alarms the PRC.[44]

Due to widespread concerns over past and future North Korean missile tests, there has been a significant change of mood among the Japanese people which has led to the parliamentary approval in 1999 of revisions to the US–Japanese Security Treaty. Among several steps that Tokyo has adopted, the most noticeable development is Tokyo's announcement that it will participate in the development of a ballistic missile defence system with the United States, known as Theatre Missile Defence (TMD). Even though the Kim Dae Jung–Kim Jong-il summit in June 2000 temporarily reduced tensions in the Korean Peninsula, the TMD plan was still ongoing.

Japan has been positive in working on a multilateral dialogue in dealing with the North Korea nuclear crisis by actively participating in the six-party talks in Beijing. Japan's growing activism in promoting a multilateral security arrangement since the early 1990s, according to Kuniko Ashizawa, stems from Japan's adoption of the "multi-tiered approach".[45] This multi-tiered approach presents a new policy perspective that packages different types of coordination among region states, including bilateral, multilateral and mini-lateral or sub-regional, in a layered, hierarchical manner. This may serve as a good starting point for Japan to move beyond single-minded, US-oriented security policy and to include players such as China and North Korea with whom it currently has few security arrangements.

Russia

As a major power across two continents, Russia's stake in Asia is only secondary compared to that in Europe. However, it has been active in terms of participating in regional integration. On the economic front, other than playing a role in the APEC framework, Russia has relied heavily on bilateral ties in the region. The best example in this regard is its oil diplomacy – that is, Russia has conducted separate negotiations with China and Japan to determine its future strategy for developing pipelines to ship its oil and natural gas to those two countries.

Russia is also a major player in East Asian international relations despite the collapse of the Soviet empire in 1990, and Beijing has worked very hard to bring Moscow on its side. At the same time, Russia is eager to secure China's support, as it has its own grudges to offset – namely, the eastern expansion of NATO, the bombing of Kosovo and the situation in Chechnya. With these two powers moving toward closer ties in political, economic and strategic dimensions, the most noteworthy development is Russia's willingness to help China modernize its military forces. In October 1999, for example, the two countries' defence ministries signed an agreement to conduct joint training and share information on the formation of military doctrine. Thus, as many as 2,000 Russian technicians were employed by Chinese military research institutes to work on advanced defence systems, such as laser technology, cruise missiles, nuclear submarines and space-based weaponry. In early 2000, China purchased two Russian-built destroyers worth $800 million each. The first destroyer has already been deployed and sailed through the Taiwan Strait in February 2000 en route to a Chinese naval base.[46] On the security front, in recent years Russia has developed close ties with China, providing it with advanced technology and weaponry systems, at the same time, participating in multilateral arrangements, such as the North Korea six-party talks and the Shanghai Security Cooperation, dealing with security issues in the Central Asia area. These developments have certainly raised concerns in Washington and elsewhere.

The two Koreas

The Koreas represent two other crucial players in the region. The Korean peninsula can be considered a good example of overlapping interests among the major powers in the area – China, Japan, Russia and the United States. South Korea has been active in seeking a multilateral security framework in dealing with the North Korean nuclear developments. Beginning in the early 1990s, Seoul pushed for four-party talks on the subject of the Korean peninsula, involving North and South Korea, the US and China, on the subject of the Korean peninsula.[47] An expanded six-party dialogue, as mentioned earlier, was later developed in 2003. South Korea has been a major advocate in creating and strengthening an East Asian community in terms of economic integration. In the late 1990s, President Kim Dae Jung proposed an East Asian Visionary Group, which was established in 1999, to study future ways for the East Asian community to integrate as a region, thereby following the lead of other regional agreements such as the EU and NAFTA.[48] Given the complex nature of political relations in the region, one suggestion is for the group o tackle economic and cultural issues first. Another idea is for it to focus on security confidence-building matters. Others have suggested that the group should discuss a code of conduct to avoid regional conflict and confrontation.[49] One of the examples of the community-building effort being made was an international symposium entitled "Cultural Conference Among Korea, China, and Japan", held in Seoul in November 2000.[50]

South Korea has greatly increased its economic interdependence on China in the past few years. With its prominent role in regional integration and, given a rivalry relationship between Tokyo and Beijing, one may speculate that Seoul may play an even greater role in providing a site for further institution-building. The major obstacle in this, however, is the unsolved problem of Pyongyang – specifically, North Korea's alleged development of nuclear weapons, as well as South Korea's voluntary revelation of its research work on nuclear weapons – all of which makes the situation more complicated.[51]

The rapidly developing political and cultural relationship with China has had a profound impact on South Korea's diplomatic and security perceptions. Some previously inconceivable questions, such as South Korea's dilemma between "eagle" and "dragon" (US and China), have been asked in the last few years.[52] As a long-time ally of the US, Seoul only normalized its relations with Beijing about a decade ago. But it indicates a degree of neutrality developing between Beijing and Washington in respect of military confrontation. This tendency towards neutrality was further reinforced with the development of anti-Americanism in South Korea under the new president Roh Myu Hun. This may actually provide greater leverage for Seoul to develop a more inclusive multilateral security regime not only with Washington and Tokyo, but also with Beijing.

As one of the most isolated societies in the world, North Korea has little economic interaction with the outside world. Its economic partners are still highly concentrated towards China and South Korea. From a security aspect, Pyongyang has rightly perceived its major protagonist to be the United States. It is therefore prudent for Pyongyang to have a bilateral dialogue with Washington and try to set up a security arrangement for North Korea, but this position was rejected by the Bush administration and Washington increasingly realized the necessity to have a multilateral approach in dealing with Pyongyang. In 2003, a multilateral arrangement for the North Korean nuclear crisis issue materialized in the form of the six-party talks between China, the United States, Japan, Russia and the two Koreas. The acceptance of this multilateral approach, however reluctantly, may prove necessary for Pyongyang as well. Ultimately, North Korea needs to deal with all of the related powers, not just one. Nevertheless, Pyongyang's eyes will still be focused on Washington, since the US is the only superpower, and perhaps the only perceived security threat to North Korea.

ASEAN

ASEAN as a whole is perhaps one of the most active players in pushing for regional economic integration. From the earlier idea of the East Asia Economic Caucus (EAEC), advocated by Malaysian Prime Minister Mahathir bin Mohamad, to the most recent development of the ASEAN-plus-three framework, the basic idea is to develop economic institutional mechanisms that are truly indigenous. It will only include players in the region, unlike APEC, which also includes such players as the US, Canada, Mexico and Russia. Obviously, economic multilateralism and regional economic integration is much in line with ASEAN's interests. But with regard to FTA arrangements with countries outside ASEAN, such as China, Japan and Korea, there are different views within the ASEAN countries.[53]

One of the most noticeable developments is the changing relationship between ASEAN and China. In October 2003, ASEAN and China signed a Treaty of Amity and Cooperation at the annual ASEAN-plus-three meeting. In addition to this treaty, China also signed a strategic partnership declaration with ASEAN. This marked the first time that China has signed such a declaration with a block of countries like ASEAN, not just with one single country.[54] Also in that meeting, Chinese Prime Minister Wen Jiabao made six specific suggestions for the future of East Asia community cooperation: first, an enhancement of political dialogue and mutual trust; second, the furthering and deepening of economic and financial cooperation, as well as a study of the feasibility of free-trade areas in the East Asia Region; third, the strengthening of security dialogue and the development of non-traditional security cooperations; fourth, a promotion of social, cultural and technological cooperation, emphasizing educational and youth exchange programmes; fifth, enhancing the development of comprehensive cooperation in all fields, such as in the development of the Mekong River; and sixth, increasing coordination among all parties to create a stable environment and finally promote integration.[55]

From the security aspect, as discussed earlier, the ASEAN countries also prefer a multilateral approach because it can strengthen each individual country's power. The best example is ASEAN's approach to have collective dialogue over the disputed South China Sea islands. But in practical terms, there are different practices for different countries with regard to multilateralism, particularly when dealing with big powers such as the United States and China. The security arrangement of the Philippines, Thailand and Singapore, vis-à-vis the United States, for example, are all bilateral in nature.

Obstacles, incentives and mechanisms for multilateralism

This chapter has examined recent trends in East Asia in terms of community building and the development of a new security framework. Major players are likely to continue to move in this direction, particularly with regard to economic integration, led by the recent move toward FTA arrangements in the context of both ASEAN-plus-three and China–Japan–Korea frameworks. Economic integration may further reduce mistrust in the region and lay a solid foundation for security cooperation. The East Asia community-building process has made some major progress in the past decade. Regional economic integration has further developed and a number of economic-oriented organizations have been more active and visible, including APEC, ASEAN, ASEAN-plus-three, and a variety of proposed packages of free trade areas among major players in the region.

Although the relative size of the economic integration and regional organizations has laid a foundation for the development of new security regimes in the region, there are nevertheless significant obstacles in the security dimension. As discussed earlier, historical legacy continues to prevent major players from further cooperation, which constantly produces what Gilbert Rozman calls "bilateral distrust".[56] Furthermore, contentious issues between China and Japan, such as oil field problems and territory disputes, have continued to jeopardize cooperation among major players,[57] virtually all of which have seen the necessity to use multilateralism for security arrangements. This belief has been enhanced by the new anti-terrorist coalition building process. We have therefore seen a switch in attitude in Beijing and a more multilateral-oriented regional approach from the US. One should nevertheless recognize the weakness of a few of the existing multilateral frameworks in the security dimension, such as the ASEAN Regional Forum (ARF), and also be careful about the changing attitude of the US towards multilateralism: it is necessary to distinguish between mere participation in a multilateral exercise, such as the six-party talks on North Korea and the actual presence of a motive for doing so.

The Asian-Pacific security environment will continue to be affected by this shift in power distribution for some time to come, despite the events of 11 September 2001. At the same time, the necessity for an anti-terrorist coalition will also provide a fresh framework for inspection of the overall dynamics of major power relationships. The spirit of this new framework may be reflected in the joint anti-terrorism statement signed by Asian-Pacific leaders in the Shanghai APEC meeting in October 2001. Along this line, the issues of management of strategic weaponry, such as nuclear proliferation and missile defence systems, appear even more crucial to regional security and stability.[58]

For the United States, this new emphasis on multilateralism is not at the expense of existing bilateral agreements. The US–Japan Security Treaty, the US–South Korea Security Alliance, and a number of other bilateral arrangements, continue to play crucial roles in the security dimension. We will therefore continue to witness a coexistence of bilateral and multilateral regimes in the region, but with a tilt toward multilateralism as a new trend. George W. Bush's whirlwind tour across Asia in October 2003 when attending the APEC summit meeting has further demonstrated this tendency.[59]

China, as a rising power, is quite different from the United States, which may be considered as an established power enjoying many well-developed bilateral security arrangements. With the new approach on its security environment, Beijing is increasingly inclined to develop multilateral security frameworks. From the Chinese perspective, therefore, the newly emerged six-party talks on the North Korea nuclear crisis may develop into mechanisms for dealing with Northeast Asian security issues. The ASEAN regional forum may deal with Southeast Asian security issues and the Shanghai Security Cooperation may deal with Central Asian security issues. On that front, Beijing has also worked with South Asian countries to improve relations. Indeed, China and India held their first joint naval exercises in November 2003, involving two Indian warships and a Chinese tanker and frigate off Shanghai. A month earlier, similar naval exercises involving China and Pakistan were held.[60] China has also looked beyond the region, cultivating its relations with Europe. Indeed, bilateral trade with the European Union is on the rise, reaching levels matching China's other two major trading partners, Japan and the United States.[61] Furthermore, the close tie between the EU and China is also reflected in political and security dimensions, as demonstrated by the clear warning issued by French President Jacques Chirac when he received the visiting Chinese president, Hu Jintao, in January 2004. Chirac called Taiwan's referendum "a grave error".[62]

It is important to pay attention to possible mechanisms for the institutional development of multilateralism in the region. One may wish to highlight the importance of incentives and opportunities for all players to develop multilateralism. For example, when faced with the international crisis of 11 September, a natural development in Washington was to establish a global anti-terrorist network. This natural reaction provided a solid foundation for other players to seize an opportunity for multilateralism and reduce incentives for US unilateralism. Major players may also wish to emphasize overlapping interests as a base for cooperation, rather than to emphasize conflicting interests. As demonstrated by the post-EPIII China–US relations, the two great powers have placed their common strategic interest above concrete disputes, which has prompted unanticipated close cooperation in a multilateral direction, as in the case of the six-party talks. This has highlighted the significance of the issue of leadership. It is still crucial for the sensible development of a regional multilateral framework to include great powers in leadership roles. Although there are still no tangible results, the very idea of bringing major powers together to deal with the North Korean crisis is already a success in terms of a multilateral security framework. The relative success of this framework has further demonstrated the importance of a leadership role by the great powers. The next mechanism is to start an institutional-building process, which is essential for any security framework to develop. When one looks at the future directions of this security framework, three possible developments may be in order.

First, the newly emerged security framework, such as the six-party negotiations over North Korea, the Shanghai Cooperation Organization, as well as the US–Japan–South Korea security alliance, may continue to develop. Second, one may anticipate a potential cross-participation in existing security regimes. For example, the US–Japan–South Korea security consultation may wish, from time to time, to invite China to participate in some of its discussion activities. Third, some sensitive issues may be opened up to a certain degree for international consultations and cooperation. This may include dialogue regarding disputed territories, as China and ASEAN countries have already been engaged in over the South China Sea islands.

With the rapid development of regional cooperation and community building, an even more clearly defined multilateral security framework may be developed. In the October 2003 ASEAN-plus-three meeting, a number of new institutions and consultation mechanisms were proposed, including permanent consultation bodies for the three Northeast Asian countries: China, Japan and South Korea. The key lesson that East Asian countries may learn from European experiences is that economic integration may gradually lead to a deeper political and strategic cooperation. In order to achieve this, East Asian countries must work hard to remove mistrust resulting from historical legacies (China and Japan, in particular)[63] and current security concerns (such as the issues surrounding Taiwan and North Korea). There are still two possibilities for future development. One the one hand, one may expect that China and the United States will continue to provide leadership, albeit in various degrees, in developing a multilateralism-oriented security framework in the region, with other key players such as Japan, Russia, the two Koreas and ASEAN also actively participating. The development may go beyond the Asia Pacific region to include Central and South Asian countries such as India and Pakistan. On the other hand, as discussed earlier, major obstacles and the uncertain attitude of the United States towards multilateralism may prevent a true multilateral security framework from forming in the Asia Pacific. In this scenario, there will perhaps be a long way to go for East Asia to reach the level of the European Union, in which there exists a well-established security organization – namely, NATO. These possibilities will actually prompt decision-makers and scholars to deliberate new security frameworks that fit the Asia–Pacific reality.

As stated at the beginning of the chapter, the development of East Asian regionalism has enormous impact on the evolution of global multilateralism in the following three ways. First, it forces the United States to rethink its unilateral approach under the second term of the Bush Jnr administration and adopt a multilateral policy in East Asia, as demonstrated in the US insistence on the six-party talks over the North Korean nuclear crisis. Second, the development of regionalism in East Asia, particularly the dynamics of the development of the East Asian summit has so far excluded the United States, and this has prompted the only superpower to pay more attention to regional development and to seek participation in multilateral setting. Third, the globalization of world politics has produced new momentum for the development of regional blocks including East Asian regionalism. In conclusion, the combined influences of global and regional settings are evident, particularly in light of the development of multilateral frameworks in East Asia.

Notes

1. Michael H. Armacost (2005) "What's ahead for US policy in Asia?", *PacNet* 1(6) (January). Accessed from listserv distributed by pacnet@hawaiibiz.r.com.
2. Ivo H. Daalder and James M. Lindsay (2003) "America unbound: the Bush revolution in foreign policy", *Brookings Review* 21(4) (Fall): 2–6.

3. Quansheng Zhao (2001) "The shift in power distribution and the change of major power relations", *Journal of Strategic Studies* 24(4) (December): 49–78.
4. "Regional briefing", *Far Eastern Economic Review*, 12 February 2004, p. 12.
5. John McBeth (2003) "Taking the helm", *Far Eastern Economic Review*, 16 October 2003, pp. 38–39.
6. "East Asia Summit of December 2005 Makes the US Uneasy", *Shijie Ribao* (*World Journal*) 16 May 2005, p. 18.
7. The most noticeable bilateral security agreements are, for example:
   - US–Japan Security Treaty (initially signed at the San Francisco Peace Conference of 1951 and renewed in 1960, and then in 1996 a new guideline was issued):
   - US–ROK Mutual Defense Treaty (signed in 1953)
   - US–Australia Defense Alliance (concluded in 1951)
   - US–New Zealand Defense Alliance (signed in 1951)
   - US–Philippines Mutual Defense Treaty (approved in 1999; until 1992, the US maintained military bases and forces pursuant to the 1947 Military Bases Agreement)
   - US–Thailand Memorandum of Understanding for Security Cooperation (signed in 1971).
8. For an excellent discussion of economic regionalism in East Asia, see Edward J. Lincoln (2004) *East Asian Economic Regionalism*, Washington, DC: Brookings Institution Press.
9. For a detailed analysis of the "ups and downs" of East Asian international relations in the post-Cold War era, see Quansheng Zhao (2001) "The shift in power distribution and the change of major power relations", *Journal of Strategic Studies* 24(4) (December): 49–78.
10. For details on American and Chinese shifts of influence in Asia, see Mark Mitchell and Michael Vatikiotis (2000) "China steps in where US fails", *Far Eastern Economic Review*, 23 November, pp. 20–22.
11. See Barry Buzan (2003) "Security architecture in Asia: the interplay of regional and global levels", *Pacific Review* 16(2): 143–174.
12. Steven C. Clemons (2001) "The Armitage Report: reading between the lines", Japan Policy Research Institute Occasional Paper No. 20 (February), p. 1.
13. See Carlyle A. Thayer (2003) "China's 'new security concept' and Southeast Asia", in David W. Lovell (ed.) *Asia–Pacific Security: Policy Challenges*, Singapore: Institute of Southeast Asian Studies, pp. 89–107.
14. For a comprehensive analysis of the US's Asian foreign policy in the post-9/11 era, see Lowell Dittmer (2002) "East Asia in the 'new era' in world politics", *World Politics* 55(1) (October): 47–57.
15. John Wong and Sarah Chan (2003) "China–ASEAN Free Trade Agreement: shaping future economic relations", *Asian Survey* 43(3) (May/June): 507–526.
16. Michael Vatikiotis and Murray Hiebert (2003) "How China is building an empire", *Far Eastern Economic Review*, 20 November, pp. 30–33.
17. For a look into the changing attitude of China from bilateralism to multilateralism, see Evans S. Medeiros and M. Taylor Fravel (2003) "China's new diplomacy", *Foreign Affairs* 82(6) (November/December): 22–35.
18. "China Briefing: Central Asia", *Far Eastern Economic Review*, 29 January 2004, p. 23.
19. "Uyghur Exile Group Forms a Government", *Far Eastern Economic Review*, 23 September 2004, p. 8.
20. An interesting example is that in July 2002, the National Defense University's (NDU) Center for the Study of Chinese Military Affairs was shut down by the Pentagon. One of the reasons, according to Larry Worzell, director of the Asian Studies Center at the Heritage Foundation, is that the NDU Center "elevated China to the center of US for-

eign and security policy. In my view, US relations with Japan are far more critical to the stability and security of Asia". See Julie Norwell (2002) "Pentagon moves to shut NDU's China center: China schism", *Original Economist*, September, p. 10.

21. Another example of this "conservative hostility" to China is the severe criticism of George W. Bush's secretary of labor, Elaine Chao, and her alleged pro-China position. See John B. Judis (2001) "The decline of principled conservative hostility to China: sullied heritage", *New Republic*, 23 April, pp. 19–25.
22. Robert Kagan (2005) "The illusion of 'managing' China", *Washington Post*, Sunday, 15 May, p. B7.
23. For an overview of various US policy options regarding the North Korean nuclear crisis, see Report of an Independent Task Force (2003) "Meeting the North Korean nuclear challenge", *Council on Foreign Relations*, New York.
24. Susan Lawrence and Jason Dean (2003) "A new threat", *Far Eastern Economic Review*, 18 December, pp. 16–18.
25. After Bush's criticism, Chen Shui-bian revised the questions for his proposed referendum. The new version asks whether Taiwan should buy more advanced weapons if China refuses to withdrawal its missiles, and whether the island should try to open talks with Beijing. Beijing rebuked both proposals as provocative. See Philip P. Pan (2004) "China Rebukes Taiwan's Leader on New Plans for Referendum, *Washington Post*, 20 January 20, p. A13.
26. Colin Powell interviews with Mike Chinoy of CNN International TV and with Anthony Yuen of Phoenix TV, China World Hotel, Beijing, China, 25 October 2004, accessed at http://www.state.gov/secretary/rm/c11020.htm.
27. For a detailed analysis of the challenges facing the US in terms of its China policy, including the issue of Taiwan, see Thomas J. Christensen (2001) "Posing problems without catching up: China's rise and challenge for US security policy", *International Security* 25(4) (Spring): 5–40.
28. Anthony Faiola (2003) "In Shift, N. Korea to Consider Bush's Security Offer", *Washington Post*, 26 October, p. A24.
29. Susan V. Lawrence and David Lague (2004) "Marching Out of Asia", *Far Eastern Economic Review*, 26 August, pp. 12–16.
30. Matt Pottinger (2004) "Own Goal", *Far Eastern Economic Review*, 19 August, p. 24.
31. Sebastien Moffett and Martin Fackler (2004) "Marching on to a New Role", *Far Eastern Economic Review*, 15 January, pp. 18–21.
32. *Qiao Bao* (*Overseas Chinese News*), 25 June 2003, p. 3.
33. Don Kirk (1999) "Seoul and Tokyo Hold Joint Naval Exercises: Maneuvers First Since End of World War II" *International Herald Tribune*, 6 August, accessed at http://www.iht.com/IHT/DK/99/dk080699.html.
34. These were well-organized, low-key, 5-day joint exercises, during which three Japanese maritime SDF destroyers, two South Korean destroyers and more than 1,000 soldiers participated. See Victor Cha, "Seoul-Tokyo Cooperation on North Korea, Tried, Tested, and True (thus far)", accessed at http://www.csis.org/pacfor/cc/993Qjapan_skorea.html.
35. Interview with Mr. Sung Joo Han, Ambassador of South Korea to the United States and former foreign minister of ROK, 6 November 2003, Washington DC.
36. Shigehiko Togo (2001) "Japan Fears Loss of Code From US Plane to China", *Washington Post*, 14 April, p. A14.
37. "Taiwan's Ex-Leader to Visit Japan", *Washington Post*, 21 April 2001, p. A13.
38. For a penetrating examination in this regard, see Eugene A. Matthews (2003) "Japan's new nationalism", *Foreign Affairs* 82(6) (November/December): 74–90.
39. See Part V of "Guidelines for US–Japan Defense Cooperation" (US–Japan Security Consultative Committee release) as follows:

V. Cooperation in Situations in Areas Surrounding Japan that Will Have an Important Influence on Japan's Peace and Security

Situations in areas surrounding Japan will have an important influence on Japan's peace and security. The concept, situations in areas surrounding Japan, is not geographic but situational. The two Governments will make every effort, including diplomatic efforts, to prevent such situations from occurring. When the two Governments reach a common assessment of the state of each situation, they will effectively coordinate their activities. In responding to such situations, measures taken may differ depending on circumstances....

When a situation in areas surrounding Japan is anticipated, the two Governments will intensify information and intelligence sharing and policy consultations, including efforts to reach a common assessment of the situation.

40. *Yomiuri Shimbun*, 18 August 1998, as quoted in Zhong Yan (2000) "Xin ri-mei fangwei hezuo zhizhen ji xiangguan lifang pingxi", ("An Analysis of the New 'Guideline for Japan–US Defense Cooperation' and Its Related Legislation") *Riben Xuekan* (*Japanese Studies*) (2): 1–12.
41. Edward Cody (2005) "China Protests US–Japan Accord", *Washington Post*, 21 February, p. A24; see also *Shijie Ribao* (*World Journal*), 19 February 2005, p. 1.
42. Paper presented by Robert Sutter (2005) "Recent convergence in China–US views – Rethinking US Policy Options", International Conference on US Taiwan Policy and the Dynamics of the Taipei–Beijing–Washington Triangle, 28 January, American University, Washington DC.
43. "Anti-Submarine Alliance Among US, Japan, and Taiwan Triangle Against PLA", *Qiao Bao* (*China Press*), 3 December 2004, p. B4.
44. Edward Cody (2005) "China Protests US–Japan Accord", *Washington Post*, Monday, 21 February, p. A24.
45. See Kuniko Ashizawa (2003) "Japan's approach toward Asian regional security: from 'hub-and-spoke' bilateralism to 'multi-tiered'", *Pacific Review* 16(3): 361–382.
46. John Pomfret (2000) "Russians Help China Modernize Its Arsenal: New Military Ties Raise US Concerns", *Washington Post*, 10 February, pp. A17–A18.
47. In 1995, South Korea suggested a four-power peace conference that included the United States, China and the two Koreas for the purpose of working out a new peace agreement to replace the armistice and thereby bring a formal end to the decades-long Korean War. Initially, Pyongyang did not want Chinese participation (Selig Harrison (1997) "Promoting a Soft Landing in Korea", *Foreign Policy* 106 (Spring)). After prolonged negotiations with the United States and South Korea in New York in July 1997, North Korea finally agreed to hold the four-power conference. The first preparatory talk was held in New York on 5 August 1997 ("Pyongyang Accepts Framework for Peace Talks", *Strait Times*, 2 July 1997, p. 21). After several on-again–off-again negotiations among the four parties, the talks broke down once more on 19 September 1997 without even agreeing an agenda for further conferences to be held in Geneva (Steven Myers (1997) "N. Korea's Talks with US Fail Over Demand for G.I. Pullout", *New York Times*, 20 September). A major previous obstacle was that the North Koreans insisted that conference participants agree in advance to discuss the removal of the 37,000 American troops stationed in South Korea (Robert Reid (1997) "Korean Peace Talks Break Down", Associated Press, 20 September 20).
48. The East Asian Vision Group was established at the suggestion of President Kim Dae Jung of South Korea in May of 1999. The first meeting was convened in November 1999 in Seoul, with former Minister of Foreign Affairs Han Sung Joo presiding. The meeting was in the so-called "10+3" format, namely the ten ASEAN members plus Japan,

China and South Korea. Each country had two representatives, one being a foreign affairs minister at the ambassador level and the other a leading scholar of Asia–Pacific international relations, making a total of 26 participants. In the future, the Vision Group may potentially be expanded to a "13+2" format in which North Korea and Mongolia will join as participants.

49. Interview with Zhang Yunling (2001) Director of Institute of Asia–Pacific Studies, Chinese Academy of Social Sciences, 2 January, in Beijing, China. Zhang Yunling was one of the PRC's representatives for the East Asian Vision Group.
50. *Renmin Ribao* (*People's Daily*), 24 November 2000, p. 6.
51. Donald Greenless and Murray Hiebert (2004) "Nuclear No-No", *Far Eastern Economic Review*, 16 September , pp. 22–25.
52. See Jae Ho Chung (2001) "South Korea between Eagle and Dragon", *Asian Survey* 45(5): 777–796.
53. For a sceptical evaluation of the future development, see Markus Hund (2003) "ASEAN Plus Three: towards a new age of Pan-East Asian regionalism?: A Skeptic's Appraisal", *Pacific Review* 16(3): 383–417.
54. *Renmin Ribao* (*People's Daily*), 9 October 2003, p. 1, and *Shijie Ribao* (*World Journal*), 9 October 2003, p. A.
55. *Renmin Ribao* (*People's Daily*), 8 October 2003, p. 1.
56. Gilbert Rozman (2004) *Northeast Asia's Stunted Regionalism Bilateral Distrust in the Shadow of Globalization*, Cambridge: Cambridge University Press.
57. Japan lodged a formal protest with the Chinese government on 12 November when Chinese submarines allegedly entered its territorial waters. See "Japan Protests To China Over Incursion by Nuclear Sub", *Washington Post*, 13 November 2004, p. A19.
58. Quansheng Zhao (2002) "Asian–Pacific International Relations in the 21st Century", in Quansheng Zhao (ed.) *Future Trends in East Asian International Relations*, London: Frank Cass, pp. 237–245.
59. "Bush Sounds Themes of Trade and Security", *Far Eastern Economic Review*, 30 October 2003, p. 14.
60. "China Briefing", *Far Eastern Economic Review*, 22 November 2003, p. 29.
61. David Murphy (2004) "It's More Than Love", *Far Eastern Economic Review*, 12 February, pp. 26–29.
62. "France Embraces China, Warns Taiwan", *Far Eastern Economic Review*, 5 February 2004, p. 22.
63. See Quansheng Zhao (2003) "China Must Shake off the Past in Ties with Japan", *Straits Times*, 7 November, p. 20.

25

Conclusions: Multilateralism under challenge or in crisis?

Edward Newman and Ramesh Thakur

The chapters in this volume suggest two key conclusions. First, the fundamental *principle* of multilateralism, with all its limitations, is not in crisis. Indeed, this principle is validated and vindicated by the demands of the contemporary world. Second, however, the values and institutions of multilateralism as *currently constituted* – and with them, the conceptual tools and presumptions with which multilateralism has been approached hitherto – are arguably under serious challenge. The distinction between the principle of multilateralism and specific forms of institutionalized multilateralism is a fundamentally important starting point.

There is no reason to conclude that the general principle of multilateralism is in crisis. Multilateralism refers to collective, cooperative action by states – when necessary, in cooperation with non-state actors – to deal with common challenges and problems when these are best managed collectively at the international level. Areas such as maintaining and promoting international peace and security, economic development and international trade, human rights, functional and technical cooperation, and the protection of the environment – amongst others – require joint action to reduce costs, and to bring order and regularity to international relations. Such common problems cannot be addressed unilaterally to optimum effectiveness. This rationale persists because all states – which remain the key although not the sole actors in international relations – face mutual vulnerabilities and share interdependence. They all need to benefit from – and thus are required to support – public goods. Even the most powerful states cannot achieve security, environmental safety and economic prosperity as effectively (if at all) in isolation or unilaterally. We have seen this demonstrated perennially, and so the international system rests upon a network of regimes, treaties, international organizations and shared practices that embody common expectations, reciprocity and equivalence of benefits. In an interdependent, globalizing world, multilateralism will continue to be a key aspect of international relations. Limitations do and always will exist, and the utility and effectiveness of formal multilateral institutions are inevitably conditioned and constrained by the exigencies of power and leadership. Powerful states may work through formal institutions at their pleasure and selectively. Some issues may defy multilateral approaches. Moreover, changing normative expectations may cast doubt upon the constitutive values of specific international institutions. But the theoretical rationale of institutionalism is broadly intact.

However, this is emphatically not to say that the values and institutions of formalized multilateralism as currently constituted are optimally effective, legitimate or normatively satisfactory. Therefore, we are confronted with specific, contextualized challenges, and of these there are very many. What is required in turn is contextual analysis, critical assessment and reasoned alternatives.

Firstly, there are what we can call structural or systemic challenges, related to the nature of the international system and its constitutive actors. Classic models of multilateralism are constituted upon regular and stable relations amongst viable sovereign states akin to a "Westphalian" model of international relations. Within this, states are by far the principal actors, and the preservation of independence and territorial integrity, and the prevention of aggression, were the primary objectives. However, this has conceptual and practical limitations. States are not necessarily all viable; state weakness and failure are characteristic of a number of regions in the developing world. Indeed, state incapacity is an underlying source of a wide range of pressing problems. Moreover, in terms of one of the principal objectives of international organizations – the maintenance of international peace and security – most instances of armed conflict are clearly domestic rather than inter-state, albeit with transborder consequences. The traditional security problematique is still very much relevant, but most violent conflicts occur outside the classic inter-state paradigm. International organizations, while not legally precluded from being involved in civil war, have had difficulty in finding a consensus or norm about the international community's role and responsibility in civil war.

In a more general and less explicit sense, sovereignty is arguably itself under challenge, with implications for multilateralism. Sovereign statehood remains a core characteristic of the international system. However, the legalist model of international politics – premised upon the primacy of sovereign autonomy, sovereign equality, non-interference and the irrelevance of domestic forms of government – is demonstrably out of touch with reality in a number of respects. International norms regarding human rights have developed an importance that significantly conditions state sovereignty and goes beyond the voluntary nature of international human rights instruments. This has given rise to a solidarist norm of "individual sovereignty", whereby the legitimacy of state sovereignty rests not only on control of territory and international recognition, but also upon fulfilling certain standards of human rights and welfare for citizens. As a corollary, the sovereignty of states which are unwilling or unable to fulfil certain basic standards may be in question. The use of military force for human protection purposes is the starkest example of this trend, although a wider range of transnational norms, institutions and processes regarding human rights and governance also underscore the normative challenge to sovereignty in this area. Sovereignty, and respect for its legitimacy, rests in part upon the recognition of other states, but the prerogative of exclusive territorial control is arguably now premised upon a broader set of criteria, including observing human rights. However, existing international organizations rest upon the basis of state sovereignty, and prioritize sovereignty and non-interference above human rights.

Some analysts may not accept that human rights are becoming a more significant factor in international politics or that they are meaningfully conditioning sovereignty. However, the evolution of sovereignty goes beyond this issue. State sovereignty traditionally implies control of territory, along with independence and reciprocal recognition. Historically, there are countless cases where this was a fiction, and yet the international community stressed the norm of sovereignty, avoiding any legal derogation of that institution. However, it is becoming increasingly difficult to uphold the idea of sovereignty in cases where states are unwilling or unable to uphold even the most basic foundations of the institution of sovereignty, especially when they can have serious negative repercussions across borders. This is represented in a number of forms: when viable public authority and control cease to exist, the rights and needs of citizens cannot be met, and relations with other international entities cannot be meaningfully pursued. Moreover, a lack of control over territory and cross-border movements of illegal activities and forced human displacement affects other states. In addition, the association of certain countries with terrorism, weapons of mass destruction and other "errant" behaviour has further challenged the Westphalian order.

The reality is that in many ways, and for different reasons, the challenge to the state, as the foundation of multilateralism, represents a challenge to formal institutionalized multilateralism. At the beginning of the twenty-first century, it is necessary to acknowledge a controversial and perhaps uncomfortable reality: the concept of equality of state legitimacy – that all states are endowed with equal rights to legal respect, sovereign prerogatives and inviolable territorial integrity – is not universally accepted.

A further problem with the state-centric nature of international organizations is that many challenges and problems are transnational and involve non-state actors. In the most extreme illustration of this, the idea of multilateralism – or even international order – as constituted by states is being challenged by terrorist non-state actors. And with respect to shaping and influencing UN policy, it would be difficult to deny that major NGOs and civil society actors such as Amnesty International, Human Rights Watch, the International Committee of the Red Cross (ICRC), Greenpeace and Transparency International have proven worthy competitors – in terms of their legitimacy and perhaps also performance – to the UN's human rights mechanisms.

Secondly, there are hegemonic challenges to contemporary multilateral institutions in the context of a unipolar international system. The US, through its economic and military pre-eminence, is in a position where it is able to exercise a certain amount of discretion in terms of its support for international organizations. According to US Defense Secretary Donald Rumsfeld, one of the most important lessons from the war against terrorism was that "the mission must determine the coalition, the coalition must not determine the mission."[1] In this context the US and its allies undertook a war against Iraq in 2003 without the authorization of the UN Security Council. In other areas of multilateralism, the US rejected the International Criminal Court and the Kyoto protocol on climate change, raised the possibility of preventive force outside the UN framework in response to latent security threats, eroded a number of multilateral arms control treaties, and has organized and leads the Proliferation Security Initiative as an alternative arrangement for dealing with illicit transfers of WMD-sensitive material.

The so-called pattern of US unilateralism has been correctly associated with the malaise of multilateralism, but it is only a partial explanation. US pre-eminence and unipolarity – which is, in any case, not an unproblematic concept – does not necessarily result in US unilateralism (and unilateralism does not necessarily result in a general decline of multilateralism). Indeed, many of the key institutions of international order established after the Second World War – including the UN and the Bretton Woods institutions – were established, through US leadership, at a time of US pre-eminence. In addition, according to hegemonic stability theory, it was *declining* US preponderance in the 1970s which was bringing multilateral institutions into question. This suggests that purely structural explanations are inadequate for identifying the relationship between power, leadership and the maintenance of multilateralism institutions.

Having observed all of this, the position of the US has brought the issue to a head and raised legitimate concerns: rigid multilateral institutions cannot hope to be respected indefinitely when their constitutive principles and performance do not meet expectations in terms of legitimacy and effectiveness. Even the most committed UN-supporter would accept this. The result is that powerful states can afford to circumvent established international organizations in matters related to critical national interests – which is nothing new – and also form alternative and sometimes ad hoc coalitions for taking action.

Third, there are normative challenges to multilateralism which concern the way that decisions are made and implemented. There are two dimensions to this. Firstly, established multilateral organizations arguably do not meet standards of accountability and representation which are considered legitimate in the twenty-first century, at least amongst democratic societies. This is a problem because international organizations are playing an increasingly prominent role in peoples' lives. A range of public practices and policy decisions have been transferred to the international level, and this raises a number of pressing normative issues which did not apply to the more narrow Westphalian origins of multilateralism. The state sovereignty basis of legitimacy is no longer sufficient in an era of popular sovereignty and democracy. This requires some elaboration.

Traditionally, ideas of political legitimacy are bounded in the state. Legitimacy in governance is usually conceived in the nature of the relationship between the government and the governed. Justice and political legitimacy bestow the right to govern and define the loss of this right in the context of the value-system and norms of a particular political community. Values and standards vary across the world, but by most definitions of political legitimacy certain foundational criteria must be met: consent, accountability and the rule of law. In the domestic context, this is embraced in many societies by the practices of democracy, and the "collective good" is defined and upheld through this process within a given political community.

There are many problems in applying ideas of political legitimacy to the international arena. The bases of political community, within which legitimacy must be constituted, is difficult to conceive at the international level. There is a far greater diversity of value systems so the roots of political legitimacy are elusive. Yet with the profile of international organizations increasing in peoples' lives there is a pressing need to apply ideas of legitimacy to the normative goals underpinning many international organizations. At a time when aspirations of leadership and governance demand legitimacy within states and democracy is expanding across the world, it is time for international organizations to embrace the spirit of this movement. In fact, democracy and legitimacy increasingly are concepts which extend beyond the domestic polity, partly as a condition of globalizing ideas and interaction amongst societies. Traditionally, the concept of legitimacy did not extend beyond the domestic arena and a different set of norms governed international relationships. This tradition has evolved into a democratic deficit in many organizations. Even in the case of those organizations which can wield enormous leverage upon the domestic policies of some states and exert a significant impact upon the lives of many millions of people, there is little transparency or public input into their policy and decision-making – or at least this is the perception. Why should international organizations be exempt from democratic accountability, transparency, public participation and judgements of legitimacy? In the absence of satisfactory answers to these questions, we have criticisms of unelected, unaccountable and inefficient international bureaucracies. In the field, also, the United Nations is facing stiff competition from NGOs, many – although not all – of which are seen as more flexible and in touch with local needs, and less steeped in political and bureaucratic constraints.

On a related level, the consensus and majoritarian manner of decision-making in some international organizations has also been questioned in terms of legitimacy. It cannot be taken as a given that all governments, in international organizations, represent their people. Why, then, should a democratic country or a group of democratic countries be obliged to act – or be constrained from acting – on critical issues according to the rules of an international organization in which non-democratic states have a vote? According to the existing rules of many multilateral organizations, the status quo – or inactivity – is acceptable if agreement to act through consensus or majority according to the rules of procedure cannot be achieved, even in situations of emergency. As Robert Keohane observes in this volume, this is no longer acceptable in the face of genocide or with the risk of terrorism combined with weapons of mass destruction. In the eyes of many contemporary observers, if international organizations cannot act in response to the most pressing global problems, then their legitimacy is questioned, even if they are following their rules of procedure. That is, their procedural legitimacy may be contributing to an erosion of their performance legitimacy. International organizations have moved far beyond the Westphalian idea of merely regulating "high politics" amongst states. It has often been accepted that formal multilateral organizations, as imperfect as they are, were legitimate relative to the feasible alternatives. This is no longer a given.

A further normative challenge relates to the constitutive values upon which international organizations, for historical reasons, are based. Many contemporary forms of institutionalized multilateralism – exemplified in the Bretton Woods organizations – reflect a particular normative heritage based upon liberal values such as the nation-state, liberal democracy and liberal human rights, and, above all, market economics and the integration of societies into free trade. However, this liberal outlook is problematic. Democracy (in terms of liberal democracy, or "polyarchy"), human rights (especially when emphasizing principally civil and political rights), market values, the integration of societies into globalization and the idea of the state are not necessarily universal values. Sometimes, these values are not appropriate for post-conflict or divided societies. Indeed, democracy and the market are arguably adversarial or even conflictual forces – appropriate in stable Western societies, but not universal. In some circumstances, some liberal values may be at odds with the attainment of sustainable peace, when, for example, they promote a neo-liberal economic agenda which may exacerbate social/economic tensions, or where democracy promotion exacerbates political conflict and sectarian divisions. Moreover, the manner in which the components of the liberal vision are promoted is, arguably, loaded in favour of the market and not social justice, and in favour of stability rather than human rights and accountability. Some aspects of contemporary conflict management associated with the liberal peace – including the role of international financial institutions, NGO work and some aspects of humanitarianism – may in fact be contributing to certain types of conflict, especially when conflicts are driven by a "war economy". There is, therefore, resistance to the values upon which established forms of multilateralism are based. As international politics intrudes increasingly into societies, international organizations have demonstrated that multilateralism is not value-free. Multilateralism has become entwined with fundamental social and political choices regarding the balance between the market and welfare, human rights, governance and democracy. This has inevitably been controversial.

Thus, in summary, we see the challenge to the values and institutions of multilateralism not only as a result of a particular distribution of power, but also systemic factors: the nature of power, the nature of security and of threats to international security, the actors which have an impact upon international peace and security, the international norms which regulate the behaviour of actors in the international arena, and the nature of the state. The reality is that the world is diverse; not all the values that "universal" multilateral organizations project and promote – or even impose, according to some observers – are accepted as truly universal.

The future of multilateralism: beyond Westphalia

If they are to be viable, multilateral values and institutions must be constituted in line with twenty-first century principles of governance and legitimacy, and capable of addressing contemporary challenges effectively. This involves moving beyond the Westphalian roots of multilateral institutions, reassessing the values upon which multilateralism is based and is promoting, and recognizing that contemporary challenges demand greater flexibility and pro-activity.

In terms of critical issues of human survival, states must recognize that sovereignty is conditional upon meeting certain standards of human welfare and human rights. There is a responsibility to protect human life. If states are unable or unwilling to meet this responsibility – in the case of genocide, for example – the international community, through multilateral organizations, should be mandated and enabled to take over this responsibility.

In terms of international peace and security, and especially weapons of mass destruction and terrorism, certain principles related to the presumption of sovereignty, non-interference and the use of force may need to be re-examined. The established rules governing the use of military force (only in self-defence, collective self-defence, or with reference to Chapter 7 of the UN Charter) have been questioned in some circumstances, especially when we are faced with the hypothetical combination of terrorism and weapons of mass destruction. The idea of preventive force in response to latent or non-imminent threats is something that has appealed to some policy analysts. When this idea has arisen, the presumption has been that such preventive force would necessarily be outside the UN framework because of the UN Charter's emphasis upon the non-use of force except in self-defence or in response to cases of aggression. The Secretary-General offered a rebuttal to this presumption in his report "In Larger Freedom" by observing that, in fact, "Where threats are not imminent but latent, the Charter gives full authority to the Security Council to use military force, including preventively, to preserve international peace and security."[2]

Nevertheless, on the basis of the Security Council's performance in the past, even in response to clear cases of large-scale aggression, it is difficult to accept that the UN at present is sufficiently constituted to authorize preventive force in response to latent threats. It will therefore not have the full confidence of some key countries in critical issues related to international security, unless it undergoes radical transformation in its rules of procedure and its definition of "threats to international peace and security". The first step should be the promotion of a threat-based system of international peace and security, in the broadest sense: including a comprehensive convention on terrorism in all its aspects, and a declaration on the responsibility to protect human life. Once members have signed-up to these core conventions, they must be enforced and the Security Council must be prepared to make decisions, including authorizing the use of coercion in response to violations.

Multilateral institutions must recognize and involve non-state actors on the basis of criteria which ensure their legitimacy and effectiveness. In particular, in the areas of social and economic welfare and humanitarianism, non-state actors are an essential component of multilateralism which must be embraced fully. In this sense, the multilateralism of the twenty-first century must not be confined to relationship amongst states; it must reflect the plurality of international relations and the key role of non-state actors.

In the past, according to the Westphalian model of multilateralism that emphasized consensus and sovereignty, ineffectiveness and status quo were tolerated according to the lowest common denominator. This resulted in perverse outcomes: the international community failed to respond to genocide and other widespread abuses of human rights, and this was legally sound according to the rules of procedure of international organizations. (Indeed, ad hoc or unilateral initiatives, even in such circumstances, could be considered illegal or illegitimate.) This cannot remain the constitutive principle of multilateralism in the twenty-first century. There is a responsibility to act in response to pressing global problems, and this should be the starting point for multilateralism. This means, amongst other things, that the principle of multilateralism must in some respects move beyond the idea of consensus.

In the social and economic realm, in light of the significant impact of multilateral decisions and institutions upon human lives, especially in developing countries, greater transparency and accountability are necessary.

Finally, we must be realistic about what the UN – and international organizations in general – can and cannot do, and recognize that many multilateral processes will work most effectively at the regional level, based upon shared values, identity and regional leadership.

Notes

1. Remarks as prepared for Secretary of Defense Donald Rumsfeld, the National Defense University in Washington, DC, Thursday, 31 January 2002, available at http://www.oft.osd.mil/library/library_files/speech_136_rumsfeld_speech_31_jan_2002.doc.
2. *In larger freedom: towards development, security and human rights for all*, Report of the Secretary-General, New York: United Nations, 21 March 2005, paragraph 125.

Index